THE YALE EDITION OF THE

SHORTER POEMS OF

# Edmund Spenser

EDITED BY WILLIAM A. ORAM

EINAR BJORVAND, RONALD BOND

THOMAS H. CAIN, ALEXANDER DUNLOP

RICHARD SCHELL

YALE UNIVERSITY PRESS

*New Haven & London*

Designed by Richard Hendel.
Set in Galliard type by
The Composing Room of Michigan, Inc.
Printed in the United States of America by
Alpine Press, Stoughton, Massachusetts.

**Library of Congress Cataloging-in-Publication Data**

Spenser, Edmund, 1552?–1599.
The Yale edition of the shorter poems
of Edmund Spenser.

Bibliography: p.
I. Oram, William A.   II. Title.
PR2352.O74 1989      821'.3      88–37852
ISBN 0–300–04244–2 (alk. paper)
ISBN 0–300–04245–0 (pbl. : alk. paper)

The paper in this book meets the guidelines for permanence and durability of
the Committee on Production Guidelines for Book Longevity of the Council
on Library Resources.

10 9 8 7 6 5 4 3 2 1

# Contents

# *Illustrations*

# Preface

᥀᥀᥀᥀᥀᥀᥀

The purpose of this edition is to make available to students the texts of Spenser's shorter poems with introductions and notes which respond to developments in Spenser criticism over the past forty years. Nearly half a century of intensive Renaissance scholarship has had its effect, and we see the poems in a different light than did the editors of the *Variorum*. We hope that a newly-annotated text of the *Shorter Poems* will make the teaching of the poems easier and their study more rewarding.

As a group we differ in our views and interests, and we have felt it right not to impose too rigorous a uniformity on our various efforts. Although we agree on many matters (such as the usefulness of seeing each published volume of the poems as a meaningful whole), the introductions and notes vary in the kind of information they provide. They differ as well in the degree to which they try to represent what particular critics have said. In annotating the poetry we have drawn freely on the rich and generous tradition of Spenserian scholarship without noting each individual indebtedness: we all stand on the shoulders of others. It should be said, however, that one of our deepest and most quietly pervasive debts is to the work of W. L. Renwick in his superb edition of the *Minor Poems* half a century ago, and to the editors of the *Spenser Variorum*. For students who want to know where to start in reading criticism on the poems, we offer brief bibliographical paragraphs at the end of the edition. Much fuller bibliographies are appended to the articles on the particular poems in the forthcoming *Spenser Encyclopedia*.

The notes are intended to provide interpretive guidance and minimal lexical information. Words judged confusing or particularly obscure and all mythological allusions have been glossed. No amount of glossing, however, could obviate the need for flexibility in reading Spenser's diction. The student is advised to consult the Oxford English Dictionary in doubtful cases. In addition there are some unfamiliar words which Spenser uses frequently in his shorter works; these appear in a list in the beginning of the book and are not normally otherwise glossed. Texts for the edition have been edited freshly; the editors as a group have tended to be conservative, keeping the readings of the copy-texts unless there are obvious misprints or the punctuation creates an active hindrance for the reader.

We would like to thank the Bodleian Library, the Houghton Library, the Huntington Library, the Smith College Library, and the Yale Library which have all generously allowed us to reproduce materials for this book. In particular we would like to thank John G. Graiff, Diane Lee, and Ruth Mortimer of the Smith Library and Thomas V. Lange of the Huntington, who went out of their way to help. The University of Nebraska Press permitted the material on the October eclogue published in Thomas H. Cain, *Praise in "The Faerie Queene"*, to appear here in somewhat different form. Financial assistance has been forthcoming from the Social Sciences and Humanities Research Council of Canada and from our various institutions: Auburn University, Laurentian University, McMaster University, Smith College, the University of Calgary, and the University of Oslo. A sabbatical leave from Smith College enabled the coordinating editor to do his job in comparative peace.

We owe many individual debts as well, only some of which we can acknowledge here. David Richardson was a founding member of our group, and after the claims of the *Spenser Encyclopedia* forced him to give up this project, he continued to contribute to it. Donald Cheney came to the assistance of the project at a critical moment. Others have responded generously in reading parts of the manuscript and suggesting changes of style and substance, including Ward S. Allen, James A. Clark, James P. Hammersmith, A. Kent Hieatt, John Hollander, Thalia A. Pandiri, and Harold Skulsky. Our student assistants have made the work much easier than it would otherwise have been, notably Donna Batyetzi, Lisa Chase, Mary Frances Nevans, Lori Paige, and Astrid Spitten, the last of whom contributed a number of suggestions to the edition of the *Amoretti*.

We are grateful as well to our editors at the Yale University Press, especially to Ellen Graham for her generous encouragement, Jay Williams for her executive skill, William Bidwell who saved us many embarrassments, and the book's designer, Richard Hendel, for his elegant work. This project originated at one of the merrie interludes of the Spenser sessions at the May meeting of the Medieval Institute at The University of Western Michigan, and was pursued at subsequent meetings; the support and encouragement of that community has been a boon.

Introductions and notes to *The Shepheardes Calender* are the work of Thomas H. Cain; text for the first six months is by Ronald Bond; text for E. K.'s Epistle and the last six months is by William A. Oram. The General Introduction to the *Complaints* and the editions of *Virgil's Gnat*, *Muiopotmos*, and Ponsonby's "Letter to the Gentle Reader" are by Ronald Bond; *The Teares of the Muses* and *Mother Hubberds Tale* were edited by William A. Oram, and *The Ruines of Time*, *The Ruines of Rome*, *Visions of Vanitie*, *Visions of Bellay*, *Visions of Petrarch*, and *The Theatre for Worldlings* by Richard Schell. *Daphnaida*, *Colin Clouts Come Home Againe*, *Astrophel*, and the Miscellaneous Short Poems were edited by William A. Oram, *Amoretti and Epithalamion* by Alexander Dunlop, and *Prothalamion* by Einar Bjorvand. Together Einar Bjorvand and Richard Schell wrote the introduction to *Fowre Hymnes*; the former prepared text and notes for the *Hymne in Honour of Love* and *An Hymne of Heavenly Love*, the latter for the *Hymne in Honour of Beautie* and *An Hymne of Heavenly Beautie*.

> *William A. Oram, Coordinating Editor*
> *Einar Bjorvand*
> *Ronald Bond*
> *Thomas H. Cain*
> *Alexander Dunlop*
> *Richard Schell*

# Word List

The dialect words and archaisms listed below are normally not glossed in the text.

*albe*: although

*als*: as; also

*annoy, anoy*: (v) harm, trouble; (n) discomfort, pain

*areade, areede*: counsel, tell, teach, decide

*assay*: (v) attempt, test; (n) attack, attempt, tribulation

*bale*: evil, woe

*bene*: are

*bewray*: reveal, expose

*careful*: dutiful, sorrowful, full of care

*cast, casten*: throw, consider, decide, plan

*compasse*: (v) plan, devise, accomplish; (n) circumference, proportion; *in compasse*: all round

*corpse*: body

*degree*: rank, order, grade

*despight*: anger, outrage, scorn, ill-will

*dight* (v): adorn, clothe, compose, prepare; (past participle): dressed

*doom(e)* (n): judgment, opinion, sentence of punishment

*earst, erst*: formerly, in the (recent) past; *at erst*: at once, at length

*eft*: after, afterward

*eftsoones*: afterward, forthwith

*eke*: also

*faine*: (adj) glad, well-pleased; (adv) gladly, willingly, eagerly

*fell* (adj): fierce, cruel, destructive, terrible

*fon*: fool

*fond*: foolish, credulous; *fondly*: foolishly

*for thy*: for this reason, therefore

*frame*: (v) fashion, prepare, perform, express; (n) structure, order

*gentle*: noble, well-bred, courteous, mild, kind

*hew, hue*: form, appearance, color

*hight* (v): call, mention, be called; (past participle): named

*ken, can, kenst*: know, recognize

*kind, kynd*: nature, species

*kindly*: (adj) natural, benevolent, proper; (adv): naturally, fittingly

*list*: wish, desire

*meed(e)*: reward, recompense

*meet*: fitting, suitable

*mote*: might

*nathelesse*: nevertheless, notwithstanding

*ne*: not, nor

*pain(e)*: difficulty, suffering, punishment

*passing* (adj): surpassing

*pleasance*: enjoyment, pleasure, delight, courtesy

*plight* (n): situation, condition

*quite, quight*: entirely, completely

*read(e), rede* (v): say, counsel, see, understand, read

*ruth*: compassion

*.s.*: Lat. *scilicet*, that is to say, namely

*sicker*: (adj) secure; (adv) without doubt

*sike*: such

*silly, seely*: helpless, innocent, simple, humble

*sith, sithens, sithence*: since, continuously

*skill*: (v) understand; (n) art, ability, understanding

*spill*: destroy, kill

*spright, sprite*: spirit

*store*: quantity, abundance, accumulation

*stound*: time, time of pain, violent noise

*stoure*: conflict, time of turmoil and stress

*straight, streight* (adv): immediately, without delay

*thilke*: this

*then/than*: are frequently not distinguished by spelling

*tho*: then, that, those

*uneath, uneth, unneath*: difficult, with difficulty

*virtue*: virtue, chastity, courage, power

*ween(e)*: think, believe

*whilome*: in past time, formerly, once upon a time

*wight*: person, creature

*wit*: intelligence, intellectual ability, a learned or clever person

*wont*: (v) to be accustomed to; (adj) accustomed to

# Edmund Spenser: Chronology

**?1554**
Birth, probably in London.

**1558**
Accession of Elizabeth I.

**?–1569**
Attends Merchant Taylor's School in London. Richard
Mulcaster, humanist and scholar, is headmaster.

**1569**
Publication of *Theatre for Worldlings* with Sp's translations.
Enters Pembroke Hall, Cambridge, as a sizar (poor stu-
dent); BA 1573; MA 1576.

**1578**
Employed by John Young, bishop of Rochester (formerly
master of Pembroke Hall).

**1579**
Sp in London by July. Employed in an unknown capacity by
the earl of Leicester. National concern over the possibility
of the queen's marriage to the French Catholic duc
D'Alençon.
Oct. 27. An Edmounde Spenser (most likely the poet) mar-
ries Machabyas Childe at St. Margaret's, Westminster.
Dec. 5. *The Shepheardes Calender* entered on the Stationers'
Register.

**1580**
Publication of the Spenser-Harvey correspondence in which
Harvey mentions having sent back "your *Faerie Queene*."

Sp leaves England as secretary to Lord Grey, governor general of Ireland; probably arrives with Lord Grey in Ireland 12 Aug. Will stay in Ireland for the next eighteen years, making occasional trips to England, and gaining various appointments in the English administration of Ireland; eventually (1589; formal grant 1590) acquires Kilcolman Castle, with an estate of 3,000 acres in Munster, which he undertakes to "plant" with English immigrants.

1582

Lord Grey recalled to England in August.

1586

Death of Sir Philip Sidney at Zutphen.

1588

Defeat of the Spanish Armada; death of the earl of Leicester.

1589

In Oct. Sp accompanies Sir Walter Ralegh to England.

Dec. 1. Ponsonby enters *The Faerie Queene* I–III on the Stationers' Register.

1590

Dec. 29. *Complaints* entered on Stationers' Register.

1591

?Publication of *Daphnaida* (dedication dated 1 January 1591).

Feb. 25. Sp receives an annual life pension of £50.

Dec. 27. Dedicatory epistle of *Colin Clouts Come Home Againe* to Sir Walter Ralegh.

1592

In July the queen discovers Ralegh's secret marriage to Elizabeth Throckmorton and imprisons him. Ralegh is eventually barred from court.

?1594

Sp marries Elizabeth Boyle on Midsummer's Day.

Nov. 19. *Amoretti and Epithalamion* entered on Stationers' Register.

1595
Publication of *Colin Clouts Come Home Againe* and *Astrophel*.

1596
Publication of *The Faerie Queene* IV–VI, *Fowre Hymnes*, and *Prothalamion*. Sp possibly in London.

1598
Sept. 30. Privy council recommends Sp for Sheriff of Cork.
Oct. Irish rebellion in Leinster spreads to Munster. Kilcolman burned.
On Dec. 24 Sp returns to England with dispatches for the privy council from Sir John Norris.

1599
Jan. 13. Sp dies. Essex pays the cost of the funeral.

1603
Death of Elizabeth I.

1609
Publication of *The Faerie Queene* with the *Cantos of Mutabilitie*.

1611
Publication of *The Faerie Queene: The Shepheards Calendar: Together with the other Works of England's Arch-Poët, Edm. Spenser.*

# The Shepheardes Calender

# THE
## Shepheardes Calender

Conteyning twelue Æglogues proportionable
to the twelue monethes.

*by E. K.*

*Entitled*
## TO THE NOBLE AND VERTV-
*ous Gentleman most worthy of all titles*
both of learning and cheualrie M.
Philip Sidney.

(∴)

AT LONDON.
*Printed by Hugh Singleton, dwelling in*
Creede Lane neere vnto Ludgate at the
figne of the gylden Tunne, and
are there to be folde.
1579.

# The Shepheardes Calender

For the culture of the Renaissance the most celebrated poet was Virgil, who had risen from modest birth to become the epic voice of the Augustan empire and the emperor's own protégé. In the lines opening the *Aeneid* in Renaissance editions readers found Virgil's summary of his poetic career from pastoral through georgic to epic. This sequence of genres coupled with Virgil's success made his career a canonical model for poets who aspired to a national role. Petrarch's laurel crown from the city of Rome in 1341, coupled with his mirroring of Virgil in Latin pastorals and epic, gave the career pattern credibility as an ongoing model. As the lines beginning *The Faerie Queene* make evident, Edmund Spenser saw his career in a Virgilian light, for they are a close adaptation of Virgil's: his "Muse whilome did maske,/As time her taught, in lowly Shepheardes weeds," but he now turns from humble pastoral to ambitious epic. So imperative is this model for Spenser that, although we know the names of poems he had already written by 1579, he publishes none before his *Calender* and none after until three books of his epic are in print.

The title Spenser chose for his pastorals serves two functions. In one sense it means "the announcement of the shepherd" (Gk *kalein*, announce) and so heralds his taking up the Virgilian role. But to organize a series of eclogues (as poems in a pastoral series are called) by a calendar design and to subordinate his speakers to the exigencies of the seasons is Spenser's innovation, with the result a structurally more intricate yet more unified pastoral sequence than Virgil's or any other previous poet's.

Pastoral is essentially literature of stasis. When something happens in pastoral it is verbal: a debate, an improvised song. When action impinges on pastoral, it is either recounted (as in the fable of the oak and briar in *Februarie*) or foretold (as with Colin's change of role in *October*). The only acts that take place in the *Calender's* present are Colin's pipe-breaking in *Januarye* and his death in *December*. Sitting and rising formulas intermittently remind us of its sedentary character. Even the immediate needs of sheep-rearing seldom affect the present of eclogue except as a concluding formula. In fact, Spenser exploits pastoral's static character to achieve a subtle variety. Stasis in the first four eclogues, for instance, modulates from Colin's frustration to the implacable opposition of *iuventus* and *senectus* to the sharing of sexual ignorance to the permanent lay praising an iconic, motionless Eliza. But this modulation does not imply progress: readers who try to find subliminal narrative development in the affair of Colin and Rosalind only betray their discomfort with the genre. *December* confirms the *Calender's* static nature for, in both form and subject, it mirrors *Januarye*. In *December* Colin's situation as poet and lover is the same as in the first eclogue; now clearly subordinate to the annual cycle, he prepares to die with the dying year. But, by making *December* recapitulate *Januarye*, Spenser also hints that the annual cycle is about to begin again. In fact, *December* is exactly twice as long as *Januarye*, suggesting that it potentially holds the succeeding January inside itself. As the concluding envoy declares, the poem is a "Calender for every yeare" (line 1). The inexorable repetitiveness inherent in the calendar design is thus a structural reflection of the pastoral stasis.

In spite of the stasis of pastoral, the *Calender* does not turn its back on the events of the great world. Even in Virgil's first eclogue two attitudes are apparent. Tityrus can enjoy an idyllic shepherd life of *otium* (leisure), nurturing his flock and in a beech's shade singing of Amaryllis. But Meliboeus, homeless and wandering, is an incidental victim of war's aftermath. Even Tityrus's *otium* is at some great man's pleasure. This capacity of pastoral to deploy the shepherd metaphor for comment on major events developed further during the Middle Ages: for the biblical image of good and bad shepherds invited pastoral allegory of church affairs. Petrarch's *Bucolicum Carmen* brought harsh satire to this allegory, and when the *Eclogues* (1486, properly *Adolescentia*) of Baptista Mantuanus became a school text they entrenched the didactic use of pastoral to criticize church and society. Under the influence of Patrick Cullen (1970) recent discussions of pastoral now use "Arcadian" and "Mantuanesque" to distinguish these idyllic and critical strains. In the *Calender* their interplay is everywhere. The three ecclesiastical eclogues are heavily Mantuanesque, though not entirely so, and none of the dominantly Arcadian eclogues (except perhaps *March* and *November*) is entirely without implicit comment on state affairs. If, as Paul McLane (1961) has argued, Rosalind's coldness to Colin reflects royal plans in 1579 for a French marriage, then all eclogues involving her share some Mantuanesque elements. In fact, the *Calender*, as Helen Cooper (1977) demonstrates, is heir to and includes features from the whole range of ancient, medieval, and Renaissance pastoral.

A glance at the physical arrangements of the *Calender* will show that only about half of it is poems. First, there is the introductory epistle and general argument by "E. K." Then for each eclogue there is a woodcut followed by E. K.'s brief "argument" or summary, the poem itself, one or more appropriate verbal tags ("emblems"), and finally E. K.'s gloss or explanatory notes.

Each woodcut shows the month's zodiacal sign and depicts the poem's scenario, often in medieval serial form. Thus in *Februarie* a shepherd and a neatherd debate while the farmer cuts down the oak and a bullock already tramples the briar. But sometimes the woodcut adds new features that aptly extend the eclogue's meaning: in *Januarye* Colin breaks his oaten pipe which in the woodcut becomes a broken bagpipe symbolic of male desire; in *October* Piers wears the laurel crown of the triumphant poet, supplying an apposite touch that the text does not have. These sensitive additions suggest that Spenser himself took some part in specifying the woodcut program.

E. K.'s arguments and glosses are a different matter indeed.

These should aim to assist the reader, but often seem to confuse, mislead, or misinform. Some arguments, as in *Februarie* and *Julye*, take up sides in debates which the poems themselves are at pains to keep unresolved, while others summarize with fair accuracy. E. K.'s glosses, however, raise unhelpful assistance to a new power. Some glosses of hard words are accurate and still useful, some are of common words Elizabethans certainly knew (e.g. "fon"), some need no gloss even today ("Belte," "Embellisht" in *Februarie*). A few seem reverse glosses designed to obfuscate an ordinary word with its Latin equivalent, as in *Januarye's* "Neighbour towne) the next towne: expressing the Latine Vicina." More conspicuous are long pedantic glosses displaying irrelevant and often inaccurate classical learning. But why should Spenser want glosses for his poem and why of so curious a sort?

One reason for the physical phenomenon of the gloss per se, irrespective of its character, was to make the eclogues of the New Poet look like those of the ancient and some Renaissance pastoralists: Virgil's eclogues had a venerable gloss by Servius, Petrarch's by Benevenuto da Imola, Mantuan's by Badius Ascensius. S. K. Heninger (1988) argues that the whole layout of the *Calender* deliberately imitated an edition of Jacopo Sannazzaro's *Arcadia* (Venice, 1571) for which Francesco Sansovino prepared glosses, woodcuts, and other paraphernalia. Some playful typography extends the *Calender's* implied claim to status as an instant classic: for the poems are printed in the neo-Gothic black letter used to lend a look of antiquity in the Tudor Chaucer folios, while the surrounding apparatus uses a modern Italian typeface, so that the New Poet appears as venerable (and as important) as the Old Poet.

But none of the previous annotators glosses so obtusely as does E. K.—which necessarily raises the question of his identity. The old proposal that E. K. is one Edwarde Kirke, a Cambridge contemporary of Spenser, seems to go nowhere through lack of information. The suggestion that E. K. is a Spenser persona has at least two bits of evidence in its favor: the transla-

Ianuarye. **Fol.1**

## Ægloga prima.

### ARGVMENT.

I N *this fyrſt Æglogue* Colin cloute *a ſhepheardes boy complaineth him
of his vnfortunate loue, being but newly (as ſemeth) enamoured of a coun-
trie laſſe called* Roſalinde: *with which ſtrong affection being very ſore tra-
ueled, he compareth his carefull caſe to the ſadde ſeaſon of the yeare, to the
froſtie ground, to the froſen trees, and to his owne winterbeaten flocke. And
laſtlye , ſynding himſelfe robbed of all former pleaſaunce and delights, hee
breaketh his Pipe in peeces, and caſteth him ſelfe to the ground.*

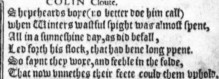

### COLIN Cloute.

A Shepheards boye (no better doe him call)
when Winters waſtful ſpight was almoſt ſpent,
All in a ſunneſhine day, as did befall,
Led forth his flock, that had bene long ypent.
So faynt they woxe, and feeble in the folde,
That now vnnethes their feete could them vphold.

All as the Sheepe, ſuch was the ſhepheards looke,
For pale and wanne he was, (alas the while,)
May ſeeme he lovd, or els ſome care he tooke:
Well couth he tune his pipe, and frame his ſtile.

A.I.

Tho

## *June.*

And thou *Menalcas*, that by trecheree
Didst vnderfong my lasse, to were so light,
Shouldest well be knowne for such thy villanee.

But since I am not, as I wish I were,
Ye gentle shepheards, which your flocks do feede,
Whether on hylls, or dales, or other where,
Beare witnesse all of thys so wicked deede:
And tell the lasse, whose flowre is woxe a weede,
And faultlesse fayth, is turned to faithlesse fere,
That she the truest shepheards hart made bleede,
That lyues on earth, and loued her most dere.

### HOBBINOL.

O carefull *Colin*, I lament thy case,
Thy teares would make the hardest flint to flowe.
Ah faithlesse Rosalind, and voide of grace,
That art the roote of all this ruthfull woe.
But now is time, I gesse, homeward to goe:
Then ryse ye blessed flocks, and home apace,
Least night with stealing steppes do: you forsloe,
And wett your tender Lambes, that by you trace.

Colins Embleme.

*Gia speme spenta.*

#### GLOSSE.

Syte) situation and place.

Paradise) A Paradise in Greeke signifieth a Garden of pleasure, or place of delights. So he compareth the soile, vvherin Hobbinoll made his abode, to that earthly Paradise, in scripture called Eden; vvherein Adam in his first creation vvas placed. VVhich of the most learned is thought to be in Mesopotamia, the most fertile and pleasaunte country in the vvorld (as may appeare by Diodorus Syculus description of it, in the hystorie of Alexanders conquest thereof.) Lying betweene the two famous Ryuers (which are sayd in scripture to flovve out of Paradise) Tygris and Euphrates, vvhereof it is so denominate.

Forsake the soyle) This is no poeticall fiction, but vnfeynedly spoken of the Poete selfe, who for speciall occasion of priuate affayres (as I haue bene partly of himselfe
informed)

tion of Cicero in the *Maye* gloss on "Tho with them" is the same as in the first of Spenser's *Three Proper Letters* to Gabriel Harvey (1580); and the obvious mistake of "Persephone" for Tisiphone in the *November* gloss on "Furies" is repeated in *Teares of the Muses* (164). S. K. Heninger (1988) has reintroduced the argument for Spenser's Cambridge associate Gabriel Harvey, who writes not only to launch his friend as poet but to also to draw attention to himself and thus further his hopes of a role at court. (Harvey's work gets fulsome praise in the apparatus). One wonders, however, whether Spenser, hoping for recognition as the English Virgil, would let major parts of his first production escape his control. It seems in fact possible that both he and Harvey had some role in producing the glosses.

In any case, the glossed *Calender* seems less curious when put in the context of Renaissance books like More's *Utopia* and Erasmus's *Praise of Folly*, playfully ironic exercises in the tradition of Lucian which force the reader to adapt and maintain a vigilantly defensive querying posture toward the text. Sidney's *Apology for Poetry* shares this ironic mode, and in *The Faerie Queene* Spenser often similarly deploys his narrator so as to keep the reader on guard. In the *Calender* he may be playfully using the accoutrements of an edition to the same effect. Indeed, an inquiring reader of the poem will learn through experience the meaning of the dictum in Renaissance literary theory that poetry must not only delight but teach. And the best teaching is not didactic but heuristic. One is tempted to see the reader's role in each eclogue as a metaphor for man's spiritual situation: above, the orienting zodiacal sign of the heavens and the lucid revelation of the woodcut; below, the invitation to wander offered by an *advocatus diaboli*. This parallels the knightly quests in *The Faerie Queene* where the questers, illuminated by the virtues of Gloriana, must find their way through a tricky milieu of temptations and perplexing signs.

In 1549 Joachim Du Bellay had published *La Deffence et Illustration de la Langue Françoyse*, the virtual manifesto of the Pléiade poets. The *Calender* performs a similar function.

Spenser sets out to prove that English, after a period of linguistic upheaval and poetic barrenness, has now become a medium capable of poetry like that of Renaissance Italy and France. Hence the determination to demonstrate as many stanza forms as possible, three of them in *August* alone. Significantly the most demanding forms (as well as the most intricate overall structures) are in those eclogues concerning the poet's role, the least demanding in the ecclesiastical eclogues.

The *Calender* did indeed inaugurate the New Poetry of England's Renaissance and in a recognized way: there were five quarto editions in the poet's lifetime. After a long critical dormancy it has once again begun to excite the perceptions of late twentieth-century readers.

Thomas H. Cain

# Using The Notes

Although E. K.'s glossing is clearly part of the text of *The Shepheardes Calender*, its presence somewhat complicates the process of using the notes. In this edition the notes are of three kinds.

First, there are the editor's notes to each poem, indicated in the usual manner by the number of the line to which reference is made.

Second, there are those glosses by E. K. that are accurate and still clear, most of them of single words. In these cases the editor has avoided double annotation by letting the original glosses do the job. Thus a reader seeking annotation for any part of the poem should first look for an editor's note and, if there is none, then look among E. K.'s glosses. Preceding each gloss there is a bracketed number, e.g. [4], indicating the line of the poem to which the gloss refers. Note, however, that E. K.'s glosses are sometimes slightly out of order: in *Januarye*, for instance, the gloss on line 61 precedes that on line 60.

Third, there are the editor's notes on E. K.'s glosses themselves. These notes are indicated by one or two bracketed numbers, e.g. [4.5], the first to indicate the number of the gloss referred to, and the second (when it occurs) to indicate the number of the prose line in the gloss that the note refers to. When the gloss occupies only one line or less, there is no second number.

11

# To His Booke.

Goe little booke: thy selfe present,
As child whose parent is unkent:
To him that is the president
Of noblesse and of chevalree,
And if that Envie barke at thee,       5
As sure it will, for succoure flee
    Under the shadow of his wing,
And asked, who thee forth did bring,
A shepheards swaine saye did thee sing,
All as his straying flocke he fedde:      10
And when his honor has thee redde,
Crave pardon for my hardyhedde.
    But if that any aske thy name,
Say thou wert base begot with blame:
For thy thereof thou takest shame.      15
And when thou art past jeopardee,
Come tell me, what was sayd of mee:
And I will send more after thee.

                         *Immeritô.*

This is the only example in Sp's works of eight-syllable lines rhyming in triplets.    1. *Goe little booke*: an envoy or "send-off" poem in the tradition of Chaucer's "Go litel bok, go litel myn tragedye" (*Troilus* 5.1786) which here does double duty as a dedication to Philip Sidney.    2. *unkent*: unknown.    3. *president*: Sidney as the ideal courtier, presiding over and also being the model (precedent) of the aristocratic virtues.    5. *barke*: A barking dog was a common image of envy, the destructive response to worthy achievement which was apparently a special anxiety of Sp's; cf. *FQ* I iv 32.    10. *All as*: while.    12. *hardyhedde*: boldness.    16. *jeopardee*: Because of its religious and political criticisms, the publication of *SC* entailed risks.    19. *Immeritô*: he who is unworthy. Sp is nowhere identified as author in the poem.

*To the most excellent and learned both*
Orator and Poete, Mayster Gabriell Harvey, his
Verie special and singular good frend E. K. commen-
deth the good lyking of this his labour,
and the patronage of the
new Poete.

($\because$)

Uncouthe unkiste, Sayde the olde famous Poete
Chaucer: whom for his excellencie and wonder-
full skil in making, his scholler Lidgate, a worthy
scholler of so excellent a maister, calleth the Loadestarre of
our Language: and whom our Colin clout in his Æglogue      5
calleth Tityrus the God of shepheards, comparing hym to
the worthines of the Roman Tityrus Virgile. Which
proverbe, myne owne good friend Ma. Harvey, as in that
good old Poete it served well Pandares purpose, for the
bolstering of his baudy brocage, so very well taketh place   10
in this our new Poete, who for that he is uncouthe (as said
Chaucer) is unkist, and unknown to most men, is regarded
but of few. But I dout not, so soone as his name shall come
into the knowledg of men, and his worthines be sounded
in the tromp of fame, but that he shall be not onely kiste,   15
but also beloved of all, embraced of the most, and won-
dred at of the best. No lesse I thinke, deserveth his wit-
tinesse in devising, his pithinesse in uttering, his com-
plaints of love so lovely, his discourses of pleasure so
pleasantly, his pastorall rudenesse, his morall wisenesse,   20
his dewe observing of Decorum everye where, in person-

---

1. *UNCOUTHE, UNKISTE*: unknown, so not kissed. Chaucer's "Unknowe,
unkist" (*Troilus* 1.809).      10. *brocage*: pimping.      20. *rudenesse*: homely,
unlearned utterance.

ages, in seasons, in matter, in speach, and generally in al
seemely simplycitie of handeling his matter, and framing
his words: the which of many thinges which in him be
straunge, I know will seeme the straungest, the words          25
them selves being so auncient, the knitting of them so
short and intricate, and the whole Periode and compasse
of speache so delightsome for the roundnesse, and so
grave for the straungenesse. And firste of the wordes to
speake, I graunt they be something hard, and of most men    30
unused, yet both English, and also used of most excellent
Authors and most famous Poetes. In whom whenas this
our Poet hath bene much traveiled and throughly redd,
how could it be, (as that worthy Oratour sayde) but that
walking in the sonne although for other cause he walked,    35
yet needes he mought be sunburnt; and having the sound
of those auncient Poetes still ringing in his eares, he
mought needes in singing hit out some of theyr tunes. But
whether he useth them by such casualtye and custome, or
of set purpose and choyse, as thinking them fittest for such   40
rusticall rudenesse of shepheards, eyther for that theyr
rough sounde would make his rymes more ragged and
rustical, or els because such olde and obsolete wordes are
most used of country folke, sure I think, and think I think
not amisse, that they bring great grace and, as one would    45
say, auctoritie to the verse. For albe amongst many other
faultes it specially be objected of Valla against Livie, and of
other against Saluste, that with over much studie they
affect antiquitie, as coveting thereby credence and honor
of elder yeeres, yet I am of opinion, and eke the best        50
learned are of the lyke, that those auncient solemne

31. English: E. K.'s extended defense of Sp's archaisms is to the point, since
it was to this feature that Sidney and Jonson objected.       34. *Oratour*:
Cicero, *De Oratore* 2.14.60.       39. *casualtye*: chance, accident.       47. *Valla*:
Laurentius Valla (c.1407–57), Italian humanist known for his careful
scrutiny of ancient texts and his standards for Latin prose style. *Livie*: Titus
Livius (Livy), Roman historian (59 B.C.–A.D. 17).       48. *Saluste*: Caius
Sallustius Crispus (Sallust), Roman historian (86–c.34 B.C.)

wordes are a great ornament both in the one and in the
other; the one labouring to set forth in hys worke an
eternall image of antiquitie, and the other carefully dis-
coursing matters of gravitie and importaunce. For if my          55
memory fayle not, Tullie in that booke, wherein he en-
devoureth to set forth the paterne of a perfect Oratour,
sayth that ofttimes an auncient worde maketh the style
seeme grave, and as it were reverend: no otherwise then
we honour and reverence gray heares for a certein re-             60
ligious regard, which we have of old age. yet nether every
where must old words be stuffed in, nor the commen
Dialecte and maner of speaking so corrupted therby, that
as in old buildings it seme disorderly and ruinous. But all
as in most exquisite pictures they use to blaze and portraict    65
not onely the daintie lineaments of beautye, but also
rounde about it to shadow the rude thickets and craggy
clifts, that by the basenesse of such parts, more excellency
may accrew to the principall; for oftimes we fynde our-
selves, I knowe not how, singularly delighted with the           70
shewe of such naturall rudenesse, and take great pleasure
in that disorderly order. Even so doe those rough and
harsh termes enlumine and make more clearly to appeare
the brightnesse of brave and glorious words. So ofentimes
a dischorde in Musick maketh a comely concordaunce: so           75
great delight tooke the worthy Poete Alceus to behold a
blemish in the joint of a wel shaped body. But if any will

---

56. *Tullie*: Marcus Tullius Cicero (106–43 B.C.), the famous Roman
rhetorician and senator, commonly referred to as Tully in the Renaissance
where his style was regarded as the model for neo-Latin prose.
57. *Oratour*: Cicero's *De Oratore* 3.38.153 and *Orator* 23.80, his other
treatise on rhetoric, together approximate what E. K. remembers.     61. *old*
*age. yet*: the punctuation here is a medial period, a curiosity of Elizabethan
practice typographically distinct from the black-letter period of the Epistle
and not followed by a capital letter. Here and elsewhere in E. K.'s
commentary it signals a rhetorical pause.     64. *all*: just.     65. *blaze*:
proclaim.     74. *brave*: splendid, showy.     76. *Alceus*: Greek lyric poet
(c.620–580 B.C.) but E. K. is citing Cicero, *De Natura Deorum* 1.28.79.

rashly blame such his purpose in choyse of old and un-
wonted words, him may I more justly blame and con-
demne, or of witlesse headinesse in judging, or of      80
heedelesse hardinesse in condemning. for not marking the
compasse of hys bent, he wil judge of the length of his cast.
for in my opinion it is one special prayse, of many whych
are dew to this Poete, that he hath laboured to restore, as
to theyr rightfull heritage such good and naturall English    85
words, as have ben long time out of use and almost cleare
disherited. Which is the onely cause, that our Mother
tonge, which truely of it self is both ful enough for prose
and stately enough for verse, hath long time ben counted
most bare and barrein of both. which default when as    90
some endevoured to salve and recure, they patched up the
holes with peces and rags of other languages, borrowing
here of the french, there of the Italian, every wherc of the
Latine, not weighing how il, those tongues accorde with
themselves, but much worse with ours: So now they have    95
made our English tongue, a gallimaufray or hodgepodge
of al other speches. Other some not so wel seene in the
English tonge as perhaps in other languages, if them hap-
pen to here an olde word albeit very naturall and signifi-
cant, crye out streight way, that we speak no English, but    100
gibbrish, or rather such, as in old time Evanders mother
spake. whose first shame is, that they are not ashamed, in
their own mother tonge straungers to be counted and
alienes. The second shame no lesse then the first, that what
so they understand not, they streight way deeme to be    105
sencelesse, and not at al to be understode. Much like to the
Mole in Æsopes fable, that being blynd her selfe, would in

80. *or*: either.    81. *hardinesse*: rudeness.    81–82. *not . . . cast*: without
noting where (an archer) aimed, the observer will criticize how far he shot.
101. *Evanders mother*: Evander had come to Rome from the wilds of Arcadia
long before Aeneas (*Aen* 8.51–54); his mother, according to Aulus Gellius,
(*Noctes Atticae* 1.10.2), spoke in archaisms.

no wise be perswaded, that any beast could see. The last
more shameful then both, that of their owne country and
natural speach, which together with their Nources milk    110
they sucked, they have so base regard and bastard judge-
ment, that they will not onely themselves not labor to
garnish and beautifie it, but also repine, that of other it
shold be embellished. Like to the dogge in the maunger,
that him selfe can eate no hay, and yet barketh at the    115
hungry bullock, that so faine would feede: whose currish
kind though cannot be kept from barking, yet I conne
them thanke that they refrain from byting.

Now for the knitting of sentences, whych they call the
joynts and members therof, and for al the compasse of the    120
speach, it is round without roughnesse, and learned wy-
thout hardnes, such indeede as may be perceived of the
leaste, understoode of the moste, but judged onely of the
learned. For what in most English wryters useth to be
loose, and as it were ungyrt, in this Authour is well    125
grounded, finely framed, and strongly trussed up to-
gether. In regard whereof, I scorne and spue out the
rakehellye route of our ragged rymers (for so themselves
use to hunt the letter) which without learning boste, with-
out judgement jangle, without reason rage and fome, as if    130
some instinct of Poeticall spirite had newly ravished them
above the meanenesse of commen capacitie. And being in
the middest of all theyr bravery, sodenly either for wont of
matter, or of ryme, or having forgotten theyr former con-
ceipt, they seeme to be so pained and traveiled in theyr    135
remembrance, as it were a woman in childebirth or as that
same Pythia, when the traunce came upon her.

Os rabidum fera corda domans etc.

128. *rakehellye*: rascally.    129. *hunt the letter*: i.e. alliterate.    134. *conceipt*:
train of thought.    137. *Pythia*: the Cumaean Sibyl compelled by Apollo to
prophecy to Aeneas as the Latin line says, "mastering her raving mouth and
fierce heart," *Aen* 6.80.

Nethelesse let them a Gods name feede on theyr owne
folly, so they seeke not to darken the beames of others       140
glory. As for Colin, under whose person the Authour selfe
is shadowed, how furre he is from such vaunted titles and
glorious showes, both him selfe sheweth, where he sayth.

Of Muses Hobbin.   I conne no skill.      And,
Enough is me to paint out my unrest, etc.                      145

And also appeareth by the basenesse of the name,
wherein, it semeth, he chose rather to unfold great matter
of argument covertly, then professing it, not suffice there-
to accordingly. which moved him rather in Æglogues,
then other wise to write, doubting perhaps his habilitie,     150
which he little needed, or mynding to furnish our tongue
with this kinde, wherein it faulteth, or following the exam-
ple of the best and most auncient Poetes, which devised
this kind of wryting, being both so base for the matter, and
homely for the manner, at the first to trye theyr habilities:  155
and as young birdes, that be newly crept out of the nest, by
little first to prove theyr tender wyngs, before they make a
greater flyght. So flew Theocritus, as you may perceive he
was all ready full fledged. So flew Virgile, as not yet well
feeling his winges. So flew Mantuane, as being not full      160
somd. So Petrarque. So Boccace; So Marot, Sanazarus,
and also divers other excellent both Italian and French
Poetes, whose foting this Author every where followeth,

144–45. See *June* below, lines 65 and 79.        158. *Theocritus*: Greek poet
(c.310–250 B.C.) who initiated literary pastoral with his *Idylls*.
160. *Mantuane*: Baptista Spagnuoli (1448–1511), usually called Mantuan,
famed for his ten satirical and moral eclogues. *full somd*: fully fledged.
161. *Petrarque*: Francesco Petrarca (1304–74) wrote twelve satirical Latin
eclogues. *Boccace*: Giovanni Boccaccio (1313–75) wrote sixteen Latin
eclogues. *Marot*: Clément Marot (1496–1544) wrote two French eclogues
imitated by Sp. *Sanazarus*: Jacopo Sannazzaro (1456–1530) wrote the
romantic prose and verse pastoral *Arcadia* and several Latin *Eclogae Piscatoriae*
with fishermen substituted for shepherds.

yet so as few, but they be wel sented can trace him out. So
finally flyeth this our new Poete, as a bird, whose princi-  165
pals be scarce growen out, but yet as that in time shall be
hable to keepe wing with the best.

Now as touching the generall dryft and purpose of his
Æglogues, I mind not to say much, him selfe labouring to
conceale it. Onely this appeareth, that his unstayed yougth  170
had long wandred in the common Labyrinth of Love, in
which time to mitigate and allay the heate of his passion,
or els to warne (as he sayth) the young shepheards .s. his
equalls and companions of his unfortunate folly, he com-
piled these xii. Æglogues, which for that they be propor-  175
tioned to the state of the xii. monethes, he termeth the
SHEPHEARDS CALENDAR, applying an olde name
to a new worke. Hereunto have I added a certain Glosse or
scholion for thexposition of old wordes and harder
phrases: which maner of glosing and commenting, well I  180
wote, wil seeme straunge and rare in our tongue: yet for
somuch as I knew many excellent and proper devises both
in wordes and matter would passe in the speedy course of
reading, either as unknowen, or as not marked, and that in
this kind, as in other we might be equal to the learned of  185
other nations, I thought good to take the paines upon me,
the rather for that by meanes of some familiar acquain-
taunce I was made privie to his counsell and secret mean-
ing in them, as also in sundry other works of his. which
albeit I know he nothing so much hateth, as to promul-  190
gate, yet thus much have I adventured upon his frendship,
him selfe being for long time furre estraunged, hoping
that this will the rather occasion him, to put forth divers
other excellent works of his, which slepe in silence, as his
Dreames, his Legendes, his Court of Cupide, and sondry  195

---

165–66. *principals*: primary feathers.    177. *olde name*: *The Calendar of
Shepherds*, a homely almanac of astrological and miscellaneous lore, reprinted
throughout the sixteenth century.    195. The poems named are lost.

others; whose commendations to set out, were verye vayne; the thinges though worthy of many, yet being knowen to few. These my present paynes if to any they be pleasurable or profitable, be you judge, mine own good Maister Harvey, to whom I have both in respect of your    200
worthinesse generally, and otherwyse upon some particular and special considerations voued this my labour, and the maydenhead of this our commen frends Poetrie, himselfe having already in the beginning dedicated it to the Noble and worthy Gentleman, the right worshipfull Ma.    205
Phi. Sidney, a special favourer and maintainer of all kind of learning, Whose cause I pray you Sir, yf Envie shall stur up any wrongful accusasion, defend with your mighty Rhetorick and other your rare gifts of learning, as you can, and shield with your good wil, as you ought, against the malice    210
and outrage of so many enemies, as I know wilbe set on fire with the sparks of his kindled glory. And thus recommending the Author unto you, as unto his most special good frend, and my selfe unto you both, as one making singuler account of two so very good and so choise frends,    215
I bid you both most hartely farwel, and commit you and your most commendable studies to the tuicion of the greatest.

> *Your owne assuredly to*
> *be commaunded* E. K.                220

*Post scr.*

Now I trust M. Harvey, that upon sight of your speciall frends and fellow Poets doings, or els for envie of so many unworthy Quidams, which catch at the garlond, which to you alone is dewe, you will    225

224. *Quidams*: so-and-sos, nonentities.

be perswaded to pluck out of the hateful darknesse, those
so many excellent English poemes of yours, which lye hid,
and bring them forth to eternall light. Trust me you doe
both them great wrong, in depriving them of the desired
sonne, and also your selfe, in smoothering your deserved     230
prayses, and all men generally, in withholding from them
so divine pleasures, which they might conceive of your
gallant English verses, as they have already doen of your
Latine Poemes, which in my opinion both for invention
and Elocution are very delicate, and superexcellent. And     235
thus againe, I take my leave of my good Mayster Harvey.
from my lodging at London thys 10. of Aprill. 1579.

# *The generall argument of*
the whole booke.

Little I hope, needeth me at large to discourse the
first Originall of Æglogues, having alreadie
touched the same. But for the word Æglogues I
know is unknowen to most, and also mistaken of some the
best learned (as they think) I wyll say somewhat thereof,      5
being not at all impertinent to my present purpose.

They were first of the Greekes the inventours of them
called Æglogai as it were αἴγον or αἰγονόμων. λόγοι. that
is Goteheards tales. or although in Virgile and others the
speakers be more shepheards, then Goteheards, yet The-      10
ocritus in whom is more ground of authoritie, then in
Virgile, this specially from that deriving, as from the first
head and welspring the whole Invencion of his Æglogues,
maketh Goteheards the persons and authors of his tales.
This being, who seeth not the grossenesse of such as by      15
colour of learning would make us beleeve that they are
more rightly termed Eclogai, as they would say, extraordi-
nary discourses of unnecessarie matter, which difinition
albe in substaunce and meaning it agree with the nature of
the thing, yet nowhit answereth with the ἀνάλυσις and      20
interpretation of the word. For they be not termed
Eclogues, but Æglogues. which sentence this authour
very well observing, upon good judgement, though in-
deede few Goteheards have to doe herein, nethelesse
doubteth not to cal them by the used and best knowen      25
name. Other curious discourses hereof I reserve to greater
occasion. These xii. Æclogues every where answering to
the seasons of the twelve monthes may be well devided

8. αἴγον . . . λόγοι: Gk *aigon* or *aigonomon logoi*, "goats'" or "goatherds'
speeches," a false etymology developed in the Middle Ages and resulting in
the common Renaissance spelling "aeglogue." Eclogue actually means "a
selection" (Gk *eklegein*, to choose).      16. *colour*: pretense.      22. *sentence*:
opinion.

into three formes orranckes. For eyther they be Plaintive,
as the first, the sixt, the eleventh, and the twelfth, or recre-    30
ative, such as all those be, which conceive matter of love,
or commendation of special personages, or Moral: which
for the most part be mixed with some Satyrical bitternesse,
namely the second of reverence dewe to old age, the fift
of coloured deceipt, the seventh and ninth of dissolute    35
shepheards and pastours, the tenth of contempt of Poetrie
and pleasaunt wits. And to this division may every thing
herein be reasonably applyed: A few onely except, whose
speciall purpose and meaning I am not privie to. And thus
much generally of these xii. Æclogues. Now will we    40
speake particularly of all, and first of the first. which he
calleth by the first monethes name Januarie: wherein to
some he may seeme fowly to have faulted, in that he er-
roniously beginneth with that moneth, which beginneth
not the yeare. For it is wel known, and stoutely main-    45
teyned with stronge reasons of the learned, that the yeare
beginneth in March. for then the sonne reneweth his fin-
ished course, and the seasonable spring refresheth the
earth, and the pleasaunce thereof being buried in the sad-
nesse of the dead winter now worne away, reliveth. This    50
opinion maynteine the olde Astrologers and Philoso-
phers, namely the reverend Andalo, and Macrobius in his
holydayes of Saturne, which accoumpt also was generally
observed both of Grecians and Romans. But saving the
leave of such learned heads, we mayntaine a custome of    55
coumpting the seasons from the moneth January, upon a
more speciall cause, then the heathen Philosophers ever
coulde conceive, that is, for the incarnation of our mighty
Saviour and eternall redeemer the L. Christ, who as then
renewing the state of the decayed world, and returning the    60
compasse of expired yeres to theyr former date and first

52. *Andalo*: Andalo di Negro (fl. 1330), who taught Boccaccio astronomy.
*Macrobius*: late Latin author (fl. 400) from whose comments on the calendar
in *Saturnalia* E. K. borrows heavily here.

commencement, left to us his heires a memoriall of his
birth in the ende of the last yeere and beginning of the
next. which reckoning, beside that eternall monument of
our salvation, leaneth also uppon good proofe of special     65
judgement. For albeit that in elder times, when as yet the
coumpt of the yere was not perfected, as afterwarde it was
by Julius Cæsar, they began to tel the monethes from
Marches beginning, and according to the same God (as is
sayd in Scripture) comaunded the people of the Jewes to      70
count the moneth Abib, that which we call March, for the
first moneth, in remembraunce that in that moneth he
brought them out of the land of Ægipt: yet according to
tradition of latter times it hath bene otherwise observed,
both in government of the church, and rule of Mightiest      75
Realmes. For from Julius Cæsar who first observed the
leape yeere which he called Bissextilem Annum, and
brought in to a more certain course the odde wandring
dayes which of the Greekes were called ὑπερβαίνοντες.
of the Romaines intercalares (for in such matter of learn-   80
ing I am forced to use the termes of the learned) the
monethes have bene nombred xii. which in the first ordi-
naunce of Romulus were but tenne, counting but CCCiiii.
dayes in every yeare, and beginning with March. But
Numa Pompilius, who was the father of al the Romain        85
ceremonies and religion, seeing that reckoning to agree
neither with the course of the sonne, nor of the Moone,
thereunto added two monethes, January and February:
wherin it seemeth, that wise king minded upon good rea-
son to begin the yeare at Januarie, of him therefore so      90
called tanquam Janua anni the gate and entraunce of the
yere, or of the name of the god Janus, to which god for
that the old Paynims attributed the byrth and beginning of
all creatures new comming into the world, it seemeth that

70. *Scripture*: Exodus 12 and 13.     84–85. *Numa Pompilius*: early Roman
king and lawgiver (715–672 B.C.).

he therfore to him assigned the beginning and first en-    95
traunce of the yeare. which account for the most part hath
hetherto continued. Notwithstanding that the Ægiptians
beginne theyr yeare at September, for that according to
the opinion of the best Rabbins, and very purpose of the
scripture selfe, God made the worlde in that Moneth, that    100
is called of them Tisri. And therefore he commaunded
them, to keepe the feast of Pavilions in the end of the
yeare, in the xv. day of the seventh moneth, which before
that time was the first.

But our Authour respecting nether the subtiltie of    105
thone parte, nor the antiquitie of thother, thinketh it fit-
test according to the simplicitie of commen understand-
ing, to begin with Januarie, wening it perhaps no de-
corum, that Shepheard should be seene in matter of so
deepe insight, or canvase a case of so doubtful judgment.    110
So therefore beginneth he, and so continueth he
throughout.

---

102. *Pavilions*: Leviticus 23.34.

# Januarye

This eclogue begins the *Calender* with pastoral in an apparently pure and simple Arcadian expression, the rejected lover's complaint made conventional by Virgil's second *Eclogue* where Corydon, a naive rustic, bewails his rejection by the boy Alexis. His situation approximates Colin's with Rosalind but only broadly. For Corydon expresses his unhappiness, then recognizes the pointlessness of his suit and decides to look elsewhere. Colin has no such emotional practicality. Instead, Spenser has couched his complaint in the Petrarchan sonneteering terms of the lover who, his beloved once seen, becomes trapped in a set of opposed emotions. Colin complains "that love should breede both joy and payne" (54) and can both "curse that carefull hower" (49) and "blesse the stoure" (51) when he saw Rosalind. This Petrarchan coloration allows Spenser to express in a fresh way the stasis intrinsic to pastoral.

He also modifies here the town-and-country motif of pastoral and countrified fable (as in the tale of the two mice). In its conventional form, which Spenser adapts for *September* from Mantuan's ninth *Eclogue*, a shepherd's trip to town gives him a new appreciation of the simple rustic life. But Colin's visit to "the neighbour towne" (50) has instead left him frustrated with the low estate of the shepherd's world and the limitations inherent in the pastoral poet's role. Scorning "rude Pan" (67), he fecklessly breaks his pipe to abjure that role. In the woodcut his back is turned to his sheep, his gaze is fixed on the townscape, and at his feet lies not the "oaten pype" (72) of the text but the bagpipe that in medieval iconography symbolized male desire and which here implies a connection between eroticism and the poet's creativity.

It is easy to take Colin's querulousness too seriously. Indeed, the voice of the frame-speaker, with his recognition that "Winters wastful spight was almost spent" (2) and that Colin is acting "halfe in despight" (76), serves to put in perspective the self-indulgent seasonal analogies and adolescent pipe-breaking. And Colin's emblem implies at least that modicum of hope available to the Petrarchan lover. This distancing hints that the pastoral phase, though confining, is temporary—a necessary stage the would-be poet of the state must pass through.

As one reads through the *Calender*, the seeming simplicity of *Januarye* begins to look in retrospect like a base line against which the poet can register his experiments in the pastoral mode, for in the succeeding eclogues he tests the limits of both Arcadian and Mantuanesque pastoral. Not till *December* does Spenser resume, though now from a changed perspective, the manner of his first eclogue.

The stanza form of *Januarye*, repeated in *December*, is the *Calender's* least adventuresome: the favorite Elizabethan stanza of quatrain and couplet with three rhymes: *ababcc*.

# *Januarye.*

*Ægloga prima.*

## ARGUMENT.

*I*N *this fyrst Æglogue* Colin cloute *a shepheardes boy complaineth him of his unfortunate love, being but newly (as semeth) enamoured of a countrie lasse called* Rosalinde: *with which strong affection being very sore traveled, he compareth his carefull case to the sadde season of the yeare, to the frostie ground, to the frosen trees, and to his owne winterbeaten flocke. And lastlye, fynding himselfe robbed of all former pleasaunce and delights, hee breaketh his Pipe in peeces, and casteth him selfe to the ground.*

              C O L I N Cloute.

A Shepeheards boye (no better doe him call)
When Winters wastful spight was almost spent,
All in a sunneshine day, as did befall,

---

A R G U M E N T. *countrie lasse*: compare "neighbour towne" (line 50).
*traveled*: travailed, burdened. *Pipe*: the panpipe or "oaten reed," symbol of
poetic composition or "song" in Theocritus and Virgil.

Led forth his flock, that had bene long ypent.
So faynt they woxe, and feeble in the folde,     5
That now unnethes their feete could them uphold.

All as the Sheepe, such was the shepeheards looke,
For pale and wanne he was, (alas the while,)
May seeme he lovd, or els some care he tooke:
Well couth he tune his pipe, and frame his stile.     10
Tho to a hill his faynting flocke he ledde,
And thus him playnd, the while his shepe there fedde.

Ye Gods of love, that pitie lovers payne,
(If any gods the paine of lovers pitie:)
Looke from above, where you in joyes remaine,     15
And bowe your eares unto my dolefull dittie.
And *Pan* thou shepheards God, that once didst love,
Pitie the paines, that thou thy selfe didst prove.

Thou barrein ground, whome winters wrath hath

                             wasted,
Art made a myrrhour, to behold my plight:     20
Whilome thy fresh spring flowrd, and after hasted
Thy sommer prowde with Daffadillies dight.
And now is come thy wynters stormy state,
Thy mantle mard, wherein thou maskedst late.

Such rage as winters, reigneth in my heart,     25
My life bloud friesing with unkindly cold:
Such stormy stoures do breede my balefull smart,
As if my yeare were wast, and woxen old.
And yet alas, but now my spring begonne,
And yet alas, yt is already donne.     30

4. *ypent*: penned up.    5. *woxe*: grew.    9. *care*: anxiety.    10. *frame his stile*: compose a poem.    11. *Tho*: then.    12. *playnd*: complained.
17. *Pan*: for his frequent erotic adventures, see Ovid, *Met*, e.g. 1.689–712.    18. *prove*: experience.    26. *unkindly*: unnatural.    27. *stoures*: upheavals, crises. *balefull smart*: painful pain (the rhetorical figure pleonasm).

You naked trees, whose shady leaves are lost,
Wherein the byrds were wont to build their bowre:
And now are clothd with mosse and hoary frost,
Instede of bloosmes, wherwith your buds did flowre:
I see your teares, that from your boughes doe raine,         35
Whose drops in drery ysicles remaine.

All so my lustfull leafe is drye and sere,
My timely buds with wayling all are wasted:
The blossome, which my braunch of youth did beare,
With breathed sighes is blowne away, and blasted,         40
And from mine eyes the drizling teares descend,
As on your boughes the ysicles depend.

Thou feeble flocke, whose fleece is rough and rent,
Whose knees are weake through fast and evill fare:
Mayst witnesse well by thy ill governement,         45
Thy maysters mind is overcome with care.
Thou weake, I wanne: thou leane, I quite forlorne:
With mourning pyne I, you with pyning mourne.

A thousand sithes I curse that carefull hower,
Wherein I longd the neighbour towne to see:         50
And eke tenne thousand sithes I blesse the stoure,
Wherein I sawe so fayre a sight, as shee.
Yet all for naught: such sight hath bred my bane.
Ah God, that love should breede both joy and payne.

It is not *Hobbinol*, wherefore I plaine,         55
Albee my love he seeke with dayly suit:
His clownish gifts and curtsies I disdaine,
His kiddes, his cracknelles, and his early fruit.
Ah foolish *Hobbinol*, thy gyfts bene vayne:
*Colin* them gives to *Rosalind* againe.         60

---

42. *depend*: hang down.    45. *ill governement*: poor care.    55. *Hobbinol*:
Gabriel Harvey, Sp's Cambridge associate.    57. *clownish*: rustic.
58. *cracknelles*: a kind of biscuit.

I love thilke lasse, (alas why doe I love?)
And am forlorne, (alas why am I lorne?)
Shee deignes not my good will, but doth reprove,
And of my rurall musick holdeth scorne.
Shepheards devise she hateth as the snake,          65
And laughes the songes, that *Colin Clout* doth make.

Wherefore my pype, albee rude *Pan* thou please,
Yet for thou pleasest not, where most I would:
And thou unlucky Muse, that wontst to ease
My musing mynd, yet canst not, when thou should:     70
Both pype and Muse, shall sore the while abye.
So broke his oaten pype, and downe dyd lye.

By that, the welked *Phœbus* gan availe,
His weary waine, and nowe the frosty *Night*
Her mantle black through heaven gan overhaile.      75
Which seene, the pensife boy halfe in despight
Arose, and homeward drove his sonned sheepe,
Whose hanging heads did seeme his carefull case to
                                             weepe.

Colins Embleme.

*Anchôra Speme.*                                    80

G L O S S E.

[1]   C O L I N Cloute) is a name not greatly used, and yet
       have I sene a Poesie of M. Skeltons under that title. But

62. *lorne*: left.       65. *devise*: song, speech, perhaps also appearance.
66. *make*: compose.       71. *the while abye*: ambiguous: pay for the time or
pay for a while.       72. *oaten pype*: Lat. *avena* means both oats and panpipe;
see *October* woodcut.       73. *welked*: faded.       74. *waine*: wagon, a homely
version of the sun god's chariot.       80. *Anchora Speme*: "still [there is] hope"
(Ital.), with pun on "anchor," the traditional symbol of hope; see *FQ* I x 14.

[1.2] *Skeltons*: John Skelton's *Colin Cloute* (1529) lampooned Cardinal
Wolsey.

indeede the word Colin is Frenche, and used of the
French Poete Marot (if he be worthy of the name of a
Poete) in a certein Æglogue. Under which name this
Poete secretly shadoweth himself, as sometime did Virgil
under the name of Tityrus, thinking it much fitter, then
such Latine names, for the great unlikelyhoode of the
language.

[6]  unnethes) scarcely.

[10]  couthe) commeth of the verbe Conne, that is, to know
or to have skill. As well interpreteth the same the worthy
Sir Tho. Smitth in his booke of goverment: wherof I
have a perfect copie in wryting, lent me by his kinseman,
and my verye singular good freend, M. Gabriel Harvey:
as also of some other his most grave and excellent
wrytings.

[49]  Sythe) time.

[50]  Neighbour towne) the next towne: expressing the
Latine Vicina.

[51]  Stoure) a fitt.   [37] Sere) withered.   [57] His
clownish gyfts) imitateth Virgils verse, Rusticus es
Corydon, nec munera curat Alexis.

[59]  Hobbinol) is a fained country name, whereby, it being
so commune and usuall, seemeth to be hidden the
person of some his very speciall and most familiar
freend, whom he entirely and extraordinarily beloved, as
peradventure shall be more largely declared hereafter. In
thys place seemeth to be some savour of disorderly love,

---

[1.4] *Marot*: Colin appears in Clément Marot's *Eclogue de Mme Loyse de
Savoye*, imitated in *November*.   [1.8] *unlikelyhoode*: conventional Lat.
(actually, usually Gk) pastoral names inconsistent with *SC's* often rustic
English.   [10.3] *Smitth*: Sir Thomas Smith whose *De Republica Anglorum*
(1556) was not published till 1581, so E. K. must have read it in MS. In
1570 Smith helped Gabriel Harvey get his fellowship at Pembroke Hall in
Cambridge; Harvey's *Smithus* (1578) was a Latin elegy on him.
[57.2] *Rusticus . . . Alexis*: "Corydon, you are a yokel, and Alexis doesn't take
to gifts."

which the learned call pæderastice: but it is gathered
beside his meaning. For who that hath red Plato his
dialogue called Alcybiades, Xenophon and Maximus
Tyrius of Socrates opinions, may easily perceive, that
such love is muche to be alowed and liked of, specially
so meant, as Socrates used it: who sayth, that in deede
he loved Alcybiades extremely, yet not Alcybiades
person, but hys soule, which is Alcybiades owne selfe.
And so is pæderastice much to be præferred before
gynerastice, that is the love whiche enflameth men with
lust toward woman kind. But yet let no man thinke, that
herein I stand with Lucian or hys develish disciple
Unico Aretino, in defence of execrable and horrible
sinnes of forbidden and unlawful fleshlinesse. Whose
abominable errour is fully confuted of Perionius, and
others.

[61] I love) a prety Epanorthosis in these two verses, and
withall a Paronomasia or playing with the word, where
he sayth (I love thilke lasse (alas etc.

[60] Rosalinde) is also a feigned name, which being wel
ordered, wil bewray the very name of hys love and
mistresse, whom by that name he coloureth. So as Ovide
shadoweth hys love under the name of Corynna, which
of some is supposed to be Julia, themperor Augustus his

[59.7] *pæderastice*: loving boys, male homosexual.    [59.7–8] *gathered . . .
meaning*: not the author's meaning.    [59.8–10] *Plato . . . opinions*: Cf.
Plato's *Alcibiades* 1.131 and Xenophon's *Symposium* 8.    [59.16] *gynerastice*:
loving women.    [59.18] *Lucian*: Greek author (c. 115–c.200) of ironic
but not notably salacious dialogues and fantasies. He was studied and
imitated by More and Erasmus, but was sometimes denounced in the
sixteenth century for his amoral detachment. In 1578 Sp wagered Harvey for
a four-volume edition of Lucian.    [59.19] *Aretino*: Pietro Aretino (1492–
1556), notorious for pornographic dialogues and comedies; much read in
Cambridge according to Harvey.    [59.21] *Perionius*: Joachim Périon
(1499?–1559), Benedictine humanist. E. K. apparently refers to his attack on
Aretino, *In Petrum Aretinum Oratio* (Paris, 1551).    [60.4] *Corynna*: Ovid,

daughter, and wyfe to Agryppa. So doth Aruntius Stella every where call his Lady Asteris and Ianthis, albe it is wel knowen that her right name was Violantilla: as witnesseth Statius in his Epithalamium. And so the famous Paragone of Italy, Madonna Cœlia in her letters envelopeth her selfe under the name of Zima: and Petrona under the name of Bellochia. And this generally hath bene a common custome of counterfeicting the names of secret Personages.

[73] Avail) bring downe.
[75] Overhaile) drawe over.

### Embleme.

His Embleme or Poesye is here under added in Italian,
Anchôra speme: the meaning wherof is, that
notwithstande his extreme passion and lucklesse love,
yet leaning on hope, he is some what recomforted.

*Amores* 1.5, 11; 2.12, 13, 17.    [60.6] *Aruntius Stella* . . .: Statius, *Epithalamium Stellae et Violentillae* in *Silvae* 1.2.197–98.
[60.10] *Madonna Coelia*: author of *Lettre Amorose* (Venice, 1562).
[60.12] *Petrona*: unidentified.

# *Februarie*

This eclogue is in two complementary sections, each an adaptation of an old form. The first exploits the static nature of the medieval poetic debate (*conflictus*), usually between two matched polar entities like the flower and the leaf, the owl and the nightingale, or, as here, youth and age (the well-worn *puer-senex* motif). The fable which balances the debate and which, as E.K. notes, is in the tradition not of Chaucer but of Aesop, is an instance of the only mode of introducing narrative into the pastoral stasis—i.e. by a shepherd's recounting events that took place somewhere else.

The debate begins when Thenot converts Cuddie's innocuous complaint about the weather into the basic man/season analogy of the *Calender* which Cuddie then applies to flocks and trees. Implicit in the debate is a series of natural contraries: spring and winter, cheerfulness and dourness, sexual vigor and aged resignation—and also contrasted superficialities: Cuddie's brash inexperience against Thenot's facile wisdom belied by too ready recourse to aphorism. Cuddie's outlook is cheerfully and simply Arcadian: "to caroll of Love" (61) and win Phyllis with gifts are enough to justify his existence. Thenot expresses his crabbed philosophy of endurance in a way that guarantees Cuddie's resistance, but it also implies, as the younger shepherd discerns, an element of envy, the urge to destroy what one can't have—in this case, "springing youngth to spil" (52): "Now thy selfe hast lost both lopp and topp/ Als my budding braunch thou wouldest cropp" (57–58). These lines hint at the subliminal presence behind the debate of the old man who cannot die except vicariously through the deaths of the young—the sinister old man of *The Pardoner's Tale* who becomes Spenser's figure of Despayre.

The mere mention of the name of the poet Tityrus, however, seems for a moment to resolve the debate and produce social harmony: Thenot learned the tale "in my youth" (92) and Cuddie applauds the wisdom of "that good old man" (97). But when the tale turns out to be an exemplum to support Thenot's argument, Cuddie cuts off its sententious moral and the impasse resumes. Nothing has changed. The eclogue ends with a depressed wintry version of the pastoral formula of closure.

The fable that balances the debate should translate Thenot's position into narrative, but in some ways it is instead an inversion of the debate. The aggressive briar instigates the situation, but in the debate this function is Thenot's and, unlike the oak, he is far from being speechless. It is the old man who would "spil" Cuddie's youth, while it is the young briar that undoes the ancient oak. Insofar as the fable's action is designed to alter the stalemate of the debate by giving Thenot points, it has no effect, except as an ironic rejoinder to Cuddie's "lopp and topp" metaphor, and does not really "applie" (100): Cuddie may scorn "Eld" but not because he is "Ambitious" (237–38). (Interestingly, the fable's central line [123], though spoken by Thenot, is in praise of the bird of love song, the nightingale.) At the same time the fable obviously does "applie" to the dangerous milieu of Elizabethan political and religious life, though exactly how is no longer clear. It may simply be a broad allegory of competition for power at court, or it may allude to a specific set of events like the displacement of the Roman church by Elizabeth's Religious Settlement. There have been several proposals but no critical consensus.

The irregular and rather free-wheeling verse form uses lines of eight to ten syllables rhymed in couplets. The ease of finding four stresses per line, these often on alliterations, makes it likely that Spenser meant to recall the old four-stress alliterative system (as in *Piers Plowman*) and so insinuate an old-fashioned rusticity.

# Februarie

*Ægloga Secunda.*

## ARGUMENT.

THis Æglogue is rather morall and generall, then bent to any
secrete or particular purpose. It specially conteyneth a discourse of
old age, in the persone of Thenot an olde Shepheard, who for his
crookednesse and unlustinesse, is scorned of Cuddie an unhappy
Heardmans boye. The matter very well accordeth with the season of
the moneth, the yeare now drouping, and as it were, drawing to his
last age. For as in this time of yeare, so then in our bodies there is a dry
and withering cold, which congealeth the crudled blood, and frieseth
the wetherbeaten flesh, with stormes of Fortune, and hoare frosts of
Care. To which purpose the olde man telleth a tale of the Oake and
the Bryer, so lively and so feelingly, as if the thing were set forth in
some Picture before our eyes, more plainly could not appeare.

ARGUMENT *crudled*: curdled, thickened. *Picture*: The poem as a verbal
picture is a common theme in Renaissance poetics, summed up in the tag *ut
pictura poesis* from Horace, *Ars Poetica* 361.

CUDDIE. THENOT.

A H for pittie, wil rancke Winters rage,
These bitter blasts never ginne tasswage?
The kene cold blowes through my beaten hyde,
All as I were through the body gryde.
My ragged rontes all shiver and shake,                    5
As doen high Towers in an earthquake:
They wont in the wind wagge their wrigle tailes,
Perke as Peacock: but nowe it avales.

THENOT.

Lewdly complainest thou laesie ladde,
Of Winters wracke, for making thee sadde.                 10
Must not the world wend in his commun course
From good to badd, and from badde to worse,
From worse unto that is worst of all,
And then returne to his former fall?
Who will not suffer the stormy time,                      15
Where will he live tyll the lusty prime?
Selfe have I worne out thrise threttie yeares,
Some in much joy, many in many teares:
Yet never complained of cold nor heate,
Of Sommers flame, nor of Winters threat:                  20
Ne ever was to Fortune foeman,
But gently tooke, that ungently came.
And ever my flocke was my chiefe care,
Winter or Sommer they mought well fare.

CUDDIE.

No marveile *Thenot*, if thou can beare                   25
Cherefully the Winters wrathfull cheare:

---

7. *wrigle*: wriggling.    8. *nowe it avales*: "it" may mean the display of tails,
hence "now their tails droop," or the wind (line 7), hence "now the wind
drops"; but cf. lines 2–3.    11–16. Apparently a cyclical view of history to
reflect the yearly cycle.    14. *former fall*: the original fall (ME *forme*,
earliest), Adam and Eve's loss of Edenic perfection.    16. *prime*: spring.

For Age and Winter accord full nie,
This chill, that cold, this crooked, that wrye.
And as the lowring Wether lookes downe,
So semest thou like good fryday to frowne.                    30
But my flowring youth is foe to frost,
My shippe unwont in stormes to be tost.

#### THENOT.

The soveraigne of seas he blames in vaine,
That once seabeate, will to sea againe.
So loytring live you little heardgroomes,                     35
Keeping your beastes in the budded broomes:
And when the shining sunne laugheth once,
You deemen, the Spring is come attonce.
Tho gynne you, fond flyes, the cold to scorne,
And crowing in pypes made of greene corne,                    40
You thinken to be Lords of the yeare.
But eft, when ye count you freed from feare,
Comes the breme winter with chamfred browes,
Full of wrinckles and frostie furrowes:
Drerily shooting his stormy darte,                            45
Which cruddles the blood, and pricks the harte.
Then is your careless corage accoied,
Your carefull heards with cold bene annoied.
Then paye you the price of your surquedrie,
With weeping, and wayling, and misery.                        50

#### CUDDIE.

Ah foolish old man, I scorne thy skill,
That wouldest me, my springing youngth to spil.
I deeme, thy braine emperished bee
Through rusty elde, that hath rotted thee:
Or sicker thy head veray tottie is,                           55

28. *wrye*: awry, twisted.     30. *good fryday*: a fast day.     35–50. Expands
Mantuan, *Eclogues* 6.19–24.     36. *broomes*: a spring-flowering shrub.
49. *surquedrie*: arrogance, presumption.     51. *skill*: reasoning.     52. *spil*:
destroy, spoil.     55. *sicker*: surely. *veray tottie*: truly dizzy.

So on thy corbe shoulder it leanes amisse.
Now thy selfe hast lost both lopp and topp,
Als my budding braunch thou wouldest cropp:
But were thy yeares greene, as now bene myne,
To other delights they would encline.                      60
Tho wouldest thou learne to caroll of Love,
And hery with hymnes thy lasses glove.
Tho wouldest thou pype of *Phyllis* prayse:
But *Phyllis* is myne for many dayes:
I wonne her with a gyrdle of gelt,                          65
Embost with buegle about the belt.
Such an one shepeheards woulde make full faine:
Such an one would make thee younge againe.

### THENOT.

Thou art a fon, of thy love to boste,
All that is lent to love, wyll be lost.                     70

### CUDDIE.

Seest, howe brag yond Bullocke beares,
So smirke, so smoothe, his pricked eares?
His hornes bene as broade, as Rainebowe bent,
His dewelap as lythe, as lasse of Kent.
See howe he venteth into the wynd.                          75
Weenest of love is not his mynd?
Seemeth thy flocke thy counsell can,
So lustlesse bene they, so weake so wan,
Clothed with cold, and hoary wyth frost.
Thy flocks father his corage hath lost:                     80
Thy Ewes, that wont to have blowen bags,
Like wailefull widdowes hangen their crags:
The rather Lambes bene starved with cold,
All for their Maister is lustlesse and old.

57. *lopp*: small branches. Loss of "lopp" and "topp" implies a tree ready for
felling.      62. *hery*: praise.      65. *gyrdle of gelt*: golden waist-band.
67. *faine*: glad, eager.      71. *brag*: proudly.      72. *smirke*: neat. *pricked*:
pointed up.      76. *Weenest*: do you think.      80. *Thy . . . lost*: your ram has
lost his sexual drive.      81. *blowen bags*: full udders.

### THENOT.

*Cuddie*, I wote thou kenst little good,                        85
So vainely tadvaunce thy headlesse hood.
For Youngth is a bubble blown up with breath,
Whose witt is weakenesse, whose wage is death,
Whose way is wildernesse, whose ynne Penaunce,
And stoopegallaunt Age the hoste of Greevaunce.        90
But shall I tel thee a tale of truth,
Which I cond of *Tityrus* in my youth,
Keeping his sheepe on the hils of Kent?

### CUDDIE.

To nought more *Thenot*, my mind is bent,
Then to heare novells of his devise:                           95
They bene so well thewed, and so wise,
What ever that good old man bespake.

### THENOT.

Many meete tales of youth did he make,
And some of love, and some of chevalrie:
But none fitter then this to applie.                           100
Now listen a while, and hearken the end.

THere grewe an aged Tree on the greene,
A goodly Oake sometime had it bene,
With armes full strong and largely displayd,
But of their leaves they were disarayde:                       105
The bodie bigge, and mightely pight,
Throughly rooted, and of wonderous hight:
Whilome had bene the King of the field,

---

85. *kenst*: understand.      86. *headlesse hood*: empty hood, thus brainless.
87–90. Wandering followed by arrival at a house of instruction is a basic
narrative scheme in *FQ*.      88. *wage is death*: Romans 6.23: "the wages of
sin is death."      90. *stoopegallaunt*: that humbles the gallant; sometimes a
low door. *Greevaunce*: grief.      92. *cond*: learned. *Tityrus*: Chaucer, as in
*June*, line 81; but in *October*, "the Romish Tityrus" (55) is Virgil. The tale is
not by Chaucer but based on Aesop.      95. *novells*: Ital. *novelle*, tales. *of his
devise*: composed by him.      106. *pight*: set.

And mochell mast to the husband did yielde,
And with his nuts larded many swine. 110
But now the gray mosse marred his rine,
His bared boughes were beaten with stormes,
His toppe was bald, and wasted with wormes,
His honor decayed, his braunches sere.
    Hard by his side grewe a bragging brere, 115
Which proudly thrust into Thelement,
And seemed to threat the Firmament.
Yt was embellisht with blossomes fayre,
And thereto aye wonned to repayre
The shepheards daughters, to gather flowres, 120
To peinct their girlonds with his colowres.
And in his small bushes used to shrowde
The sweete Nightingale singing so lowde:
Which made this foolish Brere wexe so bold,
That on a time he cast him to scold, 125
And snebbe the good Oake, for he was old.
    Why standst there (quoth he) thou brutish blocke?
Nor for fruict, nor for shadowe serves thy stocke:
Seest, how fresh my flowers bene spredde,
Dyed in Lilly white, and Cremsin redde, 130
With Leaves engrained in lusty greene,
Colours meete to clothe a mayden Queene.
Thy wast bignes but combers the grownd,
And dirks the beauty of my blossomes rownd.
The mouldie mosse, which thee accloieth, 135
My Sinamon smell too much annoieth.
Wherefore soone I rede thee, hence remove,
Least thou the price of my displeasure prove.
So spake this bold brere with great disdaine:

---

109. *mochell mast*: many acorns. *husband*: farmer.    116. *Thelement*: the
air.    119. *wonned to repayre*: were accustomed to come.    126. *snebbe*:
reprove.    132. *Colours . . . Queene*: Elizabeth was heir to the Tudor union
of the red and white roses of Lancaster and York.    134. *dirks*: darkens.

Little him answered the Oake againe,                                    140
But yielded, with shame and greefe adawed,
That of a weede he was overcrawed.

  Yt chaunced after upon a day,
The Husbandman selfe to come that way,
Of custome for to servewe his grownd,                                   145
And his trees of state in compasse rownd.
Him when the spitefull brere had espyed,
Causlesse complained, and lowdly cryed
Unto his Lord, stirring up sterne strife:
O my liege Lord, the God of my life,                                    150
Pleaseth you ponder your Suppliants plaint,
Caused of wrong, and cruell constraint,
Which I your poore Vassall dayly endure:
And but your goodnes the same recure,
Am like for desperate doole to dye,                                     155
Through felonous force of mine enemie.

  Greatly aghast with this piteous plea,
Him rested the goodman on the lea,
And badde the Brere in his plaint proceede.
With painted words tho gan this proude weede,                           160
(As most usen Ambitious folke:)
His colowred crime with craft to cloke.

  Ah my soveraigne, Lord of creatures all,
Thou placer of plants both humble and tall,
Was not I planted of thine owne hand,                                   165
To be the primrose of all thy land,
With flowring blossomes, to furnish the prime,
And scarlot berries in Sommer time?
How falls it then, that this faded Oake,
Whose bodie is sere, whose braunches broke,                             170

---

142. *overcrawed*: exulted over. This is the reading of the third Quarto and
adopted by most editors. The first Quarto has "overawed."    151. *ponder*:
weigh.    155. *doole*: distress.    158. *Him*: himself.    160. *painted*:
deceitful.    162. *crime*: accusation.    163–65. Possibly hinting at the
new aristocracy created by the Tudors.    167. *prime*: spring.

Whose naked Armes stretch unto the fyre,
Unto such tyrannie doth aspire:
Hindering with his shade my lovely light,
And robbing me of the swete sonnes sight?
So beate his old boughes my tender side,                    175
That oft the bloud springeth from wounds wyde:
Untimely my flowres forced to fall,
That bene the honor of your Coronall.
And oft he lets his cancker wormes light
Upon my braunches, to worke me more spight:                180
And oft his hoarie locks downe doth cast,
Where with my fresh flowretts bene defast.
For this, and many more such outrage,
Craving your goodlihead to aswage
The ranckorous rigour of his might,                        185
Nought aske I, but onely to hold my right:
Submitting me to your good sufferance,
And praying to be garded from greevance.
    To this the Oake cast him to replie
Well as he couth: but his enemie                           190
Had kindled such coles of displeasure,
That the good man noulde stay his leasure,
But home him hasted with furious heate,
Encreasing his wrath with many a threate.
His harmefull Hatchet he hent in hand,                     195
(Alas, that it so ready should stand)
And to the field alone he speedeth.
(Ay little helpe to harme there needeth)
Anger nould let him speake to the tree,
Enaunter his rage mought cooled bee:                       200
But to the roote bent his sturdy stroke,
And made many wounds in the wast Oake.
The Axes edge did oft turne againe,

182. *defast*: defaced, spoiled.    187. *sufferance*: choice, decision.
190. *couth*: knew how to.    192. *noulde . . . leasure*: would not wait.

As halfe unwilling to cutte the graine:
Semed, the sencelesse yron dyd feare, 205
Or to wrong holy eld did forbeare.
For it had bene an auncient tree,
Sacred with many a mysteree,
And often crost with the priestes crewe,
And often halowed with holy water dewe. 210
But sike fancies weren foolerie,
And broughten this Oake to this miserye.
For nought mought they quitten him from decay:
For fiercely the good man at him did laye.
The blocke oft groned under the blow, 215
And sighed to see his neare overthrow.
In fine the steele had pierced his pitth,
Tho downe to the earth he fell forthwith:
His wonderous weight made the grounde to quake,
Thearth shronke under him, and seemed to shake. 220
There lyeth the Oake, pitied of none.
    Now stands the Brere like a Lord alone,
Puffed up with pryde and vaine pleasaunce:
But all this glee had no continuaunce.
For eftsones Winter gan to approche, 225
The blustring Boreas did encroche,
And beate upon the solitarie Brere:
For nowe no succoure was seene him nere.
Now gan he repent his pryde to late:
For naked left and disconsolate, 230
The byting frost nipt his stalke dead,
The watrie wette weighed downe his head,
And heaped snowe burdned him so sore,
That nowe upright he can stand no more:
And being downe, is trodde in the durt 235

206. *eld*: old age.     207–12. These lines associate the oak with traditional
Catholicism.     213. *quitten*: save. *decay*: destruction.     217. *In fine*: in
the end.

Of cattell, and brouzed, and sorely hurt.
Such was thend of this Ambitious brere,
For scorning Eld—

### CUDDIE.

Now I pray thee shepheard, tel it not forth:
Here is a long tale, and little worth.                            240
So longe have I listened to thy speche,
That graffed to the ground is my breche:
My hartblood is welnigh frorne I feele,
And my galage growne fast to my heele:
But little ease of thy lewd tale I tasted.                        245
Hye thee home shepheard, the day is nigh wasted.


Thenots Embleme.

*Iddio perche è vecchio,*
*Fa suoi al suo essempio.*


Cuddies Embleme.                                                   250

*Niuno vecchio,*
*Spaventa Iddio .*


### GLOSSE.

[3]    Kene) sharpe.
[4]    Gride) perced: an olde word much used of Lidgate,
       but not found (that I know of) in Chaucer.
[5]    Ronts) young bullockes.
[10]   Wracke) ruine or Violence, whence commeth
       shipwracke: and not wreake, that is vengeaunce or
       wrath.
[21]   Foeman) a foe.


236. *brouzed*: browsed on.    242. *graffed*: grafted. *breche*: breeches.
248–49. *Iddio . . . essempio*: "Because God is an old man, take him for
example" (Ital.).    251–52. *Niuno . . . Iddio*: "No old man fears God"
(Ital.).

[25]   Thenot) the name of a shepheard in Marot his
       Æglogues.

[33]   The soveraigne of Seas) is Neptune the God of the
       seas. The saying is borowed of Mimus Publianus,
       which used this proverb in a verse.
       Improbè Neptunum accusat, qui iterum naufragium
       facit.

[35]   Heardgromes) Chaucers verse almost whole.

[39]   Fond Flyes) He compareth carelesse sluggardes
       or ill husbandmen to flyes, that so soone as the
       sunne shineth, or yt wexeth any thing warme,
       begin to flye abroade, when sodeinly they be
       overtaken with cold.

[42]   But eft when) A verye excellent and lively
       description of Winter, so as may bee indifferently
       taken, eyther for old Age, or for Winter season.

[43]   Breme) chill, bitter.   [43] Chamfred) chapt, or
       wrinckled.

[47]   Accoied) plucked downe and daunted.
       [49] Surquedrie) pryde.

[54]   Elde) olde age.   [55] Sicker) sure.   [55] Tottie)
       wavering.

[56]   Corbe) crooked.   [62] Herie) worshippe.

[63]   Phyllis) the name of some mayde unknowen,
       whom Cuddie, whose person is secrete, loved.
       The name is usuall in Theocritus, Virgile, and
       Mantuane.

[66]   Belte) a girdle or wast band.   [69] A fon) a
       foole.   [74] lythe) soft and gentile.

---

[25] *Thenot*: in Marot's *Eclogue de Mme Loyse de Savoye*.     [33.2] Mimus
Publianus: The *Sententiae* or proverbs of Publius (Publilius) Syrus were
edited by Erasmus as *Mimi Publiani* (*Opuscula Aliquot*, Basel, 1514).
[33.4–5] *Improbe . . . facit*: "He who is shipwrecked twice should not blame
Neptune."     [35] *Chaucers verse*: *House of Fame*, 1224–26.
[63.3] *Phyllis*: not used by Theocritus.

[75] Venteth) snuffeth in the wind.  [80] Thy flocks Father) the Ramme. [82] Crags) neckes.

[83] Rather Lambes) that be ewed early in the beginning of the yeare.

[87] Youth is) A verye moral and pitthy Allegorie of youth, and the lustes thereof, compared to a wearie wayfaring man.

[92] Tityrus) I suppose he meane Chaucer, whose prayse for pleasaunt tales cannot dye, so long as the memorie of hys name shal live, and the name of Poetrie shal endure.

[96] Well thewed) that is, Bene moratæ, full of morall wisenesse.

[102] There grew) This tale of the Oake and the Brere, he telleth as learned of Chaucer, but it is cleane in another kind, and rather like to Æsopes fables. It is very excellente for pleasaunt descriptions, being altogether a certaine Icon or Hypotyposis of disdainfull younkers.

[118] Embellisht) beautified and adorned.  [119] To wonne) to haunt or frequent.  [126] Sneb) checke.

[127] Why standst) The speach is scorneful and very presumptuous.  [131] Engrained) dyed in grain.

[135] Accloieth) encombreth.  [141] Adawed) daunted and confounded.

[146] Trees of state) taller trees fitte for timber wood. [149] Sterne strife) said Chaucer .s. fell and sturdy.  [150] O my liege) A maner of supplication, wherein is kindly coloured the affection and speache of Ambitious men.

[96] *Well thewed*: like *Bene moratæ*, means "of good character"; E. K.'s reading produces tautology.  [102.5] *Icon or Hypotyposis*: picture or type.  [149] *said Chaucer*: the beginning of the pseudo-Chaucerian *Plowman's Tale*, accepted as Chaucer's by his Tudor editors.

[178] Coronall) Garlande.  [182] Flourets) young
blossomes.

[166] The Primrose) The chiefe and worthiest.

[171] Naked armes) metaphorically ment of the bare
boughes, spoyled of leaves. This colourably he
speaketh, as adjudging hym to the fyre.

[176] The blood) spoken of a blocke, as it were of a
living creature, figuratively, and (as they saye)
κατ' εἰκασμόν.

[181] Hoarie lockes) metaphorically for withered
leaves.

[195] Hent) caught.  [199] Nould) for would not.
[198] Ay) evermore.

[202] Wounds) gashes.  [200] Enaunter) least that.

[209] The priestes crewe) holy water pott, wherewith
the popishe priest used to sprinckle and hallowe
the trees from mischaunce. Such blindnesse was
in those times, which the Poete supposeth, to
have bene the finall decay of this auncient Oake.

[215] The blocke oft groned) A livelye figure, whiche
geveth sence and feeling to unsensible creatures,
as Virgile also sayeth: Saxa gemunt gravido etc.

[226] Boreas) The Northerne wynd, that bringeth the
moste stormie weather.

[224] Glee) chere and jollitie.

[238] For scorning Eld) And minding (as shoulde
seme) to have made ryme to the former verse, he
is conningly cutte of by Cuddye, as disdayning to
here any more.

[244] Galage) a startuppe or clownish shoe.

---

[176.3] κατ' εἰκασμόν: Gk *kat' eikasmon*, as a comparison.
[215.2–3] *Virgile also sayeth*: not in Virgil. *Saxa gemunt gravido*: "the stones
groaned at the heavy blow."

Embleme.

This embleme is spoken of Thenot, as a moral of his
former tale: namelye, that God, which is himselfe most
aged, being before al ages, and without beginninge,
maketh those, whom he loveth like to himselfe, in
heaping yeares unto theyre dayes, and blessing them
wyth longe lyfe. For the blessing of age is not given to
all, but unto those, whome God will so blesse: and
albeit that many evil men reache unto such fulnesse of
yeares, and some also wexe olde in myserie and
thraldome, yet therefore is not age ever the lesse
blessing. For even to such evill men such number of
yeares is added, that they may in their last dayes repent,
and come to their first home. So the old man checketh
the rashheaded boy, for despysing his gray and frostye
heares. Whom Cuddye doth counterbuff with a byting
and bitter proverbe, spoken indeede at the first in
contempt of old age generally. for it was an old opinion,
and yet is continued in some mens conceipt, that men of
yeares have no feare of god at al, or not so much as
younger folke. For that being rypened with long
experience, and having passed many bitter brunts and
blastes of vengeaunce, they dread no stormes of
Fortune, nor wrathe of Gods, nor daunger of menne, as
being eyther by longe and ripe wisedome armed against
all mischaunces and adversitie, or with much trouble
hardened against all troublesome tydes: lyke unto the
Ape, of which is sayd in Æsops fables, that oftentimes
meeting the Lyon, he was at first sore aghast and
dismayed at the grimnes and austeritie of hys
countenance, but at last being acquainted with his
lookes, he was so furre from fearing him, that he would
familiarly gybe and jest with him: Suche longe

[Embleme. 30] *Erasmus*: not in his *Adagia*.

experience breedeth in some men securitie. Although it
please Erasmus a great clerke and good old father, more
fatherly and favourablye to construe it in his Adages for
his own behoofe, That by the proverbe Nemo Senex
metuit Jovem, is not meant, that old men have no feare
of God at al, but that they be furre from superstition
and Idolatrous regard of false Gods, as is Jupiter. But
his greate learning notwithstanding, it is to plaine, to be
gainsayd, that olde men are muche more enclined to
such fond fooleries, then younger heades.

# *March*

ᘒᕼᕼᘒᕼᕼᘒᕼᕼᘒᕼᕼᘒᕼᕼᘒᕼᕼᘒ

After *Februarie's* brush with death, *March* gives a delightful vignette of befuddled pubescence, deftly adjusted to the earliest beginnings of spring, as Willye and Thomalin compare their information about Cupid. The rollicking verse form accommodates this situation to the ear and makes it difficult for us to take the eclogue very seriously. Spenser borrowed the stanza, sometimes called tail rhyme or *rime couée*, from Chaucer's romance parody *Sir Thopas* which the host cuts short because its "rym doggerel" hurts his ears.

The structure of the eclogue is notable. Two parts of equal length balance on a three-line fulcrum touching on past and future, with the center line ("That is to come, let be forecast," [59]) looking toward the new season and growth in knowledge of love.

The dialogue of the first section is in the goliardic tradition of *Floret silva* ("the woods are blooming"), the medieval student songs that move from celebration of springing shoots to search for sexual adventures. Willye proposes, now the hawthorn is budding, that they awake Cupid to "leaden our daunce" (24), apparently with little sense of what that dance might entail. Like a true adolescent Thomalin lays claim to better knowledge—the "previe marks" (35) or secret signs that reveal Cupid.

In the second section Thomalin's story of what happened when he went hunting for birds expands *Idyll* 4 of the Greek pastoralist Bion where a boy bird-catcher sees a big bird but can't net him, only to be told by his old mentor to avoid that bird: it will come by itself all too soon. (Spenser knew perhaps not the Greek text but likely the Latin translation of Angelo Poliziano and the French paraphrase by Ronsard.) Bion's boy is very young. Spenser transfers the bird-catching situation to the stage of intrigued but mixed awareness about sex and combines it with the adolescent need to know-it-all among peers. But Thomalin eventually realizes that Cupid is the hunter not the hunted (there is an underlying pun between Latin *venator*, hunter, and Venus, as well as the same ambivalence in Chaucer's word *venerye*), and that his wound—the traditional sign of love's onset—is increasingly rankling. The Petrarchan way from the wound of Cupid leads either to Cuddie's winning Phyllis or Colin's impasse with Rosalind—an erotic sequence in reverse if one looks backward over the first three eclogues.

The first forty-two lines of each section match descriptions of the awakening year and the discovery of Cupid. And the last fifteen lines of each section also correspond. The news of the "wanton" ewe that can't be restrained in the first (44–57) balances Willye's account in the second (104–17) of his father's catching Cupid in a crow net: wandering lust set against Cupid restrained. But the pronominal confusions in the latter passage make it unclear whether father or Cupid will be avenged on the other. In fact, the pear tree recalls the scene of adultery in *The Merchant's Tale*, and, this being the month of Mars, the netting of Cupid hints at Vulcan's mode of trapping the adulterous Mars and Venus. These, along with Willye's "stepdame whott as fyre" (41), suggest that the wayward ewe and Willye's family situation may have something in common and point to complex workings of Cupid that these young shepherds have barely begun to sense. There are two ways for adolescents to learn about sexual love: by experience and by hearsay. Thomalin's Cupid story involves the first, Willye's the second, but both lead here only to bemused comprehension. Note how in the woodcut the two stories are balanced.

# March.

*Ægloga Tertia.*

## ARGUMENT

IN this Æglogue two shepheards boyes taking occasion of the season,
beginne to make purpose of love and other plesaunce, which to
springtime is most agreeable. The speciall meaning hereof is, to give
certaine markes and tokens, to know Cupide the Poets God of Love.
But more particularlye I thinke, in the person of Thomalin is meant
some secrete freend, who scorned Love and his knights so long, till at
length him selfe was entangled, and unwares wounded with the dart
of some beautifull regard, which is Cupides arrowe.

WILLYE     THOMALIN.

THomalin, why sytten we soe,
  As weren overwent with woe,
   Upon so fayre a morow?
The joyous time now nigheth fast,

ARGUMENT *purpose*: topic of conversation. *knights*: attendants, devotees.
*regard*: sight.

That shall alegge this bitter blast,                                      5
   And slake the winters sorowe.

THOMALIN.

Sicker Willye, thou warnest well:
For Winters wrath beginnes to quell,
   And pleasant spring appeareth.
The grasse nowe ginnes to be refresht,                                    10
The Swallow peepes out of her nest,
   And clowdie Welkin cleareth.

WILLYE.

Seest not thilke same Hawthorne studde,
How bragly it beginnes to budde,
   And utter his tender head?                                   15
*Flora* now calleth forth eche flower,
And bids make ready *Maias* bowre,
   That newe is upryst from bedde.
Tho shall we sporten in delight,
And learne with Lettice to wexe light,                                    20
   That scornefully lookes askaunce,
Tho will we little Love awake,
That nowe sleepeth in *Lethe* lake,
   And pray him leaden our daunce.

THOMALIN.

Willye, I wene thou bee assott:                                           25
For lustie Love still sleepeth not,
   But is abroad at his game.

---

9. *Sicker*: surely.   13. *studde*: stem.   14. *bragly*: showily,
bravely.   15. *utter*: put forth.   20. *Lettice*: probably from Lat. *laetitia*,
joy, appropriate to the season (compare parallel word formation in "flowre
Delice," *Aprill*, line 144, glossed as from *flos delitiarum*); also an allusion to
Lettice Knolles, countess of Essex, whose secret marriage to Leicester early in
1579 infuriated the queen. *wexe light*: become wanton.   25. *assott*:
bewildered.   26. *still sleepeth not*: never sleeps.

#### WILLYE.

How kenst thou, that he is awoke?
Or hast thy selfe his slomber broke?
 Or made previe to the same?       30

#### THOMALIN.

No, but happely I hym spyde,
Where in a bush he did him hide,
 With winges of purple and blewe.
And were not, that my sheepe would stray,
The previe marks I would bewray,      35
 Whereby by chaunce I him knewe.

#### WILLYE.

Thomalin, have no care for thy,
My selfe will have a double eye,
 Ylike to my flocke and thine:
For als at home I have a syre,       40
A stepdame eke as whott as fyre,
 That dewly adayes counts mine.

#### THOMALIN.

Nay, but thy seeing will not serve,
My sheepe for that may chaunce to swerve,
 And fall into some mischiefe.      45
For sithens is but the third morowe,
That I chaunst to fall a sleepe with sorowe,
 And waked againe with griefe:
The while thilke same unhappye Ewe,
Whose clouted legge her hurt doth shewe,    50
 Fell headlong into a dell,
And there unjoynted both her bones:

31. *happely*: by chance.   35. *bewray*: reveal.   37. *for thy*: therefore.
43. *seeing*: overseeing.   46. *sithens . . . morowe*: only three days ago.
49. *thilke*: that.   50. *clouted*: bandaged.

Mought her necke bene joynted attones,
   She shoulde have neede no more spell.
Thelf was so wanton and so wood,          55
(But now I trowe can better good)
   She mought ne gang on the greene,

WILLYE.

Let be, as may be, that is past:
That is to come, let be forecast.
   Now tell us, what thou hast seene.         60

THOMALIN.

It was upon a holiday,
When shepheardes groomes han leave to playe,
   I cast to goe a shooting.
Long wandring up and downe the land,
With bowe and bolts in either hand,         65
   For birds in bushes tooting:
At length within an Yvie todde
(There shrouded was the little God)
   I heard a busie bustling.
I bent my bolt against the bush,         70
Listening if any thing did rushe,
   But then heard no more rustling.
Tho peeping close into the thicke,
Might see the moving of some quicke,
   Whose shape appeared not:         75
But were it faerie, feend, or snake,
My courage earnd it to awake,
   And manfully thereat shotte.

---

53–54. *Mought . . . spell*: If at the same time she had broken her neck, she would have no more need of healing charms.    55. *Thelf*: the elf (ewe). *wood*: crazy.    56. *trowe*: trust, believe. *can*: knows.    57. *mought . . . greene*: would not stay on the common pasture.    59. *forecast*: planned.    62. *groomes*: helpers.    65. *bolts*: arrows.    66. *tooting*: searching, looking.    73. *thicke*: thicket.    74. *some quicke*: something alive.    77. *earnd*: yearned.

With that sprong forth a naked swayne,
With spotted winges like Peacocks trayne,               80
   And laughing lope to a tree.
His gylden quiver at his backe,
And silver bowe, which was but slacke,
   Which lightly he bent at me.
That seeing I, levelde againe,                          85
And shott at him with might and maine,
   As thicke, as it had hayled.
So long I shott, that al was spent:
Tho pumie stones I hastly hent,
   And threwe: but nought availed:                  90
He was so wimble, and so wight,
From bough to bough he lepped light,
   And oft the pumies latched.
Therewith affrayd I ranne away:
But he, that earst seemd but to playe,                  95
   A shaft in earnest snatched,
And hit me running in the heele:
For then I little smart did feele:
   But soone it sore encreased.
And now it ranckleth more and more,                     100
And inwardly it festreth sore,
   Ne wote I, how to cease it.

### WILLYE.

Thomalin, I pittie thy plight.
Perdie with love thou diddest fight:
   I know him by a token.                          105
For once I heard my father say,
How he him caught upon a day,
   (Whereof he wilbe wroken)

---

81. *lope*: lept.     85. *levelde*: aimed.     89. *pumie*: pumice. *hastly hent:*
quickly picked up.     91. *wimble . . . wight*: nimble and agile.     95. *earst*:
at first.     104. *Perdie*: surely.     105. *token*: sign, example.

Entangled in a fowling net,
Which he for carrion Crowes had set, 110
   That in our Peeretree haunted.
Tho sayd, he was a winged lad,
But bowe and shafts as then none had:
   Els had he sore be daunted.
But see the Welkin thicks apace, 115
And stouping *Phebus* steepes his face:
   Yts time to hast us homeward.


Willyes Embleme.
*To be wise and eke to love,*
*Is graunted scarce to God above.* 120


Thomalins Embleme.
*Of Hony and of Gaule in love there is store*:
*The Honye is much, but the Gaule is more.*


GLOSSE.

THIS Æglogue seemeth somewhat to resemble that same of
    Theocritus, wherein the boy likewise telling the old
    man, that he had shot at a winged boy in a tree, was by
    hym warned, to beware of mischiefe to come.
[2]   Over went) overgone.   [5] Alegge) to lessen or
    aswage.
[8]   To quell) to abate.   [12] Welkin) the skie.
[11]  The swallow) which bird useth to be counted the
    messenger, and as it were, the fore runner of springe.


111. *haunted*: frequented.   112. *Tho*: then.   116. *steepes*: bathes, i.e.
sinks into the western ocean.   119–20. from Publius (Publilius) Syrus,
*Sententiae* A.20.   122–23. from Plautus, *Cistellaria* 1.68–70, but a
commonplace in the Renaissance.   122. *Gaule*: twice spelled "gall" in FQ
IV x 1 where the same commonplace occurs; an apparent warning about the
queen's impending French marriage (cf. E. K.'s gloss on youth and age).

[E. K.'s comment] Theocritus: actually from Bion, *Idyll* 4.

[16] Flora) the Goddesse of flowres, but indede (as saith
Tacitus) a famous harlot, which with the abuse of her
body having gotten great riches, made the people of
Rome her heyre: who in remembraunce of so great
beneficence, appointed a yearely feste for the memoriall
of her, calling her, not as she was, nor as some doe
think, Andronica, but Flora: making her the Goddesse
of all floures, and doing yerely to her solemne sacrifice.

[17] Maias bowre) that is the pleasaunt fielde, or rather the
Maye bushes. Maia is a Goddes and the mother of
Mercurie, in honour of whome the moneth of Maye is
of her name so called, as sayth Macrobius.

[20] Lettice) the name of some country lasse.

[21] Ascaunce) askewe or asquint.     [37] For thy) therefore.

[23] Lethe) is a lake in hell, which the Poetes call the lake of
forgetfulnes. For Lethe signifieth forgetfulnes.
Wherein the soules being dipped, did forget the cares
of their former lyfe. So that by love sleeping in Lethe
lake, he meaneth he was almost forgotten and out of
knowledge, by reason of winters hardnesse, when al
pleasures as it were, sleepe and weare oute of mynde.

[25] Assotte) to dote.

[29] His slomber) To breake Loves slomber, is to exercise
the delightes of Love and wanton pleasures.

[33] Winges of purple) so is he feyned of the Poetes.

[40] For als) he imitateth Virgils verse.
Est mihi namque domi pater, est injusta noverca etc.

[51] A dell) a hole in the ground.

[54] Spell) is a kinde of verse or charme, that in elder tymes
they used often to say over every thing, that they
would have preserved, as the Nightspel for theeves, and

[16.2] *Tacitus*: rather from Boccaccio, *Genealogia Deorum* 4.61.
[16.7] *Andronica*: unidentified.     [17.4] *Macrobius*: *Saturnalia* 1.12.19.
[23.1] *Lethe . . . lake*: rather, a river; souls drank from it but were not
dipped.     [40.2] *Est . . . noverca*: "For at home there's my father and my
harsh stepmother," Virgil, *Ecl* 3.33.

the woodspell. And herehence I thinke is named the gospell, as it were Gods spell or worde. And so sayth Chaucer, Listeneth Lordings to my spell.

[57] Gange) goe. [67] An Yvie todde) a thicke bushe.

[79] Swaine) a boye: For so is he described of the Poetes, to be a boye .s. alwayes freshe and lustie: blindfolded, because he maketh no difference of Personages: wyth divers coloured winges, .s. ful of flying fancies: with bowe and arrow, that is with glaunce of beautye, which prycketh as a forked arrowe. He is sayd also to have shafts, some leaden, some golden: that is, both pleasure for the gracious and loved, and sorow for the lover that is disdayned or forsaken. But who liste more at large to behold Cupids colours and furniture, let him reade ether Propertius, or Moschus his Idyllion of wandring love, being now most excellently translated into Latine by the singuler learned man Angelus Politianus: whych worke I have seene amongst other of thys Poets doings, very wel translated also into Englishe Rymes.

[91] Wimble and wighte) Quicke and deliver.

[97] In the heele) is very Poetically spoken, and not without speciall judgement. For I remember, that in Homer it is sayd of Thetis, that shee tooke her young babe Achilles being newely borne, and holding him by the heele, dipped him in the River of Styx. The vertue whereof is, to defend and keepe the bodyes washed therein from any mortall wound. So Achilles being washed al over, save onely his hele, by which his mother held, was in the rest invulnerable: therfore by Paris was feyned to bee shotte with a poysoned arrowe in the heele, whiles he was busie about the marying of

[54.6] *Chaucer*: in *Sir Thopas*, at the beginning of second "fit", but misquoted. [79.11] *Propertius*: 2.12. [79.11] *Moschus*: *Idyll* 1. [79.13] *Politianus*: *Epigrammata*. [79.14] *thys Poets*: i.e. Sp's. [97.2] *Homer*: not in Homer but from Boccaccio, *Genealogia Deorum* 12.52, who uses Fulgentius, *Mythologiae* 3.7; Boccaccio is E. K.'s source for most of this gloss.

Polyxena in the temple of Apollo. which mysticall fable
Eustathius unfolding, sayth: that by wounding in the
hele, is meant lustfull love. For from the heele (as say
the best Phisitions) to the previe partes there passe
certaine veines and slender synnewes, as also the like
come from the head, and are carryed lyke little pypes
behynd the eares: so that (as sayth Hipocrates) yf those
veynes there be cut a sonder, the partie straighte
becommeth cold and unfruiteful. which reason our
Poete wel weighing, maketh this shepheards boye of
purpose to be wounded by Love in the heele.

[93]    Latched) caught.    [108] Wroken) revenged.

[106] For once) In this tale is sette out the simplicitye of
shepheards opinion of Love.

[116] Stouping Phæbus) Is a Periphrasis of the sunne setting.

## Emblcmc.

Hereby is meant, that all the delights of Love, wherein
wanton youth walloweth, be but follye mixt with
bitternesse, and sorow sawced with repentaunce. For
besides that the very affection of Love it selfe
tormenteth the mynde, and vexeth the body many
wayes, with unrestfulnesse all night, and wearines all
day, seeking for that we can not have, and fynding that
we would not have: even the selfe things which best
before us lyked, in course of time and chaung of ryper
yeares, whiche also therewithall chaungeth our wonted
lyking and former fantasies, will then seeme lothsome
and breede us annoyaunce, when yougthes flowre is
withered, and we fynde our bodyes and wits aunswere
not to suche vayne jollitie and lustful pleasaunce.

---

[97.13] *Eustathius*: a twelfth-century allegorizer of Homer whose
commentary was printed in the Rome (1542–50) and Basel editions (1560)
of Homer; but E. K.'s source is still Boccaccio.    [116] *Periphrasis*:
circumlocution.

# *Aprill*

꧁꧂꧁꧂꧁꧂꧁꧂꧁꧂꧁꧂꧁꧂

S penser would approve the long-standing recognition of *Aprill* as the *Calender's* tour de force, for his purpose here is clearly self-promotion. By placing Eliza's praise in his fourth eclogue he evokes Virgil's famous fourth ("Messianic") eclogue with its prophecy of an ideal reign and so lays claim to the role of Virgil's English successor. But in the dialogue framing his lay the speakers compare Colin's genius to that of the primordial poet Orpheus—not only in supreme poetic talent (16) but also in the irony of Orpheus's failure in erotic self-control (19–20). By his reaction to the cruel mistress Rosalind, Colin participates in this irony and so undermines the Virgilian career pattern, while in the lay Eliza empowers its fulfillment.

The lay's uniquely intricate stanza is set off sharply by the rustic dialogue. But Spenser does not overdo the contrast. Instead of the rugged couplets and diction of *Februarie*, Hobbinol and Thenot speak in alliterative-verse quatrains. And the nearly impenetrable dialect of the initial "what garres thee greete" only imputes a rudeness to the dialogue's language without actually carrying it through, for the speakers are connoisseurs sophisticated enough to recognize when "ditties bene so trimly dight" (29) even if they are not the lay's ultimate audience.

Renaissance humanists commonly distinguished two stages in the poet's creativity: their term *poeta* (Gk: maker) denoted the active artificer of verse; *vates* (Lat.: seer, prophet) the passive receptor of imaginative impulses (Aristotle's *enthousiasmos*). For the *vates's* inspiration to occur, the *poeta's* skill and effort must precede. This distinction underlies the overall structure of Colin's lay: it is a poem enacting the process of composing a poem. For the lay celebrates the activity of the poet as well as the deification of Eliza; the two are in fact complementary.

In the lay's first six stanzas (37–90) Colin acting as *poeta* organizes the queen's encomium by deploying the praise topics he had learned in school from Aphthonius's *Progymnasmata* (in the Argument E. K. punningly notes Colin's "laudable exercises"). Through this process, which culminates in better-than-the-best comparison (*comparatio in maius*), Eliza emerges as a "goddess" who outshines Phoebus and Cynthia. The *poeta's* verbs organizing the lay's first half (37–90) are characteristically imperative ("For sake your watry bowres," [39]). But in the second half (100–53) Colin for three stanzas (100–26) plays the role of *vates* and observes with admiration the transcendence of his art as Muses, graces, and nymphs come to crown the queen of victory, love, and peace. Here his verbs are those of a spectator—indicative and interrogative. But in the last three stanzas (127–53) he resumes his organizing role, Anglicizing the series of mythological coronations by calling in English shepherd girls to present the ordinary flowers of Tudor gardens and meadows.

Two further patterns of correspondence weld the halves of the lay into a complex, if recondite, structure. One pairs stanzas by topic, images, or phrases in parallel sequence so that, for example, the invocation of muses in stanza 1 (37–45) matches their arrival in stanza 8 (100–08). The other pattern pairs stanzas in symmetrical sequence so that the invocation of "Ye dayntye Nymphs" (37) in stanza 1 corresponds to the dismissal of "ye daintie Damsells" (147) in stanza 13 (145–53). Both patterns continue throughout the lay.

Though now impotent as poet, Colin's past achievement remains as *monumentum*—an unalterable fact. The equilibrium of its structures renders pastoral stasis in yet another way, as does the icon of Eliza. Seemingly before the lay begins she already "sits upon the grassie greene" (55), throughout "shee is in place" (131), and only at its end does she "ryse up" (145)—the very formulas for initiating, continuing, and concluding an eclogue. Thus the "Queene of shepheardes all" (34) becomes the genius of pastoral itself. In fact as child of Pan and Syrinx she is identical with the oaten reeds or panpipe that conventionally symbolizes the pastoral poet's ability to compose. In this sense *Aprill* is entirely Arcadian.

But in the stanza that is central to all patterns (91–99) the pairing of "my goddesse plaine" (97) and "I her shepherds swayne" (98), with its hinted plighting of troths, goes beyond Arcadian celebration to political statement. The suddenly down-home diction of "Albee forswonck and forswatt" (99)— where "Albee" may pun on Albion, i.e. England—presents Colin as Eliza's rustic English lover and so affirms the concept of the mystical marriage of Virgin Queen and England that Elizabeth herself had initiated. As a national epithalamium the lay speaks, though indirectly, against the queen's possible marriage to the French prince Alençon which in the late 1570s seemed all too probable. The marriage scheme was intensely unpopular in England, hence the assertions of rustic Englishness in the lay. Significantly, Spenser centers this encomium of Eliza on the most paradoxical of her celebratory cults developed during the 1570s, i.e. Virgin-Venus (e.g. "The flowre of Virgins" [48], who is also like Venus amid the Graces [113–17]), but weighs the balance somewhat in favor of the virginal (although April is Venus's month).

*Aprill* serves to predict the heroic poem that was already being composed. Thus in the woodcut Colin's pipe is the cornett, a Renaissance instrument used for royal salute in situations inappropriate for the trumpet which was proper to the epic poet (as in *The Faerie Queene* I Proem 1).

# Aprill.

*Ægloga Quarta.*

## ARGUMENT.

THis Æglogue is purposely intended to the honor and prayse of our most gracious sovereigne, Queene Elizabeth. The speakers herein be Hobbinoll and Thenott, two shepheardes: the which Hobbinoll being before mentioned, greatly to have loved Colin, is here set forth more largely, complayning him of that boyes great misadventure in Love, whereby his mynd was alienate and with drawen not onely from him, who moste loved him, but also from all former delightes and studies, aswell in pleasaunt pyping, as conning ryming and singing, and other his laudable exercises. Whereby he taketh occasion, for proofe of his more excellencie and skill in poetrie, to recorde a songe, which the sayd Colin sometime made in honor of her Majestie, whom abruptely he termeth Elysa.

ARGUMENT *recorde*: Lat. *recordari*, remember. *abruptely*: by way of abbreviation.

### THENOT. HOBBINOLL.

TEll me good Hobbinoll, what garres thee greete?
What? hath some Wolfe thy tender Lambes ytorne?
Or is thy Bagpype broke, that soundes so sweete?
Or art thou of thy loved lasse forlorne?

Or bene thine eyes attempred to the yeare,                    5
Quenching the gasping furrowes thirst with rayne?
Like April shoure, so stremes the trickling teares
Adowne thy cheeke, to quenche thy thristye payne.

### HOBBINOLL.

Nor thys, nor that, so muche doeth make me mourne,
But for the ladde, whome long I lovd so deare,              10
Nowe loves a lasse, that all his love doth scorne:
He plongd in payne, his tressed locks dooth teare.

Shepheards delights he dooth them all forsweare,
Hys pleasaunt Pipe, whych made us meriment,
He wylfully hath broke, and doth forbeare                  15
His wonted songs, wherein he all outwent.

### THENOT.

What is he for a Ladde, you so lament?
Ys love such pinching payne to them, that prove?
And hath he skill to make so excellent,
Yet hath so little skill to brydle love?                   20

### HOBBINOLL.

*Colin* thou kenst, the Southerne shepheardes boye:
Him Love hath wounded with a deadly darte.
Whilome on him was all my care and joye,
Forcing with gyfts to winne his wanton heart.

---

8. *thristye*: thirsty.    16. *outwent*: surpassed.    18. *prove*: experience
it.    21. *Southerne shepheardes boye*: Sp in 1578 was secretary to John
Young, bishop of Rochester, formerly Master of Pembroke Hall, Cambridge
(Sp's college).    24. *Forcing*: attempting.

But now from me hys madding mynd is starte,                    25
And woes the Widdowes daughter of the glenne:
So nowe fayre *Rosalind* hath bredde hys smart,
So now his frend is chaunged for a frenne.

THENOT.

But if hys ditties bene so trimly dight,
I pray thee *Hobbinoll*, recorde some one:                     30
The whiles our flockes doe graze about in sight,
And we close shrowded in thys shade alone.

HOBBINOL.

Contented I: then will I singe his laye
Of fayre *Elisa*, Queene of shepheardes all:
Which once he made, as by a spring he laye,                    35
And tuned it unto the Waters fall.

YE dayntye Nymphs, that in this blessed Brooke
     doe bathe your brest,
For sake your watry bowres, and hether looke,
     at my request:                                           40
And eke you Virgins, that on *Parnasse* dwell,
Whence floweth *Helicon* the learned well,
          Helpe me to blaze
          Her worthy praise,
Which in her sexe doth all excell.                            45

Of fayre *Elisa* be your silver song,
     that blessed wight:
The flowre of Virgins, may shee florish long,
     In princely plight.
For shee is *Syrinx* daughter without spotte,                 50
Which *Pan* the shepheards God of her begot:

25. *madding . . . starte*: frenzied mind has turned away.     29. *trimly dight*:
neatly or intricately composed or ornamented.     43. *blaze*: proclaim.
47. *wight*: creature, person.     49. *plight*: condition.     50–51. For Pan
and Syrinx, see Ovid, *Met* 1.689–712.

So sprong her grace
   Of heavenly race,
No mortall blemishe may her blotte.

See, where she sits upon the grassie greene,                55
   (O seemely sight)
Yclad in Scarlot like a mayden Queene,
   And Ermines white.
Upon her head a Cremosin coronet,
With Damaske roses and Daffadillies set:                    60
   Bayleaves betweene,
   And Primroses greene
Embellish the sweete Violet.

Tell me, have ye seene her angelick face,
   Like *Phœbe* fayre?                                       65
Her heavenly haveour, her princely grace
   can you well compare?
The Redde rose medled with the White yfere,
In either cheeke depeincten lively chere.                   70
   Her modest eye,
   Her Majestie,
Where have you seene the like, but there?

I sawe *Phœbus* thrust out his golden hedde,
   upon her to gaze:
But when he sawe, how broade her beames did spredde,        75
   it did him amaze.
He blusht to see another Sunne belowe,
Ne durst againe his fyrye face out showe:
   Let him, if he dare,
   His brightnesse compare                                  80
With hers, to have the overthrowe.

---

66. *haveour*: bearing.     68. *yfere*: together.     69. *depeincten*: depict.
73–81. The lady outshining the sun is a Petrarchan motif, as in *Rime* 115.

Shewe thy selfe *Cynthia* with thy silver rayes,
    and be not abasht:
When shee the beames of her beauty displayes,
    O how art thou dasht? 85
But I will not match her with *Latonaes* seede,
Such follie great sorow to *Niobe* did breede.
    Now she is a stone,
    And makes dayly mone,
Warning all other to take heede. 90

*Pan* may be proud, that ever he begot
    such a Bellibone,
And *Syrinx* rejoyse, that ever was her lot
    to beare such an one.
Soone as my younglings cryen for the dam, 95
To her will I offer a milkwhite Lamb:
    Shee is my goddesse plaine,
    And I her shepherds swayne,
Albee forswonck and forswatt I am.

I see *Calliope* speede her to the place, 100
    where my Goddesse shines:
And after her the other Muses trace,
    with their Violines.
Bene they not Bay braunches, which they doe beare,
All for *Elisa* in her hand to weare? 105
    So sweetely they play,
    And sing all the way,
That it a heaven is to heare.

Lo how finely the graces can it foote
    to the Instrument: 110

86. *I . . . not match*: he has already done so. *Latonaes seede*: Apollo and Diana,
i.e. Phoebus and Phoebe (Cynthia). 92. *Bellibone*: suggests the Platonic
model of virtue joined to beauty (Fr. *belle*, beautiful, *bonne*, good).
99. *Albee . . . forswatt*: although tired with work and sweaty (or perhaps
sunburnt). 110. *Instrument*: shepherd's pipe.

They dauncen deffly, and singen soote,
    in their meriment.
Wants not a fourth grace, to make the daunce even?
Let that rowme to my Lady be yeven:
      She shalbe a grace,               115
      To fyll the fourth place,
And reigne with the rest in heaven.

And whither rennes this bevie of Ladies bright,
    raunged in a rowe?
They bene all Ladyes of the lake behight,       120
    that unto her goe.
*Chloris*, that is the chiefest Nymph of al,
Of Olive braunches beares a Coronall:
      Olives bene for peace,
      When wars doe surcease:        125
Such for a Princesse bene principall.

Ye shepheards daughters, that dwell on the greene,
    hye you there apace:
Let none come there, but that Virgins bene,
    to adorne her grace.          130
And when you come, whereas shee is in place,
See, that your rudenesse doe not you disgrace:
      Binde your fillets faste,
      And gird in your waste,
For more finesse, with a tawdrie lace.      135

Bring hether the Pincke and purple Cullambine,
    With Gelliflowres:

---

111. *deffly*: deftly. *soote*: sweetly.    114. *yeven*: given.    116. *fourth place*:
a position usually given to Venus.    118. *rennes*: runs.    123. *Coronall*:
wreath.    126. *principall*: of prime importance. Elizabeth was celebrated in
the 1570s for the continuous peace her reign had brought.    128. *hye*:
hurry.    131. *whereas*: where.    133. *fillets*: hair ribbons.    135. *tawdrie
lace*: a silk band.    137. *Gelliflowres*: gilly flowers, i.e. clove pinks.

Bring Coronations, and Sops in wine,
    worne of Paramoures.
Strowe me the ground with Daffadowndillies,         140
And Cowslips, and Kingcups, and loved Lillies:
    The pretie Pawnce,
    And the Chevisaunce,
Shall match with the fayre flowre Delice.

Now ryse up *Elisa*, decked as thou art,         145
    in royall aray:
And now ye daintie Damsells may depart
    echeone her way.
I feare, I have troubled your troupes to longe:
Let dame *Eliza* thanke you for her song.         150
    And if you come hether,
    When Damsines I gether,
I will part them all you among.

THENOT.
And was thilk same song of *Colins* owne making?
Ah foolish boy, that is with love yblent:         155
Great pittie is, he be in such taking,
For naught caren, that bene so lewdly bent.

HOBBINOL.
Sicker I hold him, for a greater fon,
That loves the thing, he cannot purchase.
But let us homeward: for night draweth on,         160
And twincling starres the daylight hence chase.

138. *Coronations*: carnations; pun on Lat. *corona*, crown. *Sops in wine*: variety
of clove pink used to flavor wine.    142. *Pawnce*: pansy.
143. *Chevisaunce*: no such plant is known. Sp uses the word in three places to
mean "knightly adventures"; deriving the sense from Fr. *chevauché*, or
"enterprise" (*Maye*, line 92; *FQ* II ix 8, III vii 45, xi 24).    144. *flowre*
*Delice*: fleur de lis or iris, the French royal emblem: Elizabeth's title
proclaimed her Queen of France.    152. *Damsines*: damsons, small blue
plums.    156. *taking*: condition.    157. *lewdly bent*: basely,
inappropriately purposed.    158. *fon*: fool.

Thenots Embleme.

*O quam te memorem virgo?*

Hobbinols Embleme.

*O dea certe.*                                        165

GLOSSE.

[1]    Gars thee greete) causeth thee weepe and complain.

[4]    Forlorne) left and forsaken.

[5]    Attempred to the yeare) agreeable to the season of the
       yeare, that is Aprill, which moneth is most bent to
       shoures and seasonable rayne: to quench, that is, to
       delaye the drought, caused through drynesse of March
       wyndes.

[10]   The Ladde) Colin Clout.   [11] The Lasse) Rosalinda.

[12]   Tressed locks) wrethed and curled.

[17]   Is he for a ladde) A straunge manner of speaking .s.
       what maner of Ladde is he?

[19]   To make) to rime and versifye. For in this word
       making, our olde Englishe Poetes were wont to
       comprehend all the skil of Poetrye, according to the
       Greeke woorde ποιεῖν to make, whence commeth the
       name of Poets.

[21]   Colin thou kenst) knowest. Seemeth hereby that Colin
       perteyneth to some Southern noble man, and perhaps
       in Surrye or Kent, the rather bicause he so often
       nameth the Kentish downes, and before, As lythe as
       lasse of Kent.

[26]   The Widowes) He calleth Rosalind the Widowes
       daughter of the glenne, that is, of a country Hamlet or

163–65. *O . . . certe*: Aeneas to Venus disguised as a huntress: "what name
shall I know you by, maiden? Surely a goddess," *Aen* l.327–28.

[5.4] *delaye*: moisten.        [19.4] ποιεῖν: Gk *poiein*, to do, make, or create.

borough, which I thinke is rather sayde to coloure and
concele the person, then simply spoken. For it is well
knowen, even in spighte of Colin and Hobbinoll, that
shee is a Gentle woman of no meane house, nor
endewed with anye vulgare and common gifts both of
nature and manners: but suche indeede, as neede
nether Colin be ashamed to have her made knowne by
his verses, nor Hobbinol be greved, that so she should
be commended to immortalitie for her rare and
singular Vertues: Specially deserving it no lesse, then
eyther Myrto the most excellent Poete Theocritus his
dearling, or Lauretta the divine Petrarches Goddesse,
or Himera the worthye Poete Stesichorus hys Idole:
Upon whom he is sayd so much to have doted, that in
regard of her excellencie, he scorned and wrote against
the beauty of Helena. For which his præsumptuous
and unheedie hardinesse, he is sayde by vengeaunce of
the Gods, thereat being offended, to have lost both his
eyes.

[28]   Frenne) a straunger. The word I thinke was first
poetically put, and afterwarde used in commen
custome of speach for forenne.

[29]   Dight) adorned.   [33] Laye) a songe. as Roundelayes
and Virelayes. In all this songe is not to be respected,
what the worthinesse of her Majestie deserveth, nor
what to the highnes of a Prince is agreeable, but what
is moste comely for the meanesse of a shepheards witte,
or to conceive, or to utter. And therefore he calleth her
Elysa, as through rudenesse tripping in her name: and

[26.13] *Myrto*: Theocritus, *Idylls* 7.97.   [26.14] *Lauretta*: form of Laura
in Petrarch, *Rime* 5.   [26.15] *Stesichorus*: ancient Greek poet who wrote a
recantation giving a positive image of a virtuous Helen. Himera was his
native town, not his mistress.   [33.1-2] *Roundelayes and Virelayes*: two Fr.
medieval lyric forms.

a shepheards daughter, it being very unfit, that a
shepheards boy brought up in the shepefold, should
know, or ever seme to have heard of a Queenes roialty.

[37]   Ye daintie) is, as it were an Exordium ad preparandos
animos.

[41]   Virgins) the nine Muses, daughters of Apollo and
Memorie, whose abode the Poets faine to be on
Parnassus, a hill in Grece, for that in that countrye
specially florished the honor of all excellent studies.

[42]   Helicon) is both the name of a fountaine at the foote
of Parnassus, and also of a mounteine in Bæotia, out of
which floweth the famous Spring Castalius, dedicate
also to the Muses: of which spring it is sayd, that when
Pegasus the winged horse of Perseus (whereby is meant
fame and flying renowme) strooke the grownde with
his hoofe, sodenly thereout sprange a wel of moste
cleare and pleasaunte water, which fro thence forth was
consecrate to the Muses and Ladies of learning.

[46]   Your silver song) seemeth to imitate the lyke in
Hesiodus ἀργυρέον μέλος.

[50]   Syrinx) is the name of a Nymphe of Arcadie, whom
when Pan being in love pursued, she flying from him,
of the Gods was turned into a reede. So that Pan
catching at the Reedes in stede of the Damosell, and
puffing hard (for he was almost out of wind) with hys
breath made the Reedes to pype: which he seeing,
tooke of them, and in remembraunce of his lost love,
made him a pype thereof. But here by Pan and Syrinx
is not to bee thoughte, that the shephearde simplye
meante those Poetical Gods: but rather supposing (as
seemeth) her graces progenie to be divine and

---

[37.1–2] *Exordium . . . animos*: "an introduction to prepare the hearers."
[46.2] ἀργυρέον μέλος: Gk *argurion melos*, i.e. silver song; not in Hesiod.

immortall (so as the Paynims were wont to judge of all
Kinges and Princes, according to Homeres saying.

Θυμὸς δὴ μέγας ἐστὶ διοτρεφέώς βασιλήως,
τιμὴ δ' ἐκ διός ἐστι, φιλεῖ δε ὁ μητίετα Ζεύς.

could devise no parents in his judgement so worthy for
her, as Pan the shepeheards God, and his best beloved
Syrinx. So that by Pan is here meant the most famous
and victorious King, her highnesse Father, late of
worthy memorye K. Henry the eyght. And by the
name, oftymes (as hereafter appeareth) be noted kings
and mighty Potentates: And in some place Christ
himselfe, who is the verye Pan and god of Shepheardes.

[59]   Cremosin coronet) he deviseth her crowne to be of the
finest and most delicate flowers, instede of perles and
precious stones, wherewith Princes Diademes use to
bee adorned and embost.

[63]   Embellish) beautifye and set out.

[65]   Phebe) the Moone, whom the Poets faine to be sister
unto Phæbus, that is the Sunne.

[68]   Medled) mingled.

[68]   Yfere) together. By the mingling of the Redde rose and
the White, is meant the uniting of the two principall
houses of Lancaster and of Yorke: by whose longe
discord and deadly debate, this realm many yeares was
sore traveiled, and almost cleane decayed. Til the
famous Henry the seventh, of the line of Lancaster,
taking to wife the most vertuous Princesse Elisabeth,
daughter to the fourth Edward of the house of Yorke,

[50.14–15] Θυμός . . . Ζεύς: Gk *Thumos* . . . *Zeus*, "For the anger of god-
upheld kings is a great matter, to whom honor and love are given from Zeus
of the counsels," *Iliad* 2.196–97.      [50.23] *Pan*: Marot uses Pan for
Francis I in *Eclogue au Roy* and *Eclogue de Mme Loyse de Savoye*; for Christ in
*Complainct d'un Pastoureau Chrestien* (see *Maye*, line 54; *Julye*, line 49).

begat the most royal Henry the eyght aforesayde, in whom was the firste union of the Whyte Rose and the Redde.

[100] Calliope) one of the nine Muses: to whome they assigne the honor of all Poetical Invention, and the firste glorye of the Heroicall verse. other say, that shee is the Goddesse of Rhetorick: but by Virgile it is manifeste, that they mystake the thyng. For there in hys Epigrams, that arte semeth to be attributed to Polymnia, saying:

Signat cuncta manu, loquiturque Polymnia gestu. which seemeth specially to be meant of Action and elocution, both special partes of Rhetorick: besyde that her name, which (as some construe it) importeth great remembraunce, conteineth another part. but I holde rather with them, which call her Polymnia or Polyhymnia of her good singing.

[104] Bay branches) be the signe of honor and victory, and therfore of myghty Conquerors worn in theyr triumphes, and eke of famous Poets, as saith Petrarch in hys Sonets.

> Arbor vittoriosa triomphale,
> Honor d'Imperadori & di Poëti, etc.

[109] The Graces) be three sisters, the daughters of Jupiter, (whose names are Aglaia, Thalia, Euphrosyne, and Homer onely addeth a fourth .s. Pasithea) otherwise called Charites, that is thanks. whom the Poetes feyned to be the Goddesses of al bountie and comelines, which

---

[100.6] *Epigrams*: *Nomina Musarum*, the fourth-century poet Ausonius's mnemonic on the nine Muses, once attributed to Virgil.    [100.8] *Signat . . . gestu*: "Polymnia indicates everything with her hand, speaking through action."    [104.5–6] *Arbor . . . Poeti*: "Victorious and triumphal tree, the honor of emperors and poets," Petrarch, *Rime* 263.

therefore (as sayth Theodontius) they make three, to wete, that men first ought to be gracious and bountiful to other freely, then to receive benefits at other mens hands curteously, and thirdly to requite them thankfully: which are three sundry Actions in liberalitye. And Boccace saith, that they be painted naked, (as they were indeede on the tombe of C. Julius Cæsar) the one having her backe toward us, and her face fromwarde, as proceeding from us: the other two toward us, noting double thanke to be due to us for the benefit, we have done.

[111] Deaffly) Finelye and nimbly.   [111] Soote) Sweete.   [112] Meriment) Mirth.

[118] Bevie) A beavie of Ladyes, is spoken figuratively for a company or troupe. the terme is taken of Larkes. For they say a Bevie of Larkes, even as a Covey of Partridge, or an eye of Pheasaunts.

[120] Ladyes of the lake) be Nymphes. For it was an olde opinion amongste the Auncient Heathen, that of every spring and fountaine was a goddesse the Soveraigne. Whiche opinion stucke in the myndes of men not manye yeares sithence, by meanes of certain fine fablers and lowd lyers, such as were the Authors of King Arthure the great and such like, who tell many an unlawfull leasing of the Ladyes of the Lake, that is, the Nymphes. For the word Nymphe in Greeke signifieth Well water, or otherwise a Spouse or Bryde.

[120] Behight) called or named.

[122] Cloris) the name of a Nymph, and signifieth greenesse, of whome is sayd, that Zephyrus the Westerne wind being in love with her, and coveting her to wyfe, gave

[109.6] *Theodontius*: a mysterious medieval Italian mythographer, known only from Boccaccio's frequent citation of him in *Genealogia Deorum*. [109.11] *Boccace*: *Genealogia Deorum* 5.35. On the iconography of the Graces, see Wind (1967), ch. 2; cf. *FQ* VI x 21–26.   [120.8] *leasing*: lie.   [122] *Cloris*: E. K. probably takes the story from Boccaccio, *Genealogia Deorum* 4.61.

her for a dowrie, the chiefedome and soveraigntye of al
flowres and greene herbes, growing on earth.

[124] Olives bene) The Olive was wont to be the ensigne of
Peace and quietnesse, eyther for that it cannot be
planted and pruned, and so carefully looked to, as it
ought, but in time of peace: or els for that the Olive
tree, they say, will not growe neare the Firre tree,
which is dedicate to Mars the God of battaile, and used
most for speares and other instruments of warre.
Whereupon is finely feigned, that when Neptune and
Minerva strove for the naming of the citie of Athens,
Neptune striking the ground with his mace, caused a
horse to come forth, that importeth warre, but at
Minervæs stroke sprong out an Olive, to note that it
should be a nurse of learning, and such peaceable
studies.

[133] Binde your) Spoken rudely, and according to
shepheardes simplicitye.

[136] Bring) all these be names of flowers. Sops in wine a
flowre in colour much like to a Coronation, but
differing in smel and quantitye. Flowre delice, that
which they use to misterme, Flowre de luce, being in
Latine called Flos delitiarum.

[92] A Bellibone) or a Bonibell. homely spoken for a fayre
mayde or Bonilasse.

[99] Forswonck and forswatt) overlaboured and
sunneburnt.

[73] I saw Phæbus) the sunne. A sensible Narration, and
present view of the thing mentioned, which they call
παρουσία.

[82] Cynthia) the Moone so called of Cynthus a hyll, where
she was honoured.

---

[124] *Olives*: probably from Boccacio, *Genealogia Deorum* 5.67.
[136.4] *Flowre de luce*: flower of light.    [136.5] *Flos delitiarum*: flower of
pleasure.    [73.1] *sensible*: graphic.    [73.3] παρουσία: Gk *parousia*,
making a thing seem present.

[86-7] Latonaes seede) Was Apollo and Diana. Whom when
as Niobe the wife of Amphion scorned, in respect of
the noble fruict of her wombe, namely her seven
sonnes, and so many daughters, Latona being
therewith displeased, commaunded her sonne Phœbus
to slea al the sonnes, and Diana all the daughters:
whereat the unfortunate Niobe being sore dismayed,
and lamenting out of measure, was feigned of the
Poetes, to be turned into a stone upon the sepulchre of
her children. for which cause the shepheard sayth, he
will not compare her to them, for feare of like
mysfortune.

[145] Now rise) is the conclusion. For having so decked her
with prayses and comparisons, he returneth all the
thanck of hys laboure to the excellencie of her Majestie.

[152] When Damsins) A base reward of a clownish giver.

[155] Yblent) Y, is a poeticall addition. blent blinded.

## Embleme.

This Poesye is taken out of Virgile, and there of him used in
the person of Æneas to his mother Venus, appearing to
him in likenesse of one of Dianaes damosells: being
there most divinely set forth. To which similitude of
divinitie Hobbinoll comparing the excelency of Elisa,
and being through the worthynes of Colins song, as it
were, overcome with the hugenesse of his imagination,
brusteth out in great admiration, (O quam te
memorem virgo?) being otherwise unhable, then by
soddein silence, to expresse the worthinesse of his
conceipt. Whom Thenot answereth with another part
of the like verse, as confirming by his graunt and
approvaunce, that Elisa is nowhit inferiour to the
Majestie of her, of whome that Poete so boldly
pronounced, O dea certe.

[86–7] *Latonaes seede*: see Ovid, *Met* 6.146–311.

# Maye

aye is the first of three ecclesiastical eclogues where shepherd now means pastor. The charmingly Anglicized Arcadianism of its opening quickly yields to debate on an urgently Mantuanesque question about the lifestyle proper to shepherds.

Piers has a clear, uncompromising answer: clergy must live like their predecessors in the early church, concerned only for the care and teaching of their flock, reliant on God's grace to supply their needs, and prepared for the Day of Judgment "When great *Pan* account of shepeherdes shall aske" (54). What Piers says closely echoes injunctions in the Gospels and in fact represents a moderate statement of the progressive Protestants' concern in the 1570s for further church reform. Unlike the emerging radical Protestants, Piers does not attack maygames or church adornment as such, nor is there any hint of their desire (expressed in the *Admonitions* controversy of the 1570s) to dismantle episcopal orders. But, by making Piers the continuing spokesman for the clerical ideals of the now silenced Archbishop Grindal ("as Algrind *used* to say" [75]), Spenser comes close to criticizing the queen's action.

Elizabethans associated the name Piers with a satirical, supposedly proto-Protestant tradition stemming from Langland, *The Plowman's Tale*, and other Chaucerian apocrypha. Palinode's name, however, merely means countersong: he reacts against Piers' initiative. Whatever E. K. intends by calling him "Catholique," he evidently represents the unreconstructed, superficially conforming Elizabethan cleric who sees in Piers's program an innovative assault on the traditional "right" (146) of clergy to an unlearned, self-serving, nearly secular lifestyle. He prizes an earthly "felicitie" (155) he knows to be transient and accepts the inevitability of "stormie stowres" (156). While Piers may hope that the ancient church "may againe retorne" (103), Palinode stolidly accepts what " may not be mended" (162). His emotional, sometimes blustering reaction to Piers's precise scripturalism indicates the difficulty of thorough reform in England. The debate may even suggest a "prophesying"—the bible-study sessions designed to produce an informed clergy which Grindal had refused to suppress.

In terms of doctrine Piers clearly wins the debate. In terms of the poem's depiction of human experience, he doesn't. For Palinode's responses, arising from tradition and human nature, must be dealt with by more than idealist preaching if reform is to succeed. Notably, the woodcut centers on bringing home the May with the wagon here drawn by winged horses, an old symbol of poetic inspiration and of a piece with Palinode's evocative account of this idyllic fete.

The debate seems to end in stalemate: Palinode appeals for "concord" (163) among church factions and Piers insists on "none accordaunce" (164). (It is worth noting that the lines focusing on the need for concord [158–59] are the central lines in the poem.) But this impasse suddenly yields to the "felowship" (172) of the tale, which adapts the Reynard-the-fox fable to contemporary purpose: the threat posed by the Jesuits' just launched Mission to reclaim English Catholics. *Februarie* and *Maye* use the same dialogue-story structure to opposite effect: in *Februarie* the fable only consolidates impasse; in *Maye* it brings concord where there had been "conteck" (163), with both speakers agreeing on the danger from foxes. It is not clear, however, that Palinode has understood what the fable portends.

# Maye.

*Ægloga Quinta.*

## ARGUMENT.

I*N this fift Æglogue, under the persons of two shepheards Piers and*
Palinodie, be represented two formes of pastoures or Ministers, or
*the protestant and the Catholique: whose chiefe talke standeth in*
*reasoning, whether the life of the one must be like the other, with*
*whom having shewed, that it is daungerous to mainteine any felow-*
*ship, or give too much credit to their colourable and feyned goodwill,*
*he telleth him a tale of the foxe, that by such a counterpoynt of*
*craftines deceived and devoured the credulous kidde.*

### PALINODE. PIERS.
I S not thilke the mery moneth of May,
When love lads masken in fresh aray?
How falles it then, we no merrier bene,

ARGUMENT *credit*: belief. *their*: this pronoun lacks reference. *colourable*:
feigned; it apparently anticipates the fable. *counterpoynt*: trick, stratagem.

Ylike as others, girt in gawdy greene?
Our bloncket liveryes bene all to sadde,                    5
For thilke same season, when all is ycladd
With pleasaunce: the grownd with grasse, the Wods
With greene leaves, the bushes with bloosming Buds.
Yougthes folke now flocken in every where,
To gather may buskets and smelling brere:                  10
And home they hasten the postes to dight,
And all the Kirke pillours eare day light,
With Hawthorne buds, and swete Eglantine,
And girlonds of roses and Sopps in wine.
Such merimake holy Saints doth queme,                      15
But we here sytten as drownd in a dreme.

PIERS.

For Younkers *Palinode* such follies fitte,
But we tway bene men of elder witt.

PALINODE.

Sicker this morrowe, ne lenger agoe,
I sawe a shole of shepeheardes outgoe,                     20
With singing, and shouting, and jolly chere:
Before them yode a lusty Tabrere,
That to the many a Horne pype playd,
Whereto they dauncen eche one with his mayd.
To see those folkes make such jouysaunce,                 25
Made my heart after the pype to daunce.
Tho to the greene Wood they speeden hem all,
To fetchen home May with their musicall:
And home they bringen in a royall throne,
Crowned as king: and his Queene attone                    30

4. *gawdy greene*: yellowish green, associated with festival (Lat. *gaudere*, rejoice, though not a correct etymology, is relevant).   17. *Younkers*: young men, youths.   18. *tway*: two.   20. *shepeheardes*: clergy. 22. *Tabrere*: tabor player, drummer.   23. *many*: company.   28. *May*: the lord of the May, the spring festival honoring the blooming of the hawthorn or "may."

Was Lady Flora, on whom did attend
A fayre flocke of Faeries, and a fresh bend
Of lovely Nymphs. (O that I were there,
To helpen the Ladyes their Maybush beare)
Ah *Piers*, bene not thy teeth on edge, to thinke,                35
How great sport they gaynen with little swinck?

### PIERS.

Perdie so farre am I from envie,
That their fondnesse inly I pitie.
Those faytours little regarden their charge,
While they letting their sheepe runne at large,                40
Passen their time, that should be sparely spent,
In lustihede and wanton meryment.
Thilke same bene shepeheards for the Devils stedde,
That playen, while their flockes be unfedde.
Well is it seene, theyr sheepe bene not their owne,                45
That letten them runne at randon alone.
But they bene hyred for little pay
Of other, that caren as little as they,
What fallen the flocke, so they han the fleece,
And get all the gayne, paying but a peece.                50
I muse, what account both these will make,
The one for the hire, which he doth take,
And thother for leaving his Lords taske,
When great *Pan* account of shepeherdes shall aske.

### PALINODE.

Sicker now I see thou speakest of spight,                55
All for thou lackest somedele their delight.
I (as I am) had rather be envied,
All were it of my foe, then fonly pitied:
And yet if neede were, pitied would be,

---

41. *sparely*: thriftily.    43. *stedde*: place.    55. *of spight*: from spite,
maliciously.    56. *somedele*: somewhat.    58. *All*: although. *fonly*:
foolishly.

Rather, then other should scorne at me:        60
For pittied is mishappe, that nas remedie,
But scorned bene dedes of fond foolerie.
What shoulden shepheards other things tend,
Then sith their God his good does them send,
Reapen the fruite thereof, that is pleasure,        65
The while they here liven, at ease and leasure?
For when they bene dead, their good is ygoe,
They sleepen in rest, well as other moe.
Tho with them wends, what they spent in cost,
But what they left behind them, is lost.        70
Good is no good, but if it be spend:
God giveth good for none other end.

### PIERS.

Ah *Palinodie*, thou art a worldes childe:
Who touches Pitch mought needes be defilde.
But shepheards (as Algrind used to say,)        75
Mought not live ylike, as men of the laye:
With them it sits to care for their heire,
Enaunter their heritage doe impaire:
They must provide for meanes of maintenaunce,
And to continue their wont countenaunce.        80
But shepheard must walke another way,
Sike worldly sovenance he must foresay.
The sonne of his loines why should he regard
To leave enriched with that he hath spard?
Should not thilke God, that gave him that good,        85
Eke cherish his child, if in his wayes he stood?
For if he mislive in leudnes and lust,

---

68. *other moe*: many more.    75. *Algrind*: anagram for Edward Grindal,
archbishop of Canterbury, suspended from exercise of his office from 1577
to 1582 by the queen's order.    77. *With . . . heire*: For laymen it is
appropriate to provide for their inheritors.    80. *wont countenaunce*:
customary or expected outward appearance.    82. *foresay*: reject.

Little bootes all the welth and the trust,
That his father left by inheritaunce:
All will be soone wasted with misgovernaunce.                    90
But through this, and other their miscreaunce,
They maken many a wrong chevisaunce,
Heaping up waves of welth and woe,
The floddes whereof shall them overflowe.
Sike mens follie I cannot compare                                95
Better, then to the Apes folish care,
That is so enamoured of her young one,
(And yet God wote, such cause hath she none)
That with her hard hold, and straight embracing,
She stoppeth the breath of her youngling.                       100
So often times, when as good is meant,
Evil ensueth of wrong entent.
    The time was once, and may againe retorne,
(For ought may happen, that hath bene beforne)
When shepeheards had none inheritaunce,                         105
Ne of land, nor fee in sufferaunce:
But what might arise of the bare sheepe,
(Were it more or lesse) which they did keepe.
Well ywis was it with shepheards thoe:
Nought having, nought feared they to forgoe.                    110
For *Pan* himselfe was their inheritaunce,
And little them served for their mayntenaunce.
The shepheards God so wel them guided,
That of nought they were unprovided,
Butter enough, honye, milke, and whay,                          115
And their flockes fleeces, them to araye.
But tract of time, and long prosperitie:
That nource of vice, this of insolencie,

84. *spard*: spared, put aside.     88. *bootes*: helps. *trust*: estate.
92. *chevisaunce*: enterprise (cf. E. K.'s gloss).     99. *straight*: tight.
106. *fee in sufferaunce*: pay for services.     109. *ywis*: I know, certainly.
110. *forgoe*: do without.     117. *tract*: passage.

Lulled the shepheards in such securitie,
That not content with loyall obeysaunce,                    120
Some gan to gape for greedie governaunce,
And match them selfe with mighty potentates,
Lovers of Lordship and troublers of states:
Tho gan shepheards swaines to looke a loft,
And leave to live hard, and learne to ligge soft:          125
Tho under colour of shepeheards, somewhile
There crept in Wolves, ful of fraude and guile,
That often devoured their owne sheepe,
And often the shepheards, that did hem keepe.
This was the first sourse of shepheards sorowe,            130
That now nill be quitt with baile, nor borrowe.

PALINODE.

Three thinges to beare, bene very burdenous,
But the fourth to forbeare, is outragious.
Wemen that of Loves longing once lust,
Hardly forbearen, but have it they must:                   135
So when choler is inflamed with rage,
Wanting revenge, is hard to asswage:
And who can counsell a thristie soule,
With patience to forbeare the offred bowle?
But of all burdens, that a man can beare,                  140
Moste is, a fooles talke to beare and to heare.
I wene the Geaunt has not such a weight,
That beares on his shoulders the heavens height.
Thou findest faulte, where nys to be found,
And buildest strong warke upon a weake ground:             145
Thou raylest on right withouten reason,
And blamest hem much, for small encheason.
How shoulden shepheardes live, if not so?

---

121. *gape for*: desire.    125. *ligge*: lie.    126. *colour*: disguise.
131. *nill . . . borrowe*: cannot be stopped by guarantee or pledge (cf. E. K.'s
gloss).    135. *Hardly forbearen*: with difficulty refrain.    137. *wanting*:
lacking.

What? should they pynen in payne and woe?
Nay sayd I thereto, by my deare borrowe,                     150
If I may rest, I nill live in sorrowe.
   Sorrowe ne neede be hastened on:
For he will come without calling anone.
While times enduren of tranquillitie,
Usen we freely our felicitie.                                155
For when approchen the stormie stowres,
We mought with our shoulders beare of the sharpe
                                              showres.

And sooth to sayne, nought seemeth sike strife,
That shepheardes so witen ech others life,
And layen her faults the world beforne,                      160
The while their foes done eache of hem scorne.
Let none mislike of that may not be mended:
So conteck soone by concord mought be ended.

### PIERS.
Shepheard, I list none accordaunce make
With shepheard, that does the right way forsake.             165
And of the twaine, if choice were to me,
Had lever my foe, then my freend he be.
For what concord han light and darke sam?
Or what peace has the Lion with the Lambe?
Such faitors, when their false harts bene hidde,             170
Will doe, as did the Foxe by the Kidde.

### PALINODE.
Now *Piers*, of felowship, tell us that saying:
For the Ladde can keepe both our flocks from straying.

### PIERS.
THilke same Kidde (as I can well devise)
Was too very foolish and unwise.                             175

---

156. *stowres*: hard times.     157. *beare of*: ward off.     170. *faitors*:
impostors.     172. *of felowship*: as a friendly act.     175. *too very*: extremely.

For on a tyme in Sommer season,
The Gate her dame, that had good reason,
Yode forth abroade unto the greene wood,
To brouze, or play, or what shee thought good.
But for she had a motherly care                      180
Of her young sonne, and wit to beware,
Shee set her youngling before her knee,
That was both fresh and lovely to see,
And full of favour, as kidde mought be:
His Vellet head began to shoote out,                 185
And his wreathed hornes gan newly sprout:
The blossomes of lust to bud did beginne,
And spring forth ranckly under his chinne.
   My sonne (quoth she) (and with that gan weepe:
For carefull thoughts in her heart did creepe)       190
God blesse thee poore Orphane, as he mought me,
And send thec joy of thy jollitee.
Thy father (that word she spake with payne:
For a sigh had nigh rent her heart in twaine)
Thy father, had he lived this day,                    195
To see the braunche of his body displaie,
How would he have joyed at this sweete sight?
But ah false Fortune such joy did him spight,
And cutte of hys dayes with untimely woe,
Betraying him into the traines of hys foe.           200
Now I a waylfull widdowe behight,
Of my old age have this one delight,
To see thee succeed in thy fathers steade,
And florish in flowres of lusty head.
For even so thy father his head upheld,              205
And so his hauty hornes did he weld.
   Tho marking him with melting eyes,

177. *her*: his.   180. *But for*: because.   181. *wit to beware*: good sense to
be cautious.   184. *favour*: grace, good looks.   185. *Vellet*: velvet.
200. *traines*: snares.   203. *steade*: place.   206. *hauty*: lofty. *weld*: wield,
present.

A thrilling throbbe from her hart did aryse,
And interrupted all her other speache,
With some old sorowe, that made a newe breache:    210
Seemed shee sawe in the younglings face
The old lineaments of his fathers grace.
At last her solein silence she broke,
And gan his newe budded beard to stroke.
    Kiddie (quoth shee) thou kenst the great care,    215
I have of thy health and thy welfare,
Which many wyld beastes liggen in waite,
For to entrap in thy tender state:
But most the Foxe, maister of collusion:
For he has voued thy last confusion.    220
For thy my Kiddie be ruld by mee,
And never give trust to his trecheree.
And if he chaunce come, when I am abroade,
Sperre the yate fast for feare of fraude:
Ne for all his worst, nor for his best,    225
Open the dore at his request.
    So schooled the Gate her wanton sonne,
That answerd his mother, all should be done.
Tho went the pensife Damme out of dore,
And chaunst to stomble at the threshold flore:    230
Her stombling steppe some what her amazed,
(For such, as signes of ill luck bene dispraised)
Yet forth shee yode thereat halfe aghast:
And Kiddie the dore sperred after her fast.
It was not long, after shee was gone,    235
But the false Foxe came to the dore anone:
Not as a Foxe, for then he had be kend,
But all as a poore pedler he did wend,
Bearing a trusse of tryfles at hys backe,
As bells, and babes, and glasses in hys packe.    240

213. *solein*: sad.    220. *confusion*: destruction.    239. *trusse*: bundle.
240. *babes, and glasses*: dolls and mirrors (see E. K.'s gloss).

A Biggen he had got about his brayne,
For in his headpeace he felt a sore payne.
His hinder heele was wrapt in a clout,
For with great cold he had gotte the gout.
There at the dore he cast me downe hys pack,                    245
And layd him downe, and groned, Alack, Alack.
Ah deare Lord, and sweete Saint Charitee,
That some good body woulde once pitie mee.
　Well heard Kiddie al this sore constraint,
And lengd to know the cause of his complaint:                    250
Tho creeping close behind the Wickets clinck,
Prevelie he peeped out through a chinck:
Yet not so previlie, but the Foxe him spyed:
For deceitfull meaning is double eyed.
　Ah good young maister (then gan he crye)                    255
Jesus blesse that sweete face, I espye,
And keepe your corpse from the carefull stounds,
That in my carrion carcas abounds.
The Kidd pittying hys heavinesse,
Asked the cause of his great distresse,                    260
And also who, and whence that he were.
Tho he, that had well ycond his lere,
Thus medled his talke with many a teare,
Sicke, sicke, alas, and little lack of dead,
But I be relieved by your beastlyhead.                    265
I am a poore Sheepe, albe my coloure donne:
For with long traveile I am brent in the sonne.
And if that my Grandsire me sayd, be true,
Sicker I am very sybbe to you:

---

241. *Biggen*: tight cap.      243. *clout*: rag.      245. *me*: the ethical dative.
249. *constraint*: distress.      250. *lengd*: longed.      251. *Wickets clinck*:
small door's keyhole.      257. *carefull stounds*: worrisome troubles.
259. *heavinesse*: depression.      264. *lack*: short.      265. *beastlyhead*: proper
animal nature (cf. "humanity").      266. *donne*: dun, dark.      267. *traveile*:
travel, effort. *brent*: burned.      269. *very sybbe*: true kin.

So be your goodlihead doe not disdayne 270
The base kinred of so simple swaine.
Of mercye and favour then I you pray,
With your ayd to forstall my neere decay.
　Tho out of his packe a glasse he tooke:
Wherein while kiddie unwares did looke, 275
He was so enamored with the newell,
That nought he deemed deare for the jewell.
Tho opened he the dore, and in came
The false Foxe, as he were starke lame.
His tayle he clapt betwixt his legs twayne, 280
Lest he should be descried by his trayne.
　Being within, the Kidde made him good glee,
All for the love of the glasse he did see.
After his chere the Pedler can chat,
And tell many lesings of this, and that: 285
And how he could shewe many a fine knack.
Tho shewed his ware, and opened his packe,
All save a bell, which he left behind
In the basket for the Kidde to fynd.
Which when the Kidde stooped downe to catch, 290
He popt him in, and his basket did latch,
Ne stayed he once, the dore to make fast,
But ranne awaye with him in all hast.
Home when the doubtfull Damme had her hyde,
She mought see the dore stand open wyde. 295
All agast, lowdly she gan to call
Her Kidde: but he nould answere at all.
Tho on the flore she sawe the merchandise,

277. *nought . . . deare*: nothing he thought too expensive.　279. *starke*:
extremely.　281. *descried . . . trayne*: identified by what trailed behind
him.　282. *made . . . glee*: received him welcome.　284. *After his chere*:
according to his mood. *can*: did.　285. *lesings*: lies.　286. *knack*:
trick.　288. *save*: except.　291. *popt*: possibly a pun on "poped" (with
reference to the Jesuit Mission).　294. *doubtfull*: worried. *hyde*: hied,
hurried.

Of which her sonne had sette to dere a prise.
What helpe? her Kidde shee knewe well was gone:          300
Shee weeped, and wayled, and made great mone.
Such end had the Kidde, for he nould warned be
Of craft, coloured with simplicitie:
And such end perdie does all hem remayne,
That of such falsers freendship bene fayne.          305

PALINODIE.
Truly *Piers*, thou art beside thy wit,
Furthest fro the marke, weening it to hit,
Now I pray thee, lette me thy tale borrowe
For our sir John, to say to morrowe
At the Kerke, when it is holliday:          310
For well he meanes, but little can say.
But and if Foxes bene so crafty, as so,
Much needeth all shepheards hem to knowe.

PIERS.
Of their falshode more could I recount.
But now the bright Sunne gynneth to dismount:          315
And for the deawie night now doth nye,
I hold it best for us, home to hye.

Palinodes Embleme.

Πὰς μὲν ἄπιστος ἀπιστεῖ.

Piers his Embleme.          320

Τίς δ' ἄρα πίστις ἀπίστω;

GLOSSE.
[1]     Thilke) this same moneth. It is applyed to the season of
        the moneth, when all menne delight them selves with
        pleasaunce of fieldes, and gardens, and garments.

303. *coloured*: disguised.      304. *perdie . . . remayne*: surely awaits all
those.      306. *beside thy wit*: missed the point.      312. *But and*: however.

[5] Bloncket liveries) gray coates. [6] Yclad) arrayed, Y, redoundeth, as before.

[9] In every where) a straunge, yet proper kind of speaking.

[10] Buskets) a Diminutive .s. little bushes of hauthorne. [12] Kirke) church. [15] Queme) please.

[20] A shole) a multitude; taken of fishe, whereof some going in great companies, are sayde to swimme in a shole.

[22] Yode) went. [25] Jouyssance) joye. [36] Swinck) labour. [38] Inly) entirely. [39] Faytours) vagabonds.

[54] Great pan) is Christ, the very God of all shepheards, which calleth himselfe the greate and good shepherd. The name is most rightly (me thinkes) applyed to him, for Pan signifieth all or omnipotent, which is onely the Lord Jesus. And by that name (as I remember) he is called of Eusebius in his fifte booke de Preparat. Evang; who thereof telleth a proper storye to that purpose. Which story is first recorded of Plutarch, in his booke of the ceasing of oracles, and of Lavetere translated, in his booke of walking sprightes. who sayth, that about the same time, that our Lord suffered his most bitter passion for the redemtion of man, certein passengers sayling from Italy to Cyprus and passing by certain Iles called Paxæ, heard a voyce calling alowde Thamus, Thamus, (now Thamus was the name of an Ægyptian, which was Pilote of the ship,) who giving eare to the cry, was bidden, when he came to Palodes, to tel, that the great Pan was dead: which he doubting to doe, yet for that when he came

[6] *redoundeth*: is redundant.    [9] *In every where*: E. K.'s comment is on the use of "where" as noun.    [54.9] *Lavatere*: All of this note is taken from Ludwig Lavater, *De Larvis*, translated by Robert Harrison, *Of Ghostes and Spirites Walking by Night* (1572), 1.19.

to Palodes, there sodeinly was such a calme of winde,
that the shippe stoode still in the sea unmoved, he was
forced to cry alowd, that Pan was dead: wherewithall
there was heard suche piteous outcryes and dreadfull
shriking, as hath not bene the like. By whych Pan,
though of some be understoode the great Satanas,
whose kingdome at that time was by Christ conquered,
the gates of hell broken up, and death by death
delivered to eternall death, (for at that time, as he
sayth, all Oracles surceased, and enchaunted spirits,
that were wont to delude the people, thenceforth held
theyr peace) and also at the demaund of the
Emperoure Tiberius, who that Pan should be, answere
was made him by the wisest and best learned, that it
was the sonne of Mercurie and Penelope, yet I thinke it
more properly meant of the death of Christ, the onely
and very Pan, then suffering for his flock.

[57]   I as I am) seemeth to imitate the commen proverb,
Malim Invidere mihi omnes quam miserescere.

[61]   Nas) is a syncope, for ne has, or has not: as nould, for
would not.

[69]   Tho with them) doth imitate the Epitaphe of the
ryotous king Sardanapalus, whych caused to be written
on his tombe in Greeke: which verses be thus
translated by Tullie.
    "  Hæc habui quæ edi, quæque exaturata libido
    "  Hausit, at illa manent multa ac præclara relicta.
which may thus be turned into English.
    "  All that I eate did I joye, and all that I greedily
gorged:

[57.1–2] Malim . . . miserescere: "I would rather have everybody envy me
than feel sorry for me." Source is unknown.    [61] *syncope*: rhetorical figure
meaning alteration of a letter or syllable of a word (also called
*metaplosmos*).    [69.4] *Tullie*: Cicero, *Tusculan Disputations* 5.35.101; the
translation, according to the first of Sp's *Three . . . Letters* to Gabriel Harvey
(1580), is Sp's.

"    As for those many goodly matters left I for others. Much like the Epitaph of a good olde Erle of Devonshire, which though much more wisedome bewraieth, then Sardanapalus, yet hath a smacke of his sensuall delights and beastlinesse. the rymes be these.

"    Ho, Ho, who lies here?

"    I the good Erle of Devonshere,

"    And Maulde my wife, that was ful deare,

"    We lived together lv. yeare.

"       That we spent, we had:

"       That we gave, we have:

"       That we lefte, we lost.

[75] Algrind) the name of a shepheard.   [76] Men of the Lay) Lay men. [78] Enaunter) least that.

[82] Sovenaunce) remembraunce.   [91] Miscreaunce) despeire or misbeliefe.

[92] Chevisaunce) sometime of Chaucer used for gaine: sometime of other for spoyle, or bootie, or enterprise, and sometime for chiefdome.

[111] Pan himselfe) God. according as is sayd in Deuteronomie, That in division of the lande of Canaan, to the tribe of Levie no portion of heritage should bee allotted, for GOD himselfe was their inheritaunce.

[121] Some gan) meant of the Pope, and his Antichristian prelates, which usurpe a tyrannical dominion in the Churche, and with Peters counterfet keyes, open a wide gate to al wickednesse and insolent government. Nought here spoken, as of purpose to deny fatherly rule and godly governaunce (as some malitiously of late

---

[69.13] *bewraieth*: reveals. *smacke*: touch, tinge.    [111.2] *Deuteronomie* 10.9. The "tribe of Levie" (Levi) was the priestly tribe.    [121.5] *Nought here spoken*: This gloss, unlike E. K.'s Argument, states clearly the opposition in the dialogue between responsible and casual predatory clergy while unmistakably rejecting the recent ultra-Protestant attack on episcopal orders.

have done to the great unreste and hinderaunce of the
Churche) but to displaye the pride and disorder of
such, as in steede of feeding their sheepe, indeede feede
of theyr sheepe.

[130] Sourse) welspring and originall.　[131] Borrowe)
pledge or suertie.

[142] The Geaunte) is the greate Atlas, whom the poetes
feign to be a huge geaunt, that beareth Heaven on his
shoulders: being in deede a merveilous highe
mountaine in Mauritania, that now is Barbarie, which
to mans seeming perceth the cloudes, and seemeth to
touch the heavens. Other thinke, and they not amisse,
that this fable was meant of one Atlas king of the same
countrye, (of whome may bee, that that hil had his
denomination) brother to Prometheus who (as the
Grekes say) did first fynd out the hidden courses of the
starres, by an excellent imagination, wherefore the
poetes feigned, that he susteyned the firmament on hys
shoulders. Many other conjectures needelesse be told
hereof.

[145] Warke) worke.　[147] Encheason) cause, occasion.

[150] Deare borow) that is our saviour, the commen pledge
of all mens debts to death.

[159] Wyten) blame.　[158] Nought seemeth) is
unseemely.　[163] Conteck) strife contention.

[160] Her) theyr, as useth Chaucer.　[168] Han) for
have.　[168] Sam) together.

[174] This tale is much like to that in Æsops fables, but the
Catastrophe and end is farre different. By the Kidde
may be understoode the simple sorte of the faythfull
and true Christians. By hys dame Christe, that hath
alreadie with carefull watchewords (as heere doth the

[121.9–10] *feede of*: feed from, on.　　[142.1] *The Geaunte*: Boccaccio,
*Genealogia Deorum* 4.31.　　[142.9] *denomination*: name.
[174.2] *Catastrophe*: denouncement, event producing final tragic result.

gote) warned his little ones, to beware of such
doubling deceit. By the Foxe, the false and faithlesse
Papistes, to whom is no credit to be given, nor
felowshippe to be used.

[177] The gate) the Gote: Northernely spoken to turne O
into A. [178] Yode) went. afforesayd.

[182] She set) A figure called Fictio. which useth to attribute
reasonable actions and speaches to unreasonable
creatures.

[187] The bloosmes of lust) be the young and mossie heares,
which then beginne to sproute and shoote foorth,
when lustfull heate beginneth to kindle.

[189] And with) A very Poeticall πάθος.

[191] Orphane) A youngling or pupill, that needeth a Tutour
and governour.

[193] That word) A patheticall parenthesis, to encrease a
carefull Hyperbaton.

[196] The braunch) of the fathers body, is the child.

[205] For even so) Alluded to the saying of Andromache to
Ascanius in Virgile.

   Sic oculos, sic ille manus, sic ora ferebat.

[208] A thrilling throb) a percing sighe. [217] Liggen) lye.

[219] Maister of collusion) .s. coloured guile, because the
Foxe of al beasts is most wily and crafty.

[224] Sperre the yate) shut the dore.

[232] For such) The gotes stombling is here noted as an evill
signe. The like to be marked in all histories: and that
not the leaste of the Lorde Hastingues in king

[174.8] *credit*: credence, belief.  [174.9] *felowshippe . . . used*: association
to be made.  [189] πάθος.: Gk *pathos*, sensitive representation of
suffering.  [193] *Hyperbaton*: change of the normal word order.
[205.1] *Andromache*: Hector's wife, comparing Aeneas' son Ascanius to her
dead son Astyanax, *Aen* 3.490.  [205.3] *Sic . . . ferebat*: "His [Astyanax's]
eyes, his hands, his face were just like yours."  [232.3] *Hastingues*:
Shakespeare, following Holinshed, cites the stumbling detail in *Richard III*
3.4.83–85.

Rycharde the third his dayes. For beside his
daungerous dreame (whiche was a shrewde prophecie
of his mishap, that folowed) it is sayd that in the
morning ryding toward the tower of London, there to
sitte uppon matters of counsell, his horse stombled
twise or thrise by the way: which of some, that ryding
with hym in his company, were privie to his neere
destenie, was secretly marked, and afterward noted for
memorie of his great mishap, that ensewed. For being
then as merye, as man might be, and least doubting any
mortall daunger, he was within two howres after, of
the Tyranne put to a shamefull deathe.

[240] As belles) by such trifles are noted, the reliques and
ragges of popish supersition, which put no smal
religion in Belles: and Babies .s. Idoles: and glasses .s.
Paxes, and such lyke trumperies.

[244] Great cold.) For they boast much of their outward
patience, and voluntarye sufferaunce as a worke of
merite and holy humblenesse.

[247] Sweete S. Charitie.) The Catholiques comen othe, and
onely speache, to have charitye alwayes in their mouth,
and sometime in their outward Actions, but never
inwardly in fayth and godly zeale.

[251] Clincke.) a key hole. Whose diminutive is clicket, used
of Chaucer for a Key.

[257] Stoundes) fittes: aforesayde.   [262] His lere) his
lesson. [263] Medled) mingled.

[265] Bestlihead.) agreeing to the person of a
beast.   [269] Sibbe.) of kynne.

[276] Newell) a newe thing.   [273] To forestall) to
prævent.   [282] Glee) chere, afforesayde.

[299] Deare a price.) his lyfe, which he lost for those toyes.

---

[240.4] *Paxes*: plates showing Crucifixion images, to be kissed devotionally
during mass. *trumperies*: deceits.   [299] *toyes*: trifles.

[304] Such ende) is an Epiphonèma, or rather the morall of
the whole tale, whose purpose is to warne the
protestaunt beware, howe he geveth credit to the
unfaythfull Catholique: whereof we have dayly proofes
sufficient, but one moste famous of all, practised of
Late yeares in Fraunce by Charles the nynth.

[305] Fayne) gladde or desyrous.

[309] Our sir John) a Popishe priest. A saying fit for the
grosenesse of a shepheard, but spoken to taunte
unlearned Priestes.

[315] Dismount) descende or set.     [316] Nye) draweth
nere.

## Embleme.

Both these Emblemes make one whole Hexametre. The first
spoken of Palinodie, as in reproche of them, that be
distrustfull, is a peece of Theognis verse, intending,
that who doth most mistrust is most false. For such
experience in falsehod breedeth mistrust in the mynd,
thinking nolesse guile to lurke in others, then in
hymselfe. But Piers thereto strongly replyeth with
another peece of the same verse, saying as in his former
fable, what fayth then is there in the faythlesse. For if
fayth be the ground of religion, which fayth they dayly
false, what hold then is there of theyr religion. And
thys is all that they saye.

[304.5–6] *but . . . nynth*: the St. Bartholemew's Day massacre of Huguenots,
August 1572.     [309] *sir John*: "sir" as a mildly contemptuous title but not
restricted to Catholic priests as Shakespeare's Sir Oliver Martext shows (*As
You Like It*). *grosenesse*: stupidity.     [Embleme.3] *Theognis*: not in
Theognis; source unknown.

# June

♦♦♦♦♦♦♦

L ike *Aprill*, *June* advertises the poet's ability. Its central
stanza (57–64) contains Hobbinol's apotheosis of Colin
as poet: though a mere shepherd his songs "confound"
and "outgoe" the Muses themselves including their chief,
Calliope. Since Calliope presides over heroic praise, what Hob-
binol has unwittingly predicted is Colin's transformation into a
poet of epic. There is, however, unconscious paradox in Hob-
binol's approach to Colin: while recognizing his superb poetic
gifts (signaled by the Orpheus formula of his charming woods
and birds [49–56]), he nevertheless tries to woo Colin back to
the secure and lovely Arcadian dales of static, unengaged
pastoral.

Hobbinol's pleasance or *locus amoenus* is for him an end in
itself, the proper site for the contented, unambitious man. But it
is also a transient June pleasance that is dependent on the sea-
sons, as *September* shows. Colin, on the other hand, is a discon-
tented climber of "hilles" (19), aware of "Wolves" (12), and
driven by a "cruell fate,/And angry Gods . . . from coste to coste"
(14–15). This unmistakable allusion to Aeneas seeking new
Troy (*Aeneid* 1.1–5) points towards Colin's ambitious but haz-
ardous role as the would-be prophetic poet of the Elizabethan
state. What Hobbinol offers is a return to clearly outgrown
"carelesse yeeres" (33) and a concomitant wooing of Rosalind
that is now pointless. Colin's "ryper age" (36) reminds us that
Spenser has nearly finished half of the first phase of the pre-
scribed Virgilian career-pattern and that pastoral itself is the way
to another genre.

Like Hobbinol's, Colin's view of his ability is also paradoxi-
cal: while ambitiously climbing hills he lays claim to only slender
talent and no ambition, notably in the eclogue's second half. He

is not like Orpheus whose song could alter reality (and twice win Eurydice), nor even like his master Tityrus (Chaucer) who at least could sing to "slake/The flames, which love within his heart had bredd" (85–86). But this topos of inability or affected modesty is in effect an indirect tactic of self-assertion. Such assertion raises the eclogue far beyond mere Arcadianism. Indeed, the introduction of Menalcas as Rosalind's new lover may (as McLane [1961: 36–40] has argued) register Spenser's further protest against the French marriage project.

The polarity of hill and dale continues to the eclogue's end and organizes the woodcut. While Colin actively gestures toward a fortified hilltop with its connotations of power and risk, Hobbinol stands by placidly as the *beatus vir* of Psalm 1.3 symbolized by the "tree planted by the rivers of water" shown behind him. Behind Colin the cheerful haycockers do their seasonal labor in which Elizabethans would see the biblical irony of mown grass as a sign of man's mortality (e.g. Psalms 90.5–6, 103.15–16, Isaiah 40.6–8). For Colin's "ryper age" limits the time for accomplishment. Now in his late twenties, Spenser was no longer young in terms of sixteenth-century life spans.

Spenser makes the unique and difficult *June* stanza itself an advertisement. Its eight lines are two mirror-image quatrains (*ababbaba*) designed to demonstrate the most daring feature of *The Faerie Queene* stanza with its four *b*-rhymes, i.e. the difficulty in English of finding quadruple rhymes for every stanza of a very long poem and one already in process of composition.

# *June.*

*Ægloga sexta.*

## ARGUMENT.

T HIS *Æglogue is wholly vowed to the complayning of Colins ill
success in his love. For being (as is aforesaid) enamoured of a
Country lasse Rosalind, and having (as seemeth) founde place in her
heart, he lamenteth to his deare frend Hobbinoll, that he is nowe
forsaken unfaithfully, and in his steed Menalcas, another shepheard
received disloyally. And this is the whole Argument of this Æglogue.*

HOBBINOL. COLIN Cloute.

L O *Collin,* here the place, whose pleasaunt syte
From other shades hath weand my wandring
mynde.
Tell me, what wants me here, to worke delyte?
The simple ayre, the gentle warbling wynde,
So calme, so coole, as no where else I fynde:            5
The grassye ground with daintye Daysies dight,

ARGUMENT *vowed*: devoted.    3. *what wants me*: what do I lack.

The Bramble bush, where Byrds of every kynde
To the waters fall their tunes attemper right.

### COLLIN.

O happy *Hobbinoll*, I blesse thy state,
That Paradise hast found, whych *Adam* lost.          10
Here wander may thy flock early or late,
Withouten dreade of Wolves to bene ytost:
Thy lovely layes here mayst thou freely boste.
But I unhappy man, whom cruell fate,
And angry Gods pursue from coste to coste,          15
Can nowhere fynd, to shroude my lucklesse pate.

### HOBBINOLL.

Then if by me thou list advised be,
Forsake the soyle, that so doth thee bewitch:
Leave me those hilles, where harbrough nis to see,
Nor holybush, nor brere, nor winding witche:          20
And to the dales resort, where shepheards ritch,
And fruictfull flocks bene every where to see.
Here no night Ravens lodge more black then pitche,
Nor elvish ghosts, nor gastly owles doe flee.

But frendly Faeries, met with many Graces,          25
And lightfote Nymphes can chace the lingring night,
With Heydeguyes, and trimly trodden traces,
Whilst systers nyne, which dwell on *Parnasse* hight,
Doe make them musick, for their more delight:
And *Pan* himselfe to kisse their christall faces,          30
Will pype and daunce, when *Phœbe* shineth bright:
Such pierlesse pleasures have we in these places.

### COLLIN.

And I, whylst youth, and course of carelesse yeeres
Did let me walke withouten lincks of love,

8. *attemper*: bring into harmony.    12. *ytost*: disturbed.    19. *me*: for my
sake (ethical dative).    20. *winding witche*: the wych elm with pliant
branches.    24. *gastly*: causing dismay. *flee*: fly.    33. *carelesse*:
carefree.    34. *lincks*: chains.

In such delights did joy amongst my peeres:     35
But ryper age such pleasures doth reprove,
My fancye eke from former follies move
To stayed steps: for time in passing weares
(As garments doen, which wexen old above)
And draweth newe delightes with hoary heares.     40

Tho couth I sing of love, and tune my pype
Unto my plaintive pleas in verses made:
Tho would I seeke for Queene apples unrype,
To give my *Rosalind,* and in Sommer shade
Dight gaudy Girlonds, was my comen trade,     45
To crowne her golden locks, but yeeres more rype,
And losse of her, whose love as lyfe I wayd,
Those weary wanton toyes away dyd wype.

HOBBINOLL.

*Colin,* to heare thy rymes and roundelayes,
Which thou were wont on wastfull hylls to singe,     50
I more delight, then larke in Sommer dayes:
Whose Echo made the neyghbour groves to ring,
And taught the byrds, which in the lower spring
Did shroude in shady leaves from sonny rayes,
Frame to thy songe their chereful cheriping,     55
Or hold theyr peace, for shame of thy swete layes.

I sawe *Calliope* wyth Muses moe,
Soone as thy oaten pype began to sound,
Theyr yvory Luyts and Tamburins forgoe:
And from the fountaine, where they sat around,     60
Renne after hastely thy silver sound.
But when they came, where thou thy skill didst showe,
They drewe abacke, as halfe with shame confound,
Shepheard to see, them in theyr art outgoe.

39. *wexen old above*: show wear on the surface.     42. *couth*: could.
43. *Queene apples*: an old variety of early apple or perhaps the quince because
of its association with Venus.     48. *toyes*: games of love.     55. *Frame to*:
fashion according to.     59. *Tamburins*: tabors, small drums.     64. *outgoe*:
surpass.

COLLIN.

Of Muses *Hobbinol*, I conne no skill:                                     65
For they bene daughters of the hyghest *Jove*,
And holden scorne of homely shepheards quill.
For sith I heard, that *Pan* with *Phœbus* strove,
Which him to much rebuke and Daunger drove:
I never lyst presume to *Parnasse* hyll,                                    70
But pyping lowe in shade of lowly grove,
I play to please my selfe, all be it ill.

Nought weigh I, who my song doth prayse or blame,
Ne strive to winne renowne, or passe the rest:
With shepheard sittes not, followe flying fame:                           75
But feede his flocke in fields, where falls hem best.
I wote my rymes bene rough, and rudely drest:
The fytter they, my carefull case to frame:
Enough is me to paint out my unrest,
And poore my piteous plaints out in the same.                             80

The God of shepheards *Tityrus* is dead,
Who taught me homely, as I can, to make.
He, whilst he lived, was the soveraigne head
Of shepheards all, that bene with love ytake:
Well couth he wayle hys Woes, and lightly slake                          85
The flames, which love within his heart had bredd,
And tell us mery tales, to keepe us wake,
The while our sheepe about us safely fedde.

Nowe dead he is, and lyeth wrapt in lead,
(O why should death on hym such outrage showe?)                          90

---

65. *conne no skill*: know nothing.          73. *prayse or blame*: the two goals of
epideictic (demonstrative) rhetoric; when applied to poetry, as in George
Puttenham's *Arte of English Poesie* (1589), the epideictic made the purpose of
each genre praise or blame.          74. *passe*: surpass.          75. *sittes not, followe*: is
not proper to pursue.          76. *falls hem best*: it is best for them to be.
79. *me*: for me (dative).          82. *make*: compose poems.          85. *couth*: knew
how to.

And all hys passing skil with him is fledde,
The fame whereof doth dayly greater growe.
But if on me some little drops would flowe,
Of that the spring was in his learned hedde,
I soone would learne these woods, to wayle my woe,          95
And teache the trees, their trickling teares to shedde.

Then should my plaints, causd of discurtesee,
As messengers of all my painfull plight,
Flye to my love, where ever that she bee,
And pierce her heart with poynt of worthy wight:          100
As shee deserves, that wrought so deadly spight.
And thou *Menalcas*, that by trecheree
Didst underfong my lasse, to wexe so light,
Shouldest well be knowne for such thy villanee.

But since I am not, as I wish I were,          105
Ye gentle shepheards, which your flocks do feede,
Whether on hylls, or dales, or other where,
Beare witnesse all of thys so wicked deede:
And tell the lasse, whose flowre is woxe a weede,
And faultlesse fayth, is turned to faithlesse fere,          110
That she the truest shepheards hart made bleede,
That lyves on earth, and loved her most dere.

### HOBBINOL.

O carefull *Colin*, I lament thy case,
Thy teares would make the hardest flint to flowe.
And faithlesse Rosalind, and voide of grace,          115
That art the roote of all this ruthfull woe.
But now is time, I gesse, homeward to goe:
Then ryse ye blessed flocks, and home apace,
Least night with stealing steppes doe you forsloe,
And wett your tender Lambes, that by you trace.          120

---

91. *passing*: surpassing, with probable pun on "pass."     103. *underfong*:
possess, seduce (E. K.'s gloss is misleading).     110. *fere*: mate.
119. *forsloe*: hinder.     120. *trace*: walk.

Colins Embleme.

*Gia speme spenta.*

GLOSSE.

[1]  Syte) situation and place.

[10]  Paradise) A Paradise in Greeke signifieth a Garden of
pleasure, or place of delights. So he compareth the
soile, wherin Hobbinoll made his abode, to that earthly
Paradise, in scripture called Eden; wherein Adam in his
first creation was placed. Which of the most learned is
thought to be in Mesopotamia, the most fertile and
pleasaunte country in the world (as may appeare by
Diodorus Syculus description of it, in the hystorie of
Alexanders conquest thereof.) Lying between the two
famous Ryvers (which are sayd in scripture to flowe
out of Paradise) Tygris and Euphrates, whereof it is so
denominate.

[18]  Forsake the soyle) This is no poetical fiction, but
unfeynedly spoken of the Poete selfe, who for speciall
occasion of private affayres (as I have bene partly of
himselfe informed) and for his more preferment
removing out of the Northparts came into the South,
as Hobbinoll indeede advised him privately.

[19]  Those hylles) that is the North countrye, where he
dwelt.  [19] N'is) is not.

[21]  The Dales) The Southpartes, where he nowe abydeth,
which thoughe they be full of hylles and woodes (for
Kent is very hyllye and woodye; and therefore so

122. *Gia speme spenta*: "hope utterly extinguished" (Ital.).

[10.8] *Diodorus Syculus (Siculus)*: *Library of History* 17.53, but the
"description" is only one sentence.  [10.12] *it so denominate*:
Mesopotamia (Gk: place amid rivers) takes its name.  [18.4] *for . . .
preferment*: to get himself a better position

called: for Kantsh in the Saxons tongue signifieth
woodie) yet in respecte of the Northpartes they be
called dales. For indede the North is counted the
higher countrye.

[23]  Night Ravens etc.) by such hatefull byrdes, hee
meaneth all misfortunes (Whereof they be tokens)
flying every where.

[25]  Frendly faeries) the opinion of Faeries and elfes is very
old, and yet sticketh very religiously in the myndes of
some. But to roote that rancke opinion of Elfes oute of
mens hearts, the truth is, that there be no such thinges,
nor yet the shadowes of the things, but onely by a sort
of bald Friers and knavish shavelings so feigned; which
as in all other things, so in that, soughte to nousell the
comen people in ignorounce, least being once
acquainted with the truth of things, they woulde in
tyme smell out the untruth of theyr packed pelfe and
Massepenie religion. But the sooth is, that when all
Italy was distraicte into the Factions of the Guelfes and
the Gibelins, being two famous houses in Florence, the
name began through their great mischiefes and many
outrages, to be so odious or rather dreadfull in the
peoples eares, that if theyr children at any time were
frowarde and wanton, they would say to them that the
Guelfe or the Gibeline came. Which words nowe from
them (as many thinge els) be come into our usage, and
for Guelfes and Gibelines, we say Elfes and Goblins.
No otherwise then the Frenchmen used to say of that
valiaunt captain, the very scourge of Fraunce, the Lord

---

[21.4] *Kantsh*: E. K.'s source, William Lambarde's *Perambulation of Kent*
(1576), says the word is British (i.e. Celtic), not Saxon.      [25.1] *opinion of*:
belief in.      [25.2] *religiously*: persistently.      [25.6] *shavelings*:
rascals.      [25.7] *nousell*: foster.      [25.12–13] *Guelfes . . . Goblins*: a
totally fanciful (though not original) derivation for "elf" and "goblin."
[25.17] *frowarde*: perverse.

Thalbot, afterward Erle of Shrewsbury; whose noblesse
bred such a terrour in the hearts of the French, that oft
times even great armies were defaicted and put to
flyght at the onely hearing of hys name. In somuch that
the French wemen, to affray theyr chyldren, would tell
them that the Talbot commeth.

[25]  Many Graces) though there be indeede but three
Graces or Charites (as afore is sayd) or at the utmost
but foure, yet in respect of many gyftes of bounty,
there may be sayde more. And so Musæus sayth, that
in Heroes eyther eye there satte a hundred graces. And
by that authoritye, thys same Poete in his Pageaunts
sayth. An hundred Graces on her eyeledde satte. etc.

[27]  Haydeguies) A country daunce or rownd. The conceipt
is, that the Graces and Nymphes doe daunce unto the
Muses, and Pan his musicke all night by Moonelight.
To signifie the pleasauntnesse of the soyle.

[35]  Peeres) Equalles and felow shepheards.

[43]  Queneapples unripe) imitating Virgils verse.
        Ipse ego cana legam tenera lanugine mala.

[52]  Neighbour groves) a straunge phrase in English, but
word for word expressing the Latine vicina nemora.

[53]  Spring) not of water, but of young trees
springing.   [57] Calliope) afforesayde. Thys staffe is
full of verie poetical invention.   [59] Tamburines) an
olde kind of instrument, which of some is supposed to
be the Clarion.

[25.23] *Thalbot*: Sir John Talbot, lst earl of Shrewsbury, commander late in
the Hundred Years' War which ended with his defeat in 1453.
[25.3–4] *Musaeus*: *de Herone et Leandro*, 63–65.   [25.6] *Pageaunts*: the
only reference to this lost work. If it ever existed it may have resembled
Petrarch's *Trionfi*. Cf. *FQ* II iii 25; *Amor* 40; *HB* 253–54.   [43] *Ipse* . . .
*mala*: "I myself will pick the pale, soft-downed quinces," *Ecl* 2.51.
[57] *staffe*: line.   [59.3] *Clarion*: a high-pitched trumpet (impossible to
confuse with a tabor which was a small drum).

[68]  Pan with Phæbus) the tale is well knowne, howe that
      Pan and Apollo striving for excellencye in musicke,
      chose Midas for their judge. Who being corrupted
      wyth partiall affection, gave the victorye to Pan
      undeserved: for which Phœbus sette a payre of Asses
      eares upon hys head etc.

[81]  Tityrus) That by Tityrus is meant Chaucer, hath bene
      already sufficiently sayde, and by thys more playne
      appeareth, that he sayth, he tolde merye tales. Such as
      be hys Canterburie tales. whom he calleth the God of
      Poetes for hys excellencie, so as Tullie calleth Lentulus,
      Deum vitæ suæ .s. the God of hys lyfe.

[82]  To make) to versifie.   [90] O why) A pretye
      Epanorthosis or correction.

[97]  Discurtesie) he meaneth the falsenesse of his lover
      Rosalinde, who forsaking hym, hadde chosen another.

[100] Poynte of worthy wite) the pricke of deserved blame.

[102] Menalcas) the name of a shephearde in Virgile; but
      here is meant a person unknowne and secrete, agaynst
      whome he often bitterly invayeth.

[103] underfonge) undermyne and deceive by false
      suggestion.

### Embleme.

You remember, that in the fyrst Æglogue, Colins
Poesie was Anchora speme: for that as then there was
hope of favour to be found in tyme. But nowe being
cleane forlorne and rejected of her, as whose hope, that
was, is cleane extinguished and turned into despeyre,
he renounceth all comfort and hope of goodnesse to
come. which is all the meaning of thys Embleme.

---

[68] *Pan with Phæbus*: Ovid, *Met* 11.153–93.     [68.4] *partiall affection*:
favoritism.     [81.5] *Tullie*: Cicero, *Post Reditum in Senatu* 4.8.
[102] *Virgile*: *Ecl* 3.5–6.

# Julye

June and Julye, the pair of eclogues at the *Calender's* center, share the upland-lowland motif. In *June* Hobbinol invites Colin to descend to the dales; in *Julye* Morrell invites Thomalin to come up a hill. Like *Februarie*, both eclogues are versions of the medieval *conflictus* or debate between polar opposites. Both focus on the danger of high aspiration, in Colin's case poetic, in Thomalin's ecclesiastic. Even the eclogues' woodcuts placed side by side form a symmetry of heights framing lowlands. In *Julye* Spenser imitates until line 93 the mountain-plain scheme of Mantuan's eighth eclogue before turning to imitate parts of his seventh.

Once again, E. K.'s Argument is off-base. Thomalin indeed says Morrell is "prowde" (1), but he does not discernibly sound so. Nor, in spite of E. K.'s first gloss, does the parable of the sheep and the goats—the redeemed and the damned—seem to apply to Morrell and his goats. In fact the ideal shepherd Abel, says Thomalin, sometimes offered "a Kidde," sometimes "a sheepe" (135) and thus found "favour" (138) with God (the kid is, significantly, Spenser's innovation: the passage he is imitating from Mantuan, *Eclogue* 7.18–19, has a sheep, calf, and lamb).

The shepherds' debate, perhaps befitting the high summer season, lacks acrimony, and its name-calling ("laesie loord" [33]; "lewde lorrell" [93]) seems to be bantering. Both shepherds freely mix biblical and classical citations in the typical Renaissance manner. They differ mainly on whether hills frequented by saints have thus become sacred sites or simply exemplary reminders of saintly lives. In fact, Thomalin's statement of the latter position (113–20) is at the poem's center. But, if Morrell is too literal in thinking that "hills bene nigher heven"

(89), Thomalin's sweeping proverb "To Kerke the narre, from God more farre" (97) has only limited application. In fact, Morrell's idea of Eden's being on a hill (65–68) from which one enters heaven (89–90) corresponds to Dante's concept in the *Purgatorio* 28.

Thomalin's scandalized account of Palinode's pilgrimage fits into the medieval and Renaissance tradition of satirizing Roman corruptions. But his aside, "if such be Rome" (183), and his ironic comment, "Sike syrlye shepheards han we none,/they keepen all the path" (203–04), hint that abuse of church office may be found closer to home.

The eclogue's ending makes its general discussion of the perils of high office suddenly specific. For the braining of Algrind by a soaring "Eagle" (222) unmistakably refers to Elizabeth's deprivation of Edward Grindal, archbishop of Canterbury—a good shepherd who could not be more "great in gree" (215)—from exercising his office. Both shepherds concur in sympathy for Algrind's plight. Morrell's name is probably an anagram for John Aylmer, bishop of London, and Thomalin's may suggest Thomas Cooper, bishop of Lincoln (see McLane 1961: 188–215). Both were notably learned bishops who supported Grindal against the queen in his refusal to suppress the "prophesyings." Criticism of the royal action is more than implicit here, and Spenser knows he is on dangerous ground. Morrell warns, though in general terms, that "harme may come of melling" (208).

*Julye's* verse-form is the divided (i.e. internally rhymed) fourteener which George Turbervile used for his translation of Mantuan (1567), and so it is apt for this recycling of Mantuan. Since Elizabethans used it as the common measure of metrical psalm versions, it had also acquired distinctly Protestant connotations.

# *Julye.*

*Ægloga septima.*

## ARGUMENT.

THis Æglogue is made in the honour and commendation of good
shepeheardes, and to the shame and disprayse of proude and
ambitious Pastours. Such as Morrell is here imagined to bee.

THOMALIN.   MORRELL.

IS not thilke same a goteheard prowde,
   that sittes on yonder bancke,
Whose straying heard them selfe doth shrowde
   emong the bushes rancke?

MORRELL.

What ho, thou jollye shepheards swayne,       5
   come up the hyll to me:
Better is, then the lowly playne,
   als for thy flocke, and thee.

THOMALIN.

Ah God shield, man, that I should clime,
  and learne to looke alofte,                                    10
This reede is ryfe, that oftentime
  great clymbers fall unsoft.
In humble dales is footing fast,
  the trode is not so tickle:
And though one fall through heedlesse hast,  15
  yet is his misse not mickle.
And now the Sonne hath reared up
  his fyriefooted teme,
Making his way betweene the Cuppe,
  and golden Diademe:                                           20
The rampant Lyon hunts he fast,
  with Dogge of noysome breath,
Whose balefull barking bringes in hast
  pyne, plagues, and dreery death.
Agaynst his cruell scortching heate                   25
  where hast thou coverture?
The wastefull hylls unto his threate
  is a playne overture.
But if thee lust, to holden chat
  with seely shepherds swayne,                           30
Come downe, and learne the little what
  that Thomalin can sayne.

MORRELL.

Syker, thous but a laesie loord,
  and rekes much of thy swinck,
That with fond termes, and weetlesse words        35
  to blere myne eyes doest thinke.

9. *shield*: forbid.    11. *reede is ryfe*: saying is widespread.    14. *trode* . . .
*tickle*: path is not so precarious.    16. *mickle*: much.    19. *Cuppe*: the
constellation Crater.    20. *Diademe*: the constellation Corona
Borealis.    24. *pyne*: distress.    29. *lust*: wish.    30. *seely*: simple,
innocent.    31. *what*: i.e. information.    33. *loord*: lout.    34. *rekes* . . .
*swink*: think highly of your work.    35. *fond*: foolish.    36. *blere*: deceive.

In evill houre thou hentest in hond
   thus holy hylles to blame,
For sacred unto saints they stond,
   and of them han theyr name.         40
S. Michels mount who does not know,
   that wardes the Westerne coste?
And of S. Brigets bowre I trow,
   all Kent can rightly boaste:
And they that con of Muses skill,        45
   sayne most what, that they dwell
(As goteheards wont) upon a hill,
   beside a lerned well.
And wonned not the great God *Pan*,
   upon mount *Olivet*:         50
Feeding the blessed flocke of *Dan*,
   which dyd himselfe beget?

THOMALIN.

O blessed sheepe, O shepheard great,
   that bought his flocke so deare,
And them did save with bloudy sweat     55
   from Wolves, that would them teare.

MORREL.

Besyde, as holy fathers sayne,
   there is a hyllye place,
Where *Titan* ryseth from the mayne,
   to renne hys dayly race.       60
Upon whose toppe the starres bene stayed,
   and all the skie doth leane,
There is the cave, where *Phebe* layed,
   the shepheard long to dreame.

---

37. *hentest*: take.    43. *S. Brigets bowre*: unidentified.    46. *sayne most
what*: most say the following.    49–51. I.e. Christ teaching as in the
Sermon on the Mount (Matthew 5–7).    52. *which . . . beget*: from which
he was begotten, i.e. Israel; or which he himself begot, i.e. the Church.

Whilome there used shepheards all 65
  to feede theyr flocks at will,
Till by his foly one did fall,
  that all the rest did spill.
And sithens shepheardes bene foresayd
  from places of delight: 70
For thy I weene thou be affrayd,
  to clime this hilles height.
Of *Synah* can I tell thee more,
  and of our Ladyes bowre:
But little needes to strow my store, 75
  suffice this hill of our.
Here han the holy *Faunes* resourse,
  and *Sylvanes* haunten rathe.
Here has the salt Medway his sourse,
  wherein the Nymphes doe bathe. 80
The salt Medway, that trickling stremis
  adowne the dales of Kent:
Till with his elder brother Themis
  his brackish waves be meynt.
Here growes *Melampode* every where, 85
  and *Teribinth* good for Gotes:
The one, my madding kiddes to smere,
  the next, to heale theyr throtes.
Hereto, the hills bene nigher heven,
  and thence the passage ethe. 90
As well can prove the piercing levin,
  that seeldome falls bynethe.

THOMALIN.

Syker thou speakes lyke a lewde lorrell,
  of Heaven to demen so:

---

74. *Ladyes bowre*: the Virgin Mary's house said to be conveyed by angels to Loretto in Italy, mentioned by Mantuan, *Eclogues* 8.52; but see E. K.'s gloss.    75. *strow my store*: further display my knowledge.    87. *madding*: frenzied.    90. *ethe*: easy.

How be I am but rude and borrell,                               95
    yet nearer wayes I knowe.
To Kerke the narre, from God more farre,
    has bene an old sayd sawe.
And he that strives to touch the starres,
    oft stombles at a strawe.                               100
Alsoone may shepheard clymbe to skye,
    that leades in lowly dales,
As Goteherd prowd that sitting hye,
    upon the Mountaine sayles.
My seely sheepe like well belowe,                               105
    they neede not *Melampode*:
For they bene hale enough, I trowe,
    and liken theyr abode.
But if they with thy Gotes should yede,
    they soone myght be corrupted:                          110
Or like not of the frowie fede,
    or with the weedes be glutted.
The hylls, where dwelled holy saints,
    I reverence and adore:
Not for themselfe, but for the sayncts,                         115
    Which han be dead of yore.
And nowe they bene to heaven forewent,
    theyr good is with them goe:
Theyr sample onely to us lent,
    that als we mought doe soe.                             120
Shepheards they weren of the best,
    and lived in lowlye leas:
And sith theyr soules bene now at rest,
    why done we them disease?
Such one he was, (as I have heard                               125
    old Algrind often sayne)
That whilome was the first shepheard,
    and lived with little gayne:

118. *goe*: gone.   119. *sample*: example.   124. *disease*: bother,
annoyance.

As meeke he was, as meeke mought be,
    simple, as simple sheepe, 130
Humble, and like in eche degree
    the flocke, which he did keepe.
Often he used of hys keepe
    a sacrifice to bring,
Nowe with a Kidde, now with a sheepe 135
    the Altars hallowing.
So lowted he unto hys Lord,
    such favour couth he fynd,
That sithens never was abhord,
    the simple shepheards kynd. 140
And such I weene the brethren were,
    that came from *Canaan*:
The brethren twelve, that kept yfere
    the flockes of mighty *Pan*.
But nothing such thilk shephearde was, 145
    whom *Ida* hyll dyd beare,
That left hys flocke, to fetch a lasse,
    whose love he bought to deare:
For he was proude, that ill was payd,
    (no such mought shepheards bee) 150
And with lewde lust was overlayd:
    tway things doen ill agree:
But shepheard mought be meeke and mylde,
    well eyed, as *Argus* was,
With fleshly follyes undefyled, 155
    and stoute as steede of brasse.
Sike one (sayd *Algrin*) *Moses* was,
    that sawe hys makers face,
His face more cleare, then Christall glasse,
    and spake to him in place. 160
This had a brother, (his name I knewe)
    the first of all his cote,

131. *in eche degree*: in every way.    143. *yfere*: together.    152. *tway*:
two.    159. *His*: God's. See Exodus 33.11.    162. *cote*: house.

A shepheard trewe, yet not so true,
    as he that earst I hote.
Whilome all these were lowe, and lief,           165
    and loved their flocks to feede,
They never stroven to be chiefe,
    and simple was theyr weede.
But now (thanked be God therefore)
    the world is well amend,                 170
Their weedes bene not so nighly wore,
    such simplesse mought them shend:
They bene yclad in purple and pall,
    so hath theyr god them blist,
They reigne and rulen over all,             175
    and lord it, as they list:
Ygyrt with belts of glitterand gold,
    (mought they good sheepeheards bene)
Theyr Pan theyr sheepe to them has sold,
    I saye as some have seene.           180
For Palinode (if thou him ken)
    yode late on Pilgrimage
To Rome, (if such be Rome) and then
    he sawe thilke misusage.
For shepeheards (sayd he) there doen leade,     185
    as Lordes done other where,
Theyr sheepe han crustes, and they the bread:
    the chippes, and they the chere:
They han the fleece, and eke the flesh,
    (O seely sheepe the while)          190
The corne is theyrs, let other thresh,
    their hands they may not file.

---

164. *hote*: named.    165. *lowe, and lief*: humble and willing.    170. *amend*:
amended.    172. *shend*: shame.    174. *blist*: blessed.    181. *Palinode*:
refers perhaps to an English visitor and informant about Rome (see McLane
1961:340–42).    182. *yode*: *went*.    184. *misusage*: abuse.    185. *leade*:
live.    190. *seely*: helpless, too simple.    192. *file*: defile.

They han great stores, and thriftye stockes,
   great freendes and feeble foes:
What neede hem caren for their flocks?       195
   theyr boyes can looke to those.
These wisards weltre in welths waves,
   pampred in pleasures deepe,
They han fatte kernes, and leany knaves,
   their fasting flockes to keepe.       200
Sike mister men bene all misgone,
   they heapen hylles of wrath:
Sike syrlye shepheards han we none,
   they keepen all the path.

MORRELL.

Here is a great deale of good matter,       205
   lost for lacke of telling,
Now sicker I see, thou doest but clatter:
   harme may come of melling.
Thou medlest more, then shall have thanke,
   to wyten shepheards welth:       210
When folke bene fat, and riches rancke,
   it is a signe of helth.
But say me, what is *Algrin* he,
   that is so oft bynempt.

THOMALIN.

He is a shepheard great in gree,       215
   but hath bene long ypent.
One daye he sat upon a hyll,
   (as now thou wouldest me:
But I am taught by *Algrins* ill,
   to love the lowe degree.)       220
For sitting so with bared scalpe,
   an Eagle sored hye,

193. *thriftye stockes*: flourishing herds.    201. *misgone*: gone astray.
210. *wyten*: censure.    211. *rancke*: plentiful.    216. *ypent*: locked
up.

That weening hys whyte head was chalke,
a shell fish downe let flye:
She weend the shell fishe to have broake,        225
but therwith bruzd his brayne,
So now astonied with the stroke,
He lyes in lingring payne.

MORRELL.

Ah good Algrin, his hap was ill,
but shall be bett in time.        230
Now farwell shepheard, sith thys hyll
thou hast such doubt to climbe.

Thomalins Embleme.

*In medio virtus.*

Morrells Embleme.        235

*In summo fœlicitas.*

GLOSSE.

[1]    A Goteheard) By Gotes in scrypture be represented the wicked and reprobate, whose pastour also must needes be such.

[2]    Banck) is a seate of honor.   [3] Straying heard) which wander out of the waye of truth.

[8]    Als) for also.   [9] Clymbe) spoken of Ambition. [12] Great clymbers) according to Seneca his verse, Decidunt celsa graviore lapsu.   [16] Mickle) much.

233–36. *In medio virtus*: "virtue is in the middle," i.e. between extremes—the "golden mean" of Aristotle's *Nicomachean Ethics. In summo fœlicitas*: "felicity is at the height"—a Platonic concept. See Edgar Wind (1967), p. 47: "Spenser expressed the union of balance and transcendence, which he knew from his study of Italian Neoplatonists . . . by juxtaposing two seemingly incompatible mottoes".

[1] *scrypture*: Matthew 25.32–33.   [12.2] *Decidunt . . . lapsu*: "Lofty things end with a heavier fall"; not in Seneca, but resembles Horace, *Odes* 2.10.10–11.

[17]   The sonne) A reason, why he refuseth to dwell on
Mountaines, because there is no shelter against the
scortching sunne. according to the time of the yeare,
whiche is the whotest moneth of all.

[19-20] The Cupp and Diademe) Be two signes in the
Firmament, through which the sonne maketh his
course in the moneth of July.

[21]   Lion) Thys is Poetically spoken, as if the Sunne did
hunt a Lion with one Dogge. The meaning wherof is,
that in July the sonne is in Leo. At which tyme the
Dogge starre, which is called Syrius or Canicula
reigneth, with immoderate heate causing Pestilence,
drougth, and many diseases.

[28]   Overture) an open place. The word is borrowed of the
French, and used in good writers.   [29] To holden
chatt) to talke and prate.

[33]   A loorde) was wont among the old Britons to signifie a
Lorde. And therefore the Danes, that long time
usurped theyr Tyrannie here in Brytanie, were called
for more dread and dignitie, Lurdanes .s. Lord Danes.
At which time it is sayd, that the insolencie and pryde
of that nation was so outragious in thys Realme, that if
it fortuned a Briton to be going over a bridge, and
sawe the Dane set foote upon the same, he muste
retorne back, till the Dane were cleane over, or els
abyde the pryce of his displeasure, which was no lesse,
then present death. But being afterwarde expelled that
name of Lurdane became so odious unto the people,
whom they had long oppressed, that even at this daye
they use for more reproche, to call the Quartane ague
the Fever Lurdane.

[34]   Recks much of thy swinck) counts much of thy
paynes.   [35] Weetelesse) not understoode.

[41]   S. Michels mount) is a promontorie in the West part of
England.

[33] *A loorde*: from Holinshed, *Chronicles* 7.3.

[47]   A hill) Parnassus afforesayd.   [49] Pan)
Christ.   [51] Dan) One trybe is put for the whole
nation per Synecdochen.

[59]   Where Titan) the Sonne. Which story is to be redde in
Diodorus Syc. of the hyl Ida; from whence he sayth, all
night time is to bee seene a mightye fire, as if the skye
burned, which toward morning beginneth to gather
into a rownd forme, and thereof ryseth the sonne,
whome the Poetes call Titan.

[64]   The Shepheard) is Endymion, whom the Poets fayne,
to have bene so beloved of Phœbe .s. the Moone, that
he was by her kept a sleepe in a cave by the space of
xxx. yeares, for to enjoye his companye.

[63]   There) that is in Paradise, where through errour of
shepheards understanding, he sayth, that all shepheards
did use to feede theyr flocks, till one, (that is Adam) by
hys follye and disobedience, made all the rest of hys
ofspring be debarred and shutte out from thence.

[73]   Synah) a hill in Arabia, where God appeared.

[74]   Our Ladyes bowre) a place of pleasure so called.

[77-78] Faunes or Sylvanes) be of Poetes feigned to be Gods
of the Woode.

[79]   Medway) the name of a Ryver in Kent, which running
by Rochester, meeteth with Thames; whom he calleth
his elder brother, both because he is greater, and also
falleth sooner into the Sea.

[84]   Meynt) mingled.   [85-86] Melampode and Terebinth)
be hearbes good to cure diseased Gotes. of thone
speaketh Mantuane, and of thother Theocritus.
        τερμίνθου τράγων ἔσχατον ἀκρέμονα.

---

[51] *per Synecdochen*: "by means of synedoche" (figure of a part for the whole,
i.e Dan for all Israel).   [59.2] *Diodorus*: *Library of History* 17.7.
[85–86.4] *Theocritus*: *Epigrams* 1.6. E. K. misquotes the Greek which should
say "[the white goat] is nibbling the ends of terebinth twigs." Even correctly
quoted the line per se would not make sense.

[89] Nigher heaven) Note the shepheards simplenesse, which supposeth that from the hylls is nearer waye to heaven.

[91] Levin) Lightning; which he taketh for an argument, to prove the nighnes to heaven, because the lightning doth comenly light on hygh mountaynes, according to the saying of the Poete. Feriuntque summos fulmina montes.

[93] Lorrell) a losell. [95] A borell.) a playne fellowe. [97] Narre) nearer.

[107] Hale) for hole. [109] Yede) goe. [111] Frowye) mustye or mossie.

[116] Of yore) long agoe. [117] Forewente) gone afore.

[127] The firste shepheard) was Abell the righteous, who (as scripture sayth) bent hys mind to keeping of sheepe, as did hys brother Cain to tilling the grownde.

[133] His keepe) hys charge s. his flocke. [137] Lowted) did honour and reverence.

[143] The brethren) the twelve sonnes of Jacob, whych were shepemaisters, and lyved onelye thereupon.

[146] Whom Ida) Paris, which being the sonne of Priamus king of Troy, for his mother Hecubas dreame, which being with child of hym, dreamed shee broughte forth a firebrand, that set all the towre of Ilium on fire, was cast forth on the hyll Ida; where being fostered of shepheards, he eke in time became a shepheard, and lastly came to knowledge of his parentage.

[147] A lasse) Helena the wyfe of Menelaus king of Lacedemonia, was by Venus for the golden Aple to her geven, then promised to Paris, who thereupon with a sorte of lustye Troyanes, stole her out of Lacedemonia, and kept her in Troye. which was the cause of the

[91.4–5] *Poete . . . montes*: Horace, *Odes* 2.10.11, "Lightnings strike the tops of mountains." But E. K. replaces (quite workably) Horace's *fulgura* (lightnings) with *fulmina* (lightnings). [93] *losell*: scoundrel. [127] *Abell*: Genesis 4.

tenne yeares warre in Troye, and the most famous citye
of all Asia most lamentably sacked and defaced.

[154] Argus) was of the Poets devised to be full of eyes, and
therefore to hym was committed the keeping of the
transformed Cow Io: So called because that in the
print of a Cowes foote, there is figured an I in the
middest of an O.

[161] His name) he meaneth Aaron: whose name for more
Decorum, the shephearde sayth he hath forgot, lest his
remembraunce and skill in antiquities of holy writ
should seeme to exceede the meanenesse of the Person.

[163] Not so true) for Aaron in the absence of Moses started
aside, and committed Idolatry.

[173] In purple) Spoken of the Popes and Cardinalles, which
use such tyrannical colours and pompous
paynting.   [177] Belts) Girdles.

[177] Glitterand) Glittering. a Participle used sometime in
Chaucer, but altogether in J. Goore.

[179] Theyr Pan) that is the Pope, whom they count theyr
God and greatest shepheard.

[181] Palinode) A shephearde, of whose report he seemeth to
speake all thys.

[197] Wisards) greate learned heads.   [197] Welter)
wallowe.   [199] Kerne) a Churle or Farmer.

[201] Sike mister men) such kinde of men.   [203] Surly)
stately and prowde.   [208] Melling) medling.

[230] Bett) better.   [214] Bynempte) named.   [215] Gree)
for degree.

[213] Algrin) the name of a shepheard afforesayde, whose
myshap he alludeth to the chaunce, that happened to
the Poet Æschylus, that was brayned with a shellfishe.

---

[154] *Argus*: Ovid, *Met* 1.568–746.   [161.2] *Decorum*: appropriateness of
style to subject and genre.   [161.4] *meanenesse . . . Person*: low social rank
of the speaker.   [163.2] *Idolatry*: see Exodus 32.   [177] *Participle*: not
used by Chaucer; occurs in *The Plowman's Tale* and in John Gower.

Embleme.

By thys poesye Thomalin confirmeth that, which in hys
  former speach by sondrye reasons he had proved. for
  being both hymselfe sequestred from all ambition and
  also abhorring it in others of hys cote, he taketh
  occasion to prayse the meane and lowly state, as that
  wherein is safetie without feare, and quiet without
  danger, according to the saying of olde Philosphers,
  that vertue dwelleth in the middest, being environed
  with two contrary vices: whereto Morrell replieth with
  continuaunce of the same Philosophers opinion, that
  albeit all bountye dwelleth in mediocritie, yet perfect
  felicitye dwelleth in supremacie. for they say, and most
  true it is, that happinesse is placed in the highest
  degree, so as if any thing be higher or better, then that
  streight way ceaseth to be perfect happines. Much like
  to that, which once I heard alleaged in defense of
  humilitye out of a great doctour, Suorum Christus
  humillimus: which saying a gentle man in the company
  taking at the rebownd, beate backe again with lyke
  saying of another Doctoure, as he sayde. Suorum deus
  altissimus.

---

[Embleme.4] *cote*: profession.     [Embleme.17] *doctour*: learned teacher of
the church. *Suorum Christus humillimus*: "Christ is the most lowly of his
own."     [Embleme.20–21] *Suorum deus altissimus*: "God is most high
among his own. The source of these Latin tags is unknown."

# *August*

It was inevitable that Spenser include a singing match in his *Calender*, for Theocritus's *Idylls* 5 and 6 and Virgil's *Eclogues* 3 and 7 and their imitators had made it a tried-and-true pastoral convention. And its necessarily high-spirited mood befits the month of harvest festivals. But Spenser goes beyond the necessary dialogue and verse-capping of the convention to incorporate Colin's sophisticated complaint and so give the eclogue three distinct verse patterns—another instance of the special concern with formal display that characterizes all eclogues focused on Colin.

The verse of the framing dialogue is a variant of *Januarye's* six-line stanza. In the first twenty-four lines where the emotionally unattached Willye playfully taunts the lovelorn Perigot, Willye takes the quatrain and Perigot the answering couplet. During the pledging (25–42) Willye has two stanzas and Perigot one. Willye's having twice as many lines as Perigot reflects his initiative in this part of the dialogue, but, as the dialogue moves closer to the match (43–50), they have an equal number of lines.

In the ensuing roundelay, however, Perigot takes the initiative to tell how a girl's glance pierced his heart. A roundelay is a form characterized by refrain and here Willye takes this secondary role, his responses either echoing or playfully mocking Perigot. But his intention is therapeutic: to help Perigot put his "fond fantsies . . . to flight" (22) by expressing them in a poem. One of the Latin terms for poem is *carmen*, meaning both song and charm, and in this case the charm seems to have worked for Perigot looks back on the roundelay as a "mery thing" (144).

The nature of a singing match is improvisation. But Colin's complaint, like his *Aprill* lay, is a permanent poem that can be recited. It carries forward from Perigot's description of Cupid's initial wound to the next stage, the lover's suffering when separated from the beloved. It is possible to take this suffering too solemnly, for Colin's extreme and melodramatic self-pity comes close to self-parody. Like the roundelay, it is a playing with lover's sorrow.

In form, however, the songs contrast sharply, for Colin's is a sestina, an intricately formed verse pattern impossible to improvise. It requires six six-line unrhymed stanzas, each line of which ends with the same end-words as the first stanza but in a different yet fixed order (i.e. first stanza 123456, second 612345, etc.), and concludes with a half-stanza that deploys all six end-words. The sestina apparently originated in Provence with Arnaut Daniel, and was taken up by Dante, Petrarch (there are eleven sestinas in his *Rime*), and the Pléiade poets. Spenser's is apparently the first English sestina, with Sidney's soon to follow. The extreme formal handicap imposed by the sestina was an invitation for the self-confident poet to display his mastery of form: Perigot, noting the line endings, can only "admire ech turning of thy verse" (191). Colin's sestina is thus one more step in Spenser's project of self-promotion.

The curious lack of gloss for the sestina may indicate that Spenser added the poem after E. K.'s work on the eclogue was complete, although the Argument certainly recognizes Colin's "proper song." Perhaps the simplicity—indeed, Petrarchan banality—of Colin's sentiments, as distinct from the intricate form of their expression, made annotation unnecessary, although absence of need for commentary did not often inhibit E. K. elsewhere in the *Calender*.

# *August.*

*Ægloga octava.*

## ARGUMENT.

IN this *Æglogue is set forth a delectable controversie, made in
imitation of that in Theocritus: whereto also Virgile fashioned his
third and seventh Æglogue. They choose for umpere of their strife,
Cuddie a neatheards boye, who having ended their cause, reciteth also
himselfe a proper song, whereof Colin he sayth was Authour.*

WILLYE.   PERIGOT.   CUDDIE.

TEll me *Perigot*, what shalbe the game,
    Wherefore with myne thou dare thy musick
                  matche?
Or bene thy Bagpypes renne farre out of frame?
Or hath the Crampe thy joynts benomd with ache?

---

ARGUMENT *delectable*: delightful. *neatheards*: cowherd's. *ended their cause*:
brought their contest to an end. *proper*: genuine, real.    2. *Wherefore*: with
which.    3. *Bagpypes*: The woodcut shows a shawm. *renne . . . frame*: not in
playable condition.

PERIGOT.

Ah *Willye*, when the hart is ill assayde,                    5
How can Bagpipe, or joynts be well apayd?

WILLYE.

What the foule evill hath thee so bestadde?
Whilom thou was peregall to the best,
And wont to make the jolly shepeheards gladde
With pyping and dauncing, didst passe the rest.          10

PERIGOT.

Ah *Willye* now I have learnd a newe daunce:
My old musick mard by a newe mischaunce.

WILLYE.

Mischiefe mote to that newe mischaunce befall,
That so hath raft us of our meriment.
But reede me, what payne doth thee so appall?           15
Or lovest thou, or bene thy younglings miswent?

PERIGOT.

Love hath misled both my younglings, and mee:
I pyne for payne, and they my payne to see.

WILLYE.

Perdie and wellawaye: ill may they thrive:
Never knewe I lovers sheepe in good plight.              20
But and if in rymes with me thou dare strive,
Such fond fantsies shall soone be put to flight.

PERIGOT.

That shall I doe, though mochell worse I fared:
Never shall be sayde that *Perigot* was dared.

---

5. *assayde*: afflicted.    6. *apayd*: contented, rewarded, pleased.    10. *passe*:
surpass.    15. *reede*: inform.    19. *wellawaye*: alas.    20 *plight*:
condition.    21. *But and*: however.    23. *mochell*: much.    24. *dared*:
did not take up a challenge.

WILLYE.

Then loe *Perigot* the Pledge which I plight:                    25
A mazer ywrought of the Maple warre:
Wherein is enchased many a fayre sight
Of Beres and Tygres, that maken fiers warre:
And over them spred a goodly wild vine,
Entrailed with a wanton Yvie twine.                             30

Thereby is a Lambe in the Wolves jawes:
But see, how fast renneth the shepheard swayne,
To save the innocent from the beastes pawes:
And here with his shepehooke hath him slayne.
Tell me, such a cup hast thou ever sene?                        35
Well mought it beseme any harvest Queene.

PERIGOT.

Thereto will I pawne yonder spotted Lambe,
Of all my flocke there nis sike another:
For I brought him up without the Dambe.
But *Colin Clout* rafte me of his brother,                      40
That he purchast of me in the playne field:
Sore against my will was I forst to yield.

WILLYE.

Sicker make like account of his brother.
But who shall judge the wager wonne or lost?

PERIGOT.

That shall yonder heardgrome, and none other,                   45
Which over the pousse hetherward doth post.

25. *plight*: put up.      26. *mazer*: wooden drinking bowl (common in
fourteenth- and fifteenth- century England; there was a famous one at Sp's
college, Pembroke Hall). *warre*: burl.      31. *Thereby*: near that.
32. *renneth*: runs.      38. *nis sike another*: is none like him.      39. *Dambe*:
dam, mother.      40. *rafte*: deprived.      41. *purchast . . . field*: won from me
on even ground, i.e. fairly.      43. *Sicker . . . brother*: Assume that the same
will occur with his brother.

WILLYE.

But for the Sunnebeame so sore doth us beate,
Were not better, to shunne the scortching heate?

PERIGOT.

Well agreed *Willy*: then sitte thee downe swayne:
Sike a song never heardest thou, but *Colin* sing.        50

CUDDIE.

Gynne, when ye lyst, ye jolly shepheards twayne:
Sike a judge, as *Cuddie*, were for a king.

| | |
|---|---|
| PERIGOT. | I T fell upon a holly eve, |
| WILLYE. | hey ho hollidaye, |
| PER. | When holly fathers wont to shrieve:        55 |
| WIL. | now gynneth this roundelay. |
| PER. | Sitting upon a hill so hye, |
| WIL. | hey ho the high hyll, |
| PER. | The while my flocke did feede thereby, |
| WIL. | the while the shepheard selfe did spill:        60 |
| PER. | I saw the bouncing Bellibone, |
| WIL. | hey ho Bonibell, |
| PER. | Tripping over the dale alone, |
| WIL. | she can trippe it very well: |
| PER. | Well decked in a frocke of gray,        65 |
| WIL. | hey ho gray is greete, |
| PER. | And in a Kirtle of greene saye, |
| WIL. | the greene is for maydens meete: |
| PER. | A chapelet on her head she wore, |
| WIL. | hey ho chapelet,        70 |
| PER. | Of sweete Violets therein was store, |
| WIL. | she sweeter then the Violet. |

47. *But for*: because.    49. *swayne*: i.e. Cuddie.    51. *Gynne*:
begin.    53. *holly*: holy.    55. *shrieve*: shrive, hear confession.    60. *selfe
did spill*: wasted his time, was idle.    61. *Bellibone*: girl (see *Aprill*, note to
line 92).    67. *Kirtle*: tunic. *saye*: good cloth.

| | |
|---|---|
| P E R . | My sheepe did leave theyr wonted foode, |
| W I L . | hey ho seely sheepe, |
| P E R . | And gazd on her, as they were wood,                   75 |
| W I L . | woode as he, that did them keepe. |
| P E R . | As the bonilasse passed bye, |
| W I L . | hey ho bonilasse, |
| P E R . | She rovde at me with glauncing eye, |
| W I L . | as cleare as the christall glasse:                     80 |
| P E R . | All as the Sunnye beame so bright, |
| W I L . | hey ho the Sunne beame, |
| P E R . | Glaunceth from *Phœbus* face forthright, |
| W I L . | so love into thy hart did streame: |
| P E R . | Or as the thonder cleaves the cloudes,            85 |
| W I L . | hey ho the Thonder, |
| P E R . | Wherein the lightsome levin shroudes, |
| W I L . | so cleaves thy soule a sonder: |
| P E R . | Or as Dame *Cynthias* silver raye |
| W I L . | hey ho the Moonelight,                                  90 |
| P E R . | Upon the glyttering wave doth playe: |
| W I L . | such play is a pitteous plight. |
| P E R . | The glaunce into my heart did glide, |
| W I L . | hey ho the glyder, |
| P E R . | Therewith my soule was sharply gryde,           95 |
| W I L . | such woundes soone wexen wider. |
| P E R . | Hasting to raunch the arrow out, |
| W I L . | hey ho Perigot, |
| P E R . | I left the head in my hart roote: |
| W I L . | it was a desperate shot.                                  100 |
| P E R . | There it ranckleth ay more and more, |
| W I L . | hey ho the arrowe, |
| P E R . | Ne can I find salve for my sore: |

79. *rovde*: roved, shot arrows at random.      87. *lightsome*: radiant.
92. *pitteous plight*: moving effect.      97. *raunch*: wrench.      99. *hart roote*:
bottom of the heart.      100. *desperate*: bringing despair.

| W I L . | love is a curelesse sorrowe. | |
| P E R . | And though my bale with death I | |
| | bought, | 105 |
| W I L . | hey ho heavie cheere, | |
| P E R . | Yet should thilk lasse not from my | |
| | thought: | |
| W I L . | so you may buye gold to deare. | |
| P E R . | But whether in paynefull love I pyne, | |
| W I L . | hey ho pinching payne, | 110 |
| P E R . | Or thrive in welth, she shalbe mine. | |
| W I L . | but if thou can her obteine. | |
| P E R . | And if for gracelesse greefe I dye, | |
| W I L . | hey ho gracelesse griefe, | |
| P E R . | Witnesse, shee slewe me with her eye: | 115 |
| W I L . | let thy follye be the priefe. | |
| P E R . | And you, that sawe it, simple shepe, | |
| W I L . | hey ho the fayre flocke, | |
| P E R . | For priefe thereof, my death shall weepe, | |
| W I L . | and mone with many a mocke. | 120 |
| P E R . | So learnd I love on a hollye eve, | |
| W I L . | hey ho holidaye, | |
| P E R . | That ever since my hart did greve. | |
| P E R . | now endeth our roundelay. | |

C U D D Y E .

Sicker sike a roundle never heard I none.                    125
Little lacketh *Perigot* of the best.
And *Willye* is not greatly overgone,
So weren his undersongs well addrest.

---

104. *curelesse*: incurable.     105. *bale*: release.     107. *should . . . not*: the
girl would not go.     108. *to*: too.     113. *gracelesse greefe*: grief caused by
a girl's refusing her grace or favor.     116. *priefe*: proof.     120. *mocke*:
derisive gesture.     125. *roundle*: roundelay.     126. *lacketh*: falls
short.     127. *overgone*: surpassed.     128. *undersongs*: burdens, sung
responses. *addrest*: done.

**WILLYE.**

Herdgrome, I feare me, thou have a squint eye:
Areede uprightly, who has the victorye? 130

**CUDDIE.**

Fayth of my soule, I deeme ech have gayned.
For thy let the Lambe be *Willye* his owne:
And for *Perigot* so well hath hym payned,
To him be the wroughten mazer alone.

**PERIGOT.**

*Perigot* is well pleased with the doome: 135
Ne can *Willye* wite the witelesse herdgroome.

**WILLYE.**

Never dempt more right of beautye I weene,
The shepheard of *Ida*, that judged beauties Queene.

**CUDDIE.**

But tell me shepherds, should it not yshend
Your roundels fresh, to heare a doolefull verse 140
Of Rosalend (who knowes not Rosalend?)
That Colin made, ylke can I you rehearse.

**PERIGOT.**

Now say it *Cuddie*, as thou art a ladde:
With mery thing its good to medle sadde.

**WILLY.**

Fayth of my soule, thou shalt ycrouned be 145
In *Colins* stede, if thou this song areede:
For never thing on earth so pleaseth me,
As him to heare, or matter of his deede.

---

130. *Areede uprightly*: say fairly.    131. *deeme*: judge. *gayned*:
won.    133. *For*: because.    134. *alone*: exclusively.    139. *should*:
would. *yshend*: put to shame.    142. *ylke*: the same.    146. *areede*:
recite.    148. *matter . . . deede*: work he has done.

C U D D I E .

Then listneth ech unto my heavy laye,
And tune your pypes as ruthful, as ye may.　　　150

YE wastefull woodes beare witnesse of my woe,
　Wherein my plaints did oftentimes resound:
Ye carelesse byrds are privie to my cryes,
Which in your songs were wont to make a part:
Thou pleasaunt spring hast luld me oft a sleepe,　　155
Whose streames my tricklinge teares did ofte
　　　　　　　　　　　　　augment.
Resort of people doth my greefs augment,
　The walled townes do worke my greater woe:
The forest wide is fitter to resound
The hollow Echo of my carefull cryes,　　　　160
I hate the house, since thence my love did part,
Whose waylefull want debarres myne eyes from
　　　　　　　　　　　　　sleepe.
Let stremes of teares supply the place of sleepe:
　Let all that sweete is, voyd: and all that may augment
My doole, drawe neare. More meete to wayle my
　　　　　　　　　　　　woe,　165
Bene the wild woddes my sorrowes to resound,
Then bedde, or bowre, both which I fill with cryes,
When I them see so waist, and fynd no part
Of pleasure past. Here will I dwell apart
　In gastfull grove therefore, till my last sleepe　170
Doe close mine eyes: so shall I not augment
With sight of such a chaunge my restlesse woe:
Helpe me, ye banefull byrds, whose shrieking sound
Ys signe of dreery death, my deadly cryes
Most ruthfully to tune. And as my cryes　　　175
　(Which of my woe cannot bewray least part)

153. *carelesse*: carefree.　161. *part*: depart.　162. *want*: lack,
absence.　164. *voyd*: go away.　165. *doole*: sorrow.　167. *bowre*:
bedchamber.　170. *gastfull*: fearsome, depressing.　174. *deadly*:
deathly, mortal.　175. *ruthfully*: pitiably.　176. *bewray*: reveal.

You heare all night, when nature craveth sleepe,
Increase, so let your yrksome yells augment.
Thus all the night in plaints, the daye in woe
I vowed have to wayst, till safe and sound                    180
She home returne, whose voyces silver sound
To cheerefull songs can chaunge my cherelesse cryes.
Hence with the Nightingale will I take part,
That blessed byrd, that spends her time of sleepe
In songs and plaintive pleas, the more taugment              185
The memory of hys misdeede, that bred her woe:
And you that feele no woe, | when as the sound
Of these my nightly cryes | ye heare apart,
Let breake your sounder sleepe | and pitie augment.

### PERIGOT.
O *Colin, Colin*, the shepheards joye,                        190
How I admire ech turning of thy verse:
And *Cuddie*, fresh *Cuddie* the liefest boye,
How dolefully his doole thou didst reherse.

### CUDDIE.
Then blowe your pypes shepheards, til you be at home:
The night nigheth fast, yts time to be gone.                  195

Perigot his Embleme.

*Vincenti gloria victi.*

Willyes Embleme.

*Vinto non vitto.*

---

183. *Nightingale*: Philomela, raped by the "misdeede" of her brother-in-law
Tereus, became a nightingale whose song expresses her sorrow. See Ovid,
*Met* 6.424–674. In the Renaissance her song symbolized the unhappy lover's
complaint.    188. *apart*: in the distance.    189. *sounder*: too
sound.    191. *turning . . . verse*: your line endings.    192. *liefest*:
dearest.    197. *Vincenti gloria victi*: "the glory of the defeated goes to the
conqueror" (Lat.).    199. *Vinto non vitto*: "conquered yet not conquered"
(Ital.).

Cuddies Embleme. 200

*Felice chi puo.*

GLOSSE.

[7] Bestadde) disposed, ordered. [8] Peregall)
equall [8] Whilome) once.

[14] Rafte) bereft, deprived. [16] Miswent) gon a
straye. [19] Ill may) according to Virgile. Infelix o
semper ovis pecus.

[26] A mazer) So also do Theocritus and Virgile feigne
pledges of their strife.

[27] Enchased) engraven. Such pretie descriptions every
where useth Theocritus, to bring in his Idyllia. For
which speciall cause indede he by that name termeth
his Æglogues: for Idyllion in Greke signifieth the shape
or picture of any thyng, wherof his booke is ful. And
not, as I have heard some fondly guesse, that they be
called not Idyllia, but Hædilia, of the Goteheards in
them.

[30] Entrailed) wrought betwene.

[36] Harvest Queene) The manner of country folke in
harvest tyme.

[46] Pousse) Pease.

[53] It fel upon) Perigot maketh hys song in prayse of his
love, to whom Willy answereth every under verse. By
Perigot who is meant, I can not uprightly say: but if it
be, who is supposed, his love deserveth no lesse prayse,
then he giveth her.

201. *Felice chi puo*: "let him be happy who can be" (Ital.).

[19] *Infelix . . . pecus*: "O that flock of sheep is always unlucky," *Ecl*
3.3. [26] *Theocritus and Virgile*: Theocritus in *Idyll* 5.20–30, Virgil in *Ecl*
3.28–51. [46] *Pease*: i.e. the pea- field.

[66] Greete) weeping and complaint. [69] Chaplet) a kind
of Garlond lyke a crowne.

[87] Leven) Lightning. [89] Cynthia) was sayd to be the
Moone. [95] Gryde) perced.

[112] But if) not unlesse. [129] Squint eye) partiall
judgement.

[131] Ech have) so saith Virgile.

> Et vitula tu dignus, et hic etc.

So by enterchaunge of gyfts Cuddie pleaseth both
partes.

[135] Doome) judgement. [137] Dempt) for deemed,
judged. [136] Wite the witelesse) blame the
blamelesse. [138] The shepherd of Ida) was sayd to
be Paris.

[138] Beauties Queene) Venus, to whome Paris adjudged the
golden Apple, as the pryce of her beautie.

#### Embleme.

The meaning hereof is very ambiguous: for Perigot by his
poesie claming the conquest, and Willye not yeelding,
Cuddie the arbiter of theyr cause, and Patron of his
own, semeth to chalenge it, as his dew, saying, that he,
is happy which can, so abruptly ending but hee
meaneth eyther him, that can win the beste, or
moderate him selfe being best, and leave of with the
best.

---

[131.2] *Et . . . hic*: "you deserve the heifer and so does he," *Ecl*
3.109. [138.2] *pryce of*: award for. [Embleme.4] *dew*: due.
[Embleme.7] *leave of*: be content with.

# September

T he third ecclesiastical eclogue is also the most satirical. Here Spenser takes up a standard motif of the genre, the great world's corruptions set against the norm of pastoral simplicity, and in his first seventy-nine lines borrows heavily from Mantuan's ninth eclogue, where a disillusioned Faustulus unveils true Rome for a new arrival Candidus. The lots of tranquil Tityrus and displaced Meliboeus in Virgil's first eclogue also underlie Spenser's juxtaposition of Diggon Davy's experience and Hobbinol's pastoral retreat.

*September* repeats the dialogue-story scheme and the rough four-beat couplets of *Februarie* and *Maye*. The dialect of its opening (like the diction beginning *Aprill*) imputes a Welsh coloration to the rest without actually carrying it through, but it helps make the association of Diggon Davy with Richard Davies, bishop of St. David's in Wales, a progressive Protestant and supporter of Grindal who was frustrated in his efforts to effect reform in his diocese. (See McLane 1961: 216–34.)

Diggon's account of his trouble is in two parts. The first (25–46, 74–101) is couched in general terms and obscure in application, although it gradually becomes likely that "forrein costes" (28) are not Rome but Britain and probably Davies's own diocese. But in the second part (104–35) Diggon's response to Hobbinol's "speake not so dirke" (102) is blunt and precise. The people say the world is now worse (presumably than before the dissolution of the monasteries) because clergy are ignorant and greedy (cf. *Maye*). But the church's disabling problem, says Diggon, is external: the easy expropriation of its lands by great courtiers ("bigge Bulles of Basan" [124]) deprives it of the revenues needed to produce proper clergy. Lord Burghley himself acquired many of his vast holdings by this means, and several such depredations, one by the earl of Leicester, had crippled reform in Davies's own diocese. It is noteworthy that Spenser places this charge and Hobbinol's caution that it is "to plaine" (136) in the central twenty lines of the eclogue. For *September* is pastoral at its most engaged. Spenser of course recognized the peril in even indirect censure of Burghley and Leicester, the two most powerful men in England, for he has Hobbinol warn that "Such il, as is forced, mought nedes be endured" (139).

Diggon's tale of Roffy and the disguised wolf refers to a different threat to reform, i.e. the Jesuit Mission, and to some particular but unidentified case of it dealt with by the watchfulness of Spenser's employer, the bishop of Rochester (*episcopus Roffensis*, hence Roffy). To deal with subtle wolves—probably secret Catholic sympathizers as well as mission priests—only constant vigilance will serve (230–35). But that rule is "too straight" (236) for men "of fleshe" (238), says Hobbinol. As in *Maye*, such ideal models run counter to human nature. Diggon has ventured among the powerful and been undone. But Hobbinol can offer no satisfactory alternative: contentment with "tryed state" (70) does not, he admits, drive off "froward fortune" (251). Even his Arcadia of *Aprill* and *June* is now attenuated: autumn winds make shelter "under the hill" (52) a prior condition of shepherd dialogue. *September* ends with a depressed version of pastoral stasis: Hobbinol's retreat is as much a failure as Diggon's blasted career.

# September.

*Ægloga Nona.*

## ARGUMENT.

HErein *Diggon Davie* is devised to be a shepheard, that in hope of more gayne, drove his sheepe into a farre countrye. The abuses whereof, and loose living of Popish prelates, by occasion of Hobbinols demaund, he discourseth at large.

HOBBINOLL. DIGGON DAVIE.

Iggon Davie, I bidde her god day:
Or Diggon her is, or I missaye.

DIGGON.

Her was her, while it was daye light,
But now her is a most wretched wight.
For day, that was, is wightly past,                     5
And now at earst the dirke night doth hast.

---

1–4 *her*: he or him as appropriate (a usage peculiar to the Welsh dialect).    2. *missaye*: am mistaken.    6. *at earst*: already.

HOBBINOLL.

Diggon areede, who has thee so dight?
Never I wist thee in so poore a plight.
Where is the fayre flocke, thou was wont to leade?
Or bene they chaffred? or at mischiefe dead?                    10

DIGGON.

Ah for love of that, is to thee moste leefe,
Hobbinol, I pray thee gall not my old griefe:
Sike question ripeth up cause of newe woe,
For one opened mote unfolde many moe.

HOBBINOLL.

Nay, but sorrow close shouded in hart                          15
I know, to kepe, is a burdenous smart.
Eche thing imparted is more eath to beare:
When the rayne is faln, the cloudes wexen cleare.
And nowe sithence I sawe thy head last,
Thrise three Moones bene fully spent and past:                 20
Sith when thou hast measured much grownd,
And wandred I wene about the world rounde,
So as thou can many thinges relate:
But tell me first of thy flocks astate.

DIGGON.

My sheepe bene wasted, (wae is me therefore)                   25
The jolly shepeheard that was of yore,
Is nowe nor jollye, nor shepehearde more.
In forrein costes, men sayd, was plentye:
And so there is, but all of miserye.
I dempt there much to have eeked my store,                     30
But such eeking hath made my hart sore.

---

7. *areede*: explain. *dight*: equipped, dressed, placed.    8. *plight*: condition.
10. *at mischiefe*: through misfortune.    11. *that . . . leefe*: a flock, which for
you is the dearest thing.    12. *gall*: chafe, abrade.    13. *ripeth up*: opens
up.    24. *astate*: condition.    25. *wasted*: strayed.    30. *dempt*: thought.
*store*: possessions.

In tho countryes, whereas I have bene,
No being for those, that truely mene,
But for such, as of guile maken gayne,
No such countrye, as there to remaine.                    35
They setten to sale their shops of shame,
And maken a Mart of theyr good name.
The shepheards there robben one another,
And layen baytes to beguile her brother.
Or they will buy his sheepe out of the cote,              40
Or they will carven the shepheards throte.
The shepheards swayne you cannot wel ken,
But it be by his pryde, from other men:
They looken bigge as Bulls, that bene bate,
And bearen the cragge so stiffe and so state,            45
As cocke on his dunghill, crowing cranck.

### HOBBINOLL.
Diggon, I am so stiffe, and so stanck,
That uneth may I stand any more:
And nowe the Westerne wind bloweth sore,
That nowe is in his chiefe sovereigntee,                 50
Beating the withered leafe from the tree.
Sitte we downe here under the hill:
Tho may we talke, and tellen our fill,
And make a mocke at the blustring blast.
Now say on Diggon, what ever thou hast.                  55

### DIGGON.
Hobbin, ah Hobbin, I curse the stounde,
That ever I cast to have lorne this grounde.
Wel-away the while I was so fonde,

---

33. *being*: way of life, livelihood.      34–35. *But . . . remaine*: But for those
who profit from guile, there is no better country to stay in.      36. *They . . .
shame*: Shamefully they put their good offices up for sale.      39. *her*:
their.      40. *cote*: shelter for sheep.      44. *bate*: fed.      46. *cranck*: boldly.
52. *under*: under the shelter of.      57. *cast*: planned.      58. *Wel-away*: alas.

To leave the good, that I had in hande,
In hope of better, that was uncouth: 60
So lost the Dogge the flesh in his mouth.
My seely sheepe (ah seely sheepe)
That here by there I whilome usd to keepe,
All were they lustye, as thou didst see,
Bene all sterved with pyne and penuree. 65
Hardly my selfe escaped thilke payne,
Driven for neede to come home agayne.

HOBBINOLL.

Ah fon, now by thy losse art taught,
That seeldome chaunge the better brought.
Content who lives with tryed state, 70
Neede feare no chaunge of frowning fate:
But who will seeke for unknowne gayne,
Ofte lives by losse, and leaves with payne.

DIGGON.

I wote ne Hobbin how I was bewitcht
With vayne desyre, and hope to be enricht. 75
But sicker so it is, as the bright starre
Seemeth ay greater, when it is farre:
I thought the soyle would have made me rich:
But nowe I wote, it is nothing sich.
For eyther the shepeheards bene ydle and still, 80
And ledde of theyr sheepe, what way they wyll:
Or they bene false, and full of covetise,
And casten to compasse many wrong emprise.
But the more bene fraight with fraud and spight,
Ne in good nor goodnes taken delight: 85

---

61. *Dogge*: traditional fable of the dog on a bridge who dropped the meat from his mouth to get the meat he saw in his reflection in the water.
65. *sterved*: dead, in process of dying. *pyne*: distress.    66. *Hardly my selfe*: even I barely.    81. *of*: by. *they*: i.e. the sheep.    83. *casten to compasse*: attempt to achieve.    84. *more bene fraight*: majority are fraught, laden.

But kindle coales of conteck and yre,
Wherewith they sette all the world on fire:
Which when they thinken agayne to quench
With holy water, they doen hem all drench.
They saye they con to heaven the high way,                    90
But by my soule I dare undersaye,
They never sette foote in that same troade,
But balk the right way, and strayen abroad.
They boast they hand the devill at commaund:
But aske hem therefore, what they han paund.                  95
Marrie that great *Pan* bought with deare borrow,
To quite it from the blacke bowre of sorrowe.
But they han sold thilk same long agoe:
For thy woulden drawe with hem many moe.
But let hem gange alone a Gods name:                         100
As they han brewed, so let hem beare blame.

### HOBBINOLL.
Diggon, I preye thee speake not so dirke.
Such myster saying me seemeth to mirke.

### DIGGON.
Then playnely to speake of shepheards most what,
Badde is the best (this english is flatt.)                   105
Their ill haviour garres men missay,
Both of their doctrine, and of their faye.
They sayne the world is much war then it wont,
All for her shepheards bene beastly and blont.
Other sayne, but how truely I note,                         110

---

89. *drench*: drown.    91. *undersaye*: say in contradiction.    93. *balk*: stray
from.    95. *paund*: pawned.    96. *Marrie*: by Mary (expletive). *that*: that
which. *borrow*: pledge, security.    97. *quite*: release.    100. *a*: in.
103. *to*: too.    104. *shepheards most what*: the topic most relevant to
shepherds.    105. *flatt*: plain.    106. *garres*: makes. *missay*: speak
against.    107. *faye*: faith, beliefs.    109. *All . . . blont*: because their
shepherds are stupid and rude (i.e. ignorant clergy).    110. *note*: do not
know.

All for they holden shame of theyr cote.
Some sticke not to say, (whote cole on her tongue)
That sicke mischiefe graseth hem emong,
All for they casten too much of worlds care,
To deck her Dame, and enrich her heyre:                    115
For such encheason, If you goe nye,
Fewe chymneis reeking you shall espye:
The fatte Oxe, that wont ligge in the stal,
Is nowe fast stalled in her crumenall.
Thus chatten the people in theyr steads,                   120
Ylike as a Monster of many heads.
But they that shooten neerest the pricke,
Sayne, other the fat from their beards doen lick.
For bigge Bulles *of Basan* brace hem about,
That with theyr hornes butten the more stoute:             125
But the leane soules treaden under foote.
And to seeke redresse mought little boote:
For liker bene they to pluck away more,
Then ought of the gotten good to restore.
For they bene like foule wagmoires overgrast,              130
That if thy galage once sticketh fast,
The more to wind it out thou doest swink,
Thou mought ay deeper and deeper sinck.
Yet better leave of with a little losse,
Then by much wrestling to leese the grosse.                135

HOBBINOLL.

Nowe Diggon, I see thou speakest to plaine:
Better it were, a little to feyne,

111. *All for*: because. *cote*: fold (or perhaps profession).    113. *graseth*: is
prevalent.    114. *casten* . . *care*: make too much of worldly things.
116. *encheason*: course, reason.    117. *reeking*: smoking.    118. *ligge*:
lie.    122. *shooten* . . . *pricke*: come close to the point.    123. *other*: others
(i.e. great courtiers).    124. *Bulles of Basan*: Psalms 22.12: "Manie yong
bulles have compassed me: mightie bulles of Bashan have closed me about."
127. *mought little boote*: would do little good.    130. *wagmoires*: quagmires.
132. *swink*: struggle, work.    135. *leese the grosse*: lose the whole.

And cleanly cover, that cannot be cured.
Such il, as is forced, mought nedes be endured.
But of sike pastoures howe done the flocks creepe? 140

DIGGON.

Sike as the shepheards, sike bene her sheepe,
For they nill listen to the shepheards voyce,
But if he call hem at theyr good choyce,
They wander at wil, and stray at pleasure,
And to theyr foldes yead at their owne leasure. 145
For they had be better come at their cal:
For many han into mischiefe fall,
And bene of ravenous Wolves yrent,
All for they nould be buxome and bent.

HOBBINOLL.

Fye on thee Diggon, and all thy foule leasing, 150
Well is knowne that sith the Saxon king,
Never was Woolfe seene many nor some,
Nor in all Kent, nor in Christendome:
But the fewer Woolves (the soth to sayne,)
The more bene the Foxes that here remaine. 155

DIGGON.

Yes, but they gang in more secrete wise,
And with sheepes clothing doen hem disguise,
They walke not widely as they were wont
For feare of raungers, and the great hunt:
But prively prolling two and froe, 160
Enaunter they mought be inly knowe.

---

139. *forced*: compelled.    140. *creepe*: manage, get along.    143. *But* . . .
*choyce*: unless he calls them when they feel like being called.    145. *yead*:
go.    146. *had be better*: would be better off to.    149. *All* . . . *nould*:
because they refused to.    150. *leasing*: lie.    154. *soth*: truth.
156. *gang*: go. *wise*: manner.    159. *raungers*: forest rangers. *great hunt*:
organized foxhunt.    160. *prolling*: prowling.    161. *inly knowe*: known
for what they really are.

HOBBINOL.

Or prive or pert yf any bene,
We han great Bandogs will teare their skinne.

DIGGON.

Indeede thy ball is a bold bigge curre,
And could make a jolly hole in theyr furre.                    165
But not good Dogges hem needeth to chace,
But heedy shepheards to discerne their face.
For all their craft is in their countenaunce,
They bene so grave and full of mayntenaunce.
But shall I tell thee what my selfe knowe,                     170
Chaunced to Roffynn not long ygoe?

HOBBINOL.

Say it out Diggon, what ever it hight,
For not but well mought him betight.
He is so meeke, wise, and merciable,
And with his word his worke is convenable.                     175
Colin clout I wene be his selfe boye,
(Ah for Colin, he whilome my joye),
Shepheards sich, God mought us many send,
That doen so carefully theyr flocks tend.

DIGGON.

Thilk same shepheard mought I well marke:                      180
He has a Dogge to byte or to barke,
Never had shepheard so kene a kurre,
That waketh, and if but a leafe sturre.
Whilome there wonned a wicked Wolfe,
That with many a Lambe had glutted his gulfe.                  185
And ever at night wont to repayre

162. *Or . . . pert*: whether secretive or open.    163. *Bandogs*: bloodhounds.
169. *maytenaunce*: bearing, deportment.    172. *hight*: means.    173. *him*
*betight*: happen to him.    175. *convenable*: consistent.    176. *selfe*:
own.    180. *marke*: draw attention to.    183. *and if but*: if only.
184. *wonned*: lived.    185. *gulfe*: voracious appetite.    186. *repayre*: go.

Unto the flocke, when the Welkin shone faire,
Ycladde in clothing of seely sheepe,
When the good old man used to sleepe.
Tho at midnight he would barke and ball,                      190
(For he had eft learned a curres call.)
As if a Woolfe were emong the sheepe.
With that the shepheard would breake his sleepe,
And send out Lowder (for so his dog hote)
To raunge the fields with wide open throte.                   195
Tho when as Lowder was farre awaye,
This Wolvish sheepe would catchen his pray,
A Lambe, or a Kidde, or a weanell wast:
With that to the wood would he speede him fast.
Long time he used this slippery pranck,                       200
Ere Roffy could for his laboure him thanck.
At end the shepheard his practise spyed,
(For Roffy is wise, and as Argus eyed)
And when at even he came to the flocke,
Fast in theyr folds he did them locke,                        205
And tooke out the Woolfe in his counterfect cote,
And let out the sheepes bloud at his throte.

### HOBBINOLL.

Marry Diggon, what should him affraye,
To take his owne where ever it laye?
For had his wesand bene a little widder,                      210
He would have devoured both hidder and shidder.

### DIGGON.

Mischiefe light on him, and Gods great curse,
Too good for him had bene a great deale worse:
For it was a perilous beast above all,
And eke had he cond the shepherds call.                       215
And oft in the night came to the shepecote,

190. *ball*: bawl, howl.     194. *hote*: was called.     202. *practise*:
stratagem.     210. *wesand*: windpipe.

And called Lowder, with a hollow throte,
As if it the old man selfe had bene.
The dog his maisters voice did it weene,
Yet halfe in doubt, he opened the dore,                           220
And ranne out, as he was wont of yore.
No sooner was out, but swifter then thought,
Fast by the hyde the Wolfe lowder caught:
And had not Roffy renne to the steven,
Lowder had be slaine thilke same even.                          225

HOBBINOLL.

God shield man, he should so ill have thrive,
All for he did his devoyr belive.
If sike bene Wolves, as thou hast told,
How mought we Diggon, hem be-hold.

DIGGON.

How, but with heede and watchfulnesse,                          230
Forstallen hem of their wilinesse?
For thy with shepheard sittes not playe,
Or sleepe, as some doen, all the long day:
But ever liggen in watch and ward,
From soddein force theyr flocks for to gard.                    235

HOBBINOLL.

Ah Diggon, thilke same rule were too straight,
All the cold season to wach and waite.
We bene of fleshe, men as other bee,
Why should we be bound to such miseree?
What ever thing lacketh chaungeable rest,                       240
Mought needes decay, when it is at best.

DIGGON.

Ah but Hobbinol, all this long tale,
Nought easeth the care, that doth me forhaile.

219. *weene*: think.   227. *devoyr*: duty.   232. *sittes not*: it is not
appropriate to.   236. *straight*: strict.   240. *chaungeable rest*: rest from
time to time.

What shall I doe? what way shall I wend,
My piteous plight and losse to amend?                              245
Ah good Hobbinol, mought I thee praye,
Of ayde or counsell in my decaye.

### HOBBINOLL.

Now by my soule Diggon, I lament
The haplesse mischief, that has thee hent,
Nethelesse thou seest my lowly saile,                              250
That froward fortune doth ever availe.
But were Hobbinoll, as God mought please,
Diggon should soone find favour and ease.
But if to my cotage thou wilt resort,
So as I can, I wil thee comfort:                                   255
There mayst thou ligge in a vetchy bed,
Till fayrer Fortune shewe forth her head.

### DIGGON.

Ah Hobbinol, God mought it thee requite.
Diggon on fewe such freends did ever lite.

Diggons Embleme.                                                   260

*Inopem me copia fecit.*

### GLOSSE.

The Dialecte and phrase of speache in this Dialogue, semeth
    somewhat to differ from the comen. The cause whereof
    is supposed to be, by occasion of the party herein
    meant, who being very freend to the Author hereof,
    had bene long in forraine countryes, and there seene
    many disorders, which he here recounteth to
    Hobbinoll.
[1]    Bidde her) Bidde good morrow. For to bidde, is to

---

249. *hent*: caught.   251. *froward*: contrary. *availe*: lower.   261. *Inopem*
. . . *fecit*: "plenty made me poor," Ovid, *Met* 3.466.

praye, whereof commeth beades for prayers, and so they say, To bidde his beades. s. to saye his prayers.

[5] Wightly) quicklye, or sodenlye. [10] Chaffred) solde. [10] Dead at mischiefe) an unusuall speache, but much usurped of Lidgate, and sometime of Chaucer.

[11] Leefe) deare. [17] Ethe) easie. [20] Thrise thre moones) nine monethes. [21] Measured) for traveled.

[25] Wae) woe Northernly. Eeked) encreased. [41] Carven) cutte. [42] Kenne) know.

[45] Cragge) neck. [45] State) stoutely. [47] Stanck) wearie or fainte.

[49] And nowe) He applieth it to the tyme of the yeare, which is in thend of harvest, which they call the fall of the leafe: at which tyme the Westerne wynde beareth most swaye.

[54] A mocke) Imitating Horace, Debes ludibrium ventis. [57] Lorne) lefte. Soote) swete.

[60] Uncouthe) unknowen. [63] Hereby there) here and there. [76] As the brighte) Translated out of Mantuane. [83] Emprise) for enterprise. Per Syncopen. [86] Contek) strife.

[92] Trode) path. [96] Marrie that) that is, their soules, which by popish Exorcismes and practises they damme to hell.

[97] Blacke) hell. [100] Gange) goe. [103] Mister) maner. [103] Mirke) obscure. [108] Warre) worse.

[119] Crumenall) purse. [124] Brace) compasse. [116] Encheson) occasion. [130] Overgrast)

---

[10.2] *usurped of*: used by. [47] *Stanck*: coined by Sp from Ital. *stanco*, weary. [54] *Debes ludibrium ventis*: "[Beware, lest] you be mocked by the winds," Horace, *Odes* 1.14.15–16. [76] *Mantuane*: *Eclogue* 7.8–9. [83] *Per Syncopen*: by way of *syncope* (abbreviation of a word by omitting some internal letters). [119] *Crumenall*: coined by Sp from Lat. *crumena*, purse.

overgrowen with grasse. [131] Galage)

shoe. [135] The grosse) the whole.

[149] Buxome and bent) meeke and obedient.

[151] Saxon king) K. Edgare, that reigned here in Brytanye in the yeare of our Lorde. which king caused all the Wolves, whereof then was store in thys countrye, by a proper policie to be destroyed. So as never since that time, there have ben Wolves here founde, unlesse they were brought from other countryes. And therefore Hobbinoll rebuketh him of untruth, for saying there be Wolves in England.

[153] Nor in Christendome) This saying seemeth to be strange and unreasonable: but indede it was wont to be an olde proverbe and comen phrase. The original whereof was, for that the most part of England in the reigne of king Ethelbert was christened, Kent onely except, which remayned long after in mysbeliefe and unchristened, So that Kent was counted no part of Christendome.

[159] Great hunt) Executing of lawes and justice.

[161] Enaunter) least that

[161] Inly) inwardly. afforesayde.    [162] Prively or pert) openly sayth Chaucer.

[171] Roffy) The name of a shepeharde in Marot his Æglogue of Robin and the Kinge. whome he here commendeth for grete care and wise governance of his flock.

[176] Colin cloute) Nowe I thinke no man doubteth but by Colin is ever meante the Authour selfe. whose especiall good freend Hobbinoll sayth he is, or more rightly

---

[151.2] *yeare . . . Lorde* : apparently a proofreading mistake; Edgar reigned 944–75. The story is from Holinshed, *Chronicles* 6.23.    [153.5] *Ethelbert*: reigned 860–65.    [162] *Chaucer*: perhaps the pseudo-Chaucerian *La Belle Dame sans Mercy*, line 175: "privie noe perte."    [171] *Roffy*: mentioned instead in Marot's *Eglogue de Mme Loyse de Savoye*, line 42.

Mayster Gabriel Harvey: of whose speciall
commendation, aswell in Poetrye as Rhetorike and
other choyce learning, we have lately had a sufficient
tryall in diverse his workes, but specially in his
Musarum Lachrymæ, and his late Gratulationum
Valdinensium which boke in the progresse at Audley in
Essex, he dedicated in writing to her Majestie.
afterward presenting the same in print unto her
Highnesse at the worshipfull Maister Capells in
Hertfordshire. Beside other his sundrye most rare and
very notable writings, partly under unknown Tytles,
and partly under counterfayt names, as hys
Tyrannomastix, his Ode Natalitia, his Rameidos, and
esspecially that parte of Philomusus, his divine
Anticosmopolita, and divers other of lyke importance.
As also by the names of other shepheardes, he covereth
the persons of divers other his familiar freendes and
best acquayntaunce.

[180-225] This tale of Roffy seemeth to coulore some
    particular Action of his. But what, I certeinlye know
    not.    [184] Wonned) haunted.    [187] Welkin) skie.
    afforesaid.

[198] A Weanell waste) a weaned youngling.    [211] Hidder
    and shidder) He and she. Male and Female.

[224] Steven) Noyse.    [227] Belive)
    quickly.    [240] What ever) Ovids verse translated.
    Quod caret alterna requie, durabile non est.

[243] Forehaile) drawe or distresse.    [256] Vetchie) of
    Pease strawe.

[176.4] *Gabriel Harvey*: In her summer progress of 1578 Elizabeth visited
Audley End near Cambridge where Harvey presented orally his *Gratulationes
Valdinenses* ("Joyful Greetings from Saffron Walden," his nearby birthplace),
a collection of poems to the queen and five great courtiers. Of the other
works mentioned, only the *Lachrymae* and the *Ode* survive. His
*Anticosmopolita*, perhaps never completed, was apparently an epic celebrating
Elizabeth's reign.    [180.1] *coloure*: disguise.    [240] *Quod . . . est*: "what
lacks periods of rest cannot last," *Heroides* 4.89.

Embleme.

This is the saying of Narcissus in Ovid. For when the foolishe boye by beholding hys face in the brooke, fell in love with his owne likenesse: and not hable to content him selfe with much looking thereon, he cryed out, that plentye made him poore, meaning that much gazing had bereft him of sence. But our Diggon useth it to other purpose, as who that by tryall of many wayes had founde the worst, and through greate plentye was fallen into great penurie. This poesie I knowe, to have been much used of the author, and to suche like effecte, as fyrste Narcissus spake it.

# *October*

᪉᪉᪉᪉᪉᪉᪉

In this eclogue Spenser follows Mantuan's fifth *Eclogue* where Candidus, a needy poet, asks Silvanus, a niggardly connoisseur of poetry, for financial help and gets instead a lecture on the poet's social role. But after line seventy-nine Spenser turns away from Mantuan to let Piers and Cuddy focus on the rising career of Colin.

In the dialogue Piers attempts to persuade the young poet Cuddy that he has Orphic potential like "the shepheard" (28) whose "musicks might the hellish hound did tame" (30). (This unmistakable allusion to Orpheus is Spenser's invention and not in Mantuan.) When Cuddy complains that poetry lacks reward, Piers directs him to heroic praise of "fayre Elisa" (45) and her knights. Cuddy recognizes the career model of "Romish Tityrus" (55) at whose heroic praises "the Heavens did quake" (60) just as Hell yielded to Orpheus's hymn. The woodcut depicts the Virgilian paradigm by showing an aged Piers as Virgil crowned with laurel and offering Cuddy the pastoral oaten reeds. On a hill behind Piers-Virgil is an empty classical temple and an Italianate palace (cf. "Princes pallace," 80 and 81). Several figures admire the temple, but one moves resolutely toward it and another climbs its steps. In the woodcut Cuddy rejects Piers's offer by pointing out the figure approaching the temple. In the poem he demurs because he can discern no contemporary material for the heroic poem and hence no relevance in the Virgilian career, for the age of the praiseworthy hero and the generous patron has gone by. At this impasse the dialogue focuses on Colin who, both agree, is the one living poet capable of heroic praise and thus of rescuing the poetic art: "For Colin fittes such famous flight to scanne" (88). Where Cuddy sees possible satire, Colin sees an "immortall mirrhor" (93)—an image of Eliza immune to calendrical time—whose apotheosis will declare him successor to the hymnic poet Orpheus and the heroic encomiast Virgil. Obviously, the figure ascending to the temple of fame is Colin.

Spenser presents the Virgilian model here because Virgil was born in October. October is the tenth month, and it is the tenth stanza that introduces "the Romish Tityrus" (55). Virgil's birthday was the ides, or midpoint, of October and allusion to him occupies the two middle stanzas (55–66). But October is also the wine-making month. When Cuddy takes the hint and describes his imaginary version of Colin's flight, he intemperately bungles the tradition that a modicum of wine aids imagination: "when with Wine the braine begins to sweate, / The nombers flowe as fast as spring doth ryse" (107–08). Cuddy's vatic spree as tragedian, however, is comically brief and only reasserts the pastoral stasis into which he falls back. But his ersatz enthousiasmos defines by contrast the extrapastoral character of Colin's flight "above the starry skie" (94).

*Enthousiasmos* or *furor poeticus* or inspiration (what we might call the unconscious or perhaps even right-brain element in creativity) is one of Spenser's preoccupations. The only thing known about his lost treatise, *The English Poete*, is that it spoke of "celestiall inspiration" "at large" (Argument to *October*). Here "teach," "lyftes," and "cause" imply that Elizabeth herself is the source of *enthousiasmos*: not only Colin's subject but also the power speaking through him (the word's root meaning suggests a god—*theos*—possessing a spokesman). By "immortall mirrhor" Spenser probably means Elizabeth as Venus Coelestis who, according to Ficino, "dwells in the highest, supercelestial zone of the universe, i.e., in the zone of the Cosmic Mind, and the beauty symbolized by her is the primary and universal beauty of divinity" (Panofsky 1962: 142). The mirror Colin admires is clearly supercelestial, drawing his imagination "above the starry skie," that is, the *coelum stellatum* or sphere of fixed stars beyond the planetary spheres and, in Ptolemaic cosmology, adjacent to the empyrean and divine primum mobile itself. This passage leads directly to the first lines of *The Faerie Queene* where a poet emerges who has laid aside "lowly Shepheards weeds" and begins deifying an empress.

The pairing of Orpheus and Colin is built into the patterning of October which (like the April ode) simultaneously matches stanzas in arrangements that are both symmetrical (i.e. stanzas 1 and 20, 2 and 19) and parallel (i.e. stanzas 1 and 11, 2 and 12). In the symmetrical pattern, stanza 5 on Orpheus matches stanza 16 on Colin's flight. The pairing makes Colin potentially superior to Orpheus, for it recalls the Boethian sense that Orpheus mismanaged *cupiditas* and implies that Colin's "love" for Venus Coelestis who "does teach him climbe so hie" (91) makes him transcend mere desire for Rosalind, the Venus Vulgaris who left him "with love so ill bedight" (89). Some other features of the patterning are worth noting. Two pairs of stanzas reflect the Virgilian career-model. Stanza 7 involves optimistic ascent from "the base and viler clowne" (37) to "those, that weld the awful crowne" (40) and the symmetrically related stanza 14 pessimistically sees no poetry in "brest of baser birth" (82) or "Princes pallace" (81). And in stanza 10 Cuddy understands how Virgil "left his Oaten reede" (56) but in the matching parallel, stanza 20, he chooses to retreat to "our slender pipes" (118). The question of reward (the main concern in Mantuan's fifth *Eclogue*) occurs twice in the symmetrical pattern: Cuddy's unrewarded peacock-poet in stanza 6 is matched in stanza 15 by Colin as transcendent singing swan. More important, the central pair of stanzas (10 and 11) focuses on Mæcenas—Virgil's patron now "yclad in claye" (61). The implication is that, just as Colin can discern the heroic subject invisible to Cuddy, so that vision of Eliza implicitly solves the question of patronage: the Faery Queen will be Colin's Mæcenas.

The October stanza is a version of the six-line stanza but uniquely rhyming abbaba.

# October.

*Ægloga decima.*

## ARGUMENT.

IN *Cuddie is set out the perfecte paterne of a Poete, which finding
no maintenaunce of his state and studies, complayneth of the
comtempte of Poetrie, and the causes thereof: Specially having bene in
all ages, and even amongst the most barbarous alwayes of singular
accounpt and honor, and being indede so worthy and commendable
an arte: or rather no arte, but a divine gift and heavenly instinct not
to bee gotten by laboure and learning, but adorned with both: and
poured into the witte by a certain* ἐνθουσιασμός. *and celestiall
inspiration, as the Author hereof els where at large discourseth, in his
booke called the English Poete, which booke being lately come to my
hands, I mynde also by Gods grace upon further advisement to
publish.*

---

ARGUMENT *instinct*: instillment. ἐνθουσιασμός.: Gk *enthusiasmos*:
enthusiasm, inspiration, possession by a divinity. *the English Poete*: the only
mention of this lost work which (if it ever actually existed) would have been
the first Renaissance treatise on poetics in English.

### PIERCE. CUDDIE.

*Cuddie,* for shame hold up thy heavye head,
And let us cast with what delight to chace:
And weary thys long lingring *Phœbus* race.
Whilome thou wont the shepheards laddes to leade,
In rymes, in ridles, and in bydding base:       5
Now they in thee, and thou in sleepe art dead.

### CUDDYE.

*Piers,* I have pyped erst so long with payne,
That all mine Oten reedes bene rent and wore:
And my poore Muse hath spent her spared store,
Yet little good hath got, and much lesse gayne.       10
Such pleasaunce makes the Grashopper so poore,
And ligge so layd, when Winter doth her straine.

The dapper ditties, that I wont devise,
To feede youthes fancie, and the flocking fry,
Delighten much: what I the bett for thy?       15
They han the pleasure, I a sclender prise.
I beate the bush, the byrds to them doe flye:
What good thereof to Cuddie can arise?

### PIRES.

*Cuddie,* the prayse is better, then the price,
The glory eke much greater than the gayne:       20
O what an honor is it, to restraine
The lust of lawlesse youth with good advice:

---

2. *chace*: pursue, run.    3. *Phoebus race*: course of the sun, i. e. day.
5. *bydding base*: the game of prisoner's base (or perhaps lowly singing
matches).    6. *Now . . . dead*: Your creative dormancy has deprived your
audience.    9. *spared*: saved up.    11. *pleasaunce*: frivolity. *Grashopper*: the
well-known Aesopic fable of the provident ant and improvident grasshopper
who sings all summer and starves in winter.    12. *straine*: constrain, put
pressure on.    15. *what . . . thy?*: how does that better me?    16. *sclender
prise*: meager reward.    19. *price*: reward.

Or pricke them forth with pleasaunce of thy vaine,
Whereto thou list their trayned willes entice.

Soone as thou gynst to sette thy notes in frame,          25
O how the rurall routes to thee doe cleave:
Seemeth thou dost their soule of sence bereave,
All as the shepheard, that did fetch his dame
From *Plutoes* balefull bowre withouten leave:
His musicks might the hellish hound did tame.              30

### CUDDIE.

So praysen babes the Peacoks spotted traine,
And wondren at bright *Argus* blazing eye:
But who rewards him ere the more for thy?
Or feedes him once the fuller by a graine?
Sike prayse is smoke, that sheddeth in the skye,          35
Sike words bene wynd, and wasten soone in vayne.

### PIERS.

Abandon then the base and viler clowne,
Lyft up thy selfe out of the lowly dust:
And sing of bloody Mars, of wars, of giusts.
Turne thee to those, that weld the awful crowne,          40
To doubted Knights, whose woundlesse armour rusts,
And helmes unbruzed wexen dayly browne.

23. *pricke*: spur. *pleasaunce . . . vaine*: the delight your talent can give; to
teach by delighting was the poet's goal according to Renaissance poetics.
24. *trayned*: drawn along, controlled.     25. *frame*: order.     26. *routes*:
crowds. *cleave*: cling.     27. *Seemeth*: it seems that.     28. *All*: just.
29. *balefull bowre*: perilous abode, i. e. the underworld.     30. *hellish hound*:
Cerberus, the three-headed dog guarding the entrance to Hades; quelled by
Orpheus's Song, he let the singer bring Eurydice out of the underworld (cf.
*FQ* IV x 58).     33. *ere*: ever, at all. *thy*: that.     35. *sheddeth*: evaporates.
37. *base . . . clowne*: low wretched rustic.     39. *giusts*: jousts.     40. *weld*:
bear, wear. *awful*: awesome.     41–42. Refers both to the lack of heroic
writing and the long peace of Elizabeth's reign, with perhaps some further
allusion to the dearth of poetic achievement in England since the time of
Chaucer.     42. *unbruzed*: undented.

There may thy Muse display her fluttryng wing,
And stretch her selfe at large from East to West:
Whither thou list in fayre *Elisa* rest,                          45
Or if thee please in bigger notes to sing,
Advaunce the worthy whome shee loveth best,
That first the white beare to the stake did bring.

And when the stubborne stroke of stronger stounds,
Has somewhat slackt the tenor of thy string:                      50
Of love and lustihead tho mayst thou sing,
And carrol lowde, and leade the Myllers rownde,
All were *Elisa* one of thilke same ring.
So mought our *Cuddies* name to Heaven sownde.

C U D D Y E .

Indeede the Romish *Tityrus,* I heare,                            55
Through his *Mecænas* left his Oaten reede,
Whereon he earst had taught his flocks to feede,
And laboured lands to yield the timely eare,
And eft did sing of warres and deadly drede,
So as the Heavens did quake his verse to here.                    60

But ah *Mecænas* is yclad in claye,
And great *Augustus* long ygoe is dead:
And all the worthies liggen wrapt in leade,
That matter made for Poets on to play:
For ever, who in derring doe were dreade,                         65
The loftie verse of hem was loved aye.

---

43. *display*: stretch out.     45. *rest*: find a subject.     47. *Advaunce*: put
forward, praise.     48. *white beare*: a bear chained to an uprooted tree stump
("stake") was the Dudley crest, hence Leicester's.     49. *stounds*: blows.
50. *tenor*: tautness.     53. *All*: although.     56. *Mecænas*: An early patron
of Horace and Virgil, Maecenas's name came to symbolize generous
patronage of poets.     58. *laboured*: plowed, tilled (i. e. the *Georgics*, literally
"poems on plowing"). *timely eare*: grain in its season.     59. *drede*: dread.
63. *liggen*: lie.     65. *dreade*: dreaded.     66. *of hem*: ambiguous: verse
about them or verse loved by them.

But after vertue gan for age to stoupe,
And mighty manhode brought a bedde of ease:
The vaunting Poets found nought worth a pease,
To put in preace emong the learned troupe.               70
Tho gan the streames of flowing wittes to cease,
And sonnebright honour pend in shamefull coupe.

And if that any buddes of Poesie,
Yet of the old stocke gan to shoote agayne:
Or it mens follies mote be forst to fayne,               75
And rolle with rest in rymes of rybaudrye:
Or as it sprong, it wither must agayne:
Tom Piper makes us better melodie.

PIERS.

O pierlesse Poesye, where is then thy place?
If nor in Princes pallace thou doe sitt:                 80
(And yet is Princes pallace the most fitt)
Ne brest of baser birth doth thee embrace.
Then make thee winges of thine aspyring wit,
And, whence thou camst, flye backe to heaven apace.

CUDDIE.

Ah *Percy* it is all to weake and wanne,                 85
So high to sore, and make so large a flight:
Her peeced pyneons bene not so in plight,
For *Colin* fittes such famous flight to scanne:

---

67. *vertue*: manliness, heroism.    68. *a bedde of*: to bed by.    69–70. *The
. . . troupe*: The ambitious poets could find no worthwhile subject that would
allow them to compete with the learned poets (of antiquity).    70. *preace*:
press, crowd.    75. *Or . . . fayne*: either it must ignore man's follies . . . .
76. *rybaudrye*: ribaldry.    78. *Tom Piper*: generic name for an ignorant
rustic rhymster.    79. *pierlesse*: peerless, with a pun on Piers's name.
84. *apace*: quickly.    87. *peeced*: pieced together, patched. *plight*: condition.
88. *fittes*: it is fitting. *famous flight*: flight that will earn the poet fame. *scanne*:
mount, climb.

He, were he not with love so ill bedight,
Would mount as high, and sing as soote as Swanne.　　　90

### PIRES.

Ah fon, for love does teach him climbe so hie,
And lyftes him up out of the loathsome myre:
Such immortall mirrhor, as he doth admire,
Would rayse ones mynd above the starry skie.
And cause a caytive corage to aspire,　　　　　　　95
For lofty love doth loath a lowly eye.

### CUDDIE.

All otherwise the state of Poet stands,
For lordly love is such a Tyranne fell:
That where he rules, all power he doth expell.
The vaunted verse a vacant head demaundes,　　　100
Ne wont with crabbed care the Muses dwell.
Unwisely weaves, that takes two webbes in hand.

Who ever casts to compasse weightye prise,
And thinks to throwe out thondring words of threate:
Let powre in lavish cups and thriftie bitts of meate,　　105
For *Bacchus* fruite is frend to *Phœbus* wise.
And when with Wine the braine begins to sweate,
The nombers flowe as fast as spring doth ryse.

Thou kenst not *Percie* howe the ryme should rage.
O if my temples were distaind with wine,　　　　　110
And girt in girlonds of wild Yuie twine,
How I could reare the Muse on stately stage,

89. *bedight*: affected.　　90. *soote*: sweet.　　91. *Ah . . . love*: O you are fool,
for it is love that. . . .　　98. *fell*: ruthless.　　100. *vaunted*: celebrated.
101. *crabbed care*: perverse worries.　　103. *compasse*: achieve. *weightye*:
major, significant.　　105. *Let . . . meate*: Let him fill cups lavishly and have
only a little food.　　106. *For . . . wise*: For wine stimulates the ability to
compose poems (Bacchus was god of wine and Phoebus Apollo led the
Muses).　　108. *nombers*: verses.

And teache her tread aloft in buskin fine,
With queint *Bellona* in her equipage.

But ah my corage cooles ere it be warme,                    115
For thy, content us in thys humble shade:
Where no such troublous tydes han us assayde,
Here we our slender pipes may safely charme.

PIRES.
And when my Gates shall han their bellies layd:
*Cuddie* shall have a Kidde to store his farme.              120

Cuddies Embleme.

*Agitante calescimus illo etc.*

GLOSSE.
This Æglogue is made in imitation of Theocritus his xvi.
Idilion, wherein hee reproved the Tyranne Hiero of
Syracuse for his nigardise towarde Poetes, in whome is
the power to make men immortal for theyr good
dedes, or shameful for their naughty lyfe. And the lyke
also is in Mantuane, The style hereof as also that in
Theocritus, is more loftye than the rest, and applyed to
the heighte of Poeticall witte.

114. *equipage*: equipment, retinue (cf. E. K.'s gloss).    115. *corage*:
emotion, wrath, excitement.    117. *troublous tydes*: i.e. times of war
(Bellona), so outside pastoral experience. *assayde*: affected.    118. *charme*:
make songs on (cf. E. K.'s gloss).    119. *Gates . . . layd*: goats have given
birth.    120. *store*: stock.    122. *Agitante . . . etc.*: part of a line in Ovid,
*Fasti* 6.5: "[there is a god in us and] when he stirs we glow."

[E. K.'s comment] *Theocritus*: Theocritus made the woes of poets without
patrons a motif of pastoral, but Sp does not imitate *Idyll* 16 here. E. K.
means to downplay Sp's imitation of Mantuan whose eclogues were familiar
to every schoolboy.

[1]   Cuddie) I doubte whether by Cuddie be specified the
      authour selfe, or some other. For in the eyght Æglogue
      the same person was brought in, singing a Cantion of
      Colins making, as he sayth. So that some doubt, that
      the persons be different.

[4]   Whilome) sometime.   [8] Oaten reedes) Avena.

[12]  Ligge so layde) lye so faynt and unlustye.
      [13] Dapper) pretye.

[14]  Frye) is a bold Metaphore, forced from the spawning
      fishes. for the multitude of young fish be called the
      frye.

[21]  To restraine.) This place seemeth to conspyre with
      Plato, who in his first booke de Legibus sayth, that the
      first invention of Poetry was of very vertuous intent.
      For at what time an infinite number of youth usually
      came to theyr great solemne feastes called Panegyrica,
      which they used every five yeere to hold, some learned
      man being more hable than the rest, for speciall gyftes
      of wytte and Musicke, would take upon him to sing
      fine verses to the people, in prayse eyther of vertue or
      of victory or of immortality or such like. At whose
      wonderful gyft al men being astonied and as it were
      ravished, with delight, thinking (as it was indeed) that
      he was inspired from above, called him vatem: which
      kinde of men afterwarde framing their verses to lighter
      musick (as of musick be many kinds, some sadder,
      some lighter, some martiall, some heroical: and so
      diversely eke affect the mynds of men) found out

---

[1.2] *author selfe*: Cuddy and Colin can hardly both be authorial personae.
Cf. E. K.'s gloss on *Januarye*, line 1.     [1.3] Cantion: song, *canzona* (the
*August* sestina resembles several of Petrarch's longer lyrics or *canzone* which
are often sestinas).     [1.4] *doubt*: think, imagine.     [21.1] *conspyre*: agree.
E. K.'s information is not in Plato's *Laws*.     [21.13] *vatem*: seer, visionary.
The distinction between *vates* and *poeta* was standard in Renaissance poetics
(see *Aprill*, Introduction).

lighter matter of Poesie also, some playing wyth love, some scorning at mens fashions, some powred out in pleasures, and so were called Poetes or makers.

[27]  Sence bereave) what the secrete working of Musick is in the myndes of men, aswell appeareth hereby, that some of the auncient Philosophers, and those the moste wise, as Plato and Pythagoras held for opinion, that the mynd was made of a certaine harmonie and musicall nombers, for the great compassion and likenes of affection in thone and in the other as also by that memorable history of Alexander: to whom when as Timotheus the great Musitian playd the Phrygian melodie, it is said, that he was distraught with such unwonted fury, that streight way rysing from the table in great rage, he caused himselfe to be armed, as ready to goe to warre (for that musick is very war like:) And immediatly whenas the Musitian chaunged his stroke into the Lydian and Ionique harmony, he was so furr from warring, that he sat as styl, as if he had bene in matters of counsell. Such might is in musick. wherefore Plato and Aristotle forbid the Arabian Melodie from children and youth. for that being altogither on the fyft and vii, tone, it is of great force to molifie and quench the kindly courage, which useth to burne in yong brests. So that it is not incredible which the Poete here sayth, that Musick can bereave the soule of sence.

[28]  The shepheard that) Orpheus: of whom is sayd, that by his excellent skil in Musick and Poetry, he recovered his wife Eurydice from hell.

[32]  Argus eyes) of Argus is before said, that Juno to him committed hir husband Jupiter his Paragon Io, bicause he had an hundred eyes: but afterwarde Mercury wyth

[27.6–7] *compassion. . . affection*: harmony and capacity for being moved.
[28.1] *Orpheus*: E. K., like Sp, ignores Orpheus's almost immediate loss of Eurydice as irrelevant to the point of the allusion.    [32.1] *Argus*: see Ovid, *Met* 1.568–747.

hys Musick lulling Argus aslepe, slew him and brought
Io away, whose eyes it is sayd that Juno for his eternall
memory placed in her byrd the Peacocks tayle. for
those coloured spots indeede resemble eyes.

[41] Woundlesse armour) unwounded in warre, doe rust
through long peace.

[43] Display) A poeticall metaphore: whereof the meaning
is, that if the Poet list showe his skill in matter of more
dignitie, then is the homely Æglogue, good occasion is
him offered of higher veyne and more Heroicall
argument, in the person of our most gratious
soveraign, whom (as before) he calleth Elisa. Or if
mater of knighthoode and chevalrie please him better,
that there be many Noble and valiaunt men, that are
both worthy of his payne in theyr deserved prayses,
and also favourers of hys skil and faculty.

[47] The worthy) he meaneth (as I guesse) the most
honorable and renowmed the Erle of Leycester, whom
by his cognisance (although the same be also proper to
other) rather then by his name he bewrayeth, being not
likely, that the names of noble princes be known to
country clowne.

[50] Slack) that is when thou chaungest thy verse from
stately discourse, to matter of more pleasaunce and
delight.

[52] The Millers) a kind of daunce.   [53] Ring) company
of dauncers.

[55] The Romish Tityrus) wel knowen to be Virgile, who
by Mecænas means was brought into the favour of the
Emperor Augustus, and by him moved to write in
loftier kinde, then he erst had doen.

[57] Whereon) in these three verses are the three severall
workes of Virgile intended. For in teaching his flocks
to feede, is meant his Æglogues. In labouring of lands,

[47.3] *cognisance*: badge, crest.   [47.4] *other*: other families.

is hys Bucoliques. In singing of wars and deadly
dreade, is his divine Æneis figured.

[65] In derring doe) In manhoode and chevalrie.

[65] For ever) He sheweth the cause, why Poetes were wont
be had in such honor of noble men; that is, that by
them their worthines and valor shold through theyr
famous Posies be commended to al posterities.
wherfore it is sayd, that Achilles had never bene so
famous, as he is, but for Homeres immortal verses.
which is the only advantage, which he had of Hector.
And also that Alexander the great comming to his
tombe in Sigeus, with naturall teares blessed him, that
ever was his hap to be honoured with so excellent a
Poets work: as so renowmed and ennobled onely by
hys meanes. which being declared in a most eloquent
Oration of Tullies, is of Petrarch no lesse worthely sette
forth in a sonet
> Giunto Alexandro a la famosa tomba
> Del fero Achille sospirando disse
> O fortunato che si chiara tromba. Trovasti etc.

And that such account hath bene alwayes made of
Poetes, aswell sheweth this that the worthy Scipio in all
his warres against Carthage and Numantia had
evermore in his company, and that in a most familiar
sort the good olde Poet Ennius: as also that Alexander
destroying Thebes, when he was enformed that the
famous Lyrick Poet Pindarus was borne in that citie,

---

[57.4] *Bucoliques*: This generic term refers to herdsmen, hence pastoral, but
the *Georgics* are clearly intended; "Bucoliques" appears in Quartos 1–2, but it
is corrected to "Georgiques" in Quartos 3–5 and Folio.    [65.13] *Oration*:
Cicero, *Pro Archia Poeta* 10.24.    [65.13–17] *Petrarch . . . tromba*: *Rime*
187: "When Alexander reached the famous tomb of fierce Achilles, he sighed
and said, 'O fortunate man who found so clear a trumpet [and one that wrote
such high things about you].'"    [65.19] *Scipio*: in Cicero, *Pro Archia Poeta*
9. 22.    [65.24] *Pindarus*: recounted by Pliny, *Natural History* 7.29.109.

not onely commaunded streightly, that no man should
upon payne of death do any violence to that house by
fire or otherwise: but also specially spared most, and
some highly rewarded, that were of hys kinne. So
favoured he the only name of a Poete. whych prayse
otherwise was in the same man no lesse famous, that
when he came to ransacking of king Darius coffers,
whom he lately had overthrowen, he founde in a little
coffer of silver the two bookes of Homers works, as
layd up there for speciall jewells and richesse, which he
taking thence, put one of them dayly in his bosome,
and thother every night layde under his pillowe. Such
honor have Poetes alwayes found in the sight of
princes and noble men. which this author here very
well sheweth, as els where more notably.

[67]   But after) he sheweth the cause of contempt of Poetry
to be idlenesse and basenesse of mynd.   [72] Pent)
shut up in slouth, as in a coope or cage.

[78] Tom Piper) An Ironicall Sarcasmus, spoken in derision
of these rude wits, whych make more account of a
ryming rybaud, then of skill grounded upon learning
and judgment.

[82] Ne brest) the meaner sort of men.   [87] Her peeced
pineons) unperfect skil. Spoken wyth humble modestie.

[90] As soote as Swanne) The comparison seemeth to be
strange: for the swanne hath ever wonne small
commendation for her swete singing: but it is sayd of
the learned that the swan a little before hir death,
singeth most pleasantly, as prophecying by a secrete
instinct her neere destinie. As well sayth the Poete
elswhere in one of his sonetts.
The silver swanne doth sing before her dying day
As shee that feeles the deepe delight that is in death etc.

[93] Immortall myrrhour) Beauty, which is an excellent

[65.31] *Darius*: ibid.      [90.8] *The silver swanne*: this sonnet is lost.

object of Poeticall spirites, as appeareth by the worthy
Petrarchs saying.
Fiorir faceva il mio debile ingegno
A la sua ombra, et crescer ne gli affanni.
[95] A caytive corage) a base and abject minde.
[96] For lofty love) I think this playing with the letter to be
rather a fault then a figure, aswel in our English tongue,
as it hath bene alwayes in the Latine, called Cacozelon.
[100] A vacant) imitateth Mantuanes saying. vacuum curis
divina cerebrum Poscit.
[105] Lavish cups) Resembleth that comen verse Fæcundi
calices quem non fecere disertum.
[110] O if my) He seemeth here to be ravished with a
Poetical furie. For (if one rightly mark) the numbers
rise so ful, and the verse groweth so big, that it
seemeth he hath forgot the meanenesse of shepheards
state and stile.
[111] Wild yuie) for it is dedicated to Bacchus and therefore
it is sayd that the Mænades (that is Bacchus franticke
priestes) used in theyr sacrifice to carry Thyrsos, which
were pointed staves or Javelins, wrapped about with
yuie.
[113] In buskin) it was the maner of Poetes and plaiers in
tragedies to were buskins, as also in Comedies to use
stockes and light shoes. So that the buskin in Poetry is
used for tragical matter, as it said in Virgile. Solo

[93.4–5] *Fiorir . . . affanni*: *Rime* 60: "[The noble tree, i.e. the laurel] made
my frail wit to flourish in its shade and grow in griefs." [96.3] *Cacozelon*:
term in rhetoric for stylistic affectation (also called *ambitio*), with reference to
the line's four-fold alliteration. [100.1–2] *vacuum . . . Poscit*: "divine
(poetry?) requires a brain freed from worries." But the line is not in
Mantuan. [105.1–2] *Faecundi . . . disertum*: "Who is the man whom
brimming cups have failed to make eloquent?" Horace, *Epistles* 1.519.
[110.2] *Poetical furie*: the furors were states of inspiration and could be
poetic, heroic, erotic, or divine. [113.3] *stockes*: stockings.
[113.4–5] *Solo . . . cothurno*: "your songs are deserving of the Sophoclean
buskin [i.e. tragedy]," *Ecl* 8.10.

sophocleo tua carmina digna cothurno. And the like in
Horace, Magnum loqui, nitique cothurno.

[114] Queint) strange Bellona; the goddesse of battaile, that
is Pallas, which may therefore wel be called queint for
that (as Lucian saith) when Jupiter hir father was in
traveile of her, he caused his sonne Vulcane with his
axe to hew his head. Out of which leaped forth lustely
a valiant damsell armed at all poyntes, whom seeing
Vulcane so faire and comely, lightly leaping to her,
proferred her some cortesie, which the Lady
disdeigning, shaked her speare at him, and threatned
his saucinesse. Therefore such straungenesse is well
applyed to her.

[114] Æquipage.) order.     [117] Tydes) seasons.

[118] Charme) temper and order. for Charmes were wont to
be made by verses as Ovid sayth. Aut si carminibus.

Embleme.

Hereby is meant, as also in the whole course of this Æglogue,
that Poetry is a divine instinct and unnatural rage
passing the reache of comen reason. Whom Piers
answereth Epiphonematicos as admiring the
excellencye of the skyll whereof in Cuddie hee hadde
alreadye hadde a taste.

[113.6] *Magnum . . . cothurno*: "[Aeschylus taught actors] to speak grandly
and walk in buskins," *Ars Poetica* 280.     [114.6–7] *whom . . . comely*:
whom, when Vulcan saw her to be so fair and comely.     [114.10] *saucinesse*:
forwardness.     [118.2] *Aut si carminibus*: "or if in songs"; but not in
Ovid.     [Embleme.4] *Epiphonematicos*: by way of *epiphonema* (*acclamatio*),
an exclamation to end a discourse.

# November

*࿓࿓࿓࿓࿓࿓࿓*

T his eclogue has the same dialogue-and-song structure as
*Aprill* but to different effect. While in both the dialogue
centers on Colin's poetic gifts, now the disabling affair of
Rosalind seems no longer relevant: Colin makes no disclaimer
of ability and readily agrees to sing, only provided that his theme
reflect the dying year. In *Aprill* the shepherds must make do with
a quoted poem; here Colin (perhaps because he has discovered
his true subject in *October*) can improvise a sophisticated lament
that will be as permanent (of "endles sovenaunce" [5]) as the
April lay. The lament has a difficult ten-line stanza with four
distinct line lengths—a form designed to advertise ability, while
even the dialogue (until the closure, which is in the *Januarye*
stanza) proceeds in eight-line units rhyming *ababbcbc*. As E. K.
notes in his Argument, Spenser here follows Clément Marot's
*Eclogue de Mme Loyse de Savoye* (1531) but "farre passing his
reache," not only in complexity of verse form (Marot uses linked
quatrains throughout) but also by transmuting a somewhat
mannered courtier's lament into a pastoral of emotional engage-
ment and intensity.

The pastoral dirge descended from Theocritus's first *Idyll* and
the laments of Moschus and Bion through Virgil's fifth *Eclogue*
to become a staple of the genre, with Petrarch and Boccaccio as
well as Marot providing examples. It has three basic themes in a
necessary order: expression of grief, praise of the dead, and
apotheosis. This pattern, which Spenser follows, has special
relevance for the Christian mourner who must somehow recon-
cile the immediate emotional urgency of loss with belief in the
life everlasting. This is the function of funeral rites and a func-
tion here fulfilled by Colin's dirge (note in the woodcut the
procession to the church). The "herse" of the refrain is easy to

*185*

misunderstand: as E. K.'s gloss indicates, it means the verbal or sung service for the dead. Only by confronting and expressing grief in "heavie herse" and "carefull verse" can "woe" be "wasted" (201) or expended and the chief mourner Lobbin come to believe that "happy herse" and "joyful verse" are the true responses to Dido's heavenly state.

In this eclogue Colin insists on the seasons (and, more broadly, time) as the limitation of earthly pastoral (and earthly life). Individual man cannot even expect to fail and recover with the yearly cycle: the field flower "lyeth buryed long in Winters bale" (84) yet in spring again "floureth fresh" (86), while for man even "vertues braunch and beauties budde,/Reliven not for any good" (88–89). This bleak recognition of the intransigence of mortality to human goodness brings the "heavie herse" to an end with an outcry (admired by E. K.) of *contemptus mundi* (153–62). Then the lament yields to consolation. For the eternal pastoral of heaven with its "fieldes ay fresh" and "grasse ay greene" (189) transcends the temporal constrictions and human limitations of man's fallen nature. Yet it does not repudiate but rather transmutes the best values of Arcadian pastoral: Dido "raignes a goddesse now emong the saintes,/That whilome was the saynt of shepheards light" (175–76). From the perspective of *November*, pastoral's validity lies in its anticipation, however faulty, of the celestial pastoral that is the soul's true home ("Make hast ye shepheards, thether to revert" [191]). The underlying perception here is broadly Augustinian.

But who is Dido? Perhaps some girl of the Dudley family, thus making Lobbin Leicester; perhaps Elizabeth herself (in Virgil, Dido's other name is Elissa), metaphorically "dead" to England during the planning of the French marriage (McLane 1961: 47–60). No identification has been generally accepted. Perhaps we should take seriously E. K.'s insistence in the Argument that "the personage is secrete."

# November.

*Ægloga undecima.*

## ARGUMENT.

IN this xi. *Æglogue he bewayleth the death of some mayden of greate bloud, whom he calleth Dido. The personage is secrete, and to me altogether unknowne, albe of him selfe I often required the same. This Æglogue is made in imitation of Marot his song, which he made upon the death of Loys the frenche Queene. But farre passing his reache, and in myne opinion all other the Eglogues of this booke.*

### THENOT. COLIN.

COlin my deare, when shall it please thee sing,
As thou were wont songs of some jouisaunce?
Thy Muse to long slombreth in sorrowing,
Lulled a sleepe through loves misgovernaunce.
Now somewhat sing, whose endles sovenaunce,                 5

ARGUMENT *bloud*: descent. *required*: asked.    3. *to*: too.
4. *misgovernaunce*: misguidance, misdirection.    5. *somewhat*:
something.

Emong the shepeheards swaines may aye remaine,
Whether thee list thy loved lasse advaunce,
Or honor *Pan* with hymnes of higher vaine.

C O L I N .

*Thenot,* now nis the time of merimake.
Nor *Pan* to herye, nor with love to playe:                    10
Sike myrth in May is meetest for to make,
Or summer shade under the cocked haye.
But nowe sadde Winter welked hath the day,
And *Phœbus* weary of his yerely taske,
Ystabled hath his steedes in lowlye laye,                      15
And taken up his ynne in *Fishes* haske.

Thilke sollein season sadder plight doth aske:
And loatheth sike delightes, as thou doest prayse:
The mornefull Muse in myrth now list ne maske,
As shee was wont in youngth and sommer dayes.                  20
But if thou algate lust light virelayes,
And looser songs of love to underfong
Who but thy selfe deserves sike Poetes prayse?
Relieve thy Oaten pypes, that sleepen long.

T H E N O T .

The Nightingale is sovereigne of song,                         25
Before him sits the Titmose silent bee:

7. *advaunce*: praise.     9. *nis*: is not.     12. *cocked*: in cocks (small
stacks).     16. *Fishes haske*: An unsolved conundrum. "Fishes haske,"
meaning the zodiacal sign Pisces, is proper to February. The woodcut shows
Sagittarius—correct for November, as is the observation of the declining sun
which would be ascending in February. One radical solution (proposed by
Renwick [1931] and others) is that "Fishes haske" is a telltale remnant of
some putative pre-calendrical stage of the poem. McLane (1961: 53–54)
argues that the fish is the dolphin and denotes Alençon, the French dauphin,
thus making the royal sun within his pannier a criticism of the French
marriage. No solution has gained broad acceptance.     17. *plight*: mood,
approach.     21. *algate*: nevertheless.     22. *underfong*: undertake.
23. *Poetes prayse*: acclamation of poet for his achievement.     24. *Relieve*:
take up once more.     26. *sits*: it is proper that. *Titmose*: tomtit.

And I unfitte to thrust in skilfull thronge,
Should *Colin* make judge of my fooleree.
Nay, better learne of hem, that learned bee,
And han be watered at the Muses well:                    30
The kindlye dewe drops from the higher tree,
And wets the little plants that lowly dwell.

But if sadde winters wrathe and season chill,
Accorde not with thy Muses meriment:
To sadder times thou mayst attune thy quill,             35
And sing of sorrowe and deathes dreeriment.
For deade is Dido, dead alas and drent,
Dido the greate shepehearde his daughter sheene:
The fayrest May she was that ever went,
Her like shee has not left behinde I weene.              40

And if thou wilt bewayle my wofull tene:
I shall thee give yond Cosset for thy payne:
And if thy rymes as rownd and rufull bene,
As those that did thy *Rosalind* complayne,
Much greater gyfts for guerdon thou shalt gayne,         45
Then Kidde or Cosset, which I thee bynempt:
Then up I say, thou jolly shepeheard swayne,
Let not my small demaund be so contempt.

CO L I N.
*Thenot* to that I choose, thou doest me tempt,
But ah to well I wote my humble vaine,                   50
And howe my rymes bene rugged and unkempt:
Yet as I conne, my conning I will strayne.

UP then *Melpomene* thou mournefulst Muse of nyne,
Such cause of mourning never hadst afore:
Up grieslie ghostes and up my rufull ryme,               55

35. *quill*: reed, pipe.    37. *drent*: drowned.    43. *rownd*: full,
perfect.    46. *Then*: than.    48. *contempt*: disdained.    50. *vaine*:
talent.    52. *conning*: cunning, knowledge. *strayne*: put into verse.
53. *Melpomene*: Muse of Tragedy.

Matter of myrth now shalt thou have no more.
For dead shee is, that myrth thee made of yore.
    *Dido* my deare alas is dead,
    Dead and lyeth wrapt in lead:
        O heavie herse,                                    60
    Let streaming teares be poured out in store:
        O carefull verse.

Shepheards, that by your flocks on Kentish downes
                                              abyde,
Waile ye this wofull waste of natures warke:
Waile we the wight, whose presence was our pryde:      65
Waile we the wight, whose absence is our carke.
The sonne of all the world is dimme and darke:
    The earth now lacks her wonted light,
    And all we dwell in deadly night,
        O heavie herse.                                  70
Breake we our pypes, that shrild as lowde as Larke,
        O carefull verse.

Why doe we longer live, (ah why live we so long)
Whose better dayes death hath shut up in woe?
The fayrest floure our gyrlond all emong,              75
Is faded quite and into dust ygoe.
Sing now ye shepheards daughters, sing no moe
    The songs that *Colin* made in her prayse,
    But into weeping turne your wanton layes,
        O heavie herse,                                  80
Now is time to dye. Nay time was long ygoe,
        O carefull verse.

Whence is it, that the flouret of the field doth fade,
And lyeth buryed long in Winters bale:
Yet soone as spring his mantle doth displaye,          85
It floureth fresh, as it should never fayle?

---

62. *carefull*: full of care, sorrowful.    64. *warke*: work.    76. *quite*:
entirely. *ygoe*: gone.    77. *moe*: more.    84. *bale*: misery.

But thing on earth that is of most availe,
  As vertues braunch and beauties budde,
Reliven not for any good.
    O heavie herse,                                    90
The braunch once dead, the budde eke needes must
                                              quaile,
    O carefull verse.

She while she was, (that was, a woful word to sayne)
For beauties prayse and plesaunce had no pere:
So well she couth the shepherds entertayne,            95
With cakes and cracknells and such country chere.
Ne would she scorne the simple shepheards swaine,
  For she would cal hem often heme
  And give hem curds and clouted Creame.
    O heavie herse,                                   100
Als *Colin cloute* she would not once disdayne.
    O carefull verse.

But nowe sike happy cheere is turnd to heavie chaunce,
Such pleasaunce now displast by dolors dint:
All Musick sleepes, where death doth leade the daunce,  105
And shepherds wonted solace is extinct.
The blew in black, the greene in gray is tinct,
  The gaudie girlonds deck her grave,
  The faded flowres her corse embrave.
    O heavie herse,                                   110
Morne nowe my Muse, now morne with teares
                                            besprint.
    O carefull verse.

O thou greate shepheard *Lobbin,* how great is thy griefe,
Where bene the nosegayes that she dight for thee:

91. *quaile*: perish.    96. *cracknells*: biscuits.    99. *clouted*:
clotted.    103. *chaunce*: circumstance.    104. *dint*: blow.    105. *death*
. . . *daunce*: the late medieval motif of the Dance of Death.    109. *embrave*:
beautify.    111. *besprint*: sprinkled.

The colourd chaplets wrought with a chiefe,                    115
The knotted rushrings, and gilte Rosemaree?
For shee deemed nothing too deere for thee.
    Ah they bene all yclad in clay,
    One bitter blast blewe all away.
        O heavie herse,                                       120
Thereof nought remaynes but the memoree.
        O carefull verse.

Ay me that dreerie death should strike so mortall stroke,
That can undoe Dame natures kindly course:
The faded lockes fall from the loftie oke,                    125
The flouds do gaspe, for dryed is theyr sourse,
And flouds of teares flowe in theyr stead perforse.
    The mantled medowes mourne,
    Theyr sondry colours tourne.
        O heavie herse,                                       130
The heavens doe melt in teares without remorse.
        O carefull verse.

The feeble flocks in field refuse their former foode,
And hang theyr heads as they would learne to weepe:
The beastes in forest wayle as they were woode,              135
Except the Wolves, that chase the wandring sheepe:
Now she is gon that safely did hem keepe,
    The Turtle on the bared braunch,
    Laments the wound, that death did launch.
        O heavie herse,                                       140
And *Philomele* her song with teares doth steepe.
        O carefull verse.

115. *chaplets*: garlands. *chiefe*: flower head.    116. *rushrings*: wreaths of
rushes. *gilte Rosemaree*: gold-variegated rosemary, apparently rare: not well
known, according to Parkinson's *Paradisus* (1629), pp. 425–26; Gerard's
*Herball* (1597) does not mention it.    124. *kindly*: natural.    127. *flouds*:
streams. *perforse*: necessarily.    138. *Turtle*: turtledove, symbol of fidelity in
love.    139. *launch*: cut, pierce.    141. *steepe*: bathe.

The water Nymphs, that wont with her to sing and
                                    daunce,
And for her girlond Olive braunches beare,
Now balefull boughes of Cypres doen advaunce:       145
The Muses, that were wont greene bayes to weare,
Now bringen bitter Eldre braunches seare:
    The fatall sisters eke repent,
    Her vitall threde so soone was spent.
        O heavie herse,                         150
Morne now my Muse, now morne with heavie cheare.
        O carefull verse.

O trustlesse state of earthly things, and slipper hope
Of mortal men, that swincke and sweate for nought,
And shooting wide, doe misse the marked scope:     155
Now have I learnd (a lesson derely bought)
That nys on earth assuraunce to be sought:
    For what might be in earthlie mould,
    That did her buried body hould.
        O heavie herse,                         160
Yet saw I on the beare when it was brought,
        O carefull verse.

But maugre death, and dreaded sisters deadly spight,
And gates of hel, and fyrie furies forse:
She hath the bonds broke of eternall night,       165
Her soule unbodied of the burdenous corpse.
Why then weepes Lobbin so without remorse?
    O Lobb, thy losse no longer lament,
    Dido nis dead, but into heaven hent.
        O happye herse,                        170
Cease now my Muse, now cease thy sorrowes sourse,
        O joyfull verse.

---

153. *slipper*: too slippery.    154. *swincke*: labor.    155. *scope*: target.
163. **maugre**: in spite of.    167. *remorse*: mitigation.    169. *hent*: taken.

Why wayle we then? why weary we the Gods with
                                                     playnts,
As if some evill were to her betight?
She raignes a goddesse now emong the saintes,        175
That whilome was the saynt of shepheards light:
And is enstalled nowe in heavens hight.
  I see thee blessed soule, I see,
  Walke in *Elisian* fieldes so free.
      O happy herse,                           180
Might I once come to thee (O that I might)
      O joyfull verse.

Unwise and wretched men to weete whats good or ill,
We deeme of Death as doome of ill desert:
But knewe we fooles, what it us bringes until,       185
Dye would we dayly, once it to expert.
No daunger there the shepheard can astert:
  Fayre fieldes and pleasaunt layes there bene,
  The fieldes ay fresh, the grasse ay greene:
      O happy herse,                           190
Make hast ye shepheards, thether to revert,
      O joyfull verse.

*Dido* is gone afore (whose turne shall be the next?)
There lives shee with the blessed Gods in blisse,
There drincks she *Nectar* with *Ambrosia* mixt,     195
And joyes enjoyes, that mortall men doe misse.
The honor now of highest gods she is,
  That whilome was poore shepheards pryde,
  While here on earth she did abyde.
      O happy herse,                           200
Ceasse now my song, my woe now wasted is.
      O joyfull verse.

---

184. *doome*: judgment. *of*: for.    185. *until*: unto.    186. *expert*:
experience.    188. *layes*: leas, meadows.    201. *wasted*: used up.

THENOT.

Ay francke shepheard, how bene thy verses meint
With doolful pleasaunce, so as I ne wotte,
Whether rejoyce or weepe for great constrainte?　　205
Thyne be the cossette, well hast thow it gotte.
Up *Colin* up, ynough thou morned hast,
Now gynnes to mizzle, hye we homeward fast.

Colins Embleme.

*La mort ny mord.*

GLOSSE.

[2]　　Jouisaunce) myrth.　　[5] Sovenaunce) remembraunce.
[10] Herie) honour.

[13]　Welked) shortned or empayred. As the Moone being in
　　　the waine is sayde of Lidgate to welk.

[15]　In lowly lay) according to the season of the moneth
　　　November, when the sonne draweth low in the South
　　　toward his Tropick or returne.

[16]　In fishes haske) the sonne, reigneth that is, in the signe
　　　Pisces all November. a haske is a wicker pad, wherein
　　　they use to cary fish.

[21]　Virelaies) a light kind of song.

[30]　Bee watred) For it is a saying of Poetes, that they have
　　　dronk of the Muses well Castalias, whereof was before
　　　sufficiently sayd.

[36]　Dreriment) dreery and heavy cheere.

[38]　The great shepheard) is some man of high degree, and
　　　not as some vainely suppose God Pan. The person both

205. *constrainte*: distress.　　208. *mizzle*: drizzle.　　210. *La . . . mord*:
"Death does not bite" (cf. 1 Corinthians 15.55, "O death, where is thy
sting!").

[38.2] *as . . . suppose*: an apparent claim that the poem has already circulated
in manuscript.

of the shephearde and of Dido is unknowen and closely
buried in the Authors conceipt. But out of doubt I am,
that it is not Rosalind, as some imagin: for he speaketh
soone after of her also.

[38]  Shene) fayre and shining.   [39] May) for
mayde.   [41] Tene) sorrow.

[45]  Guerdon) reward.   [46] Bynempt)
bequethed.   [46] Cosset) a lambe brought up without
the dam.   [51] Unkempt) Incompti Not comed, that
is rude and unhansome.

[53]  Melpomene) The sadde and waylefull Muse used of
Poets in honor of Tragedies: as saith Virgile
Melpomene Tragico proclamat mæsta boatu.

[55]  Up griesly gosts) The maner of Tragicall Poetes, to call
for helpe of Furies and damned ghostes: so is Hecuba
of Euripedes, and Tantalus brought in of Seneca. And
the rest of the rest.   [60] Hersc) is the solemne
obsequie in funeralles.

[64]  Wast of) decay of so beautifull a peece.   [66] Carke)
care.

[73]  Ah why) an elegant Epanorthosis. as also soone after.
nay time was long ago.

[83]  Flouret) a diminutive for a little floure. This is a
notable and sententious comparison A minore ad
maius.

[89]  Reliven not) live not againe .s. not in theyr earthly
bodies: for in heaven they enjoy their due reward.

[38.4] *conceipt*: knowledge.   [51.1] *Incompti Not comed*: "unkempt"
(Lat.), not combed.   [53.3] *Melpomene . . . boatu*: "Melpomene cries
aloud with the echoing voice of gloomy tragedy"; once attributed to Virgil
but actually Ausonius's epigram *Nomina musarum*.   [55.2–3] *Hecuba . . .
Seneca*: Polydorus's ghost appears in Euripides' *Hecuba* and Tantalus's in
Seneca's *Thyestes*.   [60.2] *obsequie*: religious service for the dead.
[73.1] *Epanorthosis*: rhetorical figure where a word is repeated as a
correction.   [83.2–3] *A . . . maius*: "from less to greater" (Lat.), a
technique of comparison in rhetoric.

[91] The braunch) He meaneth Dido, who being, as it were
the mayne braunch now withered the buddes that is
beautie (as he sayd afore) can nomore flourish.

[96] With cakes) fit for shepheards bankets. [98] Heame)
for home. after the northerne pronouncing.

[107] Tinct) deyed or stayned.

[108] The gaudie) the meaning is, that the things, which
were the ornaments of her lyfe, are made the honor of
her funerall, as is used in burialls.

[113] Lobbin) the name of a shepherd, which seemeth to
have bene the lover and deere friende of
Dido.  [116] Rushrings) agreeable for such base
gyftes.

[125] Faded lockes) dryed leaves. As if Nature her selfe
bewayled the death of the Mayde.

[126] Sourse) spring.  [128] Mantled medowes) for the
sondry flowres are like a Mantle or coverlet wrought
with many colours.

[141] Philomele) the Nightingale. whome the Poetes faine
once to have bene a Ladye of great beauty, till being
ravished by hir sisters husbande, she desired to be
turned into a byrd of her name. whose complaintes be
very well set forth of Ma. George Gaskin a wittie
gentleman, and the very chefe of our late rymers, who
and if some partes of learning wanted not (albee it is
well knowen he altogyther wanted not learning) no
doubt would have attayned to the excellencye of those
famous Poets. For gifts of wit and naturall
promptnesse appeare in hym aboundantly.

[145] Cypresse) used of the old Paynims in the furnishing of
their funerall Pompe. and properly the signe of all
sorow and heavinesse.

[148] The fatall sisters) Clotho Lachesis and Atropos,

[141.5] *Gaskin*: George Gascoyne (1525?–77) in his *Complainte of
Philumene*.    [145.1] *Paynims*: pagans, i.e. Greeks and Romans.

daughters of Herebus and the Nighte, whom the Poetes fayne to spinne the life of man, as it were a long threde, which they drawe out in length, till his fatal howre and timely death be come; but if by other casualtie his dayes be abridged, then one of them, that is Atropos, is sayde to have cut the threde in twain. Hereof commeth a common verse.

Clotho colum baiulat, lachesis trahit, Atropos occat.

[153] O trustlesse) a gallant exclamation moralized with great wisedom and passionate wyth great affection.

[161] Beare) a frame, wheron they use to lay the dead corse.

[164] Furies) of Poetes be feyned to be three, Persephone Alecto and Megera, which are sayd to be the Authours of all evill and mischiefe.

[165] Eternall night) Is death or darknesse of hell.

[174] Betight) happened.

[178] I see) A lively Icon, or representation as if he saw her in heaven present.

[179] Elysian fields) be devised of Poetes to be a place of pleasure like pleasure like Paradise, where the happye soules doe rest in peace and eternal happynesse.

[186] Dye would) The very expresse saying of Plato in Phædone.

[187] Astert) befall unwares.

[195] Nectar and Ambrosia) be feigned to be the drink and foode of the gods: Ambrosia they liken to Manna in scripture and Nectar to be white like Creme, whereof is a proper tale of Hebe, that spilt a cup of it, and stayned the heavens, as yet appeareth. But I have already discoursed that at large in my Commentarye upon the

[148.9] *Clotho . . . occat*: "Clotho manages the distaff, Lachesis draws out the thread, Atropos snips it."  [164.1] *Persephone*: mistake for Tisiphone, repeated in *TM* 164.  [186] *Plato*: not in *Phaedo*.  [195.4] *Hebe*: source unknown.  [195.6] *Commentarye*: both it and the *Dreames* are lost.

dreames of the same Authour.   [203] Meynt)
Mingled.

### Embleme.

Which is as much to say, as death biteth not. For although by
course of nature we be borne to dye, and being ripened
with age, as with a timely harvest, we must be gathered
in time, or else of our selves we fall like rotted ripe
fruite fro the tree: yet death is not to be counted for
evil, nor (as the Poete sayd a little before) as doome of
ill desert. For though the trespasse of the first man
brought death into the world, as the guerdon of sinne,
yet being overcome by the death of one, that dyed for
al, it is now made (as Chaucer sayth) the grene path
way to lyfe. So that it agreeth well with that was sayd,
that Death byteth not (that is) hurteth not at all.

[Embleme.7] *first man*: Adam.

# December

In this concluding, purely Arcadian eclogue Spenser imitates Marot's *Eclogue au Roy* (1539) in which the aging poet, styling himself Robin, surveys the stages of his life in terms of the seasons of the year, from youth's happy spring through frustrated harvest to anxious winter, and appeals to Francis I, styled Pan, for assistance that, at the poem's end, the king grants. Spenser recognized in Marot's scheme an apposite ending for his own, one which would neatly encapsulate the *Calender's* conceit of man as a creature of the seasons. He recycles parts of Marot's eclogue closely throughout *December* so that Thomas Warton (1752) thought it a translation. But it is instead a sensitive and discriminating adaptation that moves toward a contrasting conclusion: the aged Robin happily accepts royal favor, while Colin sinks into death.

The *Eclogue au Roy* is in couplets, but Spenser gives his last eclogue the stanza of his first, so that the *Calender's* ending echoes its beginning in form as well as in matter. Both eclogues are largely monologues by Colin, both begin as prayers to Pan, both center on the sorrows of love. But in *Januarye* those sorrows are immediate and intense, and Colin's voice is petulant; in *December* they are distanced, even abstract, and Colin's voice, though melancholy, is tranquil. Colin mentions Rosalind but she is now a marginal concern: "The loser Lasse I cast to please nomore" (119). Spenser catches movingly here an aged sense of regret combined with acceptance: in terms of emotions Colin seems genuinely old.

This darkened serenity is entirely unlike the affectively heightened dirge of *November*, although in a sense *December* is Colin's own obsequy. Insofar as Colin is a creature of the year he must die with the year, though one suspects that with the new year his cycle will repeat. Insofar as Colin is a persona of Spenser he must be decently disposed of, for he has fulfilled his function: the mandatory first stage of the Virgilian career-pattern is now handsomely complete, and pastoral, at least for the time being, has no further relevance. Significantly, in *Januarye* Colin breaks his pipe; in *December* he hangs it up with respect for the job it has done: "never pype of reede did better sounde" (142). (The woodcut, however, shows a broken pipe.) This sense of accomplishment underlies the contentedness of *December*: Spenser knows that he has launched the New Poetry with verve and authority.

Despite the heading for it and E. K.'s gloss on it, Colin's emblem is missing. Though Hughes's conjecture as to what it might be is impressive (see note to line 157), there is no contesting the stark fact that the five quartos (all published during Spenser's life) and the folio have white space where this emblem should be. The omission (so obvious that Spenser surely knew of it) may be a final touch in the *Calender's* bookmaking: Colin has no emblem because with the eclogue's last line he dies.

# December.

*Ægloga Duodecima.*

## ARGUMENT.

THis Æglogue (even as the first beganne) is ended with a complaynte of Colin to God Pan. wherein as weary of his former wayes, he proportioneth his life to the foure seasons of the yeare, comparing hys youthe to the spring time, when he was fresh and free from loves follye. His manhoode to the sommer, which he sayth, was consumed with greate heate and excessive drouth caused throughe a Comet or blasinge starre, by which hee meaneth love, which passion is comenly compared to such flames and immoderate heate. His riper yeares hee resembleth to an unseasonable harveste wherein the fruites fall ere they be rype. His latter age to winters chyll and frostie season, now drawing neare to his last ende.

THe gentle shepheard satte beside a springe,
All in the shadowe of a bushye brere,
That *Colin* hight, which wel could pype and singe,

3. *which*: who.

For he of *Tityrus* his songs did lere.
There as he satte in secreate shade alone,                                     5
Thus gan he make of love his piteous mone.

O soveraigne *Pan* thou God of shepheards all,
Which of our tender Lambkins takest keepe:
And when our flocks into mischaunce mought fall,
Doest save from mischiefe the unwary sheepe:                              10
    Als of their maisters hast no lesse regarde,
    Then of the flocks, which thou doest watch and ward:

I thee beseche (so be thou deigne to heare,
Rude ditties tund to shepheards Oaten reede,
Or if I ever sonet song so cleare,                                             15
As it with pleasaunce mought thy fancie feede)
    Hearken awhile from thy greene cabinet,
    The rurall song of carefull Colinet.

Whilome in youth, when flowrd my joyfull spring,
Like Swallow swift I wandred here and there:                              20
For heate of heedlesse lust me so did sting,
That I of doubted daunger had no feare.
    I went the wastefull woodes and forest wyde,
    Withouten dreade of Wolves to bene espyed.

I wont to raunge amydde the mazie thickette,                              25
And gather nuttes to make me Christmas game:
And joyed oft to chace the trembling Pricket,
Or hunt the hartlesse hare, til shee were tame.
    What wreaked I of wintrye ages waste,
    Tho deemed I, my spring would ever laste.                             30

How often have I scaled the craggie Oke,
All to dislodge the Raven of her neste:

4. *lere*: learn.    12. *Then*: than.    15. *sonet*: short lyric.    17. *cabinet*:
little cabin, i.e. grove.    22. *doubted*: fearsome.    27. *Pricket*: buck in
second year with unbranched horns.    28. *hartlesse*: timid.    29. *wreaked*:
thought.    32. *All*: just. *of*: off.

Howe have I wearied with many a stroke,
The stately Walnut tree, the while the rest
   Under the tree fell all for nuts at strife: 35
For ylike to me was libertee and lyfe.

And for I was in thilke same looser yeares,
(Whether the Muse, so wrought me from my birth,
Or I tomuch beleeved my shepherd peres)
Somedele ybent to song and musicks mirth, 40
   A good olde shephearde, *Wrenock* was his name,
Made me by arte more cunning in the same.

Fro thence I durst in derring doe compare
With shepheards swayne, what ever fedde in field:
And if that *Hobbinol* right judgement bare, 45
To *Pan* his owne selfe pype I neede not yield.
   For if the flocking Nymphes did folow *Pan*,
The wiser Muses after *Colin* ranne.

But ah such pryde at length was ill repayde,
The shepheards God (perdie God was he none) 50
My hurtlesse pleasaunce did me ill upbraide,
My freedome lorne, my life he lefte to mone.
   Love they him called, that gave me checkmate,
But better mought they have behote him Hate.

Tho gan my lovely Spring bid me farewel, 55
And Sommer season sped him to display
(For love then in the Lyons house did dwell)
The raging fyre, that kindled at his ray.
   A comett stird up that unkindly heate,
That reigned (as men sayd) in *Venus* seate. 60

37. *for*: because.　40. *Somedele ybent*: somewhat given.　41. *Wrenock*:
probably Sp's headmaster at the Merchant Taylors' School, Richard
Mulcaster (c.1530–1611).　43. *derring doe*: daring deeds, usually knightly
but here singing matches.　51. *hurtlesse*: harmless.　52. *lorne*: lost.
53. *gave me checkmate*: made a winning move against me as in chess.
54. *behote*: named.　59. *unkindly*: unnatural.　60. *reigned*: was
dominant. *seate*: house (both astrological terms).

Forth was I ledde, not as I wont afore,
When choise I had to choose my wandring waye:
But whether luck and loves unbridled lore
Would leade me forth on Fancies bitte to playe:
    The bush my bedde, the bramble was my bowre,    65
    The Woodes can witnesse many a wofull stowre.

Where I was wont to seeke the honey Bee,
Working her formall rowmes in Wexen frame:
The grieslie Todestoole growne there mought I se
And loathed Paddocks lording on the same.    70
    And where the chaunting birds luld me a sleepe,
    The ghastlie Owle her grievous ynne doth keepe.

Then as the springe gives place to elder time,
And bringeth forth the fruite of sommers pryde:
Also my age now passed youngthly pryme,    75
To thinges of ryper reason selfe applyed.
    And learnd of lighter timber cotes to frame,
    Such as might save my sheepe and me fro shame.

To make fine cages for the Nightingale,
And Baskets of bulrushes was my wont:    80
Who to entrappe the fish in winding sale
Was better seene, or hurtful beastes to hont?
    I learned als the signes of heaven to ken,
    How *Phœbe* fayles, where *Venus* sittes and when.

And tryed time yet taught me greater thinges,    85
The sodain rysing of the raging seas:
The soothe of byrds by beating of their wings,
The power of herbs, both which can hurt and ease:
    And which be wont tenrage the restlesse sheepe,
    And which be wont to worke eternall sleepe.    90

---

63. *whether*: whither. *unbridled*: unrestrained.    64. *bitte*: bit, mouthpiece on the bridle for controlling a horse.    65. *bowre*: bedroom.    68. *formall rowmes*: symmetrically designed combs.    70. *Paddocks*: toads. 81. *winding*: woven.

But ah unwise and witlesse *Colin cloute,*
That kydst the hidden kinds of many a wede:
Yet kydst not ene to cure thy sore hart roote,
Whose ranckling wound as yet does rifelye bleede.
  Why livest thou stil, and yet hast thy deathes wound?    95
  Why dyest thou stil, and yet alive art founde?

Thus is my sommer worne away and wasted,
Thus is my harvest hastened all to rathe:
The eare that budded faire, is burnt and blasted,
And all my hoped gaine is turnd to scathe.    100
  Of all the seede, that in my youth was sowne,
  Was nought but brakes and brambles to be mowne.

My boughes with bloosmes that crowned were at firste,
And promised of timely fruite such store,
Are left both bare and barrein now at erst:    105
The flattring fruite is fallen to grownd before,
  And rotted, ere they were halfe mellow ripe:
  My harvest wast, my hope away dyd wipe.

The fragrant flowres, that in my garden grewe,
Bene withered, as they had bene gathered long.    110
Theyr rootes bene dryed up for lacke of dewe,
Yet dewed with teares they han be ever among.
  Ah who has wrought my *Rosalind* this spight
  To spil the flowres, that should her girlond dight,

And I, that whilome wont to frame my pype,    115
Unto the shifting of the shepheards foote:
Sike follies nowe have gathered as too ripe,
And cast hem out, as rotten and unsoote.
  The loser Lasse I cast to please nomore,
  One if I please, enough is me therefore.    120

93. *ene*: one.    94. *rifelye*: copiously.    98. *to rathe*: too quickly.
102. *brakes*: stands of bracken, a coarse fern.    105. *now at erst*: already.
114. *spil*: destroy.    115. *frame*: tune, fit.    118. *unsoote*: not sweet,
insipid.    119. *loser*: too loose.

And thus of all my harvest hope I have
Nought reaped but a weedye crop of care:
Which, when I thought have thresht in swelling sheave,
Cockel for corne, and chaffe for barley bare.
    Soone as the chaffe should in the fan be fynd,         125
    All was blowne away of the wavering wynd.

So now my yeare drawes to his latter terme,
My spring is spent, my sommer burnt up quite:
My harveste hasts to stirre up winter sterne,
And bids him clayme with rigorous rage hys right.       130
    So nowe he stormes with many a sturdy stoure,
    So now his blustring blast eche coste doth scoure.

The carefull cold hath nypt my rugged rynde,
And in my face deepe furrowes eld hath pight:
My head besprent with hoary frost I fynd,           135
And by myne eie the Crow his clawe dooth wright.
    Delight is layd abedde, and pleasure past,
    No sonne now shines, cloudes han all overcast.

Now leave ye shepheards boyes your merry glee,
My Muse is hoarse and weary of thys stounde:       140
Here will I hang my pype upon this tree,
Was never pype of reede did better sounde.
    Winter is come, that blowes the bitter blaste,
    And after Winter dreerie death does hast.

Gather ye together my little flocke,             145
My little flock, that was to me so liefe:
Let me, ah lette me in your folds ye lock,
Ere the breme Winter breede you greater griefe.
    Winter is come, that blowes the balefull breath,
    And after Winter commeth timely death.         150

124. *Cockel*: corn cockle, according to Gerard's *Herball* (1597), pp. 1086–87,
"a common and hurtfull weede in our corne" (i.e. wheat); it made flour
inedible.   125. *fynd*: sifted, refined.   127. *terme*: limit.   134. *eld*: old
age.   135. *besprent*: sprinkled.   136. *And . . . wright*: And the crow has
drawn his claw by my eye (i.e. crowfoot wrinkles).   146. *liefe*: deare.

Adieu delightes, that lulled me asleepe,
Adieu my deare, whose love I bought so deare:
Adieu my little Lambes and loved sheepe,
Adieu ye Woodes that oft my witnesse were:
Adieu good *Hobbinol,* that was so true,                    155
Tell *Rosalind,* her *Colin* bids her adieu.

Colins Embleme.

GLOSSE.

[4]    Tityrus) Chaucer: as hath bene oft sayd.
[8] Lambkins) young lambes.
[11]    Als of their) Semeth to expresse Virgils verse
Pan curat oves oviumque magistros.
[13]    Deigne) voutchsafe.    [17-8] Cabinet) Colinet)
diminutives.
[25]    Mazie) For they be like to a maze whence it is hard to
get out agayne.
[39]    Peres) felowes and companions.
[40]    Musick) that is Poetry as Terence sayth Qui artem
tractant musicam, speking of Poetes.
[43]    Derring doe) aforesayd.
[57]    Lions house) He imagineth simply that Cupid, which
is love, had his abode in the whote signe Leo, which is
in middest of somer; a pretie allegory, whereof the
meaning is, that love in him wrought an extraordinarie
heate of lust.

157. *Colins Embleme*: lacking, perhaps intentionally. J. Hughes in his edition
of 1715 conjectured that the missing emblem was *Vivitur ingenio, caetera
mortis erunt* ("He lives on in his works, the rest was mortal"), from an
epigram once attributed to Virgil. This fits E. K.'s gloss nicely.

[11.2] *Pan . . . magistros*: "Pan looks after sheep and the keepers of sheep,"
*Ecl* 2.33.    [40.1–2] *Qui . . . musicam*: "those who practice musical skills,"
*Phormio*, pro.17.

[58] His ray) which is Cupides beame or flames of Love.

[59] A Comete) a blasing starre, meant of beautie, which was the cause of his whote love.

[60] Venus) the goddesse of beauty or pleasure. Also a signe in heaven, as it is here taken. So he meaneth that beautie, which hath alwayes aspect to Venus, was the cause of all his unquietnes in love.

[67] Where I was) a fine discription of the chaunge of hys lyfe and liking; for all things nowe seemed to hym to have altered their kindly course.

[70] Lording) Spoken after the maner of Paddocks and Frogges sitting which is indeed Lordly, not removing nor looking once a side, unlesse they be sturred.

[73] Then as) The second part. That is his manhoode.

[77] Cotes) sheepecotes. for such be the exercises of shepheards.

[81] Sale) or Salow a kind of woodde like Wyllow, fit to wreath and bynde in leapes to catch fish withall.

[84] Phæbe fayles) The Eclipse of the Moone, which is alwayes in Cauda or Capite Draconis, signes in heaven.

[84] Venus) .s. Venus starre otherwise called Hesperus and Vesper and Lucifer, both because he seemeth to be one of the brightest starres, and also first ryseth and setteth last. All which skill in starres being convenient for shepheardes to knowe as Theocritus and the rest use.

[86] Raging seaes) the cause of the swelling and ebbing of the sea commeth of the course of the Moone, sometime encreasing, sometime wayning and decreasing.

[87] Sooth of byrdes) A kind of sooth saying used in elder tymes, which they gathered by the flying of byrds; First (as is sayd) invented by the Thuscanes, and from them derived to the Romanes, who (as is sayd in Livie) were

---

[84.2] *Cauda . . . Draconis*: in the tail or head of the dragon.

[87.4] *Livie*: E. K. actually cites Cicero, *De Devinatione* 1.41.

so supersticiously rooted in the same, that they agreed
that every Noble man should put his sonne to the
Thuscanes, by them to be brought up in that
knowledge.

[88]   Of herbes) That wonderous thinges be wrought by
herbes, aswell appeareth by the common working of
them in our bodies, as also by the wonderful
enchauntments and sorceries that have bene wrought
by them; insomuch that it is sayde that Circe a famous
sorceresse turned men into sondry kinds of beastes and
Monsters, and onely by herbes: as the Poete sayth Dea
sæva potentibus herbis etc.

[92]   Kidst) knewest.   [99] Eare) of corne.   [100] Scathe)
losse hinderaunce.

[112]  Ever among) ever and anone.

[97-8] Thus is my) The thyrde parte wherein is set forth his
ripe yeres as an untimely harvest, that bringeth little
fruite.

[109]  The fragraunt flowres) sundry studies and laudable
partes of learning, wherein how our Poete is seene, be
they witnesse which are privie to his study.

[127]  So now my yeere) The last part, wherein is described
his age by comparison of wyntrye stormes.

[133]  Carefull cold) for care is sayd to coole the
blood.   [139] Glee) mirth.

[135]  Hoary frost) A metaphore of hoary heares scattred lyke
to a gray frost.

[148]  Breeme) sharpe and bitter.

[151]  Adiew delights) is a conclusion of all. where in sixe
verses he comprehendeth briefly all that was touched in
this booke. In the first verse his delights of youth
generally. in the second, the love of Rosalind, in the
thyrd, the keeping of sheepe, which is the argument of

[88.7–8] *Dea . . . herbis*: "the savage goddess with powerful herbs [turned
men to beasts]," Virgil, *Aen* 7.19.

all Æglogues. In the fourth his complaints. And in the last two his professed frendship and good will to his good friend Hobbinoll.

## Embleme.

The meaning wherof is that all thinges perish and come to theyr last end, but workes of learned wits and monuments of Poetry abide for ever. And therefore Horace of his Odes a work though ful indede of great wit and learning, yet of no so great weight and importaunce boldly sayth.

> Exegi monimentum ære perennius,
> Quod nec imber nec aquilo vorax etc.

Therefore let not be envied, that this Poete in his Epilogue sayth he hath made a Calendar, that shall endure as long as time etc. folowing the ensample of Horace and Ovid in the like.

> Grande opus exegi quod nec Iovis ira nec ignis,
> Nec ferrum poterit nec edax abolere vetustas etc.

[Embleme.7–8] *Exegi . . . vorax:* "I have built a monument more lasting than bronze which neither rainstorm nor raging north wind [can destroy]," Horace, *Odes* 3.30. 1–3, misquoted.      [Embleme.7–8] *Grande . . . vetustas:* "I have built a great work which neither Jove's wrath nor fire nor sword nor eroding time can efface," Ovid, *Met* 15.871–72, misquoted.

Loe I have made a Calender for every yeare,
That steele in strength, and time in durance shall
                                        outweare:
And if I marked well the starres revolution,
It shall continewe till the worlds dissolution.
To teach the ruder shepheard how to feede his sheepe,          5
And from the falsers fraud his folded flocke to keepe.
  Goe lyttle Calender, thou hast a free passeporte,
Goe but a lowly gate emongste the meaner sorte.
Dare not to match thy pype with Tityrus hys style,
  Nor with the Pilgrim that the Ploughman playde
                                        a whyle:   10
But followe them farre off, and their high steppes
                                        adore,
The better please, the worse despise, I aske nomore.

*Merce non mercede.*

EPILOGUE: This is a "square poem" with twelve lines of twelve syllables each, appropriately building the poem out of the number of months and squaring it "for every yeare." Puttenham, *The Arte of English Poesie* (1589), 2.11, associates poems that use "no moe verses then your verse is of sillables" with the solid steadiness of the earth and, on the authority of Aristotle's *Ethics*, with the "constant minded man . . . *hominem quadratum*, a square man."   4. *worlds dissolution*: i.e. the end of time.   5. *teach . . . shepheard*: with reference to the ecclesiastical eclogues, but perhaps also a book giving instruction by example in the New Poetry.   8. *lowly gate*: appropriate to pastoral decorum but also to a poem by "Immerito."   9. *Tityrus*: Chaucer.   10. *Pilgrim . . . Ploughman*: either Langland or the author of *The Plowman's Tale*. *playde*: Sp may have known the tale to be pseudo-Chaucerian.   13. *Merce non mercede*: "[judge] by the goods, not the price."

# Complaints

# Complaints.

## Containing sundrie small Poemes of the Worlds Vanitie.

VVhereof the next Page maketh menti-
on.

By Ed. Sp.

LONDON.
Imprinted for VVilliam
Ponsonbie, dwelling in Paules
Churchyard at the signe of
the Bishops head.

1591.

# Complitaints

S
penser's *Complaints* was published in 1591, the year fol-
lowing the "setting foorth" ("The Printer to the Gentle
Reader" 1) of the first part of *The Faerie Queene*. It is likely
that Spenser himself had a hand in publishing the volume, even
though the printer, William Ponsonby, leads us to believe that
he has assembled the nine "smale Poemes" ("The Printer to the
Gentle Reader" 4) in the collection without their author's help.
Spenser's direct involvement emerges in the careful disposition
of the material into sections with discrete title pages and sepa-
rate dedications, and in various minor textual changes he seems
to have authorized in some of the copies printed in 1591. The
book, then, is more than Ponsonby's bid to capitalize on the
popularity of *The Faerie Queene*: Spenser himself must have
realized that the time was ripe for making more of his work
available to the public, even though he may originally have
intended at least some of that work for coterie audiences only.

In one way, *Complaints* appears to be an anthology of fugitive
pieces and hitherto uncollected poems previously "disperst
abroad in sundrie hands" ("The Printer to the Gentle Reader"
5.) Some of the poems in it are juvenilia: the *Visions of Bellay* and
the *Visions of Petrarch* having been anonymously translated in
1569 for *The Theatre for Worldlings*; *Mother Hubberds Tale* "long
sithens composed" in the "raw conceipt" of Spenser's youth
(*MHT* Dedication); and *Virgils Gnat*, which presumably dates
from 1579, "long since dedicated" to the earl of Leicester (*VG*
Dedicatory Sonnet). Although the first two sets of poems un-
derwent revision before appearing in *Complaints*, and *Mother
Hubberd* was probably expanded to make its satire more point-
ed, the inclusion of patently early work contributes to the retro-
spection of the volume. The early poems join *Muiopotmos*, whose

very sophistication implies maturity, *The Ruines of Time*, which could have been completed only after April, 1590, when Walsingham ("Meliboe") died, and an assortment of poems that cannot with confidence be dated, to produce a Spenserian sampler.

As Ponsonby himself emphasizes, however, in his allusion to the volume's title, these "sundrie Poemes" share "like matter of argument in them: being all complaints" ("The Printer to the Gentle Reader" 10). Distinguished more than anything else by its plangent and querulous tone, the complaint was a popular minor genre during the Middle Ages. It was a form responsible for a remarkable range of effects, since its expression of lamentation edged into elegy on one side and satire on the other. The amorous complaints common in medieval French poetry and prevalent in the work of some of Spenser's English contemporaries present a solitary speaker who contemplates ruefully the lover's unhappy lot. Spenser may well have admired Chaucer's experiments in this vein in poems such as *Anelida and Arcite*, the complaints given to Mars and Venus, and the witty parody of the jilted lover's distress in "The Complaint of Chaucer to his Purse." He may also have been familiar with the laments uttered in many medieval lyrics by the forlorn Christ or the sorrowful Mary. The medieval version of the form closest to his practice in *Complaints*, however, was the impersonal "censure of the times," as Curtius (1973) calls it. Lacking the acerbic wit and the sharp focus of satire, this sort of sober, moralizing commentary on man's wretchedness in a fickle and inconstant world could approximate the visionary and apocalyptic despair of the Old Testament prophets, for whom life itself is the vanity of vanities. Despite their diversity, Spenser's sundry complaints are all reflections on the "careful" condition of mankind, all "meditations of the worlds vanitie, verie grave and profitable" ("The Printer to the Gentle Reader" 10–11). The book reminds us that Spenser included four plaintive eclogues in *The Shepheardes Calender* ("Januarye," "June," "November," "December"), that he used the genre for Alcyon's monologue in *Daphnaida*, and that he assigned complaints to characters such as Arthur, Britomart, Cymoent, Timias, Scudamour, and, most strikingly, Dame Mutabilitie in *The Faerie Queene*. Complaint, in various guises, was an appealing form to Spenser from the beginning to the end of his career, but only in *Complaints* proper do we see him concentrating on it, subordinating gestures toward other genres to the plaintive kind. Because of the proximity in the publication dates of *Complaints* and *The Faerie Queene*, we can speculate that as gall complements honey and blame complements praise, so these two books complement one another and reveal two sides of the poet's rhetorical skill.

The fragility of human achievement, the folly of pride, the futility of aspiring to lofty heights when the world's state is "tickle" and "trustless": these are the austere themes of "like argument" that hold the disparate poems called *Complaints* together. The most imposing of Spenser's symbols of the vanity of human wishes is Rome, the eternal city reduced to ruin, the type of Verulame, its English equivalent, and the type, too, of all fallen cities and civilizations. Rome—its proud towers and noble monuments fragmented into dust by "injurious time" (*Ruines of Rome* Sonnet 27)—dominates the volume as an image of the destruction that awaits imperial and, for a Protestant, irreligious power. But Rome has its imperial counterparts in the animal kingdom. Consider, for example, the "mightie Crocodile," the "kingly" eagle, the towering cedar, and the "mighty Lyon" (*Worlds Vanitie*), whose sway is undermined by creatures as small and seemingly trivial as the little mite rudely brushed aside by the shepherd in *Virgils Gnat*. Clarion, the gorgeous butterfly in *Muiopotmos*, is, like Rome, an emblem of "vaine worlds glorie, flitting too and fro" (*Visions of Petrarch* Sonnet 7): he is deprived of the "kingly ioyaunce" to which he soars (*Muiopotmos* 208), just as the Fox and the Ape of *Mother Hubberd*, having advanced to the apex of political power, are deprived of any enduring success.

Spenser complicates our response to monuments of surquedry, then, by reminding us that they appear in natural, as well as in cultural and social forms. Hierarchy and status, always vulnerable, are not just human constructs. The ambivalence apparent in "Julye," where Spenser weighs the merits of ambition against the merits of contentment with a humble station, is found also in *Complaints*, which never express total acceptance of the *contemptus mundi* philosophy we might expect to find in them. In 1591, as *Colin Clout* reminds us, Spenser was still living in Ireland, deprived of a place at court, and relegated to the fringes of the exalted society he wished to join. Perhaps for that reason the proud and mighty in these poems inspire a mixed reaction—scorn, disdain and indignation, but admiration and envy too. In fact Spenser complains specifically about the predicament of the lowly poet, who like those held in "meane regard" at the beginning of *Mother Hubberd* (60) is "Still wayting to preferment up to clime, / Whilest others alwayes have before me stept" (76–77). By dedicating the poems in the volume to Lady Sidney and the three daughters of Sir John Spencer of Althorpe, the humbly born Spenser sought, after all, to ingratiate himself with well-placed patrons.

A concern for poets and the right relationship between poets and patrons is prominent in Spenser's "censure of the times" in *Complaints*. *The Ruines of Time*, for example, contrasts the razed monuments of cities with the durable "moniment of . . . praise" (683) constructed by the author for Sidney, the "hope of all learned men, and the Patron of my young Muses" (Dedication). But if the eternizing power claimed for poets in *Time* intimates that "all thinges perish and come to theyr last end, but workes of learned wits and monuments of Poetry abide for ever" (as E. K. puts the Horatian dictum in *The Shepheardes Calender*), poetry can prosper only in a society that honors poets. *The Teares of the Muses* bemoans the "wildernesse" (287) England has become for writers and exempts only Elizabeth from its comprehensive indictment of those who have failed to sustain literature. *Virgils Gnat* expresses the frustration of the diminuitive poet-gnat that his voice is so little esteemed, and *Mother Hubberd* qualifies the earlier praise of Elizabeth with its depiction of a sleeping monarch so heedless and secure before Mercury (eloquence) wakens him that the Fox and the Ape easily usurp imperial power. In these poems Spenser suggests that the civilizing poet builds "moniments" of admonition as well as of praise. That the great are disinclined to hear the small and to heed warnings emphasizes Calliope's embittered verdict that "the rich fee which Poets wont divide, / Now Parasites and Sycophants doo share"(*Teares* 471–72).

While regretting and reproving the neglect of poets and poetry in several poems, Spenser advertises his own literary artistry throughout the volume. He intersperses translations or imitations of Petrarch, Virgil, and especially Du Bellay, for instance, with the more or less original work found, say, in *Mother Hubberds Tale* and *Muiopotmos*. This mixture implies the enduring and problematic hold exerted over the poet's present by his literary past. The refractions of Petrarch's *Rime* 323 through Marot's translation and Du Bellay's "Songe" into both Spenser's own translations and his own visions of vanity are an indication of how the poet can respond to his literary forebears. Intertextual complexity figures as well in *Muiopotmos*, which revises fable and myth; the ruins poems, which engage with Du Bellay's *Les Antiquitez de Rome*; *Virgils Gnat*, which curiously appropriates a pseudo-Virgilian poem for a matter of personal urgency; and *The Teares of the Muses*, which ironically reworks Du Bellay's *La Musagnoeomachie*. In *Complaints* generally, "translation" is important: the humanists' notions of *translatio imperii* and *translatio studii*, which refer to the migrations westward of empire and learning, respectively, sort readily with the other metamorphic processes presented implicitly or explicitly in the poems. As in the *Cantos of Mutabilitie*, these processes are both a curse and a consolation.

By altering his verse forms frequently, Spenser further displays what it takes to be a poet. For *Time* he uses rhyme royale, recommended by Puttenham and other rhetoricians for dignified poetry, and found later in the *Fowre Hymnes*, perhaps Spenser's most philosophical works. The loud "hart-breaking mone" of the Muses, on the other hand, is expressed in the humble sixaine, earlier employed in "Januarye" and "December," two of the plaintive eclogues in *The Shepheardes Calender*. In *Gnat* and *Muiopotmos*, both of which make heroes of insects, Spenser practises ottava rima, the epic stanza of Ariosto's *Orlando Furioso*, while in *Mother Hubberds Tale*, his one experiment in formal satire, he produces polished couplets, despite the "base" style and "meane" matter of the poem (44). The rest of the poems are sonnet sequences. Spenser relies on the English, or Shakespearean, sonnet for his translations from Du Bellay and Petrarch. When he creates his imitation of their "vision-poems," he develops a new form, the so-called Spenserian sonnet, usually associated with the *Amoretti*. It may be particularly telling that Spenser wrote several sonnet sequences for the book, since the sonnet was the usual vehicle of Petrarchan poetry. As Wayne Rebhorn (1980) has shown, the attraction and repulsion that the Petrarchan lover feels for his mistress are akin to Du Bellay's ambivalence toward Rome in the *Antiquitez*, clearly a poem that loomed large in Spenser's imagination as he composed *Complaints*. In any case, the diversity of versecraft found in the book proves that Spenser was interested in "wise wordes taught in numbers for to runne" (*Time* 402) not just in his grave and profitable arguments. He is a poetic maker as well as a vatic seer in the "spectacles" he bids us to contemplate.

Modern readers of Spenser probably find *Mother Hubberds Tale* and *Muiopotmos* the most attractive and accessible poems in the collection. Both tell stories. But the juxtaposition of fluid narrative and relatively stable emblematic description characteristic of *Complaints* shows Spenser grappling with techniques that are fused in the continuous allegory of *The Faerie Queene*. It is tempting to read excerpts from the book as if it were merely an anthology of sundry poems. It is more challenging and ultimately more useful to read the volume as an integrated whole that sheds light both on the themes and arguments important to Spenser and on various ways in which they might be pleasingly presented.

*Ronald Bond*

A note of the sundrie Poemes contained in this Volume.

The Printer to the *Gentle Reader.*

SINCE my late setting foorth of the *Faerie Queene*,
finding that it hath found a favourable passage
amongst you; I have sithence endevoured by all good
meanes (for the better encrease and accomplishment of
your delights,) to get into my handes such smale          5
Poemes of the same Authors; as I heard were disperst
abroad in sundrie hands, and not easie to bee come by,
by himselfe; some of them having bene diverslie
imbeziled and purloyned from him, since his departure
over Sea. Of the which I have by good meanes gathered    10
togeather these fewe parcels present, which I have
caused to bee imprinted altogeather, for that they al
seeme to containe like matter of argument in them:
being all complaints and meditations of the worlds
vanitie; verie grave and profitable. To which effect I    15

1. *late setting foorth*: Ponsonby published the first three books of *FQ* early in
1590; *Compl* was registered on 29 December 1590 and published early in
1591.     9–10. *departure over Sea*: The phrase is ambiguous: it may refer to
Sp's return to Ireland after his trip to England in 1590, a trip recorded
poetically in *CCCHA*; it is more likely that it refers to his original departure
for Ireland in 1580. In any case, it is probable that Sp himself helped
Ponsonby gather the material for the volume.     15–23. An important
source of information about various Spenserian poems no longer
extant.

understand that he besides wrote sundrie others,
namelie *Ecclesiastes*, and *Canticum canticorum* translated,
*A senights slumber*, *The hell of lovers*, his *Purgatorie*, being
all dedicated to Ladies; so as it may seeme he ment
them all to one volume. Besides some other Pamphlets    20
looselie scattered abroad: as *The dying Pellican*, *The
howers of the Lord*, *The sacrifice of a sinner*, *The seven
Psalmes*, *&c.* which when I can either by himselfe, or
otherwise attaine too, I meane likewise for your favour
sake to set foorth. In the meane time praying you    25
gentlie to accept of these, and graciouslie to entertaine
the new Poet. *I take leave.*

17. *Ecclesiastes . . . translated*: Poetic paraphrases of scripture were common in
Renaissance England, but Sp would have been attracted to Ecclesiastes for its
meditation on vanity and to the Song of Songs for its vivid allegory.
18. *A senights slumber*: probably the "pamphlet" to which Sp refers in his *Two
. . . Letters* (1580) as *My Slomber*; Sp there considered dedicating it to Sidney
or to Edward Dyer, though Ponsonby suggests that it was offered, like the
poems in *Compl*, to a lady. The work may be related to Sp's "vision" poems
or to the trope of sleep used in *VG* and *MHT*. *senights*: seven nights'.
*The hell . . . Purgatorie*: Whether Ponsonby refers to two distinct works is
uncertain, but the material seems to have been a lover's complaint similar to
passages in *Amor* and *HL*.    21. *The dying Pellican*: a poem linked in *Three
. . . Letters* (1580) with the lost *Dreames*; the work is probably a religious
piece in which the pelican is an emblem of Christ. But cf. E. K.'s gloss to line
90 of *SC* "October" and *RT* 589–602.    21–23. *The howers . . . Psalmes*:
all religious works, most likely of a penitential cast. The seven penitential
psalms (6, 32, 38, 51, 102, 130, 143) were versified as well by Sir Philip
Sidney and the countess of Pembroke.    27. *new Poet*: one of E. K.'s terms
for the anonymous author of *SC*.

# The Ruines of Time

S penser finished *The Ruines of Time* between the death of Sir Francis Walsingham in April 1590 (alluded to in lines 435–41) and the publication of the *Complaints* the following winter. He may have made use of earlier work—a lament for Verulamium, an elegy for Sir Philip Sidney, some early *Dreames* mentioned by E. K. in his dedication to *The Shepheardes Calender*—but he imposed a remarkable thematic unity on his various materials. He further made this first poem in the *Complaints* an introduction to the larger collection. Touching on the book's characteristic concern with loss and the instability of worldly greatness, the work suggests a double response to the mutability it laments: earthly fame memorialized in poetry and divine reward. In so doing it introduces the characteristic forms of the volume, the complaint and the vision.

The poem contains three episodes: (1) a lament by the Genius of the Roman city Verulamium for the city's destruction and the attendant mocking of man's endeavours (lines 1–175); (2) a lament for the earl of Leicester, Robert Dudley, and various of his highly-placed relations including Sir Philip Sidney (lines 176–343); (3) a eulogy on the "eternizing" powers of poetry (lines 344–490). These are followed by two pageant sequences of sonnet-like pairs of seven-line stanzas somewhat in the manner of the three groups of *Visions* sonnets which end the *Complaints*, the first a series of emblems of time's power over civilization, the second suggesting Sidney's celestial apotheosis. A partial model for *The Ruines of Time* comes from Du Bellay whose *Antiquitez de Rome* and *Songe*, both translated by Spenser later in the volume, stand behind the lament for a ruined city and the pageant sequences. But the poem takes energies from other sources, religious, literary, and personal.

The chief speaker of the work is the spirit of the ancient city Verulamium, a deeply ambivalent figure, made suspect by her Roman associations. Many Elizabethan Protestants saw the English as a people chosen by God, the true successor to the Hebrew nation, and found in Old Testament history a foreshadowing of their own. The nations whose fate Verlame laments— Assyria, Persia, Greece, and finally Rome itself—were all conquerors and overlords of the Hebrew people, and as such prefigure the Roman church's menace to England as former enslaver and present threat. Protestant tradition, as it appears in John Foxe's *Book of Martyrs* and the notes to the Geneva Bible, saw the Rome of Revelation referring by implication to the Roman church and its pope, and Rome became a recapitulative metaphor for all demonically-inspired works of city- and empire-building: Egypt, Babylon, and Rome are all symbolically one with Rome's church. Verlame's lament is ironically undercut by her associations with worldly tyranny.

But there is another side. Verlame's tragedy is also a particularly English one: despite her Roman connection, she is a large part of the little early English history Renaissance antiquarians knew. The ruins eschew Roman partiality, for they include a monument to a conquering Saxon general. Their faded past greatness is England's as well as Rome's, and Verulamium becomes a mythic center of imperialism which perhaps foreshadows the aspirations of the Elizabethan: "There also where the winged ships were seene/In liquid waves to cut their fomie waie . . . " (lines 148–49). The legend that the Thames once flowed through Verulamium (lines 134–47) emphasizes the connection between the ancient city and Spenser's London.

This ambivalence in the treatment of Verlame is associated with a larger ambivalence about the degree to which any city-building is suspect. The irony of Israel's history, that the God who destroyed the cities of her enemies also allowed Jerusalem's fall, is transcended in the Epistle to the Hebrews, almost a text for *The Ruines of Time*: "For here we have no continuing citie: but we seke one to come" (Hebrews 13.14). Later, St. Augustine writes of "two cities that in this world lie confusedly together": the City of God recapitulates the Holy City, Hebrews' city outside history, and the City of Destruction recapitulates the demonic energies that build on pride and thus produce what can only end in ruin. This dichotomy provides a source of ambivalence at the root of Spenser's vision: the conflict between nostalgic failed empire on the one hand and otherworldly "sic transit gloria mundi" on the other is hardly more resolved for Spenser than it is for Verlame's Genius. What is gone was a House of Pride, but to forget history (and history's God) would be to build a proverbial house on sand and to court the same fate. History is a wheel of fortune for even the highest of personal and national aspirations.

The Spenser who worked on *A Theatre for Worldlings* in his impressionable youth knew this (as did so many of his contemporaries) from the melancholy tones of Ecclesiastes. By 1590 he was to know it more inwardly. The tragedy of Verlame is also Spenser's own tragedy: his ambitious career had been pursued in contradiction to a heady youthful piety which professed the crumbling unreliability of this-worldliness, and *The Ruines of Time* looks back to that early piety. The poem records the shock of returning to England after a decade's absence, time's ruinousness fully apparent. Old friends and patrons were simply *not there*: Sidney dead in 1586, Leicester in 1588, and Walsingham in 1590. New circles of power provided less hope: Spenser was not so near to their centers, and he knew that he never would be. Loss thus links Verlame's lament and the more personal concern of the necrological episode whose roots go back to Spenser's secretaryship to Leicester and to his project for a *Stemmata Dudleiana*. The concern for personal loss of friends and patrons which accompanies the public themes of the poem looks toward the gloomy perplexity of *The Teares of the Muses* and the plea to Leicester which prefaces *Virgils Gnat*.

It also informs the praise of immortalizing poetry in the third major section of the work. The creation of enduring art is one of the few available escapes from time's ravages, at least outside the

realm of religious aspiration. For Spenser the former must sup-
plement the latter, a characteristic Renaissance synthesis. Both
the poet and the antiquarian in Spenser intuitively find lack of
monument and memory of the past to be unthinkable. Tradition
held that the Golden Age left no monuments and that the earth-
ly Eden was washed away with the Flood. Yet a failure to re-
member the past is a failure to recognize the sources of one's
own identity. In his monumental compendium of British histo-
ry and geography, *Britannia*, Camden (whom Spenser praises as
the "nourice of antiquitie") works to redeem what past there
was to be rediscovered, cherishing its parts, articulating names
with an innocent freshness that reiterates Adam's function in
Eden. Thus beyond the inconsolable loss that the poem laments
and the sense of time's mockery comes the seed of something
that redeems.

The final part of the poem consists of two seven-part se-
quences, each with six visions followed by a seventh section
which elaborates the moral. The subject matter of the first se-
quence is reminiscent of Du Bellay's *Songe* and Petrarch's *Rime*
323 which Spenser translated for *A Theatre for Worldlings*. Four
of the traditional Seven Wonders of the World are suggested
obliquely, but in each case the emphasis shifts to related biblical
imagery, designed to warn the reader of the unreliability of what
the image stands for. The fifth image (Xerxes' bridge over the
Hellespont) is an ancient symbol of overweening pride; the
sixth (the two bears) seems to apply topically to the Dudleys.
Commentaries on Ecclesiastes (Luther's was one of the few of
his works available in English in Spenser's time) suggest the
strategy of this sequence: the world is seen as a series of vanities
from which the only sane course is a turning away towards the
kingdom of God. Love, foiled of attaching itself to the things of
this world, can only reasonably attach itself to Christ.

In the second sequence, each vision begins with a convention-
al mythological image, which is made to relate in some way to
Sir Philip Sidney, and is then given an apotheosis among the
constellations. Each such apotheosis is accompanied by the re-

ligious language of joy. The central dilemma of how to value the great deeds of this world is passed over for a purer looking to the world beyond. The poem's earlier solution is thus seen as the *ad hoc* arrangement that it is, with a limited validity in the arena of history, since heaven alone fully escapes from worldly vanity. It is perhaps significant that while the praise of earthly glory is Verlame's, the vision of heavenly glory is the Christian narrator's.

Number symbolism built on sevens reinforces the poem's meaning: the rhyme-royal stanzas have seven lines, the main sequence has seventy stanzas, and is followed by two sequences of seven two-stanza visions. Seventy years was the prophesied period of slave-service to Babylon (Jeremiah 25.11; Daniel 9) and some of the other sevens have demonic, or at least worldly, associations: the seven-headed beast of Rome, the seven-fold gates of hell, and the seven-year seige of Verulamium. On the other hand, the sevens of the vision sequences suggest the cycle of perfection with their six-plus-one patterning (see Nelson 1963:68–69): the first sequence builds up to the Old Testament vision of Ecclesiastes; the second to the more Christian apotheosis of the Envoy.

*Richard Schell*

# Dedicated
## To the right Noble and beauti-
## *full Ladie, the La. Marie*
## Countesse of Pembrooke.

MOST *Honourable and bountifull Ladie, there bee long sithens deepe sowed in my brest, the seede of most entire love and humble affection unto that most brave Knight your noble brother deceased; which taking roote began in his life time somewhat to bud forth: and to shew themselves to him, as then in the weakenes of their first spring: And would in their riper strength (had it pleased high God till then to drawe out his daies) spired forth fruit of more perfection. But since God hath disdeigned the world of that most noble Spirit, which was the hope of all learned men, and the Patron of my young* Muses; *togeather with him both their hope of anie further fruit was cut off: and also the tender delight of those their first blossoms nipped and quite dead. Yet sithens my late cumming into* England, *some frends of mine (which might much prevaile with me, and indeede commaund me) knowing with howe straight bandes of duetie I was tied to him: as also bound unto that noble house, (of which the chiefe hope then rested in him) have sought to revive them by upbraiding me: for that I have not shewed anie thankefull remembrance towards him or any of them; but suffer their names to sleep in silence and forgetfulnesse. Whome chieflie to satisfie, or els to avoide that fowle blot of unthankefulnesse, I have conceived this small Poeme, intituled by a generall name of the* worlds Ruines: *yet speciallie intended to the renowming of that noble race, from which both you and he sprong, and to the eternizing of some of the chiefe of*

DEDICATION: *La. Marie*: Lady Mary Sidney (1561–1621), poetess and patron of poets, sister to Sir Philip Sidney, niece to Robert Dudley, earl of Leicester, countess of Pembroke on marriage to Henry Herbert, 2d earl of Pembroke.      *that most brave Knight*: Sir Philip Sidney in 1577.      *spired forth*: produced.      *my late cumming*: in 1589; Sp had been gone since 1580. He stayed in England until 1591 (possibly returning to Ireland briefly in 1590).

*them late deceased. The which I dedicate unto your La. as whome it most speciallie concerneth: and to whome I acknowledge my selfe bounden, by manie singular favours and great graces. I pray for your Honourable happinesse: and so humblie kisse your handes.*

Your Ladiships ever
humblie at commaund.
*E. S.*

# The Ruines of Time

I
T chaunced me on day beside the shore
Of silver streaming *Thamesis* to bee,
Nigh where the goodly *Verlame* stood of yore,
Of which there now remaines no memorie,
Nor anie little moniment to see,                                5
By which the travailer, that fares that way,
This once was she, may warned be to say.

---

T I T L E : *Ruines*: Lat. *ruit*, it falls; cf. Donne's pun on the fall of man: "We are borne ruinous" (*Anatomy of the World* 95).

---

1. *on*: one.    2. *silver streaming Thamesis*: The phrase recurs in *Proth* 11. The Thames, of course, does not flow anywhere near Verulamium, but according to one tradition it had changed its course: "Because certain ankers were in our remembrance digged up, divers have verily thought . . . that the river *Tamis* sometimes had his course and chanell this way" (Camden, *Britannia*, p.411).    3. *Verlame*: "From *Hertford* twelve miles Westward, stood VEROLAMIUM, a Citie in times past much renowned, and as greatly frequented . . . . Neither hath it as yet lost that ancient name, for commonly they call it *Verulam*, although there remaineth nothing of it to be seene, beside the few remaines of ruined walles, the checkered pavements, and peeces of Roman coine other whiles digged up there . . . . In *Nero* his time it was counted a MUNICIPIUM . . . . These *Municipia* were townes endowed with the right of Romane Citizens . . . . In the reigne of the same *Nero*, when *Bunduica* or *Boadicea* Queene of the *Icenes* in her deepe love of her country, and conceived bitter hatred against the Romans, raised bloudy and mortall war upon them, it was rased and destroyed by the Britains . . . . Neverthelesse it flourished againe and became exceeding famous and passing well frequented . . . " (Camden, *Britannia*, pp.408–09).    4–7. In Drayton's *Polyolbion* song 16, Selden's "illustrations" note that the abbots of St. Albans carried off the stones of Verulamium; cf. note to lines 85–98 below.    4. For Renaissance writers loss of memory is often a sign of the fall of man, as in the "sicke world" of Donne's *Anatomy* 23 which has lost its "sense and memory."    5. *moniment*: recalls Horace's "monumentum aere perennius" (*Odes* 3.30), poetry as a monument more enduring than bronze; it also puns pointedly on (ad)monishment (cf. "warned" in line 7 below).

There on the other side, I did behold
A Woman sitting sorrowfullie wailing,
Rending her yeolow locks, like wyrie golde,                    10
About her shoulders careleslie downe trailing,
And streames of teares from her faire eyes forth railing.
In her right hand a broken rod she held,
Which towards heaven shee seemd on high to weld.

Whether she were one of that Rivers Nymphes            15
Which did the losse of some dere love lament,
I doubt; or one of those three fatall Impes,
Which draw the dayes of men forth in extent;
Or th'auncient *Genius* of that Citie brent:
But seeing her so piteouslie perplexed,                        20
I (to her calling) askt what her so vexed.

Ah what delight (quoth she) in earthlie thing,
Or comfort can I wretched creature have?
Whose happines the heavens envying,
From highest staire to lowest step me drave,               25

8–21. The woman recalls the Genius of fallen Rome who speaks to the poet
on the Tiber bank in *VB* 1 and a host of similar figures: the weeping virgin in
*VB* 10, fallen Jerusalem as weeping widow in Lamentations 1–2, and the
Psalmist weeping by the rivers of Babylon for the lost Jerusalem (Psalm 137).
Cf. *TW* Sonnet 8 and accompanying woodcut.        10. *yeolow . . . golde*: so
the sun-like bride in *Epith* 154 and Belphœbe (*FQ* II iii 30).        12. *railing*:
rolling, flowing.        13. *broken rod*: fallen authority; cf. the rod as an Old
Testament symbol of prophetic authority.        17. *I doubt*: I wonder. *three
fatall Impes*: Clotho, Lacheis, and Atropos, who spin, measure, and snip the
thread of life.        19. *th'auncient Genius*: Aeneas prays to the *genium loci* (*Aen*
7.136). In *FQ* II xii 46–49, Agdistes is a "Genius" or god of generation. Cf.
the porter in the Garden of Adonis (*FQ* III vi 31–33). *brent*: burned.
20. *perplexed*: biblical word, implying inability to grasp what faith
comprehends easily; cf. Isaiah 22.5 and Luke 21.25: "perplexitie" is said to
accompany the fall of Jerusalem; also cf. *VP* 26.        21. *vexed*: cf. Ecclesiastes
1.14, etc.: "All *is* vanitie, and vexacion of the spirit."        22. *earthlie thing*:
biblical diction; Verlame misses the implicit contrast with "heavenly."
23. *wretched creature*: cf. Romans 7.24.

And have in mine owne bowels made my grave,
That of all Nations now I am forlorne,
The worlds sad spectacle, and fortunes scorne.

Much was I mooved at her piteous plaint,
And felt my heart nigh riven in my brest                    30
With tender ruth to see her sore constraint,
That shedding teares a while I still did rest,
And after did her name of her request.
Name have I none (quoth she) nor anie being,
Bereft of both by Fates unjust decreeing.                   35

I was that Citie, which the garland wore
Of *Britaines* pride, delivered unto me
By *Romane* Victors, which it wonne of yore;
Though nought at all but ruines now I bee,
And lye in mine owne ashes, as ye see:                      40
*Verlame* I was; what bootes it that I was,
Sith now I am but weedes and wastfull gras?

O vaine worlds glorie, and unstedfast state
Of all that lives, on face of sinfull earth,
Which from their first untill their utmost date             45
Tast no one hower of happines or merth,
But like as at the ingate of their berth,

---

26. *bowels . . . grave*: Gk. folklore aphorism *soma sema*, a pun meaning "The
body is a tomb"; cf. Plato, *Phaedrus* 250c and *RT* 48–49 below.
27. *Nations*: Old Testament word.       28. *world's . . . scorne*: The language is
common in complaint tradition from Chaucer through the *Mirror for
Magistrates*, etc.       42. *wastfull gras*: "All flesh *is* grasse . . . . The grasse
withereth, ye floure fadeth: but the worde of our God shal stand for ever"
(Isaiah 40.6–8).       43–77. Renwick (1928:191) sees the theme coming
from the Wisdom of Solomon 2.4: "Our life shal passe away as the trace of a
cloude, & come to naught as the mist that is driven away with ye beaumes of
the sunne, and cast downe with the heat thereof. Our name also shal be
forgotten in time, and no man shal have our workes in remembrance."
43–44. Amplification of Ecclesiastes' theme: "All is vanitie."       47. *ingate*:
entrance.

They crying creep out of their mothers woomb,
So wailing backe go to their wofull toomb.

Why then dooth flesh, a bubble glas of breath,       50
Hunt after honour and advauncement vaine,
And reare a trophee for devouring death,
With so great labour and long lasting paine,
As if his daies for ever should remaine?
Sith all that in this world is great or gaie,       55
Doth as a vapour vanish, and decaie.

Looke backe, who list, unto the former ages,
And call to count, what is of them become:
Where be those learned wits and antique Sages,
Which of all wisedome knew the perfect somme:       60
Where those great warriors, which did overcomme
The world with conquest of their might and maine,
And made one meare of th'earth and of their raine?

What nowe is of th'*Assyrian* Lyonesse,
Of whome no footing now on earth appeares?       65

48–49. The womb/tomb cycle is pervasive: cf. *Romeo and Juliet* 2.3.9–10.
The ultimate source is perhaps Genesis 3.19 ("Til thou returne to the earth:
for out of it wast thou taken, because thou art dust, and to dust shalt thou
returne").    53. Psalm 90.10: "The time of our life *is* threscore yeres & ten,
and if they be of strength, foure score yeres: yet their strength *is* but labour
and sorowe: for it is cut of quickely, and we flee away."    56. *vapour*: Cf.
James 4.14: "And yet ye can not tel what *shal be* to morowe. For what is your
life? It is even a vapour that appeareth for a litle time, and afterwarde
vanisheth away."    57–77. Develops the traditional *Ubi sunt?* (Where are
they?) topos.    59. *Sages*: Solomon would be foremost among these.
63. *meare*: boundary; with a pun on mire. Cf. the pun on *raine*.
64–70. *Assyrian Lyonesse . . . Persian Beares . . . Grecian Libbard*: as identified
in Geneva Bible notes to Daniel 7.3–7, and marking the Hebrew nation's
three successive overlords which Rome was later to follow as a fourth (cf.
Revelation 13.2). The leopard is Alexander the Great. Jan van der Noot's *A
Theatre for Worldlings* (hereafter cited as Noot *TW*) 12v mentions "*Assyrians,
Egiptians, Persians,* or *Medians, Grecians,* or *Jewes, Romaines*" as all subject to
excessive devotion to the things of the world.

What of the *Persian* Beares outragiousnesse,
Whose memorie is quite worne out with yeares?
Who of the *Grecian* Libbard now ought heares,
That overran the East with greedie powre,
And left his whelps their kingdomes to devoure?          70

And where is that same great seven headded beast,
That made all nations vassals of her pride,
To fall before her feete at her beheast,
And in the necke of all the world did ride?
Where doth she all that wondrous welth nowe hide?          75
With her own weight down pressed now shee lies,
And by her heaps her hugenesse testifies.

O *Rome* thy ruine I lament and rue,
And in thy fall my fatall overthrowe,
That whilom was, whilst heavens with equall vewe          80
Deignd to behold me, and their gifts bestowe,
The picture of thy pride in pompous shew:
And of the whole world as thou wast the Empresse,
So I of this small Northerne world was Princesse.

To tell the beawtie of my buildings fayre,          85
Adornd with purest golde, and precious stone;
To tell my riches, and endowments rare
That by my foes are now all spent and gone:

71. *seven headded beast*: in Reformation tradition, Rome, and therefore the
Roman church (see Revelation 13 and Geneva Bible notes).     80. *whilst*
. . . *vewe*: Matthew 5.45 betrays the irony: "Your Father that is in heaven . . .
maketh his sunne to arise on the evil, and the good, and sendeth raine on the
juste, & unjuste."     84. *small Northerne world*: The mantle passes from
Assyria to Persia to Greece to Rome and thence ironically to England as a
little Rome.     85–98. Sp follows Camden: "If I were disposed upon the
report of the common people to reckon up what great store of Romane
peeces of coine, how many cast images of gold and silver, how many vessels,
what a sort of modules or Chapiters of pillars, and how many wonderful
things of antique worke, have beene digged up, my words would not carry
credit: The thing is so incredible" (*Britannia*, p.411).

To tell my forces matchable to none,
Were but lost labour, that few would beleeve,                    90
And with rehearsing would me more agreeve.

High towers, faire temples, goodly theaters,
Strong walls, rich porches, princelie pallaces,
Large streetes, brave houses, sacred sepulchers,
Sure gates, sweete gardens, stately galleries,                    95
Wrought with faire pillours, and fine imageries,
All those (ô pitie) now are turnd to dust,
And overgrowen with blacke oblivions rust.

Theretoo for warlike power, and peoples store,
In *Britannie* was none to match with mee,                    100
That manie often did abie full sore:
Ne *Troynovant*, though elder sister shee,
With my great forces might compared bee;
That stout *Pendragon* to his perill felt,
Who in a siege seaven yeres about me dwelt.                    105

But long ere this *Bunduca* Britonnesse
Her mightie hoast against my bulwarkes brought,
*Bunduca*, that victorious conqueresse,

100–01. Harrison writes: "It should seeme when these ancient cities
flourished, that the same towne, which we now call saint Albons, did most of
all excell: but cheefelie in the Romans time, and was not onelie nothing
inferior to London it selfe, but rather preferred before it, because it was
newer, and made a Municipium of the Romans, whereas the other was old
and ruinous, and inhabited onelie by the Britons . . . " ("Description of
England" 2.13).      102. *Troynovant*: London; the tradition goes back
to Geoffrey of Monmouth's *History of the Kings of Britain* 1.17.
104–05. "Not long after, the English-Saxons wonne it: but *Uther* the Britan
surnamed for his serpentine wisdome, *Pendragon*, by a sore seige and a long
recovered it. After whose death, it fell againe into their hands" (Camden,
*Britannia*, p.410).      106–12. Bunduca (Boadicea) *did* sack and destroy
Verulamium, *RT* 112 notwithstanding (see Tacitus, *Annals* 14.33; Camden,
*Britannia*, p.409). Nevertheless, the city flourished again (as Camden notes).
See also *FQ* II x 54–56.

That lifting up her brave heroïck thought
Bove womens weaknes, with the *Romanes* fought,      110
Fought, and in field against them thrice prevailed:
Yet was she foyld, when as she me assailed.

And though at last by force I conquered were
Of hardie *Saxons*, and became their thrall;
Yet was I with much bloodshed bought full deere,      115
And prizde with slaughter of their Generall:
The moniment of whose sad funerall,
For wonder of the world, long in me lasted;
But now to nought through spoyle of time is wasted.

Wasted it is, as if it never were,      120
And all the rest that me so honord made,
And of the world admired ev'rie where,
Is turnd to smoake, that doth to nothing fade;
And of that brightnes now appeares no shade,
But greislie shades, such as doo haunt in hell      125
With fearfull fiends, that in deep darknes dwell.

Where my high steeples whilom usde to stand,
On which the lordly Faulcon wont to towre,
There now is but an heap of lyme and sand,
For the Shriche-owle to build her balefull bowre:      130
And where the Nightingale wont forth to powre
Her restles plaints, to comfort wakefull Lovers,
There now haunt yelling Mewes and whining Plovers.

---

120–33. The lines generally reflect the apocalyptic tone of Isaiah 34 with its
imagery of chaos returned and its ruin-haunting birds and animals of prey.
The Geneva Bible notes see this as an image of destruction falling on all
enemies of the church.    123. *smoake*: Cf. the smoke of the day of the
Lord's vengeance on Israel's traditional enemy, Edom (Isaiah 34.10).
130. *Shriche-owle*: See the screech-owl or Lilith of Isaiah 34.14, a ruin-
haunting storm or wind spirit connected with the destruction of Edom.
133. *Mewes*: gulls. *Plovers*: a family of wading birds.

And where the christall *Thamis* wont to slide
In silver channell, downe along the Lee,                    135
About whose flowrie bankes on either side
A thousand Nymphes, with mirthfull jollitee
Were wont to play, from all annoyance free;
There now no rivers course is to be seene,
But moorish fennes, and marshes ever greene.               140

Seemes, that that gentle River for great griefe
Of my mishaps, which oft I to him plained;
Or for to shunne the horrible mischiefe,
With which he saw my cruell foes me pained,
And his pure streames with guiltles blood oft stained,      145
From my unhappie neighborhood farre fled,
And his sweete waters away with him led.

There also where the winged ships were seene
In liquid waves to cut their fomie waie,
And thousand Fishers numbred to have been,                 150
In that wide lake looking for plenteous praie
Of fish, which they with baits usde to betraie,
Is now no lake, nor anie fishers store,
Nor ever ship shall saile there anie more.

They all are gone, and all with them is gone,              155
Ne ought to me remaines, but to lament
My long decay, which no man els doth mone,
And mourne my fall with dolefull dreriment.
Yet it is comfort in great languishment,
To be bemoned with compassion kinde,                       160
And mitigates the anguish of the minde.

But me no man bewaileth, but in game,
Ne sheddeth teares from lamentable eie:

134–54. See note to line 2 on the Thames's disappearance.    148–54. The
imagery suggests a fairy-like empire vanished into the past.

Nor anie lives that mentioneth my name
To be remembred of posteritie,                          165
Save One that maugre fortunes injurie,
And times decay, and envies cruell tort,
Hath writ my record in true-seeming sort.

*Cambden* the nourice of antiquitie,
And lanterne unto late succeeding age,                  170
To see the light of simple veritie,
Buried in ruines, through the great outrage
Of her owne people, led with warlike rage,
*Cambden*, though time all moniments obscure,
Yet thy just labours ever shall endure.                 175

But whie (unhappie wight) doo I thus crie,
And grieve that my remembrance quite is raced
Out of the knowledge of posteritie,
And all my antique moniments defaced?
Sith I doo dailie see things highest placed,            180
So soone as fates their vitall thred have shorne,
Forgotten quite as they were never borne.

It is not long, since these two eyes beheld
A mightie Prince, of most renowmed race,

---

166–75. William Camden (1551–1623), whose *Britannia* was first
published in 1586, was to become headmaster of Westminster School,
Clarenceux King of Arms, and author of *The History of . . . Elizabeth*. Sp may
have known him personally.    166. *maugre*: in spite of.    167. *tort*:
wrong.    176–343. Sp here begins the second section of the poem, a
lament for the Dudley family, which may derive from the *Stemmata
Dudleiana* mentioned in his April 1580 letter to Harvey. The lament
mentions not only Robert Dudley, the earl of Leicester, but various of his
highly-placed relations (his brother and sister married into the families of the
earls of Bedford and of Pembroke respectively). It comes to a climax in the
lament for Sir Philip Sidney who after his death became in popular
imagination the ideal Protestant knight.    181. Cf. lines 17–18 above.
184. *A mightie Prince*: Robert Dudley, earl of Leicester (1532?–88), courtier,
soldier, and supporter of the Protestant left, favorite and intimate of
Elizabeth, who was enraged by his secret (third) marriage in 1578 (tactfully

Whom *England* high in count of honour held,                    185
And greatest ones did sue to gaine his grace;
Of greatest ones he greatest in his place,
Sate in the bosome of his Soveraine,
And *Right and loyall* did his word maintaine.

I saw him die, I saw him die, as one                            190
Of the meane people, and brought foorth on beare,
I saw him die, and no man left to mone
His dolefull fate, that late him loved deare:
Scarse anie left to close his eylids neare;
Scarse anie left upon his lips to laie                          195
The sacred sod, or *Requiem* to saie.

O trustlesse state of miserable men,
That builde your blis on hope of earthly thing,
And vainly thinke your selves halfe happie then,
When painted faces with smooth flattering                      200
Doo fawne on you, and your wide praises sing,
And when the courting masker louteth lowe,
Him true in heart and trustie to you trow.

All is but fained, and with oaker dide,
That everie shower will wash and wipe away,                    205
All things doo change that under heaven abide,
And after death all friendship doth decaie.
Therefore what ever man bearst worldlie sway,
Living, on God, and on thy selfe relie;
For when thou diest, all shall with thee die.                  210

---

unmentioned in *RT*) to Lettice Knollys, countess of Essex and mother (by
previous marriage) of Penelope Devereux, the Stella of Sidney's *Astrophil and
Stella*. Leicester died deeply in debt after leading an unsuccessful English
mission to aid the Low Countries in their war against Spain.     188. *bosome*:
Cf. the intimacy of Sapience in God's bosom (*HHB* 183).     189. *Right and
loyall*: Leicester's motto was *Droict et Loyal*.     190. Not literally: Leicester
died at Cornebury-lodge, Oxfordshire, 4 September 1588.     197–203. Cf.
the vanities cited in Ecclesiastes.     202. *louteth*: bows.     204. *oaker*:
ochre; yellow earth-derived pigment here used for cosmetic purposes.

He now is dead, and all is with him dead,
Save what in heavens storehouse he uplaid:
His hope is faild, and come to passe his dread,
And evill men now dead, his deeds upbraid:
Spite bites the dead, that living never baid.          215
He now is gone, the whiles the Foxe is crept
Into the hole, the which the Badger swept.

He now is dead, and all his glorie gone,
And all his greatnes vapoured to nought,
That as a glasse upon the water shone,                 220
Which vanisht quite, so soone as it was sought:
His name is worne alreadie out of thought,
Ne anie Poet seekes him to revive;
Yet manie Poets honourd him alive.

Ne doth his *Colin*, carelesse *Colin Cloute*,          225
Care now his idle bagpipe up to raise,
Ne tell his sorrow to the listning rout
Of shepherd groomes, which wont his songs to praise:
Praise who so list, yet I will him dispraise,
Untill he quite him of this guiltie blame:             230
Wake shepheards boy, at length awake for shame.

And who so els did goodnes by him gaine,
And who so els his bounteous minde did trie,

---

211. Cf. similar mythic hyperbole of Elizabeth Drury in Donne's
*Anniversaries*.          212. "But lay up treasures for your selves in heaven . . . "
(Matthew 6.20).          214–15. Leicester's intimacy with Elizabeth, his two
secret marriages, and the suspicious deaths of his first two wives and the
husband of this third wife (and others) led to considerable unfavorable
publicity. Cf. *RR* 187–90 and the Blatant Beast of *FQ* V–VI.          215. *living
never baid*: i.e. that never attacked the living who could defend themselves;
"baid" means barked.          216. *Foxe*: William Cecil, Lord Burghley, able to
further consolidate his power on council with Leicester dead. Leicester was
Burghley's major rival.          224. Roger Ascham, Gabriel Harvey, and
Geoffrey Whitney, among others.          225–31. Like the friends referred to in
the dedication above, Verlame upbraids Sp.

Whether he shepheard be, or shepheards swaine,
(For manie did, which doo it now denie)                    235
Awake, and to his Song a part applie:
And I, the whilest you mourne for his decease,
Will with my mourning plaints your plaint increase.

He dyde, and after him his brother dyde,
His brother Prince, his brother noble Peere,              240
That whilste he lived, was of none envyde,
And dead is now, as living, counted deare,
Deare unto all that true affection beare:
But unto thee most deare, ô dearest Dame,
His noble Spouse, and Paragon of fame.                   245

He whilest he lived, happie was through thee,
And being dead is happie now much more;
Living, that lincked chaunst with thee to bee,
And dead, because him dead thou dost adore
As living, and thy lost deare love deplore.              250
So whilst that thou, faire flower of chastitie,
Dost live, by thee thy Lord shall never die.

Thy Lord shall never die, the whiles this verse
Shall live, and surely it shall live for ever:
For ever it shall live, and shall rehearse               255
His worthie praise, and vertues dying never,
Though death his soule doo from his bodie sever.
And thou thy selfe herein shalt also live;
Such grace the heavens doo to my verses give.

Ne shall his sister, ne thy father die,                  260
Thy father, that good Earle of rare renowne,

---

239. *his brother*: Ambrose Dudley, 1st earl of Warwick, Leicester's elder
brother, died 20 February 1590, without issue.      244. *dearest Dame*: his
last wife, Anne Russell.      260. *his sister*: Mary Dudley; see note to
dedication above. *thy father*: Francis Russell, 2d earl of Bedford (1527?–85),
member of parliament for Buckinghamshire, soldier, diplomat.

And noble Patrone of weake povertie;
Whose great good deeds in countrey and in towne
Have purchast him in heaven an happie crowne;
Where he now liveth in eternall blis,                    265
And left his sonne t'ensue those steps of his.

He noble bud, his Grandsires livelie hayre,
Under the shadow of thy countenaunce
Now ginnes to shoote up fast, and flourish fayre
In learned artes and goodlie governaunce,                270
That him to highest honour shall advaunce.
Brave Impe of *Bedford*, grow apace in bountie,
And count of wisedome more than of thy Countie.

Ne may I let thy husbands sister die,
That goodly Ladie, sith she eke did spring              275
Out of this stocke, and famous familie,
Whose praises I to future age doo sing,
And foorth out of her happie womb did bring
The sacred brood of learning and all honour;
In whom the heavens powrde all their gifts upon her.   280

Most gentle spirite breathed from above,
Out of the bosome of the makers blis,
In whom all bountie and all vertuous love
Appeared in their native propertis,
And did enrich that noble breast of his,               285
With treasure passing all this worldes worth,
Worthie of heaven it selfe, which brought it forth.

His blessed spirite full of power divine
And influence of all celestiall grace,

262. A reference perhaps to his foundation of a free school at Woburn.
266. *his sonne*: in fact his grandson, Edward Russell, 3d earl of Bedford
(1573–1627).        274. *husbands sister*: Mary Dudley.        279. Sir Philip
Sidney (1554–86).        281. *breathed from above*: The language combines
biblical and Neoplatonic associations.        282. Cf. Christ in *HHL* 134, and
Sapience, as Word of God, in *HHB* 183.

Loathing this sinfull earth and earthlie slime,                    290
Fled backe too soone unto his native place,
Too soone for all that did his love embrace,
Too soone for all this wretched world, whom he
Robd of all right and true nobilitie.

Yet ere his happie soule to heaven went                            295
Out of this fleshlie goale, he did devise
Unto his heavenlie maker to present
His bodie, as a spotles sacrifise;
And chose, that guiltie hands of enemies
Should powre forth th'offring of his guiltles blood:              300
So life exchanging for his countries good.

O noble spirite, live there ever blessed,
The worlds late wonder, and the heavens new joy,
Live ever there, and leave me here distressed
With mortall cares, and cumbrous worlds anoy.                     305
But where thou dost that happines enjoy,
Bid me, ô bid me quicklie come to thee,
That happie there I maie thee alwaies see.

Yet whilest the fates affoord me vitall breath,
I will it spend in speaking of thy praise,                        310
And sing to thee, untill that timelie death
By heavens doome doo ende my earthlie daies:
Thereto doo thou my humble spirite raise,
And into me that sacred breath inspire,
Which thou there breathest perfect and entire.                    315

290. Platonic world of matter; cf. Pauline salvation "from the bodie of this
death" (Romans 7.24).        291. *too soone*: Sidney died at thirty-two on 17
October 1586 of wounds received at Zutphen a month earlier. *native place*:
Cf. men as "strangers and pilgremes on the earth" who "seke a countrey"
(Hebrews 11.13–14).        293. *wretched*: Pauline word for man's fallen state
(Romans 7.24, etc).        296. *goale*: jail.        298. *spotles sacrifise*: a sacrifice
worthy of God, like Christ's "as of a Lambe undefiled, & without spot"
(1 Peter 1.19).        299. *hands of enemies*: ubiquitous Old Testament
phrase.        300. *guiltles blood*: Christ-like.

Then will I sing, but who can better sing,
Than thine owne sister, peerles Ladie bright,
Which to thee sings with deep harts sorrowing,
Sorrowing tempered with deare delight,
That her to heare I feele my feeble spright          320
Robbed of sense, and ravished with joy,
O sad joy made of mourning and anoy.

Yet will I sing, but who can better sing,
Than thou thy selfe, thine owne selfes valiance,
That whilest thou livedst, madest the forrests ring,     325
And fields resownd, and flockes to leap and daunce,
And shepheards leave their lambs unto mischaunce,
To runne thy shrill *Arcadian* Pipe to heare:
O happie were those dayes, thrice happie were.

But now more happie thou, and wretched wee,          330
Which want the wonted sweetnes of thy voice,
Whiles thou now in *Elisian* fields so free,
With *Orpheus*, and with *Linus*, and the choice
Of all that ever did in rimes rejoyce,
Conversest, and doost heare their heavenlie layes,     335
And they heare thine, and thine doo better praise.

So there thou livest, singing evermore,
And here thou livest, being ever song

---

317. *sister*: Mary Sidney, countess of Pembroke.     318–22. Mary Sidney
translated the Psalms (started by Sir Philip Sidney); she may have written
"Clorinda" (printed with *Ast*).     322. *anoy*: discomfort.     324. *thy selfe*:
Sir Philip Sidney.     325–29. Reference to Sidney's *Arcadia*.
328. *Arcadian*: Arcady in mid-Peloponnesus is the pastoral symbol of quiet
rustic life and the setting for Sidney's *Arcadia*.     332. *Elisian fields*: the part
of the underworld reserved for the blessed; for Renaissance writers,
synonymous with Heaven (*Aen* 6.540–43). Cf. *FQ* IV x 23.
333. *Orpheus . . . Linus*: see Virgil, *Ecl* 4.55–57. Orpheus was archetypal
poet-musician and first-mentioned inhabitant of Virgil's Elisium; his playing
charmed and animated all nature. In Plato's *Apology* Socrates anticipates his
company in the afterlife. Linus was his brother.

Of us, which living loved thee afore,
And now thee worship, mongst that blessed throng          340
Of heavenlie Poets and Heroes strong.
So thou both here and there immortall art,
And everie where through excellent desart.

But such as neither of themselves can sing,
Nor yet are sung of others for reward,          345
Die in obscure oblivion, as the thing
Which never was, ne ever with regard
Their names shall of the later age be heard,
But shall in rustie darknes ever lie,
Unles they mentiond be with infamie.          350

What booteth it to have been rich alive?
What to be great? what to be gracious?
When after death no token doth survive,
Of former being in this mortall hous,
But sleepes in dust dead and inglorious,          355
Like beast, whose breath but in his nostrels is,
And hath no hope of happinesse or blis.

How manie great ones may remembred be,
Which in their daies most famouslie did florish?
Of whome no word we heare, nor signe now see,          360
But as things wipt out with a sponge to perishe,
Because they living, cared not to cherishe
No gentle wits, through pride or covetize,
Which might their names for ever memorize.

---

344–490. The death of the poet-knight Sidney leads naturally into the third
section of the poem, a defense of poetry and the secular immortality that
poetry can give, commonplaces which Sp often uses: cf. *SC* "October"
61–66; *TM* 97–108, 457–62; *RR* 451–58          351. *booteth*: be of profit or
value.          354. *this mortall hous*: Ecclesiastes 12.3–7: "When the kepers of
the house shal tremble . . . . for man goeth to the house of his age . . . . And
dust [shall] returne to the earth . . . ."          356. "The man whose breath is in
his nostrelles," i.e. "whose life is so fraile, that if his nose be stopped, he is
dead" (Isaiah 2.22 and Geneva Bible note).

Provide therefore (ye Princes) whilst ye live,      365
That of the *Muses* ye may friended bee,
Which unto men eternitie do give;
For they be daughters of Dame memorie,
And *Jove* the father of eternitie,
And do those men in golden thrones repose,      370
Whose merits they to glorifie do chose.

The seven fold yron gates of grislie Hell,
And horrid house of sad *Proserpina*,
They able are with power of mightie spell
To breake, and thence the soules to bring awaie      375
Out of dread darkenesse, to eternall day,
And them immortall make, which els would die
In foule forgetfulnesse, and nameles lie.

So whilome raised they the puissant brood
Of golden girt *Alcmena*, for great merite,      380
Out of the dust, to which the *Oetæan* wood
Had him consum'd, and spent his vitall spirite:
To highest heaven, where now he doth inherite
All happinesse in *Hebes* silver bowre,
Chosen to be her dearest Paramoure.      385

So raisde they eke faire *Ledaes* warlick twinnes,
And interchanged life unto them lent,

---

368–71. The Muses were traditionally daughters of Mnemosyne (memory)
and Jove.    373. *Proserpina*: Latin goddess of underworld; cf. E. K.'s note
to *SC* "November" 163–64.    379–85. Hercules, having failed to remove
the burning shirt of Nessus, had himself immolated on Mount Oeta (*Met*
9.229–39). He was eventually removed to the isles of the blest or
(alternatively) was given an apotheosis among the stars.    380. *Alcmena*:
Hercules' mother; "golden girt" echoes Seneca, *Hercules Furens* 543.
381. *Oetæan*: of Mt. Oeta.    384. Hebe was wife to Hercules, daughter of
Zeus, and cupbearer to the gods.    386. *Ledaes warlick twinnes*: Castor and
Pollux, who became the zodiac constellation Gemini. When Pollux asked to
die with Castor, Zeus granted that they might both spend alternate days in
heaven and in the underworld.

That when th'one dies, th'other then beginnes
To shew in Heaven his brightnes orient;
And they, for pittie of the sad wayment,                          390
Which *Orpheus* for *Eurydice* did make,
Her back againe to life sent for his sake.

So happie are they, and so fortunate,
Whom the *Pierian* sacred sisters love,
That freed from bands of impacable fate,                          395
And power of death, they live for aye above,
Where mortall wreakes their blis may not remove:
But with the Gods, for former vertues meede,
On *Nectar* and *Ambrosia* do feede.

For deeds doe die, how ever noblie donne,                         400
And thoughts of men do as themselves decay,
But wise wordes taught in numbers for to runne,
Recorded by the Muses, live for ay;
Ne may with storming showers be washt away,
Ne bitter breathing windes with harmfull blast,                   405
Nor age, nor envie shall them ever wast.

In vaine doo earthly Princes then, in vaine
Seeke with Pyramides, to heaven aspired;
Or huge Colosses, built with costlie paine;

---

390–92. See Virgil, *Aen* 6.119–20.        390. *wayment*: lamentation.
394. *Pierian sacred sisters*: the Muses.        395. *impacable*: implacable.
398. *meede*: reward.        399. *Nectar and Ambrosia*: drink and food of the
gods, giving immortality.        400–02. The thought/ word/ deed paradigm is
from the general confession to the communion service in *The Boke of Common
Prayer*.        404–06. Cf. *SC* "November" for seeing man's mortality
symbolized by the inclement weather of oncoming winter.        407–20. Cf.
*RR* son.2, where the "Seven *Romane* Hils" are sung, and cf. Du Bellay,
*Deffence et illustration de la langue françoyse* 2.5 (cited by Renwick 1928:197):
"Ce qu'avient a tous ceux qui mettent l'asseurance de leur immortalité au
Marbre, au Cuyvre, aux Collosses, aux Pyramides, aux laborieux Edifices, et
autres choses non moins subjectes aux injures du Ciel et du Tens, de la
Flamme, et du fer, que de frais excessifs, et perpetuelle sollicitude."

Or brasen Pillours, never to be fired,                    410
Or Shrines, made of the mettall most desired;
To make their memories for ever live:
For how can mortall immortalitie give?

Such one *Mausolus* made, the worlds great wonder,
But now no remnant doth thereof remaine:                  415
Such one *Marcellus*, but was torne with thunder:
Such one *Lisippus*, but is worne with raine:
Such one King *Edmond*, but was rent for gaine.
All such vaine moniments of earthlie masse,
Devour'd of Time, in time to nought doo passe.            420

But fame with golden wings aloft doth flie,
Above the reach of ruinous decay,
And with brave plumes doth beate the azure skie,
Admir'd of base-borne men from farre away:
Then who so will with vertuous deeds assay               425
To mount to heaven, on *Pegasus* must ride,
And with sweete Poets verse be glorifide.

For not to have been dipt in *Lethe* lake,
Could save the sonne of *Thetis* from to die;
But that blinde bard did him immortall make             430
With verses, dipt in deaw of *Castalie*:

414. *Mausolus*: hence "mausoleum," after his monumental tomb at
Halicarnassus.       416. Various temples were struck by lightning when
Marcellus illegally dedicated a temple jointly to two gods; see Plutarch's *Life
of Marcellus* 28.       417. *Lisippus*: sculptor of Alexander.       418. Camden's
description of the abbey at Bury St. Edmonds, suppressed by Henry VII,
attacks the king's advisers who suppressed the monastery for their own
enrichment (*Britannia*, p.461).       421–24. The image of love as winged is
ubiquitous in *FH*; cf. *RT* 645–58 below.       426. *Pegasus*: the winged horse
that struck the earth of Mt. Helicon with its foot, raising the fount of
Hippocrene, thus becoming the favorite of the Muses and a symbol of poetic
creativity.       428–29. Thetis dipped Achilles in Styx, not Lethe, the water
of oblivion.       430. *blinde bard*: Homer.       431. *Castalie*: substituted for
Hippocrene; see Boccaccio, *Genealogia Deorum* 10.27.

Which made the Easterne Conquerour to crie,
O fortunate yong-man, whose vertue found
So brave a Trompe, thy noble acts to sound.

Therefore in this halfe happie I doo read                    435
Good *Melibæ* that hath a Poet got,
To sing his living praises being dead,
Deserving never here to be forgot,
In spight of envie, that his deeds would spot:
Since whose decease, learning lies unregarded,          440
And men of armes doo wander unrewarded.

Those two be those two great calamities,
That long agoe did grieve the noble spright
Of *Salomon* with great indignities;
Who wilome was alive the wisest wight.                       445
But now his wisedome is disprooved quite;
For he that now welds all things at his will,
Scorns th'one and th'other in his deeper skill.

O griefe of griefes, ô gall of all good heartes,
To see that vertue should dispised bee                        450
Of him, that first was raisde for vertuous parts,
And now broad spreading like an aged tree,

432. *Easterne Conquerour*: Alexander: see E. K.'s gloss to *SC* "October"
65.      433–34. As Alexander said of Achilles' celebration by Homer
(Cicero, *Pro Archia* 24).      436. *Melibæ*: Sir Francis Walsingham, secretary
of state, recently dead (6 April 1590). *a Poet*: Thomas Watson praised
Walsingham in his Latin *Melibæus* and its English version, *An Eglogue Upon
the death of . . . Walsingham* (1590), and returned Sp's compliment (*FQ* III vi
45) on his *Amyntas* (1585); see Ringler (1954).      440. Sp had described
Walsingham as "the great *Mecenas* of this age" (*FQ* Dedicatory Sonnet 12)
after Horace's patron.      442–44. See Ecclesiasticus 26.29.      446. Ironic:
by "disproving" Solomon's wisdom Burghley really only more forcefully
demonstrates its applicability.      447–53. Allusions to Burghley, Leicester's
enemy, disappear from the 1611 Folio. Lines 447–48 are changed to "For
such as now have most the world at will,/ Scorn . . .in their deeper skill" and
the specific reference of line 451 "him, that first was" becomes "Such as first
were . . . ." See also textual notes.

Lets none shoot up, that nigh him planted bee:
O let the man, of whom the Muse is scorned,
Nor alive, nor dead be of the Muse adorned.                    455

O vile worlds trust, that with such vaine illusion
Hath so wise men bewitcht, and overkest,
That they see not the way of their confusion,
O vainesse to be added to the rest,
That do my soule with inward griefe infest:                    460
Let them behold the piteous fall of mee:
And in my case their owne ensample see.

And who so els that sits in highest seate
Of this worlds glorie, worshipped of all,
Ne feareth change of time, nor fortunes threate,               465
Let him behold the horror of my fall,
And his owne end unto remembrance call;
That of like ruine he may warned bee,
And in himselfe be moov'd to pittie mee.

Thus having ended all her piteous plaint,                      470
With dolefull shrikes shee vanished away,
That I through inward sorrowe wexen faint,
And all astonished with deepe dismay,
For her departure, had no word to say:
But sate long time in sencelesse sad affright,                 475
Looking still, if I might of her have sight.

Which when I missed, having looked long,
My thought returned greeved home againe,
Renewing her complaint with passion strong,
For ruth of that same womans piteous paine;                    480
Whose wordes recording in my troubled braine,
I felt such anguish wound my feeble heart,
That frosen horror ran through everie part.

456–59. In Ecclesiastes, the Preacher considers worldly works and finds their
pursuit vain.    457. *overkest*: overcast.    481. *recording*: remembering,
from Ital. *ricordari*.

So inlie greeving in my groning brest,
And deepelie muzing at her doubtfull speach,                485
Whose meaning much I labored foorth to wreste,
Being above my slender reasons reach;
At length by demonstration me to teach,
Before mine eies strange sights presented were,
Like tragicke Pageants seeming to appeare.                  490

*1*

I saw an Image, all of massie gold,
Placed on high upon an Altare faire,
That all, which did the same from farre beholde,
Might worship it, and fall on lowest staire.
Not that great Idoll might with this compaire,               495
To which th'*Assyrian* tyrant would have made
The holie brethren, falslie to have praid.         ·

But th'Altare, on the which this Image staid,
Was (ô great pitie) built of brickle clay,

491–end. "The 'pageants' which follow are "demonstrations' setting the
fallen city, in emblematic terms, against the restored city, figured in
microcosm as Sidney in the glass of art" (MacLure 1973:17). Reference is
made to "Dreames" by E. K. in the *SC* epistle dedicatory and by Sp in the
Harvey letter of April 1580, and to "Pageaunts" by E. K. again in his gloss
on *SC* "June" 25. It has been suggested that parts of these lost works show
up here in *RT*.     491–574. Of the traditional Seven Wonders of the
World, four appear here: Phidias's statue of Zeus at Olympia, the Pharos
(lighthouse) at Alexandria, the walls of Babylon with the hanging gardens of
Semiramus, and the Colossus at Rhodes. The other three were the Pyramids
(mentioned in line 408 above), the Temple of Diana at Ephesus (mentioned
in *RR* 17), and the Mausoleum by Artemis at Halicarnassus (mentioned in
line 414 above).     491. *Image*: the image of gold from Daniel 3, but Zeus's
statue perhaps provides the hint.     496. *Assyrian tyrant*: Nebuchadnezzar,
who commanded all to worship his golden image (Daniel 3). The "holy
brethren" (line 497), Shadrach, Meshack, and Abednego, refused to do
so.     498–504. Nebuchadnezzar's image is broken up by the stone "cut
without hands" (which the Geneva Bible notes take to mean Christ) and
floats away as chaff on the wind (Daniel 3).     499. *brickle*: fragile. *clay*:
Nebuchadnezzar's image had feet of clay.

That shortly the foundation decaid,                                    500
With showres of heaven and tempests worne away,
Then downe it fell, and low in ashes lay,
Scorned of everie one, which by it went;
That I it seing, dearelie did lament.


### 2

Next unto this a statelie Towre appeared,                              505
Built all of richest stone, that might bee found,
And nigh unto the Heavens in height upreared,
But placed on a plot of sandie ground:
Not that great Towre, which is so much renownd
For tongues confusion in holie writ,                                   510
King *Ninus* worke, might be compar'd to it.

But ô vaine labours of terrestriall wit,
That buildes so stronglie on so frayle a soyle,
As with each storme does fall away, and flit,
And gives the fruit of all your travailes toyle,                       515
To be the pray of Tyme, and Fortunes spoyle:
I saw this Towre fall sodainlie to dust,
That nigh with griefe thereof my heart was brust.


505. *Towre*: The Seven Wonders *schema* indicates the Pharos of Ptolemy II at
Alexandria.        507. Hints of Babel, whose builders "were moved with pride
and ambition, thinking to preferre their own glorie to Gods honour"
(Geneva Bible note to Genesis 11.4).        508. *sandie ground*: where the
foolish build (Matthew 7.26–27).        509–11. Tower of Babel; Babel was
linked by Hebrew folk-etymology to Babylon, which for symbolic purposes is
here equivalent to Egypt and Rome as archetypal center of entrenched
worldly resistance to God.        511. *Ninus*: by folk-etymology the founder of
Ninevah, hence confused with Nimrod, founder (in the Bible) of both
Ninevah and Babel. Thus Sp makes him the builder of the Tower of Babel;
cf. *FQ* II ix 21.        517. *dust*: whither man, in the end, returns (Genesis
3.19).

### 3

Then did I see a pleasant Paradize,
Full of sweete flowres and daintiest delights,                    520
Such as on earth man could not more devize,
With pleasures choyce to feed his cheerefull sprights;
Not that, which *Merlin* by his Magicke slights
Made for the gentle squire, to entertaine
His fayre *Belphœbe*, could this gardine staine.                  525

But ô short pleasure bought with lasting paine,
Why will hereafter anie flesh delight
In earthlie blis, and joy in pleasures vaine,
Since that I sawe this gardine wasted quite,
That where it was scarce seemed anie sight?                       530
That I, which once that beautie did beholde,
Could not from teares my melting eyes with-holde.

### 4

Soone after this a Giaunt came in place,
Of wondrous power, and of exceeding stature,
That none durst vewe the horror of his face,                      535
Yet was he milde of speach, and meeke of nature.
Not he, which in despight of his Creatour
With railing tearmes defied the Jewish hoast,
Might with this mightie one in hugenes boast.

For from the one he could to th'other coast,                      540
Stretch his strong thighes, and th'Occæan overstride,
And reatch his hand into his enemies hoast.
But see the end of pompe and fleshlie pride;

519–32. Negligible associations with the hanging garden of Semiramus,
many with the archetypal garden as *hortus conclusus*; cf. the garden where
Timias sees Belphœbe (*FQ* III v 39–40), the Garden of Adonis (*FQ* III vi
29–54), and *HL* 280–93.    525. *staine*: outshine.    533. *Giaunt*: the
Colossus at Rhodes.    537–39. Goliath.    538. *tearmes*: terms.
540–42. The (mistaken) belief that the Colossus, representing Apollo,
bestrode the entrance to the harbor at Rhodes.

One of his feete unwares from him did slide,
That downe hee fell into the deepe Abisse,                    545
Where drownd with him is all his earthlie blisse.

### 5

Then did I see a Bridge, made all of golde,
Over the Sea from one to other side,
Withouten prop or pillour it t'upholde,
But like the coulored Rainbowe arched wide:                  550
Not that great Arche, which *Trajan* edifide,
To be a wonder to all age ensuing,
Was matchable to this in equall vewing.

But (ah) what bootes it to see earthlie thing
In glorie, or in greatnes to excell,                         555
Sith time doth greatest things to ruine bring?
This goodlie bridge, one foote not fastned well,
Gan faile, and all the rest downe shortlie fell,
Ne of so brave a building ought remained,
That griefe thereof my spirite greatly pained.              560

### 6

I saw two Beares, as white as anie milke,
Lying together in a mightie cave,
Of milde aspect, and haire as soft as silke,
That salvage nature seemed not to have,
Nor after greedie spoyle of blood to crave:                 565
Two fairer beasts might not elswhere be found,
Although the compast world were sought around.

But what can long abide above this ground
In state of blis, or stedfast happinesse?

547. *Bridge*: Xerxes' bridge over the Hellespont. Starnes and Talbert
(1955:285), cite Herodotus (7.33), and Sephanus's and Calepine's
dictionaries. Xerxes had the sea scourged when a storm destroyed his
bridge.    551–53. Trajan's bridge over the Danube (see Dio, *History*
68.13).    551. *edifide*: built.    561–67. Possibly the earls of Leicester
and Warwick (Renwick 1928:201); cf. the Bear and Ragged Staff on the
Dudley crest.

The Cave, in which these Beares lay sleeping sound,                    570
Was but earth, and with her owne weightinesse
Upon them fell, and did unwares oppresse,
That for great sorrow of their sudden fate,
Henceforth all worlds felicitie I hate.

¶Much was I troubled in my heavie spright,                            575
At sight of these sad spectacles forepast,
That all my senses were bereaved quight,
And I in minde remained sore agast,
Distraught twixt feare and pitie; when at last
I heard a voyce, which loudly to me called,                          580
That with the suddein shrill I was appalled.

Behold (said it) and by ensample see,
That all is vanitie and griefe of minde,
Ne other comfort in this world can be,
But hope of heaven, and heart to God inclinde;                       585
For all the rest must needs be left behinde:
With that it bad me, to the other side
To cast mine eye, where other sights I spide.

*1*

¶Upon that famous Rivers further shore,
There stood a snowie Swan of heavenly hiew,                           590
And gentle kinde, as ever Fowle afore;

575–88. The whole passage echoes *VB* 1. "That all is vanitie and griefe of
minde" echoes Ecclesiastes 1.2.    585. "Enclyne youre hert unto the
Lorde the God of Israel" (Joshua 24.23, Coverdale's translation).
586. Ecclesiastes 5.14: "As he came forthe of his mothers belly, he shal
returne naked to go as he came, & shal beare away nothing of his labour . . .
. " Cf. Job 1.21, 1 Timothy 6.7, and "The Ordre for the Buriall of the Dead"
in *The Boke of Common Prayer*.    589–672. Sp depicts Sidney's apotheosis
through a series of visions, some traditional, some of a more improvised
nature. The apocalyptic symbolism of the ingathering of the faithful in the
marriage of the church and the Lamb in the fourth vision is perhaps
central.    589. *further shore*: symbolic of the afterlife.    590. *Swan*:
traditionally symbolic as singer before its own death; associated with Apollo,
god of music.

A fairer one in all the goodlie criew
Of white *Strimonian* brood might no man view:
There he most sweetly sung the prophecie
Of his owne death in dolefull Elegie.                    595

At last, when all his mourning melodie
He ended had, that both the shores resounded,
Feeling the fit that him forewarnd to die,
With loftie flight above the earth he bounded,
And out of sight to highest heaven mounted:              600
Where now he is become an heavenly signe;
There now the joy is his, here sorrow mine.


                            2
Whilest thus I looked, loe adowne the *Lee*,
I sawe an Harpe stroong all with silver twyne,
And made of golde and costlie yvorie,                    605
Swimming, that whilome seemed to have been
The harpe, on which *Dan Orpheus* was seene
Wylde beasts and forrests after him to lead,
But was th'Harpe of *Philisides* now dead.

At length out of the River it was reard                  610
And borne above the cloudes to be divin'd,
Whilest all the way most heavenly noyse was heard
Of the strings, stirred with the warbling wind,
That wrought both joy and sorrow in my mind:

---

593. *Strimonian*: River Strymon in Thrace where swans lament Bion as the
Dorian Orpheus (Moschus, *Lament for Bion* 14–18).     594–95. Suggestive
of Sidney's poetic career and early death.     599–602. The constellation
Cygnus.     603. *Lee*: The River Lee flows through Cork.     607. *Dan
Orpheus*: Chaucerian usage.     609. *Philisides*: star (or constellation) lover:
Sir Philip Sidney, from the shepherd-knight of the *Arcadia*.     610. The
head and lyre of the dismembered Orpheus float down the Hebrus to the sea
(*Met* 11.50–55).     611. *divin'd*: made divine.     612. *heavenly noyse*:
music of the spheres.

So now in heaven a signe it doth appeare,                               615
The Harpe well knowne beside the Northern Beare.


3

Soone after this I saw on th'other side,
A curious Coffer made of *Heben* wood,
That in it did most precious treasure hide,
Exceeding all this baser worldes good:                                  620
Yet through the overflowing of the flood
It almost drowned was, and done to nought,
That sight thereof much griev'd my pensive thought.

At length when most in perill it was brought,
Two Angels downe descending with swift flight,                          625
Out of the swelling streame it lightly caught,
And twixt their blessed armes it carried quight
Above the reach of anie living sight:
So now it is transform'd into that starre,
In which all heavenly treasures locked are.                             630


4

Looking aside I saw a stately Bed,
Adorned all with costly cloth of gold,
That might for anie Princes couche be red,
And deckt with daintie flowres, as if it shold
Be for some bride, her joyous night to hold:                            635
Therein a goodly Virgine sleeping lay;
A fairer wight saw never summers day.


616. The constellations are *not* "beside" each other, but the point is to
associate the lyre of Sidney's poetry with the Bear of the Dudley
family.      618. *curious Coffer*: Sidney's coffin. Or perhaps the Black
Pinnacle, Sidney's official ship as governor of Flushing; but the context
suggests a more etherialized vessel. *Heben*: ebony.      629. *that starre*: Vega,
in the constellation Lyra.      631–44. The symbolic bride and bridegroom
allude to the marriage of the church and the Lamb and the gathering of the
faithful into God's presence in Revelation 19–21.      633. *red*: taken.

I heard a voyce that called farre away
And her awaking bad her quickly dight,
For lo her Bridegrome was in readie ray 640
To come to her, and seeke her loves delight:
With that she started up with cherefull sight,
When suddeinly both bed and all was gone,
And I in languor left there all alone.

5

Still as I gazed, I beheld where stood 645
A Knight all arm'd, upon a winged steed,
The same that was bred of *Medusaes* blood,
On which *Dan Perseus* borne of heavenly seed,
The faire *Andromeda* from perill freed:
Full mortally this Knight ywounded was, 650
That streames of blood foorth flowed on the gras.

Yet was he deckt (small joy to him alas)
With manie garlands for his victories,
And with rich spoyles, which late he did purchas
Through brave atcheivements from his enemies: 655
Fainting at last through long infirmities,
He smote his steed, that straight to heaven him bore,
And left me here his losse for to deplore.

6

Lastly I saw an Arke of purest golde
Upon a brazen pillour standing hie, 660
Which th'ashes seem'd of some great Prince to hold,
Enclosde therein for endles memorie

645–58. Cf. lines 421–27 above.     646. *A Knight*: Sidney at Zutphen. *a winged steed*: Pegasus, the constellation.     647. Pegasus was so born, when Perseus decapitated Medusa (*Theogony* 280–86; *Met* 4.765–86).
657–58. Perseus and Pegasus became constellations.     659. *Arke*: sacred vessel; the Ark of the Covenant is obliquely suggested, heightening the sense of ceremony and ritual.     661. The return of Sidney's corpse to England.

Of him, whom all the world did glorifie:
Seemed the heavens with the earth did disagree,
Whether should of those ashes keeper bee.　　　　665

At last me seem'd wing footed *Mercurie*,
From heaven descending to appease their strife,
The Arke did beare with him above the skie,
And to those ashes gave a second life,
To live in heaven, where happines is rife:　　　　670
At which the earth did grieve exceedingly,
And I for dole was almost like to die.

#### L: *Envoy.*

Immortall spirite of *Philisides*,
Which now art made the heavens ornament,
That whilome wast the worlds chiefst riches;　　　675
Give leave to him that lov'de thee to lament
His losse, by lacke of thee to heaven hent,
And with last duties of this broken verse,
Broken with sighes, to decke thy sable Herse.

And ye faire Ladie th'honor of your daies,　　　680
And glorie of the world, your high thoughts scorne;
Vouchsafe this moniment of his last praise,
With some few silver dropping teares t'adorne:
And as ye be of heavenlie off spring borne,
So unto heaven let your high minde aspire,　　　685
And loath this drosse of sinfull worlds desire.

F I N I S .

666. *Mercurie*: As messenger of the gods he conducted mortals into the
afterlife.　　684. Hence of true beauty.　　684–86. Cf. *HHB* 43–49.

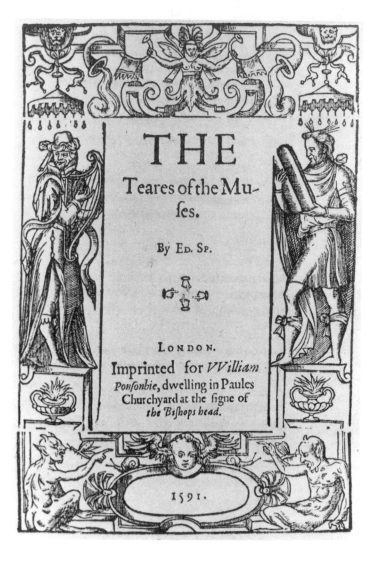

# THE

## Teares of the Mu-
ses.

By Ed. Sp.

LONDON.

Imprinted for *William*
*Ponsonbie*, dwelling in Paules
Churchyard at the signe of
*the Bishops head.*

1591.

# The Teares of the Muses

T**he** *Teares of the Muses* comes second in the *Complaints-*
volume of 1591 and it throws an ironic light on the praise
of poetry in the preceding *Ruines of Time*. If in the earlier
poem Verlame holds up learning and poetry as a means of "re-
storing the ruines" of the past, the Muses representing that
cultural memory here complain that their truth is scorned and
that barbarous ignorance has taken its place. This seems a sur-
prisingly gloomy view of Elizabethan culture in 1590, and al-
though the dedication makes no reference to its being an early
work, many critics have felt compelled to date its composition
about 1580. Renwick (1928) comments that a complaint about
the low condition of poetry in England "would seem strange if it
were uttered by the man who, in the poem which recounted his
experience during this English visit of 1590 [*Colin Clouts Come
Home Againe*], praised eleven poets of his acquaintance and
might have praised as many more" (p. 182).

Yet much suggests that Spenser's view of Elizabethan culture
in the 1590s was not our own. When one penetrates its general
rhetorical enthusiasm to the discussion of particulars, Colin's
account in *Colin Clouts Come Home Againe* presents a discourag-
ing picture of poetry at the royal court. Of the twelve poets he
mentions there, two are already dead, two are old (one "quite
hoarse" [399]), another skillful but envious, two more engaged
in work beneath their powers, and another able but "meanly
waged" (382). Only four living poets receive unqualified praise:
Spenser's patron Ralegh, Aetion (possibly Drayton), and two
newcomers—Alabaster and Daniel—so unknown at court that
Spenser cannot give them pastoral pseudonyms. Similarly the
Muses' description of their exile in *The Teares* corresponds
closely to Colin's comment in the later poem that "single Truth

and simple honestie/ Do wander up and downe despys'd of all"
(CCCHA 727–28). We know now that the glories of Sidney
and Marlowe were to be surpassed by an extraordinary flour-
ishing of poetry and drama over the next twenty-five years.
Spenser lacked the advantage of our hindsight. He was a court
poet, concerned with court verse, and we have no evidence that
the development of the popular English stage made a strong
impression on him. While Marlowe adapted a piece of *The Fa-
erie Queene* for *Tamberlaine*, Spenser never returned the compli-
ment. For him the main light of contemporary English poetry—
other than himself—would have been Sir Philip Sidney, whose
sonnet sequence had set a fashion, and whose *Arcadia* did many
of the things Spenser hoped to do with his own romance-epic.
But Sidney was untimely dead, and his death was shortly fol-
lowed by that of his uncle the earl of Leicester, the patron
Spenser had looked to in 1579. (For a fuller account of the date
see Stein 1934:42-53.)

Indeed, *The Teares of the Muses* is as much about the absence of
patrons as it is about the absence of poetry in England. Its
concern with patronage links it on the one hand to *The Ruines of
Time* with its lament for the deaths of Sidney and Leicester, and
on the other hand to *Virgils Gnat* with its obscure, desperate
appeal to Leicester himself. The poem does not seem to lament a
barbarism extending from the gothic times of the Middle
Ages—a standard topic of continental humanism—but a com-
paratively recent change. Terpsichore compares herself to one
who has been "long time luld, and fed with pleasures sweet" and
who has abruptly to face "Fortunes spight" (302–03) for no
fault of her own. It is not clear how literally we should take this,
but with the late 1580s began the final period of Elizabeth's
rule, marked by an intense competition for what seemed to be an
increasingly limited number of court prizes. While Spenser
would be comparatively successful as a poet, receiving in 1591 a
pension of £50 from the queen, he was nonetheless vulnerable.
His loss of the patrons he had counted on in the 1580s must
have been intensely felt, and the presence of Ralegh could not

have made up for them. Even at his most powerful, Ralegh was never as established as Leicester or even Sidney, Leicester's sometime heir.

As Gerald Snare (1969) has pointed out, Spenser's concern in *The Teares* goes beyond what a modern reader would think of as literary criticism because literature in the poem is a species of rhetoric, a spur and guide to human action. Poetry is a primary means of education, and the Muses are presented in terms of their contributions to man's moral and political life. Melpomene, Muse of Tragedy, stresses the part of understanding in arming "the brest with constant patience/ Against the bitter throwes of dolours darts . . . ." (133–34). Without her, man is "like a ship in midst of tempest left/ Withouten helme or Pilot her to sway" (141–42). Erato laments not so much the decline of love-poetry as the decline of love: her lament has affinities with Colin's bitter denunciation of "courting vaine" in *Colin Clout*. Human love should be a means of reaching toward the divine, but it has been allowed to remain mere physical desire. Without the Muses to teach them, mortals are blind.

*The Teares* owes something in its conception to Du Bellay's *La Musagnœomachie* which sets a monster, Ignorance, against the forces of cultural renewal. But where Du Bellay's strident call to arms envisions the monster retreating from the combined attack of learned men and their royal patrons, Spenser's myth laments a civilization in which the ruling class has abandoned its cultural mission. It looks forward to Pope's greater treatment of a similar theme in *The Dunciad*, and the two poems share a common vocabulary and common images. Ignorance rising out of its black abyss (an image developed from Du Bellay) looks forward in turn to Dullness causing universal darkness to cover all.

The myth appears most elaborately and explicitly in the fifth—hence the central—lament, that of Terpsichore, the Muse originally associated with the dance. The image of dance, however, a familiar Renaissance emblem of harmony, is here remarkable for its absence. Instead, Terpsichore tells of a usurpation. Originally the Muses held their "royall thrones . . . In th'hearts of men to rule them carefully . . ." (313–14). The idea of rule appears in many of the other speeches, always in association with the Muses' power to discipline men, guide them, enable them to keep proper *measure* in their lives. This measure is the product of the Muses' capacity to enlighten man about his own nature and his proper relation to God. Now, however, "Ignorance our kingdome did confound" (311) and her off-spring, "Blind Error, scornefull Follie, and base Spight" (317), reign in the Muses' place—in court, in the schools, in the countryside. Pleasure is divorced from instruction, the nobility told that learning is worthless, and the whole kingdom is left rudderless while the Muses wander in exile. The same charge is repeated in different contexts: Euterpe treats it in pastoral terms; Calliope laments the loss of heroic ideals which poetry preaches and commemorates; and Polyhymnia describes a profaning of the poet's sacred art.

The only break in the lament comes at the end in two stanzas (571–82) of Polyhymnia's speech which praise Queen Elizabeth and except her from the general charge that "now nor Prince nor Priest doth [Poetry] maintayne" (565). This is of course a picture of Elizabeth as her poets and learned men would have liked her to be, not as she was, and it attempts by mirroring her ideal self to persuade her to live up to it. Like Mercury waking the sleeping Lion in *Mother Hubberds Tale*, Spenser attempts through the Muse of rhetoric to remind Elizabeth of her true nature.

The elaborately formal style of *The Teares* is reemphasized by the similarity of the transitional stanza at the end of each speech, and the largely unvaried tone of the whole. There are local stylistic variations: Euterpe as a pastoral Muse speaks somewhat more simply, Calliope as an epic Muse and Urania as a Muse of religious poetry speak in somewhat higher style than most. Occasionally there is a satiric drop in the language as when Erato addresses Venus: "Faire *Cytheree* the Mother of delight,/ And Queene of beautie, now thou maist go pack" (397–98). But on the whole Spenser achieves a comparatively uniform high style appropriate to the impersonal dignity of the lament. The numerology of the poem adds to the impression of elaborate artifice: the poem contains one hundred six-line stanzas, divided in ten parts—an introduction and nine laments. Yet the pattern is imperfect, for while eight of the Muses speak ten stanzas apiece, Euterpe, the fourth, is given eleven stanzas and the introduction reduced to nine. Like the world it portrays, the form of the complaint is broken.

*William Oram*

# TO THE RIGHT HONORABLE
## the Ladie *Strange*.

*M*Ost *brave and noble Ladie, the things that make ye so much honored of the world as ye bee, are such, as (without my simple lines testimonie) are throughlie knowen to all men; namely, your excellent beautie, your vertuous behavior, and your noble match with that most honourable Lord the verie Paterne of right Nobilitie: But the causes for which ye have thus deserved of me to be honoured (if honour it be at all) are, both your particular bounties, and also some private bands of affinitie, which it hath pleased your Ladiship to acknowledge. Of which whenas I found my selfe in no part worthie, I devised this last slender meanes, both to intimate my humble affection to your Ladiship and also to make the same universallie knowen to the world; that by honouring you they might know me, and by knowing me they might honor you. Vouchsafe noble Lady to accept this simple remembrance, thogh not worthy of your self, yet such, as perhaps by good acceptance therof, ye may hereafter cull out a more meet and memorable evidence of your own excellent deserts. So recommending the same to your Ladiships good liking, I humbly take leave.*

Your La: humbly ever.

Ed. Sp.

D E D I C A T I O N: *the Ladie Strange*: Alice Spencer, wife of Ferdinando Stanley Lord Strange, was a daughter of Sir John Spencer of Althorp with whom Sp here and elsewhere claimed kinship ("some private bands of affinitie"). Sp would celebrate her with her sisters Anne and Elizabeth in *CCCHA* 536–71.

# The Teares of the Muses.

R Ehearse to me ye sacred Sisters nine:
The golden brood of great *Apolloes* wit,
Those piteous plaints and sorowfull sad tine,
Which late ye powred forth as ye did sit
Beside the silver Springs of *Helicone*,                                    5
Making your musick of hart-breaking mone.

T I T L E: The title appears to derive from a book of Latin verse by Sp's friend
Garbriel Harvey, *Smithus, vel musarum lacrymæ pro obitu T. Smithi* (1578), men-
tioned by E. K. in the notes to *SC* "September".

1–2. References to the Muses—goddesses presiding over poetry and other
intellectual skills—go back as far as Homer and Hesiod, and they are regular
topics in Renaissance mythological handbooks and dictionaries. There were
nine Muses, the daughters, according to most sources, of Zeus (Jupiter) and
Mnemosyne (Memory). Sp, with his usual freedom, makes them the
daughters of Apollo whose association with poetry would fit him to be their
father. The importance of Apollo here may have been suggested by some
pseudo-Virgilian Latin verses about the Muses which Sp almost certainly
knew, and which list the Muses in the order he follows here. The verses view
Apollo as a central creative source from which the individual Muses, like their
various arts, take their being: "The force of Apollo's mind moves the Muses
in all ways/ Phoebus remaining at the center embraces them all" (see Bennett
1932:200–02). In some cases the functions of individual Muses changed and
overlapped during the millennia of literary production before Sp, and it is
still unclear, for instance, just how he distinguished the functions of Clio,
Muse of History, and Calliope, Muse of Epic, both of whom commemorate
heroic action.     1. *rehearse*: repeat.     3. *tine*: loss.     5. *silver . . .
Helicone*: the well of Hippocrene on Mount Helicon (called "horsefoot
Helicon" at line 271 because the well was supposed to have been created
when Pegasus's foot struck the side of the mountain) was sacred to the Muses
and Apollo. Cf. Hesiod, *Theogony* 1–6.

For since the time that *Phœbus* foolish sonne
Ythundered through *Joves* avengefull wrath,
For traversing the charret of the Sunne
Beyond the compasse of his pointed path,                    10
Of you his mournfull Sisters was lamented,
Such mournfull tunes were never since invented.

Nor since that faire *Calliope* did lose
Her loved Twinnes, the dearlings of her joy,
Her *Palici*, whom her unkindly foes                        15
The fatall Sisters, did for spight destroy,
Whom all the Muses did bewaile long space;
Was ever heard such wayling in this place.

For all their groves, which with the heavenly noyses
Of their sweete instruments were wont to sound,            20
And th'hollow hills, from which their silver voyces
Were wont redoubled Echoes to rebound,

---

7. *Phœbus . . . sonne*: Phaethon, the son of Apollo and the mortal woman
Clymene.      7–12. When Phaethon asked his father to let him drive his
sun-chariot across the heavens, Apollo—against his better judgment—
allowed him to do so. Unable to control his father's horses, Phaethon left the
fixed path of the sun and began to burn heaven and earth; Jupiter was forced
to destroy him with a thunderbolt (Ovid, *Met* 2.1–326). In Ovid he is
mourned not by the Muses but by his sisters the Heliades (*Met* 2.240–43).
Having made the Muses the daughters of Apollo in the first stanza, Sp makes
them Phaethon's sisters here. In the Renaissance the story of Phaethon was
often taken as an instance of overweening ambition (see e.g. *FQ* I iv 9), and
Phaethon's inability to observe proper *measure* here looks forward to the loss
of proper proportion in the world the Muses will describe.      8. *Ythundered*:
i.e. slain by a thunderbolt.      9–10. *traversing . . . Beyond the compasse of*:
driving . . . beyond the due limits of.      10. *pointed*: appointed.
13–18. This is another piece of Spenserian myth-making. Calliope's son was
Orpheus, not the Palici, who were the twins of Jupiter and the nymph (not
the Muse) Thalia.      18. *this place*: i.e. on earth.      19–30. These stanzas
create the opposition, familiar in pastoral elegy, between the natural harmony
of the groves, winds, hills, and waters cooperating joyously together and the
discord of the same forces under the influence of present grief. Cf. e.g.
*CCCHA* 22–31.      20. *wont*: accustomed.

Did now rebound with nought but ruefull cries,
And yelling shrieks throwne up into the skies.

The trembling streames which wont in chanels cleare 25
To romble gently downe with murmur soft,
And were by them right tunefull taught to beare
A Bases part amongst their consorts oft;
Now forst to overflowe with brackish teares,
With troublous noyse did dull their daintie eares. 30

The joyous Nymphes and lightfoote Faeries
Which thether came to heare their musick sweet,
And to the measure of their melodies
Did learne to move their nimble shifting feete;
Now hearing them so heavily lament, 35
Like heavily lamenting from them went.

And all that els was wont to worke delight
Through the divine infusion of their skill,
And all that els seemd faire and fresh in sight,
So made by nature for to serve their will, 40
Was turned now to dismall heavinesse,
Was turned now to dreadfull uglinesse.

Ay me, what thing on earth that all thing breeds,
Might be the cause of so impatient plight?
What furie, or what feend with felon deeds 45
Hath stirred up so mischievous despight?
Can griefe then enter into heavenly harts,
And pierce immortall breasts with mortall smarts?

Vouchsafe ye then, whom onely it concernes,
To me those secret causes to display; 50
For none but you, or who of you it learnes
Can rightfully aread so dolefull lay.

---

28. *consorts*: groups of musical instruments (i.e. the natural instruments of
groves, hills, and waters).    30. *daintie*: delicate.    33. *measure*:
rhythm.    37. *els*: otherwise.    44. *plight*: condition.    52. *aread*: utter.

Begin thou eldest Sister of the crew,
And let the rest in order thee ensew.

### Clio

Heare thou great Father of the Gods on hie          55
That most art dreaded for thy thunder darts:
And thou our Syre that raignst in *Castalie*
And mount *Parnasse*, the God of goodly Arts:
Heare and behold the miserable state
Of us thy daughters, dolefull desolate.          60

Behold the fowle reproach and open shame,
The which is day by day unto us wrought
By such as hate the honour of our name,
The foes of learning, and each gentle thought;
They not contented us themselves to scorne,          65
Doo seeke to make us of the world forlorne.

Ne onely they that dwell in lowly dust,
The sonnes of darknes and of ignoraunce;
But they, whom thou great *Jove* by doome unjust
Didst to the type of honour earst advaunce;          70
They now puft up with sdeignfull insolence,
Despise the brood of blessed Sapience.

The sectaries of my celestiall skill,
That wont to be the worlds chiefe ornament,
And learned Impes that wont to shoote up still,          75
And grow to hight of kingdomes government
They underkeep, and with their spredding armes
Doo beat their buds, that perish through their harmes.

---

54. *ensew*: follow.          55–114. As the Muse of History, Clio was associated
with the recounting of heroic deeds.          57. *Castalie*: The Castalian spring,
sacred to Apollo and the Muses, was located on Mount Parnassus.
64. *gentle*: noble.          66. *forlorne*: abandoned.          69. *doome*: judgment.
70. *type*: highest point.          72. *Sapience*: wisdom.          73. *sectaries*:
followers.          75. *Impes*: shoots, i.e. offspring. Sp's familiar flower metaphor
continues for the rest of the stanza.

It most behoves the honorable race
Of mightie Peeres, true wisedome to sustaine,                    80
And with their noble countenaunce to grace
The learned forheads, without gifts or gaine:
Or rather learnd themselves behoves to bee;
That is the girlond of Nobilitie.

But (ah) all otherwise they doo esteeme                          85
Of th'heavenly gift of wisdomes influence,
And to be learned it a base thing deeme;
Base minded they that want intelligence:
For God himselfe for wisedome most is praised,
And men to God thereby are nighest raised.                       90

But they doo onely strive themselves to raise
Through pompous pride, and foolish vanitie;
In th'eyes of people they put all their praise,
And onely boast of Armes and Auncestrie:
But vertuous deeds, which did those Armes first give             95
To their Grandsyres, they care not to atchive.

So I, that doo all noble feates professe
To register, and sound in trump of gold;
Through their bad dooings, or base slothfulnesse,
Finde nothing worthie to be writ, or told:                      100
For better farre it were to hide their names,
Than telling them to blazon out their blames.

So shall succeeding ages have no light
Of things forepast, nor moniments of time,
And all that in this world is worthie hight                     105
Shall die in darknesse, and lie hid in slime:
Therefore I mourne with deep harts sorrowing,
Because I nothing noble have to sing.

With that she raynd such store of streaming teares,
That could have made a stonie heart to weep,                    110

94. *Armes*: heraldic insignia; hence, external trappings of rank.
102. *blazon out*: proclaim.

And all her Sisters rent their golden heares,
And their faire faces with salt humour steep.
So ended shee: and then the next anew
Began her grievous plaint as doth ensew.

### Melpomene.

O who shall powre into my swollen eyes                    115
A sea of teares that never may be dryde,
A brasen voice that may with shrilling cryes
Pierce the dull heavens and fill the ayer wide,
And yron sides that sighing may endure,
To waile the wretchednes of world impure?                 120

Ah wretched world the den of wickednesse,
Deformd with filth and fowle iniquitie;
Ah wretched world the house of heavinesse,
Fild with the wreaks of mortall miserie;
Ah wretched world, and all that is therein,                125
The vassals of Gods wrath, and slaves of sin.

Most miserable creature under sky
Man without understanding doth appeare;
For all this worlds affliction he thereby,
And Fortunes freakes is wisely taught to beare:            130
Of wretched life the onely joy shee is,
And th'only comfort in calamities.

She armes the brest with constant patience,
Against the bitter throwes of dolours darts,
She solaceth with rules of Sapience                        135
The gentle mind, in midst of worldlie smarts:
When he is sad, shee seeks to make him merie,
And doth refresh his sprights when they be werie.

But he that is of reasons skill bereft,
And wants the staffe of wisedome him to stay,             140

112. *humour*: liquid, i.e. tears.    115–74. Melpomene is the Muse of
Tragedy.    123. *heavinesse*: sorrow.    130. *freakes*: changes.
133. *patience*: the capacity to suffer uncomplainingly.

Is like a ship in midst of tempest left
Withouten helme or Pilot her to sway,
Full sad and dreadfull is that ships event:
So is the man that wants intendiment.

Whie then doo foolish men so much despize          145
The precious store of this celestiall riches?
Why doo they banish us, that patronize
The name of learning? Most unhappie wretches,
The which lie drowned in deep wretchednes,
Yet doo not see their owne unhappines.          150

My part it is and my professed skill
The Stage with Tragick buskin to adorne,
And fill the Scene with plaint and outcries shrill
Of wretched persons, to misfortune borne:
But none more tragick matter I can finde          155
Than this, of men depriv'd of sense and minde.

For all mans life me seemes a Tragedy,
Full of sad sights and sore Catastrophees;
First comming to the world with weeping eye,
Where all his dayes like dolorous Trophees,          160
Are heapt with spoyles of fortune and of feare,
And he at last laid forth on balefull beare.

So all with rufull spectacles is fild
Fit for *Megera* or *Persephone*;
But I that in true Tragedies am skild,          165
The flowre of wit, finde nought to busie me:
Therefore I mourne, and pitifully mone,
Because that mourning matter I have none.

---

143. *dreadfull*: to be dreaded. *event*: fate.     144. *intendiment*:
understanding.     147. *that* . . . : ref. to "they."     152. *Tragick buskin*: i.e.
tragic drama. The actors of Greek tragedies wore a boot, the *cothurnus*, which
Renaissance writers Englished as "buskin."     160. *Trophees*: memorials.
164. *Megera*: one of the three Furies. *Persephone*: the consort of Hades, the
god of the underworld.

Then gan she wofully to waile, and wring
Her wretched hands in lamentable wise;                    170
And all her Sisters thereto answering,
Threw forth lowd shrieks and drerie dolefull cries.
So rested she: and then the next in rew,
Began her grievous plaint as doth ensew.

### *Thalia.*

Where be the sweete delights of learnings treasure,      175
That wont with Comick sock to beautefie
The painted Theaters, and fill with pleasure
The listners eyes, and eares with melodie;
In which I late was wont to raine as Queene,
And maske in mirth with Graces well beseene?             180

O all is gone, and all that goodly glee,
Which wont to be the glorie of gay wits,
Is layd abed, and no where now to see;
And in her roome unseemly Sorrow sits,
With hollow browes and greisly countenaunce,             185
Marring my joyous gentle dalliaunce.

And him beside sits ugly Barbarisme,
And brutish Ignorance, ycrept of late
Out of dredd darknes of the deep Abysme,
Where being bredd, he light and heaven does hate:        190
They in the mindes of men now tyrannize,
And the faire Scene with rudenes foule disguize.

All places they with follie have possest,
And with vaine toyes the vulgare entertaine;
But me have banished, with all the rest                  195
That whilome wont to wait upon my traine,

---

175–234. Thalia is the Muse of Comedy.    180. *Graces*: the three
goddesses, often associated with the Muses, who preside over all civilized
activity, bestowing on men "all gracious gifts . . . Which decke the body or
adorne the mynde" (*FQ* VI x 23).    184. *roome*: place.    192. *rudenes*:
barbarousness, incivility.

Fine Counterfesaunce and unhurtfull Sport,
Delight and Laughter deckt in seemly sort.

All these, and all that els the Comick Stage
With seasoned wit and goodly pleasance graced;        200
By which mans life in his likest image
Was limned forth, are wholly now defaced;
And those sweete wits which wont the like to frame,
Are now despizd, and made a laughing game.

And he the man, whom Nature selfe had made        205
To mock her selfe, and Truth to imitate,
With kindly counter under Mimick shade,
Our pleasant *Willy*, ah is dead of late:
With whom all joy and jolly meriment
Is also deaded, and in dolour drent.        210

In stead thereof scoffing Scurrilitie,
And scornfull Follie with Contempt is crept,
Rolling in rymes of shameles ribaudrie
Without regard, or due Decorum kept,
Each idle wit at will presumes to make,        215
And doth the Learneds taske upon him take.

But that same gentle Spirit, from whose pen
Large streames of honnie and sweete Nectar flowe,
Scorning the boldnes of such base-borne men,
Which dare their follies forth so rashlie throwe;        220
Doth rather choose to sit in idle Cell,
Than so himselfe to mockerie to sell.

197. *Fine Counterfesaunce*: artful impersonation.    202. *limned*:
portrayed.    206. *mock*: imitate.    207. *kindly counter*: lifelike
imitation.    208. The identity of *Willy* is unknown; it is possibly a pastoral
pseudonym for Sir Philip Sidney who died in 1587.    211–16. The
exaggerated alliteration of this stanza parodies the "rhymes" of the poets
Thalia mocks.    217. *that . . . Spirit*: It is not known whom Thalia refers to
here; he is probably not the dead Willy of lines 205–10 since he is living but
silent. Renwick (1928) pp. 210–11 suggests Sp is referring to himself.
222. *himselfe . . . sell*: to allow himself to be mocked.

So am I made the servant of the manie,
And laughing stocke of all that list to scorne,
Not honored nor cared for of anie; 225
But loath'd of losels as a thing forlorne:
Therefore I mourne and sorrow with the rest,
Untill my cause of sorrow be redrest.

Therewith she lowdly did lament and shrike,
Pouring forth streames of teares abundantly, 230
And all her Sisters with compassion like,
The breaches of her singulfs did supply.
So rested shee: and then the next in rew
Began her grievous plaint, as doth ensew.

*Euterpe.*
Like as the dearling of the Summers pryde, 235
Faire *Philomele*, when winters stormie wrath
The goodly fields, that earst so gay were dyde
In colours divers, quite despoyled hath,
All comfortlesse doth hide her chearlesse head
During the time of that her widowhead: 240

So we, that earst were wont in sweet accord
All places with our pleasant notes to fill,
Whilest favourable times did us afford
Free libertie to chaunt our charmes at will:
All comfortlesse upon the bared bow, 245
Like wofull Culvers doo sit wayling now.

For far more bitter storme than winters stowre
The beautie of the world hath lately wasted,

---

226. *losels*: good-for-nothings.    232. *singulfs*: sobs.
235–300. Euterpe's instrument, the flute, became associated with the
shepherd's pipe of pastoral poetry. Sp accordingly gives her speech a pastoral
coloring.    236. *Philomele*: the nightingale.    241. *accord*: harmony.
244. *charmes*: songs.    246. *Culvers*: doves.    247. *stowre*: storm, turmoil.

And those fresh buds, which wont so faire to flowre,
Hath marred quite, and all their blossoms blasted:           250
And those yong plants, which wont with fruit t'abound,
Now without fruite or leaves are to be found.

A stonie coldnesse hath benumbd the sence
And livelie spirits of each living wight,
And dimd with darknesse their intelligence,                 255
Darknesse more than *Cymerians* daylie night:
And monstrous error flying in the ayre,
Hath mard the face of all that semed fayre.

Image of hellish horrour Ignorance,
Borne in the bosome of the black *Abysse*,                  260
And fed with furies milke, for sustenaunce
Of his weake infancie, begot amisse
By yawning Sloth on his owne mother Night;
So hee his sonnes both Syre and brother hight.

He armd with blindnesse and with boldnes stout,             265
(For blind is bold) hath our fayre light defaced;
And gathering unto him a ragged rout
Of *Faunes* and *Satyres*, hath our dwellings raced
And our chast bowers, in which all vertue rained,
With brutishnesse and beastlie filth hath stained.          270

The sacred springs of horsefoot *Helicon*,
So oft bedeawed with our learned layes,
And speaking streames of pure *Castalion*,
The famous witnesse of our wonted praise,
They trampled have with their fowle footings trade,         275
And like to troubled puddles have them made.

---

256. *Cymerians daylie night*: In the *Odyssey* 11.14–19 the Cimmerians are said
to live in a land at the end of the world, shrouded in perpetual darkness and
mist.          259–64. This stanza echoes Du Bellay's "La Musagnœmachie" lines
37–44.          268. *raced*: i.e. razed.          271. *horsefoot Helicon*: See note to line
5 above.          273. *pure Castalion*: See note on *Castalie*, line 57 above.

Our pleasant groves, which planted were with paines,
That with our musick wont so oft to ring,
And arbors sweet, in which the Shepheards swaines
Were wont so oft their Pastoralls to sing,                    280
They have cut downe and all their pleasaunce mard,
That now no pastorall is to bee hard.

In stead of them fowle Goblins and Shriekowles,
With fearfull howling do all places fill;
And feeble *Eccho* now laments and howles,                    285
The dreadfull accents of their outcries shrill.
So all is turned into wildernesse,
Whilest ignorance the Muses doth oppresse.

And I whose joy was earst with Spirit full
To teach the warbling pipe to sound aloft,                    290
My spirits now dismayd with sorrow dull,
Doo mone my miserie in silence soft.
Therefore I mourne and waile incessantly,
Till please the heavens affoord me remedy.

Therewith she wayled with exceeding woe                       295
And pitious lamentation did make,
And all her sisters seeing her doo soe,
With equall plaints her sorrowe did partake.
So rested shee: and then the next in rew,
Began her grievous plaint as doth ensew.                      300

*Terpsichore.*
Who so hath in the lap of soft delight
Beene long time luld, and fed with pleasures sweet,
Feareles through his own fault or Fortunes spight,
To tumble into sorrow and regreet,
Yf chaunce him fall into calamitie,                           305
Findes greater burthen of his miserie.

301–60. Terpsichore is the Muse of Dance, but here this traditional function
is not mentioned. See Introduction.    303. *Feareles*: not fearing.

So wee that earst in joyance did abound
And in the bosome of all blis did sit,
Like virgin Queenes with laurell garlands cround,
For vertues meed and ornament of wit;⁣    310
Sith ignorance our kingdome did confound,
Bee now become most wretched wightes on ground:

And in our royall thrones which lately stood
In th'hearts of men to rule them carefully,
He now hath placed his accursed brood,    315
By him begotten of fowle infamy;
Blind Error, scornefull Follie, and base Spight,
Who hold by wrong, that wee should have by right.

They to the vulgar sort now pipe and sing,
And make them merrie with their fooleries,    320
They cherelie chaunt and rymes at randon fling,
The fruitfull spawne of their ranke fantasies:
They feede the eares of fooles with flattery,
And good men blame, and losels magnify:

All places they doo with their toyes possesse,    325
And raigne in liking of the multitude,
The schooles they fill with fond newfanglenesse,
And sway in Court with pride and rashnes rude;
Mongst simple shepheards they do boast their skill,
And say their musicke matcheth *Phœbus* quill.    330

The noble hearts to pleasures they allure,
And tell their Prince that learning is but vaine,
Faire Ladies loves they spot with thoughts impure,
And gentle mindes with lewd delights distaine:
Clerks they to loathly idlenes entice,    335
And fill their bookes with discipline of vice.

310. *meed*: reward. 311. *confound*: overthrow. 322. *fantasies*:
imaginations. 324. *losels*: scoundrels. 325. *toyes*: trivial
productions. 327. *The schooles*: the universities. *newfanglenesse*: worthless
innovation. 336. *discipline of*: teaching in.

So every where they rule and tyrannize,
For their usurped kingdomes maintenaunce,
The whiles we silly Maides, whom they dispize,
And with reprochfull scorne discountenaunce,                    340
From our owne native heritage exilde,
Walk through the world of every one revilde.

Nor anie one doth care to call us in,
Or once vouchsafeth us to entertaine,
Unlesse some one perhaps of gentle kin                          345
For pitties sake compassion our paine,
And yeeld us some reliefe in this distresse:
Yet to be so reliev'd is wretchednesse.

So wander we all carefull comfortlesse,
Yet none doth care to comfort us at all;                        350
So seeke we helpe our sorrow to redresse,
Yet none vouchsafes to answere to our call:
Therefore we mourne and pittilesse complaine,
Because none living pittieth our paine.

With that she wept and wofullie waymented,                      355
That naught on earth her griefe might pacifie;
And all the rest her dolefull din augmented,
With shrikes and groanes and grievous agonie.
So ended shee: and then the next in rew,
Began her piteous plaint as doth ensew.                         360

*Erato.*
Ye gentle Spirits breathing from above,
Where ye in *Venus* silver bowre were bred,

---

339. *silly*: helpless, innocent.     353. *pittilesse*: unpitied.     355. *waymented*:
lamented.     361–420. Erato's instrument is the lyre; she is accordingly
associated with love-poetry.     361–66. "Thoughts" (363) is the direct
object of "breathing" (361) which means "voicing." The poet-lovers of this
stanza are "bred" in "Venus . . . bowre" (362) because their souls originally
derive from the central creative source she embodies, but also perhaps
because they are educated in the discipline of love. (Cf. the related treatment

Thoughts halfe devine full of the fire of love,
With beawtie kindled and with pleasure fed,
Which ye now in securitie possesse,                              365
Forgetfull of your former heavinesse:

Now change the tenor of your joyous layes,
With which ye use your loves to deifie,
And blazon foorth an earthlie beauties praise,
Above the compasse of the arched skie:                          370
Now change your praises into piteous cries,
And Eulogies turne into Elegies.

Such as ye wont whenas those bitter stounds
Of raging love first gan you to torment,
And launch your hearts with lamentable wounds                   375
Of secret sorrow and sad languishment,
Before your Loves did take you unto grace;
Those now renew as fitter for this place.

For I that rule in measure moderate
The tempest of that stormie passion,                            380
And use to paint in rimes the troublous state
Of Lovers life in likest fashion,
Am put from practise of my kindlie skill,
Banisht by those that Love with leawdnes fill.

Love wont to be schoolmaster of my skill,                       385
And the devicefull matter of my song;
Sweete Love devoyd of villanie or ill,
But pure and spotles, as at first he sprong
Out of th'Almighties bosome, where he nests;
From thence infused into mortall brests.                        390

of Cupid in *CCCHA* 840.) The passage is lightly Neoplatonic in its
language, though lines 365–66 minimize any other-worldly emphasis,
recalling the vision of satisfied earthly lovers in *HL* 273–93. The first line of
this stanza resembles the simpler line of *RT* 281 describing Sir Philip Sidney
as "Most gentle spirit breathed from above"; it is unclear which version came
first.      370. *compasse*: circle.      373. *stounds*: pangs, feelings.
375. *launch*: pierce.

Such high conceipt of that celestiall fire,
The base-borne brood of blindnes cannot gesse,
Ne ever dare their dunghill thoughts aspire
Unto so loftie pitch of perfectnesse,
But rime at riot, and doo rage in love;                    395
Yet little wote what doth thereto behove.

Faire *Cytheree* the Mother of delight,
And Queene of beautie, now thou maist go pack;
For lo thy Kingdome is defaced quight,
Thy scepter rent, and power put to wrack;                   400
And thy gay Sonne, that winged God of Love,
May now goe prune his plumes like ruffed Dove.

And ye three Twins to light by *Venus* brought,
The sweete companions of the Muses late,
From whom what ever thing is goodly thought                 405
Doth borrow grace, the fancie to aggrate;
Go beg with us, and be companions still
As heretofore of good, so now of ill.

For neither you nor we shall anie more
Finde entertainment, or in Court or Schoole:                410
For that which was accounted heretofore
The learneds meed, is now lent to the foole;
He sings of love, and maketh loving layes,
And they him heare, and they him highly prayse.

With that she powred foorth a brackish flood                415
Of bitter teares, and made exceeding mone;
And all her Sisters seeing her sad mood,
With lowd laments her answered all at one.
So ended she: and then the next in rew
Began her grievous plaint, as doth ensew.                   420

392. *gesse*: reckon.     395. *at riot*: "a term of venery, used of ill-trained
hounds" (Renwick 1928:213).     397. *Cytheree*: Venus.     401. *thy gay
Sonne*: i.e. Cupid.     403. *ye three Twins*: the Graces. See the note to line
180 above.     412. *lent*: given.

*Calliope.*

To whom shall I my evill case complaine,
Or tell the anguish of my inward smart,
Sith none is left to remedie my paine,
Or deignes to pitie a perplexed hart;
But rather seekes my sorrow to augment          425
With fowle reproach, and cruell banishment.

For they to whom I used to applie
The faithfull service of my learned skill,
The goodly off-spring of *Joves* progenie,
That wont the world with famous acts to fill;    430
Whose living praises in heroïck style,
It is my chiefe profession to compyle.

They all corrupted through the rust of time,
That doth all fairest things on earth deface,
Or through unnoble sloth, or sinfull crime        435
That doth degenerate the noble race;
Have both desire of worthie deeds forlorne,
And name of learning utterly doo scorne.

Ne doo they care to have the auncestrie
Of th'old Heroës memorizde anew,                  440
Ne doo they care that late posteritie
Should know their names, or speak their praises dew;
But die forgot from whence at first they sprong,
As they themselves shalbe forgot ere long.

What bootes it then to come from glorious         445
Forefathers, or to have been nobly bredd?
What oddes twixt *Irus* and old *Inachus*,
Twixt best and worst, when both alike are dedd;
If none of neither mention should make,
Nor out of dust their memories awake?             450

---

421–80. Calliope is the Muse of Epic and hence, with Clio, a recorder of
great deeds.

Or who would ever care to doo brave deed,
Or strive in vertue others to excell;
If none should yeeld him his deserved meed,
Due praise, that is the spur of dooing well?
For if good were not praised more than ill,                    455
None would choose goodnes of his owne freewill.

Therefore the nurse of vertue I am hight,
And golden Trompet of eternitie,
That lowly thoughts lift up to heavens hight,
And mortall men have powre to deifie:                          460
*Bacchus* and *Hercules* I raisd to heaven,
And *Charlemaine*, amongst the Starris seaven.

But now I will my golden Clarion rend,
And will henceforth immortalize no more:
Sith I no more finde worthie to commend                        465
For prize of value, or for learned lore:
For noble Peeres whom I was wont to raise,
Now onely seeke for pleasure, nought for praise.

Their great revenues all in sumptuous pride
They spend, that nought to learning they may spare;            470
And the rich fee which Poets wont divide,
Now Parasites and Sycophants doo share:
Therefore I mourne and endlesse sorrow make,
Both for my selfe and for my Sisters sake.

With that she lowdly gan to waile and shrike,                  475
And from her eyes a sea of teares did powre,
And all her sisters with compassion like,
Did more increase the sharpnes of her showre.
So ended she: and then the next in rew
Began her plaint, as doth herein ensew.                        480

---

466. *prize of value*: i.e. a proof of warlike prowess.

### Urania.

What wrath of Gods, or wicked influence
Of Starres conspiring wretched men t'afflict,
Hath powrd on earth this noyous pestilence,
That mortall mindes doth inwardly infect
With love of blindnesse and of ignorance,                                485
To dwell in darkenesse without sovenance?

What difference twixt man and beast is left
When th'heavenlie light of knowledge is put out,
And th'ornaments of wisdome are bereft?
Then wandreth he in error and in doubt,                                 490
Unweeting of the danger hee is in,
Through fleshes frailtie and deceipt of sin.

In this wide world in which they wretches stray,
It is the onelie comfort which they have,
It is their light, their loadstarre and their day;                        495
But hell and darkenesse and the grislie grave
Is ignorance, the enemie of grace,
That mindes of men borne heavenlie doth debace.

Through knowledge we behold the worlds creation,
How in his cradle first he fostred was;                                  500
And judge of Natures cunning operation,
How things she formed of a formelesse mas;
By knowledge wee do learne our selves to knowe,
And what to man, and what to God wee owe.

481–540. Urania was traditionally the Muse of Astronomy; she thus
becomes a Christian Muse, associated with religious poetry. Cf. Du Bartas,
*L'Uranie ou Muse Celeste* (1574).     483. *noyous*: harmful.
486. *sovenance*: remembrance.     489. *ornaments . . . bereft*: One might read
the line "[when] learned poets are left destitute." But in line 487 Sp seems to
ask what will distinguish man from beast when *humankind* is bereft of the
divine poets ("th'ornaments of wisdome") who voice divine knowledge and
wisdom.     495. *loadstarre*: guiding star.

From hence wee mount aloft unto the skie,                     505
And looke into the Christall firmament,
There we behold the heavens great *Hierarchie*,
The Starres pure light, the Spheres swift movement,
The Spirites and Intelligences fayre,
And Angels waighting on th'Almighties chayre.                 510

And there with humble minde and high insight,
Th'eternall Makers majestie wee viewe,
His love, his truth, his glorie, and his might,
And mercie more than mortall men can vew.
O soveraigne Lord, ô soveraigne happinesse                   515
To see thee, and thy mercie measurelesse:

Such happines have they, that doo embrace
The precepts of my heavenlie discipline;
But shame and sorrow and accursed case
Have they, that scorne the schoole of arts divine,           520
And banish me, which do professe the skill
To make men heavenly wise, through humbled will.

How ever yet they mee despise and spight,
I feede on sweet contentment of my thought,
And please my selfe with mine owne selfe-delight,            525
In contemplation of things heavenlie wrought:
So loathing earth, I looke up to the sky,
And being driven hence I thether fly.

Thence I behold the miserie of men,
Which want the blis that wisedom would them breed,           530
And like brute beasts doo lie in loathsome den,
Of ghostly darkenes, and of gastlie dreed:
For whom I mourne and for my selfe complaine,
And for my Sisters eake whom they disdaine.

With that shee wept and waild so pityouslie,                 535
As if her eyes had beene two springing wells:

518. *discipline*: teaching.     520. *schoole*: i.e. knowledge, discipline.
530. *them breed*: create for them.

And all the rest her sorrow to supplie,
Did throw forth shrieks and cries and dreery yells.
So ended shee, and then the next in rew,
Began her mournfull plaint as doth ensew.          540

*Polyhymnia.*
A dolefull case desires a dolefull song,
Without vaine art or curious complements,
And squallid Fortune into basenes flong,
Doth scorne the pride of wonted ornaments.
Then fittest are these ragged rimes for mee,          545
To tell my sorrowes that exceeding bee:

For the sweet numbers and melodious measures,
With which I wont the winged words to tie,
And make a tunefull Diapase of pleasures,
Now being let to runne at libertie          550
By those which have no skill to rule them right,
Have now quite lost their naturall delight.

Heapes of huge words uphoorded hideously,
With horrid sound though having little sence,
They thinke to be chiefe praise of Poëtry;          555
And thereby wanting due intelligence,
Have mard the face of goodly Poësie,
And made a monster of their fantasie:

Whilom in ages past none might professe
But Princes and high Priests that secret skill,          560
The sacred lawes therein they wont expresse,
And with deepe Oracles their verses fill:

541–600. Polyhymnia is the Muse of Rhetoric; here she deals specifically
with bad poetry.          542. *curious complements*: ingenious
elaborations.          549. *Diapase*: diapason, a consonance of the highest and
lowest notes. More generally "diapese" would be associated (through the idea
of a musically-constructed, harmonious cosmos) with the fullness and
perfection of the created world.          553. *uphoorded*: heaped up.
556. *intelligence*: understanding.

Then was shee held in soveraigne dignitie,
And made the noursling of Nobilitie.

But now nor Prince nor Priest doth her maintayne,     565
But suffer her prophaned for to be
Of the base vulgar, that with hands uncleane
Dares to pollute her hidden mysterie.
And treadeth under foote hir holie things,
Which was the care of Kesars and of Kings.     570

One onelie lives, her ages ornament,
And myrrour of her Makers majestie;
That with rich bountie and deare cherishment,
Supports the praise of noble Poësie:
Ne onelie favours them which it professe,     575
But is her selfe a peereles Poëtresse.

Most peereles Prince, most peereles Poëtresse,
The true *Pandora* of all heavenly graces,
Divine *Elisa*, sacred Emperesse:
Live she for ever, and her royall P'laces     580
Be fild with praises of divinest wits,
That her eternize with their heavenlie writs.

Some few beside, this sacred skill esteme,
Admirers of her glorious excellence,
Which being lightned with her beawties beme,     585
Are thereby fild with happie influence:
And lifted up above the worldes gaze,
To sing with Angels her immortall praize.

---

564. *noursling*: i.e. the care, charge.     571. *One onelie lives*: Elizabeth I.
578. *Pandora*: a woman created by the gods with all gifts. Natalis Comes
(*Mythologiae* 4.7) explains her name as a combination of *Pan* (= all) and
*doron* (= gifts).     586. *influence*: divine impression. Elizabeth is compared
with the moon whose astral "influence" affects the characters and the lives of
human beings.

But all the rest as borne of salvage brood,
And having beene with Acorns alwaies fed;                    590
Can no whit savour this celestiall food,
But with base thoughts are into blindnesse led,
And kept from looking on the lightsome day:
For whome I waile and weepe all that I may.

Eftsoones such store of teares shee forth did powre,         595
As if shee all to water would have gone;
And all her sisters seeing her sad stowre,
Did weep and waile and made exceeding mone,
And all their learned instruments did breake.
The rest untold no loving tongue can speake.                 600

FINIS.

595. *Eftsoones*: again.

# Virgils Gnat

**V**irgils Gnat is Spenser's version of the *Culex*, one of the minor poems (*opuscula*) included in the Virgilian appendix. Most modern scholars doubt that Virgil in fact wrote the poem and attribute it instead to Ovid or to an anonymous parodist writing in post-Augustan Rome. But for Spenser and his contemporaries the *Culex* was unquestionably the work of Tityrus, as Virgil is called deferentially throughout *The Shepheardes Calender*. Both his humanist education and his familiarity with the theories of the Pléiade would have impressed upon Spenser that the poem was accordingly a piece of literature intrinsically worth close study, imitation, and even translation. Since Suetonius had stated, in a comment regularly found in Renaissance editions of Virgil, that the *Culex* had been composed when the poet was only sixteen and since the poem itself alludes to its author's projected epic, Spenser may have been especially drawn to it during the late 1570s when, as a fledgling poet writing eclogues for *The Shepheardes Calender*, he was conscious of establishing the pattern for his own Virgilian career. In 1628 William Lisle remarked that "Master Spencer long since translated the Gnat, (a little fragment of Virgil's excellence), giving the world peradventure to conceive, that hee would at one time or other have gone through the rest of this poet's workes" (Cummings 1971:146–47). Spenser, of course, translated no more Virgil, but by passing, like Virgil, from pastoral poetry (the *Calender* and the *Gnat*) to epic verse (*The Faerie Queene*), he did "go through" a major portion of that poet's works imaginatively.

To describe the *Culex* is in the main to describe *Virgils Gnat*, since Spenser offers a fairly faithful rendering of the Latin text established by Pietro Bembo in his *Dialogue on the Culex and*

*Terence* (1530) and published at Antwerp in the 1542 Dumaeus edition of Virgil's works. Virgil's poem is only ostensibly a pastoral. Shepherd and flock, serpent and flea—typical appurtenances of bucolic poetry—do occupy a rustic landscape and figure exclusively in its naive plot. But the *Culex*, as its opening says plainly, is primarily a jest and a sport. It plays with its story and toys with its audience in producing a classical equivalent of a shaggy-dog story.

So mannered, in fact, is the poem's style and so meandering is the poet's tracing of the plot that we may lose the thread of the narrative line. The heroic and mythological allusions and the obtrusive display of learning, evident principally in elegant circumlocutions, constantly distract our attention from the basic story as a sequential chain of incidents. As the poem begins, the author abjures the "bigger notes" (11) of epic, but even as he does so he emphasizes what he will not do rather than what he will, using the rhetorical ploy of *occupatio*. Then, as the narrative proceeds, he seizes every opportunity to amplify and elevate "This Gnats small Poeme" (5) much as Spenser's narrator does also in *Muiopotmos*. He cannot comment on the happiness of the shepherd's carefree rural life without expatiating on the life of urbane luxury; he mythologizes at great length the shady grove in which the flock seeks rest; most obviously, he devotes almost half the poem to the gnat's complaint, which, because it describes many inhabitants of the underworld (both Hades and the Elysian fields), manages to insinuate into the poem a roll-call of celebrities, a whole anthology of little subordinate stories. This fabulous material, which disrupts the pastoral serenity of the poem, touches on tragic figures such as Sisyphus and Tantalus, enduring punishment in Tartarus, various chaste women (Alcestis, Penelope, Eurydice) who epitomize heroic love, the military heroes from both sides of the Trojan War (Hector, Ajax, Achilles, etc.), and, finally, some worthies venerated for their service to the Roman state. When we reach the end of the *Culex* we realize that, despite his disclaimers, the playful poet, "weaving slenderly" (3) has spun a very sophisticated yarn, and that the genre of the poem is an enigmatic fusion of pastoral, heroic, mock-heroic, and elegiac kinds that can scarcely be unravelled as readily as the introduction would have us believe.

The real enigma of Spenser's version of the *Culex* concerns the unusual interpretation that its dedicatory sonnet simultaneously urges on and withholds from us. Without the sonnet, we might well rest content with the notion that Spenser translated the *Culex* as an exercise preliminary to the effort of overgoing Virgil in epic. But the sonnet reveals publicly and overtly that Spenser saw in the *Culex* a way of expressing and yet concealing intensely private and covert meanings. It is even possible that in applying the poem to his own condition Spenser was tapping an allegorical undercurrent in the *Culex* itself. Thomas Lodge and John Dryden both hinted that Renaissance readers may have taken the *Culex* itself as a political allegory.

Decoding the "riddle rare" implicit in Spenser's appropriation of the *Culex* is by no means easy, though the coterie audience that may have read it before its publication probably grasped Spenser's purposes without difficulty. One possibility is that the action refers to Spenser's relationship with the earl of Leicester. In that case, the poem records the ingratitude shown Spenser (the plaintive gnat) by Leicester (the negligent shepherd), when Spenser warned Leicester in 1579 about the dangers facing the English flock in the proposed Alençon marriage (the snake in the grass). According to this interpretation, Spenser so offended Leicester that his employer and would-be patron sent him off to Ireland with Lord Grey. A second possibility is that the poem is Spenser's complaint against the queen's ingratitude to those who admonished her against the French match. In that case, the shepherd sleeping in his shady grove is an emblem of the false security everywhere decried in the *Complaints* and an anticipation of the slumbering regal lion in *Mother Hubberds Tale*. Accordingly, the shepherd's violent reaction to the gnat's well-motivated warning represents Elizabeth's harsh treatment of Walsingham, Sidney, and even, perhaps, Leicester (the group commemorated in *The Ruines of Time*) for daring to oppose her. Whatever the precise significance of the enigmatic allegory Spenser derives from the *Culex*, it is important that the poem juxtaposes the Virgil-Augustus relationship with the gnat-shepherd relationship. It is important, too, especially given Spenser's interest in poets, patrons, and fame in the two poems preceding *Virgils Gnat* in the *Complaints*-volume that at the end the shepherd raises a monument to the gnat. Since, like *The Teares of the Muses*, *Virgils Gnat* deals with the interdependence between the lowly poet and the sponsors who authorize his writing, the erection of that monument suggests that the patron is capable of conferring fame on the author just as much as the author is capable of "eternizing" the patron: "Professing thee I lifted am aloft" (33). As Spenser's reclamation of the *Culex* itself indicates, even humble literary monuments can outlast the civilizations that gave them their being and can bring enduring fame to those who crafted them.

*Ronald Bond*

## Virgils Gnat.
## Long since dedicated
### To the most noble and excellent Lord,
## the Earle of Leicester, late
## deceased.

W Rong'd, yet not daring to expresse my paine,
To you (great Lord) the causer of my care,
In clowdie teares my case I thus complaine
Unto your selfe, that onely privie are:
 But if that any Oedipus unware                                    5
Shall chaunce, through power of some divining spright,

D E D I C A T I O N: Lacking a title page, the work is ushered in by this dedication,
and a dedicatory poem addressed not just to the dedicatee, but to the inquisitive
general reader. The teasing sonnet makes clear only that Sp's translation of the
*Culex* is more than a mere poetic exercise.    *Long since dedicated*: Like the
phrase used in the dedication of *MHT*—"long sithens composed in the raw
conceipt of my youth"—this helps us to date the poem, and helps both to
exonerate the mature Sp of the 1590s from the charge that the poem is unworthy
of him and to distance him from the political events to which it alludes covertly.
*VG* was probably written in 1579 during the Alençon crisis, when Sp was intent
upon finding a suitable patron for *SC*, eventually offered to Sir Philip Sidney,
only after the earl of Leicester had been considered as a candidate. In the first of
*Two . . . Letters* (1580), written in October, 1579, Sp advises Gabriel Harvey
that the time is ripe for advancement, "when occasion is so fairely offered of
Estimation and Preferment," but also notes that it is folly "not to regarde
aforehande the inclination and qualitie of him, to whome wee dedicate oure
Bookes." By August, 1580, Sp had left the employ of the earl of Leicester, in
whose service he had expected to go to France, and had taken up an appointment
as secretary to Lord Grey in Ireland.    *Earle of Leicester*: Robert Dudley, leader
of a puritan wing of politicians, was a favorite patron of writers, especially
historians, translators, and religious writers. *VG* is the only work Sp dedicated to
him, although complimentary allusions to him occur in *SC* "October," *RT*, and
*CCCHA*. In the lost *Stemmata Dudleiana*, Sp celebrated the Leicester fam-
ily.    *late deceased*: Leicester died in 1588.

D E D I C A T O R Y   P O E M:    3. *case*: plight.    5. *Oedipus*: who solved the
riddle of the Sphinx.

To reade the secrete of this riddle rare,
And know the purporte of my evill plight,
   Let him rest pleased with his owne insight,
Ne further seeke to glose upon the text:          10
For griefe enough it is to grieved wight
To feele his fault, and not be further vext.
   But what so by my selfe may not be showen,
May by this Gnatts complaint be easily knowen.

WE now have playde (*Augustus*) wantonly,
    Tuning our song unto a tender Muse,
And like a cobweb weaving slenderly,
Have onely playde: let thus much then excuse
This Gnats small Poeme, that th'whole history     5
Is but a jest, though envie it abuse:
But who such sports and sweet delights doth blame,
Shall lighter seeme than this Gnats idle name.

Hereafter, when as season more secure
Shall bring forth fruit, this Muse shall speak to thee     10
In bigger notes, that may thy sense allure,
And for thy worth frame some fit Poesie,

7. *reade*: discover.    10. *glose*: comment.    11. *wight*: person.

1–64. The poem opens with an elaborate *recusatio*, a rhetorical device that
enables the poet to reject formally the blandishments of epic poetry, the
highest kind, for the simpler charms of the pastoral genre.    1–2. The
initial lines resemble the spurious beginning of the *Aen*, imitated by Sp at the
outset of *FQ*.    1. *Augustus*: Augustus Caesar, the first emperor of Rome.
Cf. "Octavius" (*VG* 35) and the "sacred childe" (*VG* 37). For Sp, the
counterpart of Augustus is Elizabeth.    2. *tender Muse*: named as Thalia in
the Latin—the Muse of comedy and "joyous gentle dalliaunce" (*TM* 186).
Since Sp's poem is a complaint, he generalizes about his Muse.    3. *cobweb*:
Sp mistakes *araneoli*, little spiders, for the spider's web.    7–8. *delights . . .
lighter*: Sp creates wordplay lacking in the original.    11. *bigger notes*:
translates *graviore sono*, a more dignified, weighty, epic theme. *sense allure*: a
traditional function of poetry, associated most often by Sp with the taming
and civilizing powers of Orpheus (cf. *VG* 455).

The golden ofspring of *Latona* pure,
And ornament of great *Joves* progenie,
*Phœbus* shall be the author of my song,                    15
Playing on yvorie harp with silver strong.

He shall inspire my verse with gentle mood
Of Poets Prince, whether he woon beside
Faire *Xanthus* sprincled with *Chimæras* blood;
Or in the woods of *Astery* abide;                          20
Or whereas mount *Parnasse*, the Muses brood,
Doth his broad forhead like two hornes divide,
And the sweete waves of sounding *Castaly*
With liquid foote doth slide downe easily.

Wherefore ye Sisters which the glorie bee                   25
Of the *Pierian* streames, fayre *Naiades*,
Go too, and dauncing all in companie,
Adorne that God: and thou holie *Pales*,
To whome the honest care of husbandrie
Returneth by continuall successe,                           30

13–14. *Latona . . . Joves progenie*: For the story of Latona's giving birth to
Phoebus (Apollo) on the island of Delos, see *FQ* II xii 13 and Ovid, *Met*
6.186–91.      16. *yvorie . . . silver*: The adjectives, added by Sp, enhance the
Virgilian description of Phoebus as "golden offspring" (*aurea proles*). In
Augustan poetry, Apollo was the god of poetry; his seven-stringed harp
symbolized the harmony of the music of the spheres.      18. *Poets Prince*: Sp
offers an ambiguity not found in the original, where Phoebus is clearly the
*princeps*, the source of poets' songs. Here there may be a reference to the
poet's prospective subject, the lofty monarch. *woon*: dwell.      19–24. These
are Phoebus's customary haunts.      19. *Xanthus*: the stream near which
Bellerophon fought with Chimaera, a beast with a lion's head, a goat's
stomach, and a dragon's limbs.      20. *Astery*: Delos, where Latona gave
birth to Phoebus.      21. *brood*: home, nest.      22. *two hornes*: the peaks
between which the Castalian spring flows on its way down Mount
Parnassus.      23–24. *Castaly*: Puns on "sounding" and "foote" underscore
the *fons Castalius* as a source of poetry. Boccaccio says that Castalia is
consecrated to the Muses. Cf. *TM* 57, *Daph* 228, and *RT* 431.
25–26. *Sisters . . . streames*: the nine Muses, called, in *RT*, " the Pierian
sacred sisters" (394); Pieria is the Muses' haunt in Thessaly.      28. *Adorne*:
translates *celebrate*. *that God*: Phoebus. *Pales*: goddess of agriculture; cf.
"fruitefull Pales" (*VG* 116).      30. *successe*: succession, increase.

Have care for to pursue his footing light;
Through the wide woods, and groves, with green leaves
                                                    dight.

Professing thee I lifted am aloft
Betwixt the forrest wide and starrie sky:
And thou most dread (*Octavius*) which oft                    35
To learned wits givest courage worthily,
O come (thou sacred childe) come sliding soft,
And favour my beginnings graciously:
For not these leaves do sing that dreadfull stound,
When Giants bloud did staine *Phlegræan* ground.             40

Nor how th'halfe horsy people, *Centaures* hight,
Fought with the bloudie *Lapithaes* at bord,
Nor how the East with tyranous despight
Burnt th'*Attick* towres, and people slew with sword;
Nor how mount *Athos* through exceeding might                45
Was digged downe, nor yron bands abord
The *Pontick* sea by their huge Navy cast,
My volume shall renowne, so long since past.

Nor *Hellespont* trampled with horses feete,
When flocking *Persians* did the *Greeks* affray;            50

---

32. *dight*: dressed.     35. *most dread*: translates *venerande*.     37. *sliding soft*: seemingly an echo of "slide downe easily" (*VG* 24).     39–50. *Culex* deliberately avoids singing of arms and the man, the military exploits of illustrious heroes, although epic material abounds in the gnat's complaint later.     39. *stound*: event.     40. A reference to the battle between Jupiter and the Giants, fought on the plain of Phlegra (cf. *FQ* V vii 10).     41–42. Lotspeich (1942), who notes other references to the Lapiths in *FQ* IV i 23 and VI x 13, remarks that Sp, following Natalis Comes, conceived of their victory over the Centaurs as a victory over evil powers (p. 77).     41. *hight*: called.     42. *at bord*: against, alongside.     43–50. Alludes to the Persian expeditions against Athens as recounted in Herodotus. Xerxes burned the Acropolis, dug a canal from Athos to the mainland, and tried, madly, to bind the sea.     46. *abord*: across.     48. *renowne*: make famous.     49–53. The contrast between trampling and tender feet is Virgilian; the sense of graceful movement conveyed, especially in line 53, is Spenserian. The stanza reiterates the poet's delight in sporting with a slender topic (cf. *VG* 1–8).

But my soft Muse, as for her power more meete,
Delights (with *Phœbus* friendly leave) to play
An easie running verse with tender feete.
And thou (dread sacred child) to thee alway,
Let everlasting lightsome glory strive,                              55
Through the worlds endles ages to survive.

And let an happie roome remaine for thee
Mongst heavenly ranks, where blessed soules do rest,
And let long lasting life with joyous glee,
As thy due meede that thou deservest best,                          60
Hereafter many yeares remembred be
Amongst good men, of whom thou oft are blest;
Live thou for ever in all happinesse:
But let us turne to our first businesse.

The fiery Sun was mounted now on hight                              65
Up to the heavenly towers, and shot each where
Out of his golden Charet glistering light;
And fayre *Aurora* with her rosie heare,
The hatefull darknes now had put to flight,
When as the shepheard seeing day appeare,                           70
His little Goats gan drive out of their stalls,
To feede abroad, where pasture best befalls.

---

54–64. The lines again praise Augustus before the poem proceeds to
its story proper. The story is in a sense unworthy of the sacred child,
but the poem has asked that its modest beginnings be favoured by
him nonetheless. The Latin text, by using the same word (*coepta*) to
describe the "beginnings" of the poet's career (*VG* 38) and the "first
businesse" of the pastoral narrative (*VG* 64), makes a point about the
poet's vocation that Sp's renderings obscure.     65–72. Phoebus, later
termed Hyperion (*VG* 156), is domesticated here as the "fiery Sun" who,
with Aurora, brings the dawn. As is typical in pastoral poetry, the
shepherd's experience is marked by the diurnal progress of the sun: in this
poem, daybreak, noonday (*VG* 153–68), and nightfall (*VG* 313–20) are
all occasions for intricate periphrases that signal different stages in the
action.     65. *hight*: high.     66. *each where*: everywhere.     68. *heare*:
hair.

To an high mountaines top he with them went,
Where thickest grasse did cloath the open hills:
They now amongst the woods and thickets ment,                    75
Now in the valleies wandring at their wills,
Spread themselves farre abroad through each descent;
Some on the soft greene grasse feeding their fills;
Some clambring through the hollow cliffes on hy,
Nibble the bushie shrubs, which growe thereby.                   80

Others the utmost boughs of trees doe crop,
And brouze the woodbine twigges, that freshly bud;
This with full bit doth catch the utmost top
Of some soft Willow, or new growen stud;
This with sharpe teeth the bramble leaves doth lop,             85
And chaw the tender prickles in her Cud;
The whiles another high doth overlooke
Her owne like image in a christall brooke.

O the great happines, which shepheards have,
Who so loathes not too much the poore estate,                   90
With minde that ill use doth before deprave,
Ne measures all things by the costly rate
Of riotise, and semblants outward brave;
No such sad cares, as wont to macerate
And rend the greedie mindes of covetous men,                    95
Do ever creepe into the shepheards den.

---

75. *ment*: mixed (past participle).    82. *brouze*: browse on.    84. *stud*:
stem.    89–152. The description of the shepherd's carefree lot follows
naturally from the account of the delight his flock takes in the variety of its
pasture. Cf. *Georgics* 2.458ff. for this commonplace of bucolic poetry. The
emphasis on the carelessness of the shepherd here and in lines 241–48 relates
him to Clarion in *Muio* and the lion in *MHT*.    92–106. The negative
constructions here and elsewhere in the passage praising the shepherd's life
recall lines 39–50 and thus suggest that as the little poem is to the heroic, so
pastoral contentment is to the life of luxury.    93. Sp expands Virgil's
*luxuriae*.    94. *macerate*: chew, lacerate.

Ne cares he if the fleece, which him arayes,
Be not twice steeped in Assyrian dye,
Ne glistering of golde, which underlayes
The summer beames, doe blinde his gazing eye.          100
Ne pictures beautie, nor the glauncing rayes
Of precious stones, whence no good commeth by;
Ne yet his cup embost with Imagery
Of *Bætus* or of *Alcons* vanity.

Ne ought the whelky pearles esteemeth hee,          105
Which are from Indian seas brought far away:
But with pure brest from carefull sorrow free,
On the soft grasse his limbs doth oft display,
In sweete spring time, when flowres varietie
With sundrie colours paints the sprincled lay;          110
There lying all at ease, from guile or spight,
With pype of fennie reedes doth him delight.

There he, Lord of himselfe, with palme bedight,
His looser locks doth wrap in wreath of vine:
There his milk dropping Goats be his delight,          115
And fruitefull *Pales*, and the forrest greene,
And darkesome caves in pleasaunt vallies pight,
Wheras continuall shade is to be seene,
And where fresh springing wells, as christall neate,
Do always flow, to quench his thirstie heate.          120

O who can lead then a more happie life,
Than he, that with cleane minde and hart sincere,
No greedy riches knowes nor bloudie strife,
No deadly fight of warlick fleete doth feare,

---

99. *underlayes*: underlies.     100. *summer beames*: i.e. sumpter beams, or
rafters.     104. *Bætus . . . Alcons*: Boethus and Alcon were known as
engravers in antiquity.     105. *whelky*: rounded.     108. *display*: stretch
out.     110. *lay*: lea.     111. *from*: removed from.     117. *pight*:
situated.     119. *neate*: pure.     123. *greedy riches*: translates literally *avidas
opes*.     124. *warlick*: warlike.

Ne runs in perill of foes cruell knife,          125
That in the sacred temples he may reare,
A trophee of his glittering spoyles and treasure,
Or may abound in riches above measure.

Of him his God is worshipt with his sythe,
And not with skill of craftsman polished:          130
He joyes in groves, and makes himselfe full blythe,
With sundrie flowers in wilde fieldes gathered;
Ne frankincens he from *Panchæa* buyth,
Sweete quiet harbours in his harmeles head,
And perfect pleasure buildes her joyous bowre,          135
Free from sad cares, that rich mens hearts devowre.

This all his care, this all his whole indevour,
To this his minde and senses he doth bend,
How he may flow in quiets matchles treasour,
Content with any food that God doth send;          140
And how his limbs, resolv'd through idle leisour,
Unto sweete sleepe he may securely lend,
In some coole shadow from the scorching heat,
The whiles his flock their chawed cuds do eate.

O flocks, O Faunes, and O ye pleasaunt springs          145
Of *Tempe*, where the countrey Nymphs are rife,
Through whose not costly care each shepheard sings
As merrie notes upon his rusticke Fife,
As that *Ascræan* bard, whose fame now rings

---

127. *trophee*: a memorial of a victory in war.    133. *Panchæa*: cf. *Georgics* 2.139; an island in the Indian Sea, known for its perfumes.    145. *Faunes*: Sp translates *Panes*, Pans, which he assimilates here with all sylvan gods.    146. *Tempe*: the secluded grove where Apollo made love to Daphne; another name for Arcadia. *countrey Nymphs*: specifically, nymphs of the forest, Hamadryads, as opposed to the water-nymphs, naiads, evoked in lines 25–26.    149. *Ascræan bard*: Hesiod, whose *Works and Days* extols the virtues of rustic life.

Through the wide world, and leads as joyfull life,                    150
Free from all troubles and from worldly toyle,
In which fond men doe all their dayes turmoyle.

In such delights whilst thus his carelesse time
This shepheard drives, upleaning on his batt,
And on shrill reedes chaunting his rustick rime,                      155
*Hyperion* throwing foorth his beames full hott,
Into the highest top of heaven gan clime,
And the world parting by an equall lott,
Did shed his whirling flames on either side,
As the great *Ocean* doth himselfe divide.                           160

Then gan the shepheard gather into one
His stragling Goates, and drave them to a foord,
Whose cærule streame, rombling in Pible stone,
Crept under mosse as greene as any goord.
Now had the Sun halfe heaven overgone,                               165
When he his heard back from that water foord,
Drave from the force of *Phœbus* boyling ray,
Into thick shadowes, there themselves to lay.

Soone as he them plac'd in thy sacred wood
(O *Delian* Goddesse) saw, to which of yore                          170
Came the bad daughter of old *Cadmus* brood,
Cruell *Agave*, flying vengeance sore
Of king *Nictileus* for the guiltie blood,

---

152. *fond*: foolish. *turmoyle*: vex.    154. *batt*: staff.    162. *drave*:
drove.    163. *cærule*: sky-blue.    169–70. Construe: "Then he saw them
placed in thy sacred wood . . . ."    170. *Delian Goddesse*: Diana, born like
Apollo of Latona at Delos. She is invoked here because she is "soveraine
queene profest of woods and forests" (*FQ* VII vi 38).    171–76. *The story
of Agave* (Ovid, *Met* 3.511ff.) involves a woman who slew her son, Pentheus,
while celebrating the rites of Bacchus (Nyctelius). Sp "confuses the passage
by imagining a Nyctilius King of Thebes, evidently her husband and father of
her son" (Renwick 1928:221).

Which she with cursed hands had shed before;
There she halfe frantick having slaine her sonne,                    175
Did shrowd herselfe like punishment to shonne.

Here also playing on the grassy greene,
Woodgods, and Satyres, and swift Dryades,
With many Fairies oft were dauncing seene.
Not so much did Dan *Orpheus* represse,                    180
The streames of *Hebrus* with his songs I weene,
As that faire troupe of woodie Goddesses
Staied thee, (O *Peneus*) powring foorth to thee,
From cheereful lookes great mirth and gladsome glee.

The verie nature of the place, resounding                    185
With gentle murmure of the breathing ayre,
A pleasant bowre with all delight abounding
In the fresh shadowe did for them prepayre,
To rest their limbs with warines redounding.
For first the high Palme trees with braunches faire,                    190
Out of the lowly vallies did arise,
And high shoote up their heads into the skyes.

And them amongst the wicked Lotos grew,
Wicked, for holding guilefully away
*Ulysses* men, whom rapt with sweetenes new,                    195
Taking to hoste, it quite from him did stay,
And eke those trees, in whose transformed hew

180. *Dan Orpheus*: Sir Orpheus, whose adventures are detailed in lines 433–
80.        181. *Hebrus*: a river subdued by Orpheus (cf. *VG* 450). *weene*:
expect.        183–84. Sp follows Bembo's emendations.        183. *Peneus*: a
river located in Tempe in *Proth* 78.        190–224. The catalogue of trees
anticipates *FQ* I i 8–9. The lowly grove in which the flock reposes is exalted
by mythological association.        193. *Lotos*: This "impious" tree's attractions
to Ulysses' men appear in Homer, *Odyssey* 9.83ff.        197. *eke*: also. *those
trees*: poplars, into which the Heliades, Apollo's daughters, were changed to
mourn the death of their arrogant brother, Phaethon. See Ovid, *Met* 1.750–
2.329 (cf. "the poplar never dry" in *FQ* I i 8).

The Sunnes sad daughters waylde the rash decay
Of *Phaeton*, whose limbs with lightening rent,
They gathering up, with sweete teares did lament.     200

And that same tree, in which *Demophoon*,
By his disloyalty lamented sore,
Eternall hurte left unto many one:
Whom als accompanied the Oke, of yore
Through fatall charmes transformd to such an one:     205
The Oke, whose Acornes were our foode, before
That *Ceres* seede of mortall men were knowne,
Which first *Triptoleme* taught how to be sowne.

Here also grew the rougher rinded Pine,
The great *Argoan* ships brave ornament     210
Whom golden Fleece did make an heavenly signe;
Which coveting, with his high tops extent,
To make the mountaines touch the starres divine,
Decks all the forrest with embellishment,
And the blacke Holme that loves the watrie vale,     215
And the sweete Cypresse signe of deadly bale.

Emongst the rest the clambring Yvie grew,
Knitting his wanton armes with grasping hold,
Least that the Poplar happely should rew
Her brothers strokes, whose boughes she doth enfold     220
With her lythe twigs, till they the top survew,

201–03. Believing that she was forsaken by Demophoon, Phyllis at her death
became an almond-tree. Sp misconstrues the Latin by making Demophoon
the tree.     205. *fatall charmes*: the allusion is to the oracle at Dodona. See
*Georgics* 1.8 and 147ff.     206–07. Ceres taught Triptolemus of Athens
how to sow corn.     209–14. Jason sought the Golden Fleece in the Argo,
a pine ship turned into a constellation after the completion of his quest (cf.
"The sayling Pine" in *FQ* I i 8).     215. *Holme*: the holm-oak, *quercus
ilex*.     220. *Her brothers strokes*: Phaethon's (see note to line 197). Sp's
pronouns are confused here, but the passage appears to mean that the ivy's
twigs enfold and restrain the wild limbs of the grief-stricken poplar.
221. *survew*: surmount.

And paint with pallid greene her buds of gold.
Next did the Myrtle tree to her approach,
Not yet unmindfull of her olde reproach.

But the small Birds in their wide boughs embowring,    225
Chaunted their sundrie tunes with sweete consent,
And under them a silver Spring forth powring
His trickling streames, a gentle murmure sent;
Thereto the frogs, bred in the slimie scowring
Of the moist moores, their jarring voyces bent;    230
And shrill grashoppers chirped them around:
All which the ayrie Echo did resound.

In this so pleasant place this Shepheards flocke
Lay everie where, their wearie limbs to rest,
On everie bush, and everie hollow rocke    235
Where breathe on them the whistling wind mote best;
The whiles the Shepheard self tending his stocke,
Sate by the fountaine side, in shade to rest,
Where gentle slumbring sleep oppressed him,
Displaid on ground, and seized everie lim.    240

Of trecherie or traines nought tooke he keep,
But looslie on the grassie greene dispredd,
His dearest life did trust to careles sleep;
Which weighing down his drouping drowsie hedd,
In quiet rest his molten heart did steep,    245
Devoid of care, and feare of all falshedd:
Had not inconstant fortune, bent to ill,
Bid strange mischance his quietnes to spill.

For at his wonted time in that same place
An huge great Serpent all with speckles pide,    250

223. *Myrtle*: sacred to Venus, who transformed Myrsine into the plant to protect her from indignity.    225–32. The lines suggest the music of the *locus amoenus* (cf. *FQ* II xii 71).    229. *scowring*: flow (noun).
241. *traines*: insidiousness, traps.    242. *dispredd*: spread out.    248. *spill*: destroy.    249–56. The description of the snake captures the sibilance of the original.    250. *pide*: mottled.

To drench himselfe in moorish slime did trace,
There from the boyling heate himselfe to hide:
He passing by with rolling wreathed pace,
With brandisht tongue the emptie aire did gride,
And wrapt his scalie boughts with fell despight,    255
That all things seem'd appalled at his sight.

Now more and more having himselfe enrolde,
His glittering breast he lifteth up on hie,
And with proud vaunt his head aloft doth holde;
His creste above spotted with purple die,    260
On everie side did shine like scalie golde,
And his bright eyes glauncing full dreadfullie,
Did seeme to flame out flakes of flashing fyre,
And with sterne lookes to threaten kindled yre.

Thus wise long time he did himselfe dispace    265
There round about, when as at last he spide
Lying along before him in that place,
That flocks grand Captaine, and most trustie guide:
Eftsoones more fierce in visage, and in pace,
Throwing his firie eyes on everie side,    270
He commeth on, and all things in his way
Full stearnly rends, that might his passage stay.

Much he disdaines, that anie one should dare
To come unto his haunt; for which intent
He inly burns, and gins straight to prepare    275
The weapons, which Nature to him hath lent;
Fellie he hisseth, and doth fiercely stare,
And hath his jawes with angrie spirits rent,

---

251. *trace*: travel.    254. *brandisht*: made to vibrate, darting. *gride*:
pierce.    255. *boughts*: coils.    259. *proud vaunt*: Sp moralizes the
physical action.    263. The alliteration matches repeated *m*'s in the
original.    265. *dispace*: move, stalk.    268. *grand*: Sp transfers the
epithet *ingens*, huge, from the snake to the shepherd.    275. *straight*:
straightway.    277. *Fellie*: fiercely.

That all his tract with bloudie drops is stained,
And all his foldes are now in length outstrained.                    280

Whom thus at point prepared, to prevent,
A litle noursling of the humid ayre,
A Gnat unto the sleepie Shepheard went,
And marking where his ey-lids twinckling rare,
Shewd the two pearles, which sight unto him lent,                    285
Through their thin coverings appearing fayre,
His little needle there infixing deep,
Warnd him awake, from death himselfe to keep.

Wherewith enrag'd, he fiercely gan upstart,
And with his hand him rashly bruzing, slewe                          290
As in avengement of his heedles smart,
That streight the spirite out of his senses flew,
And life out of his members did depart:
When suddenly casting aside his vew,
He spide his foe with felonous intent,                              295
And fervent eyes to his destruction bent.

All suddenly dismaid, and hartles quight,
He fled abacke, and catching hastie holde
Of a yong alder hard beside him pight,
It rent, and streight about him gan beholde,                        300
What God or Fortune would assist his might.
But whether God or Fortune made him bold
Its hard to read: yet hardie will he had
To overcome, that made him lesse adrad.

The scalie backe of that most hideous snake                         305
Enwrapped round, oft faining to retire,

280. *outstrained*: outstretched.     281. *at point*: suitably, perhaps with a play
on the gnat's needle.     282. *litle noursling*: The contrast between the "huge
great Serpent"(*VG* 250) and the miniscule gnat is Virgilian, though Sp
emphasizes it by repeating "little" in line 287.     292. *spirite*:
monosyllabic.     295. *felonous*: fierce.     299. *pight*: rooted, placed.
303. *read*: comprehend.     304. *adrad*: afraid.

And oft him to assaile, he fiercely strake
Whereas his temples did his creast-front tyre;
And for he was but slowe, did slowth off shake,
And gazing ghastly on (for feare and yre          310
Had blent so much his sense, that lesse he feard;)
Yet when he saw him slaine, himselfe he cheard.

By this the night forth from the darksome bowre
Of *Herebus* her teemed steedes gan call,
And laesie *Vesper* in his timely howre          315
From golden *Oeta* gan proceede withall,
Whenas the Shepheard after this sharpe stowre,
Seing the doubled shadowes low to fall,
Gathering his straying flocke, does homeward fare,
And unto rest his wearie joynts prepare.          320

Into whose sense so soone as lighter sleepe
Was entered, and now loosing everie lim,
Sweete slumbring deaw in carelesnesse did steepe,
The Image of that Gnat appeard to him,
And in sad tearmes gan sorrowfully weepe,          325
With greislie countenaunce and visage grim,
Wailing the wrong which he had done of late,
In steed of good hastning his cruell fate.

Said he, what have I wretch deserv'd, that thus
Into this bitter bale I am outcast,          330
Whilest that thy life more deare and precious
Was than mine owne, so long as it did last?

---

308. *tyre*: attire.     309. *slowth*: the spelling reinforces the play on
"slow/sloth."     311. *blent*: blinded.     313–20. The coming of Night,
whose home is Hell, introduces the visitation from and description of the
underworld.     314. *Herebus*: husband of Night.     315. *Vesper*: Hesperus,
the Evening Star.     316. *golden Oeta*: cf. Virgil, *Ecl* 8.30: a mountain range
in Thessaly.     317. *stowre*: crisis.     324. *Image*: spectre, translating
*effigies*.     325–28. Emerson (1918) remarks that Sp spins three lines out of
one so that the gnat's complaint can begin a stanza.     326. *greislie*: horrible.

I now in lieu of paines so gracious,
Am tost in th'ayre with everie windie blast:
Thou safe delivered from sad decay,                                          335
Thy careles limbs in loose sleep dost display.

So livest thou, but my poore wretched ghost
Is forst to ferrie over *Lethes* River,
And spoyled of *Charon* too and fro am tost.
Seest thou, how all places quake and quiver                                   340
Lightned with deadly lamps on everie post?
*Tisiphone* each where doth shake and shiver
Her flaming fire brond, encountring me,
Whose lockes uncombed cruell adders be.

And *Cerberus*, whose many mouthes doo bay,                                   345
And barke out flames, as if on fire he fed;
Adowne whose necke in terrible array,
Ten thousand snakes cralling about his hed
Doo hang in heapes, that horribly affray,
And bloodie eyes doo glister firie red;                                       350
He oftentimes me dreadfullie doth threaten,
With painfull torments to be sorely beaten.

Ay me, that thankes so much should faile of meed,
For that I thee restor'd to life againe,
Even from the doore of death and deadlie dreed.                               355
Where then is now the guerdon of my paine?
Where the reward of my so piteous deed?
The praise of pitie vanisht is in vaine,

---

333. *in lieu of*: in compensation for.     338–39. Following his source, Sp
confuses the rivers Lethe and Styx; Charon's boat usually traverses the latter
to gain entry to Hades.     339. *spoyled of*: carried off by.     342. *Tisiphone*:
one of the Furies at the threshold of Hell whose snaky hair was legendary in
antiquity.     345. *Cerberus*: the many-headed hound at the portals of Hell; a
prototype for the Blatant Beast in *FQ* VI. *bay*: bark.     353. *meed*:
reward.     356. *guerdon*: reward.     357–58. *piteous . . . pitie*: translates
*pietatis . . . pietatis.*

And th'antique faith of Justice long agone
Out of the land is fled away and gone.                    360

I saw anothers fate approaching fast,
And left mine owne his safetie to tender;
Into the same mishap I now am cast,
And shun'd destruction doth destruction render:
Not unto him that never hath trespast,                   365
But punishment is due to the offender.
Yet let destruction be the punishment,
So long as thankfull will may it relent.

I carried am into waste wildernesse,
Waste wildernes, amongst *Cymerian* shades,              370
Where endles paines and hideous heavinesse
Is round about me heapt in darksome glades.
For there huge *Othos* sits in sad distresse,
Fast bound with serpents that him oft invades;
Far of beholding *Ephialtes* tide,                       375
Which once assai'd to burne this world so wide.

And there is mournfull *Tityus* mindefull yet
Of thy displeasure, O *Latona* faire;
Displeasure too implacable was it,
That made him meat for wild foules of the ayre:          380
Much do I feare among such fiends to sit;
Much do I feare back to them to repayre,
To the black shadowes of the *Stygian* shore,
Where wretched ghosts sit wailing evermore.

---

359–60. *Justice . . . fled*: cf. *FQ* V Proem. In the protracted list of infernal
torments (*VG* 369ff.), the punishment fits the offense. The gnat protests his
innocence and thus the injustice of his being taken to Hell.    369. *waste
wildernesse*: Ireland, if we accept an application of the poem to Sp's
rustication.    370. *Cymerian shades*: hellish darkness.    373–76 Othos
and Ephialtes are brothers consigned to Hell in *Aen* 6.582–84.    375. *Far
of . . . tide*: Far off . . . tied.    377–80. Tityus was a giant whose liver
vultures devoured as punishment for his attack on Latona.

There next the utmost brinck doth he abide,      385
That did the bankets of the Gods bewray,
Whose throat through thirst to nought nigh being dride
His sense to seeke for ease turnes every way:
And he that in avengement of his pride,
For scorning to the sacred Gods to pray,      390
Against a mountaine rolls a mightie stone,
Calling in vaine for rest, and can have none.

Go ye with them, go cursed damosells,
Whose bridale torches foule *Erynnis* tynde,
And *Hymen* at your Spousalls sad, foretells      395
Tydings of death and massacre unkinde:
With them that cruell *Colchid* mother dwells,
The which conceiv'd in her revengefull minde,
With bitter woundes her owne deere babes to slay,
And murdred troupes upon great heapes to lay.      400

There also those two *Pandionian* maides,
Calling on *Itis*, *Itis* evermore,
Whom wretched boy they slew with guiltie blades;
For whome the *Thracian* king lamenting sore,
Turn'd to a Lapwing, fowlie them upbraydes,      405
And fluttering round about them still does sore:
There now they all eternally complaine
Of others wrong, and suffer endles paine.

---

385–92. These lines refer to Tantalus and Sisyphus, respectively.
386. *bankets*: banquets.     393–96. The cursed damsels are the Danaids;
Erinnys is a fiery Fury; Hymen is the god of marriage, who predicted that
Danaus's daughters would kill their cousins.     394. *tynde*: kindled.
397–400. The "Colchid mother" is Medea, who was punished in Hades for
murdering her children.     401–08 .The maids are Philomela and Procne,
daughters of Pandion; they killed Itys, son of Tereus, the Thracian king. In
Hades, Philomela was a nightingale, Procne, a swallow, and Tereus, a
hoopoe. In making Tereus a lapwing, Sp may be following Golding's
rendering of *epops* in *Met* 6.674.

But the two brethren borne of *Cadmus* blood,
Whilst each does for the Soveraignty contend,                    410
Blinde through ambition, and with vengeance wood
Each doth against the others bodie bend
His cursed steele, of neither well withstood,
And with wide wounds their carcases doth rend;
That yet they both doe mortall foes remaine,                     415
Sith each with brothers bloudie hand was slaine.

Ah (waladay) there is no end of paine,
Nor chaunge of labour may intreated bee:
Yet I beyond all these am carried faine,
Where other powers farre different I see,                        420
And must passe over to th'*Elisian* plaine:
There grim *Persephone* encountring mee,
Doth urge her fellow Furies earnestlie,
With their bright firebronds me to terrifie.

These chast *Alceste* lives inviolate,                           425
Free from all care, for that her husbands daies
She did prolong by changing fate for fate,
Lo there lives also the immortall praise
Of womankinde, most faithfull to her mate,
*Penelope*: and from her farre awayes                            430
A rulesse rout of yongmen, which her woo'd
All slaine with darts, lie wallowed in their blood.

409–16. Sp enlarges on his source, which refers to the strife between
Eteocles and Polynices.    411. *wood*: mad.    417. *waladay*: alas.
421. *Elisian plaine*: the region of the Virgilian underworld reserved for the
blessed; the "Heroës" (*VG* 480) encountered by the gnat there are thus "farre
different" (*VG* 420) from those he has just met.    422. *Persephone*: like
Tisiphone (*VG* 342), a Fury; not to be confused in Sp with Proserpina,
queen of hell.    425–27. Alcestis went to her death so that her husband,
Admetus, might live.    428–32. Penelope resisted successive suitors ("rout
of yongmen") for the sake of her mate, Odysseus.    431. *rulesse*: either
"rueless" (lacking in pity) or "ruleless" (unruly).

And sad *Eurydice* thence now no more
Must turne to life, but there detained bee,
For looking back, being forbid before:                          435
Yet was the guilt thereof, *Orpheus*, in thee.
Bold sure he was, and worthie spirite bore,
That durst those lowest shadowes goe to see,
And could beleeve that anie thing could please
Fell *Cerberus*, or Stygian powres appease.                     440

Ne feard the burning waves of *Phlegeton*,
Nor those same mournfull kingdomes, compassed
With rustie horrour and fowle fashion,
And deep digd vawtes, and Tartar covered
With bloodie night, and darke confusion,                        445
And judgement seates, whose Judge is deadlie dred,
A judge, that after death doth punish sore
The faults, which life hath trespassed before.

But valiant fortune made *Dan Orpheus* bolde:
For the swift running rivers still did stand,                   450
And the wilde beasts their furie did withhold,
To follow *Orpheus* musicke through the land:
And th'Okes deep grounded in the earthly molde
Did move, as if they could him understand;
And the shrill woods, which were of sense bereav'd,             455
Through their hard barke his silver sound receav'd.

And eke the Moone her hastie steedes did stay,
Drawing in teemes along the starrie skie,
And didst (ô monthly Virgin) thou delay
Thy nightly course, to heare his melodie?                       460

---

433–80. Like *Culex* 268–96, the poem dwells on the story of Orpheus and
Eurydice, also prominent in *Georgics* 4.453–529.    440. *Stygian*: see note
to lines 338–39.    441. *Phlegeton*: the infernal river constantly in flames;
used by Sp in connection with Pyrochles and Cymochles in *FQ* II iv
41.    442. *mournfull kingdomes*: the region of Dis.    444. *Tartar*:
Tartarus, a metonym for Hades.    457–60. The Moon, or Cynthia, travels
in a chariot drawn by black and white steeds.

The same was able with like lovely lay
The Queene of hell to move as easily,
To yeeld *Eurydice* unto her fere,
Backe to be borne, though it unlawfull were.

She (Ladie) having well before approoved,                    465
The feends to be too cruell and severe,
Observ'd th'appointed way, as her behooved,
Ne ever did her ey-sight turne arere,
Ne ever spake, ne cause of speaking mooved:
But cruell *Orpheus*, thou much crueller,                    470
Seeking to kisse her, brok'st the Gods decree,
And thereby mad'st her ever damn'd to be.

Ah but sweete love of pardon worthie is,
And doth deserve to have small faults remitted;
If Hell at least things lightly done amis                    475
Knew how to pardon, when ought is omitted:
Yet are ye both received into blis,
And to the seates of happie soules admitted.
And you, beside the honourable band
Of great Heroës doo in order stand.                          480

There be the two stout sonnes of *Aeacus*,
Fierce *Peleus*, and the hardie *Telamon*,
Both seeming now full glad and joyeous
Through their Syres dreadfull jurisdiction,
Being the Judge of all that horrid hous:                     485
And both of them by strange occasion,

461–64. Orpheus persuaded Proserpina, queen of hell, to release Eurydice
from the underworld.    463. *fere*: mate.    465–72. Orpheus broke the
decree and lost Eurydice when he looked back at her.    473–80. Sp
elaborates on the justice of their being placed among the blest in recognition
of the power of their love.    481–85. Aeacus, son of Jove himself, was a
judge in the underworld, and hence his sons have the fortune to dwell among
the happy souls. These allusions provide an oblique introduction to the
history of the Trojan War.

Renown'd in choyce of happie marriage
Through *Venus* grace, and vertues cariage.

For th'one was ravisht of his owne bondmaide,
The faire *Hesione* captiv'd from *Troy*:                              490
But th'other was with *Thetis* love assaid,
Great *Nereus* his daughter, and his joy.
On this side them there is a yongman layd,
Their match in glorie, mightie, fierce and coy;
That from th'Argolick ships, with furious yre,                        495
Bett back the furie of the Trojan fyre.

O who would not recount the strong divorces
Of that great warre, which Trojanes oft behelde,
And oft beheld the warlike Greekish forces,
When *Teucrian* soyle with bloodie rivers swelde,                     500
And wide *Sigæan* shores were spred with corses,
And *Simois* and *Xanthus* blood outwelde,
Whilst *Hector* raged with outragious minde,
Flames, weapons, wounds in *Greeks* fleete to have tynde.

For *Ida* selfe, in ayde of that fierce fight,                        505
Out of her mountaines ministred supplies,
And like a kindly nourse, did yeeld (for spight)
Store of firebronds out of her nourseries,
Unto her foster children, that they might
Inflame the Navie of their enemies,                                   510
And all the *Rhetæan* shore to ashes turne,
Where lay the ships, which they did seeke to burne.

---

487–96. Telamon married Hesione; they were parents to Ajax. Peleus
married Thetis; they were parents to Nereus and Achilles.    493. *yongman*:
Ajax, not Achilles.    495. *Argolick*: Greek.    496. *Bett*: beat.
500. *Teucrian*: Trojan; similar circumlocutions, carrying the same meaning,
follow in "Sigæan" (*VG* 501), "Rhetæan" (*VG* 511), "Phrygian" (*VG* 526),
"Iliack" (*VG* 549), and "Ericthonian" (*VG* 562).    501. *corses*:
corpses.    502. *Simois and Xanthus*: rivers near Troy.    503. *Hector*: the
principal Trojan hero—"the glorie of the Trojan field" (*VG*
516).    504. *tynde*: kindled.    505. *Ida*: Mount Ida, near Troy.

Gainst which the noble sonne of *Telamon*
Oppos'd himselfe and thwarting his huge shield,
Them battell bad, gainst whom appeard anon 515
*Hector*, the glorie of the *Trojan* field:
Both fierce and furious in contention
Encountred, that their mightie strokes so shrild,
As the great clap of thunder, which doth ryve
The ratling heavens, and cloudes asunder dryve. 520

So th'one with fire and weapons did contend
To cut the ships, from turning home againe
To *Argos*, th'other strove for to defend
The force of *Vulcane* with his might and maine.
Thus th'one *Aeacide* did his fame extend: 525
But th'other joy'd, that on the *Phrygian* playne
Having the blood of vanquisht *Hector* shedd,
He compast *Troy* thrice with his bodie dedd.

Againe great dole on either partie grewe,
That him to death unfaithfull *Paris* sent; 530
And also him that false *Ulysses* slewe,
Drawne into danger through close ambushment:
Therefore from him *Lartes* sonne his vewe
Doth turne aside, and boasts his good event
In working of *Strymonian Rhæsus* fall, 535
And efte in *Dolons* slye surprysall.

Againe the dreadfull *Cycones* him dismay,
And blacke *Lestrigones*, a people stout:

513–20. Hector's adversary was Ajax, renowned for his sevenfold shield.
514. *thwarting*: laying across.     521. *th'one*: i.e. Ajax; so too in line 525.
523. *th'other*: Hector.     524. *Vulcane*: god of fire.     526. *th'other*:
Achilles.     530–34. Paris killed Achilles; Ulysses, Laertës' son, was
indirectly responsible for the suicide of Ajax.     535. *Strymonian Rhæsus*: i.e.
Troy. Strymon is a river near the Thracian border.     536. *Dolons*: Before
killing Dolon, Ulysses extracted from him privileged information on the
Trojans.     537–44. The stanza provides detail on Ulysses' fate after the
sack of Troy, culminating with his arrival in Hell.     537. *Cycones*: the
Trojans' Thracian allies who routed Ulysses' troops at Ismarus.
538. *Lestrigones*: gigantic cannibals who destroyed all the ships of Ulysses'
fleet except his own.

Then greedie *Scilla*, under whom there bay
Manie great bandogs, which her gird about:                          540
Then doo the *Aetnean* Cyclops him affray,
And deep *Charybdis* gulphing in and out:
Lastly the squalid lakes of *Tartarie*,
And griesly Feends of hell him terrifie.

There also goodly *Agamemnon* bosts,                               545
The glorie of the stock of *Tantalus*,
And famous light of all the Greekish hosts,
Under whose conduct most victorious,
The *Dorick* flames consum'd the *Iliack* posts.
Ah but the *Greekes* themselves more dolorous,                     550
To thee, ô *Troy*, paid penaunce for thy fall,
In th'*Hellespont* being nigh drowned all.

Well may appeare by proofe of their mischaunce,
The chaungfull turning of mens slipperie state,
That none, whom fortune freely doth advaunce,                      555
Himselfe therefore to heaven should elevate:
For loftie type of honour through the glaunce
Of envies dart, is downe in dust prostrate;
And all that vaunts in worldly vanitie,
Shall fall through fortunes mutabilitie.                           560

Th'*Argolicke* power returning home againe,
Enricht with spoyles of th'*Ericthonian* towre,

---

539–41. In *Odyssey* 12, Ulysses meets Scylla, an enormous creature ringed
with hounds, and Charybdis, a raging whirlpool. Homer had placed the
episode involving the one-eyed Cyclops in Book 9.     543. *Tartarie*:
Tartarus.     545. *Agamemnon*: king of Mycenae; leader of the Greek
("Dorick") expedition against Troy.     550–52. The Greek navy was
shipwrecked not in the Hellespont *per se*, but in the Aegean Sea near Euboea.
A detailed account of its demise occurs in lines 561–92.     553–60. Sp
expands on *Culex* to insist on the theme of invidious Fortune, a
commonplace of *de casibus* tragedy. Cf. *Muio* 217–32.     562. *Ericthonian*:
Trojan. Ericthonius was the father of Tros, king of the Trojans.

Did happie winde and weather entertaine,
And with good speed the fomie billowes scowre:
No signe of storme, no feare of future paine,                           565
Which soone ensued them with heavie stowre.
*Nereis* to the Seas a token gave,
The whiles their crooked keeles the surges clave.

Suddenly, whether through the Gods decree,
Or haplesse rising of some froward starre,                              570
The heavens on everie side enclowded bee:
Black stormes and fogs are blowen up from farre,
That now the Pylote can no loadstarre see,
But skies and seas doo make most dreadfull warre;
The billowes striving to the heavens to reach,                          575
And th'heavens striving them for to impeach.

And in avengement of their bold attempt,
Both Sun and starres and all the heavenly powres
Conspire in one to wreake their rash contempt,
And downe on them to fall from highest towres:                         580
The skie in pieces seeming to be rent,
Throwes lightning forth, and haile, and harmful
                                                      showres
That death on everie side to them appeares
In thousand formes, to worke more ghastly feares.

Some in the greedie flouds are sunke and drent,                        585
Some on the rocks of *Caphareus* are throwne;
Some on th'*Euboick* Cliffs in pieces rent;
Some scattred on the *Hercæan* shores unknowne;
And manie lost, of whom no moniment

---

564. *scowre*: pass rapidly over.    566. *stowre*: disturbance.    567. *Nereis*:
one of the Nereids, water-nymphs who presided over the sea.    568. *clave*:
cleaved.    570. *froward*: perverse.    576. *impeach*: prevent.
579. *wreake*: avenge.    585. *drent*: drowned.    586. *Caphareus*: a
promontory off Euboea, where the Greek navy went down.
588. *Hercæan*: Emerson (1918) points out that Sp adds "unknowne" as if to
express his ignorance of the place.

Remaines, nor memorie is to be showne:                     590
Whilst all the purchase of the *Phrigian* pray
Tost on salt billowes, round about doth stray.

Here manie other like Heroës bee,
Equall in honour to the former crue,
Whom ye in goodly seates may placed see,                   595
Descended all from *Rome* by linage due,
From *Rome*, that holds the world in sovereigntie,
And doth all Nations unto her subdue:
Here *Fabii* and *Decii* doo dwell,
*Horatii* that in vertue did excell.                       600

And here the antique fame of stout *Camill*
Doth ever live, and constant *Curtius*,
Who stifly bent his vowed life to spill
For Countreyes health, a gulph most hideous
Amidst the Towne with his owne corps did fill,             605
T'appease the powers; and prudent *Mutius*,
Who in his flesh endur'd the scorching flame,
To daunt his foe by ensample of the same.

And here wise *Curius*, companion
Of noble vertues, lives in endles rest;                    610
And stout *Flaminius*, whose devotion
Taught him the fires scorn'd furie to detest;

591. *pray*: prey, booty.     599–600. Fabii, Decii, and Horatii are family
names of famous Romans.       601. *Camill*: Marcus Furius Camillus, who re-
founded Rome after the Gallic invasion (387 B.C.).     602–06. *Curtius*: a
youth who rode his horse into a chasm in the Forum ("gulph most hideous")
and disappeared in the water.     606–08. *Mutius*: who plunged his hand
into a flame as a gesture of defiance to his enemy, Porsenna.
609–10. *Curius*: Manius Curius Dentatus, victor over the Sabines.
611–12. *Flaminius*: The allusion is obscure, but *Culex's* play on *Flaminius*
. . . *flammae* suggests that the name may be a nickname for a person who
heroically exposed his body to fire. Badius Ascensius, in a Renaissance
commentary on *Culex*, identifies him as Lucius Metellus, who lost his sight
while rescuing the Palladium from the burning Temple of Vesta.

And here the praise of either *Scipion*
Abides in highest place above the best,
To whom the ruin'd walls of *Carthage* vow'd,                615
Trembling their forces, sound their praises lowd.

Live they for ever through their lasting praise:
But I poore wretch am forced to retourne
To the sad lakes, that *Phœbus* sunnie rayes
Doo never see, where soules doo alwaies mourne,            620
And by the wayling shores to waste my dayes,
Where *Phlegeton* with quenchles flames doth burne;
By which just *Minos* righteous soules doth sever
From wicked ones, to live in blisse forever.

Me therefore thus the cruell fiends of hell                625
Girt with long snakes, and thousand yron chaynes,
Through doome of that their cruell Judge, compell
With bitter torture and impatient paines,
Cause of my death, and just complaint to tell.
For thou art he, whom my poore ghost complaines           630
To be the author of her ill unwares,
That careles hear'st my intollerable cares.

Them therefore as bequeathing to the winde,
I now depart, returning to thee never,
And leave this lamentable plaint behinde.                 635
But doo thou haunt the soft downe rolling river,
And wilde greene woods, and fruitful pastures minde,
And let the flitting aire my vaine words sever.

---

613–16. Sp's syntax is tortured as he attempts to make sense of a corrupt
passage in his original. The lines refer to the victories of P. Cornelius Scipio
and Scipio Aemilianus over the Carthaginians in the second and third Punic
Wars.    623–24. Minos, mythical king of Crete, appears in his traditional
role as judge in Hades.    627. *doome*: verdict.    632. *careles . . . cares*:
This wordplay, which is Sp's not Virgil's, emphasizes the contrast between
the sylvan repose of the shepherd and the images of violence and heroic effort
that are everywhere implied in the gnat's description of the underworld.

Thus having said, he heavily departed
With piteous crie, that anie would have smarted.                    640

Now, when the sloathfull fit of lifes sweete rest
Had left the heavie Shepheard, wondrous cares
His inly grieved minde full sore opprest;
That baleful sorrow he no longer beares,
For that Gnats death, which deeply was imprest:                    645
But bends what ever power his aged yeares
Him lent, yet being such, as through their might
He lately slue his dreadfull foe in fight.

By that same River lurking under greene,
Eftsoones he gins to fashion forth a place,                        650
And squaring it in compasse well beseene,
There plotteth out a tombe by measured space:
His yron headed spade tho making cleene,
To dig up sods out of the flowrie grasse,
His worke he shortly to good purpose brought,                     655
Like as he had conceiv'd it in his thought.

An heape of earth he hoorded up on hie,
Enclosing it with banks on everie side,
And thereupon did raise full busily
A little mount, of greene turffs edifide;                          660

---

639. *Thus having said*: translates *dixit*, he said; a clue that the gnat's
complaint is conceived as an epic oration. *heavily*: woefully.      640. *smarted*:
wounded.      641. *fit*: condition.      644–48. Activity succeeds sloth: the
shepherd does not languish in mere sorrow, but exerts his strength,
previously responsible for killing the snake, to make amends to the
gnat.      650. *eftsoones*: forthwith.      651. *squaring . . . compasse*: translates
*hunc in orbem destinat*, which suggests more clearly that the gnat's tumulus is
round. *well beseene*: pleasant to behold.      653–54. Sp's rendering tends to
blur the contrast between the shepherd's earlier carelessness and his
carefulness here. The comparable lines in *Culex* (394–98) use *cura* twice to
point the contrast. See note to line 632.      653. *tho*: then.      657. *hoorded*:
piled.      660. *edifide*: built.

And on the top of all, that passers by
Might it behold, the toomb he did provide
Of smoothest marble stone in order set,
That never might his luckie scape forget.

And round about he taught sweete flowres to growe,   665
The Rose engrained in pure scarlet die,
The Lilly fresh, and Violet belowe,
The Marigolde, and cherefull Rosemarie,
The *Spartan* Mirtle, whence sweet gumb does flowe,
The purple Hyacinthe, and fresh Costmarie,   670
And Saffron sought for in *Cilician* soyle,
And Lawrell th'ornament of *Phœbus* toyle.

Fresh *Rhododaphne*, and the *Sabine* flowre
Matching the wealth of th'auncient Frankincence,
And pallid Yvie building his owne bowre,   675
And Box yet mindfull of his olde offence,
Red *Amaranthus*, lucklesse Paramour,
Oxeye still greene, and bitter Patience;
Ne wants there pale *Narcisse*, that in a well
Seeing his beautie, in love with it fell.   680

And whatsoever other flowre of worth,
And whatso other hearb of lovely hew
The joyous Spring out of the ground brings forth,
To cloath herselfe in colours fresh and new;

664. *scape*: escape.   665–80. Sp rearranges the list of flowers, which is a
lovely match for the catalogue of trees (*VG* 190–224). Cf. *Muio* 187–
200.   671. *Saffron*: the crocus.   672. The laurel is associated with
Phoebus in his guise as Apollo, god of poetry.   673. *Rhododaphne*:
oleander. *Sabine flowre*: the savin, *juniperus sabina*.   676. *Box*: bocchus;
named from Bocchus, the Libyan king who sacrificed his son, Jugurtha, to
preserve peace with the Romans.   677. *lucklesse Paramour*: In Thomas
Watson's *Amyntas* (1580), Amaranthus was the flower into which Amyntas
was transformed when he died of grief for Phyllis.   679. Narcissus fell in
love with his own reflection and gave his name to the pale flower.

He planted there, and reard a mount of earth,        685
In whose high front was writ as doth ensue.

> *To thee, small Gnat, in lieu of his life saved,*
> *The Shepheard hath thy deaths record engraved.*

FINIS.

---

688. *record*: from Lat. *recordare*, to remember: the epitaph is the gnat's memorial which confers on him the fame he desired.

# *Prosopopoia:* Or
# *Mother Hubberds Tale*

W̲e know little for certain about the composition of
*Prosopopoia: or Mother Hubberds Tale*. It was printed
with the *Complaints* of 1591 and Spenser's Dedica-
tory epistle mentions that the poem had been "long sithens
composed in the raw conceipt of . . . youth"; it was almost
certainly revised before publication. Modern commentators
agree that the picture of the Fox as courtier in the last two
episodes of the poem glances at Lord Burghley, and the topical
satire may have caused Spenser trouble. In 1592 Spenser's
friend Gabriel Harvey commented in passing that "Mother
Hubbard in the heat of chollar, forgetting the pure sanguine of
her sweete Feary Queene, wilfully over-shot her malcontented
selfe" (Harvey 1592), and later that year Thomas Nashe men-
tioned that the poem had kindled "sparkes of displeasure"
(Nashe 1592). Thirteen years after the publication of the *Com-
plaints*, Middleton (1604) referred to the poem's having been
"called in"—a term for the government's impounding unsold
copies of an offensive work. It was not reprinted with the rest of
the *Complaints* in the 1611 edition of Spenser's works, probably
for fear of antagonizing Robert Cecil, earl of Salisbury, Burgh-
ley's son. After Cecil's death it was reprinted with the second
edition of the *Works*.

What we know of contemporary reference to *Mother Hub-
berds Tale* suggests that the particular political targets of the
allegory were obscure even when it was published. Most mod-
ern commentators agree that the political allegory is largely
concentrated in the last episode of the work, and the most wide-
ly accepted account of the allegory is still Edwin Greenlaw's

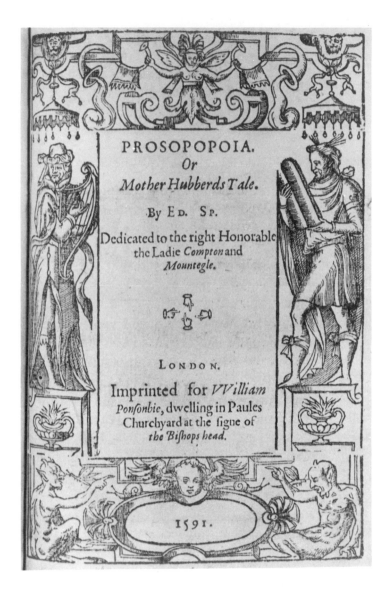

PROSOPOPOIA.
Or
*Mother Hubberds Tale.*

By ED. SP.

Dedicated to the right Honorable
the Ladie *Compton* and
*Mountegle.*

LONDON.

Imprinted for *William
Ponsonbie,* dwelling in Paules
Churchyard at the signe of
the *Bishops head.*

1591.

(1932)—that the final episode was originally written in 1579 to protest the possibility of a marriage between the queen and the French duke D'Alençon. Spenser's portrait of the Ape, Greenlaw argued, refers to the duke's envoy Simier to whom Elizabeth gave the pet name of "my monkey," or perhaps to a composite of Simier and Alençon. The injustices that the Fox and the Ape wreak in the Lion's kingdom predict what England would suffer were Alençon to become Elizabeth's consort. But, as Stein (1934) points out, it is possible to apply the fable of the Ape's assumption of the Lion's skin to many different situations: all particular interpretation is likely to remain conjectural.

The disagreement about the political allegory of the poem has distracted critical attention from the work itself. Yet *Mother Hubberds Tale* repays scrutiny: for all the studied offhandedness of its style, it is an extraordinary poem. Its complexity is signaled by its mixture of genres. As many critics have noted, it is Spenser's most Chaucerian work, beginning with an astrological *incipit* and participating in two recognizably medieval traditions. The first is that of estate satire, in which a writer presented a picture of the vices typical of a particular class or profession. Here the first three episodes of the poem present us with satiric pictures of the familiar three estates of peasantry, clergy, and (in the picture of court life) nobility. The easy roughness of the verse, the plainness and pithiness of the language (which Spenser announces will be "base" from the start) reinforces the work's satiric cast.

The second medieval kind is the quasi-allegorical beast-fable whose insistence on the similarity between men and animals has been compelling for audiences in all periods. Spenser draws in particular on the cycle of poems in French, German, and Dutch about Renard the Fox who appears as an embodiment of human skill, intelligence, and ruthless greed. But Spenser mixes his medieval materials with others which are more typically Renaissance: the picture of the perfect courtier (718–93) derives from courtesy-books like Castiglione's *The Courtier*, and the extraordinary appearance of Mercury in the poem is a topos taken from classical epic. It is this mixing of disparate materials, the setting of one generic world against another, that is typical of Spenser, and it enriches and complicates the satire.

Even what Spenser takes from his medieval models is transformed. In the Renard cycle the Fox is an important nobleman, an independent vassal of the Lion-king who has friends and "kin" at court, and whose hole is also a castle. He presents his prince with the typically medieval political problem of what to do about the powerful nobleman who thumbs his nose at his titular lord. But the social structure of Spenser's poem differs. The Fox and Ape are not nobility: they are nobodies who, in thoroughly Renaissance fashion, *make* themselves into Beggar, Shepherd, Priest, Courtier, and, eventually, King. The rogues display the social mobility which troubled and fascinated Renaissance writers. A positive vision of this mobility appears in Castiglione's *The Courtier* with its stress on the capacity of the individual to learn the skills of the court, and an analogue to it lies at the heart of Pico della Mirandola's famous *Oration on the Dignity of Man* with its vision of Man's limitless capacity to choose his own nature.

The Fox and the Ape act out a debased parodic version of this choice. Their self-fashioning is entirely a matter of clothes and gesture, a concern for externals only. (Whether or not he refers to Alençon's representative Simier, the Ape, as the proverbial imitator of human gesture, is a fitting companion for the Fox.) As such it demonstrates the ease with which spiritual beasts can imitate the outward graces of pulpit and court. As Kent Van den Berg (1978) points out, Spenser's generic title may have several relevant meanings. As a standard rhetorical term *prosopopoia* is simply a form of personification. "If ye will attribute any humane quality, as reason or speech to dombe creatures or other insensible things, & do study . . . to give them a humane person, it is . . . *Prosopopeia*" writes Puttenham (1589). But Puttenham calls the figure of *Prosopopoia* the "Counterfeit in personation," and this stress on false impersonation is central to a poem in which not only the poet but his rogues go about "counterfeiting" a series of imaginary persons.

This counterfeiting is particularly easy in the world of the poem, a world which is "Continuallie subject unto chaunge" (92) (Greene 1963). This change the narrator associates at the opening of the poem with the fall. The astrological *incipit* reminds us that Astrea, goddess of justice, has left our world for the heavens: perfect justice is no longer possible on earth. Astrea's departure was by tradition the end of the Golden Age: the iron world we now face is full of "plague, pestilence, and death" (8). Yet for the Fox and the Ape, "sonnes of the world so wide" (135), this mutability promises opportunity. The Fox comments that "Abroad where change is, good may gotten bee" (101), and a world where nothing is stable gives an advantage to the quick-change artist free to repudiate any present role for a more advantageous one. Ironically, the Fox makes even his lament about the loss of the Golden Age into grist for his rhetorical mill: he invokes it to justify community of goods and hence his right to steal whatever he wants. He and the Ape repeatedly call one another "brother" in the manner of harmless Golden Age shepherds, though their subsequent quarrel over who will wear the lion skin suggests that this rhetoric, like most of the language they use, is no more than a cloak for their private ambitions. The traditional matter of the *Complaints*-volume is thus given a peculiarly ironic slant.

The plot of the poem would seem to suggest a conservative moral: that while earthly evil may triumph temporarily, it will be overcome in the long run. Although in each case the Fox and the Ape manage successfully to pass themselves off as what they are not, their own greed eventually leads them to expose themselves; as they rise higher their punishment grows increasingly severe. In the first episode they escape entirely unpunished after gorging on slaughtered sheep; in the second they are forced to sell their living to a neighboring priest for a few pence; in the third the Fox is rusticated and the Ape, left without a servant to deal for him, falls into rags and is scorned from the court; in the fourth the Ape has his ears cropped and loses his tail. It would seem as if their very desire for unfettered freedom, their instinct to gratify their own appetites at the expense of society, leads to their being more vigorously suppressed. Yet the view of evil that the poem offers is more ambivalent. The very fact of the repeated cycle reminds us that the companions are not stopped: they possess a demonic energy which may enable them to continue in their metamorphic career long after the poem has ended.

This impression is strengthened by the intrusion of Mercury in the final episode. In the earlier incidents the impersonators were exposed by their own greed: the system worked. But in this episode it is necessary for a god to be dispatched to set things right: the false security that is so pervasive a theme in the *Complaints*-volume here shows the lion-monarch asleep during the gradual perversion of his rule. Mercury's descent balances and recalls Astrea's departure at the opening, and its obvious fantasy stresses the unlikeliness of the resolution. And even this resolution is double-edged. Commentators have often noted that the Fox escapes unpunished in this final episode, but it is equally important that the punishment of the Ape has a cosmetic value. Without his tail and with his ears cropped he will be harder to unmask because he will resemble all the more closely the human beings he imitates.

Mercury's descent also stands out as Spenser's most daring instance of generic mixing in the poem. Critics have pointed to the extraordinary stylistic indecorum of the episode: Spenser inserts a topos from classical epic into a medieval beast-fable, punctuating the "base" colloquial style of the surrounding poem with the more elaborate and complex syntax of the lines (225–56) in which Jove looks down to earth. Greene (1963) sees Spenser's inclusion of Mercury here as typical of his willingness to mix stylistic models with a freedom and an impurity that would have been anathema to more doctrinaire humanists of the Continent. Van den Berg (1978), on the other hand, suggests that the stylistic discontinuity is Spenser's means of drawing attention to Mercury's disquieting function in the poem as a representative artist. Traditionally Mercury, as messenger god, makes heaven's will known on earth, guiding and aiding the heroes of classical epic. He is thus associated by Renaissance mythographers with the power of language and his caduceus with the power of concord: he would seem to embody a harmonious and civilizing use of language opposed to the lying that characterizes the Fox and Ape. Yet Mercury himself seems uncomfortably to resemble the rogues. In mentioning his "cunning theeveries" (1287) Spenser reminds us that he is a patron of thieves, and in stressing his capacity to change himself into many shapes (1266, 1271, 1279–90) he suggests the amorality of human art, including verbal art.

Of crucial importance in understanding the work is the narrator—a figure who, like Mercury, is an artist but who, unlike the Fox and the Ape, is not a con-man. Atchity (1973) suggests that the speaker attempts to amend the disorder of the world; Mother Hubberd is offering the poem's moral medicine for its sickness. Van den Berg's (1978) more complex and problematic reading distinguishes the learned narrator from Mother Hubberd, and sees the poem as his conscious literate *revision* of the old woman's oral narrative. In his retelling of the story the narrator temporarily loses control of his subject as the pressure of his own bitter experience at court leads him to praise an unrealizable ideal courtier and to bewail his own experience as a suitor, but he recovers with the last episode—easy, undigressive, distanced, humorous. It is this complex use of the narrator that links *Mother Hubberds Tale* most clearly with Spenser's later poetry.

*William Oram*

# To the right Honourable, the
## Ladie *Compton* and
## Mountegle.

MOst *faire and vertuous Ladie; having often sought oppor-tunitie by some good meanes to make knowen to your Ladiship, the humble affection and faithfull duetie, which I have alwaies pro-fessed, and am bound to beare to that House, from whence yee spring, I have at length found occasion to remember the same, by making a simple present to you of these my idle labours; which having long sithens composed in the raw conceipt of my youth, I lately amongst other papers lighted upon, and was by others, which liked the same, mooved to set them foorth. Simple is the device, and the composition meane, yet carrieth some delight, even the rather because of the simplicitie and meannesse thus personated. The same I beseech your Ladiship take in good part, as a pledge of that profession which I have made to you, and keepe with you untill with some other more worthie labour, I do redeeme it out of your hands, and discharge my utmost dutie. Till then wishing your Ladiship all increase of honour and happinesse, I humblie take leave.*

*Your La: ever*
*humbly;*
*Ed. Sp.*

D E D I C A T I O N : *Ladie Compton and Mountegle*: Anne, fifth daughter of Sir John Spenser of Althorp whom Sp also praises as "Charillis" in *CCCHA* 548–63; she was married first to William Stanley, Lord Mounteagle, and later to Henry, Lord Compton, who died in 1589.     *conceipt*: understanding, judgment.

# *Prosopopoia:* or
# *Mother Hubberds Tale.*

IT was the month, in which the righteous Maide,
  That for disdaine of sinfull worlds upbraide,
Fled back to heaven, whence she was first conceived,
Into her silver bowre the Sunne received;
And the hot *Syrian* Dog on him awayting,            5
After the chafed Lyons cruell bayting,
Corrupted had th'ayre with his noysome breath,
And powr'd on th'earth plague, pestilence, and death.
Emongst the rest a wicked maladie
Raign'd emongst men, that manie did to die,        10
Depriv'd of sense and ordinarie reason;
That it to Leaches seemed strange and geason.
My fortune was mongst manie others moe,
To be partaker of their common woe;
And my weake bodie set on fire with griefe,       15
Was rob'd of rest, and naturall reliefe.
In this ill plight, there came to visite mee
Some friends, who sorie my sad case to see,
Began to comfort me in chearfull wise,
And meanes of gladsome solace to devise.         20

---

TITLE: *Prosopopoia*: personification, whether of an abstract concept or of an animal. See Introduction.

1–8: The month is August in which the Sun (with Sirius, the dog-star) leaves the house of Leo ("the chafed Lyon") and enters the house of Virgo (associated by Ovid and others with Astrea, "the righteous Maide"; see *Met* 1.149–50). Astrea's departure from this corrupt world at the end of the Golden Age is mentioned in *FQ* V i xi. The elaborate astrological opening of the poem echoes the works of Chaucer and his fifteenth-century imitators.
2. *upbraide*: verbal attack.    10. *did* caused.    12. *geason*: extraordinary.
15. *griefe*: pain.    19. *wise*: manner.

But seeing kindly sleep refuse to doe
His office, and my feeble eyes forgoe,
They sought my troubled sense how to deceave
With talke, that might unquiet fancies reave;
And sitting all in seates about me round,                              25
With pleasant tales (fit for that idle stound)
They cast in course to waste the wearie howres:
Some tolde of Ladies, and their Paramoures;
Some of brave Knights, and their renowned Squires;
Some of the Faeries and their strange attires;                         30
And some of Giaunts hard to be beleeved,
That the delight thereof me much releeved.
Amongst the rest a good old woman was,
Hight Mother *Hubberd*, who did farre surpas
The rest in honest mirth, that seem'd her well:                        35
She when her turne was come her tale to tell,
Tolde of a strange adventure, that betided
Betwixt the Foxe and th'Ape by him misguided;
The which for that my sense it greatly pleased,
All were my spirite heavie and diseased,                               40
Ile write in termes, as she the same did say,
So well as I her words remember may.
No Muses aide me needes heretoo to call;
Base is the style, and matter meane withall.
     ¶Whilome (said she) before the world was civill,                  45
The Foxe and th'Ape disliking of their evill
And hard estate, determined to seeke
Their fortunes farre abroad, lyeke with his lyeke:
For both were craftie and unhappie witted;

22. *forgoe*: forsake.     23. *deceave*: beguile.     24. *fancies reave*: i.e. distract
from unpleasant fantasies.     26. *idle stound*: time of inaction.     27. *waste*:
pass, occupy.     34. *Hight*: named.     35. *seem'd*: befitted.     41. *termes*:
words.     44. *meane*: low, vulgar.     45. *civill*: civilized. The tale is set in a
"barbarous" past which resembles remarkably the narrator's own age.
47. *estate*: status, condition in life.     49. *unhappie witted*: apt to cause
trouble.

Two fellowes might no where be better fitted.                           50
The Foxe, that first this cause of griefe did finde,
Gan first thus plaine his case with words unkinde.
Neighbor Ape, and my Goship eke beside,
(Both two sure bands in friendship to be tide,)
To whom may I more trustely complaine                                   55
The evill plight, that doth me sore constraine,
And hope thereof to finde due remedie?
Heare then my paine and inward agonie.
Thus manie yeares I now have spent and worne,
In meane regard, and basest fortunes scorne,                            60
Dooing my Countrey service as I might,
No lesse I dare saie than the prowdest wight;
And still I hoped to be up advaunced,
For my good parts; but still it hath mischaunced.
Now therefore that no lenger hope I see,                                65
But froward fortune still to follow mee,
And losels lifted up on high, where I did looke,
I meane to turne the next leafe of the booke.
Yet ere that anie way I doo betake,
I meane my Gossip privie first to make.                                 70
Ah my deare Gossip, (answer'd then the Ape,)
Deeply doo your sad words my wits awhape,
Both for because your griefe doth great appeare,
And eke because my selfe am touched neare:
For I likewise have wasted much good time,                              75
Still wayting to preferment up to clime,
Whilest others alwayes have before me stept,
And from my beard the fat away have swept;
That now unto despaire I gin to growe
And meane for better winde about to throwe.                             80
Therefore to me, my trustie friend, aread

50. *fitted*: provided, i.e. found (ironic).   52. *unkinde*: unnatural,
bad.   53. *Goship*: friend.   55. *complaine*: lament.   66. *froward*:
contrary.   67. *losels*: nobodies, good for nothings.   72. *awhape*:
confound, amaze.   81. *aread*: declare.

Thy councell: two is better than one head.
Certes (said he) I meane me to disguize
In some straunge habit, after uncouth wize,
Or like a Pilgrime, or a Lymiter,                                          85
Or like a *Gipsen,* or a Juggeler,
And so to wander to the worlds ende,
To seeke my fortune, where I may it mend:
For worse than that I have, I cannot meete.
Wide is the world I wote, and everie streete                               90
Is full of fortunes, and adventures straunge,
Continuallie subject unto chaunge.
Say my faire brother now, if this device
Doth like you, or may you to like entice.
Surely (said th'Ape) it likes me wondrous well;                            95
And would ye not poore fellowship expell,
My selfe would offer you t'accompanie
In this adventures chauncefull jeopardie.
For to wexe olde at home in idlenesse,
Is disadventrous, and quite fortunelesse:                                  100
Abroad where change is, good my gotten bee.
The Foxe was glad, and quickly did agree:
So both resolv'd, the morrow next ensuing,
So soone as day appeard to peoples vewing,
On their intended journey to proceede;                                     105
And over night, whatso theretoo did neede,
Each did prepare, in readines to bee.
The morrow next, so soone as one might see
Light out of heavens windowes forth to looke,
Both their habiliments unto them tooke,                                    110
And put themselves (a Gods name) on their way.
Whenas the Ape beginning well to wey

---

85. *Lymiter*: begging friar.    86. *Gipsen*: Gypsy.    94. *like*: please.
96. *expell*: refuse.    100. *disadventrous*: unfortunate. *fortunelesse*: lacking in
fortune, unrewarding.

This hard adventure, thus began t'advise;
Now read Sir Reynold, as ye be right wise,
What course ye weene is best for us to take,                    115
That for our selves we may a living make.
Whether shall we professe some trade or skill?
Or shall we varie our device at will,
Even as new occasion appeares?
Or shall we tie our selves for certaine yeares              120
To anie service, or to anie place?
For it behoves ere that into the race
We enter, to resolve first hereupon.
Now surely brother (said the Foxe anon)
Ye have this matter motioned in season:                    125
For everie thing that is begun with reason
Will come by readie meanes unto his end;
But things miscounselled must needs miswend.
Thus therefore I advize upon the case,
That not to anie certaine trade or place,                  130
Nor anie man we should our selves applie;
For why should he that is at libertie
Make himselfe bond? sith then we are free borne,
Let us all servile base subjection scorne;
And as we bee sonnes of the world so wide,                 135
Let us our fathers heritage divide,
And chalenge to our selves our portions dew
Of all the patrimonie, which a few
Now hold in hugger mugger in their hand,
And all the rest doo rob of good and land.                 140
For now a few have all and all have nought,
Yet all be brethren ylike dearly bought:

113. *advise*: consider.    114. *read*: say, counsel.    119. *occasion*:
opportunity.    121. *anie*: i.e. any one.    125. *motioned*: brought
up.    128. *miswend*: go astray.    137. *chalenge to*: claim for.    139. *in
hugger mugger*: secretly, i.e. privately.

There is no right in this partition,
Ne was it so by institution
Ordained first, ne by the law of Nature,                    145
But that she gave like blessing to each creture
As well of worldly livelode as of life,
That there might be no difference nor strife,
Nor ought cald mine or thine: thrice happie then
Was the condition of mortall men.                           150
That was the golden age of *Saturne* old,
But this might better be the world of gold:
For without golde now nothing wilbe got.
Therefore (if please you) this shalbe our plot,
We will not be of anie occupation,                          155
Let such vile vassalls borne to base vocation
Drudge in the world, and for their living droyle
Which have no wit to live withouten toyle.
But we will walke about the world at pleasure
Like two free men, and make our ease our treasure.         160
Free men some beggers call, but they be free,
And they which call them so more beggers bee:
For they doo swinke and sweate to feed the other,
Who live like Lords of that which they doo gather,
And yet doo never thanke them for the same,                165
But as their due by Nature doo it clame.
Such will we fashion both our selves to bee,
Lords of the world, and so will wander free
Where so us listeth, uncontrol'd of anie.
Hard is our hap, if we (emongst so manie)                   170
Light not on some that may our state amend;
Sildome but some good commeth ere the end.
Well seemd the Ape to like this ordinaunce:
Yet well considering of the circumstaunce,

143–72. The Fox's invocation of a golden age as part of an attack on the
present division of property recurs in the speech of the egalitarian giant of
*FQ* V ii 37–38.    147. *livelode*: livelihood.    157. *droyle*: slave.
173. *ordinaunce*: arrangement, direction.

As pausing in great doubt, awhile he staid,                    175
And afterwards with grave advizement said;
I cannot, my lief brother, like but well
The purpose of the complot which ye tell:
For well I wot (compar'd to all the rest
Of each degree) that Beggers life is best:                    180
And they that thinke themselves the best of all,
Oft-times to begging are content to fall.
But this I wot withall that we shall ronne
Into great daunger like to bee undonne,
Thus wildly to wander in the worlds eye,                      185
Without pasport or good warrantye,
For feare least we like rogues should be reputed,
And for eare marked beasts abroad be bruted:
Therefore I read, that we our counsells call,
How to prevent this mischiefe ere it fall,                    190
And how we may with most securitie,
Beg amongst those that beggers doo defie.
Right well deere Gossip ye advized have,
(Said then the Foxe) but I this doubt will save:
For ere we farther passe, I will devise                       195
A pasport for us both in fittest wize,
And by the names of Souldiers us protect;
That now is thought a civile begging sect.
Be you the Souldier, for you likest are
For manly semblance, and small skill in warre:               200
I will but wayte on you, and as occasion
Falls out, my selfe fit for the same will fashion.
The Pasport ended, both they forward went,
The Ape clad Souldierlike, fit for th'intent,
In a blew jacket with a crosse of redd                        205
And manie slits, as if that he had shedd

186. *pasport*: Elizabethan vagrants needed to have passports issued by the
appropriate authorities. See Renwick (1928) pp.235–36 for contemporary
commentary on discharged soldiers. *warrantye*: official
authorization.      192. *defie*: distrust.      198. *civile*: well-ordered.
203. *ended*: finished.

Much blood throgh many wounds therein receaved,
Which had the use of his right arme bereaved;
Upon his head an old Scotch cap he wore,
With a plume feather all to peeces tore:                    210
His breeches were made after the new cut,
*Al Portugese*, loose like an emptie gut;
And his hose broken high above the heeling,
And his shooes beaten out with traveling.
But neither sword nor dagger did he beare,                  215
Seemes that no foes revengement he did feare;
In stead of them a handsome bat he held,
On which he leaned, as one farre in elde.
Shame light on him, that through so false illusion,
Doth turne the name of Souldiers to abusion,               220
And that, which is the noblest mysterie,
Brings to reproach and common infamie.
Long they thus travailed, yet never met
Adventure, which might them a working set:
Yet manie waies they sought, and manie tryed;              225
Yet for their purposes none fit espyed.
At last they chaunst to meete upon the way
A simple husbandman in garments gray;
Yet though his vesture were but meane and bace,
A good yeoman he was of honest place,                      230
And more for thrift did care than for gay clothing:
Gay without good, is good hearts greatest loathing.
The Foxe him spying, bad the Ape him dight
To play his part, for loe he was in sight,
That (if he er'd not) should them entertaine,             235
And yeeld them timely profite for their paine.
Eftsoones the Ape himselfe gan up to reare,
And on his shoulders high his bat to beare,
As if good service he were fit to doo;

213. *broken*: torn.    217. *bat*: stick.    220. *abusion*: abuse,
misuse.    233. *dight*: prepare.

But little thrift for him he did it too:                                    240
And stoutly forward he his steps did straine,
That like a handsome swaine it him became:
When as they nigh approached, that good man
Seeing them wander loosly, first began
T'enquire of custome, what and whence they were?        245
To whom the Ape, I am a Souldiere,
That late in warres have spent my deerest blood,
And in long service lost both limbs and good,
And now constrain'd that trade to overgive,
I driven am to seeke some meanes to live:                        250
Which might it you in pitie please t'afford,
I would be readie both in deed and word,
To doo you faithfull service all my dayes.
This yron world (that same he weeping sayes)
Brings downe the stowtest hearts to lowest state:        255
For miserie doth bravest mindes abate,
And make them seeke for that they wont to scorne,
Of fortune and of hope at once forlorne.
The honest man, that heard him thus complaine,
Was griev'd, as he had felt part of his paine;                   260
And well disposd' him some reliefe to showe,
Askt if in husbandrie he ought did knowe,
To plough, to plant, to reap, to rake, to sowe,
To hedge, to ditch, to thrash, to thetch, to mowe;
Or to what labour els he was prepar'd?                           265
For husbands life is labourous and hard.
Whenas the Ape him hard so much to talke
Of labour, that did from his liking balke,
He would have slipt the coller handsomly,
And to him said; good Sir, full glad am I,                       270
To take what paines may anie living wight:

---

244. *loosly*: carelessly.     248. *good*: property.     256. *abate*: beat
down.     268. *balke*: lie out of the way.     269. *slipt the coller*: drawn back
from this task. *handsomly*: gracefully (ironic).

But my late maymed limbs lack wonted might
To doo their kindly services, as needeth:
Scarce this right hand the mouth with diet feedeth,
So that it may no painfull worke endure,                    275
Ne to strong labour can it selfe enure.
But if that anie other place you have,
Which askes small paines, but thriftines to save,
Or care to overlooke, or trust to gather,
Ye may me trust as your owne ghostly father.               280
With that the husbandman gan him avize
That it for him were fittest exercise
Cattell to keep, or grounds to oversee;
And asked him, if he could willing bee
To keep his sheep, or to attend his swyne,                 285
Or watch his mares, or take his charge of kyne?
Gladly (said he) what ever such like paine
Ye put on me, I will the same sustaine:
But gladliest I of your fleecie sheepe
(Might it you please) would take on me the keep.           290
For ere that unto armes I me betooke,
Unto my fathers sheepe I usde to looke,
That yet the skill thereof I have not loste:
Thereto right well this Curdog by my coste
(Meaning the Foxe) will serve, my sheepe to gather,        295
And drive to follow after their Belwether.
The Husbandman was meanly well content,
Triall to make of his endevourment,
And home him leading, lent to him the charge
Of all his flocke, with libertie full large,              300
Giving accompt of th'annuall increce
Both of their lambes, and of their woolly fleece.

---

275. *painfull*: laborious.    276. *enure*: accustom.    283. *Cattell*:
beasts.    287. *paine*: labor.    288. *sustaine*: support, carry out.

Thus is this Ape become a shepheard swaine
And the false Foxe his dog. (God give them paine)
For ere the yeare have halfe his course out-run,               305
And doo returne from whence he first begun,
They shall him make an ill accompt of thrift.
Now whenas Time flying with winges swift,
Expired had the terme, that these two javels
Should render up a reckning of their travels               310
Unto their master, which it of them sought,
Exceedingly they troubled were in thought,
Ne wist what answere unto him to frame,
Ne how to scape great punishment, or shame,
For their false treason and vile theeverie.               315
For not a lambe of all their flockes supply
Had they to shew: but ever as they bred,
They slue them, and upon their fleshes fed:
For that disguised Dog lov'd blood to spill,
And drew the wicked Shepheard to his will.               320
So twixt them both they not a lambkin left,
And when lambes fail'd the old sheepes lives they reft;
That how t'acquite themselves unto their Lord,
They were in doubt, and flatly set abord.
The Foxe then counsel'd th'Ape, for to require               325
Respite till morrow, t'answere his desire:
For times delay new hope of helpe still breeds.
The goodman granted, doubting nought their deeds,
And bad, next day that all should readie be.
But they more subtill meaning had than he:               330
For the next morrowes meed they closely ment,
For feare of afterclaps for to prevent.

---

309. *javels*: rogues.   310. *travels*: labors.   323. *t'acquite themselves*: to
make their accounting.   324. *flatly*: completely. *set abord*: "at sea."
328. *doubting*: suspecting.   330. *meaning*: intention.   331. *closely*:
secretly.   332. *prevent*: anticipate.

And that same evening, when all shrowded were
In careles sleep, they without care or feare,
Cruelly fell upon their flock in folde,                                335
And of them slew at pleasure what they wolde:
Of which whenas they feasted had their fill,
For a full complement of all their ill,
They stole away, and tooke their hastie flight,
Carried in clowdes of all-concealing night.                            340
So was the husbandman left to his losse,
And they unto their fortunes change to tosse.
After which sort they wandered long while,
Abusing manie through their cloaked guile;
That at the last they gan to be descryed                               345
Of everie one, and all their sleights espyed.
So as their begging now them failed quyte;
For none would give, but all men would them wyte:
Yet would they take no paines to get their living,
But seeke some other way to gaine by giving,                           350
Much like to begging but much better named;
For manie beg, which are thereof ashamed.
And now the Foxe had gotten him a gowne,
And th'Ape a cassoke sidelong hanging downe;
For they their occupation meant to change,                             355
And now in other state abroad to range:
For since their souldiers pas no better spedd,
They forg'd another, as for Clerkes booke-redd.
Who passing foorth, as their adventures fell,
Through manie haps, which needs not here to tell;                      360
At length chaunst with a formall Priest to meete,

342. *And . . . tosse*: The implicit metaphor is that of fortune as a changing sea
with the Fox and the Ape as sailors.     344. *Abusing*: deceiving.
348. *wyte*: blame.     358. *Clerkes booke- redd*: The association between
literacy and the clergy is a medieval commonplace; in this context it rapidly
becomes ironic. The priest whom the Fox and Ape meet is unable to read
their passport.     361. *formall*: dignified.

Whom they in civill manner first did greete,
And after askt an almes for Gods deare love.
The man straight way his choler up did move,
And with reproachfull tearmes gan them revile,                    365
For following that trade so base and vile;
And askt what license, or what Pas they had?
Ah (said the Ape as sighing wondrous sad)
Its an hard case, when men of good deserving
Must either driven be perforce to sterving,                        370
Or asked for their pas by everie squib,
That list at will them to revile or snib:
And yet (God wote) small oddes I often see
Twixt them that aske, and them that asked bee.
Natheles because you shall not us misdeeme,                        375
But that we are as honest as we seeme,
Yee shall our pasport at your pleasure see,
And then ye will (I hope) well mooved bee.
Which when the Priest beheld, he vew'd it nere,
As if therein some text he studying were,                          380
But little els (God wote) could therof skill:
For read he could not evidence, nor will,
Ne tell a written word, ne write a letter,
Ne make one title worse, ne make one better:
Of such deep learning little had he neede,                         385
Ne yet of Latine, ne of Greeke, that breede
Doubts mongst Divines, and difference of texts,

368. *sad*: heavily.    371. *squib*: low fellow.    372. *snib*:
reproach.    375. *misdeeme*: misjudge, think evil of.    379–95. The priest
typifies the abuses in the Anglican church alleged by stricter Protestants: he is
unlearned and unconcerned either with theological issues or with the care of
his flock, preferring to read the official homilies on Sundays instead of
preaching, and to spend his time at the "plays" which Puritans despised. See
Renwick (1928) pp.236–38 for extracts from contemporary pamphlets
attacking these abuses.    381. *skill*: understand, do.    382. *evidence*: i.e.
testimonial.

From whence arise diversitie of sects,
And hatefull heresies, of God abhor'd:
But this good Sir did follow the plaine word,                    390
Ne medled with their controversies vaine;
All his care was, his service well to saine,
And to read Homelies upon holidayes:
When that was done, he might attend his playes;
An easie life, and fit high God to please.                       395
He having overlookt their pas at ease,
Gan at the length them to rebuke againe,
That no good trade of life did entertaine,
But lost their time in wandring loose abroad,
Seeing the world, in which they bootles boad,                    400
Had wayes enough for all therein to live;
Such grace did God unto his creatures give.
Said then the Foxe; who hath the world not tride,
From the right way full eath may wander wide.
We are but Novices, new come abroad,                             405
We have not yet the tract of anie troad,
Nor on us taken anie state of life,
But readie are of anie to make preife.
Therefore might please you, which the world have
                                            proved,
Us to advise, which forth but lately moved,                      410
Of some good course, that we might undertake;
Ye shall for ever us your bondmen make.
The Priest gan wexe halfe proud to be so praide,
And thereby willing to affoord them aide;
It seemes (said he) right well that ye be Clerks,                415
Both by your wittie words, and by your werks.

---

400. *bootles*: profitlessly. *boad*: abode.    404. *eath*: easily.    408. *preife*:
proof.    412. *bondmen*: i.e. debtors.    415–542. Throughout the
following "discourse" the priest cheerfully and indiscriminately mixes
Anglican and Puritan attitudes, adopting whatever will aid his worldly
comfort and advancement.

Is not that name enough to make a living
To him that hath a whit of Natures giving?
How manie honest men see ye arize
Daylie thereby, and grow to goodly prize?        420
To Deanes, to Archdeacons, to Commissaries,
To Lords, to Principalls, to Prebendaries;
All jolly Prelates, worthie rule to beare,
Who ever them envie: yet spite bites neare.
Why should ye doubt then, but that ye likewise        425
Might unto some of those in time arise?
In the meane time to live in good estate,
Loving that love, and hating those that hate;
Being some honest Curate, or some Vicker
Content with little in condition sicker.        430
Ah but (said th'Ape) the charge is wondrous great,
To feed mens soules, and hath an heavie threat.
To feede mens soules (quoth he) is not in man:
For they must feed themselves, doo what we can.
We are but charg'd to lay the meate before:        435
Eate they that list, we need to doo no more.
But God it is that feedes them with his grace,
The bread of life powr'd downe from heavenly place.
Therefore said he, that with the budding rod
Did rule the Jewes, *All shalbe taught of God.*        440
That same hath Jesus Christ now to him raught,

---

420. *grow to*: rise by degrees to. *prize*: i.e. worth, importance.
421. *Commissaries*: Officers of a bishop entrusted with the ecclesiastical jurisdiction of particular parts of a diocese.    422. *Principalls*: heads of religious houses. *Prebendaries*: canons of a church or cathedral receiving a particular stipend or *preband*.    424. *yet . . . neare*: "whatever spiteful men may say" (Renwick 1928).    440. *All . . . God*: Isaiah 54.13. Renwick (1928) p.237 notes that the priest in his ignorance refers the text to Aaron. The priest here misuses the Protestant emphasis on the importance of the relation between God and the individual believer to avoid responsibility for the souls of his parishioners.    441. *That same*: i.e. the bread of life. *raught*: reached, taken.

By whom the flock is rightly fed, and taught:
He is the Shepheard, and the Priest is hee;
We but his shepheard swaines ordain'd to bee.
Therefore herewith doo not your selfe dismay;                    445
Ne is the paines so great, but beare ye may;
For not so great as it was wont of yore,
It's now a dayes, ne halfe so straight and sore:
They whilome used duly everie day
Their service and their holie things to say,                     450
At morne and even, besides their Anthemes sweete,
Their penie Masses, and their Complynes meete,
Their Dirges, their Trentals, and their shrifts,
Their memories, their singings, and their gifts.
Now all those needlesse works are laid away;                     455
Now once a weeke upon the Sabbath day,
It is enough to doo our small devotion,
And then to follow any merrie motion.
Ne are we tyde to fast, but when we list,
Ne to weare garments base of wollen twist,                       460
But with the finest silkes us to aray,
That before God we may appeare more gay,
Resembling *Aarons* glorie in his place:
For farre unfit it is, that person bace
Should with vile cloaths approach Gods majestie,                 465
Whom no uncleannes may approachen nie:
Or that all men, which anie master serve,
Good garments for their service should deserve;
But he that serves the Lord of hoasts most high,

---

442. *By whom*: Christ.     451–54. These various "works" are identified with
the Roman rite. *Anthemes* are antiphonal singing; *Complynes* are the final
ritual of the day; *Dirges* are services for the dead; *Trentals* a set of thirty
requiem masses; *shrift* is private confession; *memories* a service of
commemoration, especially of the departed.     458. *motion*: inclination,
impulse.     463. *Aarons glorie*: Aaron's elaborate priestly costume is
prescribed in Exodus 28.1–43. Puritan critics frequently attacked the
Anglican establishment for its retention of elaborate clerical vestments.

And that in highest place, t'approach him nigh,                    470
And all the peoples prayers to present
Before his throne, as on ambassage sent
Both too and fro, should not deserve to weare
A garment better, than of wooll or heare.
Beside we may have lying by our sides                              475
Our lovely Lasses, or bright shining Brides:
We be not tyde to wilfull chastitie,
But have the Gospell of free libertie.
By that he ended had his ghostly sermon,
The Foxe was well induc'd to be a Parson;                          480
And of the Priest eftsoones gan to enquire,
How to a Benefice he might aspire.
Marie there (said the Priest) is arte indeed.
Much good deep learning one thereout may reed,
For that the ground-worke is, and end of all,                     485
How to obtaine a Beneficiall.
First therefore, when ye have in handsome wise
Your selfe attyred, as you can devise,
Then to some Noble man your selfe applye,
Or other great one in the worldes eye,                            490
That hath a zealous disposition
To God, and so to his religion:
There must thou fashion eke a godly zeale,
Such as no carpers may contrayre reveale:
For each thing fained, ought more warie bee.                      495
There thou must walke in sober gravitee,
And seeme as Saintlike as Saint *Radegund*:
Fast much, pray oft, looke lowly on the ground,
And unto everie one doo curtesie meeke:
These lookes (nought saying) doo a benefice seeke,                500

477. *wilfull*: perverse, unreasonable.     479. *ghostly*: religious, spiritual.
484. *thereout*: about that. *reed*: teach, utter.     486. *Beneficiall*: a benefice, an
ecclesiastical living (or a letter presenting such a benefice).
491–93. *zealous* here has pronounced Puritan overtones.     499. *curtesie*:
obeisance.

And be thou sure one not to lacke or long.
But if thee list unto the Court to throng,
And there to hunt after the hoped pray,
Then must thou thee dispose another way:
For there thou needs must learne, to laugh, to lie,          505
To face, to forge, to scoffe, to companie,
To crouche, to please, to be a beetle stock
Of thy great Masters will, to scorne, or mock:
So maist thou chaunce mock out a Benefice,
Unlesse thou canst one conjure by device,          510
Or cast a figure for a Bishoprick:
And if one could, it were but a schoole-trick.
These be the wayes, by which without reward
Livings in Court be gotten, though full hard.
For nothing there is done without a fee:          515
The Courtier needes must recompenced bee
With a Benevolence, or have in gage
The *Primitias* of your Parsonage:
Scarse can a Bishoprick forpas them by,
But that it must be gelt in privitie.          520
Doo not thou therefore seeke a living there,
But of more private persons seeke elswhere,
Whereas thou maist compound a better penie,
Ne let thy learning question'd be of anie.
For some good Gentleman that hath the right          525
Unto his Church for to present a wight,
Will cope with thee in reasonable wise;
That if the living yerely doo arise
To fortie pound, that then his yongest sonne
Shall twentie have, and twentie thou hast wonne:          530
Thou hast it wonne, for it is of franke gift,

501. *or*: ere.     507. *beetle stock*: literally the handle of a hammer; an
instrument.     510. *conjure by device*: obtain by magic.     511. *cast a figure*:
draw up a horoscope.     517. *Benevolence*: a gift of money. *in gage*: in
pledge.     518. *Primitias*: first year's income.     520. *gelt*: gilded.
527. *cope*: bargain.     531. *franke*: free, unrestricted.

And he will care for all the rest to shift;
Both that the Bishop may admit of thee,
And that therein thou maist maintained bee.
This is the way for one that is unlern'd                     535
Living to get, and not to be discern'd.
But they that are great Clerkes, have nearer wayes,
For learning sake to living them to raise:
Yet manie eke of them (God wote) are driven,
T'accept a Benefice in peeces riven.                          540
How saist thou (friend) have I not well discourst
Upon this Common place (though plaine, not wourst)?
Better a short tale, than a bad long shriving.
Needes anie more to learne to get a living?
Now sure and by my hallidome (quoth he)                       545
Ye a great master are in your degree:
Great thankes I yeeld you for your discipline,
And doo not doubt, but duly to encline
My wits theretoo, as ye shall shortly heare.
The Priest him wisht good speed, and well to fare.            550
So parted they, as eithers way them led.
But th'Ape and Foxe ere long so well them sped,
Through the Priests holesome counsell lately tought,
And throgh their own faire handling wisely wroght,
That they a Benefice twixt them obtained;                     555
And craftie Reynold was a Priest ordained;
And th'Ape his Parish Clarke procur'd to bee.
Then made they revell route and goodly glee.
But ere long time had passed, they so ill
Did order their affaires, that th'evill will                  560
Of all their Parishners they had constraind;
Who to the Ordinarie of them complain'd,

540. *in peeces riven*: by division between himself and his patron.
542. *Common place*: familiar topic.     561. *constraind*: i.e. drawn on
themselves, compelled.     562–74. The Fox and Ape eventually cause their
parishioners to complain to the *Ordinary* who would be a judge empowered
to deal with ecclesiastical cases; he sends *Pursuivants* or official messengers

How fowlie they their offices abusd',
And them of crimes and heresies accusd';
The Pursivants he often for them sent:                    565
But they neglected his commaundement.
So long persisted obstinate and bolde,
Till at the length he published to holde
A Visitation, and them cyted thether:
Then was high time their wits about to geather;          570
What did they then, but made a composition
With their next neighbor Priest for light condition,
To whom their living they resigned quight
For a few pence, and ran away by night.
So passing through the Countrey in disguize,             575
They fled farre off, where none might them surprize,
And after that long straied here and there,
Through everie field and forrest farre and nere;
Yet never found occasion for their tourne,
But almost sterv'd, did much lament and mourne.          580
At last they chaunst to meete upon the way
The Mule, all deckt in goodly rich aray,
With bells and bosses, that full lowdly rung,
And costly trappings, that to ground downe hung.
Lowly they him saluted in meeke wise,                    585
But he through pride and fatnes gan despise
Their meanesse; scarce vouchsafte them to requite.
Whereat the Foxe deep groning in his sprite,
Said, Ah sir Mule, now blessed be the day,
That I see you so goodly and so gay                      590

with warrants for the Fox and Ape to appear before him; when they fail to
do so he announces that he will hold a *Visitation* or official inquiry into the
state of the parish. Such visitations might precede the dispossession of an
unfit incumbent. To anticipate this the Fox and the Ape make a *composition*
with a neighboring priest, an agreement whereby the priest will take over the
living in exchange for "a few pence."     569. *cyted*: summoned.     572. *for*
*light condition*: i.e. the "few pence" of line 574.     573. *quight*:
entirely.     579. *tourne*: trickery.     587. *requite*: return [the greeting].

In your attyres, and eke your silken hyde
Fil'd with round flesh, that everie bone doth hide.
Seemes that in fruitfull pastures ye doo live,
Or fortune doth you secret favour give.
Foolish Foxe (said the Mule) thy wretched need          595
Praiseth the thing that doth thy sorrow breed.
For well I weene, thou canst not but envie
My wealth, compar'd to thine owne miserie,
That art so leane and meagre waxen late,
That scarse thy legs uphold thy feeble gate.          600
Ay me (said then the Foxe) whom evill hap
Unworthy in such wretchednes doth wrap,
And makes the scorne of other beasts to bee:
But read (faire Sir, of grace) from whence come yee?
Or what of tidings you abroad doo heare?          605
Newes may perhaps some good unweeting beare.
From royall Court I lately came (said he)
Where all the braverie that eye may see,
And all the happinesse that heart desire,
Is to be found; he nothing can admire,          610
That hath not seene that heavens portracture:
But tidings there is none I you assure,
Save that which common is, and knowne to all,
That Courtiers as the tide doo rise and fall.
But tell us (said the Ape) we doo you pray,          615
Who now in Court doth beare the greatest sway.
That if such fortune doo to us befall,
We may seeke favour of the best of all.
Marie (said he) the highest now in grace,

619–30. A much-disputed local reference. The "Lyon" here is probably the
queen, the female "Liege" of line 628. The "wilde beasts that swiftest are in
chase" have variously been identified as the earl of Leicester, the earl of Essex,
and Sir Walter Ralegh. In the case of both Leicester and Essex it has been
argued that the "late chayne" is the secret marriage each contracted which,
when known, provoked the queen's fury. See Mounts (1950). Certainty in
this case is impossible to come by but the gossipy tone of this account of
"who's in, who's out" is unmistakable.

Be the wilde beasts, that swiftest are in chase;                    620
For in their speedie course and nimble flight
The Lyon now doth take the most delight:
But chieflie, joyes on foote them to beholde,
Enchaste with chaine and circulet of golde:
So wilde a beast so tame ytaught to bee,                            625
And buxome to his bands is joy to see.
So well his golden Circlet him beseemeth:
But his late chayne his Liege unmeete esteemeth;
For so brave beasts she loveth best to see,
In the wilde forrest raunging fresh and free.                      630
Therefore if fortune thee in Court to live,
In case thou ever there wilt hope to thrive,
To some of these thou must thy selfe apply:
Els as a thistle-downe in th'ayre doth flie,
So vainly shalt thou too and fro be tost,                          635
And loose thy labour and thy fruitles cost.
And yet full few, which follow them I see,
For vertues bare regard advaunced bee,
But either for some gainfull benefit,
Or that they may for their owne turnes be fit.                     640
Nath'les perhaps ye things may handle soe,
That ye may better thrive than thousands moe.
But (said the Ape) how shall we first come in,
That after we may favour seeke to win?
How els (said he) but with a good bold face,                       645
And with big words, and with a stately pace,
That men may thinke of you in generall,
That to be in you, which is not at all:
For not by that which is, the world now deemeth,
(As it was wont) but by that same that seemeth.                    650
Ne do I doubt, but that ye well can fashion
Your selves theretoo, according to occasion:
So fare ye well, good Courtiers may ye bee;

---

626. *buxome*: obedient. *bands*: bonds.     636. *cost*: expenditure.
640. *turnes*: tricks, maneuvers.

So proudlie neighing from them parted hee.
Then gan this craftie couple to devize,                          655
How for the Court themselves they might aguize:
For thither they themselves meant to addresse,
In hope to finde there happier successe.
So well they shifted, that the Ape anon
Himselfe had cloathed like a Gentleman,                          660
And the slie Foxe, as like to be his groome,
That to the Court in seemly sort they come.
Where the fond Ape himselfe uprearing hy
Upon his tiptoes, stalketh stately by,
As if he were some great *Magnifico*,                           665
And boldlie doth amongst the boldest go.
And his man Reynold with fine counterfesaunce
Supports his credite and his countenaunce.
Then gan the Courtiers gaze on everie side,
And stare on him, with big lookes basen wide,                   670
Wondring what mister wight he was, and whence:
For he was clad in strange accoustrements,
Fashion'd with queint devises never seene
In Court before, yet there all fashions beene:
Yet he them in newfanglenesse did pas:                          675
But his behaviour altogether was
*Alla Turchesca*, much the more admyr'd,
And his lookes loftie, as if he aspyr'd
To dignitie, and sdeign'd the low degree;
That all which did such strangenesse in him see,                680
By secrete meanes gan of his state enquire,
And privily his servant thereto hire:
Who throughly arm'd against such coverture,

---

656. *aguize*: dress.     658. *successe*: result.     667. *counterfesaunce*:
imposture.     668. *credite*: good reputation. *countenaunce*:
appearance.     670. *basen wide*: deeply amazed.     673. *queint devises*:
elaborate designs.     677. *Alla Turchesca*: in the Turkish fashion.
680. *strangenesse*: coolness, aloofness.     681. *state*: rank, position.
682. *hire*: bribe.

Reported unto all, that he was sure
A noble Gentleman of high regard,                    685
Which through the world had with long travel far'd,
And seene the manners of all beasts on ground;
Now here arriv'd, to see if like he found.
Thus did the Ape at first him credit gaine,
Which afterwards he wisely did maintaine              690
With gallant showe, and daylie more augment
Through his fine feates and Courtly complement;
For he could play, and daunce, and vaute, and spring,
And all that els pertaines to reveling,
Onely through kindly aptnes of his joynts.           695
Besides he could doo manie other poynts,
The which in Court him served to good stead:
For he mongst Ladies could their fortunes read
Out of their hands, and merie leasings tell,
And juggle finely, that became him well:             700
But he so light was at legier demaine,
That what he toucht, came not to light againe;
Yet would he laugh it out, and proudly looke,
And tell them, that they greatly him mistooke.
So would he scoffe them out with mockerie,           705
For he therein had great felicitie;
And with sharp quips joy'd others to deface,
Thinking that their disgracing did him grace:
So whilst that other like vaine wits he pleased,
And made to laugh, his heart was greatly eased.      710
But the right gentle minde would bite his lip,
To heare the Javell so good men to nip:
For though the vulgar yeeld an open eare,
And common Courtiers love to gybe and fleare
At everie thing, which they heare spoken ill,        715

689. *credit*: good name.    692. *complement*: ceremony, courtesy.
693. *vaute*: leap.    695. *kindly*: natural.    699. *leasings*: lies.
700. *juggle*: entertain (with overtones of trickery and deception).
714. *gybe*: jeer. *fleare*: laugh mockingly, grimace.

And the best speaches with ill meaning spill;
Yet the brave Courtier, in whose beauteous thought
Regard of honour harbours more than ought,
Doth loath such base condition, to backbite
Anies good name for envie or despite: 720
He stands on tearmes of honourable minde,
Ne will be carried with the common winde
Of Courts inconstant mutabilitie,
Ne after everie tattling fable flie;
But heares, and sees the follies of the rest, 725
And thereof gathers for himselfe the best:
He will not creepe, nor crouche with fained face,
But walkes upright with comely stedfast pace,
And unto all doth yeeld due curtesie;
But not with kissed hand belowe the knee, 730
As that same Apish crue is wont to doo:
For he disdaines himselfe t'embase theretoo.
He hates fowle leasings, and vile flatterie,
Two filthie blots in noble Gentrie;
And lothefull idlenes he doth detest, 735
The canker worme of everie gentle brest;
The which to banish with faire exercise
Of knightly feates, he daylie doth devise:
Now menaging the mouthes of stubborne steedes,
Now practising the proofe of warlike deedes, 740
Now his bright armes assaying, now his speare,
Now the nigh aymed ring away to beare;
At other times he casts to sew the chace
Of swift wilde beasts, or runne on foote a race,
T'enlarge his breath (large breath in armes most
                  needfull); 745
Or els by wrestling to wex strong and heedfull,
Or his stiffe armes to stretch with Eughen bowe,
And manly legs, still passing too and fro,

---

716. *meaning*: purpose, intention. *spill*: vitiate, spoil.

Without a gowned beast him fast beside;
A vaine ensample of the *Persian* pride,                    750
Who after he had wonne th'*Assyrian* foe,
Did ever after scorne on foote to goe.
Thus when this Courtly Gentleman with toyle
Himselfe hath wearied, he doth recoyle
Unto his rest, and there with sweete delight        755
Of Musicks skill revives his toyled spright,
Or els with Loves, and Ladies gentle sports,
The joy of youth, himselfe he recomforts:
Or lastly, when the bodie list to pause,
His minde unto the Muses he withdrawes;              760
Sweete Ladie Muses, Ladies of delight,
Delights of life, and ornaments of light:
With whom he close confers with wise discourse,
Of Natures workes, of heavens continuall course,
Of forreine lands, of people different,               765
Of kingdomes change, of divers government,
Of dreadfull battailes of renowmed Knights;
With which he kindleth his ambitious sprights
To like desire and praise of noble fame,
The onely upshot whereto he doth ayme:               770
For all his minde on honour fixed is,
To which he levels all his purposis,
And in his Princes service spends his dayes,
Not so much for to gaine, or for to raise
Himselfe to high degree, as for his grace,           775
And in his liking to winne worthie place;
Through due deserts and comely carriage,
In whatso please employ his personage,
That may be matter meete to gaine him praise;

749. *gowned beast*: i.e. an elaborately caparisoned horse.    754. *recoyle*:
retire.    762–67. The Muses here are the representatives of all learning,
including natural science ("nature's works"), astronomy, geography, history,
government, as well as "dreadfull battailes of renowmed Knights."
770. *upshot*: mark.    775. *his grace*: i.e. his prince.    776. *his liking*: i.e.
his prince's liking.

For he is fit to use in all assayes,                                    780
Whether for Armes and warlike amenaunce,
Or else for wise and civill governaunce.
For he is practiz'd well in policie,
And thereto doth his Courting most applie:
To learne the enterdeale of Princes strange,          785
To marke th'intent of Counsells, and the change
Of states, and eke of private men somewhile,
Supplanted by fine falshood and faire guile;
Of all the which he gathereth, what is fit
T'enrich the storehouse of his powerfull wit,         790
Which through wise speaches, and grave conference
He daylie eekes, and brings to excellence.
Such is the rightfull Courtier in his kinde:
But unto such the Ape lent not his minde;
Such were for him no fit companions,                     795
Such would descrie his lewd conditions:
But the yong lustie gallants he did chose
To follow, meete to whom he might disclose
His witlesse pleasance, and ill pleasing vaine.
A thousand wayes he them could entertaine,           800
With all the thriftles games, that may be found
With mumming and with masking all around,
With dice, with cards, with balliards farre unfit,
With shuttelcocks, misseeming manlie wit,
With courtizans, and costly riotize,                        805
Whereof still somewhat to his share did rize:
Ne, them to pleasure, would he sometimes scorne
A Pandares coate (so basely was he borne);
Thereto he could fine loving verses frame,
And play the Poet oft. But ah, for shame               810

---

781. *amenaunce*: conduct.      783. *policie*: statecraft, political sagacity.
784. *applie*: devote.      785. *enterdeale*: negotiation, intercourse. *strange*:
foreign.      799. *pleasance*: pleasing manner.      802. *mumming*:
disguising.      803. *balliards*: billiards.

Let not sweete Poets praise, whose onely pride
Is vertue to advaunce, and vice deride,
Be with the worke of losels wit defamed,
Ne let such verses Poetrie be named:
Yet he the name on him would rashly take,                    815
Maugre the sacred Muses, and it make
A servant to the vile affection
Of such, as he depended most upon,
And with the sugrie sweete thereof allure
Chast Ladies eares to fantasies impure.                      820
To such delights the noble wits he led
Which him reliev'd, and their vaine humours fed
With fruitles follies, and unsound delights.
But if perhaps into their noble sprights
Desire of honor, or brave thought of armes                   825
Did ever creepe, then with his wicked charmes
And strong conccipts he would it drive away,
Ne suffer it to house there halfe a day.
And whenso love of letters did inspire
Their gentle wits, and kindly wise desire,                   830
That chieflie doth each noble minde adorne,
Then would he scoffe at learning, and eke scorne
The Sectaries thereof, as people base
And simple men, which never came in place
Of worlds affaires, but in darke corners mewd,               835
Muttred of matters, as their bookes them shewd,
Ne other knowledge ever did attaine,
But with their gownes their gravitie maintaine.
From them he would his impudent lewde speach
Against Gods holie Ministers oft reach,                      840
And mocke Divines and their profession:
What else then did he by progression,
But mocke high God himselfe, whom they professe?

813. *losels*: profligates, rakes.    817. *affection*: lust.    822. *reliev'd*: i.e. provided him with money.    826. *charmes*: songs.    827. *conceipts*: forceful language, ideas.    833. *Sectaries*: i.e. scholars.    843. *professe*: acknowledge, teach.

But what car'd he for God, or godlinesse?
All his care was himselfe how to advaunce,  845
And to uphold his courtly countenaunce
By all the cunning meanes he could devise;
Were it by honest wayes, or otherwise,
He made small choyce: yet sure his honestie
Got him small gaines, but shameles flatterie,  850
And filthie brocage, and unseemly shifts,
And borowe base, and some good Ladies gifts:
But the best helpe, which chiefly him sustain'd,
Was his man Raynolds purchase which he gain'd.
For he was school'd by kinde in all the skill  855
Of close conveyance, and each practise ill
Of coosinage and cleanly knaverie,
Which oft maintain'd his masters braverie.
Besides he usde another slipprie slight,
In taking on himselfe in common sight,  860
False personages fit for everie sted,
With which he thousands cleanly coosined:
Now like a Merchant, Merchants to deceave,
With whom his credite he did often leave
In gage, for his gay Masters hopelesse dett:  865
Now like a Lawyer, when he land would lett,
Or sell fee-simples in his masters name,
Which he had never, nor ought like the same:
Then would he be a Broker, and draw in
Both wares and money, by exchange to win:  870
Then would he seeme a Farmer, that would sell
Bargaines of woods, which he did lately fell,
Or corne, or cattle, or such other ware,

849. *he . . . choyce*: it mattered little to him.    851. *brocage*: pimping. *shifts*:
contrivances.    852. *borowe*: surety, pledge.    854. *purchase*: winnings,
loot. *he*: the Ape.    855. *he*: the Fox.    856. *close conveyance*:
underhanded trickery, transmission.    857. *cleanly*: artful.    858. *braverie*:
ostentation, finery.    861. *personages*: false characters, roles. *sted*:
circumstance.    862. *coosined*: tricked.    866. *lett*: rent.    867. *fee-
simples*: landed estates.

Thereby to coosin men not well aware;
Of all the which there came a secret fee                    875
To th'Ape, that he his countenaunce might bee.
Besides all this, he usd' oft to beguile
Poore suters, that in Court did haunt some while:
For he would learne their busines secretly,
And then informe his Master hastely,                        880
That he by meanes might cast them to prevent,
And beg the sute, the which the other ment.
Or otherwise false Reynold would abuse
The simple Suter, and wish him to chuse
His Master, being one of great regard                       885
In Court, to compas anie sute not hard,
In case his paines were recompenst with reason:
So would he worke the silly man by treason
To buy his Masters frivolous good will,
That had not power to doo him good or ill.                   890
So pitifull a thing is Suters state.
Most miserable man, whom wicked fate
Hath brought to Court, to sue for had ywist,
That few have found, and manie one hath mist;
Full little knowest thou that hast not tride,               895
What hell it is in suing long to bide:
To loose good dayes, that might be better spent;
To wast long nights in pensive discontent;
To speed to day, to be put back to morrow;
To feed on hope, to pine with feare and sorrow;             900
To have thy Princes grace, yet want her Peeres;
To have thy asking, yet waite manie yeeres;
To fret thy soule with crosses and with cares;
To eate thy heart through comfortlesse dispaires;
To fawne, to crowche, to waite, to ride, to ronne,          905
To spend, to give, to want, to be undonne.

876. *countenaunce*: protector, backer.    881. *prevent*: come before,
anticipate.    882. *ment*: had in mind.    888. *treason*: betrayal of trust.
893. *had ywist*: proverbial, "if I had known. . . ."

Unhappie wight, borne to desastrous end,
That doth his life in so long tendance spend.
Who ever leaves sweete home, where meane estate
In safe assurance, without strife or hate,                     910
Findes all things needfull for contentment meeke;
And will to Court for shadowes vaine to seeke,
Or hope to gaine, himselfe will a daw trie:
That curse God send unto mine enemie.
For none but such as this bold Ape unblest,                    915
Can ever thrive in that unluckie quest;
Or such as hath a Reynold to his man,
That by his shifts his Master furnish can.
But yet this Foxe could not so closely hide
His craftie feates, but that they were descride               920
At length, by such as sate in justice seate,
Who for the same him fowlie did entreate;
And having worthily him punished,
Out of the Court for ever banished.
And now the Ape wanting his huckster man,                      925
That wont provide his necessaries, gan
To growe into great lacke, ne could upholde
His countenaunce in those his garments olde;
Ne new ones could he easily provide,
Though all men him uncased gan deride,                         930
Like as a Puppit placed in a play,
Whose part once past all men bid take away:
So that he driven was to great distresse,
And shortly brought to hopelesse wretchednesse.
Then closely as he might he cast to leave
The Court not asking any passe or leave;                       935
But ran away in his rent rags by night,
Ne ever stayd in place, ne spake to wight,

908. *tendance*: waiting in expectation.     909. *meane*: low, undistinguished.
913. *will . . . trie*: will act like a fool.     922. *entreate*: treat, i.e. punish.

Till that the Foxe his copesmate he had found,
To whome complayning his unhappy stound, 940
At last againe with him in travell joynd,
And with him far'd some better chaunce to fynde.
So in the world long time they wandered,
And mickle want and hardnesse suffered;
That them repented much so foolishly 945
To come so farre to seeke for misery,
And leave the sweetnes of contented home,
Though eating hipps, and drinking watry fome.
Thus as they them complayned too and fro,
Whilst through the forest rechlesse they did goe, 950
Lo where they spide, how in a gloomy glade,
The Lyon sleeping lay in secret shade,
His Crowne and Scepter lying him beside,
And having doft for heate his dreadfull hide:
Which when they sawe, the Ape was sore afrayde, 955
And would have fled with terror all dismayde.
But him the Foxe with hardy words did stay,
And bad him put all cowardize away:
For now was time (if ever they would hope)
To ayme their counsels to the fairest scope, 960
And them for ever highly to advaunce,
In case the good which their owne happie chaunce
Them freely offred, they would wisely take.
Scase could the Ape yet speake, so did he quake,
Yet as he could, he askt how good might growe, 965
Where nought but dread and death do seeme in show.
Now (sayd he) whiles the Lyon sleepeth sound,
May we his Crowne and Mace take from the ground,
And eke his skinne the terror of the wood,
Wherewith we may our selves (if we thinke good) 970

---

939. *copesmate*: accomplice.    940. *stound*: time of trouble.    945. *them
repented*: they regretted.    954. *dreadfull*: terrifying.    960. *scope*: mark,
end, purpose.

Make Kings of Beasts, and Lords of forests all,
Subject unto that powre imperiall.
Ah but (sayd the Ape) who is so bold a wretch,
That dare his hardy hand to those outstretch:
When as he knowes his meede, if he be spide,   975
To be a thousand deathes, and shame beside?
Fond Ape (sayd then the Foxe) into whose brest
Never crept thought of honor, nor brave gest,
Who will not venture life a King to be,
And rather rule and raigne in soveraign see,   980
Than dwell in dust inglorious and bace,
Where none shall name the number of his place?
One joyous houre in blisfull happines,
I chose before a life of wretchednes.
Be therefore counselled herein by me,   985
And shake off this vile harted cowardree.
If he awake, yet is not death the next,
For we may coulor it with some pretext
Of this, or that, that may excuse the cryme:
Else we may flye; thou to a tree mayst clyme,   990
And I creepe under ground; both from his reach:
Therefore be rul'd to doo as I doo teach.
The Ape, that earst did nought but chill and quake,
Now gan some courage unto him to take,
And was content to attempt that enterprise,   995
Tickled with glorie and rash covetise.
But first gan question, whither should assay
Those royall ornaments to steale away?
Marie that shall your selfe (quoth he theretoo)
For ye be fine and nimble it to doo;   1000
Of all the beasts which in the forrests bee,
Is not a fitter for this turne than yee:
Therefore, mine owne deare brother take good hart,

---

980. *see*: throne.  988. *coulor it*: excuse or disguise our attempt.
997. *whither*: which.

And ever thinke a Kingdome is your part.
Loath was the Ape, though praised, to adventer,　　　1005
Yet faintly gan into his worke to enter,
Afraid of everie leafe, that stir'd him by,
And everie stick, that underneath did ly;
Upon his tiptoes nicely he up went,
For making noyse, and still his eare he lent　　　1010
To everie sound, that under heaven blew;
Now went, now stept, now crept, now backward drew,
That it good sport had been him to have eyde:
Yet at the last (so well he him applyde,)
Through his fine handling, and cleanly play,　　　1015
He all those royall signes had stolne away,
And with the Foxes helpe them borne aside,
Into a secret corner unespide.
Whether whenas they came, they fell at words,
Whether of them should be the Lord of Lords:　　　1020
For th'Ape was stryfull, and ambicious;
And the Foxe guilefull, and most covetous,
That neither pleased was, to have the rayne
Twixt them divided into even twaine,
But either (algates) would be Lords alone:　　　1025
For Love and Lordship bide no paragone.
I am most worthie (said the Ape) sith I
For it did put my life in jeopardie:
Thereto I am in person, and in stature
Most like a man, the Lord of everie creature;　　　1030
So that it seemeth I was made to raigne,
And borne to be a Kingly soveraigne.
Nay (said the Foxe) Sir Ape you are astray:
For though to steale the Diademe away
Were the worke of your nimble hand, yet I　　　1035

---

1005. *adventer*: attempt, adventure.　　1010. *For*: in order to avoid.
1021. *stryfull*: contentious.　　1025. *algates*: any way.　　1026. *paragone*:
rival.

Did first devise the plot by pollicie;
So that it wholly springeth from my wit:
For which also I claime my selfe more fit
Than you, to rule: for gouvernment of state
Will without wisedome soone be ruinate.                   1040
And where ye claime your selfe for outward shape
Most like a man, Man is not like an Ape
In his chiefe parts, that is, in wit and spirite;
But I therein most like to him doo merite
For my slie wyles and subtill craftinesse,                   1045
The title of the Kingdome to possesse.
Nath'les (my brother) since we passed are
Unto this point, we will appease our jarre,
And I with reason meete will rest content,
That ye shall have both crowne and gouvernment,             1050
Upon condition, that ye ruled bee
In all affaires, and counselled by mee;
And that ye let none other ever drawe
Your minde from me, but keepe this as a lawe:
And hereupon an oath unto me plight.                        1055
The Ape was glad to end the strife so light,
And thereto swore: for who would not oft sweare,
And oft unsweare a Diademe to beare?
Then freely up those royall spoyles he tooke,
Yet at the Lyons skin he inly quooke;                       1060
But it dissembled, and upon his head
The Crowne, and on his backe the skin he did,
And the false Foxe him helped to array.
Then when he was all dight he tooke his way
Into the forest, that he might be seene                     1065
Of the wilde beasts in his new glory sheene.
There the two first, whome he encountred, were
The sheepe and th'Asse, who striken both with feare
At sight of him, gan fast away to flye,

1062. *did*: put.

But unto them the Foxe alowd did cry,                    1070
And in the Kings name bad them both to stay,
Upon the payne that thereof follow may.
Hardly naythles were they restrayned so,
Till that the Foxe forth toward them did goe,
And there disswaded them from needlesse feare,          1075
For that the King did favour to them beare;
And therefore dreadles bad them come to Corte:
For no wild beasts should do them any torte
There or abroad, ne would his majestye
Use them but well, with gracious clemencye,              1080
As whome he knew to him both fast and true;
So he perswaded them, with homage due
Themselves to humble to the Ape prostrate,
Who gently to them bowing in his gate,
Receyved them with chearefull entertayne.                1085
Thenceforth proceeding with his princely traync,
He shortly met the Tygre, and the Bore,
Which with the simple Camell raged sore
In bitter words, seeking to take occasion,
Upon his fleshly corpse to make invasion:                1090
But soone as they this mock-King did espy,
Their troublous strife they stinted by and by,
Thinking indeed that it the Lyon was:
He then to prove, whether his powre would pas
As currant, sent the Foxe to them streight way,          1095
Commaunding them their cause of strife bewray;
And if that wrong on eyther side there were,
That he should warne the wronger to appeare
The morrow next at Court, it to defend;
In the meane time upon the King t'attend.                1100
The subtile Foxe so well his message sayd,

1073. *Hardly*: barely.     1078. *torte*: wrong.     1085. *entertayne*: treatment.
1090. *invasion*: assault.     1094. *prove*: test.     1096. *bewray*: declare.
1099. *defend*: make a legal defense of it.

That the proud beasts him readily obayd:
Whereby the Ape in wondrous stomack woxe,
Strongly encorag'd by the crafty Foxe;
That King indeed himselfe he shortly thought,                    1105
And all the Beasts him feared as they ought:
And followed unto his palaice hye,
Where taking Conge, each one by and by
Departed to his home in dreadfull awe,
Full of the feared sight, which late they sawe.                  1110
The Ape thus seized of the Regall throne,
Eftsones by counsell of the Foxe alone,
Gan to provide for all things in assurance,
That so his rule might lenger have endurance.
First to his Gate he pointed a strong gard,                      1115
That none might enter but with issue hard:
Then for the safegard of his personage,
He did appoint a warlike equipage
Of forreine beasts, not in the forest bred,
But part by land, and part by water fed;                         1120
For tyrannie is with strange ayde supported.
Then unto him all monstrous beasts resorted
Bred of two kindes, as Griffons, Minotaures,
Crocodiles, Dragons, Beavers, and Centaures:
With those himselfe he strengthned mightelie,                    1125
That feare he neede no force of enemie.
Then gan he rule and tyrannize at will,
Like as the Foxe did guide his graceles skill,
And all wylde beasts made vassals of his pleasures,
And with their spoyles enlarg'd his private treasures.          1130
No care of justice, nor no rule of reason,
No temperance, nor no regard of season
Did thenceforth ever enter in his minde,

---

1103. *stomack*: i.e. pride.     1108. *Conge*: leave.     1116. *issue*:
action.     1124. As amphibious creatures the crocodile and beaver are "bred
of two kinds."

But crueltie, the signe of currish kinde,
And sdeignfull pride, and wilfull arrogaunce;                    1135
Such followes those whom fortune doth advaunce.
But the false Foxe most kindly plaid his part:
For whatsoever mother wit, or arte
Could worke, he put in proofe: no practise slie,
No counterpoint of cunning policie,                            1140
No reach, no breach, that might him profit bring,
But he the same did to his purpose wring.
Nought suffered he the Ape to give or graunt,
But through his hand must passe the Fiaunt.
All offices, all leases by him lept,                           1145
And of them all whatso he likte, he kept.
Justice he solde injustice for to buy,
And for to purchase for his progeny.
Ill might it prosper, that ill gotten was,
But so he got it, little did he pas.                           1150
He fed his cubs with fat of all the soyle,
And with the sweete of others sweating toyle,
He crammed them with crumbs of Benefices,
And fild their mouthes with meeds of malefices,
He cloathed them with all colours save white,                  1155
And loded them with lordships and with might,
So much as they were able well to beare,
That with the weight their backs nigh broken were;
He chaffred Chayres in which Churchmen were set,
And breach of lawes to privie ferme did let;                   1160
No statute so established might bee,
Nor ordinaunce so needfull, but that hee
Would violate, though not with violence,

1137. *kindly*: naturally (with ironic contradiction of the sense "benevolently").
1140. *counterpoint*: the metaphor is musical, suggesting various actions (like
lines of music) placed against one another.     *policie*: dissimulation,
stratagem.        1144. *Fiaunt*: warrant.        1145. *lept*: passed.        1150. *little
. . . pas*: he cared little.        1154. *meeds*: rewards.     *malefices*: evil deeds.
1159. The fox sells the sees of bishops.

Yet under colour of the confidence
The which the Ape reposd' in him alone,                    1165
And reckned him the kingdomes corner stone.
And ever when he ought would bring to pas,
His long experience the platforme was:
And when he ought not pleasing would put by,
The cloke was care of thrift, and husbandry,             1170
For to encrease the common treasures store;
But his owne treasure he encreased more
And lifted up his loftie towres thereby,
That they began to threat the neighbour sky;
The whiles the Princes pallaces fell fast               1175
To ruine: (for what thing can ever last?)
And whilest the other Peeres for povertie
Were forst their auncient houses to let lie,
And their olde Castles to the ground to fall,
Which their forefathers famous over all                 1180
Had founded for the Kingdomes ornament,
And for their memories long moniment.
But he no count made of Nobilitie,
Nor the wilde beasts whom armes did glorifie,
The Realmes chiefe strength and girlond of the crowne.  1185
All these through fained crimes he thrust adowne,
Or made them dwell in darknes of disgrace:
For none, but whom he list might come in place.
Of men of armes he had but small regard,
But kept them lowe, and streigned verie hard.            1190
For men of learning little he esteemed;
His wisedome he above their learning deemed.
As for the rascall Commons least he cared;
For not so common was his bountie shared;
Let God (said he) if please, care for the manie,        1195
I for my selfe must care before els anie:

1168. *platforme*: i.e. basis of his argument.    1190. *streigned*: restrained.
1192. *deemed*: judged, considered.

So did he good to none, to manie ill,
So did he all the kingdome rob and pill,
Yet none durst speake, ne none durst of him plaine;
So great he was in grace, and rich through gaine.      1200
Ne would he anie let to have accesse
Unto the Prince, but by his owne addresse:
For all that els did come, were sure to faile,
Yet would he further none but for availe.
For on a time the Sheepe, to whom of yore      1205
The Foxe had promised of friendship store,
What time the Ape the kingdome first did gaine,
Came to the Court, her case there to complaine,
How that the Wolfe her mortall enemie
Had sithence slaine her Lambe most cruellie;      1210
And therefore crav'd to come unto the King,
To let him knowe the order of the thing.
Soft Gooddie Sheepe (then said the Foxe) not soe:
Unto the King so rash ye may not goe,
He is with greater matter busied,      1215
Than a Lambe,or the Lambes owne mothers hed.
Ne certes may I take it well in part,
That ye my cousin Wolfe so fowly thwart,
And seeke with slaunder his good name to blot:
For there was cause, els doo it he would not.      1220
Therefore surcease good Dame, and hence depart.
So went the Sheepe away with heavie hart.
So manie moe, so everie one was used,
That to give largely to the boxe refused.
Now when high *Jove*, in whose almightie hand      1225
The care of Kings, and power of Empires stand,
Sitting one day within his turret hye,
From whence he vewes with his blacklidded eye,
Whatso the heaven in his wide vawte containes,
And all that in the deepest earth remaines,      1230
The troubled kingdome of wilde beasts behelde,

1218. *thwart*: oppose.      1224. *boxe*: money box.      1229. *vawte*: vault.

Whom not their kindly Sovereigne did welde,
But an usurping Ape with guile suborn'd,
Had all subverst, he sdeignfully it scorn'd
In his great heart, and hardly did refraine,                     1235
But that with thunder bolts he had him slaine,
And driven downe to hell, his dewest meed:
But him avizing, he that dreadfull deed
Forbore, and rather chose with scornfull shame
Him to avenge, and blot his brutish name                         1240
Unto the world, that never after anie
Should of his race be voyd of infamie:
And his false counsellor, the cause of all,
To damne to death, or dole perpetuall,
From whence he never should be quit, nor stal'd.                 1245
Forthwith he *Mercurie* unto him cal'd,
And bad him flie with never resting speed
Unto the forrest, where wilde beasts doo breed,
And there enquiring privily, to learne
What did of late chaunce to the Lyon stearne,                    1250
That he rul'd not the Empire, as he ought;
And whence were all those plaints unto him brought
Of wrongs and spoyles, by salvage beasts committed;
Which done, he bad the Lyon be remitted
Into his seate, and those same treachours vile                   1255
Be punished for their presumptuous guile.
The Sonne of *Maia* soone as he receiv'd
That word, streight with his azure wings he cleav'd
The liquid clowdes, and lucid firmament;
Ne staid, till that he came with steep descent                   1260
Unto the place, where his prescript did showe.
There stouping like an arrowe from a bowe,
He soft arrived on the grassie plaine,
And fairly paced forth with easie paine,

1233. *suborn'd*: assisted.          1237. *dewest*: rightful, most fitting.
1254. *remitted*: Lat. "sent back."          1257. *Sonne of Maia*:
Mercury.          1261. *prescript*: directions.

Till that unto the Pallace nigh he came.                    1265
Then gan he to himselfe new shape to frame,
And that faire face, and that Ambrosiall hew,
Which wonts to decke the Gods immortall crew,
And beautefie the shinie firmament,
He doft, unfit for that rude rabblement.                    1270
So standing by the gates in strange disguize,
He gan enquire of some in secret wize,
Both of the King, and of his government,
And of the Foxe, and his false blandishment:
And evermore he heard each one complaine                    1275
Of foule abuses both in realme and raine.
Which yet to prove more true, he meant to see,
And an ey-witnes of each thing to bee.
Tho on his head his dreadfull hat he dight,
Which maketh him invisible in sight,                        1280
And mocketh th'eyes of all the lookers on,
Making them thinke it but a vision.
Through power of that, he runnes through enemies
                                          swerds;
Through power of that, he passeth through the herds
Of ravenous wilde beasts, and doth beguile                  1285
Their greedie mouthes of the expected spoyle;
Through power of that, his cunning theeveries
He wonts to worke, that none the same espies;
And through the power of that, he putteth on,
What shape he list in apparition.                           1290
That on his head he wore, and in his hand
He tooke *Caduceus* his snakie wand,

---

1270. *rabblement*: crowd, disorderly assembly.     1283. *runnes through*:
passes by.     1291–99. Cf. Cartari, in Lynche's translation, "[Mercury] hath
. . . in one of his hands a slender white wand, about the which two serpents
doe annodate and entwine themselves, whose heads doe meet together even
just at the top thereof, as their tailes also do meet at the lower end, and the
one of them is male, and the other female. And this depincturance with them
was called *Concordia*, or *Signum pacis*." (*The Fountaine of Ancient Fiction*
[1599]: Mercury).

With which the damned ghosts he governeth,
And furies rules, and Tartare tempereth.
With that he causeth sleep to seize the eyes,                    1295
And feare the harts of all his enemyes;
And when him list, an universall night
Throughout the world he makes on everie wight;
As when his Syre with *Alcumena* lay.
Thus dight, into the Court he tooke his way,                     1300
Both through the gard, which never him descride,
And through the watchmen, who him never spide:
Thenceforth he past into each secrete part,
Whereas he saw, that sorely griev'd his hart;
Each place abounding with fowle injuries,                        1305
And fild with treasure rackt with robberies:
Each place defilde with blood of guiltles beasts,
Which had been slaine, to serve the Apes beheasts;
Gluttonie, malice, pride, and covetize,
And lawlesnes raigning with riotize;                             1310
Besides the infinite extortions,
Done through the Foxes great oppressions,
That the complaints thereof could not be tolde.
Which when he did with lothfull eyes beholde,
He would no more endure, but came his way,                      1315
And cast to seeke the Lion, where he may,
That he might worke the avengement for this shame,
On those two caytives, which had bred him blame.
And seeking all the forrest busily,
At last he found, where sleeping he did ly:                     1320
The wicked weed, which there the Foxe did lay,
From underneath his head he tooke away,
And then him waking, forced up to rize.
The Lion looking up gan him avize,
As one late in a traunce, what had of long                      1325

1294. *Tartare*: Tartarus, the infernal region of Greek myth. *tempereth*:
rules.      1299. Jove lay with *Alcumena* and to prolong his pleasure would
not let the sun rise for the space of three nights.      1313. *tolde*: counted.
1314. *lothfull*: reluctant.

Become of him: for fantasie is strong.
Arise (said *Mercurie*) thou sluggish beast,
That here liest senseles, like the corpse deceast,
The whilste thy kingdome from thy head is rent,
And thy throne royall with dishonour blent:                    1330
Arise, and doo thy selfe redeeme from shame,
And be aveng'd on those that breed thy blame.
Thereat enraged, soone he gan upstart,
Grinding his teeth, and grating his great hart,
And rouzing up himselfe, for his rough hide               1335
He gan to reach; but no where it espide.
Therewith he gan full terribly to rore,
And chafte at that indignitie right sore.
But when his Crowne and scepter both he wanted,
Lord how he fum'd and sweld, and rag'd, and panted;      1340
And threatned death, and thousand deadly dolours
To them that had purloyn'd his Princely honours.
With that in hast, disroabed as he was,
He toward his owne Pallace forth did pas;
And all the way he roared as he went,                         1345
That all the forrest with astonishment
Thereof did tremble, and the beasts therein
Fled fast away from that so dreadfull din.
At last he came unto his mansion,
Where all the gates he found fast lockt anon,                1350
And manie warders round about them stood:
With that he roar'd alowd, as he were wood,
That all the Pallace quaked at the stound,
As if it quite were riven from the ground,
And all within were dead and hartles left;                   1355
And th'Ape himselfe, as one whose wits were reft,
Fled here and there, and everie corner sought,
To hide himselfe from his owne feared thought.
But the false Foxe when he the Lion heard,
Fled closely forth, streightway of death afeard,            1360
And to the Lion came, full lowly creeping,

With fained face, and watrie eyne halfe weeping,
T'excuse his former treason and abusion,
And turning all unto the Apes confusion:
Nath'les the royall Beast forbore beleeving,                    1365
But bad him stay at ease till further preeving.
Then when he saw no entrance to him graunted,
Roaring yet lowder that all harts it daunted,
Upon those gates with force he fiercely flewe,
And rending them in pieces, felly slewe                         1370
Those warders strange, and all that els he met.
But th'Ape still flying, he no where might get:
From rowme to rowme, from beame to beame he fled
All breathles, and for feare now almost ded:
Yet him at last the Lyon spide, and caught,                     1375
And forth with shame unto his judgement brought.
Then all the beasts he causd' assembled bee
To heare their doome, and sad ensample see:
The Foxe, first Author of that treacherie,
He did uncase, and then away let flie.                          1380
But th'Apes long taile (which then he had) he quight
Cut off, and both eares pared of their hight;
Since which, all Apes but halfe their eares have left,
And of their tailes are utterlie bereft.
     So Mother *Hubberd* her discourse did end:                 1385
Which pardon me, if I amisse have pend,
For weake was my remembrance it to hold,
And bad her tongue that it so bluntly tolde.

                         F I N I S .

---

1363. *abusion*: imposture, outrage, wrong.     1364. *confusion*: discomfiture,
ruin.     1366. *stay at ease*: remain free.     1378. *doome*: judgment.
1380. *uncase*: strip.

# Ruines of Rome: by Bellay

T he original for Spenser's *Ruines of Rome* translation was published in 1558 as *Les Antiquitez de Rome contenant une generale description de sa grandeur, et comme une deploration de sa ruine: plus un songe ou vision sur le mesme subject.* Its author, Joachim Du Bellay (1522–60), was a brilliant Latinist of distinguished birth and an outstanding early champion of the literary potential of the French language, as Spenser was of the English: the *Antiquitez de Rome's* untranslated sonnet dedicatory to the king of France yearns to recreate ("rebastir") the glory of classical Rome in the French tongue. Du Bellay's pained disenchantment with the corruption of the modern Rome where he went to study in 1553 heightened his homesickness and contrasted sharply with his admiration for the ancient ruins and the civilization and literature they represented, thus giving the *Antiquitez* a poignancy that arguably makes it his most appealing work.

Central to the *Antiquitez de Rome's* appeal to Spenser was its tense and ambiguous concern with Rome's poets. The invention of printing and the concomitant revolution in education had made the literature of Greece and Rome *the* central experience of the imagination for Spenser's contemporaries. And the *Antiquitez* not only values that culture enormously; it also uses it to probe the mysteries of poetic creativity itself, beginning with a vatic summoning of the spirits of the buried culture that is sensitive to a kind of poetic enthusiasm that shades off into magic. Virgil is preeminent here, the empire's greatest poet, but also the agent of its legitimation, the dreamer of its dreams and the creator of its imperial mythology. Like his own Aeneas, who catches his vision of Rome's imperial future in the underworld, this Virgil has mysterious powers derived from mysterious sources. For Du Bellay it is as if Rome *is* Virgil's creation, and Rome's fall challenges his poetic authority, and by extension poetic authority in general. Exhuming the carcass and reviving the spirit of Rome are essential to repossessing the living poet.

But this necromancy has its dangers. The Rome that was the object of enormous antiquarian affection for Petrarch, Poggio, and Du Bellay, was also the Rome of Revelation, the new archetypal tyranny subsuming Old Testament Babylon, enormously powerful, apparently eternal, but in fact a shadowy and transient parody to the ultimate reality of the City of God. Such a Rome should not be resuscitated, for its life was a perversion in the first place. The world of Horatian *monumentum* is also, by Spenserean pun, moniment—an admonition. And the inescapable extension of the Roman empire for Spenser and for his English contemporaries is its survival in the Roman church. While this identification remains largely latent in Spenser's *Ruines of Rome*, it is never completely absent.

Du Bellay's other great appeal to Spenser is his Petrarchanism, the more intriguing in the *Antiquitez* because the object of sensuous interest is not a woman but a city. Long identified as the first Renaissance sonnet sequence on a subject other than love, the *Antiquitez* has, however, recently been seen (as in Rebhorn 1980) to present Rome itself as an "imperial mistress" and object of the poet's courtly love, the motifs of whose presentation rely heavily on Petrarch's Laura. Rome, like Laura, turns to dust, and Du Bellay's return to Rome's ruins is reminiscent of Petrarch's return to the sacred places of his memories of Laura. At the same time, Petrarch's professed unworthiness of the angelic Laura is answered by Du Bellay's more ambiguous relation to Rome. On one hand, we see fascinated pagan admiration of Rome's former glories and a yearning for Orphic powers to call them back. The simpler traditional sonnet style gives way to a style more elaborate and archaic, appropriate to the tone of the frequently imitated Virgil, from whom Du Bellay (and Spenser) implicitly claim symbolic descent. On the other hand, an overtly Christian recoil from Rome's seductive allurements joins with a sense of the poet's symbolic infidelity to his native land (Ferguson 1982:29). That significant features of Du Bellay's and Spenser's imperial mistress, Rome, become part of Shakespeare's treatment of his beloved in his *Sonnets* has been argued (by Hieatt 1983) on the basis of an elaborate set of significant verbal echoes.

Rome is presented in the *Antiquitez* through a diverse range of *personae* or identities, primarily female: famous offspring swarming about her, she is compared to her divine progenetrix, Cybele (sonnet 6); she is the maternal bosom into which her Gothic invaders make a destructive return (sonnet 11); she is a Pandora, indiscriminately hoarding good things and evil alike (sonnet 19); she is Tethys, titaness queen and mother of oceans and rivers (sonnet 20); she is the harlot spirit, St. Augustine's Rome as mistress of the world, more straightforwardly revealing her true nature in the modern Rome (sonnet 27); and she is the aged oak tree shamelessly displaying (in Spenser's version, at least) her ravaged body (sonnet 28). In Du Bellay's *Songe* the range of response to Rome, from fascinated observation to total dissociation, is wider yet, and she seems for a moment (see *VB* sonnet 14) to be the New Jerusalem, but her foundations of sand betray her true identity to be demonic, and rightfully doomed to be struck down by heavenly thunder in sonnet 15. For Spenser the relevance of these diverse morals to his own time derives directly from Du Bellay's sense that Rome is the world in epitome: "Le plan de Rome est la carte du monde" (*Antiquitez* 26.14).

Du Bellay's original is clearly a more sophisticated achievement than Spenser's generally accurate translation. Du Bellay's distress over contemporary Rome is "restrained by ceremonious patterning and controlled gesture" (Prescott 1978:48), which Spenser's somewhat shrill addiction to mutability themes and literal emblematic effect cannot duplicate very accurately. Spenser's version is undatable, apart from the reference to Du Bartas's *Uranie* of 1579 in the Envoy which, as Spenser's own addition to the sequence (and with its differing rhyme scheme), could be of later date. Nevertheless the brooding melancholy of Du Bellay's Roman sonnets haunts Spenser's imagination from his apprentice days on, and it is arguable that these early visions of Rome's fate have a determining role in his continuing inability to be completely confident that any other civilization is likely to do better. Later, in *The Shepheardes Calender*, Cuddie bemoans an inferior age, Rome's wealthy patrons Maecenas and Augustus long ago dead, no heroic worthies left "for Poets on to play" ("October" 61–72).

Spenser's detachment of the *Antiquitez* from the more overtly religious *Songe*, which appears later in the *Complaints* as *The Visions of Bellay*, emphasizes its secular perspective. The *Songe's* range, "from a distanced, matter-of-fact depiction of Rome's demise to a real horror at its monstrousness" (Rebhorn 1980:618), is de-emphasized in the name of a what is more of a "distinctly human continuum . . . . the fullest extent of worldly achievement, good as well as bad" (Manley 1982:211). Rome falls not so much because of the divine nemesis that is the deserved lot of a demonic tyranny, but because of a more humanistic failure of civic virtue, a failure to hold its self-destructive energies in check. Spenser's recurrent encounters with Du Bellay's poems betray a deepening awareness of the ambiguity of his relationship with them: a continuing sense of deep indebtedness is balanced by increasingly subtle criticism. The further exploration of the themes from *Ruines of Rome* comes in *The Ruines of Time* and (especially) in *The Faerie Queene* where a strenuous and patriotic exertion of the creative imagination is aimed at preserving Elizabeth's Troynovant from the same fate.

*Richard Schell*

# Ruines of Rome: by Bellay.

### 1

YE heavenly spirites, whose ashie cinders lie
　Under deep ruines, with huge walls opprest,
But not your praise, the which shall never die
Through your faire verses, ne in ashes rest;
　If so be shrilling voyce of wight alive　　　　　　5
May reach from hence to depth of darkest hell,
Then let those deep Abysses open rive,
That ye may understand my shreiking yell.
　Thrice having seene under the heavens veale
Your toombs devoted compasse over all,　　　　　　10
Thrice unto you with lowd voyce I appeale,
And for your antique furie here doo call,
　The whiles that I with sacred horror sing
　Your glorie, fairest of all earthly thing.

### 2

　Great *Babylon* her haughtie walls will praise,　　15
And sharped steeples high shot up in ayre;
*Greece* will the olde *Ephesian* buildings blaze;

SONNET 1: Invocation of the "antique furie" of Rome's own obsolete
animistic incantation rituals to summon the dead city back to life. Cf.
Aeneas's prayer for the right to tell what he has heard in the underworld (*Aen*
6.266–67). 2. *opprest*: weighed down; suggests the torture of
"pressing." 5. *shrilling*: sounding in shrill tone. 7. *rive*: crack or
split. 9–12. The ritual triple repetition is folklore convention; cf. Virgil,
*Ecl* 8.73–75. 9. *veale*: veil. 10. *devoted*: consecrated.
SONNET 2: Sp's audience would not miss the irony that this catalogue
of great cities to which Rome is preferred begins with Babylon, archetype of
demonic tyranny in Ezekiel and Daniel. In Revelation, Babylon denotes
Rome and (for Sp's English Protestant contemporaries) the bogey of the
feared and hated Roman church. 15 Cf. Daniel 4.30 (Geneva Bible
4.27). 16. *sharped steeples*: suggests the Tower of Babel; Babel was linked
by folk etymology to Babylon. 17. *Ephesian buildings*: temple to Diana; in
Acts 19 the scene of a significant uproar against Paul and his Christian
teachings. *blaze*: proclaim with a trumpet; or describe heraldically.

And *Nylus* nurslings their Pyramides faire;
  The same yet vaunting *Greece* will tell the storie
Of *Joves* great Image in *Olympus* placed,                    20
*Mausolus* worke will be the *Carians* glorie,
And *Crete* will boast the Labyrinth, now raced;
  The antique *Rhodian* will likewise set forth
The great Colosse, erect to Memorie;
And what els in the world is of like worth,                     25
Some greater learned wit will magnifie.
  But I will sing above all moniments
  Seven *Romane* Hils, the worlds seven wonderments.


                          3
    Thou stranger, which for *Rome* in *Rome* here
                                              seekest,
And nought of *Rome* in *Rome* perceiv'st at all,              30
These same olde walls, olde arches, which thou seest,
Olde Palaces, is that which *Rome* men call.
  Behold what wreake, what ruine, and what wast,
And how that she, which with her mightie powre
Tam'd all the world, hath tam'd herselfe at last,             35
The pray of time, which all things doth devowre.

18. *Nylus*: Nile.    20. *Olympus*: actually Olympia, principal Greek sanctuary
of Zeus (Roman Jupiter).    21. *Mausolus*: fourth-century B.C. satrap of the
*Carians*; his great (unfinished) tomb was the prototype of the word
mausoleum.    22. *Labyrinth*: the original, from which by legend no one
could escape, was constructed by Daedalus at Cnossos for King Minos of
Crete. *raced*: razed, levelled to the ground.    24. *Colosse*: the enormous
statue of Zeus in the harbor at Rhodes; one of the Seven Wonders of the
Ancient World.    28. *wonderments*: the traditional Seven Wonders of the
World; on the superiority of Roman lands, see Propertius, *Elegy* 3.22.
S O N N E T 3:    Savage irony here: ancient Rome is the real Rome, and the
measure to which sixteenth-century Rome in no way matches up. This sonnet
is modelled on a popular fourteen-line Latin epigram attributed to Janus
Vitalis: "Qui Romam in media quaeris, novus advena, Roma,/ Et Romae in
Roma nil reperis media . . . " (see Du Bellay 1966:275).    31. *olde arches*:
triumphal arches.    36. *time . . . devowre*: The word combination is colored
by Old Testament apocalyptic import (as in Daniel 7.23). On Shakespeare's
appropriation of this phrase and others from *RR*, see Hieatt (1983).

*Rome* now of *Rome* is th'onely funerall,
And onely *Rome* of *Rome* hath victorie;
Ne ought save *Tyber* hastning to his fall
Remaines of all: O worlds inconstancie.                                40
   That which is firme doth flit and fall away,
   And that is flitting, doth abide and stay.

### 4

   She, whose high top above the starres did sore,
One foote on *Thetis*, th'other on the Morning,
One hand on *Scythia*, th'other on the *More*,                          45
Both heaven and earth in roundnesse compassing,
   *Jove* fearing, least if she should greater growe,
The old Giants should once againe uprise,
Her whelm'd with hills, these seven hils, which be nowe
Tombes of her greatnes, which did threate the skies:                    50
   Upon her head he heapt Mount *Saturnal*,
Upon her bellie th'antique *Palatine*,
Upon her stomacke laid Mount *Quirinal*,
On her left hand the noysome *Esquiline*,
   And *Cælian* on the right; but both her feete                 55
Mount *Viminal* and *Aventine* doo meete.

### 5

   Who lists to see, what ever nature, arte,
And heaven could doo, O *Rome*, thee let him see,
In case thy greatnes he can gesse in harte,

S O N N E T 4:    44. *Thetis*: mother of Achilles and goddess of the sea for
which she often stood.    45. *Scythia*: once great invaders from northeast of
the Black Sea, by Roman times much diminished as a threat. *More*: in
antiquity the inhabitants of Mauretania (in northwest Africa).    48. *old
Giants*: the Titans (cf. Ovid, *Met* 1.151-62).    49. *these seven hils*: with the
ford over Tiber (see line 183), the strategic basis for Rome's location.
50. *threate the skies*: as the Titans did; also suggests blasphemy in Christian
context.    51–56. Cf. body as analogy for community in 1 Corinthians 12.
S O N N E T 5:    57–58. Cf. the hyperbolic praise of Laura in Petrarch,
*Rime* 248.

By that which but the picture is of thee.                          60
　　*Rome* is no more: but if the shade of *Rome*
May of the bodie yeeld a seeming sight,
It's like a corse drawne forth out of the tombe
By Magicke skill out of eternall night:
　　The corpes of *Rome* in ashes is entombed,                  65
And her great spirite rejoyned to the spirite
Of this great masse, is in the same enwombed;
But her brave writings, which her famous merite
　　In spight of time, out of the dust doth reare,
　　Doo make her Idole through the world appeare.             70

6

　　Such as the *Berecynthian* Goddesse bright
In her swift charret with high turrets crownde,
Proud that so manie Gods she brought to light;
Such was this Citie in her good daies fownd:
　　This Citie, more than that great *Phrygian* mother         75
Renowm'd for fruite of famous progenie,
Whose greatnes by the greatnes of none other,
But by her selfe her equall match could see:
　　*Rome* onely might to *Rome* compared bee,
　　And onely *Rome* could make great *Rome* to tremble:       80

---

60. Platonic contempt for artistic imitations which are seen to exist only at
various removes from reality.　　61. *shade*: the spirit of the dead, conceived
of in classical terms as an insubstantial image.　　63. *corse*: body.　　69. *out
of the dust*: Cf. the dust from which man is created (Genesis 2.7); see also the
"dust to dust" in "Buriall of the Dead," *The Boke of Common Prayer.*
70. *Idole*: likeness (Gk. *eidolon*).
S O N N E T 6:　　This sonnet develops the comparison of Rome to Cybele,
the great "Mother goddess" in *Aen* 6.784–87.　　71. *Berecynthian Goddesse*:
Cybele, goddess of Phrygia, which is the location of both Berecynthia (one of
the summits of Mt. Ida) and Troy, in legend the ancestral home of the
Romans.　　72. *turrets*: Cybele first taught men to fortify cities, and is
traditionally depicted wearing a crown crenellated like a castle.　　74. *fownd*:
found, in the sense of discovered upon inspection.　　75. *Phrygian mother*:
Cybele.　　76. *famous progenie*: the rulers of Rome.

So did the Gods by heavenly doome decree,
That other earthlie power should not resemble
  Her that did match the whole earths puissaunce,
  And did her courage to the heavens advaunce.

### 7

  Ye sacred ruines, and ye tragick sights,                        85
Which onely doo the name of *Rome* retaine,
Olde moniments, which of so famous sprights
The honour yet in ashes doo maintaine:
  Triumphant Arcks, spyres neighbours to the skie,
That you to see doth th'heaven it selfe appall,                   90
Alas, by little ye to nothing flie,
The peoples fable, and the spoyle of all:
  And though your frames do for a time make warre
Gainst time, yet time in time shall ruinate
Your workes and names, and your last reliques marre.             95
My sad desires, rest therefore moderate:
  For if that time make ende of things so sure,
  It als will end the paine, which I endure.

### 8

  Through armes and vassals *Rome* the world
                                    subdu'd,
That one would weene, that one sole Cities strength             100
Both land and sea in roundnes had survew'd,
To be the measure of her bredth and length:
  This peoples vertue yet so fruitfull was

---

S O N N E T 7:   Du Bellay loosely translates Castiglione's "Superbi colli."
87. *Olde moniments*: memorials, records, means of recognition, evidences of
fact.   89. Cf. the impious aspirations of the Tower of Babel.
94. *ruinate*: bring to destruction.   98. Suggests suicidal desperation of a
rejected lover.
S O N N E T 8:   101. *roundnes*: thoroughness. *survew'd*: overlooked,
commanded a view of.

Of vertuous nephewes, that posteritie
Striving in power their grandfathers to passe,                    105
The lowest earth, join'd to the heaven hie;
   To th'end that having all parts in their power,
Nought from the Romane Empire might be quight,
And that though time doth Commonwealths devowre,
Yet no time should so low embase their hight,                     110
   That her head earth'd in her foundations deep,
   Should not her name and endles honour keep.

9

   Ye cruell starres, and eke ye Gods unkinde,
Heaven envious, and bitter stepdame Nature,
Be it by fortune, or by course of kinde                           115
That ye doo weld th'affaires of earthlie creature;
   Why have your hands long sithence traveiled
To frame this world, that doth endure so long?
Or why were not these Romane palaces
Made of some matter no lesse firme and strong?                    120
   I say not, as the common voyce doth say,
That all things which beneath the Moone have being
Are temporall, and subject to decay:
But I say rather, though not all agreeing
   With some, that weene the contrarie in thought;  125
   That all this whole shall one day come to nought.

104. *nephewes*: descendants of remote and unspecified relation.
108. *Nought*: no one. *quight*: freed, delivered from.   109. See note to line
36 above.
S O N N E T 9:   115. *by course of kinde*: in the normal course of
nature.   116. *weld*: wield.   117. *sithence*: continuously. *traveiled*: toiled,
labored, worked hard.   118. *frame*: construct. The application of this
analogy from carpentry to the creating God is a commonplace.
121–26. Cf. the theme of the *Mutabilitie Cantos*.   126. The death (or
decay) of the world is a Renaissance commonplace; see studies by Jones
(1961) and Macklem (1958) and Donne's *Anniversaries*; cf. *FQ* V Proem.

## 10

As that brave sonne of *Aeson*, which by charmes
Atcheiv'd the golden Fleece in *Colchid* land,
Out of the earth engendred men of armes
Of Dragons teeth, sowne in the sacred sand;                 130
   So this brave Towne, that in her youthlie daies
An *Hydra* was of warriours glorious,
Did fill with her renowmed nourslings praise
The firie sunnes both one and other hous:
   But they at last, there being then not living      135
An *Hercules*, so ranke seed to represse;
Emongst themselves with cruell furie striving,
Mow'd downe themselves with slaughter mercilesse;
   Renewing in themselves that rage unkinde,
Which whilom did those earthborn brethren blinde.           140

## 11

*Mars* shaming to have given so great head
To his off-spring, that mortall puissaunce
Puft up with pride of Romane hardiehead,
Seem'd above heavens powre it selfe to advaunce;
   Cooling againe his former kindled heate,            145

S O N N E T 10:   *127. sonne of Aeson*: Jason. *charmes*: Medea's magical
charms enabled Jason to perform the labors set for him by her father and so
to win the Golden Fleece.   *128. Colchid land*: to the east of the Black Sea,
legendary home of Medea and goal of Jason's Argonaut expedition.
*129–30.* So in *Met* 7.121–31 where the teeth sewn by Jason grow in the
earth to become antagonistic warriors.   *132. Hydra*: venomous, many-
headed, life-destroying monster, reared by Hera as a menace to Heracles
(Hercules) and killed by him as his second labor; Sp compares the Blatant
Beast to it (*FQ* VI xii 32).   *134. both . . . hous*: heaven and earth?
*136. Hercules*: Most of his legendary twelve labors involve destroying
monsters of various kinds.   *140. earthborn brethren*: the "terrigenae
fratres" of *Met* 7.141.
S O N N E T 11: The theme of Rome's blasphemous overweening pride is
developed by continuing the Titan image from sonnet 4.

With which he had those Romane spirits fild;
Did blowe new fire, and with enflamed breath,
Into the Gothicke colde hot rage instil'd:
    Then gan that Nation, th'earths new Giant brood,
To dart abroad the thunder bolts of warre,                    150
And beating downe these walls with furious mood
Into her mothers bosome, all did marre;
        To th'end that none, all were it *Jove* his sire
        Should boast himselfe of the Romane Empire.

### 12

    Like as whilome the children of the earth          155
Heapt hils on hils, to scale the starrie skie,
And fight against the Gods of heavenly berth,
Whiles *Jove* at them his thunderbolts let flie;
    All suddenly with lightning overthrowne,
The furious squadrons downe to ground did fall,          160
That th'earth under her childrens weight did grone,
And th'heavens in glorie triumpht over all:
        So did that haughtie front which heaped was
        On these seven Romane hils, it selfe upreare
Over the world, and lift her loftie face          165
Against the heaven, that gan her force to feare.
        But now these scorned fields bemone her fall,
        And Gods secure feare not her force at all.

### 13

    Nor the swift furie of the flames aspiring,
Nor the deep wounds of victours raging blade,          170

149. *new Giant brood*: The Gothic invaders are seen as a new race of
Titans.    153. *all were it*: although it were. *Jove his sire*: Jupiter's father was
Saturn, a Titan.
SONNET 12:    155. *children of the earth*: the Titans; but with hints of the
builders of Babel (Genesis 11). This time it is the Romans who are compared
to the Titans.

Nor ruthlesse spoyle of souldiers blood-desiring,
The which so oft thee (*Rome*) their conquest made;
    Ne stroke on stroke of fortune variable,
Ne rust of age hating continuance,
Nor wrath of Gods, nor spight of men unstable,                    175
Nor thou opposd' against thine owne puissance;
    Nor th'horrible uprore of windes high blowing,
Nor swelling streames of that God snakie-paced,
Which hath so often with his overflowing
Thee drenched, have thy pride so much abaced;                     180
    But that this nothing, which they have thee left,
    Makes the world wonder, what they from thee reft.

*14*

    As men in Summer fearles passe the foord,
Which is in Winter lord of all the plaine,
And with his tumbling streames doth beare aboord                  185
The ploughmans hope, and shepheards labour vaine:
    And as the coward beasts use to despise
The noble Lion after his lives end,
Whetting their teeth, and with vaine foolhardise
Daring the foe, that cannot him defend:                          190
    And as at *Troy* most dastards of the Greekes
Did brave about the corpes of *Hector* colde;
So those which whilome wont with pallid cheekes
The Romane triumphs glorie to behold,
    Now on these ashie tombes shew boldnesse vaine,              195
    And conquer'd dare the Conquerour disdaine.

S O N N E T 13:    178. *snakie-paced*: appropriate to the Tiber's sluggish
current and winding course.
S O N N E T 14:    185. *aboord*: normally means to land; *OED* suggests that
Sp here means adrift.    189. *foolhardise*: foolhardiness, cowardice.
191–92. Greek warriors of lesser prowess than Achilles gathered round to
stab Hector's corpse (*Iliad* 22.369–75). The comparison is in the Virgilian
tradition of Rome as reincarnation of Troy; cf. *FQ* II x 46.

### 15

Ye pallid spirits, and ye ashie ghoasts,
Which joying in the brightnes of your day,
Brought foorth those signes of your presumptuous
boasts
Which now their dusty reliques do bewray;          200
   Tell me ye spirits (sith the darksome river
Of *Styx*, not passable to soules returning,
Enclosing you in thrice three wards for ever,
Doo not restraine your images still mourning)
   Tell me then (for perhaps some one of you      205
Yet here above him secretly doth hide)
Doo ye not feele your torments to accrewe,
When ye sometimes behold the ruin'd pride
   Of these old *Romane* works built with your hands,
   Now to become nought els, but heaped sands?      210

### 16

Like as ye see the wrathfull Sea from farre,
In a great mountaine heap't with hideous noyse,
Eftsoones of thousand billowes shouldred narre,
Against a Rocke to breake with dreadfull poyse:
   Like as ye see fell *Boreas* with sharpe blast,      215
Tossing huge tempests through the troubled skie,
Eftsoones having his wide wings spent in wast,
To stop his wearie cariere suddenly:
   And as ye see huge flames spred diverslie,
Gathered in one up to the heavens to spyre,      220
Eftsoones consum'd to fall downe feebily:
So whilom did this Monarchie aspyre
   As waves, as winde, as fire spred over all,
   Till it by fatall doome adowne did fall.

S O N N E T 15:    200. *bewray*: expose to discredit.    203. Styx flowed
nine times around the borders of Hades.
S O N N E T 16:    213. *shouldred*: pushed roughly or insolently. *narre*: near,
close.    214. *poyse*: weight.    215. *Boreas*: the north wind in Greek
mythology.    218. *cariere*: career, river course.

### 17

So long as *Joves* great Bird did make his flight,          225
Bearing the fire with which heaven doth us fray,
Heaven had not feare of that presumptuous might,
With which the Giaunts did the Gods assay.
  But all so soone, as scortching Sunne had brent
His wings, which wont the earth to overspredd,          230
The earth out of her massie wombe forth sent
That antique horror, which made heaven adredd.
  Then was the Germane Raven in disguise
That Romane Eagle seene to cleave asunder,
And towards heaven freshly to arise          235
Out of these mountaines, now consum'd to pouder.
  In which the foule that serves to beare the lightning,
  Is now no more seen flying, nor alighting.

### 18

These heapes of stones, these old wals which ye see,
Were first enclosures but of salvage soyle;          240
And these brave Pallaces which maystred bee
Of time, were shepheards cottages somewhile.
  Then tooke the shepheards Kingly ornaments
And the stout hynde arm'd his right hand with steele:
Eftsoones their rule of yearely Presidents          245
Grew great, and six months greater a great deele;
  Which made perpetuall, rose to so great might,
That thence th'Imperiall Eagle rooting tooke,
Till th'heaven it selfe opposing gainst her might,

S O N N E T 17:          225. *Joves great Bird*: the eagle, sacred to Zeus, often sent by him as an omen, appeared when he was considering war with the Titans. 226. Cf. the bird which carries the thunderbolts in *Met* 12.560. *fray*: frighten, attack.          229. *brent*: burned.          233. *Germane Raven*: the invading Goths (see line 148 above).
S O N N E T 18:          239–42. On the tradition of the humble beginnings of Rome, see Propertius, *Elegies* 4.1–78; Ovid, *Fastes* 5.93–94.          245. *yearely Presidents*: Roman consuls ruled one year.          246. *sixe months*: term of a Roman dictatorship prior to Caesar, who made it perpetual.          248. *rooting tooke*: took root.

Her power to *Peters* successor betooke;                    250
   Who shepheardlike, (as fates the same foreseeing)
   Doth shew, that all things turne to their first being.

### 19

  All that is perfect, which th'heaven beautefies;
All that's imperfect, borne belowe the Moone;
All that doth feede our spirits and our eies;            255
And all that doth consume our pleasures soone;
  All the mishap, the which our daies outweares,
All the good hap of th'oldest times afore,
*Rome* in the time of her great ancesters,
Like a *Pandora*, locked long in store.                    260
  But destinie this huge *Chaos* turmoyling,
In which all good and evill was enclosed,
Their heavenly vertues from these woes assoyling,
Caried to heaven, from sinfull bondage losed:
   But their great sinnes, the causers of their paine,   265
   Under these antique ruines yet remaine.

### 20

  No otherwise than raynie cloud, first fed
With earthly vapours gathered in the ayre,
Eftsoones in compas arch't, to steepe his hed,
Doth plonge himselfe in *Tethys* bosome faire;            270

250. *Peters successor*: The passing of Rome's power from emperor to pope is seen as an act of heavenly retribution.

S O N N E T 19:    260. *Pandora*: Zeus avenged the theft of fire by the creation of Pandora whose dowry jar released evils of all kinds. Natalis Comes, *Mythologia* 4.6, uses the story as a parable for the way in which luxury, greed, and ambition have produced all subsequent woes of mankind. On the *Roma Prima Pandora* theme, see Panofsky (1962) ch.5.

263. *assoyling*: releasing.

S O N N E T 20:    267–70. The rainbow is an ideal image of the fragility of all the earthly things men wonder at.    270. *Tethys*: a Titaness who married her brother Oceanus and became mother of the world's rivers and three thousand Oceanids. Du Bellay mentions Thetis (mother of Achilles). Natalis Comes, *Mythologia* 8.2, conflates the two.

And mounting up againe, from whence he came,
With his great bellie spreds the dimmed world,
Till at the last dissolving his moist frame,
In raine, or snowe, or haile he forth is horld;
    This Citie, which was first but shepheards shade,    275
Uprising by degrees, grewe to such height,
That Queene of land and sea her selfe she made.
At last not able to beare so great weight,
    Her power disperst, through all the world did vade;
    To shew that all in th'end to nought shall fade.    280

### 21

    The same which *Pyrrhus*, and the puissaunce
Of *Afrike* could not tame, that same brave Citie,
Which with stout courage arm'd against mischaunce,
Sustein'd the shocke of common enmitie;
    Long as her ship tost with so manie freakes,    285
Had all the world in armes against her bent,
Was never seene, that anie fortunes wreakes
Could breake her course begun with brave intent.
    But when the object of her vertue failed,
Her power it selfe against it selfe did arme;    290
As he that having long in tempest sailed,
Faine would arive, but cannot for the storme,
    If too great winde against the port him drive,
    Doth in the port it selfe his vessell rive.

---

279. *vade*: disappear.
SONNET 21:    281. *Pyrrhus*: third-century B.C. king of Epirus who
executed several substantial military incursions into Roman
territories.    281–82. *puissaunce/ Of Afrike*: Carthage, Rome's traditional
enemy.    285. *freakes*: whims, vagaries.    289–90. On Rome as author
of its own woe, see Horace, *Epodes* 16.1–2 ("Already another generation is
being killed off by civil war, and Rome herself is falling to ruin at her own
hands"), Augustine, *The City of God*, and Lucan, *De Bello Civili* 1.1–32.
294. On the proverbial shame of shipwreck before even leaving the harbour,
see Erasmus, *Adagia* 1.5.76.

### 22

When that brave honour of the Latine name,                    295
Which mear'd her rule with *Africa*, and *Byze*,
With *Thames* inhabitants of noble fame,
And they which see the dawning day arize;
   Her nourslings did with mutinous uprore
Harten against her selfe, her conquer'd spoile,              300
Which she had wonne from all the world afore,
Of all the world was spoyl'd within a while.
   So when the compast course of the universe
In sixe and thirtie thousand yeares is ronne,
The bands of th'elements shall backe reverse                305
To their first discord, and be quite undonne:
    The seedes, of which all things at first were bred,
    Shall in great *Chaos* wombe againe be hid.

### 23

O warie wisedome of the man, that would
That *Carthage* towres from spoile should be forborne,      310
To th'end that his victorious people should
With cancring laisure not be overworne;
   He well foresaw, how that the Romane courage,
Impatient of pleasures faint desires,
Through idlenes would turne to civill rage,                 315
And be her selfe the matter of her fires.
   For in a people given all to ease,
Ambition is engendred easily;
As in a vicious bodie, grose disease

---

SONNET 22:    296. *mear'd*: marked out the boundaries of. *Byze*:
Byzantium.    297. *Thames inhabitants*: the Britons.    298 Presumably
the Parthians at the eastern extreme of the empire.    300. *Harten*: take
courage.    304. The Platonic or Great Year; calculations of its length
varied greatly. See Boccaccio, *Genealogia Deorum* 8.2.    305. *bands*: uniting
forces.    307–08. Lucretian atomism; see *De Rerum Natura* passim. Ovid,
*Met* 1.7–10, and Lucan, *De Bello Civili* 1.72–78.
SONNET 23:    309. *the man*: Scipio Nasica; see Plutarch, *Marcus Cato*
27.    312. *laisure*: leisure.

Soone growes through humours superfluitie.    320
That came to passe, when swolne with plenties pride,
Nor prince, nor peere, nor kin they would abide.

### 24

If the blinde furie, which warres breedeth oft,
Wonts not t'enrage the hearts of equall beasts,
Whether they fare on foote, or flie aloft,    325
Or armed be with clawes, or scalie creasts;
   What fell *Erynnis* with hot burning tongs,
Did grype your hearts, with noysome rage imbew'd,
That each to other working cruell wrongs,
Your blades in your owne bowels you embrew'd?    330
   Was this (ye *Romanes*) your hard destinie?
Or some old sinne, whose unappeased guilt
Powr'd vengeance forth on you eternallie?
Or brothers blood, the which at first was spilt
   Upon your walls, that God might not endure,    335
   Upon the same to set foundation sure?

### 25

O that I had the *Thracian* Poets harpe,
For to awake out of th'infernall shade
Those antique *Cæsars*, sleeping long in darke,
The which this auncient Citie whilome made:    340
   Or that I had *Amphions* instrument,

320. i.e. through an imbalance of the four primal bodily fluids.
SONNET 24:    323. *blinde furie*: the uncontrolled spirit that causes civil
strife, as in Horace, *Epodes* 7.    327. *Erynnis*: a Fury; cf. Lucan, *De Bello
Civili* 1.1–7, 4.187.    332. *some old sinne*: Horace, *Epodes* 7.17–20, makes
the murder of the blameless Remus a kind of original sin which haunts the
Romans like a bitter fate.    334. *brothers blood*: Romulus's murder of
Remus for leaping over the walls of the new town.    336. Luke 6.49 likens
those unresponsive to God's word to the man who "buylt an house upon the
earth without foundacion."
SONNET 25:    337. *Thracian Poets*: Orpheus's; see *VG* 433–80.
341. *Amphions*: Amphion was a builder of Thebes; the walls were said to
erect themselves as he played his harp.

To quicken with his vitall notes accord,
The stonie joynts of these old walls now rent,
By which th'*Ausonian* light might be restor'd:
  Or that at least I could with pencill fine, 345
Fashion the pourtraicts of these Palacis,
By paterne of great *Virgils* spirit divine;
I would assay with that which in me is,
  To builde with levell of my loftie style,
  That which no hands can evermore compyle. 350

### 26

  Who list the Romane greatnes forth to figure,
Him needeth not to seeke for usage right
Of line, or lead, or rule, or squaire, to measure
Her length, her breadth, her deepnes, or her hight,
  But him behooves to vew in compasse round 355
All that the Ocean graspes in his long armes;
Be it where the yerely starre doth scortch the ground,
Or where colde *Boreas* blowes his bitter stormes.
  *Rome* was th'whole world, and al the world was *Rome*,
And if things nam'd their names doo equalize, 360
When land and sea ye name, then name ye *Rome*;
And naming *Rome* ye land and sea comprize:
  For th'auncient Plot of *Rome* displayed plaine,
  The map of all the wide world doth containe.

### 27

  Thou that at *Rome* astonisht dost behold 365
The antique pride, which menaced the skie,
These haughtie heapes, these palaces of olde,

344. *Ausonian*: Italian, from the name of an ancient southern Italian tribe.
S O N N E T 26: 351. *figure*: imagine, represent by diagram or
picture. 357. *yerely starre*: the year-round tropical sun? 358. *Boreas*:
the north wind, the god of the north wind, and (by extension)
winter. 360. *equalize*: match, come up to.
S O N N E T 27: 367. *heapes*: biblical word for ruins (e.g. see Isaiah 25.2
and Jeremiah 49.2); it thus also suggests weakness of spiritual foundations.

These wals, these arcks, these baths, these temples hie;
  Judge by these ample ruines vew, the rest
The which injurious time hath quite outworne,        370
Since of all workmen helde in reckning best,
Yet these olde fragments are for paternes borne:
  Then also marke, how Rome from day to day,
Repayring her decayed fashion,
Renewes herselfe with buildings rich and gay;       375
That one would judge, that the *Romaine Dæmon*
  Doth yet himselfe with fatall hand enforce,
Againe on foote to reare her pouldred corse.

### 28

  He that hath seene a great Oke drie and dead,
Yet clad with reliques of some Trophees olde,       380
Lifting to heaven her aged hoarie head,
Whose foote in ground hath left but feeble holde;
  But halfe disbowel'd lies above the ground,
Shewing her wreathed rootes, and naked armes,
And on her trunke all rotten and unsound       385
Onely supports herselfe for meate of wormes;
  And though she owe her fall to the first winde,
Yet of the devout people is ador'd,
And manie yong plants spring out of her rinde;
Who such an Oke hath seene, let him record       390

368. *arcks*: arches.    372. *borne*: sustained.    373–75. The Augustinian image of Rome as mistress of the world, absent at this point in Du Bellay, is rendered decidedly sleazy by Sp, in line with the biblical tradition of the Scarlet Whore.    375. *rich and gay*: Sp's phrase suggests the earthly luxury of the new buildings; Du Bellay speaks devoutly of "*œuvres divines*."
376. *Romaine Dæmon*: Genius of Rome; cf. the genius of the place in *Aen* 5.95, 7.136; *RT* 19.    378. *pouldred*: pulverized, reduced to powder or dust.
S O N N E T 28: For the comparison of Pompey to an old oak, see Lucan, *De Bello Civili* 1.136–43. Du Bellay stresses the majesty of the ravaged oak, Sp the essential decay and rottenness which leave it useful only as "meate of wormes."    388. *devout*: ironic; cf. Devotion's Mart in *FQ* I iii.

That such this Cities honour was of yore,
And mongst all Cities florished much more.

### 29

All that which *Aegypt* whilome did devise,
All that which *Greece* their temples to embrave,
After th'Ionicke, Atticke, Doricke guise,                    395
Or *Corinth* skil'd in curious workes to grave;
   All that *Lysippus* practike arte could forme,
*Apelles* wit, or *Phidias* his skill,
Was wont this auncient Citie to adorne,
And the heaven it selfe with her wide wonders fill;          400
   All that which *Athens* ever brought forth wise,
All that which *Afrike* ever brought forth strange,
All that which *Asie* ever had of prise,
Was here to see. O mervelous great change:
   *Rome* living, was the worlds sole ornament,            405
   And dead, is now the worlds sole moniment.

### 30

Like as the seeded field greene grasse first showes,
Then from greene grasse into a stalke doth spring,
And from a stalke into an eare forth-growes,
Which eare the frutefull graine doth shortly bring;          410
   And as in season due the husband mowes
The waving lockes of those faire yeallow heares,
Which bound in sheaves, and layd in comely rowes,

---

SONNET 29:    397. *Lysippus*: fourth-century B.C. Greek sculptor noted for precision of detail and a new and slender proportion of figure. *practike*: highly skilled.    398. *Apelles*: fourth-century B.C. Greek painter famous for the verisimilitude of his paintings. *Phidias*: fifth-century B.C. Greek sculptor whose Olympian Zeus at Elis was one of the Seven Wonders of the Ancient World.    401–03. Proverbial.
SONNET 30:    407–10. "For the earth bringeth forthe frute of her self, first the blade, then the eares, after that ful corne in the eares" (Mark 4.28).
411. *husband*: husbandman, farmer.    412. *heares*: ears.

Upon the naked fields in stackes he reares:
  So grew the Romane Empire by degree,          415
Till that Barbarian hands it quite did spill,
And left of it but these olde markes to see,
Of which all passers by doo somewhat pill:
  As they which gleane, the reliques use to gather,
  Which th'husbandman behind him chanst to scater.   420

### 31

  That same is now nought but a champian wide,
Where all this worlds pride once was situate.
No blame to thee, whosoever dost abide
By *Nyle*, or *Gange*, or *Tygre*, or *Euphrate*,
  Ne *Afrike* thereof guiltie is, nor *Spaine*,         425
Nor the bolde people by the *Thamis* brincks,
Nor the brave warlicke brood of *Alemaine*,
Nor the borne Souldier which *Rhine* running drinks:
  Thou onely cause, ô Civill furie, art
Which sowing in th'*Aemathian* fields thy spight,     430
Didst arme thy hand against thy proper hart;
To th'end that when thou wast in greatest hight
  To greatnes growne, through long prosperitie,
  Thou then adowne might'st fall more horriblie.

### 32

  Hope ye my verses that posteritie          435
Of age ensuing shall you ever read?

418. *pill*: pillage, plunder.    419. *gleane*: i.e. learn Rome's lessons.
S O N N E T 31:    421. *champian*: field, open country.    424. By tradition
the four rivers of Eden, thus suggesting the bounds of the known world (see
Genesis 2.11–14).    426. The British.    427. *Alemaine*: Germany.
428. Gideon chose for soldiers those who lapped water (Judges 7.4–8).
429–32. See note to lines 289–90 above.    430. Aemathian fields:
Thessalian fields, alluding to the battle at Pharsalia (in Thessaly) between
Caesar and Pompey; see Lucan, *De Bello Civili* 1.1.
S O N N E T 32: Cf. the "Exegi monumentum aere perennius" of Horace, *Ode*
3.30; cf. also *RT* 400–06.

Hope ye that ever immortalitie
So meane Harpes worke may chalenge for her meed?
    If under heaven anie endurance were,
These moniments, which not in paper writ,                    440
But in Porphyre and Marble doo appeare,
Might well have hop'd to have obtained it.
    Nath'les my Lute, whom *Phœbus* deignd to give,
Cease not to sound these olde antiquities:
For if that time doo let thy glorie live,                    445
Well maist thou boast, how ever base thou bee,
    That thou art first, which of thy Nation song
    Th'olde honour of the people gowned long.


*L'Envoy.*
    *Bellay*, first garland of free Poësie
That *France* brought forth, though fruitfull of brave
                                                wits,        450
Well worthie thou of immortalitie,
That long hast traveld by thy learned writs,
    Olde *Rome* out of her ashes to revive,
And give a second life to dead decayes:
Needes must he all eternitie survive,                        455
That can to other give eternall dayes.
    Thy dayes therefore are endles, and thy prayse
Excelling all, that ever went before;
And after thee, gins *Bartas* hie to rayse

443. Phoebus Apollo, the sun god, was also god of music and
poetry.        447. *thou art first*: restatement of Horace's boast.        448. *people
gowned long*: "gentem . . . togatam" (*Aen* 1.282).
L'E n v o y: For this there is no original in Du Bellay, but, with the
dropping of his dedicatory sonnet, its addition restores the numerological
potential of the original total of thirty-three sonnets. Sp departs from the
rhyme scheme of the thirty-two translated sonnets.        452. *traveld*: worked,
studied. *writs*: writings.        459. *Bartas*: The reference is presumably to Du
Bartas's *Uranie* (1579). The presence of Du Bartas in the envoy to a
translation of Du Bellay has been seen to suggest the need for a Protestant
correction or completion to the latter.

His heavenly Muse, th'Almightie to adore.                    460
   Live happie spirits, th'honour of your name,
   And fill the world with never dying fame.

FINIS.

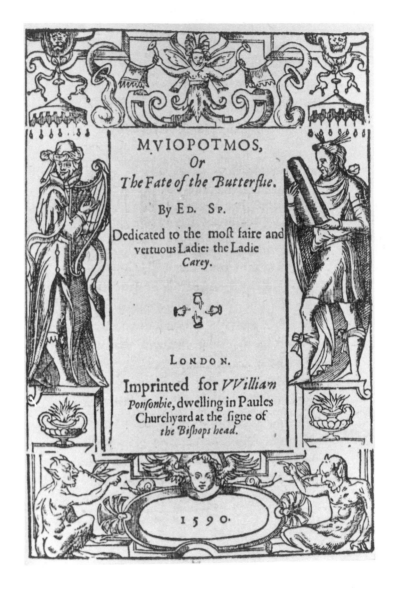

MVIOPOTMOS,
Or
*The Fate of the Butterflie.*

BY ED. SP.

Dedicated to the moſt faire and
vertuous Ladie: the Ladie
*Carey.*

LONDON.

Imprinted for *William
Ponſonbie,* dwelling in Paules
Churchyard at the ſigne of
the *Biſhops head.*

1590.

# *Muiopotmos*

❧❧❧❧❧❧❧

M uiopotmos is a carefully fabricated poem, a "curious
networke" (368) of luxurious description, heroic allu-
sion, sententious declamation, and mythological dila-
tion—all adumbrating a slight fable of a butterfly's entrapment
by a spider. Spenser spins together these strands to produce a
verbal tapestry admirable for its fine design and variegated rhe-
torical colors. That Spenser here is a poet who "weaving slen-
derly/ Has onely playde" (*VG* 3–4) is an idea that appeals to
readers impressed by the exquisite texture of the work: for them
the poem is essentially a *jeu d'esprit*. Others, however, see it not
as a tapestry but as a veil, through which we can discern, if only
dimly, meanings allegorically presented. But there is no consen-
sus about the purport of the allegory. Perhaps, like *Mother Hub-
berds Tale* or *Virgils Gnat*, *Muiopotmos* reflects on the political
maneuverings of some of Spenser's contemporaries whom it
begs us to identify. Or perhaps its mirroring of the contempo-
rary scene involves a disillusioned but general analysis of the
place-seeking and envy-ridden court that Spenser had visited
shortly before the poem was published. Finally, however, the
focus of *Muiopotmos* may be not so much on history as it is on the
making of art. If so, it self-reflexively figures forth the beauty of
which art is capable, while warning against the false security of
oblivious absorption in the enjoyment of that beauty.

An assertive narrator imbues the poem with significance, just
as Chaucer's narrator in the "Nun's Priest's Tale" invests the
commonplace events of a barnyard with meaning not intrin-
sically there. He begins with austere dignity, as he proposes an
action of epic proportions and promises a theme suffused with
such tragic implications that he must call on Melpomene for
inspiration. Here the Muse of Tragedy has presumably found

*407*

the "mourning matter" (*TM* 168) she claims to lack in *The Teares of the Muses*. Only with the beginning of the story proper do we realize that in fact the poem trifles with the fortunes of a fly. Courting bathos, Spenser thus draws our attention to the narrator's mannered style and his magnification of the small and inconsequential throughout the poem. In the passage describing the arming of Clarion, Spenser's aim is apparent: not only is the narrator reminded of the heroes of old when he contemplates Clarion's body, but he is compelled to apologize for daring to compare a butterfly's wings to Cupid's. The effect is humorous, but Spenser implies here and elsewhere when the obtrusive and sometimes pretentious voice interrupts or embellishes the narrative line that the teller of the tale constructs meaning as well as art from seemingly mundane materials. The narrator delivers, then, a fictive world changed utterly from the brazen and amoral world of entomological reality. The "spectacle of care" (440) he causes us to see is a dynamic version of the somewhat static emblematic world met in the "visions" poems that follow *Muiopotmos* in the *Complaints*.

Some conventional associations lie behind Spenser's choice of spider and butterfly as protagonists. In emblem books, butterflies stand for triviality or for ephemeral felicity. "Too lively a pleasure leads to death" and "A brief and destructive pleasure" are typical mottoes. Spiders, according to traditional iconology, are symbols of envy, since they convert whatever they touch into poison, and of calumny, since they weave flimsy webs from themselves in precisely the way that detractors manufacture their false tales (cf. *FQ* V xii 36). But rather than simply defer to these received codes of significance, the narrator attempts to invent meaningful contexts for the natural phenomena he describes. Not content with Nature's *données*, he is drawn to causal explanations for the facts that butterflies are beautiful and spiders catch butterflies. In each instance he must "digress" to locate the "roote whereof" (9) in the domain of myth. The poem contributes, then, to the etiological tradition of Callimachus's

*Aetia*, Ovid's *Metamorphoses*, and such nugatory pieces as Herrick's "How roses came red" or "Why flowers change colour."

As William Keach (1977) has emphasized, this tradition allowed and encouraged the poet's freedom of invention. It must have appealed particularly to Spenser at this stage of his career when he was revising, rejuvenating, and creating myths for *The Faerie Queene*. In any case, scholars have been unable to establish a source for the episode of Astery, which the poem attributes, facetiously, to "Report" (113): the story is in fact Spenser's own. The interpolated myth of Arachne, moreover, which comes from Ovid's account in the *Metamorphoses*, Book 6, does not simply repeat Ovid's version or redactions of it "as in stories it is written found" (258); rather, Spenser refashions the myth to make it his own.

In each case, the myth complicates the main action. In the first, Astery, a mortal, is the victim of a goddess, who transforms her into a butterfly. The text in no way suggests, however, that Astery deserves to be punished; indeed, excellence in gathering flowers "crime none were" (143). Instead, Astery, innocent to the end, is caught in a tissue of envy, detraction, and jealousy. Venus gives an ear to Astery's detractors because they convince her that her son, Cupid, may be forming a liaison with Astery that resembles his amour with Psyche, but the allegation goes unproved. Clarion is both like and unlike Astery. Each feels the full power of "heavenly might" (137) in that Venus humbles Astery, and Jove, Clarion, "heavens" (241) having ordained the presence of Aragnoll in the garden. But Clarion, though ignorant of his fate, is not as innocent as his prototype: his "vauntfull" (54) temperament, his indulgence of his "glutton sense" (179) as he flies from flower to flower, his final repose in "riotous suffisaunce" (207) after his spoiling of the garden in which his "wavering wit" (160) takes pleasure imply the narrator's doubts about his character. Provoking questions about Clarion's innocence and culpability and about the determinism to which he is subject, the Astery story, then, is more than fanciful decoration. The allusion to Psyche in fact suggests to D. C. Allen (1956) that Spenser conceives of Clarion as psyche, or the rational soul, and that the poem is in effect a "paradise lost."

Extended pictorial description characterizes the second myth, which treats the artistic competition between Minerva and Arachne, but the episode teases us to explore the differences between the mortal and divine perspectives implicit in it. Arachne was for many medieval commentators on Ovid a warning "that folk should not contend/ Against their betters, nor persist in error too the end" (Golding 1961:3). A mere mortal, she is presumptuous in challenging Minerva to a spinning contest and her subject—Jove's victimizing of Europa—subversively condemns the gods for their violence. To Arachne the gods are terrifying. Like boys with flies, they capriciously sport and make wanton with humankind. Minerva, on the other hand, chooses as her subject a synod of the gods in which she herself is the beneficiary of divine justice. The peaceful olive rather than the warlike steed epitomizes her claim to Athens, and the gods, preferring peace to strife, rule against Neptune in her favor. As Spenser concludes the story, adding to Ovid's description of Minerva's tapestry the gorgeous butterfly, he seems to prod the reader to appreciate the unity of his poem. But we are still left with mysteries, doubts, and uncertainties. Does Arachne envy just the excellence of Minerva's finely spun handiwork or does she resent the immunity art gives the serenely secure butterfly from the ravages of the gods? Applied to the main story, the question is this: does Aragnoll envy Clarion's beauty or his freedom?

Neither Clarion nor Aragnoll, of course, is aware of the mythological antecedents that the narrator uses to extend the scope of the story he recounts. As part of a Sidneyan "groundplot" they are obtuse to the "profitable invention" for which they serve as stimulus. If, for all that, *Muiopotmos* remains a beguiling and amusing poem, it is because Spenser proceeds here *serio ludens*, mingling delight and even laughter, so unusual in the *Complaints*-volume, with sententious moralizing, here gently mocked. Clarion's vanity and his carefree lack of vigilance clearly link *Muiopotmos* to the "argument" sustained by its companion pieces in the book, and ultimately the mixture of pleasure and pain evoked by the poem is germane to Spenser's ambivalence when he meditates on the glory of Rome and other flitting things.

*Ronald Bond*

# To the right worthy and vertuous
## Ladie; the La: *Carey*

MOst *brave and bountifull La: for so excellent favours as I have received at your sweet handes, to offer these fewe leaves as in recompence, should be as to offer flowers to the Gods for their divine benefites. Therefore I have determined to give my selfe wholy to you, as quite abandoned from my selfe, and absolutely vowed to your services: which in all right is ever held for full recompence of debt or damage to have the person yeelded. My person I wot wel how little worth it is. But the faithfull minde and humble zeale which I beare unto your La: may perhaps be more of price, as may please you to account and use the poore service thereof; which taketh glory to advance your excellent partes and noble vertues, and to spend it selfe in honouring you: not so much for your great bounty to my self, which yet may not be un-minded; nor for name or kindreds sake by you vouchsafed, beeing also regardable; as for that honorable name, which yee have by your brave deserts purchast to your self, and spred in the mouths of al men: with which I have also presumed to grace my verses, and under your name to commend to the world this smal Poëme, the which beseeching your La: to take in worth, and of all things therein according to your wonted graciousnes to make a milde construction, I humbly pray for your happines.*

Your La: ever
humbly;
E: S.

DEDICATION: *Lady Carey*: (1557–1618); she was one of the Spencers of Althorpe with whom Sp claimed a connection: "the noble familie,/ Of which I meanest boast my selfe to be" (*CCCHA* 537–38). She had married Sir George Carey in 1574 and was a patron of Nashe and others. In the sixteenth dedicatory sonnet to *FQ*, addressed to Lady Carey, Sp had promised to celebrate her "in ampler wise." *take in worth*: accept kindly. *milde construction*: Sometimes held to be Sp's way of discouraging allegorical interpretations and sometimes his way of encouraging them, the phrase in all likelihood simply asks Lady Carey to indulge the work with her "wonted graciousnes."

# *Muiopotmos*: or
## *The Fate of the Butterflie.*

I Sing of deadly dolorous debate,
  Stir'd up through wrathfull *Nemesis* despight,
Betwixt two mightie ones of great estate,
Drawne into armes, and proofe of mortall fight,
Through prowd ambition, and hartswelling hate,           5
Whilest neither could the others greater might
And sdeignfull scorne endure; that from small jarre
Their wraths at length broke into open warre.

TITLE PAGE:    1590: Since the signatures show that *Muio* is part of the *Compl*, entered in the Stationers' Register on 29 December 1590, it is probable that "1590" is either a printer's error, or an indication that the volume was completely printed before the end of 1590, Old Style. This is the fourth and last title page in the volume and the only one that bears the date 1590, rather than 1591.

TITLE:    *Muiopotmos*: As the first sign of mock-heroic deflation in the poem, Sp translates the Greek title in his subtitle. Allen (1956) points out that "-potmos" was "reserved by the Greeks for the fatal destiny of great heroes."

1–16. A mock epic frame, concluding with an epic question that echoes Virgil, *Aen* 1.11, introduces the poem proper. Some critics view the frame as an example of conspicuous irrelevance. According to Allen (1956), however, the "two mightie ones" are Minerva and Venus, the deities involved in the Arachne and Astery stories respectively and known as rivals in ancient times.    1. The alliteration makes the line ponderously grave.    2. Cartari notes in *The Fountaine of Ancient Fiction* (1559), that Nemesis was for Pausanias "the most severe and cruell punisher of arrogancie and vainglory," and for Macrobius "the revenger and cheefe enemie of pride, insolencie, and haughtiness." He further observes that "Among the Antients and among the old writers, Fortune and Nemesis were oftentimes taken to bee all one." *despight*: malevolence.

The roote whereof and tragicall effect,
Vouchsafe, O thou the mournfulst Muse of nyne,                    10
That wontst the tragick stage for to direct,
In funerall complaints and waylfull tyne,
Reveale to me, and all the meanes detect,
Through which sad *Clarion* did at last declyne
To lowest wretchednes; And is there then                         15
Such rancour in the harts of mightie men?

Of all the race of silver-winged Flies
Which doo possesse the Empire of the aire,
Betwixt the centred earth, and azure skies,
Was none more favourable, nor more faire                         20
Whilst heaven did favour his felicities,
Then *Clarion*, the eldest sonne and haire
Of *Muscaroll*, and in his fathers sight
Of all alive did seeme the fairest wight.

With fruitfull hope his aged breast he fed                        25
Of future good, which his yong toward yeares,
Full of brave courage and bold hardyhed,
Above th'ensample of his equall peares,
Did largely promise, and to him forered
(Whilst oft his heart did melt in tender teares)                 30
That he in time would sure prove such an one,
As should be worthie of his fathers throne.

10–15. Melpomene inspires tragedy, which is conceived of in Chaucerian
terms as a decline from prosperity to wretchedness. Cf. *Muio*209–40 and the
emphasis on the fall from glory in the "ruins" poems.     12. *tyne*: sorrow.
17. *Flies*: insects in general.     22. *Clarion*: The name denotes a trumpet, an
instrument associated with the murmuring of gnats in *FQ* II ix 16, and with
Calliope and fame in *TM* 457–63. Fame's trumpet is an iconographical
commonplace.     23. *Muscaroll*: a diminutive of Lat. *musca*, fly. Cf.
"Aragnoll."     24. *wight*: one.     26. *toward*: promising.
28. Anticipating the Astery story (*Muio* 119), Sp emphasizes that Clarion
excels his peers.

The fresh yong flie, in whom the kindly fire
Of lustfull yongth began to kindle fast,
Did much disdaine to subject his desire                    35
To loathsome sloth, or houres in ease to wast;
But joy'd to range abroad in fresh attire
Through the wide compas of the ayrie coast,
And with unwearied wings each part t'inquire
Of the wide rule of his renowmed sire.                     40

For he so swift and nimble was of flight,
That from this lower tract he dar'd to stie
Up to the clowdes, and thence with pineons light,
To mount aloft unto the Christall skie,
To vew the workmanship of heavens hight:                   45
Whence downe descending he along would flie
Upon the streaming rivers, sport to finde;
And oft would dare to tempt the troublous winde.

So on a Summers day, when season milde
With gentle calme the world had quieted,                   50
And high in heaven *Hyperions* fierie childe
Ascending, did his beames abroad dispred,
Whiles all the heavens on lower creatures smilde;
Yong *Clarion* with vauntfull lustie head,
After his guize did cast abroad to fare;                   55
And theretoo gan his furnitures prepare.

His breastplate first, that was of substance pure,
Before his noble heart he firmely bound,

---

33–40. Almost a parody of Neoplatonic ascent: see *HL* 64–70.
33. *kindly*: natural.      42. *stie*: ascend.      51. *Hyperions fierie childe*: Apollo.
This is one of many examples of periphrasis in the poem.      52. *dispred*:
spread out.      55. *cast*: resolve.      56. *furnitures*: armour, accoutrements.
The account of the arming of the hero (*Muio* 57–110) burlesques an epic
convention (cf. Homer, *Iliad* 11.15–46). The next five stanzas create, as they
dissect, a butterfly's anatomy.

That mought his life from yron death assure,
And ward his gentle corpes from cruell wound:                    60
For it by arte was framed, to endure
The bit of balefull steele and bitter stownd,
No lesse than that, which *Vulcane* made to sheild
*Achilles* life from fate of *Troyan* field.

And then about his shoulders broad he threw           65
An hairie hide of some wilde beast, whom hee
In salvage forrest by adventure slew,
And reft the spoyle his ornament to bee:
Which spredding all his backe with dreadfull vew,
Made all that him so horrible did see,                         70
Thinke him *Alcides* with the Lyons skin,
When the *Næmean* Conquest he did win.

Upon his head his glistering Burganet,
The which was wrought by wonderous device,
And curiously engraven, he did set:                             75
The mettall was of rare and passing price;
Not *Bilbo* steele, nor brasse from *Corinth* fet,
Nor costly *Oricalche* from strange *Phœnice*;
But such as could both *Phœbus* arrowes ward,
And th'hayling darts of heaven beating hard.            80

---

62. *stownd*: stroke.      63–64. Cf. *Iliad* 18.369ff.; *Aen* 8.407ff. Clarion's
"Achilles' heel" is a spot under his left wing (*Muio* 387).      69. *spredding*:
covering.      71–72. Sp alludes to the first of the twelve labors of Hercules
(Alcides). A vivid account of Hercules' victory over the Nemean lion appears
in Theocritus, *Idyll* 25.200ff.      73. *Burganet*: a helmet worn by pikemen.
75. *curiously*: carefully.      76. *passing*: surpassing.      77. *Bilbo*: Bilbao, in
Spain, known for its well-tempered steel. *Corinth fet*: fetched from Corinth,
a city known, largely from Pliny's *Natural History*, for its brass.
78. *Oricalche*: Turnus is armed in orichalcum, literally "mountain-copper," in
*Aen* 12.87; Servius commented that it was the most precious of all metals. As
Knowlton (1980) suggests, in associating the substance with Phoenicia, Sp
may have known ancient descriptions of the making of orichalcum from
cadmean, that is, Phoenician earth.      79. *Phoebus*: the sun.

Therein two deadly weapons fixt he bore,
Strongly outlaunced towards either side,
Like two sharpe speares, his enemies to gore:
Like as a warlike Brigandine, applyde
To fight, layes forth her threatfull pikes afore,               85
The engines which in them sad death doo hyde:
So did this flie outstretch his fearefull hornes,
Yet so as him their terrour more adornes.

Lastly his shinie wings as silver bright,
Painted with thousand colours, passing farre               90
All Painters skill, he did about him dight:
Not halfe so manie sundrie colours arre
In *Iris* bowe, ne heaven doth shine so bright,
Distinguished with manie a twinckling starre,
Nor *Iunoes* Bird in her ey-spotted traine               95
So manie goodly colours doth containe.

Ne (may it be withouten perill spoken)
The Archer God, the sonne of *Cytheree*,
That joyes on wretched lovers to be wroken,
And heaped spoyles of bleeding harts to see,               100
Beares in his wings so manie a changefull token.
Ah my liege Lord, forgive it unto mee,
If ought against thine honour I have tolde;
Yet sure those wings were fairer manifolde.

---

84. *Brigandine*: a small armed galley, used especially for espionage and
reconnoitering.     88–101. The butterfly's wings are reserved for the climax
because they are its most conspicuous and artful feature and because, envied
by the court ladies, they suggest to the narrator the tale of Astery. Ironically,
they prove to be not weapons, but encumbrances in the fight against
Aragnoll (*Muio* 425–30).     93. *Iris bowe*: the rainbow. Cf. *Aen* 4.700–01.
95. *Iunoes Bird*: the peacock.     98. *sonne of Cytheree*: Cupid, son of
Venus—the "liege Lord" of line 102. His wings are described by E. K., in a
gloss on *SC* "March," as "divers coloured."     98–99. The triumphs of
Cupid appear in *FQ* III xi 29–52 in a passage indebted to Ovid, *Met* 6.103–
28, Sp's source for the Arachne story.     99. *wroken*: avenged.

Full manie a Ladie faire, in Court full oft                    105
Beholding them, him secretly envide,
And wisht that two such fannes, so silken soft,
And golden faire, her Love would her provide;
Or that when them the gorgeous Flie had doft,
Some one that would with grace be gratifide,       110
From him would steale them privily away,
And bring to her so precious a pray.

Report is that dame *Venus* on a day,
In spring when flowres doo clothe the fruitful ground,
Walking abroad with all her Nymphes to play,         115
Bad her faire damzels flocking her arownd,
To gather flowres, her forhead to array:
Emongst the rest a gentle Nymph was found,
Hight *Astery*, excelling all the crewe
In curteous usage, and unstained hewe.               120

Who being nimbler joynted than the rest,
And more industrious, gathered more store
Of the fields honour, than the others best;
Which they in secret harts envying sore,
Tolde *Venus*, when her as the worthiest              125
She praisd', that *Cupide* (as they heard before)
Did lend her secret aide, in gathering
Into her lap the children of the spring.

Whereof the Goddesse gathering jealous feare,
Not yet unmindfull, how not long agoe                 130
Her sonne to *Psyche* secrete love did beare,

113–44. In rehearsing the "report" of Astery's transformation, Sp draws on
no known source. He creates an analogue to rather than a version of the
Cupid and Psyche myth, to which he refers in lines 131–33. Sp underscores
the innocence of Astery (star-queen?) who is caught, quite unwittingly, in a
web of envy, detraction, and the hasty credence that Venus, like the
husbandman in *SC* "Februarie," gives to false report.    119. *Hight*:
called.    131. *Psyche*: The word means both "soul" and "butterfly." In
Apuleius's account of Cupid's involvement with Psyche (*The Golden Ass*,
Books 7–9), only the former meaning applies.

And long it close conceal'd, till mickle woe
Thereof arose, and manie a rufull teare;
Reason with sudden rage did overgoe,
And giving hastie credit to th'accuser,                    135
Was led away of them that did abuse her.

Eftsoones that Damzel by her heavenly might,
She turn'd into a winged Butterflie,
In the wide aire to make her wandring flight;
And all those flowres, with which so plenteouslie          140
Her lap she filled had, that bred her spight,
She placed in her wings, for memorie
Of her pretended crime, though crime none were:
Since which that flie them in her wings doth beare.

Thus the fresh *Clarion* being readie dight,              145
Unto his journey did himselfe addresse,
And with good speed began to take his flight:
Over the fields in his franke lustinesse,
And all the champion he soared light,
And all the countrey wide he did possesse,                150
Feeding upon their pleasures bounteouslie,
That none gainsaid, nor none did him envie.

The woods, the rivers, and the medowes green,
With his aire-cutting wings he measured wide,
Ne did he leave the mountaines bare unseene,              155
Nor the ranke grassie fennes delights untride.
But none of these, how ever sweete they beene,
Mote please his fancie, nor him cause t'abide:
His choicefull sense with everie change doth flit.
No common things may please a wavering wit.               160

To the gay gardins his unstaid desire
Him wholly caried, to refresh his sprights:

132. *mickle*: much.    137. *Eftsoones*: presently.    145. *dight*: dressed.
148. *franke*: free, vigorous.    149. *champion*: plain.    159–60. Like his
wings (*Muio* 101), Clarion is "changefull" and fickle.    161. *unstaid*:
flighty, capricious.

There lavish Nature in her best attire,
Powres forth sweete odors, and alluring sights;
And Arte with her contending, doth aspire                165
T'excell the naturall, with made delights:
And all that faire or pleasant may be found,
In riotous excesse doth there abound.

There he arriving, round about doth flie,
From bed to bed, from one to other border,              170
And takes survey with curious busie eye,
Of everie flowre and herbe there set in order;
Now this, now that he tasteth tenderly,
Yet none of them he rudely doth disorder,
Ne with his feete their silken leaves deface;           175
But pastures on the pleasures of each place.

And evermore with most varietie,
And change of sweetnesse (for all change is sweete)
He casts his glutton sense to satisfie,
Now sucking of the sap of herbe most meete,             180
Or of the deaw, which yet on them does lie,
Now in the same bathing his tender feete:
And then he pearcheth on some braunch thereby,
To weather him, and his moyst wings to dry.

And then again he turneth to his play,                  185
To spoyle the pleasures of that Paradise:
The wholsome Saulge, and Lavender still gray,

165. Art's contention with Nature suggests that Clarion revels in a bower of
bliss. Cf. *FQ* II xii 50 and 59.    178. *all* . . . *sweete*: a maxim undercut by
the poem's metamorphoses, and inconsistent with Sp's usual attitudes to
mutability.    184. *weather*: expose to the air.    187–200. This set-piece
should be compared with a similar passage in *VG* 665–86. Sp follows
sixteenth-century herbals when mentioning the medicinal properties of many
of the plants he describes: hence, the bathetic inclusion of colworts
(cabbages), lettuce, and dill, the last of which was an antidote to hiccups.
This garden is a boon for men and for butterflies in quite different ways.
187. *Saulge*: sage, "much esteemed formerly as a medicinal herb" (OED).
*Lavender*: oil of lavender was a nostrum.

Ranke smelling Rue, and Cummin good for eyes,
The Roses raigning in the pride of May,
Sharpe Isope, good for greene wounds remedies,          190
Faire Marigoldes, and Bees alluring Thime,
Sweete Marjoram, and Daysies decking prime.

Coole Violets, and Orpine growing still,
Embathed Balme, and chearfull Galingale,
Fresh Costmarie, and breathfull Camomill,              195
Dull Poppie, and drink-quickning Setvale,
Veyne-healing Verven, and hed-purging Dill,
Sound Savorie, and Bazill hartie-hale,
Fat Colworts, and comforting Perseline,
Colde Lettuce, and refreshing Rosmarine.               200

And whatso else of vertue good or ill
Grewe in this Gardin, fetcht from farre away,
Of everie one he takes, and tastes at will,
And on their pleasures greedily doth pray.
Then when he hath both plaid, and fed his fill,        205
In the warme Sunne he doth himselfe embay,

---

188. *Rue*: "A perennial evergreen shrub . . . having bitter, strong-scented
leaves, which were formerly much used for medicinal purposes"
(OED).          190. *Isope*: hyssop, balm for bruises.          191. *Marigoldes*: used,
according to Lyte's *Herbal* (1578), to cure palpitations of the heart.
192. *prime*: spring-time.          193. *Orpine*: live-long, sometimes used in a
plaster for superficial wounds.          194. *Galingale*: an aromatic root used in
cases of dyspepsia.          195. Both costmary and camomil were thought to
have medicinal properties; the latter was held to assist in the expulsion of
phlegm (Renwick 1928).          196. *Setvale*: setwall, "whose roote the
Phistions use to gather in Sommer" (OED).          197. Verven: vervain,
valued as a drug to counteract fevers and fistulae.          198. Bazill: Renwick
(1928) notes that according to Lyte, basil "doth fortifie and strengthen the
harte."          199. *Perseline*: parsley. Renwick (1928) cites Elyot (1539): "It is
very convenient to the stomake."          200. *Rosmarine*: rosemary.
201. *vertue . . . ill*: Cf. *SC* "December" 68, which remarks on "The power of
herbs, both which can hurt and ease," and cf. the Friar's comments in *Romeo
and Juliet* 2.3.6–30.          206. *embay*: bathe.

And there him rests in riotous suffisaunce
Of all his gladfulnes, and kingly joyaunce.

What more felicitie can fall to creature,
Than to enjoy delight with libertie,                             210
And to be Lord of all the workes of Nature,
To raine in th'aire from earth to highest skie,
To feed on flowres, and weeds of glorious feature,
To take what ever thing doth please the eie?
Who rests not pleased with such happines,                        215
Well worthie he to taste of wretchednes.

But what on earth can long abide in state?
Or who can him assure of happie day;
Sith morning faire may bring fowle evening late,
And least mishap the most blisse alter may?                      220
For thousand perills lie in close awaite
About us daylie, to worke our decay;
That none, except a God, or God him guide,
May them avoyde, or remedie provide.

And whatso heavens in their secret doome                         225
Ordained have, how can fraile fleshly wight
Forecast, but it must needs to issue come?
The sea, the aire, the fire, the day, the night,
And th'armies of their creatures all and some
Do serve to them, and with importune might                       230
Warre against us the vassals of their will.
Who then can save, what they dispose to spill?

Not thou, O *Clarion*, though fairest thou
Of all thy kinde, unhappie happie Flie,

207. *riotous suffisaunce*: an oxymoron. Cf. "riotous excesse" (*Muio*
168).     209–40 The disquisition on Fortune is also a vision of the world's
vanity. Cf. Chaucer, *The Nun's Priest's Tale*: "Lo, how fortune turneth
sodeinly/ The hope and pride eek of hir enemy" (637–38).     212. *raine*:
reign.     229. *all and some*: one and all.     230. *importune*: weighty.
232. *spill*: destroy, kill.     234. *unhappie happie*: The oxymoron, with
submerged puns on "hap", connects Clarion's misfortune with his felicity.

Whose cruell fate is woven even now                          235
Of *Joves* owne hand, to worke thy miserie:
Ne may thee helpe the manie hartie vow,
Which thy olde Sire with sacred pietie
Hath powred forth for thee, and th'altars sprent:
Nought may thee save from heavens avengement.               240

It fortuned (as heavens had behight)
That in this gardin, where yong *Clarion*
Was wont to solace him, a wicked wight
The foe of faire things, th'author of confusion,
The shame of Nature, the bondslave of spight,              245
Had lately built his hatefull mansion,
And lurking closely, in awayte now lay,
How he might anie in his trap betray.

But when he spide the joyous Butterflie
In this faire plot dispacing too and fro,                  250
Fearles of foes and hidden jeopardie,
Lord how he gan for to bestirre him tho,
And to his wicked worke each part applie:
His heart did earne against his hated foe,
And bowels so with ranckling poyson swelde,                255
That scarce the skin the strong contagion helde.

The cause why he this Flie so maliced,
Was (as in stories it is written found)

235–36. Sp transfers the spinning of man's destiny, usually attributed to
Fortune or the three Fates, to Jove himself.     239. *sprent*: sprinkled.
241. *It fortuned*: Sp thus makes Aragnoll, whose name he defers until line
385, an instrument of Fortune and an agent for "heavens avangement."
*behight*: ordained.     243–46. The cumulative force of this passage makes
Aragnoll satanic.     251. Serena is vulnerable to the Blatant Beast when she
is "Without suspect of ill or daungers dred" (*FQ* VI iii 23 12) and Timias, to
Despetto, Decetto, and Defetto when he is "Nether of envy, nor of chaunge
afeard" (*FQ* VI v 12 5). Sp enlarges on Clarion's security in lines 377–84.
252. *tho*: then.     254. *earne*: yearn.     257–352. The story of Arachne
appears in Ovid, *Met* 6.1–145. Sp significantly alters Ovid's tale by
presenting Arachne's work before Minerva's, by inventing the butterfly that
distinguishes Minerva's tapestry, and by attributing Arachne's transformation

For that his mother which him bore and bred,
The most fine fingred workwoman on ground,                    260
*Arachne*, by his meanes was vanquished
Of *Pallas*, and in her owne skill confound,
When she with her for excellence contended,
That wrought her shame, and sorrow never ended.

For the *Tritonian* Goddesse having hard                      265
Her blazed fame, which all the world had fil'd,
Came down to prove the truth, and due reward
For her prais-worthie workmanship to yeild
But the presumptuous Damzel rashly dar'd
The Goddesse selfe to chalenge to the field,                  270
And to compare with her in curious skill
Of workes with loome, with needle, and with quill.

*Minerva* did the chalenge not refuse,
But deign'd with her the paragon to make:
So to their worke they sit, and each doth chuse               275
What storie she will for her tapet take.
*Arachne* figur'd how *Jove* did abuse
*Europa* like a Bull, and on his backe
Her through the sea did beare; so lively seene,
That it true Sea, and true Bull ye would weene.               280

She seem'd still backe unto the land to looke,
And her play-fellowes aide to call, and feare
The dashing of the waves, that up she tooke

into a spider (cf. Malbecco's transformation into Gelosie in *FQ* III x 59–60)
to the debilitating effects of poisonous envy rather than to divine power over
mortals.     265. *Tritonian Goddesse*: Minerva, or Pallas Athene, who had
been the ward of the sea-god, Triton, and whom Ovid calls Tritonia at the
outset of the Arachne story (cf. *Muio* 286). *hard*: heard.     272. *quill*:
bobbin.     277. *figur'd*: depicted.     281–99. In Ovid Arachne depicts
twenty-one encounters between gods and mortals. Sp selects the first of these
and expands it, perhaps recalling *Met* 2.846–75 and Moschus's Idyll about
Europa and the Bull. Some critics, impressed by the vividness of the
description, think that Sp must have known an actual painting or tapestry
that served as his model for these lines.

Her daintie feete, and garments gathered neare:
But (Lord) how she in everie member shooke,     285
When as the land she saw no more appeare,
But a wilde wildernes of waters deepe:
Then gan she greatly to lament and weepe.

Before the Bull she pictur'd winged Love,
With his yong brother Sport, light fluttering     290
Upon the waves, as each had been a Dove;
The one his bowe and shafts, the other Spring
A burning Teade about his head did move,
As in their Syres new love both triumphing:
And manie Nymphes about them flocking round,     295
And manie *Tritons*, which their hornes did sound.

And round about, her worke she did empale
With a faire border wrought of sundrie flowres,
Enwoven with an Yvie winding trayle:
A goodly worke, full fit for Kingly bowres,     300
Such as Dame *Pallas*, such as Envie pale,
That al good things with venemous tooth devowres,
Could not accuse. Then gan the Goddesse bright
Her selfe likewise unto her worke to dight.

She made the storie of the olde debate,     305
Which she with *Neptune* did for *Athens* trie:

289. *Love*: the Alexandrian Cupid, the same boy to whom the narrator had
been deferential in lines 97–99.    290. *Sport*: one of the "legions of loves"
(*Amor* 16) that often accompany Cupid. "Iocus" appears with Cupid in
Horace, *Odes* 1.2.34. Sp intends a contrast between divine joviality and
human terror.    292. *Spring*: boy.    293. *Teade*: torch.    297. *empale*:
encircle.    299. *Yvie*: Ivy, sacred to Bacchus, is emblematic of the orgiastic
scene just described. Similarly, Acrasia's bower is "Framed of wanton Yvie"
(*FQ* II v 29).    301. *pale*: Ovid's Envy is "pale" (*Met* 2.775). The word
may hint at a pun on Pallas, whose association with Envy in the Aglauros
episode is intimate.    302. *venemous tooth*: a commonplace derived from
Ovid, *Tristia* 4.10.124.    304. *dight*: prepare.    305. Cf. the "dolorous
debate" in line 1. Minerva displays the gods in council, and her image of Jove
in majesty succeeds Arachne's of Jove in love.

Twelve Gods doo sit around in royall state,
And *Jove* in midst with awfull Majestie,
To judge the strife betweene them stirred late:
Each of the Gods by his like visnomie                    310
Eathe to be knowen; but *Jove* above them all,
By his great lookes and power Imperiall.

Before them stands the God of Seas in place,
Clayming that sea-coast Citie as his right,
And strikes the rockes with his three-forked mace;        315
Whenceforth issues a warlike steed in sight,
The signe by which he chalengeth the place,
That all the Gods, which saw his wondrous might
Did surely deeme the victorie his due:
But seldome seene, forejudgement proveth true.            320

Then to her selfe she gives her *Aegide* shield,
And steelhed speare, and morion on her hedd,
Such as she oft is seene in warlicke field:
Then sets she forth, how with her weapon dredd
She smote the ground, the which streight foorth did
                                                 yield    325
A fruitfull Olyve tree, with berries spredd,
That all the Gods admir'd; then all the storie
She compast with a wreathe of Olyves hoarie.

306. *trie*: strive. Each claims patronage of the city, but Pallas Athene, as her name suggests, eventually prevails: her victory over Neptune anticipates her victory over Arachne, whose tapestry is a seascape.    311. *Eathe*: easy.    315. *three-forked mace*: Neptune's symbol of authority is his trident.    318–20. Sp adds these lines to Ovid's account.    321. *Aegide*: Following Natalis Comes's *Mythologia* (1551), Sp conflates Minerva's shield and aegis.    322. *morion*: helmet. Golding's translation of Ovid (1567) uses this word in its description of Minerva's headpiece.    323. Minerva, in her guise of Bellona, goddess of war.    327–28. Ovid modifies olive with "pacalibus" and thus confirms the tree's association with peace; cf. E. K.'s gloss on *SC* "April" line 124. Georg Sabinus, in his commentary on the *Met* (1555), distinguishes the peace and public tranquillity symbolized by the olive from the turbulence and perturbation symbolized by Neptune's sea, but the olive contrasts as well, of course, with the ivy that borders Arachne's tapestry.

Emongst those leaves she made a Butterflie,
With excellent device and wondrous slight,                                    330
Fluttring among the Olives wantonly,
That seem'd to live, so like it was in sight:
The velvet nap which on his wings doth lie,
The silken downe with which his backe is dight,
His broad outstretched hornes, his hayrie thies,                              335
His glorious colours, and his glistering eies.

Which when *Arachne* saw, as overlaid,
And mastered with workmanship so rare,
She stood astonied long, ne ought gainesaid,
And with fast fixed eyes on her did stare,                                    340
And by her silence, signe of one dismaid,
The victorie did yeeld her as her share:
Yet did she inly fret, and felly burne,
And all her blood to poysonous rancor turne.

That shortly from the shape of womanhed                                       345
Such as she was, when *Pallas* she attempted,
She grew to hideous shape of dryrihed,
Pined with griefe of follie late repented:
Eftsoones her white streight legs were altered
To crooked crawling shankes, of marrowe empted,                              350
And her faire face to fowle and loathsome hewe,
And her fine corpes to a bag of venim grewe.

This cursed creature, mindfull of that olde
Enfestred grudge, the which his mother felt,
So soone as *Clarion* he did beholde,                                         355
His heart with vengefull malice inly swelt;
And weaving straight a net with manie a folde
About the cave, in which he lurking dwelt,

330. *slight*: sleight, artifice.        333–36. Cf. *Muio* 57–90.        341. Arachne's
dismay results eventually in her being dis-maid when she becomes a
spider.        343. *felly*: fiercely.        347. *dryrihed*: sorrow. The spelling may
reflect the traditional belief that coldness and dryness were symptoms of
envy.        349–52. Arachne, dehumanized, becomes *arakhne*, Greek for
spider.        358. *cave*: the abode of Envy in *Met* 2.761.

With fine small cords about it stretched wide,
So finely sponne, that scarce they could be spide.          360

Not anie damzell, which her vaunteth most
In skilfull knitting of soft silken twyne;
Nor anie weaver, which his worke doth boast
In dieper, in damaske, or in lyne;
Nor anie skil'd in workmanship embost;                       365
Nor anie skil'd in loupes of fingring fine,
Might in their divers cunning ever dare,
With this so curious networke to compare.

Ne doo I thinke, that that same subtil gin,
The which the *Lemnian* God framde craftilie,               370
*Mars* sleeping with his wife to compasse in,
That all the Gods with common mockerie
Might laugh at them, and scorne their shamefull sin,
Was like to this. This same he did applie,
For to entrap the careles *Clarion*,                         375
That rang'd each where without suspition.

Suspition of friend, nor feare of foe,
That hazarded his health, had he at all,
But walkt at will, and wandred too and fro,
In the pride of his freedome principall:                     380
Litle wist he his fatall future woe,
But was secure, the liker he to fall.
He likest is to fall into mischaunce,
That is regardles of his governaunce.

---

361–74. Aragnoll's web is thus the only unchallengeable piece of weaving in
the poem. Through the repeated negative comparisons, the net becomes the
rhetorical equivalent of Clarion's wings (*Muio* 92–101).     364. Diaper and
linen are fine fabrics.     369. *gin*: snare.     370. *Lemnian God*: Vulcan,
who lived on the island of Lemnos, and who tried to capture with a net the
adulterous Venus and Mars in a story told both by Homer and by Ovid, *Met*
4.176–89. He is sometimes a type of jealousy.     379. *wandred*: perhaps
suggesting "erred," as in "the wandring wood . . . Errours den" (*FQ* I i 13).
380. *principall*: princely; original (with theological connotations).
381. *wist*: knew.

Yet still *Aragnoll* (so his foe was hight)        385
Lay lurking covertly him to surprise,
And all his gins that him entangle might,
Drest in good order as he could devise.
At length the foolish Flie without foresight,
As he that did all daunger quite despise,        390
Toward those parts came flying careleslie,
Where hidden was his hatefull enemie.

Who seeing him, with secrete joy therefore
Did tickle inwardly in everie vaine,
And his false hart fraught with all treasons store,        395
Was fil'd with hope, his purpose to obtaine:
Himselfe he close upgathered more and more
Into his den, that his deceiptfull traine
By his there being might not be bewraid,
Ne anie noyse, ne anie motion made.        400

Like as a wily Foxe, that having spide,
Where on a sunnie banke the Lambes doo play,
Full closely creeping by the hinder side,
Lyes in ambushment of his hoped pray,
Ne stirreth limbe, till seeing readie tide,        405
He rusheth forth, and snatcheth quite away
One of the little yonglings unawares:
So to his worke *Aragnoll* him prepares.

Who now shall give unto my heavie eyes
A well of teares, that all may overflow?        410
Or where shall I finde lamentable cryes,
And mournfull tunes enough my griefe to show?
Helpe O thou Tragick Muse, me to devise

385. *hight*: called.    394. *tickle*: tingle.    399. *bewraid*: betrayed.
402. The simile places *Muio* in the Aesopic tradition (cf. *SC* "May"
174–305).    403. *hinder*: If Aragnoll, like the Fox, attacks from the rear,
Sp may be emphasizing his affinity with envy and detraction; Sp thus
dramatizes backbiting when he describes several of the invidious characters in
*FQ*: Corflambo (IV viii 41), Sclaunder (IV viii 36), Envy (V xii 39), Defetto
(VI v 20), and Turpine (VI vi 26).    405. *tide*: opportunity.

Notes sad enough, t'expresse this bitter throw:
For loe, the drerie stownd is now arrived,      415
That of all happines hath us deprived.

The luckles *Clarion*, whether cruell Fate,
Or wicked Fortune faultles him misled,
Or some ungracious blast out of the gate
Of *Aeoles* raine perforce him drove on hed,      420
Was (O sad hap and howre unfortunate)
With violent swift flight forth caried
Into the cursed cobweb, which his foe
Had framed for his finall overthroe.

There the fond Flie entangled, strugled long,      425
Himselfe to free thereout; but all in vaine.
For striving more, the more in laces strong
Himselfe he tide, and wrapt his winges twaine
In lymie snares the subtill loupes among;
That in the ende he breathelesse did remaine,      430
And all his yougthly forces idly spent,
Him to the mercie of th'avenger lent.

Which when the greisly tyrant did espie,
Like a grimme Lyon rushing with fierce might
Out of his den, he seized greedelie      435
On the resistles pray, and with fell spight,
Under the left wing stroke his weapon slie
Into his heart, that his deepe groning spright
In bloodie streames foorth fled into the aire,
His bodie left the spectacle of care.      440

FINIS.

415. *stownd*: moment.      416. *us*: Sp thus broadens the significance of
Clarion's fall.      420. *Aeoles*: Aeolus is the wind, which Clarion has dared
to tempt (*Muio* 48).      422–24. Alliteration and enjambment help capture
the swiftness of Clarion's flight to death.      425. *fond*: silly, foolish.
431. *idly*: He had earlier disdained "loathsome sloth" (*Muio* 36).
434. *Lyon*: Cf. Psalms 21.22 and 1 Peter 5.8.      440. An echo of the final
line of the *Aen* which describes the demise of Turnus.

# Visions of the Worlds Vanitie

Three series of *Visions* end the *Complaints*: this is the only one which is original, neither a translation nor a paraphrase. Its title suggests two sources of inspiration: the vision sonnets of Du Bellay and Petrarch which Spenser translated for *A Theatre for Worldlings* (and re-translated as *The Visions of Bellay* and *The Visions of Petrarch*) and the heady melancholy of Ecclesiastes: "Vanitie of vanities saith ye Preacher . . . all *is* vanitie" (1.2). Another influence is the late medieval *de casibus* tradition, in which, as with Lydgate and Sackville, fascination with power, fame, and beauty is coupled with a sense of the inevitability of their destruction. And behind all this is the tradition of the medieval vision poem, in which a dreamer sees truth revealed in symbolic or emblematic form.

The *Visions* sonnets all show delight in the paradoxical powers of the weak to injure the strong. In *The Visions of Bellay* the moral is at the expense of Rome and in *A Theatre for Worldlings* at the expense of the Roman church. Here the references are more oblique: the crocodile of sonnet 3 and the leviathan of sonnet 5 do carry overtones of the Egyptian tyrant which in biblical symbolism is code for *all* tyrants. This lends a certain mythologizing political relevance, but it is not allowed to become specific. Recurrent understated reference to the Beatitudes gives these poems a more personal tone, and there is frequent emphasis on the speaker's being astonished, moved, and distressed. It is possible here to see the demarcations of political disappointment and the rendering of political opponents back into their mythic archetypes. But the strongest note is the deeply-ingrained defense learned early from Ecclesiastes: not to expect security from the external things of a world in which "so small thing his happines may varie" (line 112), and where man will assuredly "finde his state most fickle and unsure" (line 168).

Though these sonnets lack woodcuts like those that accompanied earlier versions of the other two *Visions* sequences, they could equally well have had them. The reductive moralistic parables of these verses also recall the moral simplicity of the clear black lines of the *Theatre* woodcuts. These sonnets have a static quality: the closing couplets of all twelve sonnets express more or less the same epigrammatic moral about the fall of the seemingly mighty and the fragility of human expectation. For this, and for unmitigated melancholy, *Visions of the Worlds Vanitie* have been seen to be early in date, while their rhyme-scheme's similarity to *Amoretti* (and difference from the rest of the *Visions* sequences) has been used to suggest otherwise. But the tone of these sonnets is a rhetorical stance, deeply ingrained in the imagination of the age, and of Spenser. With their freshness of enthusiasm and with their intuitively emblematic modes of thought, they could be by no one but Spenser, and with these skills they contain the seeds of his mature poetic talents.

*Richard Schell*

# *Visions of the worlds vanitie.*

### 1

ONe day, whiles that my daylie cares did sleepe,
  My spirit, shaking off her earthly prison,
Began to enter into meditation deepe
Of things exceeding reach of common reason;
  Such as this age, in which all good is geason,       5
And all that humble is and meane debaced,
Hath brought forth in her last declining season,
Griefe of good mindes, to see goodnesse disgraced.
  On which when as my thought was throghly placed,
Unto my eyes strange showes presented were,          10
Picturing that, which I in minde embraced,
That yet those sights empassion me full nere.
  Such as they were (faire Ladie) take in worth,
  That when time serves, may bring things better forth.


### 2

  In Summers day, when *Phœbus* fairly shone,      15
I saw a Bull as white as driven snowe,
With gilden hornes embowed like the Moone,
In a fresh flowring meadow lying lowe:

SONNET 1:   Cf. *RT* 477–90 and *Proth* 1–18.   2. Body is the soul's
prison.   5. *geason*: exhausted.   6. *meane*: of low rank, poor. *debaced*:
vilified.   7. *last declining season*: a reference to the belief that the world is
aging and in a state of final dissolution (see *RR* 126 and note).
9. *throghly*: fully.   10. *strange showes*: cf. the *Dreames* and *Pageaunts*
mentioned in the note to *RT* 491–end.   12. *empassion*: inflame with
passion. *nere*: near, i.e. deeply.   13. *Ladie*: unidentified; cf. *VP* 7.9. *in*
*worth*: for what they are worth.
SONNET 2:   16–17. Cf. Virgil, *Georgics* 1.217–18 (Renwick
1928:256).   17. *embowed*: convex, bowlike.

*433*

Up to his eares the verdant grasse did growe,
And the gay floures did offer to be eaten;                    20
But he with fatnes so did overflowe,
That he all wallowed in the weedes downe beaten,
  Ne car'd with them his daintie lips to sweeten:
Till that a Brize, a scorned little creature,
Through his faire hide his angrie sting did threaten,         25
And vext so sore, that all his goodly feature,
  And all his plenteous pasture nought him pleased:
  So by the small the great is oft diseased.


### 3

    Beside the fruitfull shore of muddie *Nile*,
Upon a sunnie banke outstretched lay                          30
In monstrous length, a mightie Crocodile,
That cram'd with guiltles blood, and greedie pray
  Of wretched people travailing that way,
Thought all things lesse than his disdainfull pride.
I saw a little Bird, cal'd *Tedula*,                          35
The least of thousands which on earth abide,
  That forst this hideous beast to open wide
The greisly gates of his devouring hell,
And let him feede, as Nature doth provide,
Upon his jawes, that with blacke venime swell.               40
  Why then should greatest things the least disdaine,
  Sith that so small so mightie can constraine?

24. *Brize*: a gadfly of a kind which annoys horses and cattle.    28. *diseased*:
deprived of ease, annoyed.
S O N N E T 3:    The identification of the crocodile with hell (line 38)
reiterates a host of biblical associations of monsters with death, hell, and the
tyrannical rulers of demonic civilizations, especially Egypt, Babylon, and
Rome. Cf. the comparison of Duessa to an Egyptian crocodile (*FQ* I v 18).
35. *Tedula*: perhaps trochilus, a small Egyptian bird held by ancient folklore
to pick the teeth of the crocodile.

### 4

The kingly Bird, that beares *Joves* thunder-clap,
One day did scorne the simple Scarabee,
Proud of his highest service, and good hap,                    45
That made all other Foules his thralls to bee:
    The silly Flie, that no redresse did see,
Spide where the Eagle built his towring nest,
And kindling fire within the hollow tree,
Burnt up his yong ones, and himselfe distrest;                50
    Ne suffred him in anie place to rest,
But drove in *Joves* owne lap his egs to lay;
Where gathering also filth him to infest,
Forst with the filth his egs to fling away:
    For which when as the Foule was wroth, said *Jove*,    55
    Lo how the least the greatest may reprove.

### 5

Toward the sea turning my troubled eye,
I saw the fish (if fish I may it cleepe)
That makes the sea before his face to flye,
And with his flaggie finnes doth seeme to sweepe      60
    The fomie waves out of the dreadfull deep,
The huge *Leviathan*, dame Natures wonder,
Making his sport, that manie makes to weep:
A sword-fish small him from the rest did sunder,
    That in his throat him pricking softly under,         65

SONNET 4:    See Alciati, *Emblemata* 182, and Aesop, *Fables*. Sp's
scarabee sets fire to the eagle's nest instead of breaking its eggs.
44. *Scarabee*: scarab; a beetle bred and nourished on dung; see Erasmus,
*Adagia* 3.7.1.
SONNET 5:    The combats of the swordfish and the whale are, curiously
enough, authentic (Renwick 1928:256-57). The fact that biblical Leviathan
is, symbolically, tyrant Egypt (Psalm 74.13–14; Ezekiel 29.1–4) gives Sp's
sonnet mythic political resonance.    58. *cleepe*: call, name.    60. *flaggie*:
soft and flabby.    63. *Making his sport*: cf. Psalm 104.26.

His wide Abysse him forced forth to spewe,
That all the sea did roare like heavens thunder,
And all the waves were stain'd with filthie hewe.
  Hereby I learned have, not to despise,
  What ever thing seemes small in common eyes.　　　　70

6

An hideous Dragon, dreadfull to behold,
Whose backe was arm'd against the dint of speare
With shields of brasse, that shone like burnisht golde,
And forkhed sting, that death in it did beare,
  Strove with a Spider his unequall peare:　　　　75
And bad defiance to his enemie.
The subtill vermin creeping closely neare,
Did in his drinke shed poyson privilie;
  Which through his entrailes spredding diversly,
Made him to swell, that nigh his bowells brust,　　　　80
And him enforst to yeeld the victorie,
That did so much in his owne greatnesse trust.
  O how great vainnesse is it then to scorne
  The weake, that hath the strong so oft forlorne.

7

High on a hill a goodly Cedar grewe,　　　　85
Of wondrous length, and streight proportion,
That farre abroad her daintie odours threwe;
Mongst all the daughters of proud *Libanon*,
  Her match in beautie was not anie one.

68. Compare the filthy vomit of the slain dragon in *FQ* I i 20. *hewe*:
appearance.
S O N N E T 6:    Job's Behemoth has bones "*like* staves of brasse" and in the
Geneva Bible his Leviathan has scales "*like* strong shields" (Job 40.13,
41.6).    75. *peare*: because "both Dragon and Spider are venomous beasts"
(Renwick 1928:257).    77. *closely*: covertly.    80. *brust*: burst.
83. *vainnesse*: foolishness, stupidity.    84. *forlorne*: destroyed.
S O N N E T 7:    Biblical cedars of Lebanon symbolize strength, splendor,
and glory. In Ezekiel 31 the cedars' fall points a political parable.

Shortly within her inmost pith there bred         90
A litle wicked worme, perceiv'd of none,
That on her sap and vitall moysture fed:
   Thenceforth her garland so much honoured
Began to die, (O great ruth for the same)
And her faire lockes fell from her loftie head,     95
That shortly balde, and bared she became.
   I, which this sight beheld, was much dismayed,
To see so goodly thing so soone decayed.

**8**

   Soone after this I saw an Elephant,
Adorn'd with bells and bosses gorgeouslie,     100
That on his backe did beare (as batteilant)
A gilden towre, which shone exceedinglie;
   That he himselfe through foolish vanitie,
Both for his rich attire, and goodly forme,
Was puffed up with passing surquedrie,     105
And shortly gan all other beasts to scorne.
   Till that a little Ant, a silly worme,
Into his nosthrils creeping, so him pained,
That casting downe his towres, he did deforme
Both borrowed pride, and native beautie stained.    110
   Let therefore nought that great is, therein glorie,
Sith so small thing his happines may varie.

**9**

   Looking far foorth into the Ocean wide,
A goodly ship with banners bravely dight,
And flag in her top-gallant I espide,     115
Through the maine sea making her merry flight:

90–92. Cf. Bartholomaeus Anglicus, *De Proprietatis Rerum* 17.23: "Cedre
. . . is never destroyed with mought [moth], neyther with Terredo, that is the
Tree worme."
SONNET 8:    101. *batteilant*: combatant.    105. *surquedrie*: arrogance.
SONNET 9:    Cf. images of ships in *VP* 2 and Alciati, *Emblemata* 50, 70.

Faire blew the winde into her bosome right;
And th'heavens looked lovely all the while,
That she did seeme to daunce, as in delight,
And at her owne felicitie did smile. 120
 All sodainely there clove unto her keele
A little fish, that men call *Remora*,
Which stopt her course, and held her by the heele,
That winde nor tide could move her thence away.
 Straunge thing me seemeth, that so small a thing 125
 Should able be so great an one to wring.

### 10

 A mighty Lyon, Lord of all the wood,
Having his hunger throughly satisfide,
With pray of beasts, and spoyle of living blood,
Safe in his dreadles den him thought to hide: 130
 His sternesse was his prayse, his strength his pride,
And all his glory in his cruell clawes.
I saw a wasp, that fiercely him defide,
And bad him battaile even to his jawes;
 Sore he him stong, that it the blood forth drawes, 135
And his proude heart is fild with fretting ire:
In vaine he threats his teeth, his tayle, his pawes,
And from his bloodie eyes doth sparkle fire;
 That dead himselfe he wisheth for despight.
 So weakest may anoy the most of might. 140

### 11

 What time the Romaine Empire bore the raine
Of all the world, and florisht most in might,
The nations gan their soveraigntie disdaine,

122. *Remora*: sucking fish (Gk. *echeneis remora*) believed by the ancients to
have the power of staying the course of any ship to which it attached itself.
Pliny, *Natural History* 32.1, includes the moral.
S O N N E T 11: 141–44. Anachronism to point a moral: Rome's
greatness dates from much later than the sacred-geese incident.

And cast to quitt them from their bondage quight:
  So when all shrouded were in silent night,         145
The *Galles* were, by corrupting of a mayde,
Possest nigh of the Capitol through slight,
Had not a Goose the treachery bewrayde.
  If then a Goose great *Rome* from ruine stayde,
And *Jove* himselfe, the patron of the place,         150
Preservd from being to his foes betrayde,
Why do vaine men mean things so much deface,
    And in their might repose their most assurance,
    Sith nought on earth can chalenge long endurance?

### 12

  When these sad sights were overpast and gone,     155
My spright was greatly moved in her rest,
With inward ruth and deare affection,
To see so great things by so small distrest:
  Thenceforth I gan in my engrieved brest
To scorne all difference of great and small,       160
Sith that the greatest often are opprest,
And unawares doe into daunger fall.
  And ye, that read these ruines tragicall
Learne by their losse to love the low degree,
And if that fortune chaunce you up to call       165
To honours seat, forget not what you be:
    For he that of himselfe is most secure,
    Shall finde his state most fickle and unsure.

FINIS.

145–48. The sacred geese saved Rome in 390 B.C. by awakening the
garrison; the story of the bribed maiden is from the earlier (eighth-century)
story of a Sabine attack (Livy, *Ab Urbe Condita* 5.47, 1.11).    152. *deface*:
discredit, defame.
SONNET 12:    Cf. the Beatitudes (Matthew 5.1–12) and Sp's attitude to
Burghley in *RT*, *MHT*, etc.    163–68. Cf. *SC* "July" 219–20.

# The Visions of Bellay

T he original of these translations, eleven of which Spenser had rendered into blank verse in *A Theatre for Worldlings*, is Du Bellay's *Songe*, a series of fifteen allegorical dream-vision sonnets appended to his *Antiquitez de Rome*. Du Bellay's inspiration has been found in Petrarch, specifically in *Rime* 323 (translated by Spenser as *The Visions of Petrarch*). This retranslation into rhyme includes the four sonnets (6, 8, 13, and 14) not translated in the *Theatre*.

Du Bellay's sonnets are notably experimental, and for other reasons besides his being the first to write sonnets on a subject other than love. Spenser would have been aware that he was translating a poet who was charting new poetic territory. The rhyme-scheme of these later translations is however not Du Bellay's, Spenser's conventional English seven rhymes replacing Du Bellay's continental system of five. Sonnet 10 (revised from *Theatre* Sonnet 8) is reduced from fifteen back to Du Bellay's fourteen lines. The more literal accuracy of the *Theatre* translations has been used to question Spenser's authorship of those originals. However the freer hand of the later translations (including perhaps some more glaring mistranslation) may be the natural concomitant of poetic maturity.

*Richard Schell*

# The Visions of Bellay.

## 1

IT was the time, when rest soft sliding downe
From heavens hight into mens heavy eyes,
In the forgetfulnes of sleepe doth drowne
The carefull thoughts of mortall miseries:
    Then did a Ghost before mine eyes appeare,         5
    On that great rivers banck, that runnes by *Rome*,
Which calling me by name, bad me to reare
My lookes to heaven whence all good gifts do come,
    And crying lowd, loe now beholde (quoth hee)
What under this great temple placed is:           10
Lo all is nought but flying vanitee.
So I that know this worlds inconstancies,
    Sith onely God surmounts all times decay,
    In God alone my confidence do stay.

## 2

    On high hills top I saw a stately frame,         15
An hundred cubits high by just assize,
With hundreth pillours fronting faire the same,
All wrought with Diamond after Dorick wize:
    Nor brick, nor marble was the wall in view,
But shining Christall, which from top to base       20

SONNET 1:     Cf. the opening of *RT*.     1–4. Echoes the "Tempus erat"
of Aeneas's dream vision of Hector (*Aen* 2.268–69).     10. *this great temple*:
the heavens.     11. Epitomizes Ecclesiastes.     12–14. Christianizes the
theme of *RR* 40–42; cf. *FQ* VII viii 2 6–9.
SONNET 2:     16. *assize*: statutory measure.     18. *Dorick wize*: Cf. the
Temple of Venus (*FQ* IV x 6 9); suggests manlike appearance (Vitruvius, *De
Architecture* 4.1.6), being based on the proportions of a man's body
(Hamilton 1977:497).     20–25. Crystal, jasper, and emerald all figure in
the imagery of God's throne and of the Holy City (Revelation 4 and 21); but
this is by contrast an earthly throne.

Out of her womb a thousand rayons threw,
One hundred steps of *Afrike* golds enchase:
 Golde was the parget, and the seeling bright
 Did shine all scaly with great plates of golde;
 The floore of *Jasp* and *Emeraude* was dight.          25
O worlds vainnesse. Whiles thus I did behold,
 An earthquake shooke the hill from lowest seat,
 And overthrew this frame with ruine great.

### 3

 Then did a sharped spyre of Diamond bright,
Ten feete each way in square, appeare to mee,          30
Justly proportion'd up unto his hight,
So far as Archer might his level see:
 The top thereof a pot did seeme to beare,
 Made of the mettall, which we most do honour,
 And in this golden vessell couched weare          35
The ashes of a mightie Emperour:
 Upon foure corners of the base were pight,
 To beare the frame, foure great Lyons of gold;
 A worthy tombe for such a worthy wight.
Alas this world doth nought but grievance hold.          40
 I saw a tempest from the heaven descend,
 Which this brave monument with flash did rend.

### 4

 I saw raysde up on yvorie pilloures tall,
Whose bases were of richest mettalls warke,
The chapters Alablaster, the fryses christall,          45
The double front of a triumphall Arke:

21. *rayons*: beams, rays (Fr. *rayon*).    22. *enchase*: inlaid.    23. *parget*:
ornamental plaster.    25. *Jasp*: jasper (Fr. *jaspe*). *dight*: constructed.
27. An earthquake is an intimation of the end in Revelation.
S O N N E T 3:    32. *level*: aim.    37. *pight*: pitched.
S O N N E T 4:    45. *chapters*: capitals.    46. Central feature of the ruins of
the Roman Forum, depicted in the woodcut to *TW* Epigram 4.

On each side purtraid was a Victorie,
Clad like a Nimph, that wings of silver weares,
And in triumphant chayre was set on hie,
The auncient glory of the Romaine Peares.          50
   No worke it seem'd of earthly craftsmans wit,
But rather wrought by his owne industry,
That thunder-dartes for *Jove* his syre doth fit.
Let me no more see faire thing under sky,
    Sith that mine eyes have seene so faire a sight          55
    With sodain fall to dust consumed quight.

5

   Then was the faire *Dodonian* tree far seene,
Upon seaven hills to spread his gladsome gleame,
And conquerours bedecked with his greene,
Along the bancks of the *Ausonian* streame:          60
   There many an auncient Trophee was addrest.
And many a spoyle, and many a goodly show,
Which that brave races greatnes did attest,
That whilome from the *Troyan* blood did flow.
   Ravisht I was so rare a thing to vew,          65
When lo a barbarous troupe of clownish fone
The honour of these noble boughs down threw,
Under the wedge I heard the tronck to grone;
    And since I saw the roote in great disdaine
    A twinne of forked trees send forth againe.          70

---

52. *his*: Vulcan's.   56. Cf. Genesis 3.19.
SONNET 5:   57. The Dodonian Oak was a shrine to Zeus in Epirus
whence Odysseus says he went for advice about his return to Ithaca.
58. *seaven hills*: as Rome had.   59. A garland of oak leaves was a military
decoration (see Pliny *Natural History* 16.7ff).   60. *Ausonian streame*: Tiber
River; Ausonia is a Virgilian name for central and southern Italy.
61. *addrest*: displayed.   64. *Troyan*: the Virgilian assumption that Rome's
founders were Trojan.   66. *fone*: foes.   68. *wedge*: tree feller's
tool.   70. Suggests the survival of Rome's spirit.

### 6

I saw a Wolfe under a rockie cave
Noursing two whelpes; I saw her litle ones
In wanton dalliance the teate to crave,
While she her neck wreath'd from them for the nones:
  I saw her raunge abroad to seeke her food,       75
And roming through the field with greedie rage
T'embrew her teeth and clawes with lukewarm blood
Of the small heards, her thirst for to asswage.
I saw a thousand huntsmen, which descended
Downe from the mountaines bordring *Lombardie*,      80
That with an hundred speares her flank wide rended.
I saw her on the plaine outstretched lie,
  Throwing out thousand throbs in her owne soyle:
  Soone on a tree uphang'd I saw her spoyle.

### 7

  I saw the Bird that can the Sun endure,      85
With feeble wings assay to mount on hight,
By more and more she gan her wings t'assure,
Following th'ensample of her mothers sight:
  I saw her rise, and with a larger flight
To pierce the cloudes, and with wide pinnneons      90
To measure the most haughtie mountaines hight,
Untill she raught the Gods owne mansions:
  There was she lost, when suddaine I behelde,
  Where tumbling through the ayre in firie fold;

SONNET 6:   71–74. As depicted on the shield of Aeneas (*Aen* 8.630–34).    72. Romulus (founder of Rome) and his brother Remus were nursed by a she-wolf.   74. *wreath'd*: turned away. *nones*: for a moment. 77. *embrew*: stain.    80. From the Alps, whence came the barbarian invaders of Rome.   83. *soyle*: place made wet by her blood. SONNET 7:   85. "The Eagle imperiall" (Noot *TW* 15r), but line 98 below suggests a phoenix.   91. *haughtie*: lofty; so the mountains, but the bird's presumptuousness is also suggested.   92. *raught*: reached.

All flaming downe she on the plaine was felde,                    95
And soone her bodie turn'd to ashes colde.
   I saw the foule that doth the light dispise,
   Out of her dust like to a worme arise.


*8*

   I saw a river swift, whose fomy billowes
Did wash the ground work of an old great wall;          100
I saw it cover'd all with griesly shadowes,
That with black horror did the ayre appall:
   Thereout a strange beast with seven heads arose,
   That townes and castles under her brest did coure,
And seem'd both milder beasts and fiercer foes          105
Alike with equall ravine to devoure.
   Much was I mazde, to see this monsters kinde
In hundred formes to change his fearefull hew,
When as at length I saw the wrathfull winde,
Which blows cold storms, burst out of *Scithian* mew          110
   That sperst these cloudes, and in so short as thought,
   This dreadfull shape was vanished to nought.


*9*

   Then all astonied with this mighty ghoast,
An hideous bodie big and strong I sawe,
With side long beard, and locks down hanging loast,          115
Sterne face, and front full of Saturnlike awe;
   Who leaning on the belly of a pot,

---

97. Suggests an owl.
S O N N E T 8:      103. The sea beast of Revelation 13 and 17; cf. *TW*
Sonnets 12 and 13 and accompanying woodcuts.      104. *coure*: cower.
107. *kinde*: form.      109–10. Barbarian invaders.
S O N N E T 9:      113–20. A personification of the River Tiber (see Noot
*TW* 15r).      115. *side long*: hanging far down. *loast*: loosed, unfastened.
116. *front . . . awe*: a face inspiring gloomy reverence.

Pourd foorth a water, whose out gushing flood
Ran bathing all the creakie shore aflot,
Whereon the *Troyan* prince spilt *Turnus* blood;      120
    And at his feete a bitch wolfe suck did yeeld
To two young babes: his left the *Palme* tree stout,
His right hand did the peacefull *Olive* wield,
And head with Lawrell garnisht was about.
    Sudden both *Palme* and *Olive* fell away,      125
    And faire greene Lawrell branch did quite decay.

### 10
    Hard by a rivers side a virgin faire,
Folding her armes to heaven with thousand throbs,
And outraging her cheekes and golden haire,
To falling rivers sound thus tun'd her sobs.      130
    Where is (quoth she) this whilom honoured face?
Where the great glorie and the auncient praise,
In which all worlds felicitie had place,
When Gods and men my honour up did raise?
    Suffisd' it not that civill warres me made      135
The whole worlds spoile, but that this Hydra new,
Of hundred *Hercules* to be assaide,
With seven heads, budding monstrous crimes anew,
    So many *Neroes* and *Caligulaes*
    Out of these crooked shores must dayly rayse?      140

---

119. *creakie*: full of creeks.    120. Aeneas kills Turnus (*Aen* 12.950–
52).    122–24. *Palme* . . . *Olive* . . . *Lawrell*: for peace, victory, and poetry
respectively.    122. *two young babes*: Romulus and Remus.    126. The
end of Latin poetry.
S O N N E T 10:    127–34. The Genius of Rome    129. *outraging* . . .
*haire*: i.e. scratching her cheeks and tearing her hair.    131–34. *Ubi sunt?*
formula; cf. *RT* 57–77. Rome's variety and cultural richness is stressed.
136–38. The hydra, whose heads sometimes numbered seven, produced two
new ones for each one cut off until Hercules had the wound cauterized with
firebrands.

### 11

Upon an hill a bright flame I did see,
Waving aloft with triple point to skie,
Which like incense of precious Cedar tree,
With balmie odours fil'd th'ayre farre and nie.
    A Bird all white, well feathered on each wing,     145
Hereout up to the throne of Gods did flie,
And all the way most pleasant notes did sing,
Whilst in the smoake she unto heaven did stie.
    Of this faire fire the scattered rayes forth threw
On everie side a thousand shining beames:     150
When sudden dropping of a silver dew
(O grievous chance) gan quench those precious flames;
    That it which earst so pleasant sent did yeld,
    Of nothing now but noyous sulphure smeld.

### 12

I saw a spring out of a rocke forth rayle,     155
As cleare as Christall gainst the Sunnie beames,
The bottome yeallow, like the golden grayle
That bright *Pactolus* washeth with his streames;
    It seem'd that Art and Nature had assembled
All pleasure there, for which mans hart could long;     160
And there a noyse alluring sleepe soft trembled,
Of manie accords more sweete than Mermaids song:
    The seates and benches shone as yvorie,
And hundred Nymphes sate side by side about;
When from nigh hills with hideous outcrie,     165
A troupe of Satyres in the place did rout,

---

SONNET 11:    141. Allegory of the corruption of the pure spirit of the early church.    142. *triple point*: papal tiara?    148. *stie*: ascend. 151. *silver dew*: simony?
SONNET 12:    155. *rayle*: flow.    157–58. The sands of the River Pactolus were turned to gold when Midas bathed in it (*Met* 11.87–126). 157. *grayle*: gravel.

Which with their villeine feete the streame did ray,
Threw down the seats, and drove the Nymphs away.

### 13

Much richer then that vessell seem'd to bee,
Which did to that sad *Florentine* appeare,                    170
Casting mine eyes farre off, I chaunst to see,
Upon the *Latine* Coast herselfe to reare:
But suddenly arose a tempest great,
Bearing close envie to these riches rare,
Which gan assaile this ship with dreadfull threat,            175
This ship, to which none other might compare.
And finally the storme impetuous
Sunke up these riches, second unto none,
Within the gulfe of greedie *Nereus*.
I saw both ship and mariners each one,                        180
And all that treasure drowned in the maine:
But I the ship saw after raisd' againe.

### 14

Long having deeply gron'd these visions sad,
I saw a Citie like unto that same,
Which saw the messenger of tidings glad;                      185
But that on sand was built the goodly frame:
It seem'd her top the firmament did rayse,
And no lesse rich than faire, right worthie sure
(If ought here worthie) of immortall dayes,
Or if ought under heaven might firme endure.                  190
Much wondred I to see so faire a wall:

---

167. *ray*: stain.
S O N N E T 13:    169–70. The Florentine is Petrarch; cf. *VP* son. 2.
179. *Nereus*: classical god, immanent in, and synonymous with, the sea.
S O N N E T 14:    183–85. Cf. the Holy City, New Jerusalem, seen by St.
John, the "messenger" (Revelation 21).    186. Cf. Jesus's parable
(Matthew 7.26).    187. *rayse*: graze.

When from the Northerne coast a storme arose,
Which breathing furie from his inward gall
On all, which did against his course oppose,
    Into a clowde of dust sperst in the aire        195
    The weake foundations of this Citie faire.

### 15

    At length, even at the time, when *Morpheus*
Most trulie doth unto our eyes appeare,
Wearie to see the heavens still wavering thus,
I saw *Typhæus* sister comming neare;         200
    Whose head full bravely with a morion hidd,
Did seeme to match the Gods in Majestie.
She by a rivers bancke that swift downe slidd,
Over all the world did raise a Trophee hie;
    An hundred vanquisht Kings under her lay,    205
With armes bound at their backs in shamefull wize;
Whilst I thus mazed was with great affray,
I saw the heavens in warre against her rize:
    Then downe she stricken fell with clap of thonder,
    That with great noyse I wakte in sudden wonder.   210

FINIS.

SONNET 15:    197. *at the time*: morning dreams are said to be more reliable.    *Morpheus*: god of dreams and sleep.    200. *Typhæus sister*: "The description suggests Bellona, but the genealogy is difficult, even for a Renaissance poem. Du Bellay probably meant Rhea, daughter, as Typhaeus was son, of Earth, and one of the patron goddesses of Rome" (Renwick 1928:259).    201. *morion*: soldier's helmet.    210. The upset terminating a dream is a bad omen.

# The Visions of Petrarch

### ⚛️⚛️⚛️⚛️⚛️⚛️⚛️

The original for *The Visions of Petrarch*, and for so much of what is emblematic in several *Complaints* poems, is Petrarch's *Rime* 323 (Canzoniere 24), a celebration of Laura. His *Secretum*, an imaginary confession to St. Augustine, tells how his love of Laura transformed his affections to a loftier level where earthly cares are displaced by heavenly desire. The presence of this spiritualized theme in *Rime* 323 is the basis for Petrarch's appeal to van der Noot, Marot, Du Bellay, and Spenser. Jan van der Noot (in whose *Theatre for Worldlings* appear Spenser's earlier versions of these translations) says that the first three sonnets represent Laura as hind, as ship, and as song-bird, and that the latter three point the lesson that in an afflicted world man's only recourse is to turn "to Godwarde" (13r–14v).

Spenser's mode of conveying his meaning is essentially ironic. The perspective of the speaker of the first six sonnets is deliberately meant to strike the reader as inadequate: the limited perspective of this world prevails, and the Christian hope that the "hidden" meaning of the symbolism suggests is pointedly missing from that perspective. This effect is incremental: the first two sonnets do not make explicit the traditional association of the ship and the hind with the church; similarly with the hints of loss of tree of life and water of life in the next two; the fifth presents an obviously incomplete version of the myth of the phoenix and the resurrection it symbolizes for Christian believers; and the sixth omits the vital part of the allusion to the heel-stinging serpent that Calvin called the first promise of salvation (*Institutes* 2.10.20). Only in the seventh sonnet (Spenser's own invention) are the wailing and complaining and the pleas for pity replaced by a properly limited valuation of the things of this world and a looking beyond to "happie rest." (Seven, the number of divine rest, is appropriate here, looking back to the sevens which end *The Ruines of Time*, the first poem of the volume.)

These revised translations (like the earlier ones in *A Theatre for Worldlings*) have been seen to be based mainly on the French version of Clément Marot (The *Theatre* states that they were made "out of the Dutch," but some possible echoes of the Flemish and of the Italian originals can be attributed to indirect influences). *Rime* 323 consists of six twelve-line stanzas and a three-line envoy. Marot radically alters the rhyme scheme, as does Spenser once again, replacing the interlocking rhymes of Petrarch and Marot with sonnets of three quatrains, each with separate rhymes, and a couplet. Here Spenser also expands all seven stanzas into sonnets: in the *Theatre* versions only 1 and 3 were sonnets and the envoy was four lines long.

*Richard Schell*

# The Visions of Petrarch;
## formerly translated.

### 1

BEing one day at my window all alone,
So manie strange things happened me to see,
As much it grieveth me to thinke thereon.
At my right hand a Hynde appear'd to mee,
  So faire as mote the greatest God delite;                    5
Two eager dogs did her pursue in chace,
Of which the one was blacke, the other white:
With deadly force so in their cruell race
  They pincht the haunches of that gentle beast,
That at the last, and in short time I spide,                   10
Under a Rocke where she alas opprest,
Fell to the ground, and there untimely dide.
  Cruell death vanquishing so noble beautie,
  Oft makes me wayle so hard a destenie.

### 2

  After at sea a tall ship did appeare,                        15
Made all of Heben and white Yvorie,
The sailes of golde, of silke the tackle were,
Milde was the winde, calme seem'd the sea to bee,
  The skie eachwhere did show full bright and faire;

SONNET 1:   4. *Hynde*: Noot *TW* 13v says the hind is Petrarch's Laura.
The hind is also an image for the perfect lover in Proverbs 5.19, and
therefore symbolic of the church.   5. *delite*: biblical diction.   6. *Two
eager dogs*: Some medieval illustrations to Psalm 42 show a hart pursued by
black and white dogs (Davis 1973:32–33). Traditional connotations of night
and day, of the "cruell race" of time (as in Noot *TW* 13v), and also of fleshly
desires.   11. *Rocke*: overtones of Christ.
SONNET 2:   Cf. *FQ* I vi 1.   15–17. The ship is Laura, the heben
(ebony) her brows, yvorie (ivory) her face, the tackle her clothes and vesture
(Noot *TW* 13v).

With rich treasures this gay ship fraighted was:        20
But sudden storme did so turmoyle the aire,
And tumbled up the sea, that she (alas)
    Strake on a rock, that under water lay,
And perished past all recoverie.
O how great ruth and sorrowfull assay,                  25
Doth vex my spirite with perplexitie,
    Thus in a moment to see lost and drown'd,
    So great riches, as like cannot be found.

### 3

    Then heavenly branches did I see arise
Out of the fresh and lustie Lawrell tree,                30
Amidst the yong greene wood: of Paradise
Some noble plant I thought my selfe to see:
    Such store of birds therein yshrowded were,
Chaunting in shade their sundric melodie,
That with their sweetnes I was ravish't nere.            35
While on this Lawrell fixed was mine eie,
    The skie gan everie where to overcast,
And darkned was the welkin all about,
When sudden flash of heavens fire out brast,
And rent this royall tree quite by the roote,            40
    Which makes me much and ever to complaine:
    For no such shadow shalbe had againe.

### 4

    Within this wood, out of a rocke did rise
A spring of water, mildly rumbling downe,

26. *vex my spirite*: See Ecclesiastes 1.14, an allusion not in Petrarch or *TW*
Epigram 2. *perplexitie*: in biblical usage the word often implies inability to
comprehend what faith comprehends easily; cf. Luke 21.25.
S O N N E T 3:        34. *Chaunting . . . melodie*: Laura's talk (Noot *TW* 14r).
38. *welkin*: sky        39. *brast*: burst (Northern form).
S O N N E T 4–6:        Seen by Noot (*TW* 14r–14v) to point the general
lesson of its own opening pages: the transitoriness of all the comforts of this
world and, therefore, the advisability of turning "to Godwarde."
S O N N E T 4:        43–46. Overtones of biblical springs of living water.

Whereto approched not in anie wise                                        45
The homely shepheard, nor the ruder clowne;
  But manie Muses, and the Nymphes withall,
That sweetly in accord did tune their voyce
To the soft sounding of the waters fall,
That my glad hart thereat did much rejoyce.                               50
  But while herein I tooke my chiefe delight,
I saw (alas) the gaping earth devoure
The spring, the place, and all cleane out of sight.
Which yet aggreeves my hart even to this houre,
  And wounds my soule with rufull memorie,                               55
  To see such pleasures gon so suddenly.


                              5
    I saw a Phœnix in the wood alone,
With purple wings, and crest of golden hewe;
Strange bird he was, whereby I thought anone,
That of some heavenly wight I had the vewe;                               60
  Untill he came unto the broken tree,
And to the spring, that late devoured was.
What say I more? each thing at last we see
Doth passe away: the Phœnix there alas
  Spying the tree destroid, the water dride,                             65
Himselfe smote with his beake, as in disdaine,
And so foorthwith in great despight he dide:
That yet my heart burnes in exceeding paine,
  For ruth and pitie of so haples plight.
  O let mine eyes no more see such a sight.                              70


---

48–49. Cf. *SC* "April" 35–36; Hollander (1971) sees in this borrowing from
Marot the origins of the music of the Bower of Bliss (see *FQ* II xii 70).
55. Cf. the fall of man as a figurative wound.
SONNET 5:    The fuller form of the myth, which eludes this grief-
stricken lover, has a new phoenix arising from the ashes of the old,
traditionally symbolizing the resurrection of Christ and the triumph of life
over death.

6

At last so faire a Ladie did I spie,
That thinking yet on her I burne and quake;
On hearbs and flowres she walked pensively,
Milde, but yet love she proudly did forsake:
    White seem'd her robes, yet woven so they were,     75
As snow and golde together had been wrought.
Above the wast a darke clowde shrouded her,
A stinging Serpent by the heele her caught;
    Wherewith she languisht as the gathered floure,
And well assur'd she mounted up to joy.     80
Alas, on earth so nothing doth endure,
But bitter griefe and sorrowfull annoy:
    Which make this life wretched and miserable,
    Tossed with stormes of fortune variable.

7

When I beheld this tickle trustles state     85
Of vaine worlds glorie, flitting too and fro,
And mortall men tossed by troublous fate
In restles seas of wretchednes and woe,
    I wish I might this wearie life forgoe,
And shortly turne unto my happie rest,     90

S O N N E T 6:     71. *Ladie*: Laura; or the church?     76. *snow and golde*:
attributes of purity.     77. *darke clowde*: the plague that took Laura?
78. The reader is meant to be aware of the prophecy of hope that eludes the
speaker here: "I wil also put enimitie betwene thee and the woman, &
betwene thy sede & her sede. He shal breake thine head, & thou shalt bruise
his heele [Satan shal sting Christ & his members, but not overcome them]"
(Genesis 3.15 and Geneva Bible note). Calvin, *Institutes* 2.10.20, calls this
verse the Old Testament's first promise of salvation.     82. *annoy*:
discomfort, vexation.
S O N N E T 7:     The images of the sea and the storm can be followed into
Sp's later works. The sonnet follows the theme of Petrarch's three-line envoy
to his canzone. The distinctively Spenserian rhyme scheme also appears in
*VG* Dedication and *Amor*.     85. *tickle*: unreliable, insecure; cf. *SC* "July"
14.

Where my free spirite might not anie moe
Be vext with sights, that doo her peace molest.
    And ye faire Ladie, in whose bounteous brest
All heavenly grace and vertue shrined is,
When ye these rythmes doo read, and vew the rest,                95
Loath this base world, and thinke of heavens blis:
    And though ye be the fairest of Gods creatures,
    Yet thinke, that death shall spoyle your goodly
                                                features.

FINIS.

91. *moe*: more.      93–94. The compliment of seeing the beloved's breast as
a repository of Platonic ideas is a Renaissance commonplace; cf. Carew,
"Song: 'Aske me no more . . . . '"      93. *faire Ladie*: presumably Mary,
countess of Pembroke, to whom Sp dedicated the *Complaints*.

# A Theatre for Worldlings

# A THEATRE

wherein be repre-
sented as wel the miseries & ca-
lamities that follow the vo-
luptuous Worldlings,

*As also the greate ioyes and
plesures which the faith-
full do enioy.*

An Argument both profitable and
delectable, to all that sincerely
loue the word of God.

*Deuised by S. Iohn van-
der Noodt .*

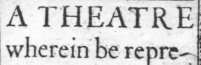 Seene and allowed according
to the order appointed.

¶ Imprinted at London by
Henry Bynneman.

Anno Domini. 1 5 6 9.

CVM PRIVILEGIO.

# A Theatre for Worldlings

᪥᪥᪥᪥᪥᪥᪥

S penser's first published work is a series of visionary emblematic translations in Jan van der Noot's *A Theatre wherein be represented as wel the miseries and calamities that follow the voluptuous Worldlings, As also the great joyes and plesures which the faithfull do enjoy.* The work had appeared in 1568 in Dutch and, weeks later, in French translation (both published in London by John Day); the English translation followed in 1569, the copper engravings replaced by woodcuts attributed variously to Marcus Gheeraerts or Lucas de Heere of Ghent (a shortened translation into German appeared in Cologne in 1572, reusing the woodcuts of the English version). Spenser at the time of the English version would have been seventeen, or nearly, and about to go up to Cambridge from the Merchant Taylors' School. His headmaster, Richard Mulcaster, who is known to have had connections with the Dutch community in London, may have nominated him for the task.

The English version of *A Theatre for Worldlings* consists of brief commendatory verses in Latin; a dedicatory epistle addressed to Queen Elizabeth; Spenser's translations as printed here, with woodcut emblems; and a long prose discourse by van der Noot. Spenser's contribution consists of "Epigrams," which translate Petrarch's *Rime* 323 (likely with reliance on Clément Marot's French rendering, *Des Visions de Pétrarque*), eleven "Sonets" translated from Du Bellay's *Songe*, and four "Sonets" of paraphrase from Revelation. Although these translations are anonymous, they can confidently be claimed for Spenser: the Epigrams, remade into full fourteen-line sonnets, reappear in his *Complaints* (1591) as *The Visions of Petrarch*, there noted as "previously translated"; the first eleven "Sonets" appear there also as *The Visions of Bellay*, the blank verse replaced by rhyme, and accompanied by the four sonnets not translated earlier for the *Theatre* from the fifteen of Du Bellay's *Songe*. The four Revelation paraphrases do not re-appear in *Complaints*, but convention (sometimes questioned: see Satterthwaite 1960:255–63) has attributed them to Spenser as well.

These four final "Sonets" are in the tradition of biblical epitome (brief summaries of biblical materials seen as essential to salvation), a genre of considerable extent in the sixteenth century. The apocalyptic beasts from Revelation, usually seen in Reformation England as coded allusions to the Roman church, are also seen by the *Theatre* as more generalized types of the sin and vice of worldlings, the totality of the fallen world being the body of Satan which receives a grievous wound through the agency of the Gospel. Borrowed largely from the biblical commentaries of two widely influential Protestant polemicists, John Bale and the Swiss Heinrich Bullinger, the main body of the *Theatre* is essentially an extended commentary on the chapters of Revelation epitomized. The voluptuous worldlings in many ways reflect the Roman church's hierarchy, whose inquisitorial activity in the Spanish Netherlands led to van der Noot's flight to London, where he rejoiced to find "the worde of God . . . purely preached" and proclaimed that "the kingdome of *Saturne*, and the Golden worlde is come againe, and the Virgin *Astrea* is desscended from heaven to builde hir a seate" (Noot *Theatre* Epistle A5v–6r). This early mythologizing eulogy of Elizabeth was to develop into a quintessential Spenserian commonplace.

The *Theatre's* searing anti-papal stance is perhaps not so unequivocally Calvinist as has been claimed; it may actually have had more to do with recovering for Christianity a spiritual basis that some thought would facilitate a broader consensus and even a reunion of the fragmented sects of the church (see Van Dorsten 1973:77–78). There may have been something of this kind of program in the peculiar Protestantism of Sir Philip Sidney and the earl of Leicester. Du Bellay had also been disgusted with the Roman church hierarchy while remaining faithfully Catholic, and van der Noot himself was soon to be reconverted to Catholicism.

The woodcuts of the English version are generally more striking than the copperplate engravings of the Dutch and French versions, their clear black lines mirroring the simplistic vision of the poems. The woodcuts reverse most of the copperplate images left-to-right (those for Epigram 6 and Sonnets 4, 5, and 7 excepted). The original English *Theatre* is an octavo with woodcuts on right-hand pages and accompanying poems on facing left-hand pages.

*Richard Schell*

# *Epigrams.*

## [1]

B Eing one day at my window all alone,
  So many strange things hapned me to see,
As much it grieveth me to thinke thereon.
At my right hande, a Hinde appearde to me,
So faire as mought the greatest God delite:          5
Two egre Dogs dyd hir pursue in chace,
Of whiche the one was black, the other white.
With deadly force so in their cruell race
They pinchte the haunches of this gentle beast,
That at the last, and in shorte time, I spied,       10
Under a rocke, where she (alas) opprest,
Fell to the grounde, and there untimely dide.
Cruell death vanquishing so noble beautie,
Oft makes me waile so harde a destinie.

E p i g r a m s  a n d  S o n n e t s:   1–11:   See the notes for the
corresponding sonnets in *VB* and *VP*. The dropping of Du Bellay's rhyme

[2]

A Fter at Sea a tall Ship dyd appere,
  Made all of Heben and white Ivorie,
The sailes of Golde, of Silke the tackle were:
Milde was the winde, calme seemed the sea to be:
The Skie eche where did shew full bright and faire.          5
With riche treasures this gay ship fraighted was.
But sodaine storme did so turmoyle the aire,
And tombled up the sea, that she, alas,
Strake on a rocke that under water lay.
O great misfortune, O great griefe, I say,          10
Thus in one moment to see lost and drownde
So great riches, as lyke can not be founde.

---

(Sonnets 1–11) may reflect a humanist value: rhyme is not found in classical
poetry. The fifteenth line added to Sonnet 8 gives the sequence of fifteen
sonnets a central line and calls numerological attention to fifteen, the number
of steps to the Temple, and hence a number of spiritual ascent. It is also the
sum of the Law and the Old Testament (seven) and the New Testament, the
Resurrection, and the New Law (eight); or of the numbers of the weekly
cycle of rotation (seven) and of the eternity in which the worldlings fail to
participate (eight); see Prescott (1978:47), following St. Augustine.

[3]

THen heavenly branches did I see arise,
  Out of a fresh and lusty Laurell tree
Amidde the yong grene wood. Of Paradise
Some noble plant I thought my selfe to see,
Suche store of birdes therein yshrouded were,                    5
Chaunting in shade their sundry melodie.
My sprites were ravisht with these pleasures there.
While on this Laurell fixed was mine eye,
The Skie gan every where to overcast,
And darkned was the welkin all aboute,                           10
When sodaine flash of heavens fire outbrast,
And rent this royall tree quite by the roote.
Which makes me much and ever to complaine,
For no such shadow shal be had againe.

[4]

Within this wood, out of the rocke did rise
 A Spring of water mildely romblyng downe,
Whereto approched not in any wise
The homely Shepherde, nor the ruder cloune,
But many Muses, and the Nymphes withall,     5
That sweetely in accorde did tune their voice
Unto the gentle sounding of the waters fall.
The sight wherof dyd make my heart rejoyce.
But while I toke herein my chiefe delight,
I sawe (alas) the gaping earth devoure     10
The Spring, the place, and all cleane out of sight.
Whiche yet agreves my heart even to this houre.

EPIGRAM 4:  6–7. John Hollander (1985) notes that this stray
alexandrine (here in an iambic pentameter context) becomes a kind of
signature trope for Sp (alexandrines close the *FQ* stanza) and his imitators.

[5]

I Saw a Phœnix in the wood alone,
With purple wings and crest of golden hew,
Straunge birde he was, wherby I thought anone,
That of some heavenly wight I had the vew:
Untill he came unto the broken tree          5
And to the spring that late devoured was.
What say I more? Eche thing at length we see
Doth passe away: the Phœnix there, alas,
Spying the tree destroyde, the water dride,
Himselfe smote with his beake, as in disdaine,          10
And so forthwith in great despite he dide.
For pitie and love my heart yet burnes in paine.

[6]

A T last so faire a Ladie did I spie,
That in thinking on hir I burne and quake,
On herbes and floures she walked pensively.
Milde, but yet love she proudely did forsake.
White seemed hir robes, yet woven so they were,          5
As snowe and golde together had bene wrought.
Above the waste a darke cloude shrouded hir,
A stinging Serpent by the heele hir caught,
Wherewith she languisht as the gathered floure:
And well assurde she mounted up to joy.          10
Alas in earth so nothing doth endure
But bitter griefe that dothe our hearts anoy.

M Y Song thus now in thy Conclusions,
Say boldly that these same six visions
Do yelde unto thy lorde a sweete request,
Ere it be long within the earth to rest.

## Sonets.

[1]

I T was the time when rest the gift of Gods
Sweetely sliding into the eyes of men,
Doth drowne in the forgetfulnesse of slepe,
The carefull travailes of the painefull day:
Then did a ghost appeare before mine eyes          5
On that great rivers banke that runnes by Rome,
And calling me then by my propre name,
He bade me upwarde unto heaven looke.
He cride to me, and loe (quod he) beholde,
What under this great Temple is containde,          10
Loe all is nought but flying vanitie.
So I knowing the worldes unstedfastnesse,
Sith onely God surmountes the force of tyme,
In God alone do stay my confidence.

[2]

ON hill, a frame an hundred cubites hie
I sawe, an hundred pillers eke about,
All of fine Diamant decking the front,
And fashiond were they all in Dorike wise.
Of bricke, ne yet of marble was the wall,                5
But shining Christall, which from top to base
Out of deepe vaute threw forth a thousand rayes
Upon an hundred steps of purest golde.
Golde was the parget: and the sielyng eke
Did shine all scaly with fine golden plates.            10
The floore was Jaspis, and of Emeraude.
O worldes vainenesse. A sodein earthquake loe,
Shaking the hill even from the bottome deepe,
Threwe downe this building to the lowest stone.

[3]

THen did appeare to me a sharped spire
Of diamant, ten feete eche way in square,
Justly proportionde up unto his height,
So hie as mought an Archer reache with sight.
Upon the top therof was set a pot                          5
Made of the mettall that we honour most.
And in this golden vessell couched were
The ashes of a mightie Emperour.
Upon foure corners of the base there lay
To beare the frame, foure great Lions of golde.            10
A worthie tombe for such a worthie corps.
Alas, nought in this worlde but griefe endures.
A sodaine tempest from the heaven, I saw,
With flushe stroke downe this noble monument.

### [4]

I Saw raisde up on pillers of Ivorie,
 Whereof the bases were of richest golde,
The chapters Alabaster, Christall frises,
The double front of a triumphall arke.
On eche side portraide was a victorie.                    5
With golden wings in habite of a Nymph.
And set on hie upon triumphing chaire,
The auncient glorie of the Romane lordes.
The worke did shewe it selfe not wrought by man,
But rather made by his owne skilfull hande            10
That forgeth thunder dartes for Jove his sire.
Let me no more see faire thing under heaven,
Sith I have seene so faire a thing as this,
With sodaine falling broken all to dust.

[5]

THen I behelde the faire Dodonian tree,
  Upon seven hilles throw forth his gladsome shade,
And Conquerers bedecked with his leaves
Along the bankes of the Italian streame.
There many auncient Trophees were erect,                    5
Many a spoile, and many goodly signes,
To shewe the greatnesse of the stately race,
That erst descended from the Trojan bloud.
Ravisht I was to see so rare a thing,
When barbarous villaines in disordred heape,                10
Outraged the honour of these noble bowes.
I hearde the tronke to grone under the wedge.
And since I saw the roote in hie disdaine
Sende forth againe a twinne of forked trees.

[6]

I Saw the birde that dares beholde the Sunne,
With feeble flight venture to mount to heaven,
By more and more she gan to trust hir wings,
Still folowing th'example of hir damme:
I saw hir rise, and with a larger flight          5
Surmount the toppes even of the hiest hilles,
And pierce the cloudes, and with hir wings to reache
The place where is the temple of the Gods,
There was she lost, and sodenly I saw
Where tombling through the aire in lompe of fire,    10
All flaming downe she fell upon the plaine.
I saw hir bodie turned all to dust,
And saw the foule that shunnes the cherefull light
Out of hir ashes as a worme arise.

[7]

THen all astonned with this nightly ghost,
I saw an hideous body big and strong,
Long was his beard, and side did hang his hair,
A grisly forehed and Saturnelike face.
Leaning against the belly of a pot                     5
He shed a water, whose outgushing streame
Ran flowing all along the creekie shoare
Where once the Troyan Duke with Turnus fought.
And at his feete a bitch Wolfe did give sucke
To two yong babes. In his right hand he bare          10
The tree of peace, in left the conquering Palme,
His head was garnisht with the Laurel bow.
Then sodenly the Palme and Olive fell,
And faire greene Laurel witherd up and dide.

[8]

HArd by a rivers side, a wailing Nimphe,
  Folding hir armes with thousand sighs to heaven
Did tune hir plaint to falling rivers sound,
Renting hir faire visage and golden haire,
Where is (quod she) this whilome honored face?          5
Where is thy glory and the auncient praise,
Where all worldes hap was reposed,
When erst of Gods and man I worshipt was?
Alas, suffisde it not that civile bate
Made me the spoile and bootie of the world,          10
But this new Hydra mete to be assailde
Even by an hundred such as Hercules,
With seven springing heds of monstrous crimes,
So many Neroes and Caligulaes
Must still bring forth to rule this croked shore.          15

[9]

UPon a hill I saw a kindled flame,
   Mounting like waves with triple point to heaven,
Which of incense of precious Ceder tree
With Balmelike odor did perfume the aire.
A bird all white, well fetherd on hir winges         5
Hereout did flie up to the throne of Gods,
And singing with most plesant melodie
She climbed up to heaven in the smoke.
Of this faire fire the faire dispersed rayes
Threw forth abrode a thousand shining leames,     10
When sodain dropping of a golden shoure
Gan quench the glystering flame. O grevous chaunge!
That which erstwhile so pleasaunt scent did yelde,
Of Sulphure now did breathe corrupted smel.

### [10]

I Saw a fresh spring rise out of a rocke,
Clere as Christall against the Sunny beames,
The bottome yellow like the shining land,
That golden Pactol drives upon the plaine.
It seemed that arte and nature strived to joyne                5
There in one place all pleasures of the eye.
There was to heare a noise alluring slepe
Of many accordes more swete than Mermaids song,
The seates and benches shone as Ivorie,
An hundred Nymphes sate side by side about,                   10
When from nie hilles a naked rout of Faunes
With hideous cry assembled on the place,
Which with their feete uncleane the water fouled,
Threw down the seats, and drove the Nimphs to flight.

[11]

AT length, even at the time when Morpheus
Most truely doth appeare unto our eyes,
Wearie to see th'inconstance of the heavens:
I saw the great Typhæus sister come,
Hir head full bravely with a morian armed,                    5
In majestie she seemde to matche the Gods.
And on the shore, harde by a violent streame,
She raisde a Trophee over all the worlde.
An hundred vanquisht kings gronde at hir feete,
Their armes in shamefull wise bounde at their backes.      10
While I was with so dreadfull sight afrayde,
I saw the heavens warre against hir tho,
And seing hir striken fall with clap of thunder,
With so great noyse I start in sodaine wonder.

[12]

I Saw an ugly beast come from the sea,
That seven heads, ten crounes, ten hornes did beare,
Having theron the vile blaspheming name.
The cruell Leopard she resembled much:
Feete of a beare, a Lions throte she had.                     5
The mightie Dragon gave to hir his power.
One of hir heads yet there I did espie,
Still freshly bleeding of a grievous wounde.
One cride aloude. What one is like (quod he)
This honoured Dragon, or may him withstande?          10
And then came from the sea a savage beast,
With Dragons speche, and shewde his force by fire,
With wondrous signes to make all wights adore
The beast, in setting of hir image up.

SONNET 12:     Summarizes Revelation 13; see Noot *TW* 20v–43v. The
woodcut shows a figure in papal tiara in the presence of the monster.
4–5. In Daniel 7 (see Noot *TW* 23v), the lion (Babylon), the bear
(the Medes), and the leopard (Persia) symbolize three consecutive demonic
tyrannies over Israel, to which the Greek and (in Revelation) the Roman were
to be a fourth and fifth.     8. The wound is the Gospel (Noot *TW* 26v).

[13]

I Saw a Woman sitting on a beast
Before mine eyes, of Orenge colour hew:
Horrour and dreadfull name of blasphemie
Filde hir with pride. And seven heads I saw,
Ten hornes also the stately beast did beare. 5
She seemde with glorie of the scarlet faire,
And with fine perle and golde puft up in heart.
The wine of hooredome in a cup she bare.
The name of Mysterie writ in hir face.
The bloud of Martyrs dere were hir delite. 10
Most fierce and fell this woman seemde to me.
An Angell then descending downe from Heaven,
With thondring voice cride out aloude, and sayd,
Now for a truth great Babylon is fallen.

SONNET 13:    See Revelation 17–18 and Noot *TW* 43v–63r. Babylon
is code for Rome (in Revelation) and the Roman church (in sixteenth-
century English Protestant polemic) and is the spiritual enslaver of the flesh
of worldlings (for van der Noot).    1. *Woman*: the Scarlet Whore of
Babylon, parody of the church as bride of Christ.    6. *seemde*: ironic.
8. See Jeremiah 51.7.    10. Eucharist parody.

[14]

THen might I see upon a white horse set
The faithfull man with flaming countenaunce,
His head did shine with crounes set therupon.
The worde of God made him a noble name.
His precious robe I saw embrued with bloud.                    5
Then saw I from the heaven on horses white,
A puissant armie come the selfe same way.
Then cried a shining Angell as me thought,
That birdes from aire descending downe on earth
Should warre upon the kings, and eate their flesh.            10
Then did I see the beast and Kings also
Joinyng their force to slea the faithfull man.
But this fierce hatefull beast and all hir traine,
Is pitilesse throwne downe in pit of fire.

SONNET 14:     See Revelation 19 and Noot *TW* 63v–77v.     10. *eate
their flesh*: The flesh of the chaos monsters (of whom tyrants are an
incarnation) will be eaten by the faithful at an apocalyptic marriage feast
(Revelation 19.17–18).

[15]

I Saw new Earth, new Heaven, sayde Saint John.
And loe, the sea (quod he) is now no more.
The holy Citie of the Lorde, from hye
Descendeth garnisht as a loved spouse.
A voice then sayde, beholde the bright abode          5
Of God and men. For he shall be their God,
And all their teares he shall wipe cleane away.
Hir brightnesse greater was than can be founde,
Square was this Citie, and twelve gates it had.
Eche gate was of an orient perfect pearle,            10
The houses golde, the pavement precious stone.
A lively streame, more cleere than Christall is,
Ranne through the mid, sprong from triumphant seat.
There growes lifes fruite unto the Churches good.

SONNET 15:       See Revelation 21–22 and Noot *TW* 77v–91r.
1–2. Re-emergence of original creation from the chaotic dragon-ridden
world of the sea which is no more.       3. *holy Citie*: prototype of which
Babylon is the now vanished parody, seemingly formidable, yet actually
transitory.       4. *spouse*: The church is the spiritual bride of Christ.
9–14. Recapitulates the imagery of the restored Temple (Ezekiel 47): from
beneath the seat of God's presence a stream flows forth turning desert into
fertile paradise.

# Daphnaïda

*Daphnaïda.*

# An Elegie vpon the

death of the noble and vertuous
Douglas Howard, *Daughter and*
heire of *Henry* Lord *Howard*, Vis-
count *Byndon*, *and wife of* Ar-
thure Gorges *Esquier.*

*Dedicated to the Right honorable the Lady*
*Helena,* Marquesse of *Northampton.*

*By* Ed. Sp.

At London
*Printed for* William Ponsonby, *dwelling in*
Paules Churchyard at the signe of the
Bishops head 1591.

# Daphnaïda

**❧❧❧❧❧❧❧**

On 13 August 1590 the nineteen-year-old Douglas Howard died, wife of Spenser's acquaintance Arthur Gorges and heir to a considerable fortune. Spenser responded with a poem dated from London the first of January, 1591. Critics have disagreed about the meaning of the date: by the old-style reckoning usual in Elizabethan England the new year begins on 25 March, and the date would thus refer to 1 January 1592. On balance, however, the evidence (including E. K.'s energetic championing of new-style dating in the Argument to *The Shepheardes Calender*) favors January, 1591, four and a half months after the death. Spenser seems not to have known Douglas Howard—in the dedication he speaks only of "the great good fame which I heard of her deceassed"—but he did know her husband Arthur Gorges, a gentleman-courtier somewhat younger than himself and a friend and kinsman of his patron Sir Walter Ralegh. He would refer to him again in *Colin Clouts Come Home Againe* as a poet overcome with grief.

The elegy Spenser wrote is one of his most experimental and least-loved works. It is unrelievedly gloomy, and despite passages of considerable beauty it often seems heavy-handed and shrill, especially the long monologue which makes up more than half the poem. The speaker of that monologue, the grieving shepherd Alcyon, is too self-involved and self-pitying to evoke much sympathy, and the poem seems in many ways a pastoral elegy manqué. The climactic vision of the dead shepherd in heaven is absent, as is the characteristic emphasis on man and nature united in a community of mourning. Alcyon seeks "alone to weepe, and dye alone" (77).

The unvaried grimness of the poem is the more surprising because it imitates, sometimes closely, Chaucer's *The Book of the*

*Duchess*, a work almost programmatically varied in its tone. Unlike *Daphnaida* Chaucer's elegy, which praises Blanche, the dead wife of John of Gaunt, suggests some consolation for the bereaved husband by setting the reality of past joy against present grief, just as it places Gaunt's surrogate, a black-clad mourner, in a radiant spring setting. Without discounting grief, *The Book of the Dutchess* makes it part of a larger whole.

In imitating Chaucer Spenser took several narrative moments from the earlier poem and reshaped them to radically different effect. In each poem the melancholy narrator meets a grieving Man in Black and asks him why he sorrows; after initially evading the narrator's questions the mourner describes his lady and admits that he grieves for her death. But Spenser avoids the movement from grief to remembered joy that characterizes Chaucer's poem, just as he avoids the careful balance of its dream-vision structure. Instead he emphasizes the one-sidedness of his own elegy in an opening which banishes the harmonious Muses and invokes the Furies in their place. Unlike the flourishing spring flowers of *The Book of the Duchess*, the flowers of *Daphnaida*, tacit emblems of Douglas Howard, have been killed by an early frost.

Spenser alters the genre of Chaucer's poem as well, recasting his work as a pastoral eclogue, and the change sets Alcyon in the context of other grieving shepherds in a tradition going back to Virgil and Theocritus. The sad shepherd is a standard pastoral type, but his characterization changes according to the nature of his sorrow. Shepherds grieving for death are the speakers of pastoral elegy: as simplified and representative beings they voice the suffering attendant on human mortality, and they are treated seriously. In Christian pastoral elegy they are often granted a consoling vision of the dead shepherd or shepherdess in heavenly bliss. Colin reaches such a vision in "November" as the speaker of *Lycidas* was later to do. Shepherds complaining for love, on the other hand, are usually presented with comic detachment: they tend to be obsessive, self-absorbed, and at times boorish. Spenser's "Shepheard boy" Colin as he usually appears

in the *Calender* is such a figure and his self-dramatizing, unre-
solved sestina in "August" epitomizes this mood. In *Daphnaida*
Spenser conflates the traditions. While Alcyon grieves for a de-
ath, he does so with the obsessive self-concern of an eclogue
lover.

Alcyon's extremity is heralded in his name, a masculine ver-
sion of Alcyone, the devoted queen who (in the version of the
story Chaucer includes in *The Book of the Duchess*) learns that her
husband has drowned and dies of grief. In Chaucer's poem such
extremity is banished to an inset tale; in Spenser's it is central
and Spenser's Alcyon revels in it. While Alcyon has just cause for
grief (the narrator of the poem feels an immediate sympathy for
his sorrow), his response is self-centered and inadequate. Angry
and rude in manner, he believes that his own anguish is unique,
and he scornfully rejects the narrator's attempts at help. The
narrator's evaluation of this behavior is quietly but recognizably
critical. He comments that his own attempts at "milde coun-
saile" are useless because Alcyon simply becomes "more empas-
sionate:/ As stubborne steed, that is with curb restrained,/ Be-
comes more fierce and fervent in his gate" (191–95). Alcyon
refuses to acknowledge the world as a mixture of bliss and woe:
for him it must be entirely perfect or entirely corrupt. His initial
picture of his love as a white lion conjures up the former, an
image of paradisal innocence in which the lion lies down with
the lamb; his extended lament (197–539) describes the latter
(Harris and Steffen 1978).

The narrator characterizes this lament as the "breaking
foorth" of Alcyon's intense grief (191–96). It is itself a recog-
nizable *complaint*, one of Spenser's last and most elaborate ex-
periments in the genre of the collection published the same year.
Here, however, the typical combination of satire and lament is
ironically undercut. While Alcyon's lament touches on the tradi-
tional subjects of the form, its dramatic context suggests that it is
the product of a fundamental impatience, an unwillingness to
submit oneself to God's will.

The most complexly ironic moment of the complaint is Alcyon's memory of Daphne's dying words. For Daphne interprets her death in accord with Christian belief: she looks with joy toward her heavenly destiny and offers Alcyon the kind of divine consolation, transcending mere pastoral comfort, with which Christian pastoral elegy frequently ends (DeNeef 1982). She further commends their child to him, counselling him to preserve her love on earth in the one way possible to mortals— through her image in her offspring. In all this she displays an exemplary Christian patience—a willingness to trust in God's will and suffer His decrees. Alcyon, significantly, chooses not to attend to her words, preferring to remember her physical pallor and weakness. The rest of his lamentation continues to curse the world for not conforming to his exalted standards.

Such a treatment of pastoral elegy makes it into the exploration of an obsessive sensibility, and it raises poetic and social problems. What is the function of such a poem? And how can one imagine Spenser's presenting Gorges with such a self-portrait? The work may in fact be didactic: as a somewhat older man who may by this time have lost his own first wife, the poet could be quietly suggesting to Gorges that grief can be carried too far (Oram 1981). Such a suggestion appears in the contrast between the narrator of the elegy and Alcyon. Although the narrator is grieving when he meets the mourner, he puts aside his own sorrow in an attempt to help his friend where Alcyon seems incapable of such self-forgetfulness.

In its combination of complaint and pastoral *Daphnaida* looks at once toward the *Complaints*-volume also published in 1591 as a summation of past work and toward his renewed experimentation with the pastoral form in the early 1590s in *Colin Clouts Come Home Againe, Astrophel*, and the sixth Book of *The Faerie Queene*. It further shares with those later works an attention to the figure of the poet. Donald Cheney (1983) has commented that the Sidney of *Astrophel*, the Ralegh of *Colin Clouts Come Home Againe*, and the Gorges of *Daphnaida* are all poets, "refractions" of Colin and ultimately of Spenser; their presence raises in different ways the problem of the poet's relation to society. In Gorges's case the man needs to master his grief if the poet is to assume his proper place and function.

The stanza of *Daphnaida* is based on the seven-line stanza of Chaucerian rhyme-royal (*ababbcc*), a stanza associated with high and formal occasion. Spenser's variation (*ababcbc*) typically avoids the neat chime of a final couplet, and integrates the last rhyme more fully into the structure of the whole. These seven-line stanzas are the basic unit of *Daphnaida's* elaborate numerology. Alcyon's lament consists of seven sections of seven stanzas—forty-nine stanzas or 443 lines. There are twenty-eight stanzas preceding the lament (4 x 7 stanzas), and four stanzas after it (4 x 7 lines). Seven has many associations in Renaissance numerology: Maren-Sofie Røstvig (1963) has stressed its connection with the ideas of justice and judgment, and the number was also associated (through the story of creation in *Genesis*) with divine rest. It seems likely that, as often happens in Renaissance texts with a numerological dimension, the perfection of the numerical scheme contrasts with the uncertain and partial grasp of truth available to the characters. The ideal form recalls that divine reality which the characters themselves cannot see.

*William Oram*

# To the right Hono-
rable and vertuous Lady *Helena*
*Marquesse of* North-hampton.

I *Have the rather presumed humbly to offer unto your Honor the dedication of this little Poëme, for that the noble and vertuous Gentlewoman of whom it is written, was by match neere alied, and in affection greatly devoted unto your Ladiship. The occasion why I wrote the same, was aswell the great good fame which I heard of her deceassed, as the particular goodwill which I beare unto her husband Master* Arthure Gorges, *a lover of learning and vertue, whose house as your Ladiship by mariage hath honoured, so doo I finde the name of them by many notable records, to be of great antiquitie in this Realm; and such as have ever borne themselves with honorable reputation to the world, and unspotted loyaltie to their Prince and Countrey: besides so linially are they descended from the* Howards, *as that the Lady* Anne Howard, *eldest daughter to* John *Duke of* Norfolke, *was wife to Sir* Edmund, *mother to Sir* Edward, *and grandmother to Sir* William *and Sir* Thomas Gorges *Knights. And therefore I doo assure my selfe that no due honour done to the white Lyon, but will be most gratefull to your Ladiship, whose husband and children*

D E D I C A T I O N:   The daughter of a Swedish knight, Helena Snackenborg came to England with Princess Cecilia of Sweden in the fall of 1565, remaining when Cecilia left the following May. Elizabeth interested herself in Helena and appointed her a maid of honor and lady of the bedchamber; in 1571, six months before his death, she was married to William Parr, marquis of Northampton. As marchioness of Northampton, she continued to hold an important position at court for the rest of Elizabeth's life: in *CCCHA*, she appears as Mansilia "best knowne by bearing up great *Cynthiaes* traine" (509). In 1591 she married Sir Thomas Gorges, the uncle of Arthur Gorges (see Sjogren 1978:597–604). Sp praises her highly in *CCCHA*, and she and her husband were on good terms with Arthur Gorges: her family position and her importance at court made her a fitting audience for the poem. The lineage Sp gives in the Dedication details the connection of the Gorges family with the Howard line through Arthur Gorges' great grandmother, the Lady Anne Howard, daughter to Sir John Howard, first duke of Norfolk (1430–1485).

*doo so neerely participate with the bloud of that noble familie. So in all duetie I recommend this Pamphlet, and the good acceptance thereof, to your honorable favour and protection.* London *this first of January.* 1591.

Your Honours humbly ever.

E. Sp.

# *Daphnaïda.*

WHat ever man he be, whose heavie minde
    With griefe of mournefull great mishap opprest,
Fit matter for his cares increase would finde:
Let reade the rufull plaint herein exprest
Of one (I weene) the wofulst man alive;             5
Even sad *Alcyon*, whose empierced brest
Sharpe sorrowe did in thousand peeces rive.

But who so else in pleasure findeth sense,
Or in this wretched life dooth take delight,
Let him be banisht farre away from hence:         10
Ne let the sacred Sisters here be hight,
Though they of sorrowe heavilie can sing;
For even their heavie song would breede delight:
But here no tunes, save sobs and grones shall ring.

In stead of them, and their sweete harmonie,     15
Let those three fatall Sisters, whose sad hands
Doo weave the direfull threds of destinie,
And in their wrath breake off the vitall bands,

---

TITLE:    Daphne + -aida. Several of Arthur Gorges's poems are written to
"Daphne," which Sp takes over as a fittingly pastoral name for Alcyon's beloved.
He adds -aida on the model of the *Aeneid* the *Franciade*, etc., keeping the Greek
accusative form, perhaps because of the "feminine" -a of the ending.

1. *heavie*: sorrowful.    2. *mishap*: misfortune.    4. *plaint*: complaint,
lament (cf. 198–539).    6. *Alcyon*: a masculine version of Alcyone, the
grieving heroine of the Ovidian and Chaucerian story of a queen whose
husband, King Ceyx, is drowned. In Ovid's version (*Met* 9.410–748) she
attempts to leap into the sea but is transformed into a Halcyon; in Chaucer's
version (*Book of the Duchess* 62–214) she dies of grief.    8. *in . . . sense*: i.e.
capable of feeling pleasure.    11. *the sacred Sisters*: the nine Muses. *hight*:
summoned.    12. *heavilie*: woefully.    16. *three fatall Sisters*: the three
Fates who spin, measure, and cut the yarn determining the length of human
lives, the "threds of destinie".    18. *bands*: i.e. the threads.

Approach hereto: and let the dreadfull Queene
Of darkenes deepe come from the Stygian strands,                    20
And grisly Ghosts to heare this dolefull teene.

In gloomie evening, when the wearie Sun
After his dayes long labour drew to rest,
And sweatie steeds now having over run
The compast skie, gan water in the west,                          25
I walkt abroade to breath the freshing ayre
In open fields, whose flowring pride opprest
With early frosts, had lost their beautie faire.

There came unto my minde a troublous thought,
Which dayly dooth my weaker wit possesse,                         30
Ne lets it rest, untill it forth have brought
Her long borne Infant, fruit of heavinesse,
Which she conceived hath through meditation
Of this worlds vainnesse and lifes wretchednesse,
That yet my soule it deepely doth empassion.                     35

So as I muzed on the miserie,
In which men live, and I of many most,
Most miserable man; I did espie
Where towards me a sory wight did cost,
Clad all in black, that mourning did bewray:                     40
And *Jaakob* staffe in hand devoutlie crost,
Like to some Pilgrim come from farre away.

19. *dreadfull Queene*: Hecate or perhaps Persephone, wife of Pluto, god of
the underworld.     20. *Stygian strands*: land of the dead, on the other side
of the river Styx.     21. *grisly*: horrible. *teene*: grief.     27. *opprest*:
crushed.     29. *troublous thought*: Oram (1981) p.158 suggests that this
thought is the memory of Sp's first wife, who may recently have died. Cf.
Wepley (1932:182–83) who argues that the narrator refers to his wife's
death when he tells Alcyon that "like wofulnesse" has given "like cause . . . to
waile and weep" (64–66). But the stanza, like Sp's first marriage, remains
obscure.     35. *yet*: still.     38–40. Cf. *The Book of the Duchess* 444–45,
457.     39. *cost*: approach.     40. *bewray*: show forth, expose.
41. *Jaakob staffe*: "The 'Jaakob-staffe' was a navigating instrument, but
Spenser here means simply a pilgrim-staff" (Renwick 1929:176).

His carelesse locks, uncombed and unshorne
Hong long adowne, and beard all over growne,
That well he seemd to be sum wight forlorne;                    45
Downe to the earth his heavie eyes were throwne
As loathing light: and ever as he went,
He sighed soft, and inly deepe did grone,
As if his heart in peeces would have rent.

Approaching nigh, his face I vewed nere,                       50
And by the semblant of his countenance,
Me seemd I had his person seene elsewhere,
Most like *Alcyon* seeming at a glaunce;
*Alcyon* he, the jollie Shepheard swaine,
That wont full merrilie to pipe and daunce,                    55
And fill with pleasance every wood and plaine.

Yet halfe in doubt because of his disguize,
I softlie sayd *Alcyon?* There with all
He lookt a side as in disdainefull wise,
Yet stayed not: till I againe did call.                        60
Then turning back he saide with hollow sound,
Who is it, that dooth name me, wofull thrall,
The wretchedst man that treades this day on ground?

One, whome like wofulnesse impressed deepe
Hath made fit mate thy wretched case to heare,                 65
And given like cause with thee to waile and weepe:
Griefe findes some ease by him that like does beare,
Then stay *Alcyon*, gentle shepheard stay,
(Quoth I) till thou have to my trustie eare
Committed, what thee dooth so ill apay.                        70

---

49. *rent*: burst.    51. *semblant*: appearance.    57–60. Recalls *The Book of
the Duchess* (502–16) only to differ. Chaucer's black knight is too sunk in
grief to hear and later apologizes courteously for his inattentiveness.
57. *disguize*: strange costume.    59. *wise*: manner.    60. *stayed*: stopped.
62. *thrall*: slave.    67. A translation of a common Latin tag, *solamen miseris
socios habuisse dolores*.    70. *apay*: please, content.

Cease foolish man (saide he halfe wrothfully)
To seeke to heare that which cannot be tolde.
For the huge anguish, which dooth multiplie
My dying paines, no tongue can well unfold:
Ne doo I care, that any should bemone               75
My hard mishap, or any weepe that would,
But seeke alone to weepe, and dye alone.

Then be it so (quoth I) that thou art bent
To die alone, unpitied, unplained,
Yet ere thou die, it were convenient               80
To tell the cause, which thee theretoo constrained:
Least that the world thee dead accuse of guilt,
And say, when thou of none shalt be maintained,
That thou for secret crime thy blood hast spilt.

Who life dooes loath, and longs to bee unbound     85
From the strong shackles of fraile flesh (quoth he)
Nought cares at all, what they that live on ground
Deeme the occasion of his death to bee:
Rather desires to be forgotten quight,
Than question made of his calamitie,               90
For harts deep sorrow hates both life and light.

Yet since so much thou seemst to rue my griefe,
And carest for one that for himselfe cares nought,
(Signe of thy love, though nought for my reliefe:
For my reliefe exceedeth living thought)           95
I will to thee this heavie case relate,
Then harken well till it to ende bee brought,
For never didst thou heare more haplesse fate.

---

77. Cf. *The Book of the Duchess* 690.     80. *convenient*: fitting, appropriate.
88. *occasion*: cause.     90. *made*: raised.     92. *rue*: pity.

Whilome I usde (as thou right well doest know)
My little flocke on westerne downes to keepe,               100
Not far from whence *Sabrinaes* streame doth flow,
And flowrie bancks with silver liquor steepe:
Nought carde I then for worldly change or chaunce,
For all my joy was on my gentle sheepe,
And to my pype to caroll and to daunce.                     105

It there befell as I the fields did range
Fearelesse and free, a faire young Lionesse,
White as the native Rose before the chaunge,
Which *Venus* blood did in her leaves impresse,
I spied playing on the grassie playne                       110
Her youthfull sports and kindlie wantonnesse,
That did all other Beasts in beawtie staine.

Much was I moved at so goodly sight;
Whose like before mine eye had seldome seene,
And gan to cast, how I her compasse might,                  115
And bring to hand, that yet had never beene:
So well I wrought with mildnes and with paine,
That I her caught disporting on the grene,
And brought away fast bound with silver chaine.

And afterwards I handled her so fayre,                      120
That though by kind shee stout and salvage were,

99–168. This passage is modeled on the Man in Black's evasion of the
narrator's questions in *The Book of the Duchess* 617–86. See Harris and Steffen
(1978) p.30.        99. *usde*: was accustomed to.        101. *Sabrinaes streame*:
the Severn river. The function of this reference is not clear. It may have a
particular, biographical significance, or may simply, as Renwick (1929)
p.177 suggests, be "an indication, discreetly vague, of the West of England.
The Gorges family was seated in Somerset and held lands in Dorset."
103–05. Cf. *The Book of the Duchess* 797–802.        103. *chaunce*: misfortune.
107. *a . . . Lionesse*: The white lion figured in the Howard coat-of-arms, and
so would be associated with Douglas Howard.        111. *kindlie wantonnesse*:
natural playfulness.        112. *staine*: excel.        115. *cast*: consider. *compasse*:
catch.        116. *bring to hand*: tame.        120. *handled*: treated.        121. *kind*:
nature. *stout*: fierce, proud.

For being borne an auncient Lions haire,
And of the race, that all wild beastes do feare;
Yet I her fram'd and wan so to my bent,
That shee became so meeke and milde of cheare,          125
As the least lamb in all my flock that went.

For she in field, where ever I did wend,
Would wend with me, and waite by me all day:
And all the night that I in watch did spend,
If cause requir'd, or els in sleepe, if nay,          130
Shee would all night by mee or watch, or sleepe;
And evermore when I did sleepe or play,
She of my flock would take full warie keepe.

Safe then and safest were my sillie sheepe,
Ne fear'd the Wolfe, ne fear'd the wildest beast:          135
All were I drown'd in carelesse quiet deepe:
My lovelie Lionesse without beheast
So carefull was for them and for my good,
That when I waked, neither most nor least
I found miscaried or in plaine or wood.          140

Oft did the Shepeheards, which my hap did heare,
And oft their lasses which my luck envide,
Daylie resort to me from farre and neare,
To see my Lyonesse, whose praises wide
Were spred abroad; and when her worthinesse          145
Much greater than the rude report they tri'de,
They her did praise, and my good fortune blesse.

---

122. *For . . . haire*: Douglas Howard was the sole heir of her father, Henry
Howard, viscount Byndon, and hence a very wealthy match for Gorges. See
Sandison (1928) pp.646–50.          124. *fram'd*: trained, influenced.
127. *wend*: go.          129. *in watch*: waking.          130. *if nay*: i.e. if there was no
reason to remain awake.          133. *warie*: careful.          134. *sillie*:
innocent.          137. *beheast*: command.          138. *good*: property, but also "my
well-being."          141. *hap*: fortune.          146. *rude*: imperfect, rough. *tri'de*:
proved, ascertained.          147. *blesse*: speak well of.

Long thus I joyed in my happinesse,
And well did hope my joy would have no end:
But oh fond man, that in worlds ficklenesse          150
Reposedst hope, or weenedst her thy frend,
That glories most in mortall miseries,
And daylie doth her changefull counsels bend:
To make new matter fit for Tragedies.

For whilest I was thus without dread or dout,          155
A cruell *Satyre* with his murdrous dart,
Greedie of mischiefe ranging all about,
Gave her the fatall wound of deadlie smart:
And reft fro me my sweete companion,
And reft fro me my love, my life, my hart,          160
My Lyonesse (ah woe is mee) is gon.

Out of the world thus was she reft awaie,
Out of the world, unworthie such a spoyle;
And borne to heaven, for heaven a fitter pray:
Much fitter than the Lyon, which with toyle          165
*Alcides* slew, and fixt in firmament;
Her now I seek throughout this earthlie soyle,
And seeking misse, and missing doe lament.

Therewith he gan afresh to waile and weepe,
That I for pittie of his heavie plight,          170
Could not abstaine mine eyes with teares to steepe:
But when I saw the anguish of his spright
Some deale alaid, I him bespake againe.
Certes *Alcyon*, painfull is thy plight,
That it in me breeds almost equall paine.          175

151–52. *her . . . That*: i.e. Fortune.    153. *counsels*: plans.    155. *dout*:
suspicion.    158. *smart*: pain.    163. *unworthie . . . spoyle*: i.e. the world
is unworthy of so valuable a creature as Daphne.    165–66. In *FQ* VII vii
36, Sp again associates the Nemean Lion which Hercules slew with the
constellation of Leo. Lotspeich (1942) p.118 cites the association in
Hygenus, *Astronomia* 2.24.    171. *abstaine*: keep from.    174. *Certes*:
certainly.

Yet doth not my dull wit well understand
The riddle of thy loved Lionesse;
For rare it seemes in reason to be skand
That man, who doth the whole worlds rule possesse
Should to a beast his noble hart embase,                    180
And be the vassall of his vassalesse:
Therefore more plaine aread this doubtfull case.

Then sighing sore, *Daphne* thou knewest (quoth he)
She now is dead; ne more endured to say:
But fell to ground for great extreamitie,                    185
That I beholding it, with deepe dismay
Was much appald, and lightly him uprearing,
Revoked life that would have fled away,
All were my self though griefe in deadly drearing.

Then gan I him to comfort all my best,                    190
And with milde counsaile strove to mitigate
The stormie passion of his troubled brest,
But he thereby was more empassionate:
As stubborne steed, that is with curb restrained,
Becomes more fierce and fervent in his gate;                    195
And breaking foorth at last, thus dearnely plained.

1 What man henceforth, that breatheth vitall ayre,
Will honour heaven, or heavenlie powers adore?
Which so unjustlie doe their judgments share;
Mongst earthlie wightes, as to afflict so sore                    200
The innocent, as those which do transgresse,

---

176–82. Cf. *The Book of the Duchess* 721–48.        177. *riddle*: obscure
saying.        178. *in . . . skand*: judging by rational standards.        180. *embase*:
"humble," with the implication of "make his heart base" by worshiping a
beast.        182. *aread*: declare.        183–84. Cf. *The Book of the Duchess* 1300–
1301, 1309.        185. *extreamitie*: violent suffering.        187. *appald*:
dismayed.        188. *Revoked*: revived, called back.        189. *drearing*: grief (a
Spenserian coinage).        193. *empassionate*: impassioned.        196. *dearnely
plained*: lamented dismally. The verb "plained" suggests the genre of the
following *complaint*.        199. *share*: apportion.        200. *so sore*: as sorely.

And doe not spare the best or fayrest more,
Than worst or fowlest, but doe both oppresse.

If this be right, why did they then create
The world so fayre, sith fairenesse is neglected?                205
Or whie be they themselves immaculate,
If purest things be not by them respected?
She faire, shee pure, most faire, most pure shee was,
Yet was by them as thing impure rejected:
Yet shee in purenesse, heaven it selfe did pas.                  210

In purenesse and in all celestiall grace,
That men admire in goodlie womankinde,
She did excell and seem'd of Angels race
Living on earth like Angell new divinde,
Adorn'd with wisedome and with chastitie:                       215
And all the dowries of a noble mind,
Which did her beautie much more beautifie.

No age hath bred (since faire *Ætræa* left
The sinfull world) more vertue in a wight,
And when she parted hence, with her she reft                    220
Great hope; and robd her race of bountie quight:
Well may the shepheard lasses now lament,
For dubble losse by her hath on them light;
To loose both her and bounties ornament.

Ne let *Elisa* royall Shepheardesse                             225
The praises of my parted love envy,
For she hath praises in all plenteousnesse

---

203. *oppresse*: crush, burden.    208–12. Cf. *The Book of the Duchess* 484–
86.    214. *divinde*: made divine.    218–19. *(since . . . world)*: With the
coming of the Iron Age, Astrea, goddess of justice, leaves the earth. In
Christian terms her retreat is thus easily associated with the fall. See Ovid,
*Met* 1.150–51, *MHT* 1–4 and *FQ* V i 5–11.    220. *reft*: took.
225. *Elisa*: Elizabeth I.

Powr'd upon her like showers of *Castaly*
By her own Shepheard, *Colin* her owne Shepherd,
That her with heavenly hymnes doth deifie,                    230
Of rustick muse full hardly to be betterd.

She is the Rose, the glorie of the day,
And mine the Primrose in the lowly shade,
Mine, ah not mine; amisse I mine did say:
Not mine but his, which mine awhile her made:                235
Mine to be his, with him to live for ay:
O that so faire a flower so soone should fade,
And through untimely tempest fall away.

She fell away in her first ages spring,
Whil'st yet her leafe was greene, and fresh her rinde,       240
And whil'st her braunch faire blossomes foorth did
                                                    bring,
She fell away against all course of kinde:
For age to dye is right, but youth is wrong;
She fel away like fruit blowne downe with winde:
Weepe Shepheard weepe to make my undersong.                  245

2. What hart so stony hard, but that would weepe,
And poure foorth fountaines of incessant teares?
What *Timon*, but would let compassion creepe
Into his breast, and pierce his frosen eares?
In stead of teares, whose brackish bitter well              250

228. *Castaly*: the Castalian spring on Mt. Parnassus, sacred to Apollo and the
Muses. Its waters are here and elsewhere associated with poetry. See *TM*
272–73.    227–30. Colin, in this case, is clearly a figure for Sp. There is
an aspect of self-advertisement here, but the reference also distinguishes
Alcyon, who is crippled by private grief, from a public poet like Colin who
celebrates the queen. In *CCCHA* Colin will encourage Alcyon to return to
the writing of his "sweet Eglantine of Meriflure" (line 389).    240. *rinde*:
bark and, by extension, "body." Cf. "this corporal rinde" in Milton's *Comus*
663.    248. *Timon*: the Athenian, famous for his misanthropy, pictured in
Plutarch's *Life of Alcibiades* and Lucian's dialogue *Timon the Misanthrope*.

I wasted have, my heart blood dropping weares,
To thinke to ground how that faire blossome fell.

Yet fell she not, as one enforst to dye,
Ne dyde with dread and grudging discontent,
But as one toyld with travaile downe doth lye, 255
So lay she downe, as if to sleepe she went,
And closde her eyes with carelesse quietnesse;
The whiles soft death away her spirit hent,
And soule assoyld from sinfull fleshlinesse.

Yet ere that life her lodging did forsake, 260
She all resolv'd and ready to remove,
Calling to me (ay me) this wise bespake;
*Alcyon*, ah my first and latest love,
Ah why does my *Alcyon* weepe and mourne,
And grieve my ghost, that ill mote him behove, 265
As if to me had chanst some evill tourne?

I, since the messenger is come for mee,
That summons soules unto the bridale feast
Of his great Lord, must needes depart from thee,
And straight obay his soveraine beheast: 270
Why should *Alcyon* then so sore lament,
That I from miserie shall be releast,
And freed from wretched long imprisonment?

Our daies are full of dolor and disease,
Our life afflicted with incessant paine, 275
That nought on earth may lessen or appease.
Why then should I desire here to remaine?
Or why should he that loves me, sorie bee
For my deliverance, or at all complaine
My good to heare, and toward joyes to see? 280

I goe, and long desired have to goe,
I goe with gladnesse to my wished rest,

259. *assoyld*: released.　265. *ghost*: spirit.　280. *toward*: future.

Whereas no worlds sad care, nor wasting woe
May come their happie quiet to molest,
But Saints and Angels in celestiall thrones                    285
Eternally him praise, that hath them blest,
There shall I be amongst those blessed ones.

Yet ere I goe, a pledge I leave with thee
Of the late love, the which betwixt us past,
My yong *Ambrosia*, in lieu of mee                             290
Love her: so shall our love for ever last.
Thus deare adieu, whom I expect ere long:
So having said, away she softly past:
Weep Shepheard weep, to make mine undersong.

3 So oft as I record those piercing words,                     295
Which yet are deepe engraven in my brest,
And those last deadly accents, which like swords
Did wound my heart and rend my bleeding chest,
With those sweet sugred speeches doo compare,
The which my soule first conquerd and possest,                 300
The first beginners of my endles care;

And when those pallid cheekes and ashy hew,
In which sad death his pourtraicture had writ,
And when those hollow eyes and deadly view,
On which the clowde of ghastly night did sit,                  305
I match with that sweet smile and chearfull brow,
Which all the world subdued unto it;
How happie was I then, and wretched now?

How happie was I, when I saw her leade
The Shepheards daughters dauncing in a rownd?                  310

290. *Ambrosia*: the actual name of Douglas Howard's daughter. Ambrosia
was the food of the gods and, according to some sources, would give
immortality. The poem's concern for the kind of immortality possible in this
world—succession through one's offspring—gives the name an additional
resonance.       294. *undersong*: accompaniment, but the line itself is an
undersong in the Spenserian sense of a refrain (see *SC* "August" 128, *Proth*
110).       309–15. Cf. *The Book of the Duchess* 848–53, 860–65.

How trimly would she trace and softly tread
The tender grasse with rosie garland crownd?
And when she list advance her heavenly voyce,
Both Nimphs and Muses nigh she made astownd,
And flocks and shepheards caused to rejoyce.      315

But now ye Shepheard lasses, who shall lead
Your wandring troupes, or sing your virelayes?
Or who shall dight your bowres, sith she is dead
That was the Lady of your holy dayes?
Let now your blisse be turned into bale,      320
And into plaints convert your joyous playes,
And with the same fill every hill and dale.

Let Bagpipe never more be heard to shrill,
That may allure the senses to delight;
Ne ever Shepheard sound his Oaten quill      325
Unto the many, that provoke them might
To idle pleasance: but let ghastlinesse
And drery horror dim the chearfull light,
To make the image of true heavinesse.

Let birds be silent on the naked spray,      330
And shady woods resound with dreadfull yells:
Let streaming floods their hastie courses stay,
And parching drougth drie up the christall wells;
Let th'earth be barren and bring foorth no flowres,
And th'ayre be fild with noyse of dolefull knells,      335
And wandring spirits walke untimely howres.

---

311. *trace*: dance.    313. *advance*: raise.    317. *virelayes*: lyrics. The word
may be used for its association with "green" or "spring" songs, fitting for the
pastoral pleasures Alcyon describes (see Gascoigne, *Certaine Notes of
Instruction*, Sect. 14).    318. *dight*: adorn.    320. *bale*: woe.    327. *idle
pleasance*: empty pleasure.    329. *heavinesse*: grief.    330–42. This
passionate desire for a world overturned is a traditional topic of pastoral
complaint, looking back to Virgil, *Ecl* 8.52–60 which in turn imitates
Theocritus, *Idyll* 1.132–36.

And Nature nurse of every living thing,
Let rest her selfe from her long wearinesse,
And cease henceforth things kindly forth to bring,
But hideous monsters full of uglinesse:                    340
For she it is, that hath me done this wrong,
No nurse, but Stepdame cruell mercilesse,
Weepe Shepheard weepe to make my under song.

4 My little flocke, whom earst I lov'd so well,
And wont to feede with finest grasse that grew,            345
Feede ye hencefoorth on bitter *Astrofell*
And stinking Smallage, and unsaverie Rew;
And when your mawes are with those weeds corrupted,
Be ye the pray of Wolves: ne will I rew,
That with your carkasses wild beasts be glutted.          350

Ne worse to you my sillie sheepe I pray,
Ne sorer vengeance wish on you to fall
Than to my selfe, for whose confusde decay
To carelesse heavens I doo daylie call:
But heavens refuse to heare a wretches cry,               355
And cruell death doth scorne to come at call,
Or graunt his boone that most desires to dye.

The good and righteous he away doth take,
To plague th'unrighteous which alive remaine:
But the ungodly ones he doth forsake,                     360

---

337–38. i.e. "And may Nature . . . rest herself from her lengthy and wearisome labors . . . ." 342. *No . . . Stepdame*: a common indictment. Cf. Ronsard's Ode "Mignonne, allons voir si la rose . . ." and du Bellay's *Regrets* 45. Renwick (1929) p.178 points to Latin forerunners in Quintilian 12.1.2 and Pliny, *Natural History* 7.1. 346. *Astrofell*: "Spenser may have thought of the yellow bog-astrophel, which was reported to be injurious to sheep; but the beauty of the word was probably the chief reason for its use" (Renwick 1929:178). 347. *Smallage*: wild parsley. *Rew*: rue. 348. *corrupted*: infected. 353–57. Cf. *The Book of the Duchess* 583–86. 353. *confusde decay*: dissolution.

By living long to multiplie their paine:
Els surely death should be no punishment,
As the great Judge at first did it ordaine,
But rather riddance from long languishment.

Therefore my *Daphne* they have tane away;  365
For worthie of a better place was she:
But me unworthie willed here to stay,
That with her lacke I might tormented be.
Sith then they so have ordred, I will pay
Penance to her according their decree,  370
And to her ghost doo service day by day.

For I will walke this wandring pilgrimage
Throughout the world from one to other end,
And in affliction wast my better age.
My bread shall be the anguish of my mind,  375
My drink the teares which fro mine eyes do raine,
My bed the ground that hardest I may finde;
So will I wilfully increase my paine.

And she my love that was, my Saint that is,
When she beholds from her celestiall throne,  380
(In which shee joyeth in eternall blis)
My bitter penance, will my case bemone,
And pitie me that living thus doo die:
For heavenly spirits have compassion
On mortall men, and rue their miserie.  385

So when I have with sorowe satisfide
Th'importune fates, which vengeance on me seeke,
And th'eavens with long languor pacifide,
She for pure pitie of my sufferance meeke,

---

379. *Saint*: blessed one. But in the context of Alcyon's desire to do "penance
to her" (370) the term may take on the associations of Catholic "sainthood"
and hence for a Protestant audience, of idolatry. See also Harris and Steffen
(1978) p.33.    387. *importune*: vexatious.    388. *languor*: suffering.

Will send for me; for which I daylie long,                    390
And will till then my painfull penance eeke:
Weep Shepheard, weep to make my under song.

5 Hencefoorth I hate what ever Nature made,
And in her workmanship no pleasure finde:
For they be all but vaine, and quickly fade,        395
So soone as on them blowes the Northern winde,
They tarrie not, but flit and fall away,
Leaving behind them nought but griefe of minde,
And mocking such as thinke they long will stay.

I hate the heaven, because it doth withhold        400
Me from my love, and eke my love from me;
I hate the earth,because it is the mold
Of fleshly slime and fraile mortalitie;
I hate the fire, because to nought it flyes,
I hate the Ayre,because sighes of it be,            405
I hate the Sea, because it teares supplyes.

I hate the day, because it lendeth light
To see all things, and not my love to see;
I hate the darknesse and the drery night,
Because they breed sad balefulnesse in mee:        410
I hate all times, because all times doo flye
So fast away, and may not stayed bee,
But as a speedie post that passeth by.

I hate to speake, my voyce is spent with crying:
I hate to heare, lowd plaints have duld mine eares:   415
I hate to tast, for food withholds my dying:
I hate to see, mine eyes are dimd with teares:
I hate to smell, no sweet on earth is left:
I hate to feele, my flesh is numbd with feares:
So all my senses from me are bereft.               420

391. *eeke*: increase.    410. *balefulnesse*: anguish.    412. *stayed*: stopped.
413. *post*: courier.

I hate all men, and shun all womankinde;
The one because as I they wretched are,
The other for because I doo not finde
My love with them, that wont to be their Starre:
And life I hate, because it will not last,                              425
And death I hate, because it life doth marre,
And all I hate, that is to come or past.

So all the world, and all in it I hate,
Because it changeth ever too and fro,
And never standeth in one certaine state,                              430
But still unstedfast round about doth goe,
Like a Mill wheele, in midst of miserie,
Driven with streames of wretchednesse and woe,
That dying lives, and living still does dye.

So doo I live, so doo I daylie die,                                    435
And pine away in selfe-consuming paine,
Sith she that did my vitall powres supplie,
And feeble spirits in their force maintaine
Is fetcht fro me, why seeke I to prolong
My wearie daies in dolor and disdaine?                                 440
Weep Shepheard weep to make my under song.

6 Why doo I longer live in lifes despight?
And doo not dye then in despight of death:
Why doo I longer see this loathsome light,
And doo in darknesse not abridge my breath,                            445
Sith all my sorrow should have end thereby,
And cares finde quiet; is it so uneath
To leave this life, or dolorous to dye?

To live I finde it deadly dolorous;
For life drawes care, and care continuall woe:                        450

---

431–34. A gloomy variation on the familiar image of Fortune's wheel.
434–36. Cf. *The Book of the Duchess* 587–88.       450. *drawes*: brings with it.

Therefore to dye must needes be joyeous,
And wishfull thing this sad life to forgoe.
But I must stay; I may it not amend,
My *Daphne* hence departing bad me so,
She bad me stay, till she for me did send.    455

Yet whilest I in this wretched vale doo stay,
My wearie feete shall ever wandring be,
That still I may be readie on my way,
When as her messenger doth come for me:
Ne will I rest my feete for feeblenesse,    460
Ne will I rest my limmes for frailtie,
Ne will I rest mine eyes for heavinesse.

But as the mother of the Gods, that sought
For faire *Eurydice* her daughter deere
Throghout the world, with wofull heavie thought;    465
So will I travell whilest I tarrie heere,
Ne will I lodge, ne will I ever lin,
Ne when as drouping *Titan* draweth neere
To loose his teeme, will I take up my Inne.

Ne sleepe (the harbenger of wearie wights)    470
Shall ever lodge upon mine ey-lids more;
Ne shall with rest refresh my fainting sprights,
Nor failing force to former strength restore,
But I will wake and sorrow all the night

453. *amend*: change, improve.    460. *Ne*: nor.    462. *heavinesse*:
drowsiness.    463–65. Sp here conflates the myth of Orpheus and Euridice
with that of Ceres and Persephone. Orpheus's wife was forced to go to the
underworld when she was stung by a serpent; Ceres' daughter when she was
seized by Hades. Ceres searched for Persephone "throughout the world" and
in Ovid's account she angrily blights the earth of Sicily (*Met* 5.477–86); her
words recall Alcyon's wish to see the world wither (330–34).    467. *lin*:
cease.    468. *Titan*: i.e. the sun.    470. *harbenger*: host. The metaphor
compares sleep to an inn-keeper. Renwick (1929) p.179 argues differently,
that "harbinger is used in its proper sense of a fore-courier who arranges
resting places. . . ."

With *Philumene*, my fortune to deplore, 475
With *Philumene*, the partner of my plight.

And ever as I see the starres to fall,
And under ground to goe, to give them light
Which dwell in darknes, I to minde will call,
How my faire Starre (that shinde on me so bright) 480
Fell sodainly, and faded under ground;
Since whose departure, day is turnd to night,
And night without a *Venus* starre is found.

But soone as day doth shew his deawie face,
And calls foorth men unto their toylsome trade, 485
I will withdraw me to some darksome place,
Or some deepe cave, or solitarie shade;
There will I sigh and sorrow all day long,
And the huge burden of my cares unlade:
Weep Shepheard, weep, to make my undersong. 490

7 Hence foorth mine eyes shall never more behold
Faire thing on earth, ne feed on false delight
Of ought that framed is of mortall moulde,
Sith that my fairest flower is faded quight:
For all I see is vaine and transitorie, 495
Ne will be helde in anie stedfast plight,
But in a moment loose their grace and glorie.

And ye fond men on fortunes wheele that ride,
Or in ought under heaven repose assurance,
Be it riches, beautie, or honors pride: 500

---

475. *Philumene*: Philomela, who was ravished and mutilated by Tereus, was
later transformed into a nightingale. Philomela is Alcyon's "partner" in being
a night-bird and a mournful one. Sp may have borrowed this version of the
name from Gascoigne's *Complaint of Philumene*.    483. *Venus starre*:
Vesper, the evening star, which figures elsewhere in Sp's works as an image
of divine beauty and guidance. Cf. *FQ* VII vi 9; *Epith* 286–94.
489. *unlade*: bring forth, unburden.    496. *plight*: condition, state.

Be sure that they shall have no long endurance,
But ere ye be aware will flit away;
For nought of them is yours, but th'onely usance
Of a small time, which none ascertaine may.

And ye true Lovers, whom desastrous chaunce          505
Hath farre exiled from your Ladies grace,
To mourne in sorrow and sad sufferaunce,
When ye doo heare me in that desert place
Lamenting lowde my *Daphnes* Elegie,
Helpe me to wayle my miserable case,          510
And when life parts, vouchsafe to close mine eye.

And ye more happie Lovers, which enjoy
The presence of your dearest loves delight,
When ye doo heare my sorrowfull annoy,
Yet pittie me in your empassiond spright,          515
And thinke that such mishap, as chaunst to me,
May happen unto the most happiest wight;
For all mens states alike unstedfast be.

And ye my fellow Shepheards, which do feed
Your carelesse flocks on hils and open plaines,          520
With better fortune, than did me succeed,
Remember yet my undeserved paines,
And when ye heare,that I am dead or slaine,
Lament my lot, and tell your fellow swaines,
That sad *Alcyon* dyde in lifes disdaine.          525

And ye faire Damsels Shepheards dere delights,
That with your loves do their rude hearts possesse,
When as my hearse shall happen to your sightes,
Vouchsafe to deck the same with Cyparesse;

---

503. *usance*: use, employment.     504. *ascertaine*: know for certain.
505. *desastrous*: unlucky, ill-starred.     507. *sufferaunce*: suffering.
514. *annoy*: distress.     515. *spright*: spirit.     525. *in lifes disdaine*: scorned
by life.     528. *happen to*: meet with.

And ever sprinckle brackish teares among,                    530
In pitie of my undeserv'd distresse,
The which I wretch, endured have thus long.

And ye poore Pilgrimes, that with restlesse toyle
Wearie your selves in wandring desert wayes,
Till that you come, where ye your vowes assoyle,         535
When passing by ye read these wofull layes
On my grave written, rue my *Daphnes* wrong,
And mourne for me that languish out my dayes:
Cease Shepheard, cease, and end thy undersong.

Thus when he ended had his heavie plaint,                 540
The heaviest plaint that ever I heard sound,
His cheekes wext pale, and sprights began to faint,
As if againe he would have fallen to ground;
Which when I saw, I (stepping to him light)
Amooved him out of his stonie swound,                       545
And gan him to recomfort as I might.

But he no waie recomforted would be,
Nor suffer solace to approach him nie,
But casting up a sdeinfull eie at me,
That in his traunce I would not let him lie,             550
Did rend his haire, and beat his blubbred face
As one disposed wilfullie to die,
That I sore griev'd to see his wretched case.

Tho when the pang was somewhat overpast,
And the outragious passion nigh appeased,               555
I him desirde, sith daie was overcast,
And darke night fast approched, to be pleased
To turne aside unto my Cabinet,
And staie with me, till he were better eased
Of that strong stownd, which him so sore beset.          560

540–45. Cf. *The Book of the Duchess* 464–503.     542. *wext*: waxed.
546. *recomfort*: give fresh comfort.     549. *sdeinfull*: disdainful.
558. *Cabinet*: rustic cottage.     560. *strong stownd*: severe pain.

But by no meanes I could him win thereto,
Ne longer him intreate with me to staie,
But without taking leave, he foorth did goe
With staggring pace and dismall lookes dismay,
As if that death he in the face had seene,                    565
Or hellish hags had met upon the way:
But what of him became I cannot weene.

FINIS.

562. *intreate*: induce.     567. *I cannot weene*: i.e. I cannot say.

*Colin Clouts*
*Come Home Againe*

COLIN CLOVTS

# Come home againe.

*By Ed. Spencer.*

LONDON

Printed for *William Ponsonbie.*

1 5 9 5.

# Colin Clouts
# Come Home Againe

In the fall of 1589 Spenser left Kilcolman with his neighbor and patron Sir Walter Ralegh to embark for England. There he must have renewed his court connections and he published the first installment of his epic; according to *Colin Clout*, he read his work to the queen and eventually, on 25 February 1591, was rewarded with an annual pension of £50. He seems to have returned to Ireland before the official grant, however, for though *Colin Clouts Come Home Againe* (somewhat revised) was not published until 1595 its Dedication is dated *"From my house of* Kilcolman, *the* 27. *of December.* 1591". In recounting his journey Spenser's poem serves his interests in several ways. It reminds the court of his presence, and acts as an elaborate thank you note, a gift in the coin only poets can mint, praising the queen for favors received and expected.

That it does more appears already in the ambiguity of its title. For if this is a poem about homecoming it is not immediately clear where "home" lies. Spenser's courtier-audience would naturally identify home with the England the poet had left for the Irish wilds ten years earlier: coming home implies a return to the center of civility which is the court. But for Colin Clout home is Ireland. The uncertain reference of the title thus suggests one of the poem's governing concerns, that of the poet's proper place in relation to the world of power—the world of Elizabeth's court. Colin's choice of two possible homes sets up the fundamental opposition of the poem, England and Ireland, court and country—an opposition appearing again in the contrast of Colin and his court double, the Shepheard of the Ocean, and that between his Irish love and his English queen.

The contrast of city (or court) and country is a familiar theme in satire and pastoral. *Colin Clout* has affinities on the one hand with English Renaissance satires like Wyatt's *Mine Owne John Poins* in which a rusticated speaker enumerates his reasons for being absent from a corrupt court, and with others like Spenser's own "September" eclogue in which a rustic describes the enormities of a city he has visited. But *Colin Clout* differs from these. Unlike them it stresses the potential for good and for evil in both country and court: in this it looks back to Virgil's first eclogue with its profoundly ambivalent view of Rome as a bestower of freedom and a source of oppression. As Kathleen Williams (1974), one of the poem's best critics, has pointed out, Spenser's art here forces the reader to take account of contradictory views of his subjects, preventing us from judging too quickly and absolutely: "Cynthia the Queen and Rosalind are both cruel and kind, the English court is both ideal and corrupt, English poets are both fine and base, Ireland is both lovely and wretched, according to where one stands at the moment and where they stand at the moment" (p.84). The sudden changes of point of view characteristic of the poem thus educate the reader as much Renaissance humanist writing does, not by giving unequivocal answers, but by arguing both sides of a case and forcing the reader to judge for himself.

The pastoral veil with which Spenser intermittently covers the persons and events he commemorates encourages such a play of perspectives. Spenser gives fictive names to actual persons and places, replacing himself with his pastoral surrogate, Colin, altering Elizabeth's poets and ladies-in-waiting to shepherds and shepherdesses, changing even the Irish landscape of the Awbeg river and the Ballyhoura Hills into Mulla and old Mole. This fiction-making has multiple effects, but most importantly it enables the poet to distance himself from his own experience. By writing a poem about Colin's journey and not his own, Spenser is freed from the need to present himself as holding unequivocally any single moral position. Yet at the same time he is enabled to invoke the particular moral standard that

Renaissance pastoral affords: the sense of community, simplicity, and "naturalness" which are surely Colin's—if not the poem's—governing ideals. Colin's loving relation to his fellow shepherds and shepherdesses appears at the opening of the poem as a model for human relationships, and it is quietly reemphasized throughout the work by the eager questions and friendly challenges of his listeners. By contrast it is the absence of true community—the duplicitous friendships, the untrustworthy language, and the elevation of outward show over inward truth—which forms the basis of Colin's satiric attack on the court.

The advantages of the pastoral form can be seen in Spenser's substitution of Colin for himself, for Colin is and is not Spenser. His journey clearly recalls that of the poet, and he is surely closer to Spenser than the immature Colin of *The Shepheardes Calender*. Yet he is not identical. Colin is by and large more one-sided and more extreme than the poet-courtier who wrote *Colin Clouts Come Home Againe*. He is, for instance, quite willing at the end of the poem to renounce hope of sexual fulfilment and worship his love Rosalind for the beauty she incarnates, where Spenser celebrates his earthly wedding and bedding in the *Epithalamion*. Equally important for the poem, he is willing to turn his back on Cynthia's court and aspire to Love's court only, where for Spenser the choice can not have been so easy or so final. Spenser can thus use Colin to dramatize impulses within himself without entirely identifying himself with them. A similar simplification occurs in Spenser's treatment of the Shepheard of the Ocean who—for all his clear identification with Sir Walter Ralegh—embodies the desire for worldly greatness which Spenser's early letters show was an important part of his own nature.

Formally, *Colin Clout* is a greatly-expanded pastoral eclogue. Its characters are rustic shepherds, and it displays the lack of action, the abundance of talk, the opposition of viewpoint, and the sudden lyrical moments that characterize the genre. Its themes—love, friendship, the uses of poetry, the choice of life—

are entirely typical of the kind. Pastoral is a humble genre, as the slightly tongue-in-cheek Dedication asserts. But it is also an unstable genre, always ready to become something else, and from Theocritus and Virgil on its humility has provided a ground for visionary moments of considerable ambitiousness. The ambition is fully evident here. *Colin Clout* is an extraordinarily long eclogue—longer than any three in *The Shepheardes Calender*—and its seemingly loose structure incorporates a variety of kinds: praise, satire, etiological myth, mythological hymn. The easy, playful style in which most of the poem is written yields at times to the terse, contemptuous denunciation of the court or rises to the intense praises of Elizabeth, Rosalind, and the God of Love. On these latter occasions Colin breaks pastoral decorum, as his auditors remind him (616–19; 823–34), and the eclogue becomes a vehicle for speculation about love, beauty, and courtiership—subjects theoretically beyond its humble bounds.

The apparent rambling of *Colin Clout* is equally deceptive. Criticism of the poem has stressed the coherence and even the tightness of its composition. The poem presents a series of variations on the theme of love (Meyer 1969) or, the related idea of concord—in the court and the state, between lovers, underlying the very elements of the universe (Burchmore 1977). David Burchmore stresses the poem's coherence by pointing to its elaborately symmetrical structure: Colin's central praise of Rosalind is bracketed by his praises of court poets and ladies which are in turn framed by double praise of Cynthia. These, finally, are enclosed by passages on friendship (Colin and the Shepheard of the Ocean) and love (Colin's mythological hymn). The political and the personal concerns of the poem merge in its underlying concern with concord: Spenser's love and his queen are "the twin anchors of personal and political stability in an uncertain universe" (Burchmore 1977:401). A second view of the poem's organization takes Colin himself as its center: the work presents Colin's transformation from the solipsistic shepherd-boy of *The Shepheardes Calender* to a "priest" of the God of

Love. By the end of the poem he has become a new Orpheus, teaching his shepherd followers, transmitting the Beauty above to the World below (Mallette 1979).

These largely compatible views of the work point to recognizable patterns in the poem, but they deal less convincingly with the problematic relation between Colin's private and public natures which appear in his devotion to Rosalind and to his Queen. It may be that, far from being twin anchors of stability, Colin's two "ladies" represent competing and mutually exclusive ideals (Cheney 1983). The patterning which Burchmore presents to prove their harmonious connection may have quite a different meaning: Rosalind seems to have displaced Cynthia from the heart of her poem, and it is noticeable that while the work begins with a praise of the queen (40–48) it ends with a praise of Rosalind (931–51). Love's court has superseded Cynthia's. Yet the praises of Elizabeth contain some of the strongest writing in the work and, unlike the strictly measured praise of Cynthia's poets or the rather formulaic tribute to her ladies, these passages strike one as deeply felt: Spenser is writing at his best. It is characteristic of the poem that this implicit conflict is not resolved.

The tension between the demands of love and the demands of society appears even in the small myth that Colin tells to the Shepheard of the Ocean, in which a lover challenges authority, this time the authority of a parent. This myth, like many of the interwoven myths in Spenser's writing, is rich in interpretive possibility and assumes a significant relation to many of the themes in the poem. Most grandly it presents us with an emblem of the one and the many in Bregog's self-division and his ultimate unification as he joins with Mulla. But at a humbler level, the wily little river suffers the watery equivalent of a ruined career by his romance: the myth suggests the price of love triumphant. It is hard to forget that this myth is told to a figure based on Sir Walter Ralegh who, at the time the poem was finally printed, had ruined *his* chances at court by his secret marriage with Elizabeth Throckmorton (Gaffney 1982). Colin significantly praises Bregog and announces that his love will last "so long/ As water doth within his bancks appeare" (94–95). The myth presents us with a world in which it is necessary to choose between competing values, and in which self-transcendence may be gained only with the loss of one's old self, and with it one's worldly name.

*Colin Clouts Come Home Againe* was printed with the group of elegies for Sir Philip Sidney headed by Spenser's own *Astrophel*. The two books are roughly equal in size (Spenser's poem runs to 954 lines, the collection to 1033). The volume as a whole might be titled the Book of the Three Poets, focussed as it is on the figures of Colin, Astrophel, and the Shepheard of the Ocean. If, as recent criticism has suggested, *Colin Clout* represents the self-conscious dramatization of a stage in Spenser's career, a temporary return to pastoral and a scrutiny of the options available to him (Shore 1985), the book as a whole widens this scrutiny to include the most famous poet-courtiers of the Elizabethan world. Astrophel/Sidney was a poet whose career was cut short by death; the strange shepheard/Ralegh had, by the time the poem was published, been ostracized from court; and Colin/Spenser, despite or because of his home in Ireland, had survived (see Cheney 1983). It is one further effect of the pastoral mode in *Colin Clout* that it unites the poem with *Astrophel* and gives the two works a common language, a basis of comparison.

*William Oram*

# TO THE RIGHT
worthy and noble Knight
Sir *Walter Raleigh*, Captaine of her Majesties
Guard, Lord Wardein of the Stanneries,
*and Lieutenant of the Countie of
Cornwall.*

(∴)

*S IR, that you may see that I am not alwaies ydle as yee thinke,
though not greatly well occupied, nor altogither undutifull,
though not precisely officious, I make you present of this simple pas-
torall, unworthie of your higher conceipt for the meanesse of the stile,
but agreeing with the truth in circumstance and matter. The which I
humbly beseech you to accept in part of paiment of the infinite debt in*

D E D I C A T I O N:    Coming from a gentry Devonshire family, Sir Walter
Ralegh gained the queen's favor and rose rapidly at court during the 1580s,
acquiring the honors that Sp mentions here as well as a number of lucrative
favors including several large grants of land in Ireland. Sp may have met him
during Ralegh's earlier Irish military service (1580–82) and they certainly
saw one another during the summer of 1589, when Ralegh, who may have
been briefly out of favor, was in Ireland. According to the poem, Sp left with
Ralegh for England where the favorite acted as his patron, advancing him
with the queen and protecting him from enemies. While the Dedication is
dated late in 1591, Sp did not publish *CCCHA* until 1595, possibly because
the disgrace attending the discovery of Ralegh's secret marriage to Elizabeth
Throckmorton (Rowse 1962) made Sp bide his time with a poem praising
Ralegh highly. The Dedication itself suggests the opposites of the work to
follow—England and Ireland, humble shepherd and great courtier, simple
truth-telling and malicious slander.    *Stanneries*: tin mines and smelting
works in Cornwall and Devon.    *not alwaies ydle*: playful exaggeration. At
the time Sp was the "undertaker" to plant Englishmen on his three-thousand
acre estate, and deputy clerk of the Council of Munster, though many of the
daily duties of this office may have been delegated.    *precisely officious*:
minutely dutiful.    *conceipt*: understanding.    *meanesse*: context suggests
"lowliness": pastoral was traditionally a low-style genre. *CCCHA* is in fact
"mean" in a second sense—it is written in a middle style which is graceful,
expansive, even decorative.

*which I acknowledge my selfe bounden unto you, for your singular favours and sundrie good turnes shewed to me at my late being in England, and with your good countenance protect against the malice of evill mouthes, which are alwaies wide open to carpe at and misconstrue my simple meaning. I pray continually for your happinesse. From my house of* Kilcolman, *the* 27. *of December.* 1591

Yours ever humbly.

*Ed. Sp.*

*late*: recent.     *protect*: protected.

# Colin Clouts
## come home againe.

THe shepheards boy (best knowen by that name)
That after *Tityrus* first sung his lay,
Laies of sweet love, without rebuke or blame,
Sate (as his custome was) upon a day,
Charming his oaten pipe unto his peres,    5
The shepheard swaines that did about him play:
Who all the while with greedie listfull eares,
Did stand astonisht at his curious skill,
Like hartlesse deare, dismayd with thunders sound.
At last when as he piped had his fill,    10
He rested him: and sitting then around,
One of those groomes (a jolly groome was he,
As ever piped on an oaten reed,
And lov'd this shepheard dearest in degree,
Hight *Hobbinol*) gan thus to him areed.    15
 *Colin* my liefe, my life, how great a losse
Had all the shepheards nation by thy lacke?
And I poore swaine of many greatest crosse:
That sith thy *Muse* first since thy turning backe
Was heard to sound as she was wont on hye,    20
Hast made us all so blessed and so blythe.
Whilest thou wast hence, all dead in dole did lie:
The woods were heard to waile full many a sythe,

---

1. *best . . . name*: SC had gone through four editions by 1591. 2. *Tityrus*:
Virgil, whose eclogues were a primary model for Renaissance pastoralists.
The "lay" would be *SC*. 5. *Charming*: playing, though lines 8–9 suggest
that the shepherds are entranced as if by magic. 6. *play*: rejoice.
7. *listfull*: eager to listen (a Spenserian coinage combining two meanings of
*list*: to desire and to listen). 8. *astonisht*: amazed. Line 9 plays on the
Latin root *extonare*: to strike with a thunderbolt. 9. *hartlesse*: dismayed,
terrified. 12. *groomes*: shepherds. 14. *dearest in degree*: most dearly of
all. 18. *crosse*: affliction.

And all their birds with silence to complaine:
The fields with faded flowers did seem to mourne,                    25
And all their flocks from feeding to refraine:
The running waters wept for thy returne,.
And all their fish with languour did lament:
But now both woods and fields, and floods revive,
Sith thou art come, their cause of meriment,                        30
That us late dead, hast made againe alive:
But were it not too painfull to repeat
The passed fortunes, which to thee befell
In thy late voyage, we thee would entreat,
Now at thy leisure them to us to tell.                              35
    To whom the shepheard gently answered thus,
*Hobbin* thou temptest me to that I covet:
For of good passed newly to discus,
By dubble usurie doth twise renew it.
And since I saw that Angels blessed eie,                            40
Her worlds bright sun, her heavens fairest light,
My mind full of my thoughts satietie,
Doth feed on sweet contentment of that sight:
Since that same day in nought I take delight,
Ne feeling have in any earthly pleasure,                            45
But in remembrance of that glorious bright,
My lifes sole blisse, my hearts eternall threasure.
Wake then my pipe, my sleepie *Muse* awake,
Till I have told her praises lasting long:
*Hobbin* desires, thou maist it not forsake,                        50
Harke then ye jolly shepheards to my song.
    With that they all gan throng about him neare,
With hungrie eares to heare his harmonie:
The whiles their flocks devoyd of dangers feare,
Did round about them feed at libertie.                              55

40. *that Angels*: Queen Elizabeth's.    42. *thoughts satietie*: the full
satisfaction of my mind's desire. The language recalls the commonplace that
only God fully satisfies human longing.    46. *bright*: brightness.
50. *forsake*: refuse.

One day (quoth he) I sat, (as was my trade)
Under the foote of *Mole* that mountaine hore,
Keeping my sheepe amongst the cooly shade,
Of the greene alders by the *Mullaes* shore:
There a straunge shepheard chaunst to find me out, 60
Whether allured with my pipes delight,
Whose pleasing sound yshrilled far about,
Or thither led by chaunce, I know not right:
Whom when I asked from what place he came,
And how he hight, himselfe he did ycleepe, 65
The shepheard of the Ocean by name,
And said he came far from the main-sea deepe.
He sitting me beside in that same shade,
Provoked me to plaie some pleasant fit,
And when he heard the musicke which I made, 70
He found himselfe full greatly pleasd at it:
Yet æmuling my pipe, he tooke in hond
My pipe before that æmuled of many,
And plaid theron; (for well that skill he cond)
Himselfe as skilfull in that art as any. 75
He pip'd, I sung; and when he sung, I piped,
By chaunge of turnes, each making other mery,
Neither envying other, nor envied,
So piped we, untill we both were weary.
There interrupting him, a bonie swaine, 80
That *Cuddy* hight, him thus atweene bespake:
And should it not thy readie course restraine,

56. *trade*: habit. Singing is, of course, the shepherd-poet's "trade" in a
vocational sense. 57. *Mole*: Sp's name for the Ballyhowra Hills in
Munster to the north of Kilcolman, his house. 59. *Mullaes shore*: Sp's
name for the river Awbeg which bordered his estate to the south and
west. 66. *shepheard . . . Ocean*: Sir Walter Ralegh's links with the ocean
were many: he was a naval authority, the Vice-Admiral of the West, an
explorer and the would-be colonizer of "Virginia." The queen's pet name for
him was "Water." 69. *Provoked*: urged. *fit*: song. 72. *æmuling*:
emulating (a Spenserian coinage). 73. *that . . . many*: that had earlier
excited the emulation of many. 82. *readie course*: narrative order.

I would request thee *Colin*, for my sake,
To tell what thou didst sing, when he did plaie.
For well I weene it worth recounting was,                                85
Whether it were some hymne, or morall laie,
Or carol made to praise thy loved lasse.
    Nor of my love, nor of my losse (quoth he)
I then did sing, as then occasion fell:
For love had me forlorne, forlorne of me,                                90
That made me in that desart chose to dwell.
But of my river *Bregogs* love I soong,
Which to the shiny *Mulla* he did beare,
And yet doth beare, and ever will, so long
As water doth within his bancks appeare.                                 95
    Of fellowship (said then that bony Boy)
Record to us that lovely lay againe:
The staie whereof, shall nought these eares annoy,
Who all that *Colin* makes, do covet faine.
    Heare then (quoth he) the tenor of my tale,                          100
In sort as I it to that shepheard told:
No leasing new, nor Grandams fable stale,
But auncient truth confirm'd with credence old.
    Old father *Mole*, (*Mole* hight that mountain gray
That walls the Northside of *Armulla* dale)                             105

---

86–87. The categories are general, but in fact the poem contains a *hymne* in
its praise of love (799–894), a *moral laie* in its tale of Bregog and Mulla (88–
155), and *carols* in its praises of Rosalind (466–79; 931–51).    90: Colin's
memory reverts to the situation he occupies in "June" of *SC*, abandoned and
desolate without Rosalind. *me . . . me*: for love had abandoned me who had
abandoned it [to grieve].    92: "Bregog flows through Spenser's land
(hence *my* river) into the Awbeg just above Doneraile. The name, which
means *deceitful* (118), and the myth here related, come from the same fact,
that the Bregog sinks underground through the limestone and reappears (in
dry weather) only some two miles lower down, a little before its confluence
with the Awbeg" (Renwick 1929:184). Myths describing the origin of a
place are common in Renaissance literature: see Gottfried (1937).
97. *Record*: repeat.    104–55. Ellrodt (1960:222) argues on the grounds
of its versification that this tale is a late addition to the poem.
105. *Armulla dale*: the Awbeg valley.

He had a daughter fresh as floure of May,
Which gave that name unto that pleasant vale;
*Mulla* the daughter of old *Mole*, so hight
The Nimph, which of that water course has charge,
That springing out of *Mole*, doth run downe right          110
To *Buttevant*, where spreading forth at large,
It giveth name unto that auncient Cittie,
Which *Kilnemullah* cleped is of old:
Whose ragged ruines breed great ruth and pittie,
To travailers, which it from far behold.          115
Full faine she lov'd, and was belov'd full faine,
Of her owne brother river, *Bregog* hight,
So hight because of this deceitfull traine,
Which he with *Mulla* wroght to win delight.
But her old sire more carefull of her good,          120
And meaning her much better to preferre,
Did thinke to match her with the neighbour flood,
Which *Allo* hight, Broad water called farre:
And wrought so well with his continuall paine,
That he that river for his daughter wonne:          125
The dowre agreed, the day assigned plaine,
The place appointed where it should be doone.
Nath'lesse the Nymph her former liking held;
For love will not be drawne, but must be ledde,
And *Bregog* did so well her fancie weld,          130
That her good will he got her first to wedde.
But for her father sitting still on hie,
Did warily still watch which way she went,
And eke from far observ'd with jealous eie,

111. *Buttevant*: "Buttevant is on the Cork-Limerick road, about three miles
from Kilcolman. The 'ragged ruines' to which Spenser refers were probably
those of the Franciscan friary there, still extant, and perhaps also those of
Ballybeg Abbey, half a mile away" (Renwick 1929:184).    118. *traine*:
stratagem.    120. *good*: well-being; property.    121. *preferre*: advance,
esp. by marriage.    123. *Allo* . . . *Broad water*: another alternation of
fictional and actual names; the Broadwater is now called the Blackwater.
131. *good will*: consent.    134. *jealous*: suspicious.

Which way his course the wanton *Bregog* bent,                    135
Him to deceive for all his watchfull ward,
The wily lover did devise this slight:
First into many parts his streame he shar'd,
That whilest the one was watcht, the other might
Passe unespide to meete her by the way;                          140
And then besides, those little streames so broken
He under ground so closely did convay,
That of their passage doth appeare no token,
Till they into the *Mullaes* water slide.
So secretly did he his love enjoy:                               145
Yet not so secret, but it was descride,
And told her father by a shepheards boy.
Who wondrous wroth for that so foule despight,
In great avenge did roll downe from his hill
Huge mightie stones, the which encomber might             150
His passage, and his water-courses spill.
So of a River, which he was of old,
He none was made, but scattred all to nought,
And lost emong those rocks into him rold,
Did lose his name: so deare his love he bought.          155
    Which having said, him *Thestylis* bespake,
Now by my life this was a mery lay:
Worthie of *Colin* selfe, that did it make.
But read now eke of friendship I thee pray,
What dittie did that other shepheard sing?                      160
For I do covet most the same to heare,
As men use most to covet forreine thing.
That shall I eke (quoth he) to you declare.
His song was all a lamentable lay,

---

136. *ward*: care, with a pun on guardianship.    141. *besides*: side by
side.    151. *spill*: destroy.    164–71. Just what poem, if any, Sp refers to
here may never be clear. Ralegh's extended lament *The 11th: and last booke of
the Ocean to Scinthia* was most probably composed in 1592, after the first

Of great unkindnesse, and of usage hard,                165
Of *Cynthia* the Ladie of the sea,
Which from her presence faultlesse him debard.
And ever and anon with singulfs rife,
He cryed out, to make his undersong
Ah my loves queene, and goddesse of my life,           170
Who shall me pittie, when thou doest me wrong?
    Then gan a gentle bonylasse to speake,
That *Marin* hight, Right well he sure did plaine:
That could great *Cynthiaes* sore displeasure breake,
And move to take him to her grace againe.              175
But tell on further *Colin*, as befell
Twixt him and thee, that thee did hence dissuade.
    When thus our pipes we both had wearied well,
(Quoth he) and each an end of singing made,
He gan to cast great lyking to my lore,                180
And great dislyking to my lucklesse lot:
That banisht had my selfe, like wight forlore,
Into that waste, where I was quite forgot.
The which to leave, thenceforth he counseld mee,
Unmeet for man, in whom was ought regardfull           185
And wend with him, his *Cynthia* to see:
Whose grace was great, and bounty most rewardfull.
Besides her peerlesse skill in making well
And all the ornaments of wondrous wit,

draft of *CCCHA* but before its revision in 1595. That poem develops out of
the imprisonment and disgrace attendant on the discovery in the summer of
1592 of Ralegh's secret marriage, and its subject—the grieving lament of the
bereft courtier—would correspond to the description given here. Sp may,
however, be referring to a lost work from the 1580s bewailing a less severe
loss of favor, or he may have no single poem in mind as he describes a kind
of poetry appropriate to the ousted shepherd's situation. The strange
shepherd's poem contrasts with Colin's in its political aim, an aim that Marin
comments on (line 173).    168. *singulfs rife*: numerous sobs.
169. *undersong*: refrain (cf. *SC* "August" 128). No extant poem of Ralegh's
has this refrain.    177. *dissuade*: divert.    180. *cast*: utter.
188. *making*: composing.

Such as all womankynd did far excell:                                    190
Such as the world admyr'd and praised it:
So what with hope of good, and hate of ill,
He me perswaded forth with him to fare:
Nought tooke I with me, but mine oaten quill:
Small needments else need shepheard to prepare.         195
So to the sea we came; the sea? that is
A world of waters heaped up on hie,
Rolling like mountaines in wide wildernesse,
Horrible, hideous, roaring with hoarse crie.
  And is the sea (quoth *Coridon*) so fearfull?             200
Fearfull much more (quoth he) then hart can fear:
Thousand wyld beasts with deep mouthes gaping
                                             direfull
Therein stil wait poore passengers to teare.
Who life doth loath, and longs death to behold,
Before he die, alreadie dead with feare,                      205
And yet would live with heart halfe stonie cold,
Let him to sea, and he shall see it there.
And yet as ghastly dreadfull, as it seemes,
Bold men presuming life for gaine to sell,
Dare tempt that gulf, and in those wandring stremes     210
Seek waies unknowne, waies leading down to hell.
For as we stood there waiting on the strond,
Behold an huge great vessell to us came
Dauncing upon the waters back to lond,
As if it scornd the daunger of the same;                      215
Yet was it but a wooden frame and fraile,
Glewed togither with some subtile matter,
Yet had it armes and wings, and head and taile,
And life to move it selfe upon the water.

190–91. *Such as . . . Such as*: refers back to "ornaments." *it*: refers to
"wondrous wit."      195. *needments*: things needed, i.e. luggage.
209. *presuming*: daring, though "wandring stremes" (210) and "down to
hell" (211) suggest "to undertake presumptuously" (Oram 1984:34–35).
210. *stremes*: currents.      217. *Glewed*: fastened. *subtile*: fine.

Strange thing, how bold and swift the monster was,                    220
That neither car'd for wynd, nor haile, nor raine,
Nor swelling waves, but thorough them did passe
So proudly, that she made them roare againe.
The same aboord us gently did receave,
And without harme us farre away did beare,                            225
So farre that land our mother us did leave,
And nought but sea and heaven to us appeare.
Then hartlesse quite and full of inward feare,
That shepheard I besought to me to tell,
Under what skie, or in what world we were,                            230
In which I saw no living people dwell.
Who me recomforting all that he might,
Told me that that same was the Regiment
Of a great shepheardesse, that *Cynthia* hight,
His liege his Ladie, and his lifes Regent.                           235
If then (quoth I) a shepheardesse she bee,
Where be the flockes and heards, which she doth keep?
And where may I the hills and pastures see,
On which she useth for to feed her sheepe?
These be the hills (quoth he) the surges hie,                        240
On which faire *Cynthia* her heards doth feed:
Her heards be thousand fishes with their frie,
Which in the bosome of the billowes breed.
Of them the shepheard which hath charge in chief,
Is *Triton* blowing loud his wreathed horne:                          245
At sound whereof, they all for their relief
Wend too and fro at evening and at morne.
And *Proteus* eke with him does drive his heard
Of stinking Seales and Porcpisces together,
With hoary head and deawy dropping beard,                            250

223. *againe*: in response.      232. *recomforting*: encouraging.
235. *Regent*: ruler.      237. *keep*: guard.      239. *useth*: is accustomed.
245. *Triton*: the herald of the sea-gods. Cf. Ovid, *Met* 1.330–42, and *FQ* IV
x 12. *wreathed*: twisted.      248. *Proteus*: here Sp stresses the sea-god's
function as a herdsman (cf. Homer, *Odyssey* Book 4).

Compelling them which way he list, and whether.
And I among the rest of many least,
Have in the Ocean charge to me assignd:
Where I will live or die at her beheast,
And serve and honour her with faithfull mind.          255
Besides an hundred Nymphs all heavenly borne,
And of immortall race, doo still attend
To wash faire *Cynthiaes* sheep, when they be shorne,
And fold them up, when they have made an end.
Those be the shepheards which my *Cynthia* serve,     260
At sea, beside a thousand moe at land:
For land and sea my *Cynithia* doth deserve
To have in her commandement at hand.
Thereat I wondred much, till wondring more
And more, at length we land far off descryde:          265
Which sight much gladed me; for much afore
I feard, least land we never should have eyde:
Thereto our ship her course directly bent,
As if the way she perfectly had knowne.
We *Lunday* passe; by that same name is ment           270
An Island, which the first to west was showne.
From thence another world of land we kend,
Floting amid the sea in jeopardie,
And round about with mightie white rocks hemd,
Against the seas encroching crueltie.                   275
Those same the shepheard told me, were the fields
In which dame *Cynthia* her landheards fed,
Faire goodly fields, then which *Armulla* yields
None fairer, nor more fruitfull to be red.
The first to which we nigh approched, was               280
An high headland thrust far into the sea,
Like to an horne, whereof the name it has,

251. *Compelling*: with Lat. force, "driving together."     *list*: chooses.
270. *Lunday*: the island of Lundy, off the north coast of Devon.
279. *red*: seen.     281–87. Colin lands in Cornwall, the etymology of which
he refers to in line 282. The "loftie mount" he mentions is St. Michael's
Mount.

Yet seemed to be a goodly pleasant lea:
There did a loftie mount at first us greet,
Which did a stately heape of stones upreare,                    285
That seemd amid the surges for to fleet,
Much greater then that frame, which us did beare:
There did our ship her fruitfull wombe unlade,
And put us all ashore on *Cynthias* land.
　What land is that thou meanst (then *Cuddy* sayd)     290
And is there other, then whereon we stand?
　Ah *Cuddy* (then quoth *Colin*) thous a fon,
That hast not seen least part of natures worke:
Much more there is unkend, then thou doest kon,
And much more that does from mens knowledge lurke.   295
For that same land much larger is then this,
And other men and beasts and birds doth feed:
There fruitfull corne, faire trees, fresh herbage is
And all things else that living creatures need.
Besides most goodly rivers there appeare,                     300
No whit inferiour to thy *Funchins* praise,
Or unto *Allo* or to *Mulla* cleare:
Nought hast thou foolish boy seene in thy daies.
But if that land be there (quoth he) as here,
And is theyr heaven likewise there all one?                    305
And if like heaven, be heavenly graces there,
Like as in this same world where we do wone?
　Both heaven and heavenly graces do much more
(Quoth he) abound in that same land, then this.
For there all happie peace and plenteous store              310
Conspire in one to make contented blisse:
No wayling there nor wretchednesse is heard,
No bloodie issues nor no leprosies,
No griesly famine, nor no raging sweard,

---

286. *fleet*: float.　　292. *thous a fon*: you're a fool (dialect).　　301–02. The
Funcheon is the actual name of a river flowing parallel to the Awbeg and
joining with the Blackwater. Cf. *FQ* VII vi 44.　　301. *praise*: worth.
305. *all one*: all the same.　　313. *issues*: sallies.

No nightly bodrags, nor no hue and cries;                                    315
The shepheards there abroad may safely lie,
On hills and downes, withouten dread or daunger:
No ravenous wolves the good mans hope destroy,
Nor outlawes fell affray the forest raunger.
There learned arts do florish in great honor,                                320
And Poets wits are had in peerlesse price:
Religion hath lay powre to rest upon her,
Advancing vertue and suppressing vice.
For end, all good, all grace there freely growes,
Had people grace it gratefully to use:                                       325
For God his gifts there plenteously bestowes,
But gracelesse men them greatly do abuse.
   But say on further, then said *Corylas*,
The rest of thine adventures, that betyded.
   Foorth on our voyage we by land did passe,                                330
(Quoth he) as that same shepheard still us guyded,
Untill that we to *Cynthiaes* presence came:
Whose glorie greater then my simple thought,
I found much greater then the former fame;
Such greatnes I cannot compare to ought:                                     335
But if I her like ought on earth might read,

315. *bodrags*: raids.     319. *affray*: attack. *raunger*: gamekeeper.
321. *price*: esteem.     322. I.e. religion can make use of secular powers.
324. *For end*: Lat. *in fine*, finally.     336. *read*: describe.     336–47. Here,
as elsewhere in the praises of the poem, Colin assumes the traditional pastoral
stance of the rustic unable fully to describe to his fellows the wonders he has
seen. But the praise of Cynthia is carefully conceived. It presents her as "the
image of the heavens in shape humane," a quasi-divine mediator between
heavenly perfection and earthly mutability. Cynthia is the image of the
heavens because her divine mind has stamped her physical form with its
heavenly beauty, but also because as queen and head of the Anglican Church,
Elizabeth I acts as God's representative on earth. Sp compares Elizabeth with
a familiar range of emblematic creatures, articulating the comparisons to
suggest that she embodies a divine union of opposites. Roses and lilies are
emblems respectively of love and purity, and the reference to a "virgin bride"
unites these in an image of loving chastity. The passage contains a series of
circles, images of perfection (cf. *FQ* VI Proem 7–8) which appear in the

I would her lyken to a crowne of lillies,
Upon a virgin brydes adorned head,
With Roses dight and Goolds and Daffadillies;
Or like the circlet of a Turtle true,                    340
In which all colours of the rainbow bee;
Or like faire *Phebes* garlond shining new,
In which all pure perfection one may see.
But vaine it is to thinke by paragone
Of earthly things, to judge of things divine:           345
Her power, her mercy, and her wisedome, none
Can deeme, but who the Godhead can define.
Why then do I base shepheard bold and blind,
Presume the things so sacred to prophane?
More fit it is t'adore with humble mind,                 350
The image of the heavens in shape humane.
   With that *Alexis* broke his tale asunder,
Saying, By wondring at thy *Cynthiaes* praise,
*Colin*, thy selfe thou mak'st us more to wonder,
And her upraising, doest thy selfe upraise.             355
But let us heare what grace she shewed thee,
And how that shepheard strange, thy cause advanced?
   The shepheard of the Ocean (quoth he)
Unto that Goddesse grace me first enhanced,
And to mine oaten pipe enclin'd her eare,               360
That she thenceforth therein gan take delight,
And it desir'd at timely houres to heare,
All were my notes but rude and roughly dight,
For not by measure of her owne great mynd,
And wondrous worth she mott my simple song,             365
But joyd that country shepheard ought could fynd
Worth harkening to, emongst the learned throng.
   Why? (said *Alexis* then) what needeth shee

crown of lilies, the "circlet" of the dove, "faire Phebes garlond," and even
(in modified form), in the rainbow, itself an image of peace, uniting heaven
with earth.    **344.** *paragone*: comparison.    **357.** *cause*: business.
**365.** *mott*: judged (preterite of *mete*).

That is so great a shepheardesse her selfe,
And hath so many shepheards in her fee, 370
To heare thee sing, a simple silly Elfe?
Or be the shepheards which do serve her laesie,
That they list not their mery pipes applie?
Or be their pipes untunable and craesie,
That they cannot her honour worthylie? 375
   Ah nay (said *Colin*) neither so, nor so:
For better shepheards be not under skie,
Nor better hable, when they list to blow
Their pipes aloud, her name to glorifie.
There is good *Harpalus* now woxen aged, 380
In faithfull service of faire *Cynthia*:
And there is *Corydon* though meanly waged,
Yet hablest wit of most I know this day.
And there is sad *Alcyon* bent to mourne,
Though fit to frame an everlasting dittie, 385
Whose gentle spright for *Daphnes* death doth tourn
Sweet layes of love to endlesse plaints of pittie.
Ah pensive boy pursue that brave conceipt,
In thy sweet Eglantine of *Merifleure*,

370. *in her fee*: in her service.   371. *Elfe*: creature.   373. *applie*:
ply.   374. *craesie*: flawed.   376–455. The pastoral naming of
Elizabeth's poets raises problems of interpretation. Presumably the court
audience for which Sp was writing would have perceived the poets Sp
mentions here by their rural pseudonyms: when he does introduce two poets
who are "knowen yet to few" he does so using their real names, Alabaster
and Daniel. But for a modern audience only four of the fictive shepherds can
be identified with complete certainty—the Shepheard of the Ocean, Astrofell,
Alcyon, and Amyntas. The other identifications depend to a greater or lesser
degree on educated guesswork. The most thorough and convincing
discussion of the matter appears in Gaffney (1982) pp.32–87.
380. *Harpalus*: ? George Turberville.   382. *Corydon*: ? Edward Dyer (see
Gaffney 1982:40–46). Abraham Fraunce has also been mentioned.
384–86. *sad Alcyon*: Sir Arthur Gorges, who lost his wife Douglas Howard
on 13 August 1590. Gorges addressed several poems to "Daphne" and Sp's
*Daphnaida* continued the pastoral pseudonym for the dead wife.
388. *conceipt*: train of thought.   389. *Eglantine of Merifiure*: an unfinished
pastoral poem of Gorges's.

Lift up thy notes unto their wonted height, 390
That may thy *Muse* and mates to mirth allure.
There eke is *Palin* worthie of great praise,
Albe he envie at my rustick quill:
And there is pleasing *Alcon*, could he raise
His tunes from laies to matter of more skill. 395
And there is old *Palemon* free from spight,
Whose carefull pipe may make the hearer rew:
Yet he himselfe may rewed be more right,
That sung so long untill quite hoarse he grew.
And there is *Alabaster* throughly taught, 400
In all this skill, though knowen yet to few,
Yet were he knowne to *Cynthia* as he ought,
His Eliseïs would be redde anew.
Who lives that can match that heroick song,
Which he hath of that mightie Princesse made? 405
O dreaded Dread, do not thy selfe that wrong,
To let thy fame lie so in hidden shade:
But call it forth, O call him forth to thee,
To end thy glorie which he hath begun:
That when he finisht hath as it should be, 410
No braver Poeme can be under Sun.
Nor *Po* nor *Tyburs* swans so much renowned,
Nor all the brood of *Greece* so highly praised,
Can match that *Muse* when it with bayes is crowned,
And to the pitch of her perfection raised. 415
And there is a new shepheard late up sprong,
The which doth all afore him far surpasse:
Appearing well in that well tuned song,

392. *Palin*: ? George Peale.    394. *Alcon*: ? Thomas Lodge (see Gaffney 1982:56-63).    396. *Palemon*: ? Thomas Churchyard.
400–11. *Alabaster*: William Alabaster had completed the first book of his *Elisaeis*, a Latin epic on the trials of Queen Elizabeth. The work was never completed and remained unpublished until 1979.    409. *glorie*: praise.    412. *Po . . . Tyburs swans*: i.e. Dante and Virgil.    415. *pitch*: height.    416. *a new shepheard*: Samuel Daniel published his sonnet sequence *Delia* in 1592; Sp may have seen it, or he may have seen the *Complaint of Rosamond* which was written in the same year.

Which late he sung unto a scornfull lasse.
Yet doth his trembling *Muse* but lowly flie,        420
As daring not too rashly mount on hight,
And doth her tender plumes as yet but trie,
In loves soft laies and looser thoughts delight.
Then rouze thy feathers quickly *Daniell*,
And to what course thou please thy selfe advance:      425
But most me seemes, thy accent will excell,
In Tragick plaints and passionate mischance.
And there that shepheard of the Ocean is,
That spends his wit in loves consuming smart:
Full sweetly tempred is that *Muse* of his      430
That can empierce a Princes mightie hart.
There also is (ah no, he is not now)
But since I said he is, he quite is gone,
*Amyntas* quite is gone and lies full low,
Having his *Amaryllis* left to mone.      435
Helpe, O ye shepheards helpe ye all in this,
Helpe *Amaryllis* this her losse to mourne:
Her losse is yours, your losse *Amyntas* is,
*Amyntas* floure of shepheards pride forlorne:
He whilest he lived was the noblest swaine,      440
That ever piped in an oaten quill:
Both did he other, which could pipe, maintaine,
And eke could pipe himselfe with passing skill.
And there though last not least is *Aetion*,

422. *tender*: youthful.    424. *rouze*: shake (a technical term from
hawking).    427. Daniel's *Tragedie of Cleopatra* was printed in
1594.    430. *tempred*: constituted, but also "balanced" and "hardened"
(appropriate for an arrowhead able to "empierce" a prince's heart).
432–35. Ferdinando Stanley, Lord Strange, fifth earl of Derby, who died on
16 April 1594. The lament for Amyntas is one of the passages clearly added
to the original draft.    435. *Amaryllis*: Alice Spenser, Lady Strange.
443. *passing*: surpassing.    444–47. *Aetion*: ? Probably Michael Drayton,
whose eclogue book *Idea, The Shepheards Garland* (1593) featured the poet-
hero Rowland; hence his Muse might "like himselfe Heroically sound." On
the other hand Shake-speare's name also sounds heroic, and the praise is
unspecific.

A gentler shepheard may no where be found:      445
Whose *Muse* full of high thoughts invention,
Doth like himselfe Heroically sound.
All these, and many others mo remaine,
Now after *Astrofell* is dead and gone:
But while as *Astrofell* did live and raine,      450
Amongst all these was none his Paragone.
All these do florish in their sundry kynd,
And do their *Cynthia* immortall make:
Yet found I lyking in her royall mynd,
Not for my skill, but for that shepheards sake.      455
   Then spake a lovely lasse, hight *Lucida*,
Shepheard, enough of shepheards thou hast told,
Which favour thee, and honour *Cynthia*:
But of so many Nymphs which she doth hold
In her retinew, thou hast nothing sayd;      460
That seems, with none of them thou favor foundest,
Or art ingratefull to each gentle mayd,
That none of all their due deserts resoundest.
   Ah far be it (quoth *Colin Clout*) fro me,
That I of gentle Mayds should ill deserve:      465
For that my selfe I do professe to be
Vassall to one, whom all my dayes I serve;
The beame of beautie sparkled from above,
The floure of vertue and pure chastitie,
The blossome of sweet joy and perfect love,      470
The pearle of peerlesse grace and modestie:
To her my thoughts I daily dedicate,
To her my heart I nightly martyrize:
To her my love I lowly do prostrate,

---

449. *Astrofell*: Sir Philip Sidney, who had died in 1586.    455. *that*
*shepheards*: i.e. the Shepherd of the Ocean.    466. *For that*: because.
467. *to one*: Rosalind. For speculation about possible historical reference see
Burchmore (1977) pp. 395–406 and Oakshott (1971) pp. 5–6.
468: Colin conceives of Rosalind's beauty in good Neoplatonic fashion as
emanating from "above."

To her my life I wholly sacrifice:                                        475
My thought, my heart, my love, my life is shee,
And I hers ever onely, ever one:
One ever I all vowed hers to bee,
One ever I, and others never none.
    Then thus *Melissa* said; Thrise happie Mayd,            480
Whom thou doest so enforce to deifie:
That woods, and hills, and valleyes thou hast made
Her name to eccho unto heaven hie.
But say, who else vouchsafed thee of grace?
    They all (quoth he) me graced goodly well,              485
That all I praise, but in the highest place,
*Urania*, sister unto *Astrofell*,
In whose brave mynd as in a golden cofer,
All heavenly gifts and riches locked are:
More rich than pearles of *Ynde*, or gold of *Opher*,        490
And in her sex more wonderfull and rare.
Ne lesse praise worthie I *Theana* read,
Whose goodly beames though they be over dight
With mourning stole of carefull wydowhead,
Yet through that darksome vale do glister bright;          495
She is the well of bountie and brave mynd,
Excelling most in glorie and great light:

477. *ever one*: The words recall the motto of Elizabeth I, *semper eadem*, always
the same (Cheney 1983).          478. This is the central line of *CCCHA*. *all*:
entirely.          481. *enforce*: strive.          485–577. The description of Cynthia's
twelve ladies-in-waiting balances that of her twelve poets. Many of the ladies
are easily identifiable, e.g. Urania as Mary Sidney, countess of Pembroke, or
the three Spensers of Althorp. Others are referred to vaguely enough that
their identities are not surely recoverable. Koller (1935:155–58) describes a
copy of *CCCHA* with annotations in a seventeenth-century hand which
identify a number of the ladies; where there is no other evidence its
identifications are offered here.          487. *Urania*: Mary Sidney, countess of
Pembroke and translator (with her brother, Sir Philip) of the Psalms. As the
Muse of Astronomy, Urania is identified as the Muse of Christian Poetry. Cf.
*TM* 481–540, and cf. du Bartas's *L'Uranie ou Muse Celeste*.          492. *Theana*:
Anne Russell, widow of Ambrose Dudley, earl of Warwick, who died 20
February 1589/90.

She is the ornament of womankind,
And Courts chief garlond with all vertues dight.
Therefore great *Cynthia* her in chiefest grace          500
Doth hold, and next unto her selfe advance,
Well worthie of so honourable place,
For her great worth and noble governance.
Ne lesse praise worthie is her sister deare,
Faire *Marian*, the *Muses* onely darling:                505
Whose beautie shyneth as the morning cleare,
With silver deaw upon the roses pearling.
Ne lesse praise worthie is *Mansilia*,
Best knowne by bearing up great *Cynthiaes* traine:
That same is she to whom *Daphnaida*                     510
Upon her neeces death I did complaine.
She is the paterne of true womenhead,
And onely mirrhor of feminitie:
Worthie next after *Cynthia* to tread,
As she is next her in nobilitie.                          515
Ne lesse praise worthie *Galathea* seemes,
Then best of all that honourable crew,
Faire *Galathea* with bright shining beames,
Inflaming feeble eyes that her do view.
She there then waited upon *Cynthia*,                     520
Yet there is not her won, but here with us
About the borders of our rich *Coshma*,
Now made of *Maa* the Nymph delitious.
Ne lesse praisworthie faire *Neæra* is,
*Neæra* ours, not theirs, though there she be,           525

505. *Marian*: ? Margaret, countess of Cumberland.     508. *Mansilia*:
Helena Snackenborg, widow of William Parr and wife of Sir Thomas Gorges.
See note to the Dedication of *Daph*.     512. *paterne*: model.
516–23. *Galathea*: ? Frances Howard, wife of Henry Fitzgerald, twelfth earl
of Kildare. "Her jointure included Croom and Adare on the Maigue, from
which the Barony of Coshma takes its name" (*Var*. VII Pt.1 p.475).
523. *Maa*: modern Maigre.     524. *Neaera*: Elizabeth Sheffield, wife of
Thomas Butler, tenth earl of Ormonde. Like the other Irish lady, Galathea,
she bears the name of a sea-nymph.

For of the famous Shure, the Nymph she is,
For high desert, advaunst to that degree.
She is the blosome of grace and curtesie,
Adorned with all honourable parts:
She is the braunch of true nobilitie,                              530
Belov'd of high and low with faithfull harts.
Ne lesse praisworthie *Stella* do I read,
Though nought my praises of her needed arre,
Whome verse of noblest shepheard lately dead
Hath prais'd and rais'd above each other starre.                  535
Ne lesse praisworthie are the sisters three,
The honor of the noble familie:
Of which I meanest boast my selfe to be,
And most that unto them I am so nie.
*Phyllis, Charillis*, and sweet *Amaryllis*,                      540
*Phyllis* the faire, is eldest of the three:
The next to her, is bountifull *Charillis*.
But th'youngest is the highest in degree.
*Phyllis* the floure of rare perfection,
Faire spreading forth her leaves with fresh delight,              545
That with their beauties amorous reflexion,
Bereave of sense each rash beholders sight.
But sweet *Charillis* is the Paragone
Of peerlesse price, and ornament of praise,
Admyr'd of all, yet envied of none,                               550

526. *the . . . Shure*: modern Suir.      532. *Stella*: the lady addressed in
Sidney's *Astrophil and Stella*, whom Sp wrongly identifies in the Dedication
to *Ast* as Sidney's wife, Frances Walsingham. See *Ast*, note to line 55, and
Friedrich (1936).      536–70. Phyllis, Charillis, and sweet Amaryllis are
Elizabeth, Anne, and Alice, the second, fifth, and sixth daughters of Sir John
Spencer of Althorp. Sp claimed relation with the Spencers and in the
*Complaints* volume he dedicated *Mui* to Elizabeth, *MHT* to Anne, and *TM* to
Alice.      544. *Phyllis*: Elizabeth Spencer, Lady Carey. The leaf and flower
imagery that follows plays with the name (Gk *phyllis*, foliage).
546. *reflexion*: image.      548. *Charillis*: Anne Spencer, Lady Compton and
Monteagle. On 4 September 1591 she married Robert Sackville who is the
"noble swaine" (552) celebrated here.

Through the myld temperance of her goodly raies.
Thrise happie do I hold thee noble swaine,
The which art of so rich a spoile possest,
And it embracing deare without disdaine,
Hast sole possession in so chaste a brest:     555
Of all the shepheards daughters which there bee,
And yet there be the fairest under skie,
Or that elsewhere I ever yet did see,
A fairer Nymph yet never saw mine eie:
She is the pride and primrose of the rest,     560
Made by the maker selfe to be admired:
And like a goodly beacon high addrest,
That is with sparks of heavenle beautie fired.
But *Amaryllis*, whether fortunate,
Or else unfortunate may I aread,     565
That freed is from *Cupids* yoke by fate,
Since which she doth new bands adventure dread.
Shepheard what ever thou has heard to be
In this or that praysd diversly apart,
In her thou maist them all assembled see,     570
And seald up in the threasure of her hart.
Ne thee lesse worthie gentle *Flavia*,
For thy chaste life and vertue I esteeme:
Ne thee lesse worthie curteous *Candida*,
For thy true love and loyaltie I deeme.     575
Besides yet many mo that *Cynthia* serve,

560. *primrose*: the primrose or cowslip is the earliest rose, but Sp puns on the
Lat. *primus*, foremost. Cf. E. K.'s gloss on "primrose" in *SC* "September"
166: "the chiefe and worthiest."    562. *addrest*: raised.    564. *Amaryllis*:
Alice Spencer, recent widow of Ferdinando Stanley, Lord Strange
("Amyntas" of 433–43).    572–75. "It is possible that Flavia and Candida
are thus introduced to obviate injured feelings among the ladies of the court
who might feel they ought to be mentioned: a maiden might wish to
recognize herself in Flavia, a matron in Candida or a blonde in Candida and a
brunette in Flavia. The characterizations such as they are are general enough
to cover all cases" (*Var.* VII Pt.1 p.477).    572. *Flavia*: Lat. yellow,
blond.    574. *Candida*: Lat. shining, white.

Right noble Nymphs, and high to be commended:
But if I all should praise as they deserve,
This sun would faile me ere I halfe had ended.
Therefore in closure of a thankfull mynd,      580
I deeme it best to hold eternally,
Their bounteous deeds and noble favours shrynd,
Then by discourse them to indignifie.
  So having said, *Aglaura* him bespake:
*Colin*, well worthie were those goodly favours      585
Bestowd on thee, that so of them doest make,
And them requitest with thy thankfull labours.
But of great *Cynthiaes* goodnesse and high grace,
Finish the storie which thou hast begunne.
  More eath (quoth he) it is in such a case      590
How to begin, then know how to have donne.
For everie gift and everie goodly meed,
Which she on me bestowd, demaunds a day;
And everie day, in which she did a deed,
Demaunds a yeare it duly to display.      595
Her words were like a streame of honny fleeting,
The which doth softly trickle from the hive:
Hable to melt the hearers heart unweeting,
And eke to make the dead againe alive.
Her deeds were like great clusters of ripe grapes,      600

583. *indignifie*: dishonor.    590–615. This praise, with its many echoes of
the Old Testament, touches on a common theme in eulogies of Elizabeth, the
discussion of the queen as a female Solomon. See Johnson (1981) pp. 75–82.
596–99. *Her . . . honny*: Honey is traditionally associated with the word of
God. Cf. Psalms 119.103: "How swete are thy promises unto my mouth!
*yea*, more then honie unto my mouth." See also Proverbs 16.24; Song of
Songs 4.11.    596. *fleeting*: flowing.    598. *unweeting*: unconsciously,
without the hearer being fully aware of what has happened.
599. This line echoes the early praise of Colin who has revived the Irish
landscape: both poet and ruler in their different ways mediate between divine
truth and earthly existence.    600–03. Cf. John 15.5, 8: "I am the vine, ye
are the branches: he that abydeth in me, and I in him, the same bringeth
forthe muche frute. For without me, can ye do nothing. . . . Herein is my
Father glorified, that ye beare much frute, and be made my disciples."

Which load the bunches of the fruitfull vine:
Offring to fall into each mouth that gapes,
And fill the same with store of timely wine.
Her lookes were like beames of the morning Sun,
Forth looking through the windowes of the East:       605
When first the fleecie cattell have begun
Upon the perled grasse to make their feast.
Her thoughts are like the fume of Franckincence,
Which from a golden Censer forth doth rise:
And throwing forth sweet odours mounts fro thence     610
In rolling globes up to the vauted skies.
There she beholds with high aspiring thought,
The cradle of her owne creation:
Emongst the seats of Angels heavenly wrought,
Much like an Angell in all forme and fashion.         615
    *Colin* (said *Cuddy* then) thou hast forgot
Thy selfe, me seemes, too much, to mount so hie:
Such loftie flight, base shepheard seemeth not,
From flocks and fields, to Angels and to skie.
    True (answered he) but her great excellence,       620
Lifts me above the measure of my might:
That being fild with furious insolence,
I feele my selfe like one yrapt in spright.
For when I thinke of her, as oft I ought,
Then want I words to speake it fitly forth:           625
And when I speake of her what I have thought,

603: *timely wine*: seasonable or opportune, but punning perhaps on the association of earthly (as opposed to eternal) wine. Cf. also Psalms 1.3 where the just man will be "like a tre planted by the rivers of waters, that wil bring forthe her frute in due season." Cf. Song of Songs 2.13.     606. *fleecie cattell*: i.e. sheep.     611. *vauted*: vaulted.     613. *The cradle*: i.e. in heaven.     615. *fashion*: bearing.     616–17. *forgot/ Thy selfe*: The high style of Cynthia's praise contrasts with Colin's pastoral humility.     618. *seemeth*: befits.     621. *measure*: limit.     622. *furious insolence*: i.e. inspired exultation, the divine madness which possesses poets, raising them to unusual heights of eloquence. See Edwards (1971) pp.53–54.     623. *yrapt in spright*: enraptured.

I cannot thinke according to her worth.
Yet will I thinke of her, yet will I speake,
So long as life my limbs doth hold together,
And when as death these vitall bands shall breake,         630
Her name recorded I will leave for ever.
Her name in every tree I will endosse,
That as the trees do grow, her name may grow:
And in the ground each where will it engrosse,
And fill with stones, that all men may it know.            635
The speaking woods and murmuring waters fall,
Her name Ile teach in knowen termes to frame:
And eke my lambs when for their dams they call,
Ile teach to call for *Cynthia* by name.
And long while after I am dead and rotten:                 640
Amongst the shepheards daughters dancing rownd,
My layes made of her shall not be forgotten,
But sung by them with flowry gyrlonds crownd.
And ye, who so ye be, that shall survive:
When as ye heare her memory renewed,                      645
Be witnesse of her bountie here alive,
Which she to *Colin* her poore shepheard shewed.
    Much was the whole assembly of those heards,
Moov'd at his speech, so feelingly he spake:
And stood awhile astonisht at his words,                  650
Till *Thestylis* at last their silence brake,
Saying, Why *Colin*, since thou foundst such grace
With *Cynthia* and all her noble crew:
Why didst thou ever leave that happie place,
In which such wealth might unto thee accrew?              655
And back returnedst to this barrein soyle,
Where cold and care and penury do dwell:
Here to keep sheepe, with hunger and with toyle,

627. *thinke*: i.e. express, unless Colin means that the act of expressing the
earlier vision dims that vision.    632. *endosse*: inscribe.    634. *each where*:
everywhere *engrosse*: write in large letters.    635. *fill*: i.e. fill in the letters.

Most wretched he, that is and cannot tell.
    Happie indeed (said *Colin*) I him hold,         660
That may that blessed presence still enjoy,
Of fortune and of envy uncomptrold,
Which still are wont most happie states t'annoy:
But I by that which little while I prooved:
Some part of those enormities did see,         665
The which in Court continually hooved,
And followd those which happie seemd to bee.
Therefore I silly man, whose former dayes
Had in rude fields bene altogether spent,
Darest not adventure such unknowen wayes,         670
Nor trust the guile of fortunes blandishment,
But rather chose back to my sheep to tourne,
Whose utmost hardnesse I before had tryde,
Then having learnd repentance late, to mourne
Emongst those wretches which I there descryde.         675
    Shepheard (said *Thestylis*) it seemes of spight
Thou speakest thus gainst their felicitie,
Which thou enviest, rather then of right
That ought in them blameworthie thou doest spie.
    Cause have I none (quoth he) of cancred will         680
To quite them ill, that me demeand so well:
But selfe-regard of private good or ill,
Moves me of each, so as I found, to tell
And eke to warne yong shepheards wandring wit,
Which through report of that lives painted blisse,         685
Abandon quiet home, to seeke for it,

---

659. "I take this to mean, most wretched he, that is wretched and cannot tell
why" (Renwick 1929:189).     664. *prooved*: experienced.     666. *hooved*:
arose, possibly punning on the shortened form of "behoove", to be fitting. It
is only at court that *enormities* (things beyond the norm) could be
fitting.     667. *followd*: i.e. afflicted.     668. *silly*: innocent.     670. Cf.
line 211. *adventure*: venture upon.     673. *hardness*: severity.     678. *of
right*: with reason.     682. *selfe-regard . . . ill*: i.e. concern for good or ill
done to me.

And leave their lambes to losse misled amisse.
For sooth to say, it is no sort of life,
For shepheard fit to lead in that same place,
Where each one seeks with malice and with strife,  690
To thrust downe other into foule disgrace,
Himselfe to raise: and he doth soonest rise
That best can handle his deceitfull wit,
In subtil shifts, and finest slights devise,
Either by slaundring his well deemed name,  695
Through leasings lewd and fained forgerie:
Or else by breeding him some blot of blame,
By creeping close into his secrecie;
To which him needs, a guilefull hollow hart,
Masked with faire dissembling curtesie,  700
A filed toung furnisht with tearmes of art,
No art of schoole, but Courtiers schoolery.
For arts of schoole have there small countenance,
Counted but toyes to busie ydle braines:
And there professours find small maintenance,  705
But to be instruments of others gaines.
Ne is there place for any gentle wit,
Unlesse to please, it selfe it can applie:
But shouldred is, or out of doore quite shit,
As base, or blunt, unmeet for melodie.  710

694–95. "There is apparently a line missing between these two. If it ran
some such way as *"His neighbor to supplant with means unfit"* then *his* in line
695, *him* in 697, would refer to the noun in the missing line. But the
unrhymed line may be a mere oversight and *his, him* may refer to *other* in
691; or, as is more likely, the pronouns are used absolutely as *one man's* and
*another man"* (Renwick 1929:189).  697. *breeding*: causing.
698. *secrecie*: confidence.  701. *filed*: smooth. See *FQ* I i 35 7. There is a
possible pun on "defiled." *tearmes of art*: artful language. The more usual
meaning of "technical expression" is contradicted by the next line.
702. *art of schoole*: learning. *schoolery*: education.  703. *countenance*:
estimation.  705. *professours*: i.e. those who would teach or practice arts of
school.  707. *wit*: learned man.  708. Cf. *FQ* VI xii 41 9.
709. *shouldred*: thrust aside *shit*: shut.  710. *unmeet*: unsuited.

For each mans worth is measured by his weed,
As harts by hornes, or asses by their eares:
Yet asses been not all whose eares exceed,
Nor yet all harts, that hornes the highest beares.
For highest lookes have not the highest mynd,                715
Nor haughtie words most full of highest thoughts:
But are like bladders blowen up with wynd,
That being prickt do vanish into noughts.
Even such is all their vaunted vanitie,
Nought else but smoke, that fumeth soone away,              720
Such is their glorie that in simple eie
Seeme greatest, when their garments are most gay.
So they themselves for praise of fooles do sell,
And all their wealth for painting on a wall;
With price whereof, they buy a golden bell,                 725
And purchace highest rowmes in bowre and hall:
Whiles single Truth and simple honestie
Do wander up and downe despys'd of all;
Their plaine attire such glorious gallantry
Disdaines so much, that none them in doth call.             730
    Ah *Colin* (then said *Hobbinol*) the blame
Which thou imputest, is too generall,
As if not any gentle wit of name,
Nor honest mynd might there be found at all.
For well I wot, sith I my selfe was there,                  735
To wait on *Lobbin* (*Lobbin* well thou knewest)
Full many worthie ones then waiting were,
As ever else in Princes Court thou vewest.
Of which, among you many yet remaine,

711–30. This passage invokes the familiar biblical topic of worldly greatness
overturned: "for whosoever wil exalt him self, shalbe broght low: and
whosoever wil humble him self shalbe exalted" (Matthew 23.12).
719. Landrum (1926) notes Psalms 68.2: "As the smoke vanisheth, so shalt
thou drive them awaie."    726. *bowre*: bedchamber.    727. *single*: plain,
honest.    736. *Lobbin*: possibly Robert Dudley, earl of Leicester, who had
died in 1588, hence the tense of "knewest."    738. *else*: elsewhere.

Whose names I cannot readily now ghesse:                          740
Those that poore Sutors papers do retaine,
And those that skill of medicine professe.
And those that do to Cynthia expound
The ledden of straunge languages in charge:
For *Cynthia* doth in sciences abound,                           745
And gives to their professors stipends large.
Therefore unjustly thou doest wyte them all,
For that which thou mislikedst in a few.
  Blame is (quoth he) more blamelesse generall,
Than that which private errours doth pursew:                     750
For well I wot, that there amongst them bee
Full many persons of right worthie parts,
Both for report of spotlesse honestie,
And for profession of all learned arts,
Whose praise hereby no whit impaired is,                         755
Though blame do light on those that faultie bee,
For all the rest do most-what fare amis,
And yet their owne misfaring will not see:
For either they be puffed up with pride,
Or fraught with envie that their galls do swell,                 760
Or they their dayes to ydlenesse divide,
Or drownded lie in pleasures wastefull well,
In which like Moldwarps nousling still they lurke,
Unmyndfull of chiefe parts of manlinesse,
And do themselves for want of other worke,                       765
Vaine votaries of laesie love professe,
Whose service high so basely they ensew,

---

741. *those . . . retaine*: i.e. intermediaries. *retaine*: remember.     744. *ledden*:
form (of speech). *in charge*: as a responsibility.     745. *sciences*: knowledge
(Lat. *scientia*).     747. *wyte*: blame.     749. Satiric condemnation is proper
when it attacks vices without naming individuals. A commonplace: cf. *As You
Like It* 2.7.70–87.     750. *private*: individual.     757. *most-what*: for the
most part.     761. *divide*: allocate.     763. *Moldwarps nousling*: moles
nuzzling. Moles are traditionally blind and lazy, creatures of the earth. *lurke*:
idle.     767. *ensew*: follow.

That *Cupid* selfe of them ashamed is,
And mustring all his men in *Venus* vew,
Denies them quite for servitors of his.                    770
　　And is love then (said *Corylas*) once knowne
In Court, and his sweet lore professed there?
I weened sure he was our God alone:
And only woond in fields and forests here.
　　Not so (quoth he) love most aboundeth there.          775
For all the walls and windows there are writ,
All full of love, and love, and love my deare,
And all their talke and studie is of it.
Ne any there doth brave or valiant seeme,
Unlesse that some gay Mistresse badge he beares:          780
Ne any one himselfe doth ought esteeme,
Unlesse he swim in love up to the eares.
But they of love and of his sacred lere,
(As it should be) all otherwise devise,
Then we poore shepheards are accustomd here,             785
And him do sue and serve all otherwise.
For with lewd speeches and licentious deeds,
His mightie mysteries they do prophane,
And use his ydle name to other needs,
But as a complement for courting vaine.                   790
So him they do not serve as they professe,
But make him serve to them for sordid uses,
Ah my dread Lord, that doest liege hearts possesse,
Avenge thy selfe on them for their abuses.

771. *once*: ever.　　772. *lore*: teaching *professed*: acknowledged.
774. *woond*: dwelt.　　776. *writ*: engraved, carved.　　778. *studie*: thought,
with an ironic invocation of the still current Latinate meaning, "zeal,
devotion."　　780. *badge*: i.e. token.　　781. *ought*: aught.　　786. *sue and
serve*: follow as servant.　　787. *lewd*: Here the obvious meaning of
"unchaste" is intensified by the older meaning of "not clerical": love is, after
all, a god whose mysteries these laymen profane.　　790. *complement*:
personal accomplishment. *courting*: pun on "wooing" and "acting like a
courtier."　　792. *uses*: purposes.　　793. *liege*: loyal.　　794. *abuses*:
violations (of love's laws).

But we poore shepheards whether rightly so,        795
Or through our rudenesse into errour led,
Do make religion how we rashly go,
To serve that God, that is so greatly dred;
For him the greatest of the Gods we deeme,
Borne without Syre or couples of one kynd,        800
For *Venus* selfe doth soly couples seeme,
Both male and female through commixture joynd.
So pure and spotlesse *Cupid* forth she brought,
And in the gardens of *Adonis* nurst:
Where growing, he his own perfection wrought,        805
And shortly was of all the Gods the first.
Then got he bow and shafts of gold and lead,
In which so fell and puissant he grew,
That *Jove* himselfe his powre began to dread,
And taking up to heaven, him godded new.        810
From thence he shootes his arrowes every where
Into the world, at randon as he will,
On us fraile men, his wretched vassals here,
Like as himselfe us pleaseth, save or spill.
So we him worship, so we him adore        815
With humble hearts to heaven uplifted hie,
That to true loves he may us evermore
Preferre, and of their grace us dignifie:

797. *Do . . . go*: are scrupulously careful about the ways in which we may act
rashly.    799–822. The Cupid of this description derives primarily from
the imperious love-god of medieval poetry, though he is the offspring of a
bisexual Venus like that of *FQ* IV x 411.    800. *couples*: sexual union.
*kynd*: nature, i.e. Venus's nature.    801. *soly*: alone. *couples*: a pair.
805. *perfection*: full development.    807: The gold shaft traditionally causes
the victim to love; the leaden one causes him to hate. Alternately they
symbolize happy and unhappy love.    810. *godded*: deified.    812. *randon*:
i.e. random.    814. *Like . . . spill*: Just as it pleases him to do with us,
sparing or destroying.    816. The paradox of elevation through humility
appears throughout this section and contrasts with the description of the
court.    818. *Preferre*: advance.    *grace*: favor, with possibly the
implication of "divine influence."    *dignifie*: make worthy. The line can be
read as either: "ennoble us by means of their gracious influence" or "make us
worthy of their grace."

Ne is there shepheard, ne yet shepheards swaine,
What ever feeds in forest or in field,                    820
That dare with evil deed or leasing vaine
Blaspheme his powre, or termes unworthie yield.
  Shepheard it seemes that some celestiall rage
Of love (quoth *Cuddy*) is breath'd into thy brest,
That powreth forth these oracles so sage,                 825
Of that high powre, wherewith thou art possest.
  But never wist I till this present day
Albe of love I alwayes humbly deemed,
That he was such an one, as thou doest say,
And so religiously to be esteemed.                        830
  Well may it seeme by this thy deep insight,
That of that God the Priest thou shouldest bee:
So well thou wot'st the mysterie of his might,
As if his godhead thou didst present see.
  Of loves perfection perfectly to speake,               835
Or of his nature rightly to define,
Indeed (said *Colin*) passeth reasons reach,
And needs his priest t'expresse his powre divine.
  For long before the world he was y'bore
And bred above in *Venus* bosome deare:                  840
For by his powre the world was made of yore,
And all that therein wondrous doth appeare.
  For how should else things so far from attone

---

822. *termes*: words.    *yield*: utter.    823. *celestiall rage*: the Neoplatonic
furor or divine madness which inspires the poet's eloquence. Cf. Ficino,
*Commentary on Plato's Symposium* 7.13–14, and Yates (1947), pp.79–94.
826. *possest*: divinely controlled.    833. *wot'st*: know. *mysterie*: divine
truth.    835–94. The Cupid that emerges here is a creator-god, responsible
for the making of the world. Ellrodt (1960:19–23, 222) argues, partly on
grounds of its versification, that this more explicitly Neoplatonic passage was
added shortly before the poem was published. In this syncretic description Sp
brings together what were already reconciled in medieval cosmogonies, a
biblical view of creation (855–70) and Pythagorean and Stoic commonplaces
about creation as the harmonization of warring elements. See *HL* 67–119 for
a more explicitly Neoplatonic version of this process.    843. *attone*: at one,
state of concord.

And so great enemies as of them bee,
Be ever drawne together into one,                                           845
And taught in such accordance to agree?
Through him the cold began to covet heat,
And water fire; the light to mount on hie,
And th'heavie downe to peize; the hungry t'eat
And voydnesse to seeke full satietie.                                        850
So being former foes, they wexed friends,
And gan by litle learne to love each other:
So being knit, they brought forth other kynds
Out of the fruitfull wombe of their great mother.
Then first gan heaven out of darknesse dread                                 855
For to appeare, and brought forth chearfull day:
Next gan the earth to shew her naked head,
Out of deep waters which her drownd alway.
And shortly after everie living wight,
Crept forth like wormes out of her slimie nature,                           860

844. *And . . . bee,*: i.e. [how should things] which are such great enemies of
one another. . . .     846. *accordance*: concord. The musical dimension of the
idea is stressed by "agree".     847–54. One can understand this passage
more clearly by reference to the fuller account in *HL*. There Love first
*distinguishes* the various elements which have lain "confused ever" (*HL* 77) in
chaos; the elements, as soon as they are separate, begin to war on each other
until Love "tempering goodly well/ Their contrary dislikes and loved
meanes,/ Did place them all in order. . ." (*HL* 85–87). Contrary elements
like water and fire find "meanes" in the intervening elements of earth and air
because these intervening elements bring together some qualities of each
contrary. Air, for instance, which is hot and moist, shares with fire (hot and
dry) the quality of heat and with water (cold and moist) the quality of
moistness. Colin touches on the distinguishing of the elements in lines 847–
50 when they take their places in the cosmic hierarchy and on the
overcoming of their enmity in lines 851–54 when they "knit" their opposites
in harmonious union, creating the world we know. But the passage does not
attempt to separate the two stages very clearly. In this elliptical description
Love becomes the binding force of the world, analogous to the Concord of
*FQ* IV x 31–36. Like Concord, Love develops out of and remains dependent
on an original and continuing opposition. See Heninger (1974) pp.149–51,
160–94.     849. *peize*: sink.     854. *their great mother*: i.e. chaos. Cf. *FQ*
III vi 36.     855–66. Cf. Genesis 1.

Soone as on them the Suns life giving light,
Had powred kindly heat and formall feature,
Thenceforth they gan each one his like to love,
And like himselfe desire for to beget,
The Lyon chose his mate, the Turtle Dove                    865
Her deare, the Dolphin his owne Dolphinet,
But man that had the sparke of reasons might,
More then the rest to rule his passion:
Chose for his love the fairest in his sight,
Like as himselfe was fairest by creation.                   870
For beautie is the bayt which with delight
Doth man allure, for to enlarge his kynd,
Beautie the burning lamp of heavens light,
Darting her beames into each feeble mynd:
Against whose powre, nor God nor man can fynd               875
Defence, ne ward the daunger of the wound,
But being hurt, seeke to be medicynd
Of her that first did stir that mortall stownd.
Then do they cry and call to love apace,
With praiers lowd importuning the skie,                     880
Whence he them heares, and when he list shew grace,
Does graunt them grace that otherwise would die.
So love is Lord of all the world by right,
And rules the creatures by his powrfull saw:
All being made the vassalls of his might,                   885
Through secret sence which therto doth them draw.
Thus ought all lovers of their lord to deeme:

861. For the sun as a bestower of life and form see Ovid, *Met* 1.416–37, and
*FQ* III vi 8.    872. *enlarge his kynd*: multiply his race. In the larger context
of Colin's love for Rosalind, the phrase may mean "expand his nature." Such
a reading is reemphasized by the next two lines with their stress on spiritual
growth.    878. *stir*: excite.    *mortall*: at once "deadly" and "human."
884. *saw*: command.    886. *secret sence*: inward faculties of perception. The
phrase admits of a specifically sexual interpretation (=sexual desire), or in the
context of Colin's love-theology an entirely spiritual one (=spiritual
awareness).

And with chaste heart to honor him alway:
But who so else doth otherwise esteeme,
Are outlawes, and his lore do disobay. 890
For their desire is base, and doth not merit,
The name of love, but of disloyall lust:
Ne mongst true lovers they shall place inherit,
But as Exuls out of his court be thrust.

So having said, *Melissa* spake at will, 895
*Colin*, thou now full deeply hast divynd:
Of love and beautie and with wondrous skill,
Hast *Cupid* selfe depainted in his kynd.
To thee are all true lovers greatly bound,
That doest their cause so mightily defend: 900
But most, all wemen are thy debtors found,
That doest their bountie still so much commend.

That ill (said *Hobbinol*) they him requite,
For having loved ever one most deare:
He is repayd with scorne and foule despite, 905
That yrkes each gentle heart which it doth heare.

Indeed (said *Lucid*) I have often heard
Faire *Rosalind* of divers fowly blamed:
For being to that swaine too cruell hard,
That her bright glorie else hath much defamed. 910
But who can tell what cause had that faire Mayd
To use him so that used her so well:
Or who with blame can justly her upbrayd,
For loving not? for who can love compell?
And sooth to say, it is foolhardie thing, 915
Rashly to wyten creatures so divine,
For demigods they be and first did spring
From heaven, though graft in frailnesse feminine.

---

893. *inherit*: receive. 896. *divynd*: explained, with a pun on "acted the divine." 910. *That*: i.e. Colin. *defamed*: proclaimed. 916. *wyten*: blame. 918. *graft*: planted. The soul is transplanted into the matter of the body which is imagined as female, earthly, and weak. Cf. *FQ* VI Proem 3.

And well I wote, that oft I heard it spoken,
How one that fairest *Helene* did revile: 920
Through judgement of the Gods to been ywroken
Lost both his eyes and so remaynd long while,
Till he recanted had his wicked rimes,
And made amends to her with treble praise:
Beware therefore, ye groomes, I read betimes, 925
How rashly blame of *Rosalind* ye raise.
  Ah shepheards (then said *Colin*) ye ne weet
How great a guilt upon your heads ye draw:
To make so bold a doome with words unmeet,
Of thing celestiall which ye never saw. 930
For she is not like as the other crew
Of shepheards daughters which emongst you bee,
But of divine regard and heavenly hew,
Excelling all that ever ye did see.
Not then to her that scorned thing so base, 935
But to my selfe the blame that lookt so hie:
So hie her thoughts as she her selfe have place,
And loath each lowly thing with loftie eie.
Yet so much grace let her vouchsafe to grant
To simple swaine, sith her I may not love: 940
Yet that I may her honour paravant,
And praise her worth, though far my wit above.
Such grace shall be some guerdon for the griefe,
And long affliction which I have endured:
Such grace sometimes shall give me some reliefe, 945

919–23. Socrates tells the story of Stesichorus's blindness and his recantation
in Plato's *Phaedrus* 343, and it became a commonplace. It appears, for
instance, in Bembo's speech in the Fourth Book of Castiglione's *The
Courtier*.    920. *Helene*: Helen of Troy.    921. *ywroken*: punished.
925. *read*: counsel. *betimes*: before it is too late.    929. *doome*:
judgment.    933. *regard*: appearance.    937. *her thoughts*: thoughts of
her.    938. *loath*: loathsome. The "lowly thing with lofty eye" is Colin for
whom full love of Rosalind amounts to a kind of overreaching.
939. *grace*: mercy.    941. *paravant*: above all others.    943. *guerdon*:
recompense.

And ease of paine which cannot be recured.
And ye my fellow shepheards which do see
And heare the languours of my too long dying,
Unto the world for ever witnesse bee,
That hers I die, nought to the world denying,                950
This simple trophe of her great conquest.
　So having ended, he from ground did rise,.
And after him uprose eke all the rest:
All loth to part, but that the glooming skies
Warnd them to draw their bleating flocks to rest.            955

FINIS.

946. *recured*: cured.　　950. *nought*: not at all.　　951. *trophe*: memorial.
952–55. A traditional eclogue-ending. Cf. Virgil *Ecl* 10.75–77 and the
endings to "Januarye" and "March" in *SC*.

# *Astrophel*
# *and*
# *The Doleful Lay of Clorinda*

I f *Colin Clouts Come Home Againe* makes a case for a pastoral
retreat from court, it is balanced by the second half of the
volume which deals with the death of a military hero. The
*Astrophel*-book is a series of elegies by various hands for Sir
Philip Sidney, whose Protestant zeal at court and eventual death
in the low countries had made him a legend. Sidney was given
one of the most elaborate funerals of the Elizabethan period and
there was an outpouring of poetical lament at the time, and so
it is puzzling that Spenser and his collaborators should have
waited nine years to publish or perhaps even to write their own
elegies. Yet Sidney may have been on Spenser's mind for several
reasons. As a poet-courtier, albeit one much more highly born,
Sidney would embody (like Ralegh) a life of courtly engage-
ment, and Spenser's early career was associated with that of
Leicester and his circle. Sidney had been part of the world which
Colin renounces.

Spenser's connection with the Sidney circle may also figure
also in his uncertain relation to the second poem in the elegy-
book. While Spenser wrote *Astrophel*, the narrative which gives
its name to the group and acts as a frame for the whole, it is
unclear whether he also composed the following elegy, *The
Doleful Lay of Clorinda*. The narrator of *Astrophel* ascribes the *Lay*
to Astrophel's sister, whose biographical counterpart would be
Mary Sidney, countess of Pembroke, and the countess, a transla-
tor with her brother of the Psalms, might well have written a
poem like the *Lay*. But the phrasing and versification recall

# ASTROPHEL.

## A Paſtorall Elegie vpon
the death of the moſt Noble and valorous
Knight, Sir *Philip Sidney.*

## Dedicated

*T o the moſt beautifull and vertuous Ladie, the Counteſſe
of* Eſſex.

Spenser's. Perhaps the *Lay* was a joint endeavor, for, whoever composed it, it is linked to *Astrophel* in many ways. Together the two poems form contrasting parts of a complex whole, and their unity of idea is reinforced by common motifs, a shared verse-form (the familiar sexain rhyming *ababcc*), and a numerological program.

As Michael O'Connell (1971) first demonstrated, *Astrophel* and *The Doleful Lay* create a diptych presenting two attitudes toward death and two kinds of consolation. The narrator of *Astrophel* is a shepherd in the tradition of classical pastoral: the only solace he can find is that afforded by Astrophel's poetry and symbolized by the flower which remains after he dies. The speaker of *The Doleful Lay*, on the other hand, follows the familiar path of Christian pastoral elegy, beginning in despondency and ending with the consolation of divine hope. Spenser had used the opposition before: *The Ruines of Time*, in which Sidney also figures importantly, opposes the despondent pagan lament of Verlame to the Christian vision of the poem's narrator. In *Astrophel* Spenser places the opposition in a pastoral context, using the shepherd-narrator to dramatize a misunderstanding of Astrophel's death.

This narrator is unable to see Astrophel's fate as more than proof of the instability of human happiness. His account blames the "cruell skies" (113) or, alternately, the shepherd's bad luck. His initial description of Astrophel states that the shepherd excelled others in all things save "That he was not so happie as the rest" (12). Astrophel's lack of happiness is not a lack of joy: his Stella accepts him and his peers give him reverence. He is unhappy because he is unlucky: the fact of his subsequent mishap darkens the early description. (A similar pun appears again when the narrator comments that he has "such felicitie,/ Or rather infelicitie" [79–80] in hunting that he pursues it constantly. The Latinate meaning of *felix* as "lucky" is very much present.) At his death Astrophel is thus a "lucklesse boy" (142), an instance of the chanciness of human affairs.

Renaissance readers trained to see God's hand in all events

would be likely to notice the discrepancy between their assumptions and the narrator's, and they might notice another discrepancy in the narrator's inability to understand Astrophel's desire to hunt. "What needeth perill to be sought abroad" he asks, "Since round about us, it doth make abroad?" (89–90). He describes Astrophel addressing himself "greedily" to the slaughter of the beasts he has captured with a tone of unmistakable reproof: "Ill mynd so much to mynd anothers ill,/ As to become unmyndfull of his owne" (111–12). The shepherd of classical pastoral is fundamentally different from the hunter: he is a herdsman enjoying his peaceful leisure by making music in the shade of a strategically-placed tree, or perhaps by dancing or engaging in inoffensive community games. Even in the less friendly pastoral surroundings of *The Shepheardes Calender* the shepherd may have a dog to keep off wolves, but he does not engage in the chase. A shepherd who does spend his time hunting is, to the narrator, simply inexplicable. Astrophel is indeed not an ordinary shepherd: he belongs to a less peaceful and more heroic world.

The meaning of Astrophel's hunting is further illuminated by the literary traditions of the Adonis myth and by the episode's relation to Sidney's biography. Spenser chose to model his elegy on the myth of Adonis, Venus's beloved who hunts a boar against her advice and is slain by it. The myth was a popular one in the Renaissance (see for instance Allen 1968:44–57). Spenser certainly knew Ovid's treatment of it in the *Metamorphoses* and adapted part of his own version from Ronsard's *Adonis*. In various Renaissance moralizations of the myth the "hard hunt" of the beast was opposed and morally superior to the "soft hunt" of love. The opposition appears strikingly in Spenser's treatment of the myth in Malecasta's tapestry (*FQ* III i 34–38) where it suggests the dangers of a love that distracts one from a life of adult responsibility in the world. Venus keeps Adonis "in secret shade," attempting to protect him from the dangers of the chase, but in doing so she keeps him a mere "Boy"

(*FQ* III i 35). By implication Astrophel's hunting is a necessary concomitant of manhood.

Further, his death possesses a meaning which would be beyond the pagan narrator's understanding. For the biographical parallel to Astrophel's fatal hunt is Sidney's death in battle against Spanish forces at Zutphen, and with that death Sidney became for his co-religionists a quasi-mythical figure, an ideal Protestant knight. His motive for fighting Elizabeth's wars was not only love of glory as the narrator implies (85–90) but love of God. The narrator's pastoral incomprehension of Astrophel's hunting becomes an analogue to the response of any reader unable to see Sidney's divinely-appointed role, or to acknowledge God's purposes in earthly events. Spenser thus makes the contrasts between the materials of his poem—pastoral elegy, the Adonis myth, the legend of Sidney's life—the basis for its meaning. The same attention to significant opposition characterizes the relation between *Colin Clouts Come Home Againe* and the *Astrophel* diptych. If in *Colin Clout* the simple pastoral community provides a standard by which to judge the court, in *Astrophel* its values—innocent gaity, peaceful contemplation— are themselves judged by the severe standard of God's service in the world.

Where *Astrophel* is narrative, the *Doleful Lay* is lyric, and presents a more immediately passionate reaction to Astrophel's death. It functions within the group of elegies as the first of the individual laments for which *Astrophel* acts as a frame and, in relation to *Astrophel*, as a corrective to its limited "pagan" vision. At the opening of the lament Clorinda's mourning leaves her even more desolate than the narrator of *Astrophel*. Her grief isolates her both from the heavens which have willed Astrophel's death, and from men who have no power to comfort her. Yet, though she resolves to sing her lament for herself only, she soon moves beyond herself to address the shepherd lasses who have also loved Astrophel (37–48), and eventually to speak for other mortals as she blesses Astrophel and laments the instability of earthly things. She has now had a vision of a world beyond the present one, in which it is possible to find "Sweet love still joyous, never feeling paine" (82). With this new vision the crucial word of the earlier poem returns transformed: "But live thou there still happie, happie spirit" (91). Here is a happiness which has nothing to do with luck, and which is full because it is "still"—unthreatened by the possibility of its ever ending. Secure in her knowledge of Astrophel's happiness, Clorinda can now recognize the human self-centeredness of her grief, blessing her brother and bidding him farewell.

The movement from a limited view to a more comprehensive one is quietly emphasized by the poem's numerology. After the three-stanza Proem which introduces them both, *Astrophel* has 216 lines (36 stanzas) and its sequel 108 lines (18 stanzas), forming a ratio of 2:1. Two is a number associated with the falsehood and uncertainty of this world; three with divine harmony. Clorinda's lay perfects what is imperfect in the previous poem, moving from the disharmonies of this world toward the perfection of eternity.

The present edition prints only the two poems in which Spenser may have had a part. The other elegies in the book—by Spenser's friend and superior in the Irish administration Lodowick Bryskett, Sidney's friend and biographer Fulke Greville, and Sir Walter Ralegh among others—are not included here.

*William Oram*

# Astrophel.

SHepheards that wont on pipes of oaten reed,
  Oft times to plaine your loves concealed smart:
And with your piteous layes have learnd to breed
Compassion in a countrey lasses hart.
Hearken ye gentle shepheards to my song,                    5
And place my dolefull plaint your plaints emong.

To you alone I sing this mournfull verse,
The mournfulst verse that ever man heard tell:
To you whose softened hearts it may empierse,
With dolours dart for death of Astrophel.                   10
To you I sing and to none other wight,
For well I wot my rymes bene rudely dight.

Yet as they been, if any nycer wit
Shall hap to heare, or covet them to read:
Thinke he, that such are for such ones most fit,            15
Made not to please the living but the dead.
And if in him found pity ever place,
Let him be moov'd to pity such a case.

T I T L E :    *Astrophel's* name derives from the name of the protagonist of
Sidney's sonnet sequence *Astrophil and Stella*. The change in the vowel quietly
substitutes for the aspiration implicit in the original name ("star-lover") the
suggestion of a star fallen, or perhaps the picture of one to whom the stars were
cruel (cf. the "cruell skies" of line 113). Sidney is lamented under this
pseudonym in *CCCHA* 449–51.

D E D I C A T I O N :     Frances Walsingham, the countess of Essex in 1595, was
Sidney's widow. See note on line 55, below.

P R O E M :     3. *breed*: cause.    9. *empierse*: pierce.    12. *bene*: are. *dight*:
composed.     13. *nycer wit*: more refined intelligence.

A Gentle Shepheard borne in *Arcady*,
  Of gentlest race that ever shepheard bore:
About the grassie bancks of *Hæmony*,
Did keepe his sheep, his litle stock and store.
Full carefully he kept them day and night,        5
In fairest fields, and *Astrophel* he hight.

Young *Astrophel* the pride of shepheards praise,
Young *Astrophel* the rusticke lasses love:
Far passing all the pastors of his daies,
In all that seemly shepheard might behove.        10
In one thing onely fayling of the best,
That he was not so happie as the rest.

For from the time that first the Nymph his mother
Him forth did bring, and taught her lambs to feed:
A sclender swaine excelling far each other,        15
In comely shape, like her that did him breed.
He grew up fast in goodnesse and in grace,
And doubly faire wox both in mynd and face.

Which daily more and more he did augment,
With gentle usage and demeanure myld:        20
That all mens hearts with secret ravishment
He stole away, and weetingly beguyld.
Ne spight it selfe that all good things doth spill,
Found ought in him, that she could say was ill.

---

1. *Arcady*: Arcadia, section of the Greek Peloponnesis, portrayed in Virgil's
*Eclogues* as a land of shepherds. Sidney was also known as the author of the
*Arcadia*, a massive romance which was first published in 1590, five years
before the appearance of *Astrophel*.    2. *gentlest race*: Sidney's mother was
sister to the earls of Leicester and Warwick, and for most of his life he was
Leicester's heir.    3. *Hæmony*: pastoral name for Greek Thessaly.
9. *pastors*: shepherds.    10. *In . . . behove*: in all that befits a shepherd.
"Seemly" can also mean "handsome."    12. *happie*: fortunate.
20. *usage*: conduct.    22. *weetingly beguyld*: skillfully charmed.    23. *spill*:
destroy, corrupt.

His sports were faire, his joyance innocent,                25
Sweet without sowre, and honny without gall:
And he himselfe seemd made for meriment,
Merily masking both in bowre and hall.
There was no pleasure nor delightfull play,
When *Astrophel* so ever was away.                          30

For he could pipe and daunce, and caroll sweet,
Emongst the shepheards in their shearing feast:
As Somers larke that with her song doth greet
The dawning day forth comming from the East.
And layes of love he also could compose,                    35
Thrise happie she, whom he to praise did chose.

Full many Maydens often did him woo,
Them to vouchsafe emongst his rimes to name,
Or make for them as he was wont to doo,
For her that did his heart with love inflame.               40
For which they promised to dight for him,
Gay chapelets of flowers and gyrlonds trim.

And many a Nymph both of the wood and brooke,
Soone as his oaten pipe began to shrill:
Both christall wells and shadie groves forsooke,            45
To heare the charmes of his enchanting skill.
And brought him presents, flowers if it were prime,
Or mellow fruit if it were harvest time.

But he for none of them did care a whit,
Yet wood Gods for them often sighed sore:                   50
Ne for their gifts unworthie of his wit,
Yet not unworthie of the countries store.

28. *masking*: taking part in a masked dance (an occupation more suitable for a nobleman than a shepherd).   38. *vouchsafe*: agree, permit, condescend. 39. *make*: compose.   41. *dight*: construct.   42. *trim*: elegantly arranged.   46. *charmes*: songs (Lat. *carmen*), but the "enchanting" plays on the magical associations of the word.

For one alone he cared, for one he sight,
His lifes desire, and his deare loves delight.

*Stella* the faire, the fairest star in skie,                    55
As faire as *Venus* or the fairest faire:
A fairer star saw never living eie,
Shot her sharp pointed beames through purest aire.
Her he did love, her he alone did honor,
His thoughts, his rimes, his songs were all upon her.    60

To her he vowd the service of his daies,
On her he spent the riches of his wit:
For her he made hymnes of immortall praise,
Of onely her he sung, he thought, he writ.
Her, and but her of love he worthie deemed,             65
For all the rest but litle he esteemed.

Ne her with ydle words alone he wowed,
And verses vaine (yet verses are not vaine)
But with brave deeds to her sole service vowed,
And bold atchievements her did entertaine.              70
For both in deeds and words he nourtred was,
Both wise and hardie (too hardie alas).

In wrestling nimble, and in renning swift,
In shooting steddie, and in swimming strong:

53. *sight*: i.e. sighed.     55. *Stella*: the lady in Sidney's sonnet sequence, *Astrophil and Stella*. Stella's equivalent in Sidney's actual biography was Penelope Devereux, who was at the time married to Lord Rich. Friedrich (1936) argues convincingly that the identification was not common knowledge until the previously-suppressed sonnets published in the 1598 version of *Astrophil and Stella* made the connection inescapable. Sp (and other writers of the *Astrophel* elegies) seem to have identified Stella with Frances Walsingham, whom Sidney married 21 September 1583. *Astrophel* (unlike the sonnet sequence) presents the hero's love as fully returned, which is explicable if Sp thought Stella had become Astrophil's wife. After Sidney's death Frances Walsingham remarried, becoming the countess of Essex; the *Astrophel* elegies are dedicated to her.     62. *wit*: mind.     65. *deemed*: judged.     67. *wowed*: wooed.     72. *hardie*: daring, bold.

Well made to strike, to throw, to leape, to lift,                    75
And all the sports that shepheards are emong.
In every one he vanquisht every one,
He vanquisht all, and vanquisht was of none.

Besides, in hunting such felicitie,
Or rather infelicitie he found:                                      80
That every field and forest far away,
He sought, where salvage beasts do most abound.
No beast so salvage but he could it kill,
No chace so hard, but he therein had skill.

Such skill matcht with such courage as he had,                       85
Did prick him foorth with proud desire of praise:
To seek abroad, of daunger nought y'drad,
His mistresse name, and his owne fame to raise.
What needeth perill to be sought abroad,
Since round about us, it doth make aboad?                            90

It fortuned, as he that perilous game
In forreine soyle pursued far away:
Into a forest wide, and waste he came
Where store he heard to be of salvage pray.
So wide a forest and so waste as this,                               95
Nor famous *Ardeyn*, nor fowle *Arlo* is.

There his welwoven toyles and subtil traines,
He laid the brutish nation to enwrap:
So well he wrought with practise and with paines,
That he of them great troups did soone entrap.                       100
Full happie man (misweening much) was hee,
So rich a spoile within his power to see.

84. *skill*: capability of accomplishing something with precision and
certainty.      87. *seek*: adventure.      94. *store*: abundance, plenty.
96. *Ardeyn*: the forest of Ardennes. Arlo: the glen of Aherlow, near Sp's
house, Kilcolman, which "Doth to this day with Wolves and Thieves
abound" (*FQ* IV vi 55).      97. *toyles and . . . traines*: nets and lures.
98. *enwrap*: entangle.

Eftsoones all heedlesse of his dearest hale,
Full greedily into the heard he thrust:
To slaughter them, and worke their finall bale,                105
Least that his toyle should of their troups be brust.
Wide wounds emongst them many one he made,
Now with his sharp borespear, now with his blade.

His care was all how he them all might kill,
That none might scape (so partiall unto none)                110
Ill mynd so much to mynd anothers ill,
As to become unmyndfull of his owne.
But pardon that unto the cruell skies,
That from himselfe to them withdrew his eies.

So as he rag'd emongst that beastly rout,                115
A cruell beast of most accursed brood
Upon him turnd (despeyre makes cowards stout)
And with fell tooth accustomed to blood,
Launched his thigh with so mischievous might,
That it both bone and muscles ryved quight.                120

So deadly was the dint and deep the wound,
And so huge streames of blood thereout did flow:
That he endured not the direfull stound,
But on the cold deare earth himselfe did throw.
The whiles the captive heard his nets did rend,                125
And having none to let, to wood did wend.

Ah where were ye this while his shepheard peares,
To whom alive was nought so deare as hee:

103. *all*: entirely. *hale*: health.    104. *greedily*: eagerly.    105. *finall bale*:
death.    106. *brust*: i.e. burst.    109. *care*: concern.    113–14. *But . . .
eies*: i.e. forgive this oversight by attributing it to heavenly powers which
turned Astrophel's eyes from his own safety to the slaughter of the beasts.
119. *Launched*: pierced. *mischievous*: harmful. Sidney was indeed wounded in
the thigh.    123. *endured*: withstood.    126. *to let*: to hinder.
127–32. Recalls a traditional apostrophe in pastoral elegy: cf. Virgil, *Ecl*
10.9–10.

And ye faire Mayds the matches of his yeares,
Which in his grace did boast you most to bee?  130
Ah where were ye, when he of you had need,
To stop his wound that wondrously did bleed?

Ah wretched boy the shape of dreryhead,
And sad ensample of mans suddein end:
Full litle faileth but thou shalt be dead,  135
Unpitied, unplaynd, of foe or frend.
Whilest none is nigh, thine eylids up to close,
And kisse thy lips like faded leaves of rose.

A sort of shepheards sewing of the chace,
As they the forest raunged on a day:  140
By fate or fortune came unto the place,
Where as the lucklesse boy yet bleeding lay.
Yet bleeding lay, and yet would still have bled,
Had not good hap those shepheards thether led.

They stopt his wound (too late to stop it was)  145
And in their armes then softly did him reare:
Tho (as he wild) unto his loved lasse,
His dearest love him dolefully did beare.
The dolefulst beare that ever man did see,
Was *Astrophel*, but dearest unto mee.  150

She when she saw her love in such a plight,
With crudled blood and filthie gore deformed:
That wont to be with flowers and gyrlonds dight,
And her deare favours dearly well adorned,
Her face, the fairest face, that eye mote see,  155
She likewise did deforme like him to bee.

Her yellow locks that shone so bright and long,
As Sunny beames in fairest somers day:

---

136. *unplaynd*: unlamented.    139. *sewing*: i.e. pursuing.    149. *beare*:
bier, litter, playing also with the idea of "burden"—that one bears (cf. line
148).

She fiersly tore, and with outragious wrong
From her red cheeks the roses rent away.                    160
And her faire brest the threasury of joy,
She spoyld thereof, and filled with annoy.

His palled face impictured with death,
She bathed oft with teares and dried oft:
And with sweet kisses suckt the wasting breath,            165
Out of his lips like lillies pale and soft.
And oft she cald to him, who answerd nought,
But onely by his lookes did tell his thought.

The rest of her impatient regret,
And piteous mone the which she for him made:              170
No toong can tell, nor any forth can set,
But he whose heart like sorrow did invade.
At last when paine his vitall powres had spent,
His wasted life her weary lodge forwent.

Which when she saw, she staied not a whit,                175
But after him did make untimely haste:
Forth with her ghost out of her corps did flit,
And followed her make like Turtle chaste.
To prove that death their hearts cannot divide,
Which living were in love so firmly tide.                 180

The Gods which all things see, this same beheld,
And pittying this paire of lovers trew:
Transformed them there lying on the field,
Into one flowre that is both red and blew.
It first growes red, and then to blew doth fade,          185
Like *Astrophel*, which thereinto was made.

162. *spoyld*: despoiled. *annoy*: mental pain.       169. *impatient*: unbearable.
172. *invade*: attack, seize, enter.       177. *Forth with*: immediately.
184–85. No flower answers to this description, which may be adapted from
Ronsard's account of the transformation in his *Adonis*.

And in the midst thereof a star appeares,
As fairly formd as any star in skyes:
Resembling *Stella* in her freshest yeares,
Forth darting beames of beautie from her eyes,      190
And all the day it standeth full of deow,
Which is the teares, that from her eyes did flow.

That hearbe of some, Starlight is cald by name,
Of others *Penthia*, though not so well:
But thou where ever thou doest finde the same,      195
From this day forth do call it *Astrophel*.
And when so ever thou it up doest take,
Do pluck it softly for that shepheards sake.

Hereof when tydings far abroad did passe,
The shepheards all which loved him full deare:      200
And sure full deare of all he loved was,
Did thether flock to see what they did heare.
And when that pitteous spectacle they vewed,
The same with bitter teares they all bedewed.

And every one did make exceeding mone,              205
With inward anguish and great griefe opprest:
And every one did weep and waile, and mone,
And meanes deviz'd to shew his sorrow best.
That from that houre since first on grassie greene,
Shepheards kept sheep, was not like mourning seen.  210

But first his sister that *Clorinda* hight,
The gentlest shepheardesse that lives this day:
And most resembling both in shape and spright
Her brother deare, began this dolefull lay.
Which least I marre the sweetnesse of the vearse,   215
In sort as she it sung, I will rehearse.

194. *Penthia*: from Gk *penthos*, sorrow.       211. *Clorinda*. Sidney's sister was
Mary Sidney, countess of Pembroke. Clorinda appears, however, to be
entirely a fictional character.

# [The Lay of Clorinda]

A Y me, to whom shall I my case complaine,
    That may compassion my impatient griefe?
Or where shall I unfold my inward paine,
That my enriven heart may find reliefe?
  Shall I unto the heavenly powres it show?      5
  Or unto earthly men that dwell below?

To heavens? ah they alas the authors were,
And workers of my unremedied wo:
For they foresee what to us happens here,
And they foresaw, yet suffred this be so.      10
  From them comes good, from them comes also il,
  That which they made, who can them warne to spill.

To men? ah they alas like wretched bee,
And subject to the heavens ordinance:
Bound to abide what ever they decree,      15
Their best redresse, is their best sufferance.
  How then can they like wretched comfort mee,
  The which no lesse, need comforted to bee?

Then to my selfe will I my sorrow mourne,
Sith none alive like sorrowfull remaines:      20
And to my selfe my plaints shall back retourne,
To pay their usury with doubled paines.
  The woods, the hills, the rivers shall resound
  The mournfull accent of my sorrowes ground.

Woods, hills and rivers, now are desolate,      25
Sith he is gone the which them all did grace:
And all the fields do waile their widow state,
Sith death their fairest flowre did late deface.

THE DOLEFULL LAY OF CLORINDA:   1. *case*: plight. *complaine*:
lament.   12. *warne*: forbid.   51. *quight*: entirely.

The fairest flowre in field that ever grew,
Was *Astrophel*; that was, we all may rew. 30

What cruell hand of cursed foe unknowne,
Hath cropt the stalke which bore so faire a flowre?
Untimely cropt, before it well were growne,
And cleane defaced in untimely howre.
   Great losse to all that ever him did see, 35
   Great losse to all, but greatest losse to mee.

Breake now your gyrlonds, O ye shepheards lasses,
Sith the faire flowre, which them adornd, is gon:
The flowre, which them adornd, is gone to ashes,
Never againe let lasse put gyrlond on. 40
   In stead of gyrlond, weare sad Cypres nowe,
   And bitter Elder, broken from the bowe.

Ne ever sing the love-layes which he made,
Who ever made such layes of love as hee?
Ne ever read the riddles, which he sayd 45
Unto your selves, to make you mery glee.
   Your mery glee is now laid all abed,
   Your mery maker now alasse is dead.

Death the devourer of all worlds delight,
Hath robbed you and reft fro me my joy: 50
Both you and me, and all the world he quight
Hath robd of joyance, and left sad annoy.
   Joy of the world, and shepheards pride was hee,
   Shepheards hope never like againe to see.

Oh death that hast us of such riches reft, 55
Tell us at least, what hast thou with it done?
What is become of him whose flowre here left
Is but the shadow of his likenesse gone.

---

52. *annoy*: disturbance, mental pain.    57–58. *What . . . gone*:
metaphorically, the flower may be Sidney's poetry, the shadow of his earthly
likeness. See O'Connell (1971) pp.32–33.

Scarse like the shadow of that which he was,
Nought like, but that he like a shade did pas.          60

But that immortall spirit, which was deckt
With all the dowries of celestiall grace:
By soveraine choyce from th'hevenly quires select,
And lineally deriv'd from Angels race,
    O what is now of it become aread.          65
    Ay me, can so divine a thing be dead?

Ah no: it is not dead, ne can it die,
But lives for aie, in blisfull Paradise:
Where like a new-borne babe it soft doth lie,
In bed of lillies wrapt in tender wise.          70
    And compast all about with roses sweet,
    And daintie violets from head to feet.

There thousand birds all of celestiall brood,
To him do sweetly caroll day and night:
And with straunge notes, of him well understood,          75
Lull him a sleep in Angelick delight;
    Whilest in sweet dreame to him presented bee
    Immortall beauties, which no eye may see.

But he them sees and takes exceeding pleasure
Of their divine aspects, appearing plaine,          80
And kindling love in him above all measure,
Sweet love still joyous, never feeling paine.
    For what so goodly forme he there doth see,
    He may enjoy from jealous rancor free.

There liveth he in everlasting blis,          85
Sweet spirit never fearing more to die:
Ne dreading harme from any foes of his,
Ne fearing salvage beasts more crueltie.

---

65. *aread*: explain.     71. *compast*: surrounded.     80. *aspects*:
appearances.     83. *forme*: shape, but with a Platonizing overtone of
"essence."

Whilest we here wretches waile his private lack,
And with vaine vowes do often call him back.      90

But live thou there still happie, happie spirit,
And give us leave thee here thus to lament:
Not thee that doest thy heavens joy inherit,
But our owne selves that here in dole are drent.
    Thus do we weep and waile, and wear our eies,      95
    Mourning in others, our owne miseries.

Which when she ended had, another swaine
Of gentle wit and daintie sweet device:
Whom *Astrophel* full deare did entertaine,
Whilest here he liv'd, and held in passing price,      100
    Hight *Thestylis*, began his mournfull tourne,
    And made the *Muses* in his song to mourne.

And after him full many other moe,
As everie one in order lov'd him best,
Gan dight themselves t'expresse their inward woe,      105
With dolefull layes unto the time addrest.
    The which I here in order will rehearse,
    As fittest flowres to deck his mournfull hearse.

---

89. *private lack*: withdrawn absence. "Private" has overtones of the Lat.
*privare*, to deprive, bereave.    90. *vowes*: prayers.    94. *dole*: grief. *drent*:
drowned.    99. *entertaine*: cherish.    100. *passing*: surpassing. *price*:
worth.    101. *Thestylis*: Ludovic Bryskytt.    105. *dight themselves*: prepare
themselves.    106. *time*: occasion.    107. *rehearse*: repeat.

# *Amoretti and Epithalamion*

TITLE PAGE: The title, *Amoretti,* means "little loves." The word was used in the late sixteenth century to designate simply love sonnets or poems, but may suggest here also earthly as opposed to heavenly love. At *Epith* 357 Sp invokes "an hundred little winged loves" to attend the consummation of his marriage. *Written not long since*: We know by the calendrical references in *Amor* and *Epith* that the period of courtship includes the period 13 February through 31 March 1594, and that the wedding occurs on St. Barnabas's day, 11 June. If the assumption is correct that the volume was intended as a wedding present (see *Epith* 427f.), then the work was probably completed in April and May of 1594 at Sp's estate in county Cork, Ireland. It was entered in the Stationers' Register in London 19 November 1594. [*Emblem*]: This is one of several marks used in various works by the printer Peter Short, whose initials appear at the bottom. Short was one of approximately 25 master printers in London at this time; he printed for Ponsonby and other important booksellers. The Latin legend *et usque ad nubes veritas tua.* may be translated "your truth [ascends] even to the heavens." *William Ponsonby*: A prominent London bookseller and publisher, Ponsonby published most of Sp's works as well as Sidney's *Arcadia* and works by Greene and others.

# AMORETTI
## AND
## Epithalamion.

*Written not long since
by Edmunde
Spenser.*

Printed for William
Ponsonby. 1595.

# Amoretti and Epithalamion

❧❧❧❧❧❧❧

In 1595 a little book entitled *AMORETTI AND Epithalamion.* appeared in London. An Elizabethan who thumbed through it might have wondered whether it contained one work or two or perhaps one or more collections of entirely separate poems. The period after the title suggests a unit, but the differing type sizes suggest two works. That *Epithalamion* looks like an extended Italian *canzone* links it with *Amoretti*, whose sonnet-form also has Italian roots, but its Greek title separates it. That sonnets and stanzas are both printed one to a page with virtually identical borders throughout suggests continuity, but *Epithalamion's* separate title page suggests disparity. The tension between wholeness and separateness already apparent in the typographical ordering is characteristic of *Amoretti and Epithalamion* in all its aspects. It suggests the many tensions the sequence dramatizes and seeks to reconcile—between dominance and mutuality in love, between the flesh and the spirit, between life in time and the timeless structures that may give life meaning.

This is not to say that Spenser sought to create tensions in his work. On the contrary it was his life's work to suggest unity and harmony beneath the multiplicity of life. His unifying vision proceeds from his identity as loyal male subject of a Protestant monarchy and it is colored in *Amoretti and Epithalamion* by continental influences related to love poetry, especially Petrarchism and Neoplatonism. At the heart of this work is the general tension between the confusion Spenser feels and the vision that permits him to deny that confusion. It is a tension that was to be felt ever more acutely in the years following 1595: by Shakespeare, by Jonson, by Milton. Reconstructing the cultural dialogue of Spenser's world may enable us to approximate in some measure the dynamic of reading this work in its own day. It is the aim of this introduction both to identify some of the systems that operate through and in *Amoretti and Epithalamion* and their inherent tensions.

1. Petrarchism. The conventions of poetic love in the Renaissance were themselves frequently in conflict. The formulations English poets inherited derived largely from the Italian poet Francis Petrarch (1304–1374) whose *Rime*, a collection of sonnets, *canzoni*, sestinas, ballads, and madrigals, became the principal subtext of European love poetry for the next several hundred years. Petrarch shares with St. Augustine a keen awareness of the frailty of human will, a taste for the pleasures of the physical world, and an introspective and troubled mind. These qualities inform Petrarch's representation of a personal drama that Dante (1265–1321) had elaborated to such acclaim in the *Vita Nuova* and the *Commedia*: that of a poet's profound passion for a distant lady. But whereas Dante had been able to sublimate his passion for his lady Beatrice in his love for God, Petrarch admits no such transcendent resolution. The love of Laura and the love of God remain in tension and the *Rime* record the effects of that tension on the lover over time. The fundamental Petrarchan tension is ultimately that between a God-centered and a self-centered universe. The only resolution is renunciation of one of these centers, and in the last poems Petrarch renounces his love for Laura, ending his long history of personal torment with a hymn to the Virgin Mary, the last word of which is "peace."

The characteristic tension of the *Rime* manifests itself in the tightly controlled rhyme scheme separating the octave (*abbaabba*) from the sestet (*cdecde*, or a variant) and reinforcing the frequently antithetical opposition between them; in the striking diction often involving sharp contrasts (tears/smiles, fire/ice, freedom/imprisonment, fear/hate, war/peace); in the shifts in the lover's moods through the sequence of poems. Though the *Rime* are generally subtly pensive and quietly affective, the tensions pile up in a few poems such as 134, "Pace non trovo," ·

which seems almost a parody of the qualities that were so widely imitated in the following centuries, as Petrarchism became the standard language of the sonnet sequence. Spenser would probably have read Sir Thomas Wyatt's free translation of "Pace non trovo" as it appears in *Tottle's Miscellany*:

> I find no peace, and all my warre is done:
> I feare, and hope: I burne, and frese like yse:
> I flye aloft, yet can I not arise:
> And nought I have, and all the worlde I season.
>
> That lockes nor loseth, holdeth me in pryson,
> And holdes me not, yet can I scape no wise:
> Nor lettes me lyve, nor dye, at my devise,
> And yet of death it geveth me occasion.
>
> Without eye I se, without tong I playne:
> I wish to perysh, yet I aske for helth:
> I love another, and thus I hate my selfe.
>
> I fede me in sorow, and laugh in all my payne.
> Lo, thus displeaseth me both death and life.
> And my delight is causer of this strife.

A glance at the diction of some of the central sonnets of *Amoretti*, e.g. XLI–XLIII, will make it clear that Spenser, who had earlier translated *Rime* 323 as *Visions of Petrarch*, is placing his sonnet sequence in the tradition of Petrarchan love-poetry. The shifts in mood of the lover, especially in the first half of the sequence, his preoccupation with his own emotions, the corresponding radical limitation of the lady's role, and the melancholy separation at the end all are Petrarchan. Yet conceptually Spenser is closer to Dante than to Petrarch, for he manages to integrate the love of his lady with the love of God. Dante overcomes the problem of Beatrice's essential human separateness from God by redefining her as part of the spiritual hierarchy by which he defines himself. He thus bypasses earthly circumstances to achieve a spiritual union in *Purgatorio* and *Paradiso*.

Spenser's love, like Dante's, ends in fulfillment, but unlike Dante's it is an earthly fulfillment in the divinely sanctioned marriage celebrated in *Epithalamion*. Where the norm for the Petrarchan scenario, arising from the inability to reconcile the tension between the physical and the spiritual, is the frustrated stalemate of, for instance, Sir Philip Sidney's *Astrophel and Stella*, Spenser enjoys a spiritualized earthly union. Dante and Spenser seek to transcend the separateness of the physical and the spiritual, Dante by having Beatrice rise, Spenser by having God reach down. Where Dante loves God through the spiritualized Beatrice, Spenser loves God through his spiritually worthy but still earthly bride, Elizabeth.

2. Neoplatonism. The inclination to transcend the gap between the physical and the spiritual suggests some affinity with Neoplatonism, an ancient philosophical system of universal transcendence, which had been revived by Florentine scholars, most notably Marsilio Ficino (1433–1499), and which remained influential through the sixteenth century. Neoplatonists held that as all beauty emanates from the One, with Whom the soul longs to reunite, earthly love may lead us upward to a contemplative or angelic love. Spenser's exploration of Neoplatonic ideas also in *Fowre Hymnes* may indicate a trend of his thought in this period. In fact, *An Hymne in Honour of Love*, the first of the *Fowre Hymnes*, describes as a general process the course of events presented as individual experience in *Amoretti*. Love stirs desire in the lover (*HL* 120–24) until he sees nothing but the lady (*HL* 131–33: *Amor* XXXV); at the same time love hardens the lady's heart (*HL* 137–39, 145–47) causing the lover to suffer (*HL* 120–55: *Amor* I–LVII); but the suffering is remedial (*HL* 165–66) and love is transcendent, rising above the physical (*HL* 176–78) and at the same time elevating the lover's thoughts (*HL* 183–88: *Amor* LXVIII); the ennobled lover again sees nothing but the lady (*HL* 204–07: *Amor* LXXVI–LXXXIII), but his love, not yet heavenly, is troubled by envy, spite, and jealousy (*HL* 259–69: *Amor* LXXXIV–LXXXVI); this disquietude is merely an entrance to a more

heavenly joy (*HL* 273–93: *Epith*). *An Hymne in Honour of Love* is in effect a program for *Amoretti and Epithalamion*. Though neither of these works is dogmatically or systematically Neoplatonic, the Neoplatonic paradigm of progressive love is clear. Yet the culmination of the work in marriage denies the Neoplatonic impulse to transcend the earthly: Spenser remains a poet of this world.

3. Protestantism. Spenser's interest in Neoplatonic ideas accords awkwardly with his English Protestantism, which emphasized man's inability to bridge the gap between himself and God. *Amoretti and Epithalamion* is even less dogmatically Protestant than Neoplatonic, but the Protestant influence is felt in several ways. Perhaps most fundamental is that Spenser is careful to contain the lover's progression within the limits of common human experience. The sense of that limit is palpable both at the end of *Amoretti*, where the lover is left awaiting, rather than striving for, what is beyond, and at the end of *Epithalamion*, where his expression of hope that his posterity may one day rise from the earth to increase the number of the blessed in heaven makes it clear that his business will be not the mystical ascent of a disembodied soul toward the One, but the engendering of an earthly posterity. A second influence of Spenser's Protestantism may be seen in his avoidance of any suggestion that the lover's progression is self-motivated. Salvation comes through grace alone, and if the lover progresses spiritually in *Amoretti and Epithalamion* it is through the influence of God and Elizabeth.

The influence of Protestantism is evident also in the lover's expression, as he approaches his betrothal (chiefly *Amor* LXV), of the ideal of mutuality in marriage. This ideal, which emerged in the sixteenth century as a feature of Protestant doctrine—no doubt partly as an alternative to monastic asceticism, remained in conflict in Elizabethan society, as it does in *Amoretti and Epithalamion*, with long-standing traditions about the relationships of men and women in courtship and marriage. One such tradition is the firmly established patriarchal structure of marriage. Another, largely literary, is the tradition of courtly love, which inverts the patriarchal order during courtship so that the lover, temporarily, becomes the "servant" of the lady. The conflicts between these influences appear clearly in the development of the lover's relation to his lady in *Amoretti and Epithalamion*. He proceeds through a courtship, Petrarchan in style and mood, in which he must subordinate himself to his lady in order to win her favor. But whereas Dante was able simply to transfer this order of courtship to the spiritual realm, Spenser is headed towards marriage. The poet's subordination to the lady in winning her favor gives way to promises of mutuality in LXV and reconciliation. Beginning with sonnet LIX the lover realizes that Elizabeth has withheld her favor not because of pride, as he thought earlier (e.g. XXVII), but because of virtue. This recognition makes possible a reversal culminating in the ritual of her submission in LXVII, their betrothal in LXVIII, and finally their wedding in *Epithalamion*.

4. The male perspective. Despite this stress on reconciliation, tensions remain. Behind these lie clear suggestions of mastery. The poet's assurances of mutual love (LXV), simple peace and joint submission to God (LXVIII) are accompanied by images of caging (LXV), binding (LXVII), conquest (LXIX), captivity, and imprisonment (LXX). Both mutuality and mastery seem inappropriate for a "sweet Saynt" (XXII) that "ought rather worshipt be" (LXI). The tension between these social paradigms imposes an artistic dilemma at the point of the betrothal (LXVIII), for to stress the lover's mastery would be to undermine the lady's elevated status established in the first part of the sequence. This difficulty may account for the fact that it is not clear to what extent Elizabeth is physically present in the sonnets after LXVIII until her reappearance in *Epithalamion*.

Similarly, in *Epithalamion*, where we might anticipate a celebration of "mutuall good will," we find rather a demonstration of mastery. The epithalamion, or wedding song, is of Greek origin in both name and form, but its most influential practitioner is the Roman Catullus (84–54 B.C.), who was actively imitated by French Renaissance poets, most notably Ronsard (1524–1585). The form includes a series of topoi which Spenser adapts, among them an invocation of Hymen, god of marriage; a description of the bride; an account of the wedding and the bedding of the couple; and a prayer that the marriage be fruitful. Spenser follows Catullus 61 both in the general plan of his poem and its social setting, but he makes more elaborate and specific the sense of hierarchy and the sense of time, and he changes the role of the narrator. The Catullan narrator is a third party, an observer and sometime orchestrator of the events of the wedding day. Spenser—the lover, the poet, and the bridegroom—sings his own wedding song and functions as director of his own wedding celebration, preserving the Petrarchan egocentrism through the very time when he is involved in merging his identity in the union with Elizabeth. On the day they institutionalize their mutual love, the bride does not speak and the bridegroom, even in the bedchamber, does not name her or even address her except very briefly to reassure her at the altar (*Epith* 238–39). Rather he summons all of the social and natural community to gaze upon her as the priest places his hands on her and she displays her vaunted modesty and humility. Some may see this as a ritual of subordination, not of mutual bonding. The integration of the ideal of mutuality into Spenser's assumptions about social and political institutions and his fundamentally hierarchical pattern of thought remains partial and problematical.

5. The historical dimension. Another kind of tension is that between the large symbolic structures of the poem and its historical particularity. In accord with the convention of the sonnet sequence, these poems are, at least in part, specifically autobiographical. This is a convention that by its nature pulls the reader in different directions—between fiction and history, between text and context—and that at the same time blurs the distinction between those poles (see Cheney 1984). We learn from the text that the lover is a poet in his early forties who has completed six books of *The Faerie Queene*; that he has a friend

and advisor named Lodowick Bryskett; that his queen, his mother, and his lady are all named Elizabeth; that he courted Elizabeth at least in part during February and March of 1594 and that their wedding occurred on 11 June. All of this accords with what we know of Spenser's life from other sources, but a reader may wonder why Spenser chose just these auto-biographical details. Why does Spenser include mention of Lodowick Bryskett, his friend and fellow civil servant in the Irish government? When Spenser identifies himself as the author of *The Faerie Queene* (XXXIII and LXXX), for which he had received acclaim and reward in London in 1590, and announces completion of the second part a year before his return to England in 1595, should we wonder whether his motives are amorous, poetical, or political? We are led to ask questions only tangentially related to the text: how long had his first wife, by whom he had a son and a daughter, been dead before he met Elizabeth? Was the connection to Elizabeth's influential kinsman Richard Boyle, later earl of Cork, advantageous? The auto-biographical detail that Spenser places in his work adds a dimension of particularity that counterbalances its symbolic structure, and at the same time breaks the plane of fiction, pulling us outward away from the pattern of unified meaning.

6. The narrative. A similar complexity exists in Spenser's treatment of the book's narrative, which relates to the auto-biographical element as does the general to the particular. The story on the simplest level is spare, in accord with the sonnet convention. Hopelessly enamored and emotionally in turmoil, the lover sets out to win his lady; sometimes he is arrogant, sometimes servile, sometimes respectful, sometimes tender, sometimes comic. The lady, perceiving his worth beneath his shortcomings, eventually accepts him. They marry and look forward to a fruitful life together. Yet the wholeness of this simple story is brought into question by the uncertainty of narrative progression from sonnet to sonnet and even from work to work, or more precisely by our inability to say with certainty whether or not the segments of *Amoretti and Epithalamion* are in

fact parts of a larger work. For example, the lover's reaction to the threat of worldly intrusion into his union with Elizabeth (*Amor* LXXXIV–LXXXVI) has neither narrative cause nor effect. The most absolute disruption of the narrative sequence is the placement between *Amoretti* and *Epithalamion* of four playful poems of trivialized mythology about Venus and Cupid in the manner of the Greek poet Anacreon (?572–?488 B.C.) whose works had been published in 1554 and imitated widely by French and Italian poets. The poems' imagery seems erotic on one level—stings and arrows healed by wrapping, application of salve, and bathing in "the well of deare delight" (Anacreontics 70; see Kaske 1978). The action, taken continuously, may also be read as an allegorical narrative. The poet is stung by a bee; then Cupid takes Diane's dart, wounds the poet's lady, and confuses her with Venus; finally, Cupid, stung by a bee and cured by Venus, wounds the poet. We note that the lady is wounded by Cupid in association with the divine Diane and subsequently appears divine; the lover is wounded by the bestial bee and then by Cupid in association with the bee. Mere bee-sting, we see, is cured by a bath in "the well of deare delight," but we do not learn how the symptoms of the two different dart wounds of opposing provenance may find a cure. The Anacreontics end in an unresolved tension. If this little allegory is intended as a paradigm of the beginning of attraction between men and women, its place in the narrative sequence should be before rather than after *Amoretti*, which describes the process of resolving the problem in love theory which is represented in the Anacreontics. The fact that the presiding deities of the Anacreontics are pagan and feminine would place them at the beginning of the progression of *Amoretti and Epithalamion* in which pagan imagery is subsumed in a Christian framework and the independent lady in a patriarchal social structure. But whatever their thematic and conceptual relationship to *Amoretti* and to *Epithalamion*, the Anacreontic verses violate the narrative continuity of the book.

7. The drama. The development of the lover's—not the

lady's—consciousness forms the general dramatic structure within the work. The sonnet sequence is a dramatic monologue: we know only what the lover tells us, and his words, of course, tell us much more about him than about her. The lady of the first part of the sequence, he reports, counters his argument with a pun in XXIX, she smiles in XXXIX and XL, and burns a paper he has sent (XLVIII), but in general she remains, in the Petrarchan tradition, consistently composed and unyielding at the prospect of the lover's histrionics. She offers little encouragement; indeed, he complains, "the more she fervent sees my fit:/ the more she frieseth in her wilfull pryde" (XXXII). In general she "lyke the Spectator ydly sits . . . beholding me with constant eye" (LIV) while he does "all the pageants play,/ disguysing diversly my troubled wits" (LIV) and "lyke *Narcissus* vaine" (XXXV) is concerned only with his own emotions. Each sonnet represents a moment in the lover's emotional development. He signals his progress during the sequence by use of familiar terms of Elizabethan psychology, which was, in general, a dualistic system of body (senses, heart) and soul (mind, wits, fancy, imagination, memory), the two mediated by the spirit. The basis and outline of the development of the lover's consciousness are discussed in relation to Neoplatonism, above. Consideration of *Amoretti and Epithalamion* as drama leads to questions of character and effect. Because we understand more about the lover than he does about himself, he is inescapably ironic. He is enmeshed in a process that profoundly affects him but of which he only gradually gains some understanding. The lover, then, is a comic figure because in his lack of self-knowledge he is made to seem temporarily inferior to the reader, and because his suffering is temporary and he is led to a felicitous ending. Yet this comic characterization is undermined by the quasi-heroic role he assumes in *Epithalamion* as winner of the lady and temporary center of universal harmony.

8. Symbolic structures. The tension between wholeness and separateness, hierarchy and mutuality, centeredness and decen-

teredness emerges most clearly and specifically in the formal and symbolic structures of *Amoretti and Epithalamion*, which express symbolically the meaning that the lover in his dramatic situation does not always see. A poet who places a sonnet announcing a new beginning (LXII) as the first poem of the second half of the volume (counting equally the eighty-nine sonnets, nine Anacreontic stanzas, and twenty-four epithalamic stanzas) is one who is keenly aware of numbers and patterns and especially of centeredness. Yet the pattern marked by this device is not concentric, but a sequence of two. If we count the four Anacreontic poems rather than the separate stanzas, then LIX, the sonnet of the lover's enabling recognition, discussed above, is the numerical center of the work. Sequential and concentric patterns coexist throughout *Amoretti and Epithalamion*.

*Amoretti and Epithalamion* is one of the most striking examples in literature of the use of time as a poetic device. Spenser is engaged in denying the meaningless sequentiality of time by identifying patterns of religious and cosmological meaning within it. His use in *Amoretti* of a framework related to Ash Wednesday and Easter removes those events from the mere sequence of history and asserts this transcendence of the personal and particular events that seem to form the sequence of historical time. The tone and imagery of XXII and LXVIII identify them as Ash Wednesday and Easter sonnets; the number of sonnets between them equals the number of days between Ash Wednesday and Easter. This group is centered in *Amoretti*, with twenty-one sonnets preceding and following and a spring sonnet two before and two after the central group. This concentric formal symbol is given specific temporal identity by the occurrence of LXII, a new year's sonnet, on the date when Easter occurred in 1594, the year *Amoretti and Epithalamion* was entered in the Stationers' Register. Yet, though this calendrical framework informs *Amoretti* in a fundamental way, it does not become the sequence. Spenser apparently does not intend for us to date each sonnet; on the contrary he uses only a few sonnets to establish the pattern. Meaning may inform time, but cannot become it, for meaning, as Spenser conceives it, is timeless, and time as he conceives it usually seems meaningless.

*Epithalamion* is a monument through time to a very particular time, St. Barnabas's day, 11 June, the longest day of the year by the calendar of Spenser's day. So precise is the association with this particular day that the phrase "now night is come" occurs in the fourth line of stanza 17, corresponding, Hieatt (1960) has pointed out, to the sixteen-and-a-fraction hours of daylight on 11 June in southern Ireland, as recorded in contemporary almanacs; all of the refrains before this are affirmative and all after it negative. The narrative of *Epithalamion* is arranged around the centrally placed church ceremonies "the which do endlesse matrimony make" (217, the central line of *Epithalamion*). Yet the centered action occurs within the centerless continuum of time. In fact, the formal structure of *Epithalamion*, with its 24 hour-related stanzas, 365 long lines, and 68 short lines which may represent the total of the weeks, months, and seasons, makes it "for short time an endlesse moniment" (*Epith* 433). This line, the last of the poem, proclaims that poetry like matrimony (*Epith* 217), may be "endlesse," but that time is "short," that these special forms of human endeavor may serve to mediate between the eternal and the temporal in imitating transcendent patterns glimpsed through the particulate, sequential medium of time.

Despite the elaborate and comprehensive symbolic patterning, no "key" has been or is likely to be found to establish a simple unity of *Amoretti and Epithalamion*. Spenser suggests that universal values inform particular experience, but to see more than a glimpse of that hierarchical unified truth would be to exceed the human experience to which this work is devoted. Spenser's several formal patterns remain in tension with each other and with the many particular details which elude or resist the patterns.

How appropriate for the book entitled *AMORETTI AND Epithalamion*. to end with a wedding song whose insistent theme of universal harmony is challenged by its equally insistent allusion to sequential time, which levels by its nature hierarchies and meanings and orders. Systematically Spenser includes every social order and every animate natural order in the celebration of his wedding. But his vision is of the wholeness and order of just a day: "let this day let this one day be myne,/ Let all the rest be thine," he implores the sun (*Epith* 125–26). This harmony, this wholeness, like Calidore's vision on Mount Acidale (*FQ* VI x 18), will dissolve into the separateness of time, leaving as monuments only Spenser's marriage and the little book *AMORETTI AND Epithalamion.*

*Alexander Dunlop*

# The Epistle Dedicatory.

To the Right Worshipfull Sir Robart Needham Knight.

SIr, to gratulate your safe return from Ireland, I had nothing so readie, nor thought any thing so meete, as these sweete conceited Sonets, the deede of that weldeserving gentleman, maister Edmond Spenser: whose name sufficiently warranting the worthinesse of the work: I do more confidently presume to publish it in his absence, under your name to whom (in my poore opinion) the patronage therof, doth in some respectes properly appertaine. For, besides your judgement and delighte in learned poesie: This gentle Muse for her former perfection long wished for in Englande, nowe at the length crossing the Seas in your happy companye, (though to your selfe unknowne) seemeth to make choyse of you, as meetest to give her deserved countenaunce, after her retourne: entertaine her, then, (Right worshipfull) in sorte best beseeming your gentle minde, and her merite, and take in worth my good will herein, who seeke no more, but to shew my selfe yours in all dutifull affection.

W.P

### G:W.senior, to the Author

DArke is the day, when *Phœbus* face is shrowded,
    and weaker sights may wander soone astray:

THE EPISTLE DEDICATORY *Sir Robart Needham*: The cavalry captain Robert Needham of Shropshire was knighted for service in Ireland on 1 September 1594 and was in England from 25 September until the following April. Sp's manuscript may have arrived in England on the same boat, possibly in a packet of mail carried by Needham. Needham's connections to Sp and/or Ponsonby are uncertain.

FIRST COMMENDATORY SONNET *G:W.senior*: The authors of the commendatory sonnets are probably Geoffrey Whitney senior and junior ("G.W.J."), who appear to have had connections to both Sp and Needham.

but when they see his glorious raies unclowded,
with steddy steps they keepe the perfect way,
So while this Muse in forraine landes doth stay,     5
invention weepes, and pens are cast aside,
the time like night, deprivd of chearefull day,
and few do write, but (ah) too soone may slide.
Then, hie thee home, that art our perfect guide,
and with thy wit illustrate Englands fame,     10
dawnting thereby our neighboures auncient pride,
that do for poesie challendge cheefest name.
So we that live and ages that succeede,
   With great applause thy learned works shall reede.


*Ah Colin, whether on the lowly plaine*
   *pyping to shepherds thy sweete roudelaies:*
   *or whether singing in some lofty vaine*
   *heroick deedes of past or present daies:*
*Or whether in thy lovely mistris praise*     5
   *thou list to exercise thy learned quill:*
   *thy muse hath got such grace, and power to please,*
   *with rare invention bewtified by skill,*
*As who therein can ever joy their fill.*
   *O therefore let that happy muse proceede*     10
   *to clime the height of vertues sacred hill,*
   *where endles honor shall be made thy meede,*
*Because no malice of succeeding daies*
   *can rase those records of thy lasting praise.*

                    *G.W.J.*


SECOND COMMENDATORY SONNET    2. *roudelaies*: A roundelay is a
simple song.    9. *who . . . fill*: Either "anyone can find therein his fill of
pleasure" or "no one can be sated with this pleasure."    12. *meede*: reward.

### SONNET. I.

HAppy ye leaves when as those lilly hands,
    which hold my life in their dead doing might
shall handle you and hold in loves soft bands,
lyke captives trembling at the victors sight.
And happy lines, on which with starry light,         5
    those lamping eyes will deigne sometimes to look
and reade the sorrowes of my dying spright,
written with teares in harts close bleeding book.
And happy rymes bath'd in the sacred brooke
of *Helicon* whence she derived is,         10
when ye behold that Angels blessed looke,
my soules long lacked foode, my heavens blis.
Leaves, lines, and rymes, seeke her to please alone,
    whom if ye please, I care for other none.

SONNET I    Sp has invented a rhyme scheme that, with its tight pattern of only five rhymes and its linked quatrains (*ababbcbccdcdee*), reflects the idea of linking and synthesis that is both the method and theme of the whole work. Sonnets I through IV are introductory.    1. The *leaves* . . . *lines* . . . *rymes* (1,5,9) are those of *Amor*, presumably presented to the lady piecemeal as the sequence progresses.    2. *dead doing might*: murderous power. 4. *captives trembling*: The lover's happy submission to the lady of himself in the form of the leaves of his poetry enacts the traditional pattern of courtly love in which the lover temporarily becomes the "servant" of the lady during courtship.    6. *lamping*: beaming.    7. *spright*: The lover claims, in hyperbolic mode, that his spirit is dying (7), his heart is bleeding (8) and his soul is starving (12). Throughout the sequence the lover observes fine distinctions among these three faculties. The rational, incorporeal soul connects man with higher angelic orders of being; the irrational, corporeal body connects man with the beasts. The heart is considered part of the body. Marsilio Ficino notes in his *Commentary on Plato's Symposium* (1484) that "three things seem to be in us: the soul, the spirit, and the body. The soul and body, which are by nature very different from each other, are joined by means of the spirit, which is a certain very thin and clear vapor produced by the heat of the heart" (6.6). See also the Introduction, above.    8. *harts* . . . *book*: the secret book of my bleeding heart.    10. *Helicon*: The winged horse Pegasus, a favorite of the Muses, created with a stamp of his hoof on Mt. Helicon the fountain Hippocrene, thenceforth a special haunt of the Muses.

## SONNET. II.

UNquiet thought, whom at the first I bred
   Of th'inward bale of my love pined hart:
and sithens have with sighes and sorrowes fed,
till greater then my wombe thou woxen art:
Breake forth at length out of the inner part,        5
   in which thou lurkest lyke to vipers brood:
and seeke some succour both to ease my smart
and also to sustayne thy selfe with food.
But if in presence of that fayrest proud
   thou chance to come, fall lowly at her feet:       10
and with meeke humblesse and afflicted mood,
pardon for thee, and grace for me intreat.
Which if she graunt, then live and my love cherish,
   if not, die soone, and I with thee will perish.

SONNET II    1. *Unquiet thought*: The psychology of the lover is an important focus in the sequence. This sonnet is addressed to his own "unquiet thought," i.e. his passion, which, it seems, he no longer controls. The distinction between himself and the "unquiet thought" is clear in the last line. Developed in his heart (2), rather than in his mind, the "unquiet thought" is sent to seek pardon for itself from the lady; the lover himself must seek grace for having had it. Further, the "unquiet thought" is "lyke to vipers brood" (6), which, when it "breake[s] forth" (5), is fatal to the mother, according to contemporary lore (*Variorum*, p.421). The logic of the metaphor is elaborate, but precise. The breaking forth of desire implies death for the lover. If the lady pardons this thought (desire), it is only the desire which will live and cherish his beloved, for he will die spiritually. If the lady does not pardon the "unquiet thought" (i.e. if she remains intransigent), the lover will die, he mistakenly believes or at least claims to believe, of the torments of love. The resolution of this dilemma is a central concern of the sequence.    2. *bale*: pain; may also suggest evil. *pined*: tormented. 3. *sithens*: since then.    4. *woxen*: past participle of the verb "to wax."

SONNET. III.

THe soverayne beauty which I doo admyre,
 witnesse the world how worthy to be prayzed:
the light wherof hath kindled heavenly fyre,
in my fraile spirit by her from basenesse raysed.
That being now with her huge brightnesse dazed,                5
 base thing I can no more endure to view:
but looking still on her I stand amazed,
 at wondrous sight of so celestiall hew.
So when my toung would speak her praises dew,
 it stopped is with thoughts astonishment:                     10
and when my pen would write her titles true,
 it ravisht is with fancies wonderment:
Yet in my hart I then both speake and write
 the wonder that my wit cannot endite.

SONNET. IIII.

NEw yeare forth looking out of Janus gate,
 Doth seeme to promise hope of new delight:
and bidding th'old Adieu, his passed date
bids all old thoughts to die in dumpish spright.

SONNET III    1. *soverayne beauty*: In II the lady was "that fayrest
proud"; here she seems almost divine. This other aspect of the lady provides
the means for the eventual resolution of the dilemma introduced in II. Such
radical shifts in attitude also show the lover's emotional confusion.
5. *dazed*: Heavenly light gives spiritual vision, but blinds one to earthly
things.    7. *amazed*: stunned.    10. *astonishment*: paralysis. Thought,
proceeding from the wit (14) is stopped, along with its instruments the
tongue and pen. At this point, he claims, his inspiration is restricted to the
heart and hence is inexpressible.    12. *fancies wonderment*: the dazing, or
paralysis, of the creative imagination. The fancy was an integrative faculty of
the spirit, combining images either from sense or from memory.
SONNET IV    1. *Janus*: the Roman god of doorways and gates and so of
beginnings, e.g. of the year, of sowing, of war. "Janus gate" and "sad winters
night" seem to suggest 1 January, but the imminence of spring (9–10) may
indicate a March new year (see *FQ* VII vii 32–43 and *SC* "generall
argument"). Perhaps the lover's claim that "lusty spring now in his timely

And calling forth out of sad Winters night,                                    5
    fresh love, that long hath slept in cheerlesse bower:
    wils him awake, and soone about him dight
    his wanton wings and darts of deadly power.
For lusty spring now in his timely howre,
    is ready to come forth him to receive:                             10
    and warnes the Earth with divers colord flowre
    to decke hir selfe, and her faire mantle weave.
Then you faire flowre, in whom fresh youth doth raine,
    prepare your selfe new love to entertaine.

### SONNET. V.

RUdely thou wrongest my deare harts desire,
    In finding fault with her too portly pride:
the thing which I doo most in her admire
is of the world unworthy most envide.
For in those lofty lookes is close implide,                                    5
    scorn of base things, and sdeigne of foule dishonor:

howre,/ is ready to come forth" (9–10) is part of his amorous strategy to
create a mood of *carpe diem*. Note, though, that the love evoked has "wanton
wings and darts of deadly power" (8), so that the earth must "decke hir selfe"
(12). "Wanton," "deadly," "lusty," and "warnes" may suggest a danger.
2. *seeme*: may suggest a specious promise.    4. *dumpish spright*:
melancholy.    7. *dight*: put on.    9. *lusty*: pleasant, but possibly also
lustful.    12. *decke*: cover or clothe.
S O N N E T  V    Sonnets V through XXI form a tableau representing the
lover's attitudes at this point toward courtship: V, XIII, and XXI show the
lover's fleeting recognition that he is being "taught and trained"; VI and XIV
are sonnets of self-encouragement; the rest of the first twenty-one show the
lover in conventional stances of courtship, either praising the lady's virtues
(VII, VIII, IX, XV, XVI, XVII), attacking her obduracy (X, XI, XII, XVIII,
XIX, XX), or recognizing the dual nature of her effect on him (V, XIII,
XXI).    1. *thou*: Here, as later in LXXXVI, the lover addresses a putative
observer who represents, he feels, an external threat. Or we may read "thou"
here as that part of himself that has yet to learn the larger meaning of love.
Other than in V and LXXXVI, the poet uses "thou" only in reference to
divinity (XXII, LXVIII) or to the lady's deified smile (XXXIX).    2. *portly*:
grand, imposing.

thretning rash eies which gaze on her so wide,
that loosely they ne dare to looke upon her.
Such pride is praise, such portlinesse is honor,
   that boldned innocence beares in hir eies:           10
   and her faire countenance like a goodly banner,
   spreds in defiaunce of all enemies.
Was never in this world ought worthy tride
   without some spark of such self-pleasing pride.

### SONNET. VI.

**B**E nought dismayd that her unmoved mind
   doth still persist in her rebellious pride:
such love, not lyke to lusts of baser kynd,
   the harder wonne, the firmer will abide.
The durefull Oake, whose sap is not yet dride,       5
   is long ere it conceive the kindling fyre:
but when it once doth burne, it doth divide
   great heat, and makes his flames to heaven aspire.
So hard it is to kindle new desire
   in gentle brest that shall endure for ever:       10
   deepe is the wound, that dints the parts entire
   with chast affects, that naught but death can sever.
Then thinke not long in taking litle paine,
   to knit the knot, that ever shall remaine.

### SONNET. VII.

**F**ayre eyes, the myrrour of my mazed hart,
   what wondrous vertue is contaynd in you

8. *ne*: not.
SONNET VI   1. *nought*: not a bit. Sp braids a series of negatives
("nought . . . not . . . not . . . naught . . . not") to produce a positive "knot,
that ever shall remaine"(14). Cf. Shakespeare's sonnet 116.   5. *durefull*:
enduring.   7. *divide*: distribute.   11. *dints*: forcefully impresses.
SONNET VII   1. *myrrour*: The lady as guide in love serves as both lamp
(11, also I.6) and mirror. Ficino (*Commentary on Plato's Symposium* 7.1)
summarizes the idea: "Just as a mirror, struck in a certain way by a ray of the

the which both lyfe and death forth from you dart
into the object of your mighty view?
For when ye mildly looke with lovely hew,                    5
    then is my soule with life and love inspired:
but when ye lowre, or looke on me askew
    then doe I die, as one with lightning fyred.
But since that lyfe is more then death desyred,
    looke ever lovely, as becomes you best,                 10
that your bright beams of my weak eies admyred,
    may kindle living fire within my brest.
Such life should be the honor of your light,
    such death the sad ensample of your might.

### SONNET. VIII.

M Ore then most faire, full of the living fire,
    Kindled above unto the maker neere:
no eies but joyes, in which al powers conspire,
    that to the world naught else be counted deare.
Thrugh your bright beams doth not the blinded guest        5
    shoot out his darts to base affections wound:
but Angels come to lead fraile mindes to rest
    in chast desires on heavenly beauty bound.
You frame my thoughts and fashion me within,
    you stop my toung, and teach my hart to speake,        10
you calme the storme that passion did begin,
    strong thrugh your cause, but by your vertue weak.

sun, shines back, and by that reflection of the splendor sets on fire a piece of
wool placed next to it, so . . . part of the soul . . . (like the mirror) is struck
by a certain image (like a ray) of beauty itself (taking the place of the sun),
taken in through the eyes; in such a way that from that it makes another
image for itself . . . by which the force of desire (like the wool) is kindled and
loves . . . ". *mazed*: bewildered, stunned (as in III.7, above).    3. *the which*:
through the power of which.    4. *object*: i.e. the speaker.
SONNET VIII    The rhyme scheme is Shakespearean (*ababcdcdefefgg*).
9–12 The lover shows awareness of the lady's function as guide in love.

Dark is the world, where your light shined never;
well is he borne, that may behold you ever.

### SONNET. IX.

L Ong-while I sought to what I might compare
those powrefull eies, which lighten my dark
spright,
yet find I nought on earth to which I dare
resemble th'ymage of their goodly light.
Not to the Sun: for they doo shine by night;                    5
nor to the Moone: for they are changed never;
nor to the Starres: for they have purer sight;
nor to the fire: for they consume not ever;
Nor to the lightning: for they still persever;
nor to the Diamond: for they are more tender;                   10
nor unto Christall: for nought may them sever;
nor unto glasse: such basenesse mought offend her;
Then to the Maker selfe they likest be,
whose light doth lighten all that here we see.

### SONNET. X.

U Nrighteous Lord of love what law is this,
That me thou makest thus tormented be:
the whiles she lordeth in licentious blisse
of her freewill, scorning both thee and me.
See how the Tyrannesse doth joy to see                          5
the huge massacres which her eyes do make:
and humbled harts brings captives unto thee,
that thou of them mayst mightie vengeance take.
But her proud hart doe thou a little shake
and that high look, with which she doth comptroll             10

SONNET IX    4. *resemble*: liken.    11. *Christall*: probably rock-crystal,
or quartz.
SONNET X    3. *licentious*: lawless.    7. *captives*: captive (adjective
modifying "harts").

all this worlds pride bow to a baser make,
and al her faults in thy black booke enroll:
That I may laugh at her in equall sort,
    as she doth laugh at me and makes my pain her sport.

### SONNET. XI.

DAyly when I do seeke and sew for peace,
    And hostages doe offer for my truth:
she cruell warriour doth her selfe addresse
to battell, and the weary war renew'th.
Ne wilbe moov'd with reason or with rewth,      5
to graunt small respit to my restlesse toile:
but greedily her fell intent poursewth,
Of my poore life to make unpitteid spoile.
Yet my poore life, all sorrowes to assoyle,
  I would her yield, her wrath to pacify:      10
but then she seekes with torment and turmoyle,
to force me live and will not let me dy.
All paine hath end and every war hath peace,
  but mine no price nor prayer may surcease.

### SONNET. XII.

ONe day I sought with her hart-thrilling eies
    to make a truce and termes to entertaine:
all fearelesse then of so false enimies,
which sought me to entrap in treasons traine.
So as I then disarmed did remaine,      5
  a wicked ambush which lay hidden long
in the close covert of her guilefull eyen,

11. *bow . . . make*: "bow" is transitive; the subject is "thou"; the object is
"look." The poet implores the "unrighteous Lord of love" to direct the lady's
look toward a less elevated possible mate, namely the poet himself.      14. an
alexandrine; also XLV.14.
SONNET XI      2. *truth*: pledge of faith in a solemn agreement, military or
marital.      5. *rewth*: pity.      9. *assoyle*: dispel.
SONNET XII      7. *close covert*: secret shelter. *eyen*: eyes (an archaic plural
form).

thence breaking forth did thick about me throng.
Too feeble I t'abide the brunt so strong,
   was forst to yeeld my selfe into their hands:        10
   who me captiving streight with rigorous wrong,
   have ever since me kept in cruell bands.
So Ladie now to you I doo complaine,
   against your eies that justice I may gaine.

### SONNET. XIII.

IN that proud port, which her so goodly graceth,
   whiles her faire face she reares up to the skie:
and to the ground her eie lids low embaseth,
   most goodly temperature ye may descry,
Myld humblesse mixt with awfull majesty,         5
   for looking on the earth whence she was borne,
   her minde remembreth her mortalitie:
   what so is fayrest shall to earth returne.
But that same lofty countenance seemes to scorne
   base thing, and thinke how she to heaven may clime:   10
   treading downe earth as lothsome and forlorne,
   that hinders heavenly thoughts with drossy slime.
Yet lowly still vouchsafe to looke on me,
   such lowlinesse shall make you lofty be.

### SONNET. XIIII.

REtourne agayne my forces late dismayd,
   Unto the siege by you abandon'd quite;
great shame it is to leave like one afrayd,
   so fayre a peece for one repulse so light.
Gaynst such strong castles needeth greater might     5

SONNET XIII   1. *port*: bearing or stance.     4. *temperature*: an equal
blend of elements; hence, a balanced temperament.    6–12. This is a
conventional Neoplatonic opposition of mortal flesh and immortal
spirit.    12. *drossy*: impure, trashy.

then those small forts which ye were wont belay;
such haughty mynds enur'd to hardy fight,
disdayne to yield unto the first assay.
Bring therefore all the forces that ye may,
  and lay incessant battery to her heart;         10
playnts, prayers, vowes, ruth, sorrow, and dismay,
those engins can the proudest love convert.
And if those fayle fall downe and dy before her,
  so dying live, and living do adore her.

### SONNET. XV.

YE tradefull Merchants that with weary toyle
  do seeke most pretious things to make your
                         gaine:
and both the Indias of their treasures spoile,
what needeth you to seeke so farre in vaine?
For loe my love doth in her selfe containe         5
  all this worlds riches that may farre be found:
if Saphyres, loe her eies be Saphyres plaine,
if Rubies, loe hir lips be Rubies sound:
If Pearles, hir teeth be pearles both pure and round;
  if Yvorie, her forhead yvory weene;        10
if Gold, her locks are finest gold on ground;
  if silver, her faire hands are silver sheene,
But that which fairest is, but few behold,
  her mind adornd with vertues manifold.

### SONNET. XVI.

ONe day as I unwarily did gaze
  on those fayre eyes my loves immortall light:

---

SONNET XIV    6. *wont belay*: accustomed to besiege.    8. *assay*:
assault.
SONNET XV    This catalogue of the lady's parts, called a blazon, was a
favorite Renaissance form.    10. *weene*: beautiful.    12. *sheene*: beautiful,
bright.

the whiles my stonisht hart stood in amaze,
through sweet illusion of her lookes delight,
I mote perceive how in her glauncing sight, 5
legions of loves with little wings did fly:
darting their deadly arrowes fyry bright,
at every rash beholder passing by.
One of those archers closely I did spy,
ayming his arrow at my very hart: 10
when suddenly with twincle of her eye,
the Damzell broke his misintended dart.
Had she not so doon, sure I had bene slayne,
yet as it was, I hardly scap't with paine.

### SONNET. XVII.

THe glorious pourtraict of that Angels face,
Made to amaze weake mens confused skil
and this worlds worthlesse glory to embase,
what pen, what pencill can expresse her fill?
For though he colours could devize at will, 5
and eke his learned hand at pleasure guide:
least trembling it his workmanship should spill,
yet many wondrous things there are beside.
The sweet eye-glaunces, that like arrowes glide,
the charming smiles, that rob sence from the hart: 10
the lovely pleasance and the lofty pride,
cannot expressed be by any art.
A greater craftesmans hand thereto doth neede,
that can expresse the life of things indeed.

SONNET XVI    6. The poet here blends the playful Anacreontic mode
(see note to Anacreontics 1) with the potentially more serious figure of the
lady's eyes as lamp, introduced in sonnet I, line 6.    14. *I hardly . . . paine*:
my escape was difficult and painful.
SONNET XVII    2. *amaze*: stun, bewilder (as at III.7; VII.1;
etc.).    7. *least . . . spill*: the slightest trembling could ruin the artist's work.

### SONNET. XVIII.

THe rolling wheele that runneth often round,
  The hardest steele in tract of time doth teare:
and drizling drops that often doe redound,
the firmest flint doth in continuance weare.
Yet cannot I with many a dropping teare,                                    5
  and long intreaty soften her hard hart:
that she will once vouchsafe my plaint to heare,
or looke with pitty on my payneful smart.
But when I pleade, she bids me play my part,
  and when I weep, she sayes teares are but water:                          10
and when I sigh, she sayes I know the art,
  and when I waile she turnes hir selfe to laughter.
So doe I weepe, and wayle, and pleade in vaine,
  whiles she as steele and flint doth still remayne.

### SONNET. XIX.

THe merry Cuckow, messenger of Spring,
  His trompet shrill hath thrise already sounded:
that warnes al lovers wayt upon their king,
who now is comming forth with girland crouned.
With noyse whereof the quyre of Byrds resounded                            5
  their anthemes sweet devized of loves prayse,
that all the woods theyr ecchoes back rebounded,
as if they knew the meaning of their layes.
But mongst them all, which did Loves honor rayse,
  no word was heard of her that most it ought,                             10
but she his precept proudly disobayes,

SONNET XVIII    3. *redound*: fall.
SONNET XIX    1. *Cuckow*: The cuckoo's raucous cry is the call of the
male during mating season. Its "trompet shrill" (2) contrasts with the
"anthemes sweet" (6) of the other birds. The lady correctly interprets the
cuckoo's cry as an "ydle message" (12). She is guiding the lover to a greater
love, and, indeed, the poet later describes the cuckoo's song as "witlesse"
(LXXXV.4).    11. *proudly*: The lover continues to misinterpret the lady's
proper modesty as pride.

and doth his ydle message set at nought.
Therefore O love, unlesse she turne to thee
ere Cuckow end, let her a rebell be.

SONNET. XX.

IN vaine I seeke and sew to her for grace,
and doe myne humbled hart before her poure:
the whiles her foot she in my necke doth place,
and tread my life downe in the lowly floure.
And yet the Lyon that is Lord of power, 5
and reigneth over every beast in field:
in his most pride disdeigneth to devoure
the silly lambe that to his might doth yield.
But she more cruell and more salvage wylde,
then either Lyon or the Lyonesse: 10
shames not to be with guiltlesse bloud defylde,
but taketh glory in her cruelnesse.
Fayrer then fayrest let none ever say,
that ye were blooded in a yeelded pray.

SONNET. XXI.

WAs it the worke of nature or of Art?
which tempred so the feature of her face:
that pride and meeknesse mixt by equall part,
doe both appeare t'adorne her beauties grace.
For with mild pleasance, which doth pride displace, 5
she to her loves doth lookers eyes allure:
and with sterne countenance back again doth chace
their looser lookes that stir up lustes impure.
With such strange termes her eyes she doth inure,
that with one looke she doth my life dismay: 10

SONNET XX 5–8. *Lyon . . . disdeigneth to devoure*: This zoological lore,
recorded by Pliny (*Natural History* 8.19), serves to valorize not only the
mercifulness of the mighty, but also the natural propriety of submission to
power. 8. *silly*: helpless, innocent.

and with another doth it streight recure;
her smile me drawes, her frowne me drives away.
Thus doth she traine and teach me with her lookes,
such art of eyes I never read in bookes.

### SONNET. XXII.

THis holy season fit to fast and pray,
   Men to devotion ought to be inclynd:
therefore, I lykewise on so holy day,
for my sweet Saynt some service fit will find.
Her temple fayre is built within my mind,        5
   in which her glorious ymage placed is,
on which my thoughts doo day and night attend
lyke sacred priests that never thinke amisse.
There I to her as th'author of my blisse,
   will builde an altar to appease her yre:       10
and on the same my hart will sacrifise,

SONNET XXI    11. *recure*: heal, restore.
SONNET XXII    Specific references enable us to identify XXII through
LXVIII as a Lenten group and also to date the courtship of *Amor* quite
precisely. References to "this holy season fit to fast and pray" (1) and to
burning suggest that XXII may be associated with Ash Wednesday. Sonnet
LXVIII is clearly an Easter sonnet, and it occurs forty-seven sonnets after
XXII—the number of days between Ash Wednesday and Easter. The New
Year's sonnet LXII permits us to attach this span to a specific date and year.
If LXII represents 25 March, the date on which the year normally changed in
England (rather than 1 January, the Julian New Year's Day), its placement
within the Lenten group requires that Easter fall on 31 March. March 31
was, in fact, the date of Easter in 1594, the year *Amor* was entered in the
Stationers' Register. This calendrical configuration occurred only one other
time in Sp's lifetime, in 1583, long before he could have written *Amor*. This
Lenten group is centered in the sequence, with twenty-one sonnets preceding
it and twenty-one following. Thematically, it is characterized by its emphasis
on the lover's distress. Sonnets XXIII through XXXVIII and XLI through
LVII all refer to the cruelty of the lady, the suffering of the lover, or both of
these.    5. *mind*: The poet is describing an internal process.    11. The
object to be sacrificed in the process of Lenten purgation is his heart, where
he bred his "unquiet thought" in II. The purgation is by fire here, but when

burning in flames of pure and chast desyre:
The which vouchsafe O goddesse to accept,
amongst thy deerest relicks to be kept.


### SONNET. XXIII.

PEnelope for her *Ulisses* sake,
   Deviz'd a Web her wooers to deceave:
in which the worke that she all day did make
the same at night she did againe unreave,
Such subtile craft my Damzell doth conceave,       5
   th'importune suit of my desire to shonne:
for all that I in many dayes doo weave,
in one short houre I find by her undonne.
So when I thinke to end that I begonne,
   I must begin and never bring to end:       10
for with one looke she spils that long I sponne,
and with one word my whole years work doth rend.
Such labour like the Spyders web I fynd,
   whose fruitlesse worke is broken with least wynd.


### SONNET. XXIIII.

WHen I behold that beauties wonderment,
   And rare perfection of each goodly part:
of natures skill the onely complement,
I honor and admire the makers art.

the lady later accepts his love, the imagery is of water rather than of fire; this
corresponds to Dante, *Purgatorio* 25–26 and 31. See also Psalms 51, an
appointed reading for the Ash Wednesday service in the first Edwardine *Book
of Common Prayer.*
SONNET XXIII   1. *Penelope*: Uncertain of the fate of her long-absent
husband Ulysses, Penelope kept suitors at bay by delaying them until she
finished weaving a shroud; after three years they discovered that each night
she had undone the progress she had made during the day (Homer, *Odyssey*
2).   4. *unreave*: unravel.   9. *that*: that which.   12. *whole years work*:
We may read this either as a declaration that the lover has been wooing for a
year, or as hyperbole.

But when I feele the bitter balefull smart,                    5
   which her fayre eyes unwares doe worke in mee:
   that death out of theyr shiny beames doe dart,
   I thinke that I a new *Pandora* see,
Whom all the Gods in councell did agree,
   into this sinfull world from heaven to send:          10
   that she to wicked men a scourge should bee,
   for all their faults with which they did offend.
But since ye are my scourge I will intreat,
   that for my faults ye will me gently beat.

### SONNET. XXV.

HOw long shall this lyke dying lyfe endure,
   And know no end of her owne mysery:
   but wast and weare away in termes unsure,
   twixt feare and hope depending doubtfully.
Yet better were attonce to let me die,                         5
   and shew the last ensample of your pride:
   then to torment me thus with cruelty,
   to prove your powre, which I too wel have tride.
But yet if in your hardned brest ye hide,
   a close intent at last to shew me grace:                10
   then all the woes and wrecks which I abide,
   as meanes of blisse I gladly wil embrace.
And wish that more and greater they might be,
   that greater meede at last may turne to mee.

SONNET XXIV   6. *unwares*: either (a)unintentionally or (b)suddenly. If we choose (b) Elizabeth becomes a more active agent of the poet's suffering, whereas (a) leaves much of the responsibility with the poet himself and shifts attention to the process of the poet's education in love. In the latter reading the first two quatrains show the dual nature, not of Elizabeth, but of the lover's perceptions.   8. *Pandora*: In retaliation for Prometheus's efforts to better the race of men, Zeus sent the first woman, Pandora, bearing, as "gifts" from the gods, all the evils that would plague mankind. The irony of the name "Pandora" (all gifts) was often ignored in the Renaissance. See *TM* 577ff.

SONNET XXV   4. *depending*: hanging.   14. *meede*: reward.

SONNET. XXVI.

SWeet is the Rose, but growes upon a brere;
  Sweet is the Junipere, but sharpe his bough;
sweet is the Eglantine, but pricketh nere;
sweet is the firbloome, but his braunches rough.
Sweet is the Cypresse, but his rynd is tough,                5
  sweet is the nut, but bitter is his pill;
sweet is the broome-flowre, but yet sowre enough;
and sweet is Moly, but his root is ill.
So every sweet with soure is tempred still,
  that maketh it be coveted the more:                       10
for easie things that may be got at will,
  most sorts of men doe set but little store.
Why then should I accoumpt of little paine
  that endlesse pleasure shall unto me gaine.

SONNET. XXVII.

FAire proud now tell me why should faire be proud,
  Sith all worlds glorie is but drosse uncleane:
and in the shade of death it selfe shall shroud,
how ever now thereof ye little weene.

SONNET XXVI    This is the first of two floral catalogues, symmetrically placed fourth after the Ash Wednesday sonnet and fourth before the Easter sonnet. Here the catalogue emphasizes the "lower" senses of taste and touch, which in each line of the octave supercede those of smell or sight, implied presumably by "sweet." According to Ficino (*Commentary on Plato's Symposium* 1.4), "the pleasures of taste and touch . . . are so violent and wild that they remove the intellect from its proper state and perturb the man." 3. *Eglantine*: a European rose with prickly stem, fragrant leaves and pink flowers, also called sweetbriar.     7. *broome-flowre*: European shrub with large yellow flowers; the twigs were used to make brooms.     8. *Moly*: a magical white flower with a black root used by Odysseus as an antidote to the sorcery of Circe (*Odyssey* 10).     13. *accoumpt*: take account of.
SONNETS XXVII–XXIX    In these sonnets the lover seeks to woo the lady with promises of poetic immortality, a common Renaissance theme introduced here for the first time in *Amor*.
SONNET XXVII    4. *how . . . weene*: though you may hardly think about, expect, or imagine that now.

That goodly Idoll now so gay beseene,      5
   shall doffe her fleshes borowd fayre attyre:
   and be forgot as it had never beene,
   that many now much worship and admire.
Ne any then shall after it inquire,
   ne any mention shall thereof remaine:      10
   but what this verse, that never shall expyre,
   shall to you purchas with her thankles paine.
Faire be no lenger proud of that shall perish,
   but that which shal you make immortall, cherish.

## SONNET. XXVIII.

THe laurell leafe, which you this day doe weare,
   gives me great hope of your relenting mynd:
for since it is the badg which I doe beare,
   ye bearing it doe seeme to me inclind:
The powre thereof, which ofte in me I find,      5
   let it lykewise your gentle brest inspire
with sweet infusion, and put you in mind
   of that proud mayd, whom now those leaves attyre:
Proud *Daphne* scorning Phæbus lovely fyre,
   on the Thessalian shore from him did flie:      10
for which the gods in theyr revengefull yre
   did her transforme into a laurell tree.
Then fly no more fayre love from Phebus chace,
   but in your brest his leafe and love embrace.

---

5. *beseene*: looking, appearing.     9–10. *Ne . . . ne*: neither . . . nor.
11–12. *but what . . . paine*: except what this eternal verse will gain you
through my unappreciated effort.
SONNET XXVIII   3. *badg . . . beare*: The laurel is the poet's sign.
7. *infusion*: the pouring in of an idea, inspiration.     9. *Proud Daphne
scorning Phæbus lovely fyre*: There are several Renaissance versions of Daphne's
rejection of the sun god's amorous passion, some of which, like the lover's
here, treat Daphne's transformation as a punishment for failure to submit
rather than a rescue from importunate pursuit, as in Ovid (*Met* 1).

### SONNET. XXIX.

S ee how the stubborne damzell doth deprave
my simple meaning with disdaynfull scorne:
and by the bay which I unto her gave,
accoumpts my selfe her captive quite forlorne.
The bay (quoth she) is of the victours borne,5
yielded them by the vanquisht as theyr meeds,
and they therewith doe poetes heads adorne,
to sing the glory of their famous deedes.
But sith she will the conquest challeng needs,
let her accept me as her faithfull thrall,10
that her great triumph which my skill exceeds,
I may in trump of fame blaze over all.
Then would I decke her head with glorious bayes,
and fill the world with her victorious prayse.

### SONNET. XXX.

M Y love is lyke to yse, and I to fyre;
how comes it then that this her cold so great
is not dissolv'd through my so hot desyre,
but harder growes the more I her intreat?
Or how comes it that my exceeding heat5
is not delayd by her hart frosen cold:
but that I burne much more in boyling sweat,
and feele my flames augmented manifold?
What more miraculous thing may be told
that fire which all thing melts, should harden yse:10
and yse which is congeald with sencelesse cold,
should kindle fyre by wonderfull devyse.

SONNET XXIXContinues the situation of XXVIII.1. *deprave*:
distort.3. *bay*: laurel.9. *sith . . . needs*: as she insists on challenging
my victory.
SONNET XXX7. *boyling sweat*: "boyling" may be a pun on Elizabeth
Boyle's name; the visual rhyme with "heat" (5) suggests a possible pun on
"sweat."10. *that*: than that.11. *sencelesse*: numbing.

Such is the powre of love in gentle mind,
that it can alter all the course of kynd.

### SONNET. XXXI.

A h why hath nature to so hard a hart,
given so goodly giftes of beauties grace?
Whose pryde depraves each other better part,
and all those pretious ornaments deface.
Sith to all other beastes of bloody race,                    5
a dreadfull countenaunce she given hath:
that with theyr terrour al the rest may chace,
and warne to shun the daunger of theyr wrath.
But my proud one doth worke the greater scath,
through sweet allurement of her lovely hew:              10
that she the better may in bloody bath
of such poore thralls her cruell hands embrew.
But did she know how ill these two accord,
such cruelty she would have soone abhord.

### SONNET. XXXII.

T he paynefull smith with force of fervent heat
the hardest yron soone doth mollify:
that with his heavy sledge he can it beat,
and fashion to what he it list apply.
Yet cannot all these flames in which I fry,              5
her hart more harde then yron soft awhit:
ne all the playnts and prayers with which I
doe beat on th'andvyle of her stubberne wit:
But still the more she fervent sees my fit:
the more she frieseth in her wilfull pryde,            10
and harder growes the harder she is smit,

SONNET XXXI   3. *depraves . . . part*: distorts her other, nobler, features
(see XXIX.1).      9. *scath*: injury.
SONNET XXXII      1. *fervent*: very hot.      4. *fashion . . . apply*: make of
it whatever he wishes.      6. *soft awhit*: soften at all.

620 : *Amoretti* and *Epithalamion*

with all the playnts which to her be applyde.
What then remaines but I to ashes burne,
and she to stones at length all frosen turne?

GReat wrong I doe, I can it not deny,
   to that most sacred Empresse my dear dred,
not finishing her Queene of faëry,
that mote enlarge her living prayses dead:
But lodwick, this of grace to me aread:             5
doe ye not thinck th'accomplishment of it
sufficient worke for one mans simple head,
all were it as the rest but rudely writ.
How then should I without another wit:
thinck ever to endure so tædious toyle,         10
sins that this one is tost with troublous fit
of a proud love, that doth my spirite spoyle.
Ceasse then, till she vouchsafe to grawnt me rest,
or lend you me another living brest.

Lyke as a ship that through the Ocean wyde
   by conduct of some star doth make her way,
whenas a storme hath dimd her trusty guyde,
out of her course doth wander far astray:

SONNET XXXIII   2. *Empresse*: Queen Elizabeth. *dred*: object of
reverence.   3. The lover is here given the specific historical identity of
Edmund Spenser, author of *FQ*.   4. *living prayses dead*: posthumous
fame.   5. *lodwick*: Lodowick Bryskett was a companion of Philip Sidney
who became a friend and admirer of Sp while he and Sp held posts in
Ireland; he contributed "A pastorall Aeglogue upon the death of Sir Phillip
Sidney Knight" to Sp's collection *Astrophel* (1595), and represented Sp with
great admiration in his *Discourse on Civil Life* (1606). *aread*: explain.   8. *all
. . . writ*: even though it may lack stylistic refinement.
SONNET XXXIV   The role of the lady as guide is defined
metaphorically in the general situation of this sonnet. The lover must see
beyond the darkening storms (of passion) to follow her (pure) light.

So I whose star, that wont with her bright ray          5
 me to direct, with cloudes is overcast,
 doe wander now in darknesse and dismay,
 through hidden perils round about me plast.
Yet hope I well, that when this storme is past
 my *Helice* the lodestar of my lyfe          10
 will shine again, and looke on me at last,
 with lovely light to cleare my cloudy grief.
Till then I wander carefull comfortlesse,
 in secret sorow and sad pensivenesse.

## SONNET. XXXV.

M Y hungry eyes through greedy covetize
 still to behold the object of their paine:
 with no contentment can themselves suffize,
 but having pine and having not complaine.
For lacking it they cannot lyfe sustayne,          5
 and having it they gaze on it the more:
 in their amazement lyke *Narcissus* vaine
 whose eyes him starv'd: so plenty makes me poore.
Yet are mine eyes so filled with the store
 of that faire sight, that nothing else they brooke,          10
 but lothe the things which they did like before,
 and can no more endure on them to looke.
All this worlds glory seemeth vayne to me,
 and all their showes but shadowes saving she.

10. *Helice*: name given to the constellation Ursa Major. Elizabeth's name
becomes a symbol of universal harmony, uniting earth (Helicon: see note to
I.10) and stars (Helice); this also epitomizes her role as guide in love.
*lodestar*: guiding star. 13. *careful*: full of care, sad.
S O N N E T  X X X V This sonnet represents a stage in the lover's
development in which he concentrates all his attention on his lady, excluding
other goals or persons. It is reprinted as LXXXIII with different meaning.
7. *Narcissus*: The proud and vain Narcissus was so enraptured with his own
image reflected in the water that he could not leave it; he died at the water's
edge and his body was transformed into a flower. 10. *brooke*: tolerate.

### SONNET. XXXVI.

TEll me when shall these wearie woes have end,
  Or shall their ruthlesse torment never cease:
but al my dayes in pining languor spend,
without hope of aswagement or release?
Is there no meanes for me to purchace peace,      5
  or make agreement with her thrilling eyes:
but that their cruelty doth still increace,
and dayly more augment my miseryes?
But when ye have shewed all extremityes,
  then thinke how litle glory ye have gayned     10
by slaying him, whose lyfe though ye despyse,
mote have your life in honour long maintayned.
But by his death which some perhaps will mone,
  ye shall condemned be of many a one.

### SONNET. XXXVII.

WHat guyle is this, that those her golden tresses
  She doth attyre under a net of gold:
and with sly skill so cunningly them dresses
that which is gold or heare may scarse be told?
Is it that mens frayle eyes, which gaze too bold,     5
  she may entangle in that golden snare:
and being caught may craftily enfold
theyr weaker harts, which are not wel aware?
Take heed therefore, myne eyes, how ye doe stare
  henceforth too rashly on that guilefull net,     10
in which if ever ye entrapped are,
out of her bands ye by no meanes shall get.
Fondnesse it were for any being free,
  to covet fetters, though they golden bee.

SONNET XXXVI   6. *thrilling*: piercing.   9. *extremityes*: severe or
violent powers.   12. *mote*: might.
SONNET XXXVII   4. *which*: which of them. See Chrétien de Troyes,
*Cligés* 1170, p.108.   13. *fondnesse*: folly.

## SONNET. XXXVIII.

A Rion, when through tempests cruel wracke,
 He forth was thrown into the greedy seas:
  through the sweet musick which his harp did make
  allur'd a Dolphin him from death to ease.
But my rude musick, which was wont to please     5
 some dainty eares, cannot with any skill
  the dreadfull tempest of her wrath appease,
  nor move the Dolphin from her stubborne will.
But in her pride she dooth persever still,
 all carelesse how my life for her decayse:     10
  yet with one word she can it save or spill;
  to spill were pitty, but to save were prayse.
Chose rather to be praysd for dooing good,
 then to be blam'd for spilling guiltlesse blood.

## SONNET. XXXIX.

S Weet smile, the daughter of the Queene of love,
 Expressing all thy mothers powrefull art:
  with which she wonts to temper angry Jove,
  when all the gods he threats with thundring dart,

SONNET XXXVIII  1. *Arion*: legendary Greek bard said to have been
rescued by a dolphin because of the beauty of the music he played before he
leapt overboard to escape death at the hands of greedy sailors (e.g. Virgil, *Ecl*
8.55–56. Sp makes no mention of the sailors and has Arion instead thrown
overboard by a storm, perhaps to conform both to the lover's complaint that
he has been victimized and to the current of tempest imagery in this part of
the sequence (e.g. XXXIV, XL, XLVI, LVI, LIX, LXIII). That the dolphin
was often a symbol of salvation in the Christian tradition may point to the
lady's spiritual function. *wracke*: violence.
SONNETS XXXIX AND XL  This pair of sonnets is an interlude of
calm and insight in the midst of the plaintive sonnets between XXII and
LVII.
SONNET XXXIX  1. *Queene of love*: Venus. The lady's smile seems to
have a spiritual significance akin to that of Dante's Beatrice (*Purgatorio* 31f.).
It expresses both mercy and wisdom (see LXXXI), and its effect is on his soul
(XXXIX.9–10) as well as on his heart (XL.13).  3. *Jove*: Jupiter or Zeus,
patriarchal ruler of the Graeco-Roman pantheon.

Sweet is thy vertue as thy selfe sweet art,        5
   for when on me thou shinedst late in sadnesse:
   a melting pleasance ran through every part,
   and me revived with hart robbing gladnesse.
Whylest rapt with joy resembling heavenly madnes,
   my soule was ravisht quite as in a traunce:      10
   feeling thence no more her sorowes sadnesse,
   fed on the fulnesse of that chearefull glaunce.
More sweet than Nectar or Ambrosiall meat
   seemd every bit, which thenceforth I did eat.

SONNET. XL.

MArk when she smiles with amiable cheare,
   And tell me whereto can ye lyken it:
when on each eyelid sweetly doe appeare
an hundred Graces as in shade to sit.
Lykest it seemeth in my simple wit      5
   unto the fayre sunshine in somers day:
   that when a dreadfull storme away is flit,
   thrugh the broad world doth spred his goodly ray:
At sight whereof each bird that sits on spray,
   and every beast that to his den was fled      10
   comes forth afresh out of their late dismay,
   and to the light lift up theyr drouping hed.
So my storme beaten hart likewise is cheared
   with that sunshine when cloudy looks are cleared.

SONNET. XLI.

IS it her nature or is it her will,
   to be so cruell to an humbled foe?

13. *Nectar . . . meat*: drink and food of the gods.
SONNET XL    4. *Graces*: three divine sisters, here hyperbolically
multiplied, who came to be associated with Venus and to represent gracious
beauty in nature, man, and the gods. For the Neoplatonists they represented
the idea of the return of love to God. See Wind 1958, also E. K.'s gloss to
*SC* "April," also *FQ* VI x 23–24.    7. *flit*: moved.

if nature, then she may it mend with skill,
if will, then she at will may will forgoe.
But if her nature and her wil be so,          5
that she will plague the man that loves her most:
and take delight t'encrease a wretches woe,
then all her natures goodly guifts are lost.
And that same glorious beauties ydle boast,
is but a bayt such wretches to beguile          10
as, being long in her loves tempest tost,
she meanes at last to make her piteous spoyle.
O fayrest fayre let never it be named,
that so fayre beauty was so fowly shamed.

### SONNET. XLII.

THe love which me so cruelly tormenteth,
So pleasing is in my extreamest paine:
that all the more my sorrow it augmenteth,
the more I love and doe embrace my bane.
Ne doe I wish (for wishing were but vaine)          5
to be acquit from my continuall smart:
but joy her thrall for ever to remayne,
and yield for pledge my poore captyved hart;
The which that it from her may never start,
let her, yf please her, bynd with adamant chayne:          10
and from all wandring loves which mote pervart,
his safe assurance strongly it restrayne.
Onely let her abstaine from cruelty,
and doe me not before my time to dy.

### SONNET. XLIII.

SHall I then silent be or shall I speake?
And if I speake, her wrath renew I shall:

SONNET XLI     10. *bayt . . . beguile*: The lady in effect functions as a bait
to guide the poet to love, but in his moments of anger, passion, confusion,
and self-pity he cannot see beyond the temporary pain. Cf. LIII.11.
SONNET XLII     4. *bane*: ruin.     7. *thrall*: captive.     10. *adamant*:
strong.     11. *pervart*: lead astray.

and if I silent be, my hart will breake,
or choked be with overflowing gall.
What tyranny is this both my hart to thrall,                                  5
and eke my toung with proud restraint to tie?
that nether I may speake nor thinke at all,
but like a stupid stock in silence die.
Yet I my hart with silence secretly
will teach to speak, and my just cause to plead:                             10
and eke mine eies with meeke humility,
love learned letters to her eyes to read.
Which her deep wit, that true harts thought can spel,
wil soone conceive, and learne to construe well.

### SONNET. XLIIII.

WHen those renoumed noble Peres of Greece,
thrugh stubborn pride amongst themselves did
jar
forgetfull of the famous golden fleece,
then Orpheus with his harp theyr strife did bar.
But this continuall cruell civill warre,                                     5
the which my selfe against my selfe doe make:
whilest my weak powres of passions warreid arre,
no skill can stint nor reason can aslake.
But when in hand my tunelesse harp I take,
then doe I more augment my foes despight:                                    10
and griefe renew, and passions doe awake,
to battaile fresh against my selfe to fight.

SONNET XLIII    5. *thrall*: bind.        8. *stupid stock*: stump or log
without feelings.    13. *true harts thought can spel*: The lover seems to be
learning to bring his heart into accord with the proper dictates of the mind
and spirit; the lady understands this. Cf. III, VIII, LXXXI.
SONNET XLIV    1. *Peres*: leaders, in this case the Argonauts, amongst
whom the legendary Greek poet Orpheus is said to have often kept peace
through the power of his music. For Orpheus see *Epith*, note to line
16.    7. *of passions warreid*: embattled by passions.    8. *aslake*:
diminish.    10. *despight*: scorn, spite.

Mongst whome the more I seeke to settle peace,
the more I fynd their malice to increace.

### SONNET. XLV.

L Eave lady in your glasse of christall clene,
 Your goodly selfe for evermore to vew:
and in my selfe, my inward selfe I meane,
most lively lyke behold your semblant trew.
Within my hart, though hardly it can shew        5
 thing so divine to vew of earthly eye:
 the fayre Idea of your celestiall hew,
 and every part remaines immortally:
And were it not that through your cruelty,
 with sorrow dimmed and deformd it were:        10
 the goodly ymage of your visnomy,
 clearer then christall would therein appere.
But if your selfe in me ye playne will see,
 remove the cause by which your fayre beames
                                        darkned be.

### SONNET. XLVI.

W Hen my abodes prefixed time is spent,
 My cruell fayre streight bids me wend my way:
but then from heaven most hideous stormes are sent
as willing me against her will to stay.
Whom then shall I or heaven or her obay?        5
 the heavens know best what is the best for me:

SONNET XLV    The poet here trivializes the concept of the lover's
function as mirror (see note to line 1 of VII). Her image in his heart is, as he
suggests, "dimmed and deformd" (10) by his sorrow; however, the proper
solution is not her submission, but his transcendence of the deforming
passions. Ironically, it is precisely her resistance that serves to "remove the
cause by which your fayre beames darkned be" (14).    4. *semblant*:
likeness.    11. *visnomy*: face.    14. an alexandrine; also X.14.
SONNET XLVI    1. *abodes*: visit's.    5. *or heaven or her*: heaven or her.

but as she will, whose will my life doth sway,
my lower heaven, so it perforce must bee.
But ye high hevens, that all this sorowe see,
    sith all your tempests cannot hold me backe:          10
aswage your stormes, or else both you and she,
    will both together me too sorely wrack.
Enough it is for one man to sustaine
    the stormes, which she alone on me doth raine.

SONNET. XLVII.

TRust not the treason of those smyling lookes,
    untill ye have theyr guylefull traynes well tryde:
for they are lyke but unto golden hookes,
    that from the foolish fish theyr bayts doe hyde:
So she with flattring smyles weake harts doth guyde          5
    unto her love and tempte to theyr decay,
whome being caught she kills with cruell pryde,
    and feeds at pleasure on the wretched pray:
Yet even whylst her bloody hands them slay,
    her eyes looke lovely and upon them smyle:          10
that they take pleasure in her cruell play,
    and dying doe them selves of payne beguyle.

8. Having artificially established a conflict between heaven and the lady, the
lover shockingly chooses his "lower heaven," still failing to understand that
the two are in concert. Ficino explains that "wrapped in its earthly body, the
soul serves the use of the body for a very long time. To this work it always
accommodates sensation, and also reason more often than it should"
(*Commentary on Plato's Symposium* 5.4). Similarly in XXXIII the poet chooses
to follow the dictates of love rather than of duty. XXXIII and XLVI are the
sixth sonnets before and after the "smile" interlude at XXXIX–XL.
SONNET XLVII    Most of the negative images introduced thus far seem
to be reunited in this bitter outburst: the spider's web of XXIII, the fish nets
of XXXVII, and the bait of XLI are joined in lines 3 and 4; the smiles
reverently celebrated in XXXIX and XL are derided in lines 5 and 6; the
association in XX and XXXI of the lady's cruelty with beastly rapacity is
repeated in lines 8 and 9.    2. *traynes*: generally, tricks or wiles; more
specifically, lines or trails of bait for luring wild animals. *tryde*: tested,
examined.    8. *pray*: prey.

O mighty charm which makes men love theyr bane,
and thinck they dy with pleasure, live with payne.

### SONNET. XLVIII.

INnocent paper whom too cruell hand
   Did make the matter to avenge her yre:
and ere she could thy cause wel understand,
did sacrifize unto the greedy fyre.
Well worthy thou to have found better hyre,           5
   then so bad end for hereticks ordayned:
yet heresy nor treason didst conspire,
   but plead thy maisters cause unjustly payned.
Whom she all carelesse of his griefe constrayned
   to utter forth th'anguish of his hart:           10
and would not heare, when he to her complayned,
   the piteous passion of his dying smart.
Yet live for ever, though against her will,
   and speake her good, though she requite it ill.

### SONNET. XLIX.

FAyre cruell, why are ye so fierce and cruell?
   Is it because your eyes have powre to kill?
then know, that mercy is the mighties jewell,
   and greater glory thinke to save, then spill.
But if it be your pleasure and proud will          5
   to shew the powre of your imperious eyes:
then not on him that never thought you ill,
   but bend your force against your enemyes.
Let them feele th'utmost of your crueltyes,
   and kill with looks as Cockatrices doo:         10

SONNET XLVIII    8. *thy . . . payned*: the cause of thy master, who has
been made to suffer unjustly.    13–14. *Yet live . . . /and speake*: The verbs
are imperatives addressed to the "innocent paper" on which he is writing his
verse.
SONNET XLIX    3–4. *mercy . . . spill*: Here again the lover trivializes a
concept of spiritual significance.    10. *Cockatrices*: fictive creatures whose
glance was supposed to have the power to kill.

but him that at your footstoole humbled lies,
with mercifull regard, give mercy too.
Such mercy shal you make admyred to be,
so shall you live by giving life to me.

SONNET. L.

L Ong languishing in double malady,
of my harts wound and of my bodies griefe:
there came to me a leach that would apply
fit medicines for my bodies best reliefe.
Vayne man (quod I) that hast but little priefe            5
in deep discovery of the mynds disease,
is not the hart of all the body chiefe?
and rules the members as it selfe doth please?
Then with some cordialls seeke first to appease
the inward languour of my wounded hart,                   10
and then my body shall have shortly ease:
but such sweet cordialls passe Physitions art.
Then my lyfes Leach doe you your skill reveale,
and with one salve both hart and body heale.

SONNET. LI.

D Oe I not see that fayrest ymages
Of hardest Marble are of purpose made?
for that they should endure through many ages,
ne let theyr famous moniments to fade.

SONNET L    There is irony here. Every Elizabethan reader understood
that the heart governs the body, but requires governance, in turn, by the
mind and spirit. The poet calls on the lady to heal his heart and body, but she
will not do so, of course, until he has attained the proper governance of his
own heart. When Macbeth asks "Canst thou not minister to a mind diseas'd?"
the doctor replies "Therein the patient/ Must minister to himself" (*Macbeth*
5.3.40–45).    5. *priefe*: experience.    9. *cordialls*: medicines to raise the
spirits or warm the heart.

Why then doe I, untrainde in lovers trade,     5
    her hardnes blame which I should more commend?
Sith never ought was excellent assayde,
    which was not hard t'atchive and bring to end.
. Ne ought so hard, but he that would attend,
    mote soften it and to his will allure:     10
so doe I hope her stubborne hart to bend,
    and that it then more stedfast will endure.
Onely my paines wil be the more to get her,
    but having her, my joy wil be the greater.


SONNET. LII.

SO oft as homeward I from her depart,
    I goe lyke one that having lost the field:
is prisoner led away with heavy hart,
    despoyld of warlike armes and knowen shield.
So doe I now my selfe a prisoner yeeld,     5
    to sorrow and to solitary paine:
from presence of my dearest deare exylde,
    longwhile alone in languor to remaine.
There let no thought of joy or pleasure vaine
    dare to approch, that may my solace breed:     10
but sudden dumps and drery sad disdayne
    of all worlds gladnesse more my torment feed.
So I her absens will my penaunce make,
    that of her presens I my meed may take.


SONNET LI     5–6. *Why . . . commend?*: The lover begins to question his
own attitude.     9. *ne ought*: nor anything. *attend*: attend to it.
10. *mote*: might. *allure*: This curious usage seems to break the plane of
metaphor, referring to his attracting the lady rather than to the softening of a
hard substance.
SONNET LII     4. *knowen*: familiar.     10. *breed*: generate (as in
II.1).     13. *penaunce*: Here he reintroduces the devotional theme of XXII.

### SONNET. LIII.

THe Panther knowing that his spotted hyde
 Doth please all beasts but that his looks them
              fray:
 within a bush his dreadfull head doth hide,
 to let them gaze whylest he on them may pray.
Right so my cruell fayre with me doth play,      5
 for with the goodly semblant of her hew:
 she doth allure me to mine owne decay,
 and then no mercy will unto me shew.
Great shame it is, thing so divine in view,
 made for to be the worlds most ornament:    10
 to make the bayte her gazers to embrew,
 good shames to be to ill an instrument.
But mercy doth with beautie best agree,
 as in theyr maker ye them best may see.

### SONNET. LIIII.

OF this worlds Theatre in which we stay,
 My love lyke the Spectator ydly sits
 beholding me that all the pageants play,
 disguysing diversly my troubled wits.
Sometimes I joy when glad occasion fits,      5
 and mask in myrth lyke to a Comedy:
 soone after when my joy to sorrow flits,
 I waile and make my woes a Tragedy.
Yet she beholding me with constant eye,
 delights not in my merth nor rues my smart:   10
 but when I laugh she mocks, and when I cry
 she laughes, and hardens evermore her hart.

SONNET LIII 2. *fray*: frighten. 10. *most*: greatest. 11. *to make*:
to make herself. *embrew*: imbrue, stain (with blood). 12. *shames*: shames
itself.
SONNET LIV 3. *pageants*: scenes. 6. *mask*: perform in a masque
(amateur theatrical performance at court); also: disguise his real feelings.

What then can move her? if nor merth nor mone,
she is no woman, but a sencelesse stone.

### SONNET. LV.

SO oft as I her beauty doe behold,
   And therewith doe her cruelty compare:
I marvaile of what substance was the mould
the which her made attonce so cruell faire.
Not earth: for her high thoghts more heavenly are;     5
  not water: for her love doth burne like fyre;
  not ayre: for she is not so light or rare;
  not fyre: for she doth friese with faint desire.
Then needs another Element inquire
  whereof she mote be made; that is the skye.     10
  for to the heaven her haughty lookes aspire:
  and eke her mind is pure immortall hye.
Then sith to heaven ye lykened are the best,
  be lyke in mercy as in all the rest.

### SONNET. LVI.

FAyre ye be sure, but cruell and unkind,
   As is a Tygre that with greedinesse
hunts after bloud, when he by chance doth find
a feeble beast, doth felly him oppresse.
Fayre be ye sure but proud and pittilesse,     5
  as is a storme, that all things doth prostrate:
  finding a tree alone all comfortlesse,
  beats on it strongly it to ruinate.
Fayre be ye sure, but hard and obstinate,
  as is a rocke amidst the raging floods:     10
  gaynst which a ship of succour desolate,
  doth suffer wreck both of her selfe and goods.

SONNET LV    9. *needs . . . inquire*: there is need to seek another element.
12. *eke*: also.
SONNET LVI    4. *felly*: cruelly.

That ship, that tree, and that same beast am I,
  whom ye doe wreck, doe ruine, and destroy.

### SONNET. LVII.

S Weet warriour when shall I have peace with you?
    High time it is, this warre now ended were:
  which I no lenger can endure to sue,
  ne your incessant battry more to beare:
So weake my powres, so sore my wounds appeare,                5
  that wonder is how I should live a jot,
  seeing my hart through launched every where
  with thousand arrowes, which your eies have shot:
Yet shoot ye sharpely still, and spare me not,
  but glory thinke to make these cruel stoures;               10
  ye cruell one, what glory can be got,
  in slaying him that would live gladly yours?
Make peace therefore, and graunt me timely grace,
  that al my wounds wil heale in little space.

### SONNET. LVIII.

*By her that is most assured to her selfe.*

W Eake is th'assurance that weake flesh reposeth
    In her owne powre and scorneth others ayde:

SONNET LVII   1. *peace*: With this sonnet the war is ended. The
emphasis on suffering and complaint disappears now until the very end of
*Amor*, where the lover suffers for different reasons.   4. *incessant battry*: In
XIV.10 the lover announced his intention to lay "incessant battery" to her
heart. Apparently he has lost the initiative that was his in the first twenty-one
sonnets; the besieger now feels besieged.   10. *stoures*: battles.
SONNET LVIII   *By her . . .* : Some readers, seeking consistency with
the preceding plaintive sonnets or uncomfortable with the poet's attribution
of this sonnet to the lady, have suggested that the superscription belongs
above LIX or that "by" may mean "concerning." The printer's reasonable care
in setting and correcting the book (see textual notes) makes the first
suggestion doubtful; the second is lexically improbable. If we read the text as
it stands and with the common meaning of "by," this declaration by

that soonest fals when as she most supposeth
her selfe assurd, and is of nought affrayd.
All flesh is frayle, and all her strength unstayd,          5
    like a vaine bubble blowen up with ayre:
    devouring tyme and changeful chance have prayd
    her glories pride that none may it repayre.
Ne none so rich or wise, so strong or fayre,
    but fayleth trusting on his owne assurance:          10
    and he that standeth on the hyghest stayre
    fals lowest: for on earth nought hath enduraunce.
Why then doe ye proud fayre, misdeeme so farre,
    that to your selfe ye most assured arre.

SONNET. LIX.

THrise happie she, that is so well assured
    Unto her selfe and setled so in hart:
    that nether will for better be allured,
    ne feard with worse to any chaunce to start,
But like a steddy ship, doth strongly part          5
    the raging waves and keepes her course aright:
    ne ought for tempest doth from it depart,
    ne ought for fayrer weathers false delight.

Elizabeth becomes an important and perfectly placed part of the lover's
process of discovery in the sonnets that follow. LVIII and LIX form a
dialogue introducing the crucial change in his attitude. In LVIII, a
condemnation of the self-assurance of the flesh, Elizabeth summarizes the
lesson she has been teaching the lover in preparation for what is to come.
The feminine pronouns in lines 1 through 8 all refer to "flesh."          7. *prayd*:
preyed upon.          13. *proud fayre*: Perhaps because it refers to the lover rather
than the lady, the familiar phrase as used elsewhere in *Amor* at II.9 and
XXVII.1 is here inverted.
SONNET LIX          We may read this as the lover's admiring response to the
wisdom of the lady expressed in LVIII. Her self-assurance, unlike his, is
above tempests and passions. Hereafter the mood shifts sharply; the nine
sonnets between LVIII and LXVIII increasingly are charged with a sense of
propitious change.          3. *nether*: neither.          4. *ne . . . start*: nor will be
frightened in any circumstance to deviate.

Such selfe assurance need not feare the spight
 of grudging foes, ne favour seek of friends:    10
but in the stay of her owne stedfast might,
nether to one her selfe nor other bends.
Most happy she that most assured doth rest,
 but he most happy who such one loves best.

SONNET. LX.

THey that in course of heavenly spheares are skild,
 To every planet point his sundry yeare:
in which her circles voyage is fulfild,
 as Mars in three score yeares doth run his spheare.
So since the winged God his planet cleare    5
 began in me to move, one yeare is spent:
the which doth longer unto me appeare,
 then al those fourty which my life outwent.
Then by that count, which lovers books invent,
 the spheare of Cupid fourty yeares containes:    10
which I have wasted in long languishment,
 that seemd the longer for my greater paines.
But let my loves fayre Planet short her wayes
 this yeare ensuing, or else short my dayes.

SONNET. LXI.

THe glorious image of the makers beautie,
 My soverayne saynt, the Idoll of my thought,

12. *nether . . . bends*: bends (herself) neither to one nor the other.
S O N N E T  LX  4. Ptolemy gives the planetary year of Mars as seventy-nine and a fraction (*Almagest* 9.3).  5. *the winged God*: Cupid.  6. *one yeare*: He has loved Elizabeth for one year. As he is already in love with Elizabeth at the beginning of *Amor*, we can make no inference from this line about time values in the sequence.  8. *fourty*: This perhaps precise, perhaps approximate, indication of the lover's age permits us to place Sp's birth date in 1554, or perhaps a bit earlier to allow for his matriculation at Cambridge in 1569 at the normal age.
S O N N E T  LXI  1. *image*: See note to line 1 of VII. Ficino adds: "There immediately appears in the intellect another species of this image, which no

dare not henceforth above the bounds of dewtie
t'accuse of pride, or rashly blame for ought.
For being as she is divinely wrought,                                    5
  and of the brood of Angels hevenly borne:
  and with the crew of blessed Saynts upbrought,
  each of which did her with theyr guifts adorne;
The bud of joy, the blossome of the morne,
  the beame of light, whom mortal eyes admyre:                          10
  what reason is it then but she should scorne
  base things that to her love too bold aspire?
Such heavenly formes ought rather worshipt be,
  then dare be lov'd by men of meane degree.

### SONNET. LXII.

THe weary yeare his race now having run,
  The new begins his compast course anew:
with shew of morning mylde he hath begun,
betokening peace and plenty to ensew,
So let us, which this chaunge of weather vew,                           5
  chaunge eeke our mynds and former lives amend;
  the old yeares sinnes forepast let us eschew,
  and fly the faults with which we did offend.
Then shall the new yeares joy forth freshly send
  into the glooming world his gladsome ray:                            10

longer seems to be a likeness of one particular human body, as it was in the
fancy, but a common Reason or definition of the whole human race equally
. . . . The latter raises him up to the angelic or contemplative life"
(*Commentary on Plato's Symposium* 7.1).      3. *dare not*: one, or perhaps even
I, dare not: the subject is elliptical.      8. *each . . . adorne*: The Pandora
image of XXIV here becomes entirely reverential.      13. *ought rather*
*worshipt be*: The lover shows an incipient awareness of the spiritual dimension
of love.
SONNET LXII      Numerically this New Year's sonnet is the first poem of
the second half of *Amor and Epith*, if we count all the sonnets, the nine
Anacreontic stanzas and the twenty-four stanzas of *Epith*.      1. *weary yeare*:
See note to XXII.      5. *vew*: apparent.      6–8. Words like "amend . . .
sinnes . . . faults . . . offend" suggest that the lover is becoming aware of his
past shortcomings.

and all these stormes which now his beauty blend,
shall turne to caulmes and tymely cleare away.
So likewise love cheare you your heavy spright,
and chaunge old yeares annoy to new delight.

### SONNET. LXIII.

AFter long stormes and tempests sad assay,
  Which hardly I endured heretofore:
in dread of death and daungerous dismay,
with which my silly barke was tossed sore,
I doe at length descry the happy shore,     5
  in which I hope ere long for to arryve,
fayre soyle it seemes from far and fraught with store
of all that deare and daynty is alyve.
Most happy he that can at last atchyve
  the joyous safety of so sweet a rest:     10
whose least delight sufficeth to deprive
remembrance of all paines which him opprest.
All paines are nothing in respect of this,
  all sorrowes short that gaine eternall blisse.

### SONNET. LXIIII.

COmming to kisse her lyps, (such grace I found)
  Me seemd I smelt a gardin of sweet flowres:

11. *blend*: conceal.
SONNET LXIII    1. *assay*: trial.    2. *hardly*: with difficulty.
3. *daungerous dismay*: fear of danger.    4. *silly . . . sore*: poor boat was
grievously tossed.    5. *descry*: espy.    6. *in*: on or at.    7–8. *fayre . . .
alyve*: from afar it seems a fair land with an abundance of all that is precious
and lovely.
SONNET LXIV    1. *Comming to kisse*: The catalogue of flowers differs
here from the catalogue at XXVI in stressing sight and smell, higher senses
than those of taste and touch. Its sensuousness is informed with the tradition
of the *Song of Songs* 4.12: "My sister my spouse is as a garden inclosed" (see
DeNeef 1982), and the first kiss is an expression of a love that is gradually
becoming spiritualized as the creation of an avenue between two souls. See

that dainty odours from them threw around
for damzels fit to decke their lovers bowres.
Her lips did smell lyke unto Gillyflowers,                    5
    her ruddy cheekes lyke unto Roses red:
    her snowy browes lyke budded Bellamoures,
    her lovely eyes lyke Pincks but newly spred,
Her goodly bosome lyke a Strawberry bed,
    her neck lyke to a bounch of Cullambynes:              10
    her brest lyke lillyes, ere theyr leaves be shed,
    her nipples lyke yong blossomd Jessemynes.
Such fragrant flowres doe give most odorous smell,
    but her sweet odour did them all excell.

### S O N N E T. L X V.

THe doubt which ye misdeeme, fayre love, is vaine,
    That fondly feare to loose your liberty;
when loosing one, two liberties ye gayne,
and make him bond that bondage earst dyd fly.
Sweet be the bands, the which true love doth tye,          5
    without constraynt or dread of any ill:
    the gentle birde feeles no captivity
    within her cage, but singes and feeds her fill.
There pride dare not approch, nor discord spill

Castiglione, *The Book of the Courtier* 4 (p.315), e.g.: "All chaste lovers covet a
kisse as a coupling of soules together."    5. *Gillyflowers*: a variety of pinks
noted for a clove-like scent.    7. *Bellamoures*: unidentified white flowers.
10. *Cullambynes*: columbines, small plants with inverted flowers often violet
in color. See *SC* "April" 136.    12. *Jessemynes*: jasmines, shrubs of southern
origin with fragrant white or yellow flowers, introduced into England in the
sixteenth century.
S O N N E T  L X V    1. *misdeeme*: mistakenly harbor.    2. *fondly*: foolishly.
3. Cf. Ficino: "O wondrous contract in which he who gives himself up for
another has the other, and does not cease to have himself!" (*Commentary on
Plato's Symposium* 2.8).    4. *make him bond*: Comparison of these lines with
I.3–4, XII.9–12, XXIX.10, or XXXVII.13–14 reveals the striking shift in the
lover's attitude; comparison with LXVIII.3–4 suggests the significance of
this shift.

the league twixt them, that loyal love hath bound:　　10
but simple truth and mutuall good will
seekes with sweet peace to salve each others wound.
There fayth doth fearlesse dwell in brasen towre,
and spotlesse pleasure builds her sacred bowre.

SONNET. LXVI.

TO all those happy blessings which ye have,
　　with plenteous hand by heaven upon you
　　　　　　　　　　　　　　thrown:
　　this one disparagement they to you gave,
　　that ye your love lent to so meane a one.
Yee whose high worths surpassing paragon,　　5
　　could not on earth have found one fit for mate,
　　ne but in heaven matchable to none,
　　why did ye stoup unto so lowly state.
But ye thereby much greater glory gate,
　　then had ye sorted with a princes pere:　　10
　　for now your light doth more it selfe dilate,
　　and in my darknesse greater doth appeare.
Yet since your light hath once enlumind me,
　　with my reflex yours shall encreased be.

SONNET. LXVII.

LYke as a huntsman after weary chace,
　　Seeing the game from him escapt away:
　　sits downe to rest him in some shady place,
　　with panting hounds beguiled of their pray,
So after long pursuit and vaine assay,　　5

11. *mutuall good will*: perhaps reflects the sixteenth-century Protestant
emphasis on mutuality in the marriage relationship. See Sinfield 1983,
especially pp.66–68.　　13. *brasen*: strong.
SONNET LXVI　1. *have*: have had.　　8–14. Sp here seems to conflate
the idea of the lady as spiritual guide with that of Christ as spiritual guide.

when I all weary had the chace forsooke,
the gentle deare returnd the selfe-same way,
thinking to quench her thirst at the next brooke.
There she beholding me with mylder looke,
sought not to fly, but fearelesse still did bide:　　　10
till I in hand her yet halfe trembling tooke,
and with her owne goodwill hir fyrmely tyde.
Strange thing me seemd to see a beast so wyld,
so goodly wonne with her owne will beguyld.

### SONNET. LXVIII.

M Ost glorious Lord of lyfe that on this day
　　Didst make thy triumph over death and sin:
and having harrowd hell didst bring away
captivity thence captive us to win,
This joyous day, deare Lord, with joy begin,　　　5
and grant that we for whom thou diddest dye
being with thy deare blood clene washt from sin,
may live for ever in felicity.
And that thy love we weighing worthily,
may likewise love thee for the same againe:　　　10
and for thy sake that all lyke deare didst buy,
with love may one another entertayne.
So let us love, deare love, lyke as we ought,
love is the lesson which the Lord us taught.

SONNET LXVII　14. *her owne will*: LXVII announces metaphorically
that the new bond of love between the lady and lover came about not
through his conquest but through her voluntary submission. Prescott (1985)
shows that the chief symbolic elements of this poem—the hart, water, and
voluntary submission—are those of the medieval liturgical tradition of the
Easter Eve baptism of the catechumens.
SONNET LXVIII　This explicitly paschal sonnet draws together several
levels of meaning in *Amor*; it relates God's love for man to the love between
the lady and the poet and it expresses the poet's new understanding of the
meaning of love.

### SONNET. LXIX.

THe famous warriors of the anticke world,
   Used Trophees to erect in stately wize:
in which they would the records have enrold,
of theyr great deeds and valarous emprize.
What trophee then shall I most fit devize,         5
   in which I may record the memory
   of my loves conquest, peerelesse beauties prise,
   adorn'd with honour, love, and chastity?
Even this verse vowd to eternity,
   shall be thereof immortall moniment:         10
   and tell her prayse to all posterity,
   that may admire such worlds rare wonderment,
The happy purchase of my glorious spoile,
   gotten at last with labour and long toyle.

### SONNET. LXX.

FResh spring the herald of loves mighty king,
   In whose cote armour richly are displayd
all sorts of flowers the which on earth do spring
in goodly colours gloriously arrayd.
Goe to my love, where she is carelesse layd,         5
   yet in her winters bowre not well awake:
   tell her the joyous time wil not be staid
   unlesse she doe him by the forelock take.
Bid her therefore her selfe soone ready make
   to wayt on love amongst his lovely crew:         10
   where every one that misseth then her make

SONNET LXIX    7. *conquest*: New problems await the lover in the last twenty-one sonnets. Here he emulates pagan tradition and also erroneously assumes he has won the lady with his own labor, when in fact she freely bestowed her favor on him. The irony here depends on the shared assumption of Elizabethan readers that God's grace transcends human understanding and human efforts.
SONNET LXX    7. Cf. *Song of Solomon* 2.10. *staid*: detained.
11. *make*: mate.

shall be by him amearst with penance dew.
Make hast therefore sweet love, whilest it is prime,
for none can call againe the passed time.

### SONNET. LXXI.

I Joy to see how in your drawen work,
 Your selfe unto the Bee ye doe compare;
and me unto the Spyder that doth lurke
in close awayt to catch her unaware.
Right so your selfe were caught in cunning snare          5
of a deare foe, and thralled to his love:
in whose streight bands ye now captived are
so firmely, that ye never may remove.
But as your worke is woven all about,
with woodbynd flowers and fragrant Eglantine:          10
so sweet your prison you in time shall prove,
with many deare delights bedecked fyne.
And all thensforth eternall peace shall see
betweene the Spyder and the gentle Bee.

### SONNET. LXXII.

OFt when my spirit doth spred her bolder winges,
 In mind to mount up to the purest sky:
it down is weighd with thoght of earthly things
and clogd with burden of mortality,

12. *amearst*: punished.     13. *make hast*: The *carpe diem* theme here
continues the worldly interests of LXIX.
SONNET LXXI     1. *drawen work*: embroidery. Cf. XXIII.     4. *in close
awayt*: covertly poised.     7. *streight*: tight.     10. *woodbynd*: probably
honeysuckle. *Eglantine*: sweetbrier, a variety of rose.
SONNET LXXII     1–3. *spirit . . . mind . . . earthly things*: See note to
I.7. In XXXIII and XLVI the lover failed to fulfill civic and spiritual
responsibilities because of the distraction of wooing; though he has won
both the lady and a deeper understanding of the spiritual dimension of love,
a tension between earthly and spiritual love remains, especially when he is in
the presence of the beloved. Her absence will become an important concern
of the last sonnets.

Where when that soverayne beauty it doth spy,                    5
  resembling heavens glory in her light:
  drawne with sweet pleasures bayt, it back doth fly,
  and unto heaven forgets her former flight.
There my fraile fancy fed with full delight,
  doth bath in blisse and mantleth most at ease:               10
  ne thinks of other heaven, but how it might
  her harts desire with most contentment please.
Hart need not wish none other happinesse,
  but here on earth to have such hevens blisse.

SONNET. LXXIII.

B Eing my selfe captyved here in care,
  My hart, whom none with servile bands can tye
  but the fayre tresses of your golden hayre,
  breaking his prison forth to you doth fly.
Lyke as a byrd that in ones hand doth spy                       5
  desired food, to it doth make his flight:
  even so my hart, that wont on your fayre eye
  to feed his fill, flyes backe unto your sight.
Doe you him take, and in your bosome bright
  gently encage, that he may be your thrall:                   10
  perhaps he there may learne with rare delight,
  to sing your name and prayses over all,
That it hereafter may you not repent,
  him lodging in your bosome to have lent.

SONNET. LXXIIII.

M Ost happy letters fram'd by skilfull trade,
  with which that happy name was first desynd:
  the which three times thrise happy hath me made,

---

10. *mantleth*: self-indulgently stretches her wings (a hawking term).
SONNET LXXIII    3. *but*: but only with.

with guifts of body, fortune and of mind.
The first my being to me gave by kind,                    5
    from mothers womb deriv'd by dew descent,
    the second is my sovereigne Queene most kind,
    that honour and large richesse to me lent.
The third my love, my lives last ornament,
    by whom my spirit out of dust was raysed:              10
    to speake her prayse and glory excellent,
    of all alive most worthy to be praysed.
Ye three Elizabeths for ever live,
    that three such graces did unto me give.

### SONNET. LXXV.

ONe day I wrote her name upon the strand,
    but came the waves and washed it a way:
agayne I wrote it with a second hand,
    but came the tyde, and made my paynes his pray.
Vayne man, sayd she, that doest in vaine assay,          5
    a mortall thing so to immortalize.
    for I my selve shall lyke to this decay,
    and eek my name bee wyped out lykewize.
Not so, (quod I) let baser things devize
    to dy in dust, but you shall live by fame:              10
    my verse your vertues rare shall eternize,
    and in the hevens wryte your glorious name,
Where whenas death shall all the world subdew,
    our love shall live, and later life renew.

SONNET LXXIV    13. *three Elizabeths*: This is Sp's only mention of his
mother's or wife's name.
SONNET LXXV    1. *strand*: shore.    14: Through its example of how
to attain true love on earth his verse will "later life renew," both spiritually
and physically. These lines provide a succinct but beautiful statement of Sp's
poetic purpose in *Amor*.

## SONNET. LXXVI.

FAyre bosome fraught with vertues richest tresure,
   The neast of love, the lodging of delight:
the bowre of blisse, the paradice of pleasure,
the sacred harbour of that hevenly spright.
How was I ravisht with your lovely sight,                      5
   and my frayle thoughts too rashly led astray?
Whiles diving deepe through amorous insight,
   on the sweet spoyle of beautie they did pray.
And twixt her paps like early fruit in May,
   whose harvest seemd to hasten now apace:                     10
they loosely did theyr wanton winges display,
   and there to rest themselves did boldly place.
Sweet thoughts I envy your so happy rest,
   which oft I wisht, yet never was so blest.

## SONNET. LXXVII

WAs it a dreame, or did I see it playne,
   a goodly table of pure yvory:
all spred with juncats, fit to entertayne
the greatest Prince with pompous roialty.
Mongst which there in a silver dish did ly                      5
   twoo golden apples of unvalewd price:
far passing those which Hercules came by,
   or those which Atalanta did entice:

SONNETS LXXVI–LXXVII    The fundamental tension of the last
twenty-one sonnets, that between the two levels of love the poet has
experienced, is most clearly expressed here. LXXVI and LXXVII are the most
sensual poems of the sequence, but that sensuality is at the same time denied
by the fact that the subject of these sonnets is not the poet, but, specifically,
his *thoughts* (LXXVI.6 and 13; LXXVII.14; LXXVIII.14).
SONNET LXXVII    3. *juncats*: sweets, delicacies.    7. *Hercules*: In his
eleventh labor, performed to atone for his crimes, Hercules through guile and
strength fetched from the end of the world the golden apples guarded by
nymphs called the Hesperides.    8. *Atalanta*: The fleet and beautiful
Atalanta promised to wed the man who could outrun her. Hippomenes

Exceeding sweet, yet voyd of sinfull vice,
   That many sought yet none could ever taste,         10
   sweet fruit of pleasure brought from paradice
   By love himselfe and in his garden plaste.
Her brest that table was, so richly spredd,
   my thoughts the guests, which would thereon have
   fedd.

## SONNET. LXXVIII.

L ackyng my love I go from place to place,
   lyke a young fawne that late hath lost the hynd:
   and seeke each where, where last I sawe her face,
   whose ymage yet I carry fresh in mynd.
I seeke the fields with her late footing synd,         5
   I seeke her bowre with her late presence deckt,
   yet nor in field nor bowre I her can fynd:
   yet field and bowre are full of her aspect,
But when myne eyes I thereunto direct,
   they ydly back returne to me agayne,         10
   and when I hope to see theyr trew object,
   I fynd my selfe but fed with fancies vayne.
Ceasse then myne eyes, to seeke her selfe to see,
   and let my thoughts behold her selfe in mee.

finally did so with Aphrodite's help by dropping three golden apples during
the race in order to distract her.
SONNET LXXVIII  1. *Lackyng my love*: Following the celebration of
Elizabeth's name in LXXIV and its washing away in LXXV, Elizabeth
appears to be absent in LXXVI–LXXVIII. Sonnets LXXXVII–LXXXIX
again specify her absence. The separation at LXXXIX serves to intensify the
reunion in *Epith*; here it may also be seen as part of the lover's program of
spiritual discovery; Castiglione explains: "The lover therefore that
considereth onely the beautie in the bodie, loseth this treasure and
happinesse, as soone as the woman beloved with her departure leaveth the
eies without their brightnesse . . . . The Courtier by the helpe of reason must
full and wholy call backe againe the coveting of the bodie to beautie alone . .
. and frame it within his imagination sundred from all matter" (*The Book of
the Courtier* 4, pp.316–17). The idea is further developed in LXXIX.
5. *synd*: signed (i.e. personally marked).

### SONNET. LXXIX.

MEn call you fayre, and you doe credit it,
　　For that your selfe ye dayly such doe see:
but the trew fayre, that is the gentle wit,
and vertuous mind, is much more praysd of me.
For all the rest, how ever fayre it be,　　　　　　　　5
　　shall turne to nought and loose that glorious hew:
but onely that is permanent and free
from frayle corruption, that doth flesh ensew.
That is true beautie: that doth argue you
　　to be divine and borne of heavenly seed:　　　　　10
deriv'd from that fayre Spirit, from whom al true
and perfect beauty did at first proceed.
He onely fayre, and what he fayre hath made,
　　all other fayre lyke flowres untymely fade.

### SONNET. LXXX.

AFter so long a race as I have run
　　Through Faery land, which those six books
　　　　　　　　　　　　　　　　　　compile,
　　give leave to rest me being halfe fordonne,
　　and gather to my selfe new breath awhile.
Then as a steed refreshed after toyle,　　　　　　　5

SONNET LXXIX　　1. *doe credit it*: do credit to it (i.e. justify the
assertion), or do believe it.　　7–9. *but onely that . . .* : The difficulty of
these lines is in determining which of the four instances of "that" are relative
pronouns and which demonstrative. One of several possible readings, all of
which convey the same general idea: only that (which) is permanent and free
from (the) frail corruption that attends the flesh, (only) that is true beauty;
only that doth argue you to be divine.　　13. *He onely fayre*: In accord with
the Neoplatonic concept that true beauty derives from God, the poet
increasingly focusses on the spiritual beauty of Elizabeth and of their love.
Yet this recognition remains in tension with the earthly love which his
human nature imposes. Sp is building towards the mythical celebration in
*Epith* of the harmony of earthly and spiritual love.
SONNET LXXX　　1–8. These lines indicate that Sp completed the sixth
book of *FQ* during or shortly before 1594 and that he definitely planned six
more books at that time.

Out of my prison I will breake anew:
and stoutly will that second worke assoyle,
with strong endevour and attention dew.
Till then give leave to me in pleasant mew,
    to sport my muse and sing my loves sweet praise:       10
    the contemplation of whose heavenly hew,
    my spirit to an higher pitch will rayse.
But let her prayses yet be low and meane,
    fit for the handmayd of the Faery Queene.

### SONNET. LXXXI.

Fayre is my love, when her fayre golden heares,
    with the loose wynd ye waving chance to marke:
fayre when the rose in her red cheekes appeares,
    or in her eyes the fyre of love does sparke.
Fayre when her brest lyke a rich laden barke,       5
    with pretious merchandize she forth doth lay:
fayre when that cloud of pryde, which oft doth dark
    her goodly light with smiles she drives away.
But fayrest she, when so she doth display
    the gate with pearles and rubyes richly dight:      10
throgh which her words so wise do make their way
    to beare the message of her gentle spright.
The rest be works of natures wonderment,
    but this the worke of harts astonishment.

7. *assoyle*: assail. Compare the lover's positive attitude here with his attitude in XXXIII, the other sonnet referring to *FQ*.    9. *mew*: cell (continuing the prison metaphor of line 6).    13. *meane*: modest.
SONNET LXXXI    9–14. Thus Castiglione: "The reasonable lover woteth well, that although the mouth be a parcell of the bodie, yet is it an issue for the wordes, that be the enterpreters of the soule, and for the inwarde breath, which is also called the soule" (*The Book of the Courtier* 4, p.315).    10. *dight*: adorned; the pearls and rubies, by color association, suggest her teeth and lips.    14. *harts astonishment*: Sonnets LXXX and LXXXI are the culmination in *Amor* of the theme of self-expression. In III the lover's thought was stopped; here it is his heart, considered part of the body (see L), that is astonished. He has accomplished the sacrifice of his heart promised in XXII.

### SONNET. LXXXII.

JOy of my life, full oft for loving you
I blesse my lot, that was so lucky placed:
but then the more your owne mishap I rew,
that are so much by so meane love embased.
For had the equall hevens so much you graced          5
in this as in the rest, ye mote invent
som hevenly wit, whose verse could have enchased
your glorious name in golden moniment.
But since ye deignd so goodly to relent
to me your thrall, in whom is little worth,          10
that little that I am, shall all be spent
in setting your immortall prayses forth.
Whose lofty argument uplifting me,
shall lift you up unto an high degree.

### SONNET. LXXXIII.

MY hungry eyes, through greedy covetize
Still to behold the object of theyr payne:
with no contentment can themselves suffize,
but having pine, and having not complayne;
For lacking it, they cannot lyfe sustayne,          5
and seeing it, they gaze on it the more:
in theyr amazement lyke Narcissus vayne
whose eyes him starv'd: so plenty makes me pore.
Yet are myne eyes so filled with the store
of that fayre sight, that nothing else they brooke:          10

SONNET LXXXII     6. *mote*: might.     7. *enchased*: enshrined.
13. *uplifting*: He recognizes that the "lofty argument" of his poems in her
praise is indeed uplifting him. See note to LXI.1.
SONNET LXXXIII     This is an almost exact reprint of XXXV. If we
assume that the repetition is intentional and that the sonnet takes new
meaning from its new context, then in XXXV the poet seems to distinguish
between different objects of beauty, i.e. between the lady and any other
aspect of earthly creation; here between different kinds of beauty, i.e.
between physical and spiritual beauty. See LXXVIII.13–14 and note.

but loath the things which they did like before,
and can no more endure on them to looke.
All this worlds glory seemeth vayne to me,
and all theyr shewes but shadowes saving she.

### SONNET. LXXXIIII.

L Et not one sparke of filthy lustfull fyre
   breake out, that may her sacred peace molest:
ne one light glance of sensuall desyre
Attempt to work her gentle mindes unrest.
But pure affections bred in spotlesse brest,       5
and modest thoughts breathd from wel tempred
sprites
goe visit her in her chast bowre of rest,
accompanyde with angelick delightes.
There fill your selfe with those most joyous sights,
the which my selfe could never yet attayne:      10
but speake no word to her of these sad plights,
which her too constant stiffenesse doth constrayn.
Onely behold her rare perfection,
and blesse your fortunes fayre election.

### SONNET. LXXXV.

T He world that cannot deeme of worthy things,
   when I doe praise her, say I doe but flatter:
so does the Cuckow, when the Mavis sings,
begin his witlesse note apace to clatter.
But they that skill not of so heavenly matter,      5

SONNETS LXXXIV–LXXXVI    In these three sonnets the lover is prey
to ill-defined fears. He becomes distraught in LXXXIV, and more so in
LXXXVI, yet he lashes out not, as in XXIII through LVII, at the lady, but at
the outer world, or conceivably even at his lower self, as he has recently, in
LXXVI through LXXVIII, developed such a distinction between his "selfe"
(e.g. LXXVIII.12) and his "thoughts" (e.g. LXXVIII.14).
SONNET LXXXV    3. *Mavis*: thrush, a songbird.

all that they know not, envy or admyre;
rather then envy let them wonder at her,
but not to deeme of her desert aspyre.
Deepe in the closet of my parts entyre,
   her worth is written with a golden quill:         10
that me with heavenly fury doth inspire,
and my glad mouth with her sweet prayses fill.
Which when as fame in her shrill trump shal thunder,
   let the world chose to envy or to wonder.

### SONNET. LXXXVI.

VEnemous toung tipt with vile adders sting,
   Of that selfe kynd with which the Furies fell
theyr snaky heads doe combe, from which a spring
of poysoned words and spitefull speeches well,
Let all the plagues and horrid paines of hell,         5
   upon thee fall for thine accursed hyre:
that with false forged lyes, which thou didst tel,
in my true love did stirre up coles of yre,
The sparkes whereof let kindle thine own fyre,
   and catching hold on thine owne wicked hed        10
consume thee quite, that didst with guile conspire
in my sweet peace such breaches to have bred.
Shame be thy need, and mischiefe thy reward.
   dew to thy selfe that it for me prepard.

### SONNET. LXXXVII.

SInce I did leave the presence of my love,
   Many long weary dayes I have outworne:

---

8. *deeme . . . aspyre*: aspire to win her favor.    9. *the closet . . . entyre*: my
innermost self.    11–12. Cf. III.9–10.    13. *trump*: trumpet.
SONNET LXXXVI    2. *Furies fell*: grim female spirits of retribution
sometimes represented with snakes for hair.    14. *dew*: due
SONNET LXXXVII–LXXXIX    The last three sonnets express the

and many nights, that slowly seemd to move
theyr sad protract from evening untill morne.
For when as day the heaven doth adorne,     5
   I wish that night the noyous day would end:
and when as night hath us of light forlorne,
   I wish that day would shortly reascend.
Thus I the time with expectation spend,
   and faine my griefe with chaunges to beguile,     10
that further seemes his terme still to extend,
   and maketh every minute seeme a myle.
So sorrow still doth seeme too long to last,
   but joyous houres doo fly away too fast.

### SONNET. LXXXVIII.

SInce I have lackt the comfort of that light,
   The which was wont to lead my thoughts astray:
I wander as in darkenesse of the night,
affrayd of every dangers least dismay.
Ne ought I see, though in the clearest day,     5
   when others gaze upon theyr shadowes vayne:
but th'onely image of that heavenly ray,
   whereof some glance doth in mine eie remayne.
Of which beholding th'Idæa playne,
   through contemplation of my purest part:     10
with light thereof I doe my selfe sustayne,
   and thereon feed my love-affamisht hart.
But with such brightnesse whylest I fill my mind,
   I starve my body and mine eyes doe blynd.

lover's distress at his separation from the lady. These sonnets, and of course
the subsequent marriage hymn, suggest that Sp felt that human nature
imposed a definite limitation on the Neoplatonic concept of spiritualized
love. The lover is not pure spirit; he misses the physical presence of the lady
and longs for reunion with her, as, on another level, the Christian longs for
reunion with Christ.
SONNET LXXXVII    4. *protract*: duration.    6. *noyous*: troublesome.
10. *faine*: must be satisfied.

### SONNET. LXXXIX.

L Yke as the Culver on the bared bough
    Sits mourning for the absence of her mate:
and in her songs sends many a wishfull vow,
for his returne that seemes to linger late,
So I alone now left disconsolate,                    5
    mourne to my selfe the absence of my love:
and wandring here and there all desolate,
seek with my playnts to match that mournful dove.
Ne joy of ought that under heaven doth hove
    can comfort me, but her owne joyous sight:         10
whose sweet aspect both God and man can move,
    in her unspotted pleasauns to delight.
Dark is my day, whyles her fayre light I mis,
    and dead my life that wants such lively blis.

### FINIS.

SONNET LXXXIX    1. *Culver*: dove. The sequence of birds in *Amor* is from the raucous cuckoo (LXXXV) to the songful mavis (LXXXV) to the dove, a bird associated with peace and the Holy Spirit.     12. *pleasauns*: charm.

# [*Anacreontics*]

## [POEM 1]

IN youth before I waxed old,
  The blynd boy Venus baby,
For want of cunning made me bold,
  In bitter hyve to grope for honny.
  But when he saw me stung and cry,          5
  He tooke his wings and away did fly.

## [POEM 2]

As Diane hunted on a day,
She chaunst to come where Cupid lay,
  his quiver by his head:

[ANACREONTICS]    These nine stanzas, which seem to form an
emblematic link between *Amor* and *Epith*, have come to be known as the
Anacreontics; their style and matter are derived from the Greek poets
Anacreon (sixth century B.C.) and Theocritus (third century B.C.), whose
works had been widely disseminated during the sixteenth century and were
often imitated, notably by Tasso, Ronsard and Baif. In the 1595 octavo,
stanzas 1 and 2 are printed together on a page, and the remaining stanzas one
to a page. There are three rhyme schemes: those of stanzas 1, 2–3, and 4–9.
Because there appear to be four narrative units corresponding with four
metric patterns (those of stanzas 1, 2, 3, and 4–9) the Anacreontics are often
treated as four separate poems, indicated by bracketed headings. Stylistically
and thematically the nine stanzas are integral, and all end with a tetrameter
couplet. Lines of the Anacreontics are numbered consecutively throughout,
rather than by poems or stanzas.
[POEM 1]    2. *baby*: Cupid.    3. *want of cunning*: The lover's boldness
in *Amor* resulted from his lack of understanding.    4. *bitter hyve . . . honny*:
The line may suggest that the lover was seeking love blindly, or that the
attainment of love is often painful.    5. *stung*: smitten, metaphorically. The
bestial origin of the lover's wound perhaps suggests the lowest kind of love,
which Pico calls irrational or bestial. But see note to Anacreontics 25, below.
[POEM 2]    7. *Diane*: goddess of hunting and chastity.

One of his shafts she stole away,                              10
And one of hers did close convay
   into the others stead:
     With that, love wounded my loves hart,
     but Diane beasts with Cupids dart.

### [ P O E M  3 ]

I Saw in secret to my Dame,                                    15
  How little Cupid humbly came:
   and sayd to her All hayle my mother.
But when he saw me laugh, for shame:
His face with bashfull blood did flame,
   not knowing Venus from the other.                      20
Then never blush Cupid (quoth I)
   for many have err'd in this beauty.

### [ P O E M  4 ]

U Pon a day as love lay sweetly slumbring,
  all in his mothers lap:
A gentle Bee with his loud trumpet murm'ring,                  25
  about him flew by hap.
Whereof when he was wakened with the noyse,
  and saw the beast so small:
Whats this (quoth he) that gives so great a voyce,

---

13. *love . . . hart*: Cupid strikes the lady's heart with Diane's arrow, an emblem of the hardening of the lady's heart in chastity.
[ P O E M  3 ]    20. *the other*: his lady. After the wound with Diane's arrow, the lady appears divinely beautiful, an emblem of the effect of chastity.
22. *err'd . . . beauty*: mistaken his lady's human beauty for divine.
[ P O E M  4 ]    25. *gentle Bee*: The bee, as beast, may represent physical love in the Anacreontics, but had also been associated with chastity and continence (Virgil, Plutarch, Bernard of Clairvaux, Dante). The coexistence of these contrary associations in the image of the bee carries the germ of a theme that will be developed in *Epith*: that of the sanctification of sexuality.
26. *hap*: chance.

that wakens men withall.                                      30
In angry wize he flyes about,
    and threatens all with corage stout.

TO whom his mother closely smiling sayd,
    twixt earnest and twixt game:
See thou thy selfe likewise art lyttle made,                 35
    if thou regard the same.
And yet thou suffrest neyther gods in sky,
    nor men in earth to rest:
But when thou art disposed cruelly,
    theyr sleepe thou doost molest.                           40
Then eyther change thy cruelty,
    or give lyke leave unto the fly.

NAthlesse the cruell boy not so content,
    would needs the fly pursue:
And in his hand with heedlesse hardiment,                     45
    him caught for to subdue.
But when on it he hasty hand did lay,
    the Bee him stung therefore:
Now out alasse (he cryde) and welaway,
    I wounded am full sore:                                   50
The fly that I so much did scorne,
    hath hurt me with his little horne.

UNto his mother straight he weeping came,
    and of his griefe complayned:
Who could not chose but laugh at his fond game,              55
    though sad to see him pained.
Think now (quod she) my sonne how great the smart
    of those whom thou dost wound:
Full many thou hast pricked to the hart,
    that pitty never found:                                   60

---

32. *corage stout*: Here and in the following stanzas there may be an
undercurrent of erotic meaning. Courage meant bravery, but another
meaning was lust.   42. *fly*: bee.   44. *needs*: of necessity (ironic).

Therefore henceforth some pitty take,
　　when thou doest spoyle of lovers make.

SHe tooke him streight full pitiously lamenting,
　　and wrapt him in her smock:
She wrapt him softly, all the while repenting,　　　　　65
　　that he the fly did mock.
She drest his wound and it embaulmed wel
　　with salve of soveraigne might:
And then she bath'd him in a dainty well,
　　the well of deare delight.　　　　　　　　　　　70
Who would not oft be stung as this,
　　to be so bath'd in Venus blis.

THe wanton boy was shortly wel recured
　　of that his malady:
But he soone after fresh againe enured　　　　　　75
　　his former cruelty.
And since that time he wounded hath my selfe
　　with his sharpe dart of love:
And now forgets the cruell carelesse elfe
　　his mothers heast to prove. So now　　　　　　80
I languish till he please
　　my pining anguish to appease.

FINIS.

64. *smock*: frock, or female undergarment; may also suggest immorality.
70. *well of deare delight*: the apparent cure for "bee sting."　　73. *wanton*:
unruly.　　77. *wounded*: The poet has suffered two wounds, the first by the
bee, the second by Cupid who has himself been wounded by the bee, perhaps
suggesting that the first wound, inflicting irrational love, is subsumed in the
second, inducing rational love. By this device the Anacreontics summarize the
lover's experience in *Amor* and point forward to *Epith*, which celebrates the
harmony of human love with the higher and lower forces of the universe.
80. *his . . . prove*: to do his mother's bidding.　　81–82: The lover is left
pining in solitude as at the end of *Amor*.

# Epithalamion

EPITHALAMION. The new title page separates this work in some measure from the preceding poems. The title designates a wedding song. The irregular stanzas resemble in some ways those of the Pindaric ode and in others those of the Petrarchan *canzone*, but here, as in *Amor*, Sp elevates form to the level of symbol, creating a symbolic framework that enlarges the concept of the poem. Various elements of creation participate in the historical experience of Sp's wedding: elements physical and spiritual, ancient and modern; plants, birds, mammals, and fish; minstrels, priests, townfolk, boys, and maidens; ghosts, goblins, screech-owls, and frogs; sun and moon, stars and planets, gods and angels. These elements play their roles during the wedding day in a pageant-like progression from the lady's maiden bedroom to the church to the nuptial bedroom. This progression may reflect Sp's awareness of the derivation of the title from *epi* (=upon) and *thalamos* (=bride chamber), but the conceptual and structural center of the work is unquestionably the wedding ceremony at the church in stanzas 12 and 13. From that spiritual experience flows the force that binds the disparate elements of Sp's world.

In the form of the stanzas there is a tension between regularity and irregularity reflecting the larger tension between universality and particularity. Like the sonnets of *Amor*, the stanzas were printed one to a page, but they vary in length from seventeen to nineteen lines (excluding the seven-line envoy) according to no pattern that has been explained. The rhyme scheme of each begins with the same pattern, then diverges. Most, but not all, are divided into four sections by the occurrence of short lines (mostly trimeter) in approximately, but not exactly, the same places. The refrain of each stanza is similar, yet subtly and significantly varied.

The narrative and thematic relationships among stanzas are multiply ordered. The progressive nature of the narrative is emphasized by its forward bias. With the exception of the wedding stanzas 12 and 13, *Epith* deals consistently with the time before the event that is its stated or implied focus at any point. Thus successively the poet anticipates the awakening of the bride as he summons attendants (stanzas 2–5), her emergence as he directs her adornment (stanzas 6–8), the wedding ceremony as she approaches the church (stanzas 9–11), withdrawal to their bedchamber as he describes the festivities (stanzas 14–16), consummation of the marriage as he invokes protective and supportive spirits (stanzas 17–20), childbirth and progeny as he asks blessings of the gods (stanzas 21–23). The anticipatory focus extends beyond the poem, implying an infinite linear progression. On the other hand this progression is framed by stanzas 1 and 24, which deal with the poem itself, and centered on stanzas 12 and 13, which directly represent the wedding ceremony itself.

# Epithalamion·

The sequence of the experiences of the wedding day progresses on a regular temporal schedule from first awakening until late at night. However, we follow the linear progression of the events not by clock time, but by the phenomena of celestial light: twilight, sunrise, sunshine, dusk, nightfall, moonlight. Indeed the poet treats the motions of sun, moon, and stars not merely as concurrent phenomena by which we measure human experience, but temporarily as active participants in the events of his wedding day, along with the various other participants from the whole range of natural and social orders. Yet this integration of natural forces with human aspirations is, the poet recogognizes, only temporary: "let this one day be myne,/ Let all the rest by thine," he implores the sun (125–26).

The coexistence of the concentric order of Sp's vision with the sequential order of daily events is expressed also in the experience of the bride and groom and in the arrangement of the stanzas. The ten stanzas between the invocation (stanza 1) and the wedding ceremony (stanzas 12 and 13) are clearly preparatory. The next ten stanzas before the envoy (stanza 24) are all legitimized by and therefore consequent to the ceremony. The basis of this concentric order is not human experience, for the groom and, immediately or approximately, the bride are present throughout. Rather it is the divine sanction through church and priest that forms the center and imparts order to the whole. This superimposition of linear and concentric orders has enabled readers to identify several patterns of matching stanzas, both concentric (see Greene 1957 and Wickert 1968) and sequential (see Hieatt 1960 and 1961, Fowler 1970, and Eade 1972).

As in *Amor* Sp underscores the personal and historical dimension of his vision through a symbolic calendrical link to a specific date and time. In identifying and elucidating that link in *Epith*, A. Kent Hieatt (1960) radically changed our understanding of this poem and imparted a new direction to Spenser studies generally. He noted that the totals of stanzas (=24-hour day) and long lines (=365-day year) symbolize calendrical units; further that Sp was married on 11 June, St. Barnabas's day (line 266) and that the phrase "now night is come" occurs after sixteen-and-a-quarter stanzas, corresponding to the indication in contemporary almanacs of sixteen-and-a-quarter hours of daylight for southern Ireland in June. Identification of other possible astronomical allusions, such as Fowler's observation (1970) that the twenty- three-and-a-half stanzas may symbolize the degrees of inclination of the ecliptic and hence the sun's midsummer declination, serve to underscore the importance of Sp's concern with time and its relationship to meaning in life.

[1]

Y E learned sisters which have oftentimes
  beene to me ayding, others to adorne:
Whom ye thought worthy of your gracefull rymes,
That even the greatest did not greatly scorne
To heare theyr names sung in your simple layes,     5
But joyed in theyr prayse:
And when ye list your owne mishaps to mourne,
Which death, or love, or fortunes wreck did rayse,
Your string could soone to sadder tenor turne,
And teach the woods and waters to lament      10
Your dolefull dreriment:
Now lay those sorrowfull complaints aside,
And having all your heads with girland crownd,
Helpe me mine owne loves prayses to resound,
Ne let the same of any be envide,         15
So Orpheus did for his owne bride,
So I unto my selfe alone will sing,
The woods shall to me answer and my Eccho ring.

[STANZA 1]  1. *learned sisters*: the nine Muses. *oftentimes/beene to me ayding*: Sp establishes his identity as poet.  3. *gracefull*: conferring grace.  4. *That*: so graceful that. *greatest*: e.g. Elizabeth I, especially in *FQ*.  5. *layes*: songs.  7. *list*: desire.  16. *Orpheus*: legendary Greek poet famed for the supernatural power of his music and for his fatally ardent devotion to his wife Eurydice whom he won, according to one tradition, by his music, but whom he failed to free from the underworld after her death because he violated the injunction not to look back at her on the way. Orpheus was widely celebrated in the Renaissance both as a mystical seer and as a poetic enchanter. The bridegroom's music in *Epith* has the Orphic power both to win his bride and to invoke the universal harmony of all the participants and the surrounding answering woods (see Cain 1971, also Allman 1980).  18. The refrain, which has a long tradition of use by Sp (e.g. *SC* "June" 52; *FQ* I iii 8; II iii 20; VI x 10) and others (e.g. Psalms 96; Petrarch, *Rime* 61; Virgil *Aen* 149), finds its consummate use here in epitomizing the central idea of *Epith*, that of universal complicity in the particular event.

### [2]

EArly before the worlds light giving lampe
His golden beame upon the hils doth spred, 20
Having disperst the nights unchearefull dampe,
Doe ye awake and with fresh lusty hed,
Go to the bowre of my beloved love,
My truest turtle dove;
Bid her awake; for Hymen is awake, 25
And long since ready forth his maske to move,
With his bright Tead that flames with many a flake,
And many a bachelor to waite on him,
In theyr fresh garments trim.
Bid her awake therefore and soone her dight, 30
For lo the wished day is come at last,
That shall for al the paynes and sorrowes past,
Pay to her usury of long delight,
And whylest she doth her dight,
Doe ye to her of joy and solace sing, 35
That all the woods may answer and your eccho ring.

### [3]

BRing with you all the Nymphes that you can heare
both of the rivers and the forrests greene:
And of the sea that neighbours to her neare,
Al with gay girlands goodly wel beseene. 40

[STANZA 2] 22. *ye*: The poet apparently is still addressing the Muses
of line 1. *lusty hed*: cheerfulness. 24. *my beloved love*: Stanza two shifts
attention from the poet himself to the bride. 25. *Hymen*: god of
marriage. 26. *maske*: pageant. 27. *Tead*: torch. *flake*: detached piece
of flaming matter. 30. *dight*: dress. 31. *day is come*: Stanzas 2 through
4 are twilight stanzas. 32. *paynes and sorrowes*: e.g. those of *Amor* XXII–
LVII and LXXXIV–LXXXIX.
[STANZA 3] 37. *Nymphes*: mythological feminine spirits inhabiting
nature whom Sp treats as lesser deities; the focus has shifted from the poet in
stanza 1 to the bride in 2 to the natural environment in 3 and 4. *you can
heare*: can hear you. 38–44. The color symbols may suggest that charity
and faith (red and white) in a setting of hope (green) are united by the bond
of loyal human love (blue). On colors, see Dante, *Purgatorio* 29.

And let them also with them bring in hand,
Another gay girland
For my fayre love of lillyes and of roses,
Bound truelove wize with a blew silke riband.
And let them make great store of bridal poses,                    45
And let them eeke bring store of other flowers
To deck the bridale bowers.
And let the ground whereas her foot shall tread,
For feare the stones her tender foot should wrong,
Be strewed with fragrant flowers all along,                       50
And diapred lyke the discolored mead.
Which done, doe at her chamber dore awayt,
For she will waken strayt,
The whiles doe ye this song unto her sing,
The woods shall to you answer and your Eccho ring.                55

[4]
YE Nymphes of Mulla which with carefull heed,
The silver scaly trouts doe tend full well,
and greedy pikes which use therein to feed,
(Those trouts and pikes all others doo excell)
And ye likewise which keepe the rushy lake,                       60
Where none doo fishes take,
Bynd up the locks the which hang scatterd light,
And in his waters which your mirror make,
Behold your faces as the christall bright,
That when you come whereas my love doth lie,                      65
No blemish she may spie.
And eke ye lightfoot mayds which keepe the dere,
That on the hoary mountayne use to towre,
And the wylde wolves which seeke them to devoure,

51. *diapred . . . mead*: strewn in a varied pattern to imitate the particolored
meadowland.     54–55. These lines end the address to the learned sisters of
line 1.
[STANZA 4]     56. *Mulla*: Irish river.     60–61. Reportedly the small
lake beside Kilcolman tower, the remains of Sp's residence in Ireland, is still
"inhospitable to fish."     67. *lightfoot mayds*: the woodland nymphs.

With your steele darts doo chace from comming neer,    70
Be also present heere,
To helpe to decke her and to help to sing,
That all the woods may answer and your eccho ring.

[5]
Wake now my love, awake; for it is time,
    The Rosy Morne long since left Tithones bed,    75
All ready to her silver coche to clyme,
And Phœbus gins to shew his glorious hed.
Hark how the cheerefull birds do chaunt theyr laies
And carroll of loves praise.
The merry Larke hir mattins sings aloft,    80
The thrush replyes, the Mavis descant playes,
The Ouzell shrills, the Ruddock warbles soft,
So goodly all agree with sweet consent,
To this dayes merriment.
Ah my deere love why doe ye sleepe thus long,    85
When meeter were that ye should now awake,
T'awayt the comming of your joyous make,
And hearken to the birds lovelearned song,
The deawy leaves among.
For they of joy and pleasance to you sing,    90
That all the woods them answer and theyr eccho ring.

[6]
My love is now awake out of her dreame,
    and her fayre eyes like stars that dimmed were
With darksome cloud, now shew theyr goodly beams

---

[STANZA 5]    74. *my love*: the first address to the bride.
75. *Tithones*: a mortal Trojan prince loved by the dawn goddess Eos, or
Aurora (the "Rosy Morne"), who asked Zeus to make him immortal but
neglected to ask also that he be made ageless and so eventually lost interest in
him.    77. *Phœbus gins to shew*: The sun begins its ascent.    80. *Larke*:
songbird associated with dawn; after the spirits of wood and water now the
birds of the air are called to join the event.    81. *Mavis*: a variety of thrush
with a mellow song.    82. *Ouzell*: blackbird. *Ruddock*: robin.
86. *meeter*: more appropriate.

More bright then Hesperus his head doth rere.                    95
Come now ye damzels, daughters of delight,
Helpe quickly her to dight,
But first come ye fayre houres which were begot
In Joves sweet paradice, of Day and Night,
Which doe the seasons of the yeare allot,                        100
And al that ever in this world is fayre
Doe make and still repayre.
And ye three handmayds of the Cyprian Queene,
The which doe still adorne her beauties pride,
Helpe to addorne my beautifullest bride                          105
And as ye her array, still throw betweene
Some graces to be seene,
And as ye use to Venus, to her sing,
The whiles the woods shal answer and your eccho ring.

[7]

NOw is my love all ready forth to come,                          110
Let all the virgins therefore well awayt,
And ye fresh boyes that tend upon her groome
Prepare your selves; for he is comming strayt.
Set all your things in seemely good aray
Fit for so joyfull day,                                          115

[STANZA 6]     95. *Hesperus*: the evening star, the planet Venus.
96. *damzels*: the bridesmaids; the gradually broadening focus now includes
human society to which are added below (98, 103) the Hours and Graces
representing qualities that may inhabit both man and nature.     97. *dight*:
attire, get ready.     98. *houres*: The Horae, Hours, are three daughters of
Zeus associated with the principle of order, more specifically with the seasons
and later with the hours of the day and identified (like Janus) as keepers of
heaven's gate. Here and at *FQ* VII vii 45, where time is a central concept, Sp
identifies their mother as Night rather than the earth goddess Themis who is
commonly named as their mother. The importance of time in *Epith* is
signaled by the fact that the hours are the first-named attendants on the
bride.     103. *handmayds of the Cyprian Queene*: the Graces. See note to
*Amor* XL.4.     106–08: I.e. the Hours and Graces should adorn and
serenade Elizabeth just as they do Venus, but visibly and audibly.
[STANZA 7]     111. *virgins*: the "damzels" of line 96.

The joyfulst day that ever sunne did see.
Faire Sun, shew forth thy favourable ray,
And let thy lifull heat not fervent be
For feare of burning her sunshyny face,
Her beauty to disgrace.                                       120
O fayrest Phœbus, father of the Muse,
If ever I did honour thee aright,
Or sing the thing, that mote thy mind delight,
Doe not thy servants simple boone refuse,
But let this day let this one day be myne,              125
Let all the rest be thine.
Then I thy soverayne prayses loud wil sing,
That all the woods shal answer and theyr eccho ring.

[8]
Arke how the Minstrels gin to shrill aloud
Their merry Musick that resounds from far,       130
The pipe, the tabor, and the trembling Croud,
That well agree withouten breach or jar.
But most of all the Damzels doe delite,
When they their tymbrels smyte,
And thereunto doe daunce and carrol sweet,        135
That all the sences they doe ravish quite,
The whyles the boyes run up and downe the street,
Crying aloud with strong confused noyce,
As if it were one voyce.
Hymen io Hymen, Hymen they do shout,               140
That even to the heavens theyr shouting shrill
Doth reach, and all the firmament doth fill,
To which the people standing all about,

---

118. *lifull*: sustaining or giving life.       121. *Phœbus*: normally Zeus was
considered father of the Muses, but see *TM* 2.       124. *boone*: favor.
[STANZA 8]       131. *pipe*: flute. *tabor*: small drum. *Croud*: stringed
instrument.       133–43. *Damzels . . . boyes . . . people standing all about*:
These are townspeople, observers, not directly of the wedding party.
134. *tymbrels* tambourines.

As in approvance doe thereto applaud
And loud advaunce her laud,                                    145
And evermore they Hymen Hymen sing,
that al the woods them answer and theyr eccho ring.

[9]

L Oe where she comes along with portly pace,
  Lyke Phœbe from her chamber of the East,
Arysing forth to run her mighty race,                        150
Clad all in white, that seemes a virgin best.
So well it her beseemes that ye would weene
Some angell she had beene.
Her long loose yellow locks lyke golden wyre,
Sprinckled with perle, and perling flowres a tweene,         155
Doe lyke a golden mantle her attyre,
And being crowned with a girland greene,
Seeme lyke some mayden Queene.
Her modest eyes abashed to behold
So many gazers, as on her do stare,                          160
Upon the lowly ground affixed are.
Ne dare lift up her countenance too bold,
But blush to heare her prayses sung so loud,
So farre from being proud.
Nathlesse doe ye still loud her prayses sing,                165
That all the woods may answer and your eccho ring.

[10]

T Ell me ye merchants daughters did ye see
  So fayre a creature in your towne before,

145. *laud*: praise.
[STANZA 9] 148. *portly*: stately.     149. *Phœbe*: the moon goddess
Diana, associated with virginity.     151. *seemes*: is appropriate to, beseems
(as in line 152).     155. *perling flowres a tweene*: studded with glistening
flowers.     165. *ye*: probably the "gazers" of line 160 who are also the
"people standing all about" of the preceding stanza.
[STANZA 10]     167. *see*: Movement (181) and even sound (183) stop
in the predominantly visual experience of this stanza. Cf. *Amor* XXVI and

So sweet, so lovely, and so mild as she,
Adornd with beautyes grace and vertues store,        170
Her goodly eyes lyke Saphyres shining bright,
Her forehead yvory white,
Her cheekes lyke apples which the sun hath rudded,
Her lips lyke cherryes charming men to byte,
Her brest like to a bowle of creame uncrudded,        175
Her paps lyke lyllies budded,
Her snowie necke lyke to a marble towre,
And all her body like a pallace fayre,
Ascending uppe with many a stately stayre,
To honors seat and chastities sweet bowre.        180
Why stand ye still ye virgins in amaze,
Upon her so to gaze,
Whiles ye forget your former lay to sing,
To which the woods did answer and your eccho ring.

[11]

B Ut if ye saw that which no eyes can see,        185
The inward beauty of her lively spright,
Garnisht with heavenly guifts of high degree,
Much more then would ye wonder at that sight,
And stand astonisht lyke to those which red
Medusaes mazeful hed.        190

LXIV. For two stanzas the bride becomes an icon where the onlookers can behold the model of beauty and goodness now in presence. The passage reworks and anglicizes the praise of the Song of Songs 4.1–8, though the sensuality of the description is finally denied in the culminating image of her body as a palace ascending "to honors seat and chastities sweet bowre." 171–76. *Saphyres . . . yvory . . . apples . . . cherryes . . . lyllies*: Cf. the bouquet of flowers in lines 38–44.  175. *uncrudded*: uncurdled, fresh. [STANZA 11]  185. *no eyes can see*: The description proceeds from the visible image of the bride to her mind, which is endowed with seven heavenly gifts: love, chastity, faith, "womanhood," honor, modesty, and, reigning over both "spright" (186) and "base affections" (196), virtue.  189. *red*: saw. 190. *Medusaes*: Medusa was a monstrous mythological figure the sight of which petrified the beholder. She was sometimes associated with chastity (see Milton, *Comus* 446–51).  *mazefull*: bewildering.

There dwels sweet love and constant chastity,
Unspotted fayth and comely womanhood,
Regard of honour and mild modesty,
There vertue raynes as Queene in royal throne,
And giveth lawes alone.                                                  195
The which the base affections doe obay,
And yeeld theyr services unto her will,
Ne thought of thing uncomely ever may
Thereto approch to tempt her mind to ill.
Had ye once seene these her celestial threasures,          200
And unrevealed pleasures,
Then would ye wonder and her prayses sing,
That al the woods should answer and your echo ring.

### [12]

OPen the temple gates unto my love,
Open them wide that she may enter in,                        205
And all the postes adorne as doth behove,
And all the pillours deck with girlands trim,
For to recyve this Saynt with honour dew,
That commeth in to you.
With trembling steps and humble reverence                   210
She commeth in, before th'almighties vew,
Of her ye virgins learne obedience,
When so ye come into those holy places,
To humble your proud faces.
Bring her up to th'high altar that she may                   215
The sacred cermonies there partake,
The which do endlesse matrimony make,
And let the roring Organs loudly play

[STANZA 12]     211. *She commeth in*: here the action is in the present
tense, the focus is direct.     217. This is the midpoint of *Epith* by line-
count. A midpoint is an ideal imposed on the flow of time, corollary to the
definition of a beginning and an end. The word "endlesse" at the center of
this line epitomizes both the synthesis of universal and particular towards
which *Amor and Epith* moves and the tensions inherent in that fragile
synthesis.

The praises of the Lord in lively notes,
The whiles with hollow throates                                    220
The Choristers the joyous Antheme sing,
That al the woods may answere and their eccho ring.

[13]

B ehold whiles she before the altar stands
Hearing the holy priest that to her speakes
And blesseth her with his two happy hands,                        225
How the red roses flush up in her cheekes,
And the pure snow with goodly vermill stayne,
Like crimsin dyde in grayne,
That even th'Angels which continually,
About the sacred Altare doe remaine,                              230
Forget their service and about her fly,
Ofte peeping in her face that seemes more fayre,
The more they on it stare.
But her sad eyes still fastened on the ground,
Are governed with goodly modesty,                                235
That suffers not one looke to glaunce awry,
Which may let in a little thought unsownd.
Why blush ye love to give to me your hand,
The pledge of all our band?
Sing ye sweet Angels, Alleluya sing,                             240
That all the woods may answere and your eccho ring.

[STANZA 13]    227. *vermill*: scarlet, red.    234. *sad*: serious, sober.
237. *thought unsownd*: Cf. the "unquiet thought" which the poet allowed to
overcome him at the beginning of *Amor*.    238. *give to me your hand*:
Probably the bride and groom have exchanged rings (perhaps line 216) and
received the priest's blessing (225); now he joins their right hands and will
pronounce them "man and wife together" before proceeding to the readings
and communion, in accord with "The Form of Solemnization of Matrimony"
of the Elizabethan *Book of Common Prayer*.    239. *pledge . . . band*: outward
sign of our mutual contract or bond.    240. *Angels*: the highest rank in the
community of celebrants that Sp has assembled.

[14]

NOw al is done; bring home the bride againe,
bring home the triumph of our victory,
Bring home with you the glory of her gaine,
With joyance bring her and with jollity.                                245
Never had man more joyfull day then this,
Whom heaven would heape with blis.
Make feast therefore now all this live long day;
This day for ever to me holy is.
Poure out the wine without restraint or stay,              250
Poure not by cups, but by the belly full,
Poure out to all that wull,
And sprinkle all the postes and wals with wine,
That they may sweat, and drunken be withall.
Crowne ye God Bacchus with a coronall,                       255
And Hymen also crowne with wreathes of vine,
And let the Graces daunce unto the rest;
For they can doo it best:
The whiles the maydens doe theyr carroll sing,
To which the woods shal answer and theyr eccho ring.   260

[15]

RIng ye the bels, ye yong men of the towne,
And leave your wonted labors for this day:
This day is holy; doe ye write it downe,
that ye forever it remember may.
This day the sunne is in his chiefest hight,                    265
With Barnaby the bright,
From whence declining daily by degrees,
He somewhat loseth of his heat and light,
When once the Crab behind his back he sees.

[STANZA 14]    255. *Bacchus*: god of wine.
[STANZA 15]    263–73. This reference to St. Barnabas's day identifies
the wedding date as 11 June; because the old calendar had gotten ten days
behind, 11 June also marked the summer solstice, the longest day of the
year.    269. The sun moves from the zodiacal house of the crab to that of
the lion in mid-June.

But for this time it ill ordained was,                                    270
To chose the longest day in all the yeare,
And shortest night, when longest fitter weare:
Yet never day so long, but late would passe.
Ring ye the bels, to make it weare away,
And bonefiers make all day,                                               275
And daunce about them, and about them sing:
that all the woods may answer, and your eccho ring.

[16]
AH when will this long weary day have end,
  and lende me leave to come unto my love?
How slowly do the houres theyr numbers spend?                            280
How slowly does sad Time his feathers move?
Hast thee O fayrest Planet to thy home
Within the Westerne fome:
Thy tyred steedes long since have need of rest.
Long though it be, at last I see it gloome,                              285
And the bright evening star with golden creast
Appeare out of the East.
Fayre childe of beauty, glorious lampe of love
That all the host of heaven in rankes doost lead,
And guydest lovers through the nights dread,                             290
How chearefully thou lookest from above,
And seemst to laugh atweene thy twinkling light
As joying in the sight
Of these glad many which for joy doe sing,
That all the woods them answer and their echo ring.                      295

273. *late*: at last. *would pass*: Here and in stanza 16 the poet, resuming the
anticipatory perspective of the stanzas before 12, looks forward with
increasing impatience to the time for the newlyweds to retire to their
bedchamber.        275. *bonefiers*: Dancing around bonfires was part of an
ancient northern celebration of the summer solstice.
[STANZA 16]        282. *fayrest Planet*: the sun, drawn in his chariot.
286. Venus is the evening star, as is Hesperus, a mythological figure often
represented as a boy rider carrying a torch, but Sp seems to have in mind
more the star itself than its mythological representation.        294. *these glad
many*: this happy throng.

[17]

Now ceasse ye damsels your delights forepast;
Enough is it, that all the day was youres:
Now day is doen, and night is nighing fast:
Now bring the Bryde into the brydall boures.
Now night is come, now soone her disaray,                    300
And in her bed her lay;
Lay her in lillies and in violets,
And silken courteins over her display,
And odourd sheetes, and Arras coverlets.
Behold how goodly my faire love does ly                      305
In proud humility,
Like unto Maia, when as Jove her tooke,
In Tempe, lying on the flowry gras,
Twixt sleepe and wake, after she weary was
With bathing in the Acidalian brooke.                        310
Now it is night, ye damsels may be gon,
And leave my love alone,
And leave likewise your former lay to sing:
The woods no more shal answere, nor your echo ring.

[18]

NOw welcome night, thou night so long expected,             315
that long daies labour doest at last defray,
And all my cares, which cruell love collected,
Hast sumd in one, and cancelled for aye:
Spread thy broad wing over my love and me,

[STANZA 17]    296. *damsels*: the bridesmaids of stanza 7.
299. *boures*: bowers, private bedrooms, as in the medieval bower-and-hall
arrangement.    300. *Now night is come*: Sp's symbolism is precise. The
placement of this phrase one-fourth through stanza 17 reflects the indication
in contemporary almanacs of 16 and one-fourth hours of daylight on 11 June
in southern Ireland (see Hieatt 1960).    304. *Arras*: northeastern French
city formerly noted for its tapestries.    307–10. The Acidalian brook is
associated with Venus. The idea here is that Hermes' mother Maia, noted in
the Homeric hymn to Hermes (lines 5–6) as retiring, remained modest even
under the influence of Venus.

that no man may us see,                                               320
And in thy sable mantle us enwrap,
From feare of perrill and foule horror free.
Let no false treason seeke us to entrap,
Nor any dread disquiet once annoy
the safety of our joy:                                                325
But let the night be calme and quietsome,
Without tempestuous storms or sad afray:
Lyke as when Jove with fayre Alcmena lay,
When he begot the great Tirynthian groome:
Or lyke as when he with thy selfe did lie,                            330
And begot Majesty.
And let the mayds and yongmen cease to sing:
Ne let the woods them answer, nor theyr eccho ring.

[19]

L Et no lamenting cryes, nor dolefull teares,
Be heard all night within nor yet without:                            335
Ne let false whispers breeding hidden feares,
Breake gentle sleepe with misconceived dout.
Let no deluding dreames, nor dreadful sights
Make sudden sad affrights;
Ne let housefyres, nor lightnings helpelesse harmes,                  340
Ne let the Pouke, nor other evill sprights,
Ne let mischivous witches with theyr charmes,

[STANZA 18]    322–25. One specific source of such fear may have
been raids by Irish guerrillas; in 1598 a concerted attack on Kilcolman forced
Sp to leave Ireland.    328–29: By one version Jove appeared to Alcmena
in a shower of gold and according to several sources he ordered the sun not
to shine so as to lengthen the night. In this tempestuous night was conceived
the "Tirynthian groome" Heracles.    330–31. In describing the allegorical
figure Majesty as the offspring of Jove and Night, Sp is apparently drawing
either on an unknown source or on his own imagination, based, perhaps, on
the non-classical assumption that Majesty must derive from royalty. Ovid
gives Honor and Reverence as parents of Majesty.    332. *mayds and
yongmen*: These seem to be the youth of the town invoked in stanza 8, as the
bridesmaids were dismissed in stanza 17, line 311.
[STANZA 19]    341. *Pouke*: hobgoblin, Puck, Robin Goodfellow.

Ne let hob Goblins, names whose sence we see not,
Fray us with things that be not.
Let not the shriech Oule, nor the Storke be heard:                345
Nor the night Raven that still deadly yels,
Nor damned ghosts cald up with mighty spels,
Nor griesly vultures make us once affeard:
Ne let th'unpleasant Quyre of Frogs still croking
Make us to wish theyr choking.                                   350
Let none of these theyr drery accents sing;
Ne let the woods them answer, nor theyr eccho ring.


[20]

B Ut let stil Silence trew night watches keepe,
That sacred peace may in assurance rayne,
And tymely sleep, when it is tyme to sleepe,                     355
May poure his limbs forth on your pleasant playne,
The whiles an hundred little winged loves,
Like divers fethered doves,
Shall fly and flutter round about your bed,
And in the secret darke, that none reproves,                     360
Their prety stealthes shal worke, and snares shal spread
To filch away sweet snatches of delight,
Conceald through covert night.
Ye sonnes of Venus, play your sports at will,
For greedy pleasure, careless of your toyes,                     365
Thinks more upon her paradise of joyes,
Then what ye do, albe it good or ill.
All night therefore attend your merry play,
For it will soone be day:
Now none doth hinder you, that say or sing,                      370
Ne will the woods now answer, nor your Eccho ring.


[STANZA 20]    356. *poure*: The image, perhaps borrowed from Virgil,
seems to be that of a god spreading his protective wings over the human field
of battle; the tone may be mock-heroic. See *Amor* XX.2.    364. *sonnes of*
*Venus*: Cupids.

## [21]

WHo is the same, which at my window peepes?
   Or whose is that faire face, that shines so bright,
Is it not Cinthia, she that never sleepes,
But walkes about high heaven al the night? 375
O fayrest goddesse, do thou not envy
My love with me to spy:
For thou likewise didst love, though now unthought,
And for a fleece of woll, which privily,
The Latmian shephard once unto thee brought, 380
His pleasures with thee wrought.
Therefore to us be favorable now;
And sith of wemens labours thou hast charge,
And generation goodly dost enlarge,
Encline thy will t'effect our wishfull vow, 385
And the chast wombe informe with timely seed,
That may our comfort breed:
Till which we cease our hopefull hap to sing,
Ne let the woods us answere, nor our Eccho ring.

## [22]

ANd thou great Juno, which with awful might 390
   the lawes of wedlock still dost patronize,

[STANZA 21] Stanzas 21 through 23 shift attention forward to
procreation and progeny.    374. *Cinthia*: The moon goddess Cynthia (also
Diana, Artemis, Selene) was associated with hunting and chastity, but also, as
Sp indicates, with childbirth, and women's interests generally.
380. *Latmian shephard*: According to legend Cynthia made love on Mount
Latmos with the handsome shepherd Endymion after he brought her,
according to post-classical sources, a fleece. In retribution Zeus made
Endymion sleep eternally.    387. *comfort*: aid, support.    388. *we*: The
lover's personal song (line 17) has now become their mutual song. The
pronoun of the last three refrains is "we." The second person plural pronoun
first appeared at line 320, shortly after night fell.    *our hopefull hap to sing*:
to sing of our hoped-for event, i.e. conception. The promise to cease to sing
of this event is fulfilled in that stanza 22 moves on from the topic of
conception to that of childbirth and 23 to that of progeny.
[STANZA 22]    390. *Juno*: Jove's consort, the chief goddess of women,
associated, like Cynthia, with marriage, childbirth and women's interests.
*awful*: awesome.

And the religion of the faith first plight
With sacred rites hast taught to solemnize:
and eeke for comfort often called art
Of women in their smart,                                          395
Eternally bind thou this lovely band,
And all thy blessings unto us impart.
And thou glad Genius, in whose gentle hand
The bridale bowre and geniall bed remaine
Without blemish or staine,                                        400
And the sweet pleasures of theyr loves delight
With secret ayde doest succour and supply
Till they bring forth the fruitfull progeny,
Send us the timely fruit of this same night.
And thou fayre Hebe, and thou Hymen free,                         405
Grant that it may so be.
Til which we cease your further prayse to sing,
Ne any woods shal answer, nor your Eccho ring.

[23]
A Nd ye high heavens, the temple of the gods,
In which a thousand torches flaming bright                        410
Doe burne, that to us wretched earthly clods
In dreadfull darknesse lend desired light;
And all ye powers which in the same remayne,
More then we men can fayne,
Poure out your blessing on us plentiously,                        415
And happy influence upon us raine,
That we may raise a large posterity,
Which from the earth, which they may long possesse,
With lasting happinesse,
Up to your haughty pallaces may mount,                            420
And for the guerdon of theyr glorious merit
May heavenly tabernacles there inherit,

398. *Genius*: a male spirit associated with fertility.      399. *geniall*: nuptial
405. *Hebe*: a daughter of Zeus and Hera, associated with youthfulness and
rejuvenation.
[STANZA 23]      414. *fayne*: imagine.      421. *guerdon*: reward.

Of blessed Saints for to increase the count.
So let us rest, sweet love, in hope of this,
And cease till then our tymely joyes to sing,          425
The woods no more us answer, nor our eccho ring.

### [24]

SOng made in lieu of many ornaments,
  With which my love should duly have bene dect,
Which cutting off through hasty accidents,
Ye would not stay your dew time to expect,          430
But promist both to recompens,
Be unto her a goodly ornament,
And for short time an endlesse moniment.

FINIS.
*Imprinted by P. S. for Wil-*
liam Ponsonby.

[STANZA 24] The envoy, or *tornata*, a brief concluding stanza addressed back to the poem itself, is characteristic of the Italian *canzone*. The passage is difficult, and may be read many ways. The lexical notes below suggest some of the possibilities. Here, for the sake of clarity and coherence, is one simple paraphrase that it is hoped may serve students in a non-prescriptive way as a starting point for interpretation: this song was made in place of the many ornaments that his bride deserved; as circumstances imposed haste, the time that ought to have been spent on the song was shortened; and so in recompense he offers the song as both an appropriate ornament to his bride and a permanent monument to fleeting time.
428. *dect*: adorned.          429. *cutting off*: preventing. *hasty*: rushed, sudden. *accidents*: occurrences, contingencies, mishaps (see Neuse 1966).          430. *Ye*: the song. *stay*: remain, wait, delay. *dew*: marking a term of fulfillment or completion; the normal course of; owed to you; owed by you; that which is owed to you; that which is owed by you. *expect*: delay, await, anticipate.
431. This is the last short line. The total of 68, Hieatt suggests (1960), may represent the total of weeks, months and seasons. *promist*: having been promised; showing promise. *both*: the bride and time; the bride and the song.          432. *goodly*: well-proportioned, well-suited, ample.          433. *for*: offered to; in honor of; in place of. *short time*: fleeting time in general, the measure of human mortality (see *FQ* VII viii 9); this particular short span of time: his wedding day and night. *endlesse*: the juxtaposition of "short" and "endlesse" in this last line restates the vision of synthesis of the particular and universal, the physical and spiritual, that underlies all of *Amor and Epith*.

# Fowre Hymnes

# Fovvre Hymnes,

MADE BY
EDM. SPENSER.

LONDON,
Printed for VVilliam Ponsonby.
1596.

# Fowre Hymnes

S penser's *Fowre Hymnes* deals with the philosophy of love
without being, in any real sense, a philosophical work.
Ideas about love, whether divine or human, were central
to Renaissance thought in general and to Spenser's poetry in
particular. Attempting, in his usual manner, not to develop
further the thought of any one of his predecessors but to bring
them all together in a new unity, a new vision of truth and
harmony, Spenser collected materials from a long tradition in-
cluding the Bible, Plato, and the whole range of writers from
Augustine through Dante and Petrarch to the Florentine Neo-
platonists. His poem is thus not reducible to the formulation of
any particular philosophical theory, and indeed on a cursory
reading the ideas and attitudes that he brings into the work seem
strangely out of consonance with each other. Certain sections of
his four-part poem are straightforwardly Petrarchan while oth-
ers seem clearly influenced by the more syncretistic bent of
Ficino and his followers. At times, as in *An Hymne of Heavenly
Love*, his song becomes a pious hymn versifying the central story
of the Gospels; at other times, as in parts of *An Hymne of Heav-
enly Beautie*, it stretches towards the divine vision of the Chris-
tian mystics. Whatever unified vision there is in the poem is
more likely to be found in the unity of Spenser's artistic creation
than any set of Neoplatonic and/or biblical ideas which have
been "together linkt" by our eclectic author.

In dedicating the carefully printed 1596 quarto to the count-
esses of Warwick and Cumberland, Spenser states that the
Hymnes of Love and Beautie were composed "in the greener
times of my youth," and that his patronesses, worried about
their moral effect on "those of like age and disposition" have
asked him to recall the poems. Since the number of extant copies

make this impossible, the poet has decided to add a second pair—the hymnes of Heavenly Love and Beautie—by way of retraction. These statements have given rise to a critical debate about the date of composition and more importantly about the relationship between the two pairs of hymns. While it seems improbable that Spenser would present his two patronesses with a lie, the literary retraction was a conventional cliché for which there were numerous precedents both in England and on the Continent. There is also internal evidence to suggest that even the first two hymns were written—or at least rewritten—after the publication of the *Amoretti* in 1595 (Ellrodt 1960).

The retraction creates a biographical-literary myth which associates youth with passionate love to be superseded, in maturity, by spiritual love. This does not mean, of course, that the mature Spenser had come to embrace a religious outlook involving the rejection of sexual love and physical beauty. After all he had recently married and he here states that he has dedicated his poem to the two countesses precisely because they are such excellent representatives of love and beauty "both in the one and the other kinde." But the Dedication announces through biographical allusion the tension which the hymns themselves will develop, and defines a major area of critical debate: the relation between the first pair of hymns and the second. Do the hymns in praise of heavenly love and beauty represent a continuation at a higher level of the argument presented in the earlier hymns? Or should the second pair be interpreted as a repudiation of the first? Do the last two hymns present the reader with a fresh start on a different journey?

Such tensions existed already in Renaissance conceptions of the hymn-form. Greek *hymnos*, a word of doubtful origin, denotes any metrical address to a god and later to heroes as well, normally comprising a recitation (originally incantatory and magical) of birth, names, epithets, deeds, and the like. Orphic hymns had initiatory functions in mystery religion. Yet Christian tradition, set by Augustine and embraced by the Protestants, inevitably limited their scope to God alone. Milton touches on both traditions in the *Reason of Church Government* when he mentions the works of Pindar and Callimachus as valuable examples of the form yet finds scriptural hymns "beyond all these" in spiritual worth. In the Renaissance the classical hymn was revived in Neo-Latin poetry, and was popular in the verse of many vernacular poets including Ronsard; it continued side by side with the dominant tradition of the Christian hymn. In *Fowre Hymnes* Spenser thus makes explicit an already-existing tension in hymnic tradition, playing upon the parallelism as well as the contrast between earthly and heavenly, pagan and Christian, mythological and scriptural, classical and modern.

Yet one may stress this tension too much. In considering the relation between the two pairs of hymns the modern reader often observes an opposition between the ideas of the pagan classics and Christian teaching that was not equally apparent to the educated Elizabethan. By modern standards Elizabethan schools were strongly religious, yet they insisted that a wide range of Greek and Latin classics should be studied by the young pupils, not only for language and style but also for content. It was popularly argued that, when studied in the proper spirit, classical literature, philosophy, and mythology would provide the reader with useful insights, both moral and religious. Thus Greco-Roman gods and mythological stories, in keeping with medieval tradition, were frequently interpreted as types and shadowy figures of biblical persons and biblical stories. By patristic sanction Plato was the most "Christian" of all the pagan philosophers. He was indeed sometimes seen as an extra-biblical prophet—a Moses Atticus. It is not surprising therefore that the coloring of the first two hymns is pervasively Platonic.

Elizabethans like Spenser commonly derived their knowledge of Plato through two channels: medieval Neoplatonism and the Florentine Neoplatonists. The ubiquity of Neoplatonic ideas in Spenser's time and milieu and his comparative unconcern with scholarly precision renders unwise the naming of any one source for what Spenser may have found in several places. In most cases the more popularly read sources would be the most likely. On the other hand, the existence of encyclopedias, translations, and the like should not lead us to the mistaken conclusion that educated Elizabethans *never* had recourse to the source itself. The only Platonic dialogue known to the Middle Ages was the *Timaeus*, Plato's dialogue of the creation, which had been handed down in Cicero's Latin translation. Other Platonic dialogues became known to the West only after the sack of Constantinople in 1453. Even then they were eagerly translated into Latin and passed on to European readers accompanied by the Neoplatonic and syncretistic ideas of Marsilio Ficino and his followers. It is quite possible that Spenser had direct knowledge of some of the Platonic dialogues—notably the *Timaeus* and the *Symposium*. But even if he read Plato's texts he would have done so with the assumptions of a Renaissance humanist, not those of a modern classical scholar. For Plato's ideas had undergone great development in the late classical period by pagan philosophers, it had been adapted to Christian belief by theologians like Origen and Augustine, and had then again been developed and reinterpreted in the syncretistic commentaries of Ficino, Pico della Mirandola, and other Florentine Neoplatonists. These ideas had in turn been popularized in the sixteenth century in a large number of literary works including Castiglione's dialogue, *The Book of the Courtier* (1528), (trans. Hoby 1561).

In the *Fowre Hymnes* these ideas are dramatically presented and tested in the lover's development. His implied progress in the first hymn from love's first kindling at the sight of the beloved, through cruel rejection, refinement of the emotions, and the self-torture of jealousy, to the triumph of erotic love symbolized by a paradisal garden of sensual delight, gathers a whole series of themes that were already commonplace to medieval love poetry and that became a source of endlessly-varied fascination to Renaissance poets. Spenser's development of these themes employs much of the language of Renaissance Neoplatonic love theory with its multistage "ladder of love"—the lover's progression from love of the body to love of the soul, and from love of the beloved's individual beauty to love of Beauty itself. Yet even in the first two hymns, Spenser's use of Neoplatonic doctrine is radically inconsistent with his major sources. The Neoplatonic account is broken by the Petrarchan images of Cupid as a feudal lord who exposes the lover to his tyranny. Further, C. S. Lewis (1954) has argued that the first two hymns are "substantially meditations on chivalrous, monogamous, English love" (p.376). For the Neoplatonists, the beautiful woman is only a starting point in an ascent to mystical ecstasy. But as many critics have noted, the first two hymns never really ascend the traditional ladder beyond the level of appreciating the mistress's beauty in her absence. The first hymns, that is, never really abandon the particular for the universal. Indeed, as is evident from his *Amoretti* and *Epithalamion* of the previous year, Spenser, with his more English and Protestant perspective, exalts matrimonial love as the supreme manifestation of lawful and harmonious union. Married love becomes the most exquisite expression of a force that extends itself from the order of nature through the private and social spheres to the cosmic level.

Rather than a continuous progression up the rungs of the Neoplatonic ladder of love many critics have discerned in the hymns a complex system of parallels and contrasts between the two pairs guiding the reader towards frequent comparison and reevaluation. Some parallels and contrasts strike the reader immediately. Each hymn praises a guardian deity: Cupid and Venus in the first pair and Christ and Sapience in the last. Thus the hymns of love are both concerned with male deities while the realm of beauty is appropriately presided over by female figures. While the male deities descend to the world of man to guide him, in strikingly different ways, to "paradise," the two female beings characteristically remain above.

It also seems possible to discern a broadly similar four-part structural scheme in all four hymns. (1) The opening stanzas (except in the *Hymne of Heavenly Love*) address the appropriate divinity (or persona of God) and invoke his (her) authority. (2) An account of the creation is given in every hymn, and while (3) the greater part of each hymn treats of its named subject, (4) they all end in a paradisal vision, a sensual paradise in the first two hymns paralleled by a spiritual paradise in the latter two.

In the first hymn love is both a beneficent and a cruel force. Cupid is a creator-god who reconciles the warring elements. He moves man to embrace "Beauties glorious beame" (*HL* 116) and thus inspires him with power and energy to "enlarge his lasting progenie" (*HL* 105) and to do great deeds to win his lady's favor (*HL* 218–37). Similarly in the *Hymne in Honour of Beautie* presided over by Venus, the lover is educated, learning to identify beauty with the "faire lampe" (*HB* 99) of the immortal soul, not with the corruptible matter in which that soul temporarily lodges. The attraction between lovers comes from a similarity of souls, not from bodily desire (*HB* 190–210). And the lover ends by creating in his mind an image of the beloved, a "more refyned forme" (*HB* 214) which mirrors the beauty of her soul, not the imperfect beauty of her body.

Yet when the poet-speaker finds himself within the domains of heavenly love and beauty, the speaker of the first two hymns appears self-centered and without perspective, his lord a cruel tyrant, and his praise of Cupid so grossly inappropriate at times as to verge on blasphemy. While the speaker of the *Hymne of Heavenly Love* is full of pity as he contemplates the sufferings of Christ, the speaker of the first hymn feels only self-pity. While Christ descended to serve man and liberate him from bondage, Cupid descends only to enslave man and be his lord. Where the speaker of the third hymn is concerned that man should show some love and compassion for his fellow men, the speaker of the first hymn is so obsessed with his desire to gain his love that his fellow beings appear primarily as rivals and competitors (*HL* 259–72).

This is perhaps the most striking example of how images in the "earthly" hymns are mirrored by images in the "heavenly" hymns. Not surprisingly images of vision seem to be particularly important in the hymns as we proceed from natural eyesight to the perception of what is "inly faire" and finally to the ecstatic vision of the soul. The images of vision are also closely linked with images of flight and ascent. The wings of Cupid in *Hymne in Honour of Love* are superseded by the "golden wings" of the "heavenly" hymns (*HHL*,st.1, and *HHB*,st.14). The link between these groups of images is clearly seen in the references to the falcon and the sharp-sighted eagle—a symbol of regeneration. The relation between physical and spiritual vision is hinted at even in the first hymn in the complex image of the blind Cupid who is both a symbol of the physical lover, groping in spiritual darkness, and an image of the seer blinding the eyes of the body for the better use of the eyes of the mind. The last two hymns are concerned with a meditation on the life of Christ and with the complex but ultimately biblical figure of Divine Sapience; they present the reader with a Christian vision transcending the illumination possible to the lover of the earthly hymns. Yet the poem would have been much poorer without them. The lover of the first two hymns has excluded the truly spiritual world of the last two hymns from his paradise of pleasures, and the ardent Christian of the last two hymns is eager to denounce the kingdom of Cupid. Yet Spenser, the poet, has included them both.

*Einar Bjorvand*
*Richard Schell*

# TO THE RIGHT HO-
# NORABLE AND MOST VER-
## tuous Ladies, the Ladie Margaret Countesse
## of Cumberland, and the Ladie Marie
## Countesse of Warwicke.

*H*Aving in the greener times of my youth, composed these former
*two Hymnes in the praise of Love and Beautie, and finding
that the same too much pleased those of like age and disposition, which
being too vehemently caried with that kind of affection, do rather
sucke out poyson to their strong passion, then hony to their honest
delight, I was moved by the one of you two most excellent Ladies,to call
in the same. But being unable so to doe, by reason that many copies
thereof were formerly scattered abroad, I resolved at least to amend,
and by way of retractation to reforme them, making in stead of those
two Hymnes of earthly or naturall love and beautie, two others of
heavenly and celestiall. The which I doe dedicate joyntly unto you two
honorable sisters, as to the most excellent and rare ornaments of all
true love and beautie, both in the one and the other kinde, humbly
beseeching you to vouchsafe the patronage of them, and to accept this
my humble service, in lieu of the great graces and honourable favours
which ye dayly shew unto me, untill such time as I may by better
meanes yeeld you some more notable testimonie of my thankfull mind
and dutifull devotion.*

    *And even so I pray for your happinesse.*
    *Greenwich this first of September.*
        1596.
        *Your Honors most bounden ever*
        *in all humble service.*
        Ed. Sp.

D E D I C A T I O N : Marie is a mistake for Anne. The Ladies Margaret and Anne
were both daughters of Francis Russell, earl of Bedford. Margaret (d. 1616) was
married to George Clifford, earl of Cumberland; and Anne (d. 1604) was the
wife of Leicester's brother, Ambrose Dudley, earl of Warwick. Both ladies were
praised in *CCCHA* (492–507), and the Lady Warwick received the poet's
compliments in *RT* (244–45).

# *An Hymne in Honour of Love.*

### [1]

LOve, that long since hast to thy mighty powre,
Perforce subdude my poore captived hart,
And raging now therein with restlesse stowre,
Doest tyrannize in everie weaker part;
Faine would I seeke to ease my bitter smart,          5
By any service I might do to thee,
Or ought that else might to thee pleasing bee.

### [2]

And now t'asswage the force of this new flame,
And make thee more propitious in my need,
I meane to sing the praises of thy name,          10

[STANZAS 1–6]     These form the introduction to the first hymn. The first three stanzas are devoted to the traditional lover's complaint and his promise to sing Cupid's praise; and the last three stanzas contain the invocation of Cupid and a call for the assistance of the Muses, nymphs, and young ladies. The introduction employs the conventional Petrarchan stance of Cupid as the cruel tyrant and the lover as his slave. This theme, which finds its classical precedent in Ovid's *Amores* 1.2, was developed by Petrarch in his *Trionfo d'Amore*. Sp also echoes the first stanza of Benivieni's *Canzone della Amore*. The Petrarchan tradition of the suffering lover, although popular in the Renaissance—particularly among the soneteers—may possibly have been felt to be somewhat outmoded by 1596, especially as it may be said to have been superseded by Sp's own *Amoretti and Epithalamion* of the previous year. If so, the Petrarchan stanzas may well be seen to be in accordance with the fiction of the dedication that the first two hymns were written "in the greener times" of the poet's youth. In so far as it is possible to see the first hymn as introducing the first steps on a ladder leading to the vision of heavenly love and beauty in the last two hymns, the Petrarchan vision of cruel love in the introductory stanzas, and again in st. 18–24 and 36–39 (lines 120–68; 245–72), may well be seen to constitute a difficulty. Sp may also be seen consciously to base his description on the contrast between Cupid who makes his followers suffer to deserve his favor and Christ who suffers in order to promote undeserving man to a state of grace (cf. *HL* 159 and *HHL* 160).

[STANZA 1]     3. *stowre*: tumult, disturbance.
[STANZA 2]     8. *asswage*: assuage, appease.

And thy victorious conquests to areed;
By which thou madest many harts to bleed
Of mighty Victors, with wyde wounds embrewed,
And by thy cruell darts to thee subdewed.

[3]
Onely I feare my wits enfeebled late,                    15
Through the sharpe sorrows, which thou hast me bred,
Should faint, and words should faile me, to relate
The wondrous triumphs of thy great godhed.
But if thou wouldst vouchsafe to overspred
Me with the shadow of thy gentle wing,                   20
I should enabled be thy actes to sing.

[4]
Come then, ô come, thou mightie God of love,
Out of thy silver bowres and secret blisse,
Where thou doest sit in *Venus* lap above,
Bathing thy wings in her ambrosiall kisse,               25
That sweeter farre then any Nectar is;
Come softly, and my feeble breast inspire
With gentle furie, kindled of thy fire.

[5]
And ye sweet Muses, which have often proved
The piercing points of his avengefull darts;             30
And ye faire Nimphs, which oftentimes have loved
The cruell worker of your kindly smarts,

11. *areed*: make known, proclaim.    13. *embrewed*: stained. Cupid is the
conqueror of conquerors. Even those who inflict wounds on others (in
battle) are themselves wounded by Cupid.
[STANZA 3]    16. *bred*: caused.
[STANZA 4]    22–26. The description of Cupid's heavenly state may be
seen to have both a spiritual and a sensual aspect. It may be compared to the
description of the lovers' paradise in lines 280–93. Thus Cupid's heavenly
state, "in Venus lap above," is also filled with sensuous delight. (Cf. *HHL*
134 and *HHB* 183–84.)    28. *furie: furor poeticus* (poetical rapture).
[STANZA 5]    29. *proved*: tried, felt.    32. *kindly*: natural.

Prepare your selves, and open wide your harts,
For to receive the triumph of your glorie,
That made you merie oft, when ye were sorie.                    35

[6]

And ye faire blossomes of youths wanton breed,
Which in the conquests of your beautie bost,
Wherewith your lovers feeble eyes you feed,
But sterve their harts, that needeth nourture most,
Prepare your selves, to march amongst his host,          40
And all the way this sacred hymne do sing,
Made in the honor of your Soveraigne king.

[7]

G Reat god of might, that reignest in the mynd,
  And all the bodie to thy hest doest frame,
Victor of gods, subduer of mankynd,                            45
That doest the Lions and fell Tigers tame,
Making their cruell rage thy scornefull game,
And in their roring taking great delight;
Who can expresse the glorie of thy might?

[8]

Or who alive can perfectly declare,                            50
The wondrous cradle of thine infancie?
When thy great mother *Venus* first thee bare,
Begot of Plentie and of Penurie,

---

[STANZA 6]    36. *wanton*: playful, wild.    39. *sterve*: starve.
[STANZA 7]    44. *hest*: command.    45. The idea that both men and
gods are subject to the rule of love comes from Plato, and Sp probably culled
it from Marsilio Ficino's influential *Commentary on Plato's Symposium* which
was largely responsible for the spread of Neoplatonic and syncretistic ideas of
love in the Renaissance.    46. *fell*: fierce, savage.
[STANZA 8]    52–53. The mystery of the birth of Love. Like Natalis
Comes (Conti), Sp tries to blend the two traditions of Cupid's parentage as
the son of Venus and the child of Penia and Porus (see below, note to lines
61–70).

Though elder then thine owne nativitie;
And yet a chyld, renewing still thy yeares;                          55
And yet the eldest of the heavenly Peares.

[9]
For ere this worlds still moving mightie masse,
Out of great Chaos ugly prison crept,
In which his goodly face long hidden was
From heavens view, and in deepe darknesse kept,                     60
Love, that had now long time securely slept
In *Venus* lap, unarmed then and naked,
Gan reare his head, by *Clotho* being waked.

[10]
And taking to him wings of his owne heate,
Kindled at first from heavens life-giving fyre,                      65
He gan to move out of his idle seate,
Weakely at first, but after with desyre
Lifted aloft, he gan to mount up hyre,
And like fresh Eagle, make his hardie flight
Through all that great wide wast, yet wanting light.                 70

[11]
Yet wanting light to guide his wandring way,
His owne faire mother, for all creatures sake,
Did lend him light from her owne goodly ray:

54–56. The paradox of Cupid's age is taken from Ficino's *Commentary*
5.10.     56. *heavenly Peares*: the gods.
[STANZAS 9–14]     The creation account given here should be
compared to those in *HB* 29–56; *HHL* 22–42; and *HHB* 29–105.
[STANZA 9]     57. *still*: continually.
[STANZAS 9–10]     61–70. In st. 4 (line 24) Cupid, as Venus's son, is
resting content in his mother's lap, i.e. Love is satisfied in union with Beauty.
As the offspring of Porus and Penia ("Plentie" and "Penurie") he is called
from the "idle seate" as Penia is called from Chaos by Porus and Clotho to
descend and become the force of Love at work in the created world.
63. *Clotho*: the daughter of Chaos. She is the Fate presiding over birth and
responsible for the spinning of the thread of life.
[STANZA 10]     69. *hardie* bold.     70. *wanting*: lacking.
[STANZA 11]     73. Ficino and Benivieni both identify beauty with light.

Then through the world his way he gan to take,
The world that was not till he did it make; 75
Whose sundrie parts he from them selves did sever,
The which before had lyen confused ever.

[12]
The earth, the ayre, the water, and the fyre,
Then gan to raunge them selves in huge array,
And with contrary forces to conspyre 80
Each against other, by all meanes they may,
Threatning their owne confusion and decay:
Ayre hated earth, and water hated fyre,
Till Love relented their rebellious yre.

[13]
He then them tooke, and tempering goodly well 85
Their contrary dislikes and loved meanes,
Did place them all in order, and compell
To keepe them selves within their sundrie raines,
Together linkt with Adamantine chaines;
Yet so, as that in every living wight 90
They mixe themselves, and shew their kindly might.

[14]
So ever since they firmely have remained,
And duly well observed his beheast;
Through which now all these things that are contained
Within this goodly cope, both most and least 95
Their being have, and dayly are increast,
Through secret sparks of his infused fyre,
Which in the barraine cold he doth inspyre.

---

[STANZAS 11–13]    76–91. Sp's account of how the elements were
separated from the disorder and confusion of chaos and arranged in
hierarchical order, each with its own sphere. And yet, paradoxically (lines
90–91), they "mixe themselves" in all living things.
[STANZA 12]    84. *relented*: abated.
[STANZA 13]    88. *raines*: domains.    91. *kindly*: natural.
[STANZA 14]    95. *cope*: canopy.    98. *inspyre*: breathe into.

[15]

Thereby they all do live, and moved are
To multiply the likenesse of their kynd,                              100
Whilest they seeke onely, without further care,
To quench the flame, which they in burning fynd:
But man, that breathes a more immortall mynd,
Not for lusts sake, but for eternitie,
Seekes to enlarge his lasting progenie.                              105

[16]

For having yet in his deducted spright,
Some sparks remaining of that heavenly fyre,
He is enlumind with that goodly light,
Unto like goodly semblant to aspyre:
Therefore in choice of love, he doth desyre                          110
That seemes on earth most heavenly, to embrace,
That same is Beautie, borne of heavenly race.

[17]

For sure of all, that in this mortall frame
Contained is, nought more divine doth seeme,
Or that resembleth more th'immortall flame                           115
Of heavenly light, then Beauties glorious beame.
What wonder then, if with such rage extreme
Fraile men, whose eyes seek heavenly things to see,
At sight thereof so much enravisht bee?

[18]

Which well perceiving, that imperious boy                            120
Doth therwith tip his sharp empoisned darts;

[STANZAS 15–16]    According to Plato (*Symposium* 208b) and Ficino
(*Commentary* 6.11) man is alone among the created beings in making love
with a purpose that transcends lust, i.e. in order to achieve an earthly
immortality through his offspring.
[STANZA 16]    106. *deducted*: reduced, weakened.    109. *semblant*:
likeness.    111. *That*: what.
[STANZA 17]    117. *rage*: passion.
[STANZA 18]    120. Love, having descended to the world of man, is
transformed into the tyrannical Cupid of the Petrarchan tradition. Stanza 18
marks a return to the rule of tyranny of the opening stanzas.

Which glancing through the eyes with countenance coy,
Rest not, till they have pierst the trembling harts,
And kindled flame in all their inner parts,
Which suckes the blood, and drinketh up the lyfe          125
Of carefull wretches with consuming griefe.

[19]
Thenceforth they playne, and make ful piteous mone
Unto the author of their balefull bane;
The daies they waste, the nights they grieve and grone,
Their lives they loath, and heavens light disdaine;          130
No light but that, whose lampe doth yet remaine
Fresh burning in the image of their eye,
They deigne to see, and seeing it still dye.

[20]
The whylst thou tyrant Love doest laugh and scorne
At their complaints, making their paine thy play;          135
Whylest they lye languishing like thrals forlorne,
The whyles thou doest triumph in their decay,
And otherwhyles, their dying to delay,
Thou doest emmarble the proud hart of her,
Whose love before their life they doe prefer.          140

[21]
So hast thou often done (ay me the more)
To me thy vassall, whose yet bleeding hart,
With thousand wounds thou mangled hast so sore

---

125–26. The suffering endured by the lovers whose hearts have been pierced
by Cupid's arrows may be seen to foreshadow the "never dead, yet ever dying
paine" of the sinners described in *HHL* st. 18. Further parallels may be
observed between the description of Cupid's slaves (*HL* st. 18–20) and fallen
man (*HHL* st. 18–20).          126. *carefull*: careworn.
[STANZA 19]          127. *playne*: complain.          128. *balefull bane*: deadly
ruin.          133. *still*: continually.
[STANZA 20]          137. *decay*: destruction.          139. *emmarble*: turn to
marble, make hard as marble.
[STANZAS 21–24]          When compared to the description of Christ in
*HHL* st. 21–24, the parallels between the sufferings of the lover and those of

That whole remaines scarse any little part,
Yet to augment the anguish of my smart, 145
Thou hast enfrosen her disdainefull brest,
That no one drop of pitie there doth rest.

### [22]

Why then do I this honor unto thee,
Thus to ennoble thy victorious name,
Since thou doest shew no favour unto mee, 150
Ne once move ruth in that rebellious Dame,
Somewhat to slacke the rigour of my flame?
Certes small glory doest thou winne hereby,
To let her live thus free, and me to dy.

### [23]

But if thou be indeede, as men thee call, 155
The worlds great Parent, the most kind preserver
Of living wights, the soveraine Lord of all,
How falles it then, that with thy furious fervour,
Thou doest afflict as well the not deserver,
As him that doeth thy lovely heasts despize, 160
And on thy subjects most doest tyrannize?

### [24]

Yet herein eke thy glory seemeth more,
By so hard handling those which best thee serve,
That ere thou doest them unto grace restore,
Thou mayest well trie if they will ever swerve, 165
And mayest them make it better to deserve,
And having got it, may it more esteeme,
For things hard gotten, men more dearely deeme.

Christ seem striking. "The parallel to the lover's anguish is that of Jesus"
(Nelson 1963:101). The injustice of Christ's executioners "Doing him die,
that never it deserved" (*HHL* st. 23) is parallelled by the injustice of Cupid
who does not scruple to "afflict as well the not deserver" (*HL* st. 23).
[STANZA 22]    151. *ruth*: pity.    153. *Certes*: certainly.
[STANZA 23]    157. *wights*: creatures.
[STANZA 24]    162. *eke*: also, moreover.

[25]

So hard those heavenly beauties be enfyred,
As things divine, least passions doe impresse, 170
The more of stedfast mynds to be admyred,
The more they stayed be on stedfastnesse:
But baseborne mynds such lamps regard the lesse,
Which at first blowing take not hastie fyre,
Such fancies feele no love, but loose desyre. 175

[26]

For love is Lord of truth and loialtie,
Lifting himselfe out of the lowly dust,
On golden plumes up to the purest skie,
Above the reach of loathly sinfull lust,
Whose base affect through cowardly distrust 180
Of his weake wings, dare not to heaven fly,
But like a moldwarpe in the earth doth ly.

[27]

His dunghill thoughts, which do themselves enure
To dirtie drosse, no higher dare aspyre,
Ne can his feeble earthly eyes endure 185
The flaming light of that celestiall fyre,
Which kindleth love in generous desyre,
And makes him mount above the native might
Of heavie earth, up to the heavens hight.

[STANZA 25]     With this stanza we move from the tyranny of Love to
the ascent to the lovers' paradise in st. 41, only broken by the purgatorial
pains described in st. 36–40.     169–172. The sense of these lines is as
follows: Those "heavenly beauties" (the ladies with marble hearts) are like
divine things in that they are not easily influenced by the passions, and the
more steadfast they are, the more are they to be admired by steadfast
minds.     169. *enfyred*: hardened by fire.     172. *stayed*: fixed.
[STANZA 26]     180. *affect*: passion.     182. *moldwarpe*: mole.
[STANZA 27]     183. *enure*: accustom.

[28]
Such is the powre of that sweet passion,                    190
That it all sordid basenesse doth expell,
And the refyned mynd doth newly fashion
Unto a fairer forme, which now doth dwell
In his high thought, that would it selfe excell;
Which he beholding still with constant sight,              195
Admires the mirrour of so heavenly light.

[29]
Whose image printing in his deepest wit,
He thereon feeds his hungrie fantasy,
Still full, yet never satisfyde with it,
Like *Tantale*, that in store doth sterved ly:             200
So doth he pine in most satiety,
For nought may quench his infinite desyre,
Once kindled through that first conceived fyre.

[30]
Thereon his mynd affixed wholly is,
Ne thinks on ought, but how it to attaine;                 205
His care, his joy, his hope is all on this,
That seemes in it all blisses to containe,
In sight whereof, all other blisse seemes vaine.
Thrise happie man, might he the same possesse;
He faines himselfe, and doth his fortune blesse.          210

[STANZAS 29–31]      Critics who argue in favor of a continuous
Neoplatonic scale of love throughout *FH* identify these stanzas as marking
the second stage of the ascent. It should be noted, however, that the lover of
the first hymn never seems to transcend love of the individual.
[STANZA 29]      200. *Tantale*: Tantalus was punished by the gods by
being made to stand in water which he was unable to drink, and to reach up
towards a cluster of grapes that would be snatched away from him at the
crucial moment.
[STANZA 30]      210. *faines*: imagines.

[31]
And though he do not win his wish to end,
Yet thus farre happie he him selfe doth weene,
That heavens such happie grace did to him lend,
As thing on earth so heavenly, to have seene,
His harts enshrined saint, his heavens queene,                    215
Fairer then fairest, in his fayning eye,
Whose sole aspect he counts felicitye.

[32]
Then forth he casts in his unquiet thought,
What he may do, her favour to obtaine;
What brave exploit, what perill hardly wrought,              220
What puissant conquest, what adventurous paine,
May please her best, and grace unto him gaine:
He dreads no danger, nor misfortune feares,
His faith, his fortune, in his breast he beares.

[33]
Thou art his god, thou art his mightie guyde,                  225
Thou being blind, letst him not see his feares,

[STANZA 31]   216. *then*: than. *fayning*: longing, eager.
[STANZA 32]   218. *casts*: considers, plans.   220. *hardly*: with
difficulty.
[STANZA 33]   This is the only stanza in *FH* which is one line short.
The fourth line, although metrically regular, exceeds the normal line length
by more than one third and is carried over into an indented fifth line, while
the fifth line proper is missing. There is, however, nothing in the syntax to
indicate that a line should be missing: it makes perfectly good sense as it
stands. Interestingly, the long fourth line is divided in the 1596 quarto
edition and later in the folio edition of 1611, in exactly the same manner as
showed here, and this produces the effect of an apparent rhyme:
"thousand"—"withstand"—"hand." Bjorvand (1975:26–28) argues that the
"error" is intentional and serves both to underline the spiritual error of the
poet-speaker in his excessive praise of Cupid, and to support the fiction of
the dedication of the first two hymns as having been composed by the young
and technically inexperienced poet.   226. Erwin Panofsky (1939;
1962:125–26) has argued that Renaissance Neoplatonists regarded the blind

But cariest him to that which he hath eyde,
Through seas, through flames, through thousand
    swords and speares:
Ne ought so strong that may his force withstand,
With which thou armest his resistlesse hand.          230

[34]
Witnesse *Leander*, in the Euxine waves,
And stout *AEneas* in the Troiane fyre,
*Achilles* preassing through the Phrygian glaives,
And *Orpheus* daring to provoke the yre
Of damned fiends, to get his love retyre:             235
For both through heaven and hell thou makest way,
To win them worship which to thee obay.

[35]
And if by al these perils and these paynes,
He may but purchase lyking in her eye,
What heavens of joy, then to himselfe he faynes,      240

Cupid as a representative of an earthly and sensual form of love in contrast to
their own spiritual and heavenly concept of love. According to Wind
(1967:62), however, Marsilio Ficino, Pico della Mirandola, and other
syncretists interpreted the blind Cupid not only as blind passion without
reason but also as a higher intellectual vision blinding the eyes of the body
only to activate the eyes of the mind.          230. *resistlesse*: irresistible.
[STANZA 34]          231. *Leander*: In his *Heroides* Ovid describes how
Leander swam across the Hellespont every night to visit his beloved Hero
until one night he was drowned and Hero threw herself into the
sea.          232. *Æneas*: Virgil (*Aen* 2) describes how Aeneas battles with the
Greeks and rescues his family from burning Troy.          233. Achilles returned
to the battle of Troy to kill Hector who had slain his friend Patroclus (*Iliad*
Bks. 18–22). *glaives*: swords.          234–35. Orpheus journeyed to Hades to
retrieve his bride Eurydice who had died after being bitten by a snake. By the
power of his music he made the lords of the underworld grant him his wish
of bringing his wife back to the world of the living. But disobeying their
orders not to turn around to look for her, he lost her forever (Virgil, *Georgics*
6.453–527; Ovid, *Met* 10.1–147).
[STANZA 35]          240. *faynes*: fashions, imagines.

Eftsoones he wypes quite out of memory,
What ever ill before he did aby:
Had it bene death, yet would he die againe,
To live thus happie as her grace to gaine.

[36]
Yet when he hath found favour to his will,                       245
He nathemore can so contented rest,
But forceth further on, and striveth still
T'approch more neare, till in her inmost brest,
He may embosomd bee, and loved best;
And yet not best, but to be lov'd alone,                         250
For love can not endure a Paragone.

[37]
The feare whereof, ô how doth it torment
His troubled mynd with more then hellish paine!
And to his fayning fansie represent
Sights never seene, and thousand shadowes vaine,                 255
To breake his sleepe, and waste his ydle braine;
Thou that hast never lov'd canst not beleeve
Least part of th'evils which poore lovers greeve.

[38]
The gnawing envie, the hart-fretting feare,
The vaine surmizes, the distrustfull showes,                     260
The false reports that flying tales doe beare,
The doubts, the daungers, the delayes, the woes,
The fayned friends, the unassured foes,
With thousands more then any tongue can tell,
Doe make a lovers life a wretches hell.                          265

[39]
Yet is there one more cursed then they all,
That cancker worme, that monster Gelosie,

241. *Eftsoones*: at once.     242. *aby*: suffer, purchase.
[STANZA 36]     246. *nathemore*: neverthemore.     251. *Paragone*: rival.
[STANZA 38]     260. *showes*: appearances.

Which eates the hart, and feedes upon the gall,
Turning all loves delight to miserie,
Through feare of loosing his felicitie.                    270
Ah Gods, that ever ye that monster placed
In gentle love, that all his joyes defaced.

### [40]
By these, ô Love, thou doest thy entrance make,
Unto thy heaven, and doest the more endeere
Thy pleasures unto those which them partake,              275
As after stormes when clouds begin to cleare,
The Sunne more bright and glorious doth appeare;
So thou thy folke, through paines of Purgatorie,
Dost beare unto thy blisse, and heavens glorie.

### [41]
There thou them placest in a Paradize                     280
Of all delight, and joyous happie rest,
Where they doe feede on Nectar heavenly wize,
With *Hercules* and *Hebe*, and the rest
Of *Venus* dearlings, through her bountie blest,
And lie like Gods in yvorie beds arayd,                    285
With rose and lillies over them displayd.

### [42]
There with thy daughter *Pleasure* they doe play
Their hurtlesse sports, without rebuke or blame,
And in her snowy bosome boldly lay
Their quiet heads, devoyd of guilty shame,                290
After full joyance of their gentle game,

[STANZA 39]    272. *defaced*: eclipsed, destroyed.
[STANZA 40]    278–79. The description of the lovers who have to go
through a Roman Catholic purgatory may be seen as a contrast to the very
clearly Protestant vision presented in *HHL*.
[STANZA 41]    283. After his death, Hercules ascended to heaven and
was married to Hebe, goddess of youth and daughter of Zeus and Hera
(Hesiod *Theogony* 950–53)    286. *displayd*: spread out.

Then her they crowne their Goddesse and their Queene,
And decke with floures thy altars well beseene.

[43]
Ay me, deare Lord, that ever I might hope,
For all the paines and woes that I endure, 295
To come at length unto the wished scope
Of my desire, or might my selfe assure,
That happie port for ever to recure.
Then would I thinke these paines no paines at all,
And all my woes to be but penance small. 300

[44]
Then would I sing of thine immortall praise
An heavenly Hymne, such as the Angels sing,
And thy triumphant name then would I raise
Bove all the gods, thee onely honoring,
My guide, my God, my victor, and my king; 305
Till then, dread Lord, vouchsafe to take of me
This simple song, thus fram'd in praise of thee.

FINIS.

[STANZA 43]   296. *scope*: object.   298. *recure*: recover.

# An Hymne in Honour of Beautie.

### [1]

AH whither, Love, wilt thou now carrie mee?
What wontlesse fury dost thou now inspire
Into my feeble breast, too full of thee?
Whylest seeking to aslake thy raging fyre,
Thou in me kindlest much more great desyre,　　　　5
And up aloft above my strength doest rayse
The wondrous matter of my fyre to prayse.

### [2]

That as I earst in praise of thine owne name,
So now in honour of thy Mother deare,
An honourable Hymne I eke should frame,　　　　10
And with the brightnesse of her beautie cleare,
The ravisht harts of gazefull men might reare,
To admiration of that heavenly light,
From whence proceeds such soule enchaunting might.

### [3]

Therto do thou great Goddesse, queene of Beauty,　　15
Mother of love, and of all worlds delight,
Without whose soverayne grace and kindly dewty,
Nothing on earth seemes fayre to fleshly sight,

[STANZAS 1–4]　　These opening stanzas contain invocations to Cupid
(lines 1–7) and to Venus (lines 8–21) and dedications to Venus (line 22)
and to the poet's mistress (lines 23–28).
[STANZA 1]　　Cf. Plato, *Phaedrus* 245a, on the madness of the Muses as
a necessary condition to poetic creativity. In Ficino, *Commentary on Plato's
Symposium* 7.13–14, poetic madness is the first step in a multi-stage ascent
culminating in the madness of love as "desire for the divine beauty and thirst
for the Good."　　1–3. Cf. Horace, *Odes* 3.25.　　1. *Love*: Cupid, son of
Venus.　　2. *wontlesse*: unaccustomed. *inspire*: breathe into.　　4. *aslake*:
mitigate, alleviate.　　7. *wondrous matter*: beauty, love of which is the
highest form of divine madness.
[STANZA 2]　　9. *Mother*: Venus.　　12. *gazefull*: gazing intently.

706

Doe thou vouchsafe with thy love-kindling light,
T'illuminate my dim and dulled eyne,                    20
And beautifie this sacred hymne of thyne.

[4]
That both to thee, to whom I meane it most,
And eke to her, whose faire immortall beame,
Hath darted fyre into my feeble ghost,
That now it wasted is with woes extreame,               25
It may so please that she at length will streame
Some deaw of grace, into my withered hart,
After long sorrow and consuming smart.

[5]
WHat time this worlds great workmaister did cast
   To make al things, such as we now behold,           30
It seemes that he before his eyes had plast
A goodly Paterne, to whose perfect mould
He fashiond them as comely as he could,
That now so faire and seemely they appeare,
As nought may be amended any wheare.                    35

[STANZA 3]     19. In Castiglione, *Courtier*, beauty is transcendent, "an heavenly shining beame" (p.313), which manifests itself in visible proportion and balance, to which love is a visual response (p.304). The love-kindling light here is also the "beame" of the planet Venus (cf. *HB* 55–56).
20. *eyne*: eyes.
[STANZA 4]     24. *ghost*: spirit or soul; but also suggesting Ovidian love-starved death.     26. *streame*: cause to flow.
[STANZAS 5–9]     The description of creation *as finished product* conforming to a formal pattern of perfect beauty parallels *HL* st.9–14 which treats creation *as a process* effected by love. The parallel recurs with creation *as process* in *HHL* st.4–6 and creation *as product* in *HHB* st.4–15.
[STANZA 5]     29. *What time*: when. *workmaister*: Cf. Plato's Demiurge in *Timaeus* 28a: "The work of the creator, whenever he looks to the unchangeable and fashions the form and nature of his work after an unchangeable pattern, must necessarily be made fair and perfect . . . ." *cast*: set out or resolve.

[6]

That wondrous Paterne wheresoere it bee,
Whether in earth layd up in secret store,
Or else in heaven, that no man may it see
With sinfull eyes, for feare it to deflore,
Is perfect Beautie which all men adore,                    40
Whose face and feature doth so much excell
All mortall sence, that none the same may tell.

[7]

Thereof as every earthly thing partakes,
Or more or lesse by influence divine,
So it more faire accordingly it makes,                     45
And the grosse matter of this earthly myne,
Which clotheth it, thereafter doth refyne,
Doing away the drosse which dims the light
Of that faire beame, which therein is empight.

[8]

For through infusion of celestiall powre,                  50
The duller earth it quickneth with delight,

[STANZA 6]    For Plato all men have seen the pattern of perfect being in
a "place beyond the heavens," but most have lost memory of it. Sp ignores
the "doctrine of reminiscence" and allows (in line 37) the looser Neoplatonic
notion that the pattern may be immanent in the world. (See Ficino,
*Commentary* 2.3: "beauty is the ray of God, infused in those four circles . . . .
This ray forms in those four circles all the species of all things. Those species
we are accustomed to call in the Mind, Ideas; in the Soul, Reasons; in
Nature, Seeds; and in Matter, Forms.")    37. *store*: storage place.
39. *deflore*: violate, desecrate.
[STANZA 7]    For beauty as the result of a transcendent victory over
"martiall and grosse nature," see Castiglione, *Courtier*, p.311. Ficino,
*Commentary* 5.4, develops the notion that things are beautiful in proportion
to their participation in divine beauty: beauty is mirrored less perfectly at
lower points on a scale that descends from God down through angelic mind,
world-soul, and nature, to corporeal matter.    44. *influence*: Cf. "influence"
of the stars in astrology.    46. *myne*: earth as a source or supply of inert
matter; cf. *FQ* III vi 36.    49. *empight*: implanted.
[STANZA 8]    50. *infusion*: Cf. astrological usage. For the notion that
beauty emanates from God, see Ficino, *Commentary* 2.5: "Beauty is a certain
act or ray from [the Good] penetrating through all things . . . ."

And life-full spirits privily doth powre
Through all the parts, that to the lookers sight
They seeme to please. That is thy soveraine might,
O *Cyprian* Queene, which flowing from the beame          55
Of thy bright starre, thou into them doest streame.

### [9]

That is the thing which giveth pleasant grace
To all things faire, that kindleth lively fyre,
Light of thy lampe, which shyning in the face,
Thence to the soule darts amorous desyre,          60
And robs the harts of those which it admyre,
Therewith thou pointest thy Sons poysned arrow,
That wounds the life, and wastes the inmost marrow.

### [10]

How vainely then doe ydle wits invent,
That beautie is nought else, but mixture made          65
Of colours faire, and goodly temp'rament
Of pure complexions, that shall quickly fade
And passe away, like to a sommers shade,
Or that it is but comely composition
Of parts well measurd, with meet disposition.          70

51. Greek informing of inert matter by transcendent idea is conflated with
Hebrew creation by God breathing life into man's clay form (Genesis 2.7).
*quickneth*: brings to life.     52. *privily*: invisibly.     55. *Cyprian Queene*:
Venus was born out of the waves near Cyprus, a region sacred to her (Hesiod,
*Theogony* 173–210).
[STANZA 9]     60–61. See note to line 19 above.     63. *wastes*:
consumes.
[STANZAS 10–16]     Physical beauty is seen to consist of more than
physical appearance—pleasing color or proportion—reflecting as it does the
light of a transcendent spirit.
[STANZAS 10–11]     "There are some who think that beauty consists
in a certain arrangement of all the parts, or, to use their own terms, in
symmetry and proportion, together with a certain agreeableness of colors"
(Ficino, *Commentary* 5.3). Sp counters this argument.
[STANZA 10]     66. *temp'rament*: proportionate mixture of elements.
67. *complexions*: humors.     69. *composition*: orderly agreement.     70. *meet*:
proper, fit. *disposition*: arrangement, order.

### [11]

Hath white and red in it such wondrous powre,
That it can pierce through th'eyes unto the hart,
And therein stirre such rage and restlesse stowre,
As nought but death can stint his dolours smart?
Or can proportion of the outward part,                    75
Move such affection in the inward mynd,
That it can rob both sense and reason blynd?

### [12]

Why doe not then the blossomes of the field,
Which are arayd with much more orient hew,
And to the sense most daintie odours yield,                80
Worke like impression in the lookers vew?
Or why doe not faire pictures like powre shew,
In which oftimes, we Nature see of Art
Exceld, in perfect limming every part.

### [13]

But ah, beleeve me, there is more then so                  85
That workes such wonders in the minds of men.
I that have often prov'd, too well it know;
And who so list the like assayes to ken,
Shall find by tryall, and confesse it then,
That Beautie is not, as fond men misdeeme,                 90
An outward shew of things, that onely seeme.

---

[STANZA 11]    73. *stowre*: combat, tumult.    74. *stint*: cut short. *his*:
its.    75–77. "Hence it happens that the Reason itself of beauty cannot be
a body, since, if beauty were corporeal, it would not be applicable to the
virtues of the soul, which are incorporeal . . . . Not only the beauty which is
in the virtues of the soul cannot be corporeal, but also that which is in bodies
and sounds" (Ficino, *Commentary* 5.3).
[STANZA 12]    78–81. Cf. Matthew 6.28–29.    79. *orient*:
resplendent.    81. *like*: similar.    83. *of*: by.    84. *limming*: depiction.
[STANZA 13]    85. *more then so*: i.e. more than the mixture of red and
white in the lady's face.    87. *prov'd*: made test.    88. *list*: desires. *assayes*:
(metallurgical) trials.    *ken*: understand.    90. *fond*: foolish, credulous.
*misdeeme*: misjudge unfavorably.

[14]
For that same goodly hew of white and red,
With which the cheekes are sprinckled, shal decay,
And those sweete rosy leaves so fairely spred
Upon the lips, shall fade and fall away                    95
To that they were, even to corrupted clay.
That golden wyre, those sparckling stars so bright
Shall turne to dust, and loose their goodly light.

[15]
But that faire lampe, from whose celestiall ray
That light proceedes, which kindleth lovers fire,        100
Shall never be extinguisht nor decay,
But when the vitall spirits doe expyre,
Unto her native planet shall retyre,
For it is heavenly borne and can not die,
Being a parcell of the purest skie.                           105

[16]
For when the soule, the which derived was
At first, out of that great immortall Spright,
By whom all live to love, whilome did pas
Downe from the top of purest heavens hight,
To be embodied here, it then tooke light                  110
And lively spirits from that fayrest starre,
Which lights the world forth from his firie carre.

[17]
Which powre retayning still or more or lesse,
When she in fleshly seede is eft enraced,

[STANZA 14]     97. *wyre*: hair.     *stars*: eyes.
[STANZA 15]     102. *vitall spirits*: Ficino speaks of spirit as a third entity
in man, mediating between body and the powers of the soul (*Commentary*
6.6); cf. Donne, *The Extasie* 61–64.     105. *parcell*: part.
[STANZA 16]     112. *carre*: conveyance, chariot.
[STANZAS 17–21]     Physical and spiritual beauty are seen to be
intimately related.
[STANZA 17]     113. *or . . . or*: either . . . or.     114. *seede*: progeny
(biblical diction). *enraced*: implanted, inborn.

Through every part she doth the same impresse,                    115
According as the heavens have her graced,
And frames her house, in which she will be placed,
Fit for her selfe, adorning it with spoyle
Of th'heavenly riches, which she robd erewhyle.

[18]
Therof it comes, that these faire soules, which have              120
The most resemblance of that heavenly light,
Frame to themselves most beautifull and brave
Their fleshly bowre, most fit for their delight,
And the grosse matter by a soveraine might
Tempers so trim, that it may well be seene,                       125
A pallace fit for such a virgin Queene.

[19]
So every spirit, as it is most pure,
And hath in it the more of heavenly light,
So it the fairer bodie doth procure
To habit in, and it more fairely dight                            130
With chearefull grace and amiable sight.
For of the soule the bodie forme doth take:
For soule is forme, and doth the bodie make.

[20]
Therefore where ever that thou doest behold
A comely corpse, with beautie faire endewed,                      135
Know this for certaine, that the same doth hold

117–19. Body as soul's dwelling place is commonplace; cf. *FQ* II ix.
117. *frames*: makes.
[S T A N Z A S  1 8 – 2 0]      The idea that physical beauty is proportional to
goodness of soul is a commonplace of Neoplatonism; cf. Castiglione,
*Courtier*, pp.310–11.
[S T A N Z A  1 8]      122. *brave*: worthy.      125. *trim*: elegantly.
[S T A N Z A  1 9]      130. *habit*: dwell.
[S T A N Z A  2 0]      135. *endewed*: endowed.

A beauteous soule, with faire conditions thewed,
Fit to receive the seede of vertue strewed.
For all that faire is, is by nature good;
That is a signe to know the gentle blood.    140

[21]

Yet oft it falles, that many a gentle mynd
Dwels in deformed tabernacle drownd,
Either by chaunce, against the course of kynd,
Or through unaptnesse in the substance fownd,
Which it assumed of some stubborne grownd,    145
That will not yield unto her formes direction,
But is perform'd with some foule imperfection.

[22]

And oft it falles (ay me the more to rew)
That goodly beautie, albe heavenly borne,
Is foule abusd, and that celestiall hew,    150
Which doth the world with her delight adorne,
Made but the bait of sinne, and sinners scorne;
Whilest every one doth seeke and sew to have it,
But every one doth seeke, but to deprave it.

137. "Beautie . . . leadeth them into the way of vertuous conditions . . . "
(Castiglione, *Courtier*, p.311). *conditions*: qualities. *thewed*: trained.
138. *strewed*: scattered.
[STANZA 21]    This is the central stanza of *HB*; see note to *HHB* st.22.
Cf. Ficino, *Commentary* 5.6, 6.6. Sp is here more charitable than Castiglione,
who sees such discrepancies between soul and body as rare (*Courtier*, p.309).
Sp's reasoning extends the logic of Platonism: the problem is seen to arise
from the inherent recalcitrance of matter.    141. *falles*: happens.
143. *kynd*: natural descent.    144. *unaptnesse*: flaw.    147. *perform'd*:
worked out.
[STANZAS 22–25]    In discussing the corruption of spiritual beauty by
lust, Sp follows Castiglione's affirmation of "the affinitie that beautie hath
with goodnesse" and his assignment of external responsibility for corruption:
"ill bringing up, the continuall provocations of lovers, tokens, povertie, hope,
deceites, fear, and a thousand other matters" (*Courtier*, p.311). But for Sp, a
soul that remains incorruptible cannot be degraded.
[STANZA 22]    153. *sew*: (pur)sue.

### [23]

Yet nathemore is that faire beauties blame,        155
But theirs that do abuse it unto ill:
Nothing so good, but that through guilty shame
May be corrupt, and wrested unto will.
Nathelesse the soule is faire and beauteous still,
How ever fleshes fault it filthy make:        160
For things immortall no corruption take.

### [24]

But ye faire Dames, the worlds deare ornaments,
And lively images of heavens light,
Let not your beames with such disparagements
Be dimd, and your bright glorie darkned quight,        165
But mindfull still of your first countries sight,
Doe still preserve your first informed grace,
Whose shadow yet shynes in your beauteous face.

### [25]

Loath that foule blot, that hellish fierbrand,
Disloiall lust, faire beauties foulest blame,        170
That base affections, which your eares would bland,
Commend to you by loves abused name;
But is indeede the bondslave of defame,
Which will the garland of your glorie marre,
And quench the light of your bright shyning starre.        175

[STANZA 23]    155. *nathemore*: not at all.    158. *corrupt*: corrupted,
spoiled.    161. Cf. 1 Corinthians 15.42,53–54.
[STANZA 24]    164. Cf. note to line 19 above. *disparagements*:
dishonorable actions.    166. "For they that say suche things, declare
plainely that they seke a [heavenly] countrey" (Hebrews 11.14).
167. The image of God is implanted at creation. *informed*: imparted.
[STANZA 25]    Ellrodt (1960:129) comments that Sp's contrast
between "loiall" love and "Disloiall lust" is essentially at variance with the
Platonic contrast between intellectual and sensual delights.    170. *blame*:
fault.    171. *bland*: flatter.    173. *defame*: defamation, slander.

[26]

But gentle Love, that loiall is and trew,
Will more illumine your resplendent ray,
And adde more brightnesse to your goodly hew,
From light of his pure fire, which by like way
Kindled of yours, your likenesse doth display,          180
Like as two mirrours by opposd reflexion,
Doe both expresse the faces first impression.

[27]

Therefore to make your beautie more appeare,
It you behoves to love, and forth to lay
That heavenly riches, which in you ye beare,          185
That men the more admyre their fountaine may,
For else what booteth that celestiall ray,
If it in darknesse be enshrined ever,
That it of loving eyes be vewed never?

[28]

But in your choice of Loves, this well advize,          190
That likest to your selves ye them select,
The which your forms first sourse may sympathize,
And with like beauties parts be inly deckt:

[STANZAS 26–27]     Fulfillment of beauty through true love.
[STANZA 26]     "There is also the fact that the lover engraves the figure
of the beloved on his own soul. And so the soul of the lover becomes a
mirror in which the image of the beloved is reflected. For that reason, when
the beloved recognizes himself in the lover, he is forced to love him" (Ficino,
*Commentary* 2.8).
[STANZA 27]     Cf. Matthew 5.14–16: "Ye are the light of the worlde.
A citie that is set on an hill, can not be hid. Nether do men light a candel,
and put it under a bushel, but on a candelsticke, & it giveth light unto all that
are in the house. Let your light so shine before men . . . . "     187. *booteth*:
profits.
[STANZAS 28–33]     The realization of true love through the matching
of the idealized image of the lover to the internalized ideal.
[STANZA 28]     190. *advize*: consider.     193. *inly*: inwardly.

For if you loosely love without respect,
It is no love, but a discordant warre,                    195
Whose unlike parts amongst themselves do jarre.

### [29]

For Love is a celestiall harmonie,
Of likely harts composd of starres concent,
Which joyne together in sweete sympathie,
To worke ech others joy and true content,                200
Which they have harbourd since their first descent
Out of their heavenly bowres, where they did see
And know ech other here belov'd to bee.

### [30]

Then wrong it were that any other twaine
Should in loves gentle band combyned bee,                 205
But those whom heaven did at first ordaine,
And made out of one mould the more t'agree:
For all that like the beautie which they see,
Streight do not love: for love is not so light,
As streight to burne at first beholders sight.           210

### [31]

But they which love indeede, looke otherwise,
With pure regard and spotlesse true intent,

194. *loosely*: immorally. *respect*: discrimination.      196. *jarre*: clash.
[S T A N Z A  2 9]      "Those who . . . are born under the same star are so
constituted that the image of the more beautiful of them, penetrating
through the eyes into the soul of the other, matches and corresponds
completely with a certain identical image which was formed in the astral
body of that soul as well as in its inner nature from its creation. The soul thus
stricken recognizes the image before it as something which is its own"
(Ficino, *Commentary* 6.6).      198. *likely*: similar. *composd of*: brought
together by. *concent*: harmony.      199–200. "Whenever two men embrace
each other in mutual affection, this one lives in that; that one, in this. Such
men exchange themselves with each other; and each gives himself to the
other in order to receive the other" (Ficino, *Commentary* 2.8).
[S T A N Z A  3 0]      205. *band*: bond, covenant.      209. *light*: trivial.
[S T A N Z A S  3 1 – 3 3]      Cf. Castiglione's sense that true love depends

Drawing out of the object of their eyes,
A more refyned forme, which they present
Unto their mind, voide of all blemishment;                          215
Which it reducing to her first perfection,
Beholdeth free from fleshes frayle infection.


[32]
And then conforming it unto the light,
Which in it selfe it hath remaining still
Of that first Sunne, yet sparckling in his sight,                   220
Thereof he fashions in his higher skill,
An heavenly beautie to his fancies will,
And it embracing in his mind entyre,
The mirrour of his owne thought doth admyre.


[33]
Which seeing now so inly faire to be,                               225
As outward it appeareth to the eye,
And with his spirits proportion to agree,
He thereon fixeth all his fantasie,
And fully setteth his felicitie,
Counting it fairer, then it is indeede,                             230
And yet indeede her fairenesse doth exceede.


upon discerning inward sight: beauty "draweth unto it mens eyes with
pleasure, and pearcing through them, imprinteth himselfe in the soule . . . "
(*Courtier*, p.304). Cf. Ficino, *Commentary* 6.6: "The soul then puts the
[beloved's] visual image beside its own interior image, and if anything is
lacking in the former . . . the soul restores it by reforming it. Then the soul
loves that reformed image as its own work." Ellrodt (1960:130–33) stresses
that Sp does not go beyond the second step of the "ladder." There is no
formation of a concept of universal beauty out of various beauties, a
development essential to Castiglione, Benevieni, and Pico.
[STANZA 31]     216. *her*: the form's.
[STANZA 32]     218. *conforming*: harmonizing.     221. *skill*:
understanding.          223. *entyre*: perfectly, intimately.
[STANZA 33]     229. *setteth*: establishes.

[34]

For lovers eyes more sharply sighted bee
Then other mens, and in deare loves delight
See more then any other eyes can see,
Through mutuall receipt of beames bright,               235
Which carrie privie message to the spright,
And to their eyes that inmost faire display,
As plaine as light discovers dawning day.

[35]

Therein they see through amorous eye-glaunces,
Armies of loves still flying too and fro,               240
Which dart at them their litle fierie launces,
Whom having wounded, backe againe they go,
Carrying compassion to their lovely foe;
Who seeing her faire eyes so sharpe effect,
Cures all their sorrowes with one sweete aspect.        245

[36]

In which how many wonders doe they reede
To their conceipt, that others never see,
Now of her smiles, with which their soules they feede,
Like Gods with Nectar in their bankets free,
Now of her lookes, which like to Cordials bee;         250
But when her words embassade forth she sends,
Lord how sweete musicke that unto them lends.

[37]

Sometimes upon her forhead they behold
A thousand Graces masking in delight,

[STANZAS 34–37]    The role of physical beauty in love.
[STANZA 34]    236. *privie*: secret.    237. *faire*: beauty.
[STANZA 35]    On the function of the eyes in love, see Castiglione,
*Courtier*, pp.246–47.    240. *loves*: cupids.    245. *aspect*: glance.
[STANZA 36]    246–47. "Let him lay aside therefore the blinde
judgement of the sense . . . " (Castiglione, *Courtier*, p.313).    246. *reede*:
discern.    247. *conceipt*: whim.    249. *bankets*: banquets. *free*:
lavish.    251. *embassade*: as ambassador.    252. *lends*: imparts.

Sometimes within her eye-lids they unfold                    255
Ten thousand sweet belgards, which to their sight
Doe seeme like twinckling starres in frostie night:
But on her lips like rosy buds in May,
So many millions of chaste pleasures play.

[38]
All those, ô *Cytherea*, and thousands more                    260
Thy handmaides be, which do on thee attend
To decke thy beautie with their dainties store,
That may it more to mortall eyes commend,
And make it more admyr'd of foe and frend;
That in mens harts thou mayst thy throne enstall,    265
And spred thy lovely kingdome over all.

[39]
Then *Iö tryumph*, ô great beauties Queene,
Advance the banner of thy conquest hie,
That all this world, the which thy vassals beene,
May draw to thee, and with dew fealtie,              270
Adore the powre of thy great Majestie,
Singing this Hymne in honour of thy name,
Compyld by me, which thy poore liegeman am.

[40]
In lieu whereof graunt, ô great Soveraine,
That she whose conquering beautie doth captive       275
My trembling hart in her eternall chaine,
One drop of grace at length will to me give,
That I her bounden thrall by her may live,

[STANZA 37]    256. *belgards*: loving looks.
[STANZAS 38–41]    Praise of Venus and of his lover and plea for
mercy.
[STANZA 39]    Cf. Ovid, *Amores* 1.2.34: "Vulgus 'io' magna voce
'triumphe!' canet." 268. *Advance*: lift up. 273. *liegeman*: faithful
follower.
[STANZA 40]    274. *In lieu whereof*: in exchange for which.

And this same life, which first fro me she reaved,
May owe to her, of whom I it receaved.                    280

[41]
And you faire *Venus* dearling, my deare dread,
Fresh flowre of grace, great Goddesse of my life,
When your faire eyes these fearefull lines shal read,
Deigne to let fall one drop of dew reliefe,
That may recure my harts long pyning griefe,           285
And shew what wondrous powre your beauty hath,
That can restore a damned wight from death.

FINIS.

279. *reaved*: robbed.
[STANZA 41]    281. *dread*: person reverenced.    285. *recure*: cure.

# An Hymne of Heavenly Love.

### [1]

LOve, lift me up upon thy golden wings,
From this base world unto thy heavens hight,
Where I may see those admirable things,
Which there thou workest by thy soveraine might,
Farre above feeble reach of earthly sight,        5
That I thereof an heavenly Hymne may sing
Unto the god of Love, high heavens king.

[STANZAS 1–3]   These form the introduction to this hymn and
consist of the "correction" in st. 1 and the recantation in st. 2–3. The
invocation proper is postponed till st. 7 (lines 43–49).
[STANZA 1]   The "golden wings" of Love in the first line may serve to
recall the wings of Cupid in *HL* 67–70 as he makes his bold flight through
the darkness of chaos, or they may be taken to echo those "golden plumes"
upon which earthly love was seen to lift itself "Above the reach of loathly
sinfull lust" in *HL* 178–79. There is no critical agreement as to whether the
"flight" introduced here should be interpreted as a contrast, a fresh start, in
relation to the first two hymns, or whether it should be seen as a more or less
direct continuation of the ascent that found its beginning in the first two
hymns. It should be noted, however, that the "golden plumes" of earthly love
only serve to lift love up from "sinfull lust." There is no suggestion in the
first hymn of leaving the realm of physical love, the sphere of Eros. Thus
several modern critics have argued that there can be little doubt that "the
object of the devotion has changed" (Welsford 1967:49), and that Sp seems
to insist that the object of his devotion in this hymn is radically different in
kind from that described in the first two hymns. Thus the first st. can be read
as an answer to the last st. of *HL*. When Sp comes to sing his "heavenly
Hymne" (*HL* 302) it is not Cupid who is his "God" and his "king" (*HL* 305)
but it is Christ who is the true "god of Love" and "high heavens king" (*HHL*
7). Sp clearly saw a parallel between the spheres of human love and divine
love, and he makes use of such parallels to enforce the unity of his work. But
just as there seems to be little reason to assume that Sp, one year after the
publication of his *Amoretti and Epithalamion*, had arrived at a position which
involved the renunciation of sensual love, so there seems to be scant evidence
for the conclusion that he regarded human love as a stepping stone in an
ascent to divine love.

### [2]

Many lewd layes (ah woe is me the more)
In praise of that mad fit, which fooles call love,
I have in th'heat of youth made heretofore,               10
That in light wits did loose affection move.
But all those follies now I do reprove,
And turned have the tenor of my string,
The heavenly prayses of true love to sing.

### [3]

And ye that wont with greedy vaine desire               15
To reade my fault, and wondring at my flame,
To warme your selves at my wide sparckling fire,
Sith now that heat is quenched, quench my blame,
And in her ashes shrowd my dying shame:
For who my passed follies now pursewes,               20
Beginnes his owne, and my old fault renewes.

### [4]

B Efore this worlds great frame, in which al things
Are now containd, found any being place,

[STANZAS 2–3]     The retraction of these two stanzas conforms with
literary convention such as that established by Petrarch in his sonnets of
repentance. This does not necessarily mean, however, that Sp is simply
paying lip service to the supposedly puritanical attitude of the two ladies of
the Dedication. The conventionality of this type of public recantation should
make it quite clear, however, that these st. cannot be used as evidence
signalling a basic change in Sp's attitude to earthly love and beauty. If that
were the case, the first pair of hymns would certainly have had to be excluded
altogether. Arguably, the recantation may be seen to indicate that the next
two hymns do not constitute a continuation from the first pair, but that the
poet is now moving to a different sphere.
[STANZA 2]     11. *affection*: passion.     13. He is now singing in a
different key, or more literally, he has tightened the strings of his harp to play
in a higher pitch.
[STANZA 3]     16. *reade*: regard.     18. *sith*: since.
[STANZAS 4–18]     This account of creation forms a structural parallel
to those given earlier in *HL* and *HB*. It includes a description of the Trinity

Ere flitting Time could wag his eyas wings
About that mightie bound, which doth embrace          25
The rolling Spheres, and parts their houres by space,
That high eternall powre, which now doth move
In all these things, mov'd in it selfe by love.

[5]

It lov'd it selfe, because it selfe was faire;
(For faire is lov'd;) and of it selfe begot          30
Like to it selfe his eldest sonne and heire,
Eternall, pure, and voide of sinfull blot,
The firstling of his joy, in whom no jot
Of loves dislike, or pride was to be found,
Whom he therefore with equall honour crownd.          35

[6]

With him he raignd, before all time prescribed,
In endlesse glorie and immortall might,
Together with that third from them derived,
Most wise, most holy, most almightie Spright,
Whose kingdomes throne no thought of earthly wight          40
Can comprehend, much lesse my trembling verse
With equall words can hope it to reherse.

and the invocation of the Holy Ghost (st. 4–7), the creation and fall of the
angels (st. 8–14), and the creation and fall of man (st. 15–18).
[STANZA 4]     24. *eyas wings*: the wings of an untrained hawk. Sp returns
again and again to the imagery of wings and flight. To the image used here
and the majestic metaphor of the first line may be added the image of angelic
wings in line 66. Compare Cupid's wings in *HL* 25 and 64, and the wings of
the falcon and of the eagle in *HHB* 26–28 and 133–40.     25–26. The
sphere of the *primum Mobile* and the fixed stars moves around the earth in
twenty-four hours bringing with it the inner spheres of the planets. The
highest sphere was divided into twenty-four "hours," each occupying fifteen
degrees so that two "hours," or thirty degrees, would be given to each of the
twelve signs of the Zodiac.
[STANZAS 4–6]     27–42. Sp's description of the Trinity may be said to
have Neoplatonic overtones, yet this type of Neoplatonic phrasing could be
found in any patristic writing.
[STANZA 6]     42. *equall*: suitable. *reherse*: recount.

[7]
Yet ô most blessed Spirit, pure lampe of light,
Eternall spring of grace and wisedome trew,
Vouchsafe to shed into my barren spright,          45
Some little drop of thy celestiall dew,
That may my rymes with sweet infuse embrew,
And give me words equall unto my thought,
To tell the marveiles by thy mercie wrought.

[8]
Yet being pregnant still with powrefull grace,     50
And full of fruitfull love, that loves to get
Things like himselfe, and to enlarge his race,
His second brood though not in powre so great,
Yet full of beautie, next he did beget
An infinite increase of Angels bright,             55
All glistring glorious in their Makers light.

[9]
To them the heavens illimitable hight,
Not this round heaven, which we from hence behold,
Adornd with thousand lamps of burning light,
And with ten thousand gemmes of shyning gold,      60
He gave as their inheritance to hold,
That they might serve him in eternall blis,
And be partakers of those joyes of his.

[10]
There they in their trinall triplicities
About him wait, and on his will depend,            65

[STANZA 7]    Sp invokes the Holy Spirit because the Holy Spirit alone
can inspire man to an understanding of the mystery of divine love (see I
Corinthians 2.9–13).    47. *infuse*: infusion.
[STANZA 8]    51. *get*: beget.
[STANZA 9]    The angels reside in the Empyrean Heaven outside the
world of time and space encircled by the crystalline sphere of the *primum
mobile*.
[STANZA 10]    64. In a popular work probably dating from the sixth

Either with nimble wings to cut the skies,
When he them on his messages doth send,
Or on his owne dread presence to attend,
Where they behold the glorie of his light,
And caroll Hymnes of love both day and night.                    70

### [11]

Both day and night is unto them all one,
For he his beames doth still to them extend,
That darknesse there appeareth never none,
Ne hath their day, ne hath their blisse an end,
But there their termelesse time in pleasure spend,              75
Ne ever should their happinesse decay,
Had not they dar'd their Lord to disobay.

### [12]

But pride impatient of long resting peace,
Did puffe them up with greedy bold ambition,
That they gan cast their state how to increase,                 80
Above the fortune of their first condition,
And sit in Gods owne seat without commission:
The brightest Angell, even the Child of light
Drew millions more against their God to fight.

century, the angels were divided into three hierarchies each consisting of
three orders of angels. Until about 1500 this work enjoyed considerable
authority because it was believed to be written by Dionysius the Areopagite
who was converted by St. Paul (Acts 17.24). In spite of the discovery that it
was of a much later date, it continued to be popular throughout the
Renaissance. (Cf. *HHB* 85–98.)
[STANZA 11]     72–73. There is a parallel here between God, extending
his light to the angels, and *HL* 72–73, where Venus "His owne faire mother,
for all creatures sake, /Did lend him light from her owne goodly ray."
72. *still*: constantly.     75. *termelesse*: endless.
[STANZA 12]     83–84. Lucifer, a leader of the highest order of angels,
rebelled against the rule of God, and as a punishment for his pride was
thrown down into Hell to become the Devil. (Cf. Isaiah 14.12.)

### [13]

Th'Almighty seeing their so bold assay,                    85
Kindled the flame of his consuming yre,
And with his onely breath them blew away
From heavens hight, to which they did aspyre,
To deepest hell, and lake of damned fyre;
Where they in darknesse and dread horror dwell,            90
Hating the happie light from which they fell.

### [14]

So that next off-spring of the Makers love,
Next to himselfe in glorious degree,
Degendering to hate fell from above
Through pride; (for pride and love may ill agree)          95
And now of sinne to all ensample bee:
How then can sinfull flesh it selfe assure,
Sith purest Angels fell to be impure?

### [15]

But that eternall fount of love and grace,
Still flowing forth his goodnesse unto all,                100
Now seeing left a waste and emptie place
In his wyde Pallace, through those Angels fall,
Cast to supply the same, and to enstall
A new unknowen Colony therein,
Whose root from earths base groundworke shold begin.       105

### [16]

Therefore of clay, base, vile, and next to nought,
Yet form'd by wondrous skill, and by his might:

[STANZAS 13 – 14] For the fate of the fallen angels, see II Peter 2.4 and
Jude 6.      85. *assay*: attempt.      94. *Degendering*: degenerating.
[STANZA 15]      100. *flowing*: pouring.      103. *Cast*: planned. *supply*:
fill.
[STANZAS 16 – 17]      The account of the creation of man resembles in
some respects Plato's account in the *Timaeus*. But the description is
nevertheless basically orthodox and based on Genesis 1.27: "Thus God
created the man in his image"; and Genesis 2.7: "And the Lord God also

According to an heavenly patterne wrought,
Which he had fashiond in his wise foresight,
He man did make, and breathd a living spright          110
Into his face most beautifull and fayre,
Endewd with wisedomes riches, heavenly, rare.

[17]

Such he him made, that he resemble might
Himselfe, as mortall thing immortall could;
Him to be Lord of every living wight,                  115
He made by love out of his owne like mould,
In whom he might his mightie selfe behould:
For love doth love the thing belov'd to see,
That like it selfe in lovely shape may bee.

[18]

But man forgetfull of his makers grace,                120
No lesse then Angels, whom he did ensew,
Fell from the hope of promist heavenly place,
Into the mouth of death to sinners dew,
And all his off-spring into thraldome threw:
Where they for ever should in bonds remaine,           125
Of never dead, yet ever dying paine.

[19]

Till that great Lord of Love, which him at first
Made of meere love, and after liked well,
Seeing him lie like creature long accurst,
In that deepe horror of despeyred hell,                130
Him wretch in doole would let no lenger dwell,
But cast out of that bondage to redeeme,
And pay the price, all were his debt extreeme.

made man of the dust of the grounde, and breathed in his face the breath of
life, and man was a living soul."      112. *Endewd*: endowed.
[STANZA 18]      121. *ensew*: follow.      123. *dew*: due.
[STANZA 19]      128. *meere*: pure.      130. *despeyred*: hopeless.
131. *doole*: misery.      133. See I Corinthians 7.23: "Ye are boght with a
price." *all*: although.

[20]

Out of the bosome of eternall blisse,
In which he reigned with his glorious syre,                    135
He downe descended, like a most demisse
And abject thrall, in fleshes fraile attyre,
That he for him might pay sinnes deadly hyre,
And him restore unto that happie state,
In which he stood before his haplesse fate.                    140

[21]

In flesh at first the guilt committed was,
Therefore in flesh it must be satisfyde:
Nor spirit, nor Angell, though they man surpas,
Could make amends to God for mans misguyde,
But onely man himselfe, who selfe did slyde.                   145
So taking flesh of sacred virgins wombe,
For mans deare sake he did a man become.

[22]

And that most blessed bodie, which was borne
Without all blemish or reprochfull blame,
He freely gave to be both rent and torne                       150
Of cruell hands, who with despightfull shame
Revyling him, that them most vile became,

[STANZA 20]    136–38. Christ "made him self of no reputation, and
toke upon him the forme of a servant, and was made like unto men and
founde in shape as a man. He humbled him self, and became obedient unto
the death, even the death of the crosse" (Philippians 2.7–8). "And the Worde
was made flesh, and dwelt among us" (John 1.14). Cf. *HL* st. 20 and note.
136. *demisse*: humiliated, submissive.        138. *hyre*: wages. ("For the wages
of sinne is death," Romans 6.23.)
[STANZA 21]    141–42. "God sending his owne Sonne, in the
similitude of sinful flesh, and for sinne, condemned sinne in the flesh"
(Romans 8.3). "For since by man came death, by man came also the
resurrection of the dead" (I Corinthians 15.21).        144. *misguyde*:
wrongdoing.
[STANZA 22]    152. *that . . . became*: that ill became them.

At length him nayled on a gallow tree,
And slew the just, by most unjust decree.

### [23]

O huge and most unspeakeable impression                    155
Of loves deepe wound, that pierst the piteous hart
Of that deare Lord with so entyre affection,
And sharply launching every inner part,
Dolours of death into his soule did dart;
Doing him die, that never it deserved,                     160
To free his foes, that from his heast had swerved.

### [24]

What hart can feele least touch of so sore launch,
Or thought can think the depth of so deare wound?
Whose bleeding sourse their streames yet never staunch,
But stil do flow, and freshly still redound,               165
To heale the sores of sinfull soules unsound,
And clense the guilt of that infected cryme,
Which was enrooted in all fleshly slyme.

### [25]

O blessed well of love, ô floure of grace,
O glorious Morning starre, ô lampe of light,               170
Most lively image of thy fathers face,
Eternall King of glorie, Lord of might,
Meeke lambe of God before all worlds behight,
How can we thee requite for all this good?
Or what can prize that thy most precious blood?            175

---

154. Cf. *HL* 153–54.
[STANZA 23]    158. *launching*: piercing.    161. *heast*: command.
[STANZA 24]    165. *redound*: overflow.
[STANZA 25]    169. *well of love*: "the water that I shal give him, shalbe
in him a well of water, springing up into everlasting life" (John 4.14). *floure
of grace*: this phrase should be contrasted with *HB* 282.    173. *behight*:
ordained.    175. *prize*: pay for.

### [26]

Yet nought thou ask'st in lieu of all this love,
But love of us for guerdon of thy paine.
Ay me; what can us lesse then that behove?
Had he required life of us againe,
Had it beene wrong to aske his owne with gaine?          180
He gave us life, he it restored lost;
Then life were least, that us so litle cost.

### [27]

But he our life hath left unto us free,
Free that was thrall, and blessed that was band;
Ne ought demaunds, but that we loving bee,          185
As he himselfe hath lov'd us afore hand,
And bound therto with an eternall band,
Him first to love, that us so dearely bought,
And next, our brethren to his image wrought.

### [28]

Him first to love, great right and reason is,          190
Who first to us our life and being gave;
And after when we fared had amisse,
Us wretches from the second death did save;
And last the food of life, which now we have,
Even himselfe in his deare sacrament,          195
To feede our hungry soules unto us lent.

### [29]

Then next to love our brethren, that were made
Of that selfe mould, and that selfe makers hand,

---

[STANZA 26]     176. *lieu*: reward, return.     177. *of*: from.
178. *behove*: befit.     180. *gaine*: advantage, interest.
[STANZA 27]     184. *band*: banned (from Heaven), damned.
187. *band*: bond.     188–89. "Thou shalt love the Lord thy God with all
thine heart, with all thy soule, and with all thy minde. . . . Thou shalt love
thy neighbour as thy self" (Matthew 22.37–39).
[STANZA 28]     196. *lent*: gave.

That we, and to the same againe shall fade,
Where they shall have like heritage of land,                    200
How ever here on higher steps we stand;
Which also were with selfe same price redeemed
That we, how ever of us light esteemed.

[30]

And were they not, yet since that loving Lord
Commaunded us to love them for his sake,                     205
Even for his sake, and for his sacred word,
Which in his last bequest he to us spake,
We should them love, and with their needs partake;
Knowing that whatsoere to them we give,
We give to him, by whom we all doe live.                      210

[31]

Such mercy he by his most holy reede
Unto us taught, and to approve it trew,
Ensampled it by his most righteous deede,
Shewing us mercie miserable crew,
That we the like should to the wretches shew,                 215
And love our brethren; thereby to approve,
How much himselfe that loved us, we love.

[32]

Then rouze thy selfe, ô earth, out of thy soyle,
In which thou wallowest like to filthy swyne,
And doest thy mynd in durty pleasures moyle,                  220
Unmindfull of that dearest Lord of thyne;

[STANZA 29]    199. *That we*: as we.
[STANZA 30]    208. *partake*: share.
[STANZA 31]    211. *reede*: precept.    212. *approve*: prove.
213. *Ensampled*: exemplified.    215. "Be ye therefore merciful, as your
Father also is merciful" (Luke 6.36).
[STANZA 32]    This description of how man is raised from the mud of
sin, forms a parallel to the description, in *HL* 176–89, of the power of love
to lift man up from the "dunghill" of lust.    218. *soyle*: dirt, mud.
220. *moyle*: defile.

Lift up to him thy heavie clouded eyne,
That thou his soveraine bountie mayst behold,
And read through love his mercies manifold.

[33]

Beginne from first, where he encradled was          225
In simple cratch, wrapt in a wad of hay,
Betweene the toylefull Oxe and humble Asse,
And in what rags, and in how base aray,
The glory of our heavenly riches lay,
When him the silly Shepheards came to see,          230
Whom greatest Princes sought on lowest knee.

[34]

From thence reade on the storie of his life,
His humble carriage, his unfaulty wayes,
His cancred foes, his fights, his toyle, his strife,
His paines, his povertie, his sharpe assayes,          235
Through which he past his miserable dayes,
Offending none, and doing good to all,
Yet being malist both of great and small.

[35]

And looke at last how of most wretched wights,
He taken was, betrayd, and false accused,          240
How with most scornefull taunts, and fell despights
He was revyld, disgrast, and foule abused,
How scourgd, how crownd, how buffeted, how brused;
And lastly how twixt robbers crucifyde,
With bitter wounds through hands, through feet and
                                    syde.          245

222. *eyne*: eyes.     224. *read*: perceive.
[STANZA 33]     225–26. Cf. the description of Cupid's cradle in *HL* st.
8.     226. *cratch*: manger. *wad*: bundle.     230. *silly*: innocent, blessed.
[STANZA 34]     233. *carriage*: bearing.     234. *cancred*:
malignant.     235. *assayes*: trials.     238. *malist*: hated.

[36]

Then let thy flinty hart that feeles no paine,
Empierced be with pittifull remorse,
And let thy bowels bleede in every vaine,
At sight of his most sacred heavenly corse,
So torne and mangled with malicious forse,　　　　　　250
And let thy soule, whose sins his sorrows wrought,
Melt into teares, and grone in grieved thought.

[37]

With sence whereof whilest so thy softened spirit
Is inly toucht, and humbled with meeke zeale,
Through meditation of his endlesse merit,　　　　　　255
Lift up thy mind to th'author of thy weale,
And to his soveraine mercie doe appeale;
Learne him to love, that loved thee so deare,
And in thy brest his blessed image beare.

[38]

With all thy hart, with all thy soule and mind,　　　　260
Thou must him love, and his beheasts embrace;
All other loves, with which the world doth blind
Weake fancies, and stirre up affections base,
Thou must renounce, and utterly displace,
And give thy selfe unto him full and free,　　　　　　265
That full and freely gave himselfe to thee.

[39]

Then shalt thou feele thy spirit so possest,
And ravisht with devouring great desire
Of his deare selfe, that shall thy feeble brest
Inflame with love, and set thee all on fire　　　　　　270

[STANZA 36]　　249. *corse*: body.
[STANZA 37]　　256. *weale*: welfare.
[STANZA 38]　　263. *affections*: passions.

With burning zeale, through every part entire,
That in no earthly thing thou shalt delight,
But in his sweet and amiable sight.

### [40]

Thenceforth all worlds desire will in thee dye,
And all earthes glorie on which men do gaze,                275
Seeme durt and drosse in thy pure sighted eye,
Compar'd to that celestiall beauties blaze,
Whose glorious beames all fleshly sense doth daze
With admiration of their passing light,
Blinding the eyes and lumining the spright.                280

### [41]

Then shall thy ravisht soule inspired bee
With heavenly thoughts, farre above humane skil,
And thy bright radiant eyes shall plainely see
Th'Idee of his pure glorie present still,
Before thy face, that all thy spirits shall fill          285
With sweete enragement of celestiall love,
Kindled through sight of those faire things above.

FINIS.

[STANZA 39]     271. *entire*: inward.     273. *amiable*: lovely.
[STANZA 40]     Compare the description of "that sweet passion" which
"all sordid basenesse doth expell" in *HL* 190–96.     279. *passing*:
surpassing.
[STANZA 41]     282. *skil*: understanding.     284. The use of the
Neoplatonic term *Idea* underlines the continued parallelism with *HL* st. 28.
The distinction between the physical beauty of the lady and the image in the
lover's mind is clearly seen as a parallel to the distinction between the view of
the historical Christ, the incarnate Christ, and the vision of the Godhead, the
ascended Christ.     284. *still*: constantly.     286. *enragement*: rapture.

# An Hymne of Heavenly Beautie.

### [1]

R Apt with the rage of mine own ravisht thought,
Through contemplation of those goodly sights,
And glorious images in heaven wrought,
Whose wondrous beauty breathing sweet delights,
Do kindle love in high conceipted sprights:          5
I faine to tell the things that I behold,
But feele my wits to faile, and tongue to fold.

### [2]

Vouchsafe then, ô thou most almightie Spright,
From whom all guifts of wit and knowledge flow,
To shed into my breast some sparkling light          10
Of thine eternall Truth, that I may show
Some litle beames to mortall eyes below,
Of that immortall beautie, there with thee,
Which in my weake distraughted mynd I see.

[STANZAS 1–3]     The enraptured speaker asks divine aid in translating
his vision into speech which will move his mortal audience to love God,
"th'eternall fountaine of that heavenly beauty."
[STANZA 1]     The poet seems to have the vision he anticipates in *HHL*
st.41.     1. *rage . . . thought*: Religious passion and poetic inspiration are
both here. The principal reminiscence is of the divinely-inspired madness of
prophets and poets in Plato, *Phaedrus* 249–50. There is an implicit echo of
and contrast with the "raging fyre" of erotic love in *HB* 4. Cf. the "goodly
fury" in *FQ* VI Proem 2 6.     2. *goodly sights*: See Revelation 21.
3. Christianized version of Platonic ideas suggesting the intimate mysteries of
God's creation, especially the notion of God's image in which (unfallen) man
is made (Genesis 1.26).     5. *high conceipted*: high-minded.     6. *faine*:
desire.
[STANZA 2]     8. *almightie Spright*: Holy Spirit.     9. "For the Lord
giveth wisdome, out of his mouth *commeth* knowledge and understanding"
(Proverbs 2.6; see also John 14.26). *wit*: intellect, reason, wisdom.
11. The gift of eternal truth is identified with the Holy Spirit in John 14.16–
17.     12. "Let your light so shine before men, that they may se your good
workes, & glorifie your Father which is in heaven" (Matthew 5.16).
13. Cf. *HHL* st.40 and *HHB* st.27 which it foreshadows.
14. *distraughted*: distracted.

[3]

That with the glorie of so goodly sight,                          15
The hearts of men, which fondly here admyre
Faire seeming shewes, and feed on vaine delight,
Transported with celestiall desyre
Of those faire formes, may lift themselves up hyer,
And learne to love with zealous humble dewty            20
Th'eternall fountaine of that heavenly beauty.

[4]

Beginning then below, with th'easie vew
Of this base world, subject to fleshly eye,
From thence to mount aloft by order dew,
To contemplation of th'immortall sky,                        25
Of the soare faulcon so I learne to fly,
That flags awhile her fluttering wings beneath,
Till she her selfe for stronger flight can breath.

[5]

Then looke who list, thy gazefull eyes to feed
With sight of that is faire, looke on the frame             30

[STANZA 3]    17–18. The distinction between "vaine delight" and
"celestiall desyre" reflects the Platonic notion of a world of becoming as
opposed to a world of being. But the diction here has buried Plato in
concerns more typical of Christian otherworldliness.
[STANZAS 4–15]    The account of creation that follows the
introductory stanzas in the other three *Hymnes* is here replaced by an account
of the order of creation, organized by the principle of ascent from creature to
Creator. Cf. Augustine, *De Trinitate* 6.10.
[STANZA 4]    Here the sense of ascent reflects Plato: "Starting from
individual beauties, the quest for the universal beauty must find him ever
mounting the heavenly ladder, stepping from rung to rung . . . until at last
he comes to know what beauty is" (*Symposium* 211c).    26. *Of*: from. *soare
faulcon*: an unmolted first-year hawk still with its first red plumage; cf. sorrel
horses. *so*: thus.    27. *flags*: allows to droop.    28. *breath*: take breath.
[STANZA 5]    Cf. Augustine, *Enarratio in Psalmos* 145.5: "On all sides
stands the beauty of the work, commending to you the artist. You admire the
creation: love the Creator."    29. *list*: chooses to.    30. *frame*:
constitution.

Of this wyde *universe*, and therein reed
The endlesse kinds of creatures, which by name
Thou canst not count, much lesse their natures aime:
All which are made with wondrous wise respect,
And all with admirable beautie deckt.                    35

### [6]

First th'Earth, on adamantine pillers founded,
Amid the Sea engirt with brasen bands;
Then th'Aire still flitting, but yet firmely bounded
On everie side, with pyles of flaming brands,
Never consum'd nor quencht with mortall hands;          40
And last, that mightie shining christall wall,
Wherewith he hath encompassed this All.

### [7]

By view whereof, it plainly may appeare,
That still as every thing doth upward tend,
And further is from earth, so still more cleare          45
And faire it growes, till to his perfect end
Of purest beautie, it at last ascend:
Ayre more then water, fire much more then ayre,
And heaven then fire appeares more pure and fayre.

---

31. *reed*: scan, count, discern.    33 *aime*: conjecture.    34. *respect*: care
and attention.
[STANZA 6]    The order is that of ascent upward through the traditional
sphere of the four elements, thence through the crystalline spheres of the
heavenly bodies (here not mentioned directly) to the all-encompassing
*primum mobile*.    36. "For the pillers of the earth are the Lords, and he
hathe set the worlde upon them" (1 Samuel 2.8). *adamantine*: unbreakable.
38. *flitting*: shifting about.    40. This suggests qualities not of the sphere
of fire but of the purer "ether" that fills all space beyond the sphere of the
moon.
[STANZA 7]    A version of the Great Chain of Being: "In Sp's version
purity, charity, or simplicity of substance is the organizing principle of the
hierarchy. Beauty, then, acts as a sort of law of gravity, holding everything in
its proper place in the universe" (Kellogg and Steele 1965:516).    46. *his*:
its.

### [8]

Looke thou no further, but affixe thine eye                     50
On that bright shynie round still moving Masse,
The house of blessed Gods, which men call *Skye*,
All sowd with glistring stars more thicke then grasse,
Whereof each other doth in brightnesse passe;
But those two most, which ruling night and day,               55
As King and Queene, the heavens Empire sway.

### [9]

And tell me then, what hast thou ever seene,
That to their beautie may compared bee,
Or can the sight that is most sharpe and keene,
Endure their Captains flaming head to see?                    60
How much lesse those, much higher in degree,
And so much fairer, and much more then these,
As these are fairer then the land and seas?

### [10]

For farre above these heavens which here we see,
Be others farre exceeding these in light,                     65
Not bounded, not corrupt, as these same bee,
But infinite in largenesse and in hight,
Unmoving, uncorrupt, and spotlesse bright,
That need no Sunne t'illuminate their spheres,
But their owne native light farre passing theirs.             70

[STANZA 8]    51. *still*: continuously, silently.    52. *Gods*: the
planets.    54. *passe*: surpass.    56. *King and Queene*: sun and moon. *sway*:
govern.
[STANZA 9]    60. *Captains flaming head*: the sun.
[STANZAS 10–11]    The passage touches on the medieval
commonplace of three worlds: a world below the moon, a world of the nine
spheres of the planets and the fixed stars, and a world beyond the limits of
the visible universe.
[STANZA 10]    69–70. "They nede no candle, nether light of ye sunne:
for the Lord God giveth them light . . . " (Revelation 22.5).

[11]
And as these heavens still by degrees arize,
Untill they come to their first Movers bound,
That in his mightie compasse doth comprize,
And carrie all the rest with him around,
So those likewise doe by degrees redound,                    75
And rise more faire, till they at last arive
To the most faire, whereto they all do strive.


[12]
Faire is the heaven, where happy soules have place,
In full enjoyment of felicitie,
Whence they doe still behold the glorious face              80
Of the divine eternall Majestie;
More faire is that, where those *Idees* on hie
Enraunged be, which *Plato* so admyred,
And pure *Intelligences* from God inspyred.


[STANZA 11]    72. *first Movers bound*: the sphere of the *primum mobile*.    73. *comprize*: enclose.    75. *redound*: swell or surge upward.
[STANZA 12]    "The assignment of the abode of the blest to the Empyrean (the sphere of the *primum mobile*, or Crystalline sphere), was a commonplace . . . . The separation of the sphere of souls and that of ideas seems to have the authority of Plato himself, in the *Phaedrus* myth. Pico devotes a chapter to the relation between the two spheres . . . " (Bennett 1931:40–41).    80–81. "Then *shal we se* face to face" (1 Corinthians 13.12; cf. Revelation 22.4).    82–84. Plato, *Phaedrus* 247c–e, speaks of "that place beyond the heavens" occupied by immortal souls: "And while [the soul] is bourne round she discerns justice, its very self, and likewise temperance, and knowledge . . . the veritable knowledge of being that veritably is." Kellogg and Steele (1965:517) suggest that Sp "means to show that the highest reaches of pagan thought do not approach in beauty and power the perfection of the God of Christianity."    84. *Intelligences*: For Aquinas an equivalent in Arabic philosophy for angels where the term seems to designate angels collectively (*Summa Theologica* 1.q.79.art.10; cf. Dante, *Paradiso* 28.76ff).

[13]

Yet fairer is that heaven, in which doe raine                    85
The soveraine *Powres* and mightie *Potentates*,
Which in their high protections doe containe
All mortall Princes, and imperiall States;
And fayrer yet, whereas the royall Seates
And heavenly *Dominations* are set,                              90
From whom all earthly governance is fet.

[14]

Yet farre more faire be those bright *Cherubins*,
Which all with golden wings are overdight,
And those eternall burning *Seraphins*,
Which from their faces dart out fierie light;                    95
Yet fairer then they both, and much more bright
Be th'Angels and Archangels, which attend
On Gods owne person, without rest or end.

[15]

These thus in faire each other farre excelling,
As to the Highest they approch more neare,                       100
Yet is that Highest farre beyond all telling,
Fairer then all the rest which there appeare,
Though all their beauties joynd together were:
How then can mortall tongue hope to expresse,
The image of such endlesse perfectnesse?                         105

[STANZAS 13 – 14]    See note to *HHL* 64. The normal hierarchy of the
angels, inherited from Dionysus the Areopagite, arranges the Bible's angelic
beings in descending order: seraphim, cherubim, thrones; dominions,
virtues, powers; principalities, archangels, angels (see Patrides 1982). Sp
abandons the traditional order, making the comparatively humble angels and
archangels attendants of God's presence.
[STANZA 13]    91. *fet*: drawn.
[STANZA 14]    93. *golden wings*: The crafted cherubim that decorate the
ark of the covenant are to be of gold (see Exodus 25.18–20; 1 Kings 6.28).
*overdight*: decked all over.
[STANZA 15]    99. *faire*: beauty.

[16]

Cease then my tongue, and lend unto my mynd
Leave to bethinke how great that beautie is,
Whose utmost parts so beautifull I fynd,
How much more those essentiall parts of his,
His truth, his love, his wisedome, and his blis,      110
His grace, his doome, his mercy and his might,
By which he lends us of himselfe a sight.

[17]

Those unto all he daily doth display,
And shew himselfe in th'image of his grace,
As in a looking glasse, through which he may      115
Be seene, of all his creatures vile and base,
That are unable else to see his face,
His glorious face which glistereth else so bright,
That th'Angels selves can not endure his sight.

[18]

But we fraile wights, whose sight cannot sustaine      120
The Suns bright beames, when he on us doth shyne,

[STANZAS 16–20]    The glory of God's presence appears in his creation: "The splendor and grace of this face . . . whether in the Angel or in the Soul, or in the Matter of the World, is to be called universal beauty. And the impulse toward that is to be called universal love." (Ficino, *Commentary* 5.4).

[STANZA 16]    Similarly Calvin compares God's revelation in his creation (*Institutes* 1.5.5–6) and through his dealings with man (1.5.7–8). 108. *utmost parts*: the essence of the creation.    109. *essentiall parts*: God's essential attributes.    111. *doome*: judgement.

[STANZA 17]    "For now we se through a glasse darkely: but then *shal we se* face to face" (1 Corinthians 13.12).    113–15. "The reason why the author of The Letter to the Hebrews elegantly calls the universe the appearance of things invisible [11.3] is that this skillful ordering of the universe is for us a sort of mirror in which we can contemplate God, who is otherwise invisible" (Calvin, *Institutes* 1.5.1).

[STANZA 18]    "But because most people, immersed in their own errors, are struck blind in such a dazzling theater, he exclaims that to weigh those works of God wisely is a matter of rare and singular wisdom [Psalms

But that their points rebutted backe againe
Are duld, how can we see with feeble eyne,
The glory of that Majestie divine,
In sight of whom both Sun and Moone are darke,          125
Compared to his least resplendent sparke?

[19]

The meanes therefore which unto us is lent,
Him to behold, is on his workes to looke,
Which he hath made in beauty excellent,
And in the same, as in a brasen booke,                 130
To reade enregistred in every nooke
His goodnesse, which his beautie doth declare,
For all thats good, is beautifull and faire.

[20]

Thence gathering plumes of perfect speculation,
To impe the wings of thy high flying mynd,             135
Mount up aloft through heavenly contemplation,
From this darke world, whose damps the soule do

                                                        blynd,

And like the native brood of Eagles kynd,

107.43], in viewing which they who otherwise seem to be extremely acute
profit nothing. And certainly however much the glory of God shines forth,
scarcely one man in a hundred is a true spectator of it!" (Calvin, *Institutes*
1.5.8).          120–23. Cf. Plato's analogy of the cave (*Republic*, bk.7).
122. *But that*: except. *rebutted*: forced back.          123. *eyne*: eyes.
[STANZA 19]          127–28. "For the invisible things of him, that is, his
eternal power and Godhead, are sene by the creation of the worlde . . . "
(Romans 1.20).          130. *brasen booke*: "an indestructible book, strong as
brass" (Welsford 1967:169).          132. "The cause . . . by which he was led
once to create all these things, and is now moved to preserve them . . . is his
goodness alone" (Calvin, *Institutes* 1.5.6).          133. Cf. *HB* 139.
[STANZA 20]          134–37. Cf. similar imagery in *RT* 421–24.
134. *plumes*: wings. *speculation*: vision, especially intelligent or
comprehending vision.          135. *impe*: falconry term: to engraft feathers.
137. Another extension of Plato's cave analogy.          138–40. Young eagles
were thought to be able to gaze steadily at the sun. In *FQ* I x 47
Contemplation's earthly eyes are dim, but the greatness of his spiritual vision

On that bright Sunne of glorie fixe thine eyes,
Clear'd from grosse mists of fraile infirmities.                    140

### [21]

Humbled with feare and awfull reverence,
Before the footestoole of his Majestie,
Throw thy selfe downe with trembling innocence,
Ne dare looke up with corruptible eye,
On the dred face of that great *Deity*,                            145
For feare, lest if he chaunce to looke on thee,
Thou turne to nought, and quite confounded be.

### [22]

But lowly fall before his mercie seate,
Close covered with the Lambes integrity,
From the just wrath of his avengefull threate,                    150
That sits upon the righteous throne on hy:
His throne is built upon Eternity,
More firme and durable then steele or brasse,
Or the hard diamond, which them both doth passe.

is suggested by comparison with eagles' eyes. In Psalms 103.5 and Isaiah
40.31 the eagle is an image of renewal, as it is in *FQ* I xi 34.
[S T A N Z A S  2 1 – 2 6]     Sp here suggests the intimacy of God's presence
mediated by traditional symbols: throne, scepter, light.
[S T A N Z A  2 1]     142. *footestoole*: biblical symbol of God's presence; see 1
Chronicles 28.2, Psalms 99.5, etc.     144–47. "Thou canst not se my face,
for there shal no man se me, and live" (Exodus 33.20).
[S T A N Z A  2 2]     The central stanza of *HHB* appropriately enters the
presence of God. Cf. the central stanza of *HB* (st.21) which features the
"deformed tabernacle" of man's body (see Bjorvand 1975:39).
148. *mercie seate*: cover of the ark of the covenant, symbolic of God's most
intimate meeting with his priests (Exodus 25–40 *passim*).     149. "In the
middes of the throne . . . stode a Lambe as thogh he had been killed . . . "
(Revelation 5.6). The Geneva commentators add: "This vision confirmeth ye
power of our Lord Jesus, which is the Lambe of God that taketh away the
sinne of the world." The "Lambes integrity" in Protestant theology refers to
the adequacy of Christ's atonement, whence merit is imputed to unworthy
man.     150. *wrath*: recurrent biblical term conveying God's power and
authority.     152. "Thy throne, ô God *is* for ever and ever . . . " (Psalms
45.6; cf. Hebrews 1.8).     154. *passe*: surpass.

### [23]

His scepter is the rod of Righteousnesse,                           155
With which he bruseth all his foes to dust,
And the great Dragon strongly doth represse,
Under the rigour of his judgement just;
His seate is Truth, to which the faithfull trust;
From whence proceed her beames so pure and bright,     160
That all about him sheddeth glorious light.

### [24]

Light farre exceeding that bright blazing sparke,
Which darted is from *Titans* flaming head,
That with his beames enlumineth the darke
And dampish aire, wherby al things are red:                    165
Whose nature yet so much is marvelled
Of mortall wits, that it doth much amaze
The greatest wisards, which thereon do gaze.

[STANZAS 23–26]     "Now you comprehend in a measure the beauty
of God, which excels all other beauties at least as much as that light of the
sun in itself, pure, single, and inviolate, surpasses the splendor of the sun
dispersed through the cloudy air, divided, stained, and obscured" (Ficino,
*Commentary* 6.17).
[STANZA 23]     155. "The scepter of thy kingdome *is* a scepter of
righteousnes" (Psalms 45.6; cf. Hebrews 1.8).     156. *bruseth*:
pounds.     157. *great Dragon*: "The great dragon, that olde serpent, called
the devil and Satan, was cast out . . . " (Revelation 12.9).
[STANZAS 24–25]     "But neither the ray proper to the eyes nor the
colors proper to the bodies suffice to bring about vision unless the one light
itself above the many, from which the many lights proper to eyes and bodies
are distributed, arrives, illuminates, arouses, and strengthens. In the same
way, the first act of all, which is called God, bestowed upon each thing, in
creating it, species and act . . . . the perpetual and invisible single light of the
divine sun is always shining over all things; it warms, brings to life,
stimulates, perfects, and strengthens" (Ficino, *Commentary* 2.2).
[STANZA 24]     163. *Titans*: the sun's.     165. *red*: seen.
166. *marvelled*: wondered at.     167. *Of*: by. *amaze*: bewilder.
168. *wisards*: sages, philosophers.

[25]

But that immortall light which there doth shine,
Is many thousand thousand times more cleare, 170
More excellent, more glorious, more divine,
Through which to God all mortall actions here,
And even the thoughts of men, do plaine appeare:
For from th'eternall Truth it doth proceed,
Through heavenly vertue, which her beames doe breed. 175

[26]

With the great glorie of that wondrous light,
His throne is all encompassed around,
And hid in his owne brightnesse from the sight
Of all that looke thereon with eyes unsound:
And underneath his feet are to be found 180
Thunder, and lightning, and tempestuous fyre,
The instruments of his avenging yre.

[27]

There in his bosome *Sapience* doth sit,
The soveraine dearling of the *Deity*,
Clad like a Queene in royall robes, most fit 185

[STANZA 25] 172–73. "For the Lord searcheth all hearts, and understandeth all the imaginacions of thoughtes" (1 Chronicles 28.9). "The light of the intellect for understanding all things is the same God himself, by whom all things are made . . ." (Ficino, *Commentary* 6.13). 175. *her*: truth's.
[STANZA 26] 176–79. The prototype for the depiction of God's throne is in Ezekiel 1 (and in its re-creation in Revelation 4). The encompassing brightness echoes Ezekiel 1.4 ("A brightnes *was* about it . . . ") and Revelation 4.3 ("There *was* a raine bowe rounde about the throne in sight like to an emeraude"). 178. *brightnesse*: God's brightness contrasts with the finally inadequate brightness of the lady's love in *HB* 178.
181. "Out of the throne proceded lightnings, and thundrings and voyces, & there were seven lampes of fyre . . ." (Revelation 4.5).
[STANZAS 27–37] Proverbs 8–9 personifies Wisdom as a female being whose conception precedes the creation. Paul (1 Corinthians 1.24) identifies Christ with Wisdom ("*We preache Christ*, the power of GOD, and

For so great powre and peerelesse majesty.
And all with gemmes and jewels gorgeously
Adornd, that brighter then the starres appeare,
And make her native brightnes seem more cleare.

the wisdome of God"), and by typological tradition Christ is read back into
Old Testament Wisdom passages, as in Augustine, *De Trinitate* 7.3
("Therefore, when anything concerning wisdom is proclaimed in Scripture
. . . the Son is indicated to us") or the note in the Geneva Bible to Proverbs
8.30 ("This Wisdome, even Christ Jesus, was equal with God his Father, and
created, preserved and stil worketh with him . . . "). Sp's Sapience also
reflects something of the Shekinah of the Talmud, which is both distinct
from and identical with God, at once a separate being and a personified
attribute, mediating between God's immanence and his otherness. The
Wisdom tradition is traced in Quitslund (1969) and Manley (1963).
[STANZA 27]    Sapience's appearance is strategically placed. This is the
153d stanza of *FH*; 153 is the sum of the first 17 numbers; 17 is the sum of
the law (10 commandments) and of grace (7 gifts of the Holy Spirit); see
Røstvig (1963:90), and Bjorvand (1975:41).    183. Wisdom is "conversant
with God" (Wisdom 8.3) and is identified with His throne (9.4,10). For her
identity with Christ as the pre-incarnate *Logos* of God, see John 1.18, where
the image of God's bosom makes the connection: "No man hathe sene God
at any time: the onely begotten Sonne, which is in the bosome of the Father,
he hathe declared him" (for Sp's awareness of this, cf. *HHL* 134–35, where
"the bosome of eternall blisse" is the place of Christ's origin). The Geneva
Bible identifies "his father's bosome" as the place where Christ receives his
revelation (note to Revelation 1.1) and connects the image of the throne
with the intimacy of the Trinity (note to Revelation 7.15).    184. *dearling*:
Wisdom says: "I was daily *his* delite rejoycing alwaie before him . . . "
(Proverbs 8.30).    185. Sapience is personified as female: see Julian of
Norwich, quoted in Ellrodt (1960:167): "I understood that the high Might
of the Trinity is our Father, and the deep Wisdom of the Trinity is our
Mother, and the great Love of the Trinity is our Lord"; see also Milton,
*Paradise Lost* 7.8–12.    186. *powre*: Wisdom has "all power" (Wisdom
7.23).    187–88. "Receive mine instruction, and not silver, and knowledge
rather then fine golde. For wisdome is better then precious stones . . . .
Riches and honour *are* with me: *even* durable riches and righteousness"
(Proverbs 8.10–11,18).    189. *brightnes*: "For she is the brightnes of the
everlasting light, the undefiled mirroure of the majestie of God, and the
image of his goodnes" (Wisdom 7.26).

[28]

And on her head a crowne of purest gold          190
Is set, in signe of highest soveraignty,
And in her hand a scepter she doth hold,
With which she rules the house of God on hy,
And menageth the ever-moving sky,
And in the same these lower creatures all,          195
Subjected to her powre imperiall.

[29]

Both heaven and earth obey unto her will,
And all the creatures which they both containe:
For of her fulnesse which the world doth fill,
They all partake, and do in state remaine,          200
As their great Maker did at first ordaine,
Through observation of her high beheast,
By which they first were made, and still increast.

[30]

The fairenesse of her face no tongue can tell,
For she the daughters of all wemens race,          205
And Angels eke, in beautie doth excell,
Sparkled on her from Gods owne glorious face,
And more increast by her owne goodly grace,

[STANZA 28]          193. Wisdom says: "My dwelling is above in the height . . . " (Ecclesiasticus 24.7).          194. *menageth*: direct the affairs of (as of a household).          195. *in the same*: in so doing.
[STANZA 29]          199. *fulnesse . . . fill*: "For the Spirit of the Lord filleth all the worlde . . . " (Wisdom 1.7); "And of his fulnes have we all received . . . " (John 1.16).          201–03. Wisdom is identified traditionally with the creating Spirit of Genesis: "The Lord by wisdome hathe laied the fundacion of the earth . . . " (Proverbs 3.19); "thy wisdome with thee . . . which also was when thou madest the worlde" (Wisdom 9.9).          203. *still increast*: continually reproduced.
[STANZA 30]          "She is more beautiful then the sunne . . . " (Wisdom 7.29). "Love pursues things which are beautiful. The most beautiful of all things is wisdom" (Ficino, *Commentary* 6.10).

That it doth farre exceed all humane thought,
Ne can on earth compared be to ought. 210

### [31]

Ne could that Painter (had he lived yet)
Which pictured *Venus* with so curious quill,
That all posteritie admyred it,
Have purtrayd this, for all his maistring skill;
Ne she her selfe, had she remained still, 215
And were as faire, as fabling wits do fayne,
Could once come neare this beauty soverayne.

### [32]

But had those wits the wonders of their dayes,
Or that sweete *Teian* Poet which did spend
His plenteous vaine in setting forth her prayse, 220
Seene but a glims of this, which I pretend,
How wondrously would he her face commend,
Above that Idole of his fayning thought,
That all the world shold with his rimes be fraught?

### [33]

How then dare I, the novice of his Art, 225
Presume to picture so divine a wight,

[STANZAS 31–32]     Venus dethroned, the failure of the hope of *HB* st.38–41 (see Bjorvand 1975:42). The Venus of earthly beauty, "had she remained still," is but an invention of "faining thought" compared to Sapience. The whole passage is colored by Plato's contempt for the poet and painter, who merely copy reality (see *Republic*, bk.10); Kellogg and Steele (1965:521) see the reality/copy analogy as the structural basis of *FH*.
[STANZA 31]     211. *that Painter*: Apelles painted Aphrodite Anadyomene (Venus) rising from the sea foam, wringing out her hair (see Pliny, *Natural History* 35.26).     212. *curious*: minutely accurate.
214. *maistring*: skillfully executed.     215. *her selfe*: i.e. Venus.
216. *fayne*: imagine.
[STANZA 32]     219. *Teian Poet*: Anacreon (born at Teios) whose *Ode* 57 describes a painting of Venus on a dish.     220. *vaine*: vein, line of thought.     221. *pretend*: put forward.     223. *fayning thought*: fantasy.     224. *fraught*: filled.

Or hope t'expresse her least perfections part,
Whose beautie filles the heavens with her light,
And darkes the earth with shadow of her sight?
Ah gentle Muse thou art too weake and faint,                    230
The pourtraict of so heavenly hew to paint.

[34]

Let Angels which her goodly face behold
And see at will, her soveraigne praises sing,
And those most sacred mysteries unfold,
Of that faire love of mightie heavens king.                     235
Enough is me t'admyre so heavenly thing,
And being thus with her huge love possest,
In th'only wonder of her selfe to rest.

[35]

But who so may, thrise happie man him hold,
Of all on earth, whom God so much doth grace,                   240
And lets his owne Beloved to behold:
For in the view of her celestiall face,
All joy, all blisse, all happinesse have place,
Ne ought on earth can want unto the wight,
Who of her selfe can win the wishfull sight.                    245

[36]

For she out of her secret threasury,
Plentie of riches forth on him will powre,

[STANZA 34]    238. *th'only wonder*: only the wonder.
[STANZAS 35 – 36]    There is something here of the lover desiring to
marry Wisdom, as in Wisdom 8.2.
[STANZA 35]    239. *thrise happie man*: the reality of which the earlier
"Thrise happy man" of *HL* 209 is the illusory version (see Bjorvand
1975:24–25).    244. *wight*: person.    245. *wishfull*: wished for,
desirable.
[STANZAS 36]    "All good things therefore came to me together with
her, and innumerable riches thorow her hands" (Wisdom 7.11).
246. *secret threasury*: "For she is an infinite treasure unto men . . . " (Wisdom
7.14); "Who hathe found out her place? or who hathe come into her
treasures?" (Baruch 3.15).    247–48. *Plentie . . . heavenly riches*: cf. "the

Even heavenly riches, which there hidden ly
Within the closet of her chastest bowre,
Th'eternall portion of her precious dowre,                   250
Which mighty God hath given to her free,
And to all those which thereof worthy bee.

### [37]

None thereof worthy be, but those whom shee
Vouchsafeth to her presence to receave,
And letteth them her lovely face to see,                     255
Wherof such wondrous pleasures they conceave,
And sweete contentment, that it doth bereave
Their soule of sense, through infinite delight,
And them transport from flesh into the spright.

### [38]

In which they see such admirable things,                     260
As carries them into an extasy,
And heare such heavenly notes, and carolings
Of Gods high praise, that filles the brasen sky,
And feele such joy and pleasure inwardly,
That maketh them all worldly cares forget,                   265
And onely thinke on that before them set.

---

unsearcheable riches of Christ" (Ephesians 3.8; cf. 2.7).    248. *which . . .
ly*: Cf. Ephesians 3.9: "the felowship of the mysterie . . . which from the
beginning of the worlde hathe bene hid in God, who hathe created all things
by Jesus Christ."    250. *dowre*: dowry.
[STANZA 37]    253–54. "For by grace are ye saved through faith, and
that not of your selves: it *is* the gifte of God . . . " (Ephesians 2.8). Some
have seen here an illusion to Calvin's doctrine of predestination, although the
idea's provenance is hardly limited to Calvinism. Cf. Ephesians 2.18: "For
through him we bothe have an entrance unto the Father by one
Spirit."    255–59. "Wisdome . . . preventeth them that desire her, that she
may first shewe her selfe unto them . . . . For she goeth about, seking suche
as are mete for her, and sheweth her self cherefully unto them in the wayes,
and meteth them in everie thoght" (Wisdom 6.12–16).    257. *bereave*:
rob.

[39]

Ne from thenceforth doth any fleshly sense,
Or idle thought of earthly things remaine,
But all that earst seemd sweet, seemes now offense,
And all that pleased earst, now seemes to paine.          270
Their joy, their comfort, their desire, their gaine,
Is fixed all on that which now they see,
All other sights but fayned shadowes bee.

[40]

And that faire lampe, which useth to enflame
The hearts of men with selfe consuming fyre,          275
Thenceforth seemes fowle, and full of sinfull blame;
And all that pompe, to which proud minds aspyre
By name of honor, and so much desyre,
Seemes to them basenesse, and all riches drosse,
And all mirth sadnesse, and all lucre losse.          280

[41]

So full their eyes are of that glorious sight,
And senses fraught with such satietie,
That in nought else on earth they can delight,
But in th'aspect of that felicitie,
Which they have written in their inward ey;          285
On which they feed, and in their fastened mynd
All happie joy and full contentment fynd.

[STANZA 39]     273. *fayned shadowes*: the false knowledge characterized
in Plato's analogy of the cave (*Republic*, bk.7).
[STANZA 40]     276. *blame*: fault.     277–80. Cf. Wisdom 7.8: "I
preferred her to scepters and thrones, & counted riches nothing in
comparison of her."     280. *all lucre losse*: "I thinke all things but losse for
the excellent knowledge sake of Christ Jesus my Lord, for whom I have
counted all things losse . . . " (Philippians 3.8).
[STANZA 41]     281–83. Ellrodt (1960:21–22) calls attention to similar
language in *CCCHA* 40–46, 344–47.     286. *fastened*: firmly fixed.

### [42]

Ah then my hungry soule, which long hast fed
On idle fancies of thy foolish thought,
And with false beauties flattring bait misled,                    290
Hast after vaine deceiptfull shadowes sought,
Which all are fled, and now have left thee nought,
But late repentance through thy follies prief;
Ah ceasse to gaze on matter of thy grief.

### [43]

And looke at last up to that soveraine light,                    295
From whose pure beams al perfect beauty springs,
That kindleth love in every godly spright,
Even the love of God, which loathing brings
Of this vile world, and these gay seeming things;
With whose sweete pleasures being so possest,                    300
Thy straying thoughts henceforth for ever rest.

[STANZA 42]    293. *prief*: experience.
[STANZA 43]    295–97. Cf. *HHL* 283–87.    295–96. "Thus the
light and beauty of God, which is utterly pure and free of all other things,
may be called . . . infinite beauty" (Ficino, *Commentary* 6.18).    295. *that
soveraine light*: Cf. the Word as light (John 1.9).

# Prothalamion

# Prothalamion

*Or*

A Spousall Verse made by
*Edm. Spenser.*

## IN HONOVR OF THE DOV-

ble mariage of the two Honorable & vertuous
*Ladies,the Ladie* Elizabeth *and the Ladie* Katherine
*Somerset*, Daughters to the Right Honourable the
Earle of *Worcester* and espoused to the two worthie
Gentlemen M. *Henry Gilford*, and
M.*William* Peter Esquyers.

AT LONDON.
Printed for William Ponsonby.
1596.

# *Prothalamion*

For this poem, published one year after his *Epithalamion*, Spenser invented a new title, *Prothalamion* (i.e. before [in time or place] the bridal chamber) because this time he was not writing to celebrate a wedding but to commemorate a betrothal ceremony. Classical literature knows several betrothal poems, and the use of songs and poems as part of the betrothal festivities was not uncommon in Elizabethan England, but the title is Spenser's own, indicating perhaps that he wished to regard the betrothal poem as a separate genre.

The poem was written to celebrate the double betrothal of Elizabeth and Katherine Somerset, the two eldest daughters of Edward Somerset, fourth earl of Worcester. In the double wedding which took place on 8 November 1596, Elizabeth married Henry Guildford of Hemsted Place, Kent, and Katherine married William Petre of Writtle. We do not know when the betrothal ceremony took place but we have to look for a date after the return of the earl of Essex from his expedition to Spain on 7 August, referred to in stanza 9, and before the court moved from Greenwich on 1 October; a date in September seems likely.

The poem professes, as the occasion demanded, an optimistic faith in a promising future. History does, however, have its ironies. Only four years later Essex, whom the poem celebrates as "Great Englands glory" (146) and its potential saviour, had fallen out of favor with his queen. During Essex's rebellion, the earl of Worcester was kept a prisoner at Essex House and later served as one of the peers for Essex's trial. Spenser died in 1599, Essex paying the funeral expenses; Essex was executed in 1601, and his great Eliza herself died in 1603.

As the first stanza makes plain, Spenser was too aware of

living in a world of mutability to write a poem that would invite a straightforward and blindly optimistic reading. Spenser's "calme" day is clearly a special one, and the harmony it exudes is precarious and of uncertain duration. The river of time acquiesces in the poet's request to "runne softly," but the acquiescence is clearly only a temporary one: "till I end my Song." The harmonious and beautiful moment captured by the poet is potentially enriching, but it bears no certain and causal relationship to the world outside the poem. Even in the description of the purity of the birds/brides as they move towards their love union, Spenser introduces more or less clear mythical references to the rapes of Proserpine, Europa, and Leda. The swans themselves seem to be representatives of the dualistic balance of flesh and spirit; they seem to be angels, but they are "bred of *Somersheat*" (67), and, with a characteristic pun, they are "Fowles so lovely" (61).

Although generally praised for its beauty and formal perfection, Spenser's *Prothalamion* has puzzled many modern readers, who cannot help feeling that their attention is too frequently diverted from what is ostensibly the main theme of the poem, the double betrothal ceremony. These objections concern Spenser's personal complaints (in stanzas 1 and 8) and the references to the history of the Temple (stanza 8) and to the military exploits of Essex (stanza 9). If we choose, however, to see these references not as discordant elements but as autonomous parts of the poem, we should perhaps begin to consider that the poem is not simply concerned with the double betrothal and the subsequent double wedding.

In Spenser's world marriage was not simply a private contract of no particular interest to anybody but the parties concerned. Marriage was a public event with a social significance as well as a symbol of harmony both in religious, social, and sexual terms. This is clearly brought out in the movement of the poem from private to social, from mythical to actual, from classical past to English present. Entering the poem in a pastoral escape from unpleasant actuality, the poet-speaker accompanies the brides as they cast off their pastoral disguise as birds and enter London. The City has become morally cleansed and socially secure as the proud Knights Templars have been superseded by the "studious Lawyers" (134)(the two bridegrooms and their father-in-law were all members of the Inner and Middle Temple), and the tragic loss of Leicester is made up for by Essex whose martial triumphs, combined with the queen's good government, provide for a great and secure future of obvious importance for the happiness of the married couples. (For further discussion of the poet-speaker's return to or reconciliation with the temporal, socio-political world of the city, see Berger [1965;1972] and Manley [1982].)

The complex structure of the *Epithalamion* is mirrored by a similar, yet simpler, structure in the *Prothalamion*. Thus the line total of 180 may be taken to suggest the 180 degrees of the sun's half-circle in its daytime movement (see Fowler 1975:66).

Spenser also uses parallels and contrasts to underscore the structural unity of his poem. Thus the poet's "discontent" because of his "long fruitlesse stay / In Princes Court" in stanza 1 contrasts with the "hearts content" and "fruitfull issue" promised to the brides in stanza 6; the poet who "Walkt forth" to the river in his escape from "Princes Court" and hot Titan in stanza 1 is paralleled by the stately bridegrooms "forth pacing to the Rivers side" under the guidance of "Radiant Hesper" in stanza 10. Just as the swans "excell / The rest" of the "foule" on the river (119–21) and seem "heavenly borne" (62) so the two "gentle Knights," replacing the fallen Knights Templars, may be observed "Above the rest" of the "great traine" and seem like "the twins of Jove" (167–73). The nymphs who gather flowers to fill their baskets "Made of fine twigs" in the mythical nature of stanza 2 are recalled in the description of Essex as "Faire branch of Honor, flower of Chevalrie, / That fillest *England* with thy triumphes fame" in the socio-political world of reality in stanza 9.

It is perhaps precisely because of the far-reaching implications of the idea of marriage that the poet can allow himself such an

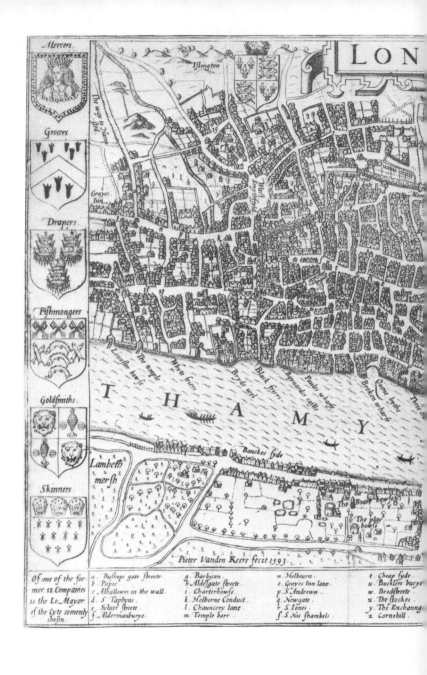

obvious presence in the poem; a presence which is, of course, not confined to the complaints in stanzas 1 and 8, but which is evident in the refrain of the last line of every stanza. Once we begin to read the poem in this way we may also come to see that precisely because the idea of marriage concerns the poet, not only in his public role but also in his private role, it also concerns us as readers.

*Einar Bjorvand*

# *Prothalamion.*

## 1

CAlme was the day, and through the trembling ayre,
  Sweete breathing *Zephyrus* did softly play
A gentle spirit, that lightly did delay
Hot *Titans* beames, which then did glyster fayre:
When I whom sullein care,                                                    5
Through discontent of my long fruitlesse stay
In Princes Court, and expectation vayne
Of idle hopes, which still doe fly away,
Like empty shaddowes, did aflict my brayne,
Walkt forth to ease my payne                                                 10
Along the shoare of silver streaming *Themmes*,
Whose rutty Bancke, the which his River hemmes,
Was paynted all with variable flowers,
And all the meades adornd with daintie gemmes,
Fit to decke maydens bowres,                                                 15
And crowne their Paramours,

STANZA 1.     1. Sp's careful choice of adjectives to suggest a mood of
momentary and precarious harmony is well illustrated by "Calme," placed in
initial position in the first line to create an inverted foot.     2. *Zephyrus*: the
west wind associated with morning and spring.     3. *delay*: allay.     4. *Hot
Titans beames*: The burning sun was commonly taken to represent unpleasant
actuality. Luther and Calvin both interpreted biblical images of the hot sun as
metaphors of the temptations and miseries of man's life.     5–10. The
complaint makes it clear just how personal this public poem is. The lines
indicate Sp's ambivalent attitude to his own political and courtly
ambitions.     10–11. The poem begins as an escape from unpleasant
actuality, but the vision is of a progress towards society rather than away
from it and so prepares for the re-entry into the world of social reality in the
last three stanzas.     12. *rutty*: rooty.     12–14. The scene is designed to
give an impression of spring, beauty, and fertility; it also serves to recall the
myth of Zephyrus and Flora: the wind-god pursued Chloris and changed her
into the fertile Flora, guardian of flowers.

Against the Brydale day, which is not long:
   Sweete *Themmes* runne softly, till I end my Song.

2

There, in a Meadow, by the Rivers side,
A Flocke of *Nymphes* I chaunced to espy,           20
All lovely Daughters of the Flood thereby,
With goodly greenish locks all loose untyde,
s each had bene a Bryde,
And each one had a little wicker basket,
Made of fine twigs entrayled curiously,           25
In which they gathered flowers to fill their flasket:
And with fine Fingers, cropt full feateously
The tender stalkes on hye.
Of every sort, which in that Meadow grew,
They gathered some; the Violet pallid blew,      30
The little Dazie, that at evening closes,
The virgin Lillie, and the Primrose trew,
With store of vermeil Roses,
To decke their Bridegromes posies,

17–18. The couplet at the end of each stanza forms a refrain. The last line, which is concerned not with the pending marriage but with the poet, remains the same throughout. The first line changes from present tense to past tense and back as it refers partly to the betrothal and partly to the future wedding; it may even be taken to indicate that, in the nature of things, the "bridal day" does not last long.

STANZA 2. The description of the nymphs gathering flowers in the meadow may be designed to recall two myths of violent sexual encounters. Ovid tells how Proserpine, attended by her maids and gathering flowers at Henna, was caught by Pluto (Ovid, *Fasti* 4.429ff., *Met* 5.391ff.). Moschus describes how Europa, gathering flowers with her friends, was carried off by Zeus in the shape of a bull (Moschus, 2.33ff.). These echoes form a sharp contrast to the general note of purity, and they prepare for the important reference to Zeus's rape of Leda in stanza three. 21. *Flood*: river. 25. *entrayled*: entwined, interlaced. 26. *flasket*: a shallow basket. 27. *feateously*: beautifully. 28. *on hye*: hurriedly. 30–33. Critical opinions vary as to whether Sp's list of flowers has significant symbolic and mythological dimensions.

Against the Brydale day, which was not long:    35
   Sweete *Themmes* runne softly, till I end my Song.

### 3

With that I saw two Swannes of goodly hewe,
Come softly swimming downe along the Lee;
Two fairer Birds I yet did never see:
The snow which doth the top of *Pindus* strew,    40
Did never whiter shew,
Nor *Jove* himselfe when he a Swan would be
For love of *Leda*, whiter did appeare:
Yet *Leda* was they say as white as he,
Yet not so white as these, nor nothing neare;    45
So purely white they were,

STANZA 3. 37. There may be several reasons why Sp chose to present the two brides as a pair of swans. The Thames was famous for its many swans. The actual procession of the brides may have taken place in barges designed to resemble swans; processions of this kind were not unusual in Elizabethan England. Sp may also have been influenced by the antiquarian poems of John Leland ("Cygnea Cantio") and William Vallans ("A Tale of Two Swannes"). These poems also refer explicitly to the classical idea of the poet as swan, a myth which gained widespread popularity in the Renaissance (cf. Whitney's *Choice of Emblems* (1586), p. 126, and *RT* 589–602), so that the unobtrusive presence of the poet as swan may be suggested as he accompanies the birds/brides on their voyage from the Lea estuary to Essex House. 38. *Lee*: This word may mean "meadow," or "riverbank," or even, it has been suggested, be a general word for "river." It may also, however, refer to the river Lea, in which case we can trace the voyage of the brides from the mouth of the Lea as it joins the Thames, past the court at Greenwich, until they arrive within the City (st. 8), pass by the Temple, and land at Essex House. 40. *Pindus*: mountains in western and north-western Greece. 42–44. According to Greek myth Jove (or Zeus) pursued Leda in many disguises and finally in the shape of a swan. As a result of this strange union Leda gave birth to two eggs (according to one version) from which came two pairs of twins: Helen and Clytemnestra, and Castor and Pollux. After their deaths, Castor and Pollux were granted immortality by Zeus as stars in the constellation Gemini (i.e. twins). This may be the second important allegory in the poem as the two bridegrooms are compared to the "twins of Jove" in st. 10.

That even the gentle streame, the which them bare,
Seem'd foule to them, and bad his billowes spare
To wet their silken feathers, least they might
Soyle their fayre plumes with water not so fayre,                    50
And marre their beauties bright,
That shone as heavens light,
Against their Brydale day, which was not long:
    Sweete *Themmes* runne softly, till I end my Song.

4

Eftsoones the *Nymphes*, which now had Flowers their
                                                            fill,     55
Ran all in haste, to see that silver brood,
As they came floating on the Christal Flood,
Whom when they sawe, they stood amazed still,
Their wondring eyes to fill,
Them seem'd they never saw a sight so fayre,                    60
Of Fowles so lovely, that they sure did deeme
Them heavenly borne, or to be that same payre
Which through the Skie draw *Venus* silver Teeme,
For sure they did not seeme
To be begot of any earthly Seede,                    65
But rather Angels or of Angels breede:
Yet were they bred of *Somers-heat* they say,
In sweetest Season, when each Flower and weede
The earth did fresh aray,
So fresh they seem'd as day,                    70

47–54. The river constitutes the link between the world of myth and purity
and the corruptible world of time.    49. *least*: lest.
S T A N Z A 4 .    56. *brood*: offspring.    63. That Venus's chariot was
drawn by two swans was a popular myth in the Renaissance, illustrated by
several painters. The classical sources for the myth are Ovid's *Met* 10.717–
18, and Horace's *Odes* 4.1.10. Vallans's poem refers to Venus's use of swans
from the Thames to draw her chariot.    65. *Seede*: source, race.
67. *Somers-heat*: a pun on summer's heat and their family name, daughters of
Edward Somerset, fourth earl of Worcester.

Even as their Brydale day, which was not long:
  Sweete *Themmes* runne softly till I end my Song.

5

Then forth they all out of their baskets drew,
Great store of Flowers, the honour of the field,
That to the sense did fragrant odours yield,        75
All which upon those goodly Birds they threw,
And all the Waves did strew,
That like old *Peneus* Waters they did seeme,
When downe along by pleasant *Tempe* shore
Scattred with Flowres, through *Thessaly* they streeme,   80
That they appeare through Lillies plenteous store,
Like a Brydes Chamber flore:
Two of those *Nymphes*, meane while, two Garlands
                        bound,
Of freshest Flowres which in that Mead they found,
The which presenting all in trim Array,        85
Their snowie Foreheads therewithall they crownd,
Whil'st one did sing this Lay,
Prepar'd against that Day,
Against their Brydale day, which was not long:
  Sweete *Themmes* runne softly till I end my Song.   90

6

Ye gentle Birdes, the worlds faire ornament,
And heavens glorie, whom this happie hower
Doth leade unto your lovers blisfull bower,

STANZA 5. In stanzas 3–5 Sp's description of nature and the brides is accompanied by classical allusions as the beauty of the mythical present, invoked by the poet, can only be compared, favorably, with the beauty of the mythical past. Conversely, in st. 8–9, the references are almost exclusively to a social and political English scene, past and present. 78–80. The river Peneus (Pineios) is the chief river of Thessaly in Greece, flowing through the Tempe valley whose beauty was praised by several poets, notably by Catullus, 64. 278–86. 85. *trim*: nice, perfect.
STANZA 6. 93. *bower*: boudoir, bedroom, room.

Joy may you have and gentle hearts content
Of your loves couplement:                                         95
And let faire *Venus*, that is Queene of love,
With her heart-quelling Sonne upon you smile,
Whose smile they say, hath vertue to remove
All Loves dislike, and friendships faultie guile
For ever to assoile.                                             100
Let endlesse Peace your steadfast hearts accord,
And blessed Plentie wait upon your bord,
And let your bed with pleasures chast abound,
That fruitfull issue may to you afford,
Which may your foes confound,                                    105
And make your joyes redound,
Upon your Brydale day, which is not long:
    Sweete *Themmes* run softlie, till I end my Song.

### 7

So ended she; and all the rest around
To her redoubled that her undersong,                             110
Which said, their bridale daye should not be long.

94. The "gentle hearts content" and prospective "fruitfull issue" (104)
promised to the birds/brides in the inlaid song, contrasts strongly with the
poet-speaker's "discontent of my long fruitlesse stay" at court (6).
95. *couplement*: union, marriage.        97. *Sonne*: Cupid, Venus's son.
98. *vertue*: power.        99. *Loves dislike*: dislike of love; an oxymoron, echoing
*IIHL* 34, as is also "friendships faultie guile." *guile*: deceit. The song
describes a world, far from that known to the poet-speaker, of perfect love
and friendship (cf. line 140).        100. *assoile*: remove.        101. *accord*:
harmonize.        104. *afford*: produce.        105. *confound*: defeat.
106. *redound*: overflow.
STANZA 7.        In this stanza nature takes part in the celebration of the
birds/ brides. The nymphs join in the song of praise repeating the first line of
the refrain (111), and nature answers with an echo (112). The rest of the
stanza presents a traditional image of Edenic harmony as nature and the
lower creatures offer their willing service to those placed higher on the *scala
creaturarum* (114–24), a relationship which is further illustrated by the
hierarchical image of Cynthia (the moon) and "the lesser starres" (121–22).
110. *undersong*: refrain.

And gentle Eccho from the neighbour ground,
Their accents did resound.
So forth those joyous Birdes did passe along,
Adowne the Lee, that to them murmurde low,     115
As he would speake, but that he lackt a tong,
Yeat did by signes his glad affection show,
Making his streame run slow.
And all the foule which in his flood did dwell
Gan flock about these twaine, that did excell     120
The rest, so far, as *Cynthia* doth shend
The lesser starres. So they enranged well,
Did on those two attend,
And their best service lend,
Against their wedding day, which was not long:     125
    Sweete *Themmes* run softly, till I end my song.

### 8

At length they all to mery *London* came,
To mery London, my most kyndly Nurse,
That to me gave this Lifes first native sourse:
Though from another place I take my name,     130
An house of auncient fame.
There when they came, whereas those bricky towres,
The which on *Themmes* brode aged backe doe ryde,
Where now the studious Lawyers have their bowers,
There whylome wont the Templer Knights to byde,     135
Till they decayd through pride:

121. *shend*: put to shame.    122. *enranged*: placed in proper order (i.e. in hierarchical harmony).
STANZA 8.    127. If the references to "Lee" in st. 3 and 7 are to the river Lea, the passage from the mouth of the Lea to the City takes place between st. 7 and the beginning of st. 8.    128–29. Sp was born and bred in London.    130–31. Sp was related to the Spencers at Althorp in Northamptonshire (the forefathers of the present Princess Diana).
132–36. This estate, still called the Temple, was owned by the Knights Templars until the order was suppressed and later dissolved, and most of the buildings were taken over by students of law.

Next whereunto there standes a stately place,
Where oft I gayned giftes and goodly grace
Of that great Lord, which therein wont to dwell,
Whose want too well, now feeles my freendles case:  140
But Ah here fits not well
Olde woes but joyes to tell
Against the bridale daye which is not long:
   Sweete *Themmes* runne softly till I end my Song.

### 9

Yet therein now doth lodge a noble Peer,  145
Great *Englands* glory and the Worlds wide wonder,
Whose dreadfull name, late through all *Spaine* did
                       thunder,
And *Hercules* two pillors standing neere,
Did make to quake and feare:
Faire branch of Honor, flower of Chevalric,  150
That fillest *England* with thy triumphes fame,
Joy have thou of thy noble victorie,
And endlesse happinesse of thine owne name
That promiseth the same:
That through thy prowesse and victorious armes,  155
Thy country may be freed from forraine harmes:
And great *Elisaes* glorious name may ring
Through al the world, fil'd with thy wide Alarmes,
Which some brave muse may sing
To ages following,  160

---

137–39. Leicester House, first occupied by the earl of Leicester who died in
1588, and in 1596 occupied by the earl of Essex.
STANZA 9. 145–47. Robert Devereux, second earl of Essex, had
returned to England on 7 August 1596 from his successful expedition against
Spain, burning the Spanish fleet and capturing Cadiz.    148. *Hercules two
pillors*: the two cliffs on both sides of the Straits of Gibraltar said to have been
erected by Hercules.    153–54. A pun on his name, Devereux, as dev(enir)
(h)eureux, i.e. to become happy.    157. *Elisaes*: Elizabeth's.
158. *Alarmes*: call to arms.

Upon the Brydale day, which is not long:
Sweete *Themmes* runne softly till I end my Song.

### 10

From those high Towers, this noble Lord issuing,
Like Radiant *Hesper* when his golden hayre
In th'*Ocean* billowes he hath Bathed fayre,                165
Descended to the Rivers open vewing,
With a great traine ensuing.
Above the rest were goodly to bee seene
Two gentle Knights of lovely face and feature
Beseeming well the bower of anie Queene,                170
With gifts of wit and ornaments of nature,
Fit for so goodly stature:
That like the twins of *Jove* they seem'd in sight,
Which decke the Bauldricke of the Heavens bright.
They two forth pacing to the Rivers side,                175
Received those two faire Brides, their Loves delight,
Which at th'appointed tyde,
Each one did make his Bryde,
Against their Brydale day, which is not long:
Sweete *Themmes* runne softly, till I end my Song.                180

FINIS.

161. The refrain, as a reference to the Somerset wedding, does not seem to
make much sense in this st.. It has been suggested that the line in this case
carries a reference to the queen's Accession Day on 17 November, shortly
after the double wedding. The unmarried queen liked to see herself as the
virgin bride of England, and her Accession Day could thus be appropriately
referred to as her wedding day.
STANZA 10. 164. *Hesper*: Hesperus, the Evening Star. 169. *Two gentle Knights*: the bridegrooms. 173. *the twins of Jove*: Castor and
Pollux, see note to lines 42–44. 174. *Bauldricke*: the Zodiac.
177. th'appointed tyde: the time appointed for the betrothal ceremony.

# Miscellaneous Short Poems

# Commendatory Sonnets

*To the right worshipfull, my singular good frend,*
*M. Gabriell Harvey, Doctor*
*of the Lawes.*

## [1]

HArvey, the happy above happiest men
  I read: that sitting like a Looker-on
Of this worldes Stage, doest note with critique pen
The sharpe dislikes of each condition:
And as one carelesse of suspition,                         5
Ne fawnest for the favour of the great:
Ne fearest foolish reprehension
Of faulty men, which daunger to thee threat.
But freely doest, of what thee list, entreat,
Like a great Lord of peerelesse liberty:                  10
Lifting the Good up to high Honours seat,
And the Evill damning evermore to dy.
For Life, and Death is in thy doomefull writing:
So thy renowme lives ever by endighting.

*Dublin: this xviii. of July: 1586.*

> *Your devoted frend, during life,*
> Edmund Spencer.

[SONNET 1].    Dedication: Gabriel Harvey was a fellow of Pembroke Hall several years older than Sp and, during the first part of his career, an important literary friend. For a study of his life and work see Stern (1979). He may have collaborated with Sp in the writing of E. K.'s notes for *SC* (Heninger, 1988). Harvey published this sonnet in his *Fowre Letters, and certaine Sonnets* . . . (1592).    1. *happy*: fortunate.    2. *read*: judge. 3. *critique*: carping.    4. *dislikes*: discords, disharmonies. *condition*: rank, estate.    5. *carelesse of*: unconcerned with.    7. *reprehension*: censure. 9. *entreat*: treat.    13. *doomefull*: judicious; also *assigning* a "doom" or judgment by praising or blaming.    14. *endighting*: composition, literary creation.

[2]

Who so wil seeke by right deserts t'attaine
  Unto the type of true Nobility,
  And not by painted shewes and titles vaine,
  Derived farre from famous Auncestrie,
Behold them both in their right visnomy                  5
  Here truly pourtray'd, as they ought to be,
  And striving both for termes of dignitie,
  To be advanced highest in degree.
And when thou doost with equall insight see
  The ods twixt both, of both then deem aright        10
  And chuse the better of them both to thee,
  But thanks to him that it deserves, behight:
To *Nenna* first, that first this worke created,
  And next to *Jones*, that truely it translated.

                                     *Ed. Spenser.*

[SONNET 2].     This sonnet is prefixed to *Nennio, Or a Treatise of Nobility: Wherein is discoursed what true Nobilitie is, and such qualities as are required in a perfect Gentleman . . . . Done into English by William Jones, Gent . . . .* (1595). Other commendatory sonnets are by George Chapman and Samuel Daniel.    2. *type*: pattern, epitome.    5. *visnomy*: physiognomy, face.    7. *termes*: conditions, state.    10. *deem*: judge.    11. *to*: for. 12. *behight*: grant.

## [3]

### UPON THE HISTORIE OF GEORGE CASTRIOT, ALIAS SCAN-DERBEG KING OF THE EPIROTS, *translated into English.*

WHerefore doth vaine antiquitie so vaunt,
    Her ancient monuments of mightie peeres,
And old Heroes, which their world did daunt
With their great deedes, and fild their childrens eares?
Who rapt with wonder of their famous praise,     5
    Admire their statues, their Colossoes great,
Their rich triumphall Arcks which they did raise,
Their huge Pyramids, which do heaven threat.
Lo one, whom later age hath brought to light,
    Matchable to the greatest of those great:     10
Great both by name, and great in power and might,
And meriting a meere triumphant seate.
    The scourge of Turkes, and plague of infidels,
    Thy acts, ô Scanderbeg, this volume tels.

                                    *Ed. Spenser.*

[SONNET 3].     Prefixed to *The Historie of George Castriot, surnamed Scanderbeg, King of Albanie. Containing his famous actes, his noble deedes of Armes, and memorable victories against the Turkes, for the Faith of Christ* . . . . (1596).     6. *Colossoes*: The enormous bronze statue of the Colossus of Rhodes stood astride the entrance to the harbor of Rhodes, and was considered one of the wonders of the ancient world.     11. *name*: reputation.     12. *meriting . . . seate*: entirely meriting a triumphal chariot.

[4]

THe antique *Babel*, Empresse of the East,
　　Upreard her buildinges to the threatned skie:
And Second *Babell* tyrant of the West,
　Her ayry Towers upraised much more high.
But with the weight of their own surquedry,　　　　　　　5
　They both are fallen, that all the earth did feare,
　And buried now in their own ashes ly,
　Yet shewing by their heapes how great they were.
But in their place doth now a third appeare,
　Fayre *Venice*, flower of the last worlds delight,　　　　10
　And next to them in beauty draweth neare,
　But farre exceedes in policie of right.
Yet not so fayre her buildinges to behold
　As *Lewkenors* stile that hath her beautie told.

　　　　　　　　　　　　　　　　*Edm. Spencer.*

---

[SONNET 4].　　Prefixed to *The Commonwealth and Government of Venice. Written by the Cardinall Gasper Contareno, and translated out of Italian into English, by Lewes Lewkenor, Esquire* (1599).　　1. *The antique Babel*: Babylon, thought to have had buildings high enough to be compared by sixteenth-century biblical commentators with the tower of Babel in Genesis 11 (Williams 1948:162). Sp makes the connection again in *FQ* II ix 21 (see Tuve 1970:98-101).　　3. *Second Babell*: Rome.　　5. *surquedry*: pride. 6. *feare*: "frighten" if the subject is "that," "fear" if the subject is "all the earth."　　10. *last* most recent, latest.

# Fragments

## [1]

See yee the blindefoulded pretie God, that feathered
           Archer,
 Of Lovers Miseries which maketh his bloodie Game?
Wote ye why, his Moother with a Veale hath coovered
          his Face?
 Trust me, least he my Loove happely chaunce to
          beholde.

## [2]

That which I eate, did I joy, and that which I greedily
          gorged,
 As for those many goodly matters leaft I for others.

## [3]
### *Iambicum Trimetrum.*

UNhappie Verse, the witnesse of my unhappie state,
 Make thy selfe fluttring wings of thy fast flying
          thought,
 And fly forth unto my Love, whersoever she be:
Whether lying reastlesse in heavy bedde, or else,       5
 Sitting so cheerelesse at the cheerfull boorde, or else
 Playing alone carelesse on hir heavenlie Virginals.
If in Bed, tell hir, that my eyes can take no reste:

[FRAGMENTS 1–2].   These passages are quoted by Sp in the first
epistle of the Spenser-Harvey correspondence, *Three Proper, and wittie,
familiar letters: lately passed between two University men* . . . . (1580) Both
writers give examples of their experiments in quantitive metre, and these
fragments, with "Iambicum trimetrum" [3] are Spenser's efforts.
[FRAGMENT 3]   *Iambicum trimetrum.*   Quoted by Sp in a section
of the Harvey-Spenser correspondence with its own title page, *Two Other very
commendable Letters* . . .   6. *Virginals*: A keyed stringed instrument like a
spinet, often referred to as "a pair of virginals."   8. *Boorde*: table. *meate*:
food.

If at Boorde, tell hir, that my mouth can eate no
                                            meate:
If at hir Virginals, tel hir, I can heare no mirth.
Asked why? say: Waking Love suffereth no sleepe:          10
    Say, that raging Love dothe appall the weake
                                        stomacke:
    Say, that lamenting Love marreth the Musicall.
Tell hir, that hir pleasures were wonte to lull me
                                        asleepe:
    Tell hir, that hir beautie was wonte to feede mine
                                        eyes:
    Tell hir, that hir sweete Tongue was wonte to make
                                        me mirth.          15
Nowe doe I nightly waste, wanting my kindely reste:
    Nowe doe I dayly starve, wanting my lively foode:
    Nowe doe I always dye, wanting thy timely mirth.
And if I waste, who will bewaile my heavy chaunce?
    And if I starve, who will record my cursed end?       20
    And if I dye, who will saye: *this was, Immerito*?

[4]
*Certaine verses* of Mr Edm. Spenser's.

A translation made *ex tempore* by Mr *Edm.
Spenser* upon this distich, written on a
Booke belonging to the right honorable
*Richard Earle* of *Corke*, etc.

NUlla dies pereat, pereat pars nulla diei,
    Ne tu sic pereas, ut periere dies.

LEt no day passe, passe no part of the day,
    Lest thou doe passe, as dayes doe passe away.

9. *mirth*: joy, pleasure.    11. *appall*: enfeeble.    16. *kindely*: natural.
[FRAGMENTS 4–5].    These pieces are from Sir James Ware's *The
Historie of Ireland* . . . . (1633), which includes Spenser's *A Vew* and

[5]
*Verses upon the said Earles Lute.*

WHilst vitall sapp did make me spring,
 And leafe and bough did flourish brave,
I then was dumbe and could not sing,
Ne had the voice which now I have:
But when the axe my life did end,
The Muses nine this voice did send.

*E.S.*

[6]
[From E. K.'s notes on *The Shepheardes Calender*]

An hundred Graces on her eyeledde satte.

The silver swanne doth sing before her dying day
As shee that feeles the deepe delight that is in death

concludes with a sampling of Sp's "Irish" poetry—the list of Irish rivers in
*FQ* IV xi 40-44 and the Faunus episode of *FQ* VII vi 38-55.

# Textual Notes

On the whole the texts for this edition are conservative though each editor has been free to make his own decisions about what was necessary to retain. Our usual practice has been to emend copy-texts in the case of obvious misprints or where the original punctuation represents an active hindrance to understanding. No attempt has been made to standardize spelling or capitalization. Abbreviations have been silently expanded and i/j, u/v modernized. In all cases the texts are based on the first edition published; particular copies used are listed in the note before the variants for each volume.

With a few exceptions the list of variants below includes only departures from copy-text; a nearly-complete list of variants is available in the *Variorum Minor Poems*. The first (italicized) item in each variant is the reading adopted for this edition. If it has appeared before, the first edition to adopt it exactly as it appears in the text, in both spelling and punctuation, is cited in parentheses; otherwise the emendation is the editor's own. The last item (in roman type) is the rejected reading of the copy-text unless it is otherwise identified.

In preparing this edition and especially in citing the work of other editors, the editors have made extensive use of the list of variants in the *Variorum*. Previous editions cited include the three folios of Spenser's collected works that appeared in 1611 (*F1*), 1617 (*F2*), and 1679 (*F3*), with (*F*) indicating agreement of all three; Hughes, 1715 (*Hu1*); Hughes, 1750 (*Hu2*); both editions of Hughes (*Hu*); Todd, 1805 (*T*); Child, 1855 (*Ch*); Collier, 1862 (*Co*); Morris and Hales, 1869 ff. (*MH*); Grosart, 1882–84 (*G*); Dodge, 1908 (*D*); de Selincourt, 1910 (*S*); Renwick, 1928 (*R*); and the *Variorum Minor Poems* 1943–47 (*V*). When—as in the case of the *Complaints* or *Colin Clout*—there is a corrected and an uncorrected version of the Quarto, they are referred to as (*cQ*) and (*uQ*).

# *Shepheardes Calender*

This edition of the poem is based on a xerox copy of the 1579 quarto (*Q1*) of *The Shepheardes Calender* (STC 23089) in the the Huntington Library. Four more quarto editions were published in 1581, 1586, 1591, and 1597; they are referred to respectively as (*Q2*), (*Q3*), (*Q4*), and (*Q5*). Occasional reference is made to the editions of the poem by Bathurst, 1732 (B), and Herford, 1895 (He).

## *Epistle*

97 *not so well seene* (Q3)   no so wel seme
98 *if them* (R)   if the
155 *habilities:* (Q3)   habilities?
166 *scarce growen* (Q2)   scarcegrowen
202 *considerations* (Q2)   cousiderations
209 *learning* (Q2)   learning.)
226 *darknesse,* (Q2)   darknesse.
235 *and Elocution* (Q2)   aud Elocution

## *Argument*

10 *more shepheards, then Goteheards* (Q5)   most shepheards, and Goteheards
13 *Invencion* (Q2)   Invericion
49 *in* (Q2)   iu
71 *Abib* (F)   Abil
75 *of the church* (Q2)   of of the church
109 *Shepheard* (Q2)   Sepheard

## *Januarye*

2. *When* (Q3)   when
49. *hower,* (Q2)   hower.

53. *such* (Q2)   snch
[75] This gloss follows "Embleme" in Q1–5

## Februarie

Argument line 10. *purpose* (Q2)   pnrpose
142. *overcrawed* (Q3)   overawed
238. *Eld—* (Hu)   Eld (with no punctuation following)
[39.5.] *cold.* (Q2)   cold:
[135.] *encombreth* (MH)   encombrerh
[166.] *worthiest.* (Q2)   worthiest
[Embleme.34.] *Erasmus* (Q2)   Erasimus

## March

4. *nigheth* (F)   nighest
95. *that* (Q3)   thast
[2.] *overgone.* (Q2)   overgone

## Aprill

113. *Wants not* (Q3)   Wants not not
143. *Chevisaunce,* (Q5)   Chevisaunce.
144. *Delice.* (F)   Delice,
148. *way.* (Q4)   way,
[50.14–15.] δε ὁ μητίετα (S) δέ ε μετίετα
[120.] *Behight* (F)   Bedight

## Maye

Argument line 1. *fift* (Q5)   firste
36. *swinck?* (MH)   swinck.
54. *great* (Q5)   gread
82. *worldly* (Q2)   wordly
113. *shepheards* (Q2)   shephears
170. *hidde,* (Q3)   hidde.
177. *reason,* (Q5)   reason.
254. *deceitfull* (Q2)   deceifull

261. *were.* (Q5)   were,
[38.] *entirely.* (Q2)   entirely
[142.11.] *imagination,* (Q2)   imagination
[145.] *worke.* (Q2)   worke:
[189.] πάθος (Co)   παθός
[247.] *Sweete S. Charitie)* (Q2)   Sweete S. Charitie
[309.] *priest.* (T)   priest,

## June

1. *Collin* (Co)   Collni
6. *ground* (Q2)   gronnd
16. *shroude* (T)   shouder
18. *doth thee* (Q2)   doth the
21. *shepheards* (Q2)   shipheards
23. *Ravens* (F)   Ravene
38. *steps:* (F)   steps.
46. *but* (Q2)   bnt
[57.] *is full* (Q2)   is is full
[103.] *undermyne* (MH)   undermynde

## Julye

12. *great* (Q4)   Great
14. *tickle* (Q5)   trickle
100. *strawe.* (Q5)   strawe,
120. *that* (Q2)   That
177. *gold,* (Q4)   gold.
208. *melling.* (Q2)   melling,
215. *gree,* (Q3)   gree.
230. *bett* (He)   better
233. *Thomalins* (Ch)   Palinodes
[12.] *Seneca* (Q2)   Sene-neca (divided between lines)
*Lapsu* (Q3)   lapsus
[51.] *Synecdochen.* (Q2)   Synecdochen
[59.6.] *Titan.* (Q3)   Titan:

[63.3.] (That is Adam) (D)    (That is Adam
[79.3.] *both* (Q2)    borh

## *August*

16a. *Perigot* (Q2)    Perigor
18. *see.* (Q2)    see,
76. *woode* (F)    Woode
84. *thy* (F)    my
104. *curelesse* (B)    carelesse
105. *bought,* (Q2)    bought.
134. *him* (Q2)    hm
148. *deede.* (Q3)    deede,
154. *a part* (Q3)    apart
[138.2.] *golden* (Q2)    goldden

## *September*

56. *Hobbin* (Q2)    hobbin
132. *Thou* (Q2)    Thon
145. *yead* (F)    yeeld
153. *Christendome* (Q2)    Chrisiendome
165. *theyr* (Q2)    thoyr
169. *They* (Q5)    The
196. *awaye,* (Q2)    awaye. (Q1 has a small round period,
quite different from the normal square black-letter version,
like the small period used to mark pauses in the prose
sections.)
201. *thanck.* (Q5)    thanck
207a. *Hobbinoll.* (Q2)    Diggon.
255. *can,* (Q3)    can:
257. *her* (cQ1)    his (uQ1)
[20.] *Thrise* (Q5)    These
[45.] *stoutely.* (Q2)    stoutely
[57.] *lefte.* (Q2)    lefte
[96.2.] *practises* (Q2)    pract-tises (divided between lines)
[124.] *Brace) compasse* (Q3)    Brace compasse

[151.5.] *here founde* (Q2)   here souude
[171.4.] *flock.* (Q2)   flock (period crowded out in Q1)
[176.14.] *unknown* (Q2)   vuknown
[Embleme.4.] *looking* (Q2)   lookng

## October

Argument line 1. *which* (Q2)   whishe
line 4. *even* (Q2)   enen
6. *dead.* (Q5)   dead?
39–40. *giusts . . . crowne,* (R)   giusts, . . . crowne.
79. *thy* (Q3)   the
96a. *Cuddie* (Q3)   (omitted in Q1-2)
100. *demaundes, . . . dwell.* (S)   demaundes. . . . dwell,
113. *buskin* (Q2)   bus-kin
[21.9.] *eyther* (Q2)   eythet
[27.17.] *matters* (Q2)   mattcs
[27.18.] *Arabian* (Q3)   Aradian
[32.1.] *Juno* (Q2)   Inno
[47.] *meaneth* (Q2)   meanerh
[50.2.] *more* (Q2)   moro
[78.1.] *Sarcasmus* (Q3)   Sacrasmus
[90.6.] *destinie.* (Q2)   destinie
[93.3.] *Petrarchs* (Q3)   Petrachs

## November

4. *misgovernaunce.* (Q5)   misgovernaunce,
14. *taske* (Q2)   tas-ke (in Q1 the same hyphenation takes
place at lines 16,17, and 27)
88. *budde,* (Co)   budde.
128–29 mourne, . . .tourne (Q3)   morune, . . . torune
132. *carefull* (Q2)   carsefull
147. *seare:* (Q5)   seare,
[30.2.] *Castalias* (Q3)   Castlias
[83.] *diminutive* (Q3)   dimumtine
[107.] *Tinct* (Q3)   Tuict
[145.2.] *The signe of* (Q3)   the of

[148.1–2.] *Atropos, daughters* (Q3)   Atrapodas, ughters
[148.7.] *Atropos* (Q3)   Atrhpos
[165.] *Eternal night* (Q3)   Eternal might
[174.] *happened.* (Q3)   happened,
[186.] *expresse* (Q2)   epresse
[Embleme.7.] *desert.* (Q2)   desert

## *December*

24. *espyed.* (Q2)   espyed,
40. *mirth,* (T)   mirth.
43. *derring doe* (D)   derring to
60. *That* (Q2)   that
64. *playe:* (V)   playe. (light period in Q1)
89. *tenrage* (Q3)   to tenrage
106. *before,* (Q4)   before.
108. *wipe.* (Q2)   wipe
113. *Rosalind* (Q2)   Rolalind
114. *dight?* (Q3)   dight,
139. *your* (Q2)   yonr
glee (Q2)   gleə
[17–18.] *Cabinet* (Q3)   Eabinet
[84.4.] *skill* (Q3)   still
[87.3.] *invented* (Q2)   nivented
[97–98.] *Thus is* (T)   This is
[109.] *fragraunt* (Q3)   flagraunt
[139.] *Glee) mirth.* (R)   Glee mirth)
[Embleme.13.] *quod* (Q3)   quae
[Embleme.14.] *ferrum* (Q3)   ferum

# *Complaints*

This edition is based on a copy of the 1591 quarto of the
*Complaints* (STC 23078) in the Beinecke Library, Yale
University. This volume was the sole printing of any of its
component poems during Spenser's lifetime. Sheets were
corrected during printing, and copies were apparently

assembled without discrimination between corrected and uncorrected sheets. The Yale copy is composed almost entirely of corrected sheets. Emendations of the copy-text are based on the authorities mentioned above, on Jortin (1734), on the Harleian MS 6910 in the British Library (*Harl*), and on variants in other copies of the quartos, notably British Library copy 239.i.1 (*BLQ*). See the Variorum VII.2 pp. 679–723 for full textual commentary.

## The Ruines of Time

Title: The Ruines of Time (running title) The Ruine of Time (title block)
Dedication *handes* (F)    hauds
84. *Princesse.* (F)    Princesse,
100. *mee,* (F)    mee;
154. *more.* (F)    more,
175. *endure.* (F)    endure,
259. *give.* (F)    give,
330. *wretched* (F)    wetched
359. *florish?* (S)    florish;
363. *covetize* (F)    covertize
413. *give?* (F2)    give.
414. *Mausolus* (F)    Mansolus
453. *him* (Q)    (changed to "them" in F)
454. *O let the man* (Q)    (changed to "O! let not those" in F)
497. *praid.* (F)    praid,
511. *worke,* (F)    worke
551. *which* (F)    with
574. *worlds* (F)    words
588. *spide.* (F)    spide?
671. *exceedingly* (F)    exceedtngly

## The Teares of the Muses

171. *answering,* (F)    answering.
197. *unhurtfull* (F)    unhurtfnll

256. *night:* (F)    night?
310. *wit;* (F2)    wit.
346–47. *paine, . . . distresse:* (F)    paine: . . . distresse,
399. *defaced* (F)    defacd
486. *sovenance* (Harl)    soverance
566. *be* (F)    beee
598–99. *mone, . . . breake.* (F)    mone: . . . breake,

## *Virgils Gnat*

122. *hart* (F)    hear
144. *eate.* (F)    eate,
149. *Ascræan* (Jortin)    Astræan
150. *life,* (Hu)    life.
233. *Shepheards* (F)    Speheards
308. *creast-front tyre* (F)    creast front-tyre
368. *relent.* (F)    relent,
387. *throat* (F)    threat
406. *fluttering* (F)    flattering
490. *Hesione* (Jortin)    Ixione
575. *billowes* (Harl)    billowe
680. *fell.* (Hu)    fell,

## *Mother Hubberds Tale*

94. *entice.* (F)    entice
121. *or* (F)    ot
160. *our treasure* (cQ)    a treasure
184. *undonne,* (F)    undonne.
251. *t'afford,* (F)    t'afford.
658. *successe.* (T)    successe,
713. *eare,* (T)    eare.
732. *himselfe* (F)    himfelfe
745. *needfull);* (V notes a semicolon after the "full" in
Newberry copy)    needfull
804. *shuttelcocks,* (F)    shuttelcocks.
1108. *Conge* (F)    Couge

1231. *The* (S)   And
1363. *abusion,* (F)   abusion.

## Ruines of Rome

21. *Mausolus* (F)   Mansolus
*glorie,* (Ch)   glorie.
32. *Palaces, is that* (Hu)   Palaces is that,
145–46. *heate, . . . fild;* (S)   heate; . . . fild,
210. *Now to become* (F)   To become
243. *ornaments* (Hu: needed for the rhyme)   ornament
414. *stackes* (F)   stalkes
435. *verses* (F)   yerses

## Muiopotmos

34. *yongth* (T)   yonght
36–37. *wast; . . . attire* (Ch)   wast, . . . attire;
196. *Dull* (cQ)   (word is omitted in uQ)
247. *lay,* (F)   lay.
250. *dispacing* (cQ)   displacing
346. *attempted,* (cQ)   attempted.
354. *Enfestred* (cQ)   Enfested
370. *framde craftilie* (cQ)   did slily frame
391. *those* (F)   thoss

## Visions of the Worlds Vanitie

110. *native* (cQ)   natures

## The Visions of Bellay

12. *inconstancies,* (Hu)   inconstancies.
26. *vainnesse* (BLQ)   vainesse
43. *pilloures* (S)   pillowes (TW Sonets 4.1 pillers)
113. *astonied* (BLQ)   astoined
117. *pot,* (F)   pot.
140. *rayse?* (F)   rayse.

### The Visions of Petrarch

27. *moment* (F)   monent (TW Epigram 2.11: moment)
29. *Then* (D)   The (TW Epigram 3.1: Then)

## A Theatre For Worldlings

This edition of the poem is based on the University
Microfilm reproduction of the 1569 Quarto (STC 18602) in
the Huntington Library.

### Sonnet 14

13. *traine,* (T)   traine.

## Daphnaïda

This edition of the poem is based on the University
Microfilm reproduction of the 1591 Quarto (STC 23079) in
the Huntington Library. A few emendations have been
adopted from the 1596 Quarto (Q2) and from subsequent
editions.

208. *faire, most* (Q2)   faire most
212. *womankinde,* (MH)   womankinde;
254. *discontent,* (Q2)   discontent
391. *till* (Hu)   tell
469. *Inne* (Q2)   Innne
524. *swaines,* (Hu)   swaines;
549. *a sdeinfull* (T)   asdeinfull

## Colin Clouts Come Home Againe

This edition of *Colin Clouts Come Home Againe*, *Astrophel*, and
*The Doleful Lay of Clorinda* is based on the corrected copy of

the 1595 Quarto of *Colin Clouts Come Home Againe* (STC 23077) in the Rare Book Room of the Smith College Library.

## Colin Clouts Come Home Againe

1. *knowen* (F)   knowne
44. *delight,* (F)   delight.
109–11. Each line in Q begins with an italic capital T.
193. *fare:* (F)   fare,
303. *daies.* (F)   daies,
353. *praise,* (F3)   praise:
378. *blow* (F)   blow,
382. *Corydon though* (Hu)   a Corydon, but
487. *Urania* (F)   Uriana
558. *see,* (T)   see.
600. *clusters* (F)   glusters
642. *forgotten,* (F)   forgotten.
737. *worthie* (F)   worrhie
743. *expound* (F)   expound,
757. *fare* (F)   far
772. *there?* (F)   there,
774. *here.* (F)   here,
775. No paragraph indentation in Q; indented in F.
776. Paragraph indentation in the Q; not indented in F.
796. *led,* (F)   led
805. *growing, he* (F)   growing he,
846. *agree?* (F)   agree.
861. *life* (F2)   like
875. *fynd* (F)   fynd,
884. *the* (F)   their
920. *revile:* (F)   revile
923–24. *rimes, . . . praise:* (F)   rimes: . . . praise,
954. *skies* (F2)   skies,

## *Astrophel*

33. *greet* (F)   greet,
50. *often* (F)   oft
72. *alas)*. (F2)   alas)
89. *needeth* (F)   need
91. *fortuned, as he* (F)   fortuned as he,
116. *brood* (F2)   brood:
154. *adorned,* (F)   adorned

## *The Doleful Lay of Clorinda*

17. *wretched* (F)   wetched
35. *Great* (F)   Creat
35. *him did see* (F)   him see

## *Amoretti and Epithalamion*

The present edition is based on a University Microfilm
reproduction of the 1595 Octavo (STC 23076) in the
Huntington Library. Typesetters worked with moderate care
on this edition, the only one published in Sp's lifetime.
Corrections made in the course of printing account for the
few minor variations in the eleven extant copies. Though lack
of standardization produced wide variations in Elizabethan
spelling, only ten characters in the Huntington Library copy
are clearly erroneous (*Amor* XVII.7, XXVIII.2, XXXVIII.4,
XLII.6, L.2, LXXVIII.6, LXXXIX.3, and *Epith* 67, 341, and
356).

Punctuation of the octavo is chaotic, reflecting not only the
looseness of Elizabethan conventions of punctuation but
probably also the habits and idiosyncrasies of various
typesetters working in the shop of the printer Peter Short. In
this regard it is instructive to compare the spelling and
punctuation of the two versions of sonnet XXXV/LXXXIII.

In general, the typesetters appear to have shared a superficial and mechanical idea of sonnet form. More than three-fourths of the sonnets, for example, have a colon at the end of the second line, irrespective of syntax. Because punctuation is more meaningful to the modern reader, the editor has made changes where the octavo reading was likely to confuse a student.

Punctuation has been added to distinguish between restrictive and non-restrictive modifiers, or to indicate the end of a grammatical element; it has been eliminated where it was found to disrupt grammatical and rhythmic units (e.g. subject and verb, verb and object, noun or verb and modifier).

## *Amoretti*

G:W.senior
12. *poesie* poesie,

G.W.J., 1. *plaine* plaine.
3. *vaine* vaine,
4. *deedes* deedes,
*past* past
daies: (F)    daies.
5. *praise* praise,
6. *quill:* quill.
8. *skill,* (F2)    skill.
11. *neighboures* (F)    neighoures
12. *meede,* meede.
13. *daies* daies,
G.W.J. Copy text has *G.W.*I. In modernizing the letter we assume that the I stands for "Junior."
I, 9. *brooke* brooke,
II, 1. *bred* bred,
4. *art:* (F)    art.
III, 13. *write* (F)    write,
IV, 11. *flowre* flowre,

V, 3. *admire* admire,
VI, 1. *mind* (F) mind,
3. *love,* love
9. *desire* desire,
VIII, 5. *guest* (F) guest,
X, 12. *enroll:* (F) enroll.
XI, 3. *addresse* (F) addresse,
XII, 1. *eies* (F) eies,
XIII, 6. *borne,* (F) borne:
7. *mortalitie:* mortalitie,
XIV, 2. *quite;* quite,
5. *might* might,
6. *belay;* (F) belay,
10. *heart;* heart,
XV, 1. *toyle* toyle,
6. *found:* (Co) found,
XVI, 4. *delight,* (Co) delight.
XVII, 7. *workmanship* (F) wormanship
XIX, 9. *rayse,* (T) rayse
XXI, 8. *impure.* (F2) impure,
11. *recure;* recure,
XXIV, 8. *see,* (F) see.
XXVI, 13. *paine* paine,
XXVIII, 2. *gives* (F) gvies
8. *attyre:* (F3) attyre
XXXI, 11. *bath* (F) bath,
XXXII, 1. *heat* heat,
XXXIII, 6. *it* it,
11. *fit* fit,
XXXIIII, 1. *wyde* wyde,
2. *way,* (F) way.
3. *guyde,* (Co) guyde.
4. *astray:* (F) astray.
5. *ray* ray,
12. *grief.* grief,
XXXV, 1. *covetize* (T) covetize,

8. *poore.* (Hu)   poore
XXXVI, 4. *release?* release.
8. *miseryes?* (T)   miseryes.
10. *gayned* (T)   gayned:
XXXVII, 1. *tresses* (F)   tresses,
3. *dresses* dresses,
4. *heare* heare,
7. *enfold* enfold,
XXXVIII, 4. *allur'd* (F)   allu'rd
6. *skill* skill,
8. *will.* (Ch)   will,
11. *spill;* spill,
XXXIX, 4. *dart,* dart.
13. *meat* meat,
XL, 3. *appeare* (F)   appeare,
8. *ray:* (F)   ray
10. *fled (S)   fled:*
13. *cheared* cheared,
XLI, 2. *foe?* (F)   foe:
9. *boast* boast,
10. *beguile* beguile:
11. *as,* as
XLII, 6. *from* (F)   fro
8. *hart;* (F)   hart
XLIV, 7. *arre,* (F)   arre.
XLV, 5. *shew* (F)   shew,
XLVI, 5. *obay?* (T)   obay,
13. *sustaine* (F)   sustaine,
XLVII, 5. *guyde* (F)   guyde,
XLVIII, 1. *hand* (F)   hand,
XLIX, 5. *will* will,
10. *kill* (F)   kill,
L, 2. *griefe* (F)   greife
5. *priefe* (Co)   priefe:
8. *please?* (F)   please.
9. *appease* (F)   appease,

LII, 9. *vaine* vaine,
11. *disdayne* (T)  disdayne,
LIII, 1. *hyde* (Co)  hyde,
6. *hew* (Ch)  hew:
LV, 5. *earth:* earth;
5. *are;* (Hu2)  are,
6. *water:* water;
*fyre;* fyre:
7. *ayre:* ayre;
rare; (Ch)  rare,
8. *fyre:* fyre;
14. *rest.* (F)  rest:
LVII, 10. *stoures;* stoures,
13. *grace,* (F)  grace.
LVIII, 1. *reposeth* (F)  reposeth,
3. *supposeth* (F)  supposeth,
7. *prayd* (Co)  prayd,
LIX, 5. *ship,* ship
9. *spight* (F)  spight,
LX, 4. *spheare.* (F)  spheare
5. *cleare* cleare,
LXI, 3. *dewtie* dewtie,
11. *scorne* (F)  scorne,
LXII, 6. *amend;* (T)  amend
9. *send* send,
LXIII, 4. *sore,* (Co)  sore.
9. *atchyve* (T)  atchyve,
11. *deprive* (F2)  deprive,
LXIV, 12. *Jessemynes.* (Co)  Jessemynes,
LXV, 1. *vaine,* (F)  vaine
2. *liberty;* liberty,
12. *wound.* (R)  wound
LXVII, 4. *pray,* (Ch)  pray.
LXVIII, 1. *day* day,
3. *away* (F)  away,
4. *win,* (Ch)  win.

6. *thou* (F)  tbou
LXIX, 8. *chastity?* chastity.
12. *wonderment,* wonderment.
LXX, 2. *displayd* (F)  displayd,
9. *make* make,
11. *make* make,
LXXI, 3. *lurke* (F)  lurke,
13. *see* (T)  see.
LXXIII, 2. *tye* (G)  tye:
9. *bright* bright,
12. *all,* all.
LXXV, 9. *devize* (S)  devize,
12. *name,* name.
LXXVII, 3. *entertayne* (F)  entertayne,
5. *ly* (F)  ly,
8. *entice:* entice.
11. *paradice* (Co)  paradice:
12 This line was printed flush left in 1595, apparently to avoid confusion with the turn-over of "fedd" in line 14.
13. *was,* was
LXXVIII, 14. *mee.* (F)  mee:
LXXX, 2. *compile,* (F)  compile
LXXXI, 9. *display* (F2)  display,
12. *spright.* (T)  spright,
LXXXII, 11. *spent* spent,
LXXXIII, 1. *covetize* covetize,
4. *complayne;* complayne
LXXXIV, 3. *desyre* (T)  desyre:
LXXXV, 6. *admyre;* admyre,
13. *thunder,* (F)  thunder
LXXXVI, 4. *well,* (Ch)  well.
LXXXVII, 3. *move* (F)  move,
LXXXIX, 1. *bough* bough,
3. *vow* (F)  vew
4. *late,* (Ch)  late.
8. *dove.* (MH)  dove
9. *hove* hove,

## [Anacreontics]

1. *old,* (F)  old.
11. *convay* convay,
13. *that,* that
20. *other.* (F1)  other,
73. *recured* (F)  recured,
75. *enured* (F)  enured,
79. *elfe* elfe,
81. *please* (F)  please,

## Epithalamion

6. *prayse:* prayse.
11. *dreriment:* (F)  dreriment.
19. *lampe* (F)  lampe,
24. *dove;* dove
49. *wrong,* (F)  wrong
61. *take,* (F)  take.
67. *dere* (Ch)  dore
70. *neer,* (V)  neer
109. *ring.* (F)  ring
116. *see.* (F)  see
129. *aloud* (F)  aloud,
158. *Queene.* (F)  Queene,
184. *ring.* (F)  ring
209. *you.* (F)  you,
210. *reverence* reverence,
214. *faces.* (Co)  faces
215. *may* (F)  may,
218. *play* (F2)  play;
220. *throates* (F)  throates.
222. *ring.* (F)  ring
237. *unsownd.* (F)  unsownd,
239. *band?* (F2)  band,
241. *ring.* ring
248. *day;* day,
249. *is.* is,

304. *coverlets.* (F)   coverlets,
306. *humility,* humility;
309. *was* was,
310. *brooke.* (F)   brooke
341. *Pouke* (Co)   Ponke
356. *poure* (4 of the 11 octavo copies read "ponre," an error apparently introduced in the process of correction)
385. *thy* (F)   they
398. *hand* hand,
399. *remaine* remaine,
401. *delight* (most 1595 copies)   delight. (Huntington copy)
402. *supply* supply,
411. *clods* (Hu)   clods:


# Fowre Hymnes

The text of the poem is based on the University Microfilm reproduction of the copy of the 1596 quarto (STC 23086) in the Huntington Library. Only a few mistakes have had to be corrected in the carefully printed quarto.


## An Hymne in Honour of Love

83. *hated* (F)   hate
120. *perceiving, . . . boy* (F2)   perceiving . . . boy,
221. *adventurous* (Hu)   aduenturons
242. *aby:* (F2)   aby,
274. *endeere* (F1)   endeere,


## An Hymne in Honour of Beautie

14. *soule* (F2)   foule
30. *behold,* (F)   behold (comma crowded off?)
32. *Paterne, . . . mould* (T)   Paterne . . . mould,

## An Hymne of Heavenly Love

238. *of great* (G) of great.
261. *embrace:* (F)   embrace,

## An Hymne of Heavenly Beautie

23. *to* (F)   ro
50. *eye* (Hu)   eye,
80. *behold* (F)   behold,
165. *And dampish* (Hu)   The dark and dampish
170. *many thousand thousand times more cleare,* (R)   many
thousand times more cleare (F has: many thousand times
more bright, more cleare)
180. *found* (F)   found,
270. *paine.* (Hu)   paine,
294. *on* (F)   no

## Prothalamion

The present edition is based on the University Microfilm
reproduction of the 1596 quarto (STC 23088) in the
Huntington Library.

75. *yield* (F)   yeild
102. *your* (F)   you
113. *resound.* (F)   resound?
114. *forth* (F)   forth,
129. *gave* (F)   gaue,
134. *bowers,* (F)   bowers

## Miscellaneous Short Poems

The occasional poems and fragments were published in a
variety of works. Most of them were first collected in Frances
G. Waldron's *Literary Museum* (1792).

## Dedicatory Sonnets

[1]. Text for the sonnet to Harvey is taken from the University Microfilm reproduction of the first quarto (1592) of Gabriall Harvey, *Fowre Letters, and certaine Sonnets* . . . . (STC 12900) in the Huntington Library.

3. *this worldes* (Waldron)   thisworldes

[2]. Text for the dedicatory sonnet printed before William Jones's 1595 translation of *Nennio, Or A Treatise of Nobility* (STC 18428) is taken from the copy in the Beinecke Library, Yale University.

2. *Unto (Waldron)* unto      10. *then (Waldron)* thē (The ē could stand for an en or an em; "then" seems more likely and less awkward than "them.")

[3]. Text for the dedicatory sonnet printed before Z. I.'s 1596 translation of J[acques] de Lavardin's *The Historie of George Castriot* (STC 15318) is taken from the copy in the Beinecke Library, Yale University.

[4]. Text for the dedicatory sonnet printed before Lewes Lewkenor's 1599 translation of *The Commonwealth and Government of Venice* (STC 15642) is taken from the copy in the Beinecke Library, Yale University.

*Sig. Edm. Spenser* (Waldron) Edw. Spenser

## Fragments

[1] and [2]. Texts for the two fragments of quantitative verse "See yee the blindefoulded. . ." and "That which I eate. . . ." published in the 1580 quarto of *Three . . . Letters* (STC 23095) were taken from the University Microfilm reproduction of the 1580 quarto in the Huntington Library.

[3]. Text for "Iambicum Trimetrum" also published in *Three
. . . Letters* (1580; STC 23095) after a separate title page, *Two
Other, very commendable Letters.* . . . is taken from the
University Microfilm reproduction of the 1580 quarto in the
Huntington Library.

2–3. *fast flying thought,* / *And.* . . . *(Davison)* fast flying /
Thought, and. . . . (In the copy-text "thought" is misplaced at
the beginning of the third line.)      21. *saye: this was,
Immerito?* (This is the reading of the copy-text. V notes that
there are eight variations on punctuation and typography of
these words in the 1580 edition.)

[4] and [5]. Texts for the two poems published in Sir James
Ware's 1633 *The Historie of Ireland* (STC 25067) were taken
from the copy in the Beinecke Library, Yale University.

# Further Reading

# Further Reading

The following paragraphs are intended to suggest first steps, some important studies a student of the shorter poems should be aware of. More extensive bibliographies can be found at the end of the relevant articles in the forthcoming *Spenser Encyclopedia*. *Edmund Spenser: An Annotated Bibliography 1937–1972* by Waldo F. McNeir and Foster Provost gives an exhaustive listing of work which is updated annually in the fall issues of the *Spenser Newsletter*.

## THE SHEPHEARDES CALENDER

Nelson (1963) offers a wise but brief introduction to *SC*; Hamilton (1956) examines the poet-pastor role, Berger (1969) surveys Sp's concern with his medium, and Heninger (1962) examines form in numerological terms. Cullen (1970) reads the *SC* in terms of opposed Arcadian vs. Mantuanesque strains, while Shore (1985) affirms their interfused nature as intrinsic to pastoral. Cooper (1977) fills in a gap admirably by exploring *SCs* background in medieval pastoral. Hoffman (1977) considers the poem's social role. Helgerson (1983) describes Sp's effort to become a professional poet of state affairs and thereby transcend prejudice against poetry as a temporary youthful folly. Montrose (1979) sees Colin's Petrarchan attitude toward figures of Elizabeth as a means to gain power in the milieu of court. Miller (1979) focusses on Sp's attempt in *SC* to forge an identity as a major poet.

Some more specialized studies follow. On the physical arrangement of *SC* as a book see Luborsky (1980 and 1981) and Heninger (1988). For the theological background of the ecclesiastical eclogues, see Hume (1984) and King (1986a, 1986b).

Collinson (1967) is the main authority on Elizabethan Protestantism and (1979) definitive on Grindal. McLane (1961) is the most effective attempt at identifying persons behind speakers, especially bishops. Harvey's works and biography are the subject of Stern (1979). Thompson (1961) and Woods (1984) analyze *SC*'s versification. On Sp's use of astrology in the Calender see Richardson (1988).

Some individual eclogues have attracted much attention; others little. On "Januarye," see Berger (1983); on "Februarie," Bond (1981); on "March," Spitzer (1950). For "April," much written on, see Cain (1978), Montrose (1980), and Johnson (1981); on "June," Bernard (1981); on "October," Hardin (1976); on "November," Lambert (1976); on "December," Reamer (1969).

## COMPLAINTS

### General

Renwick's edition (1928) contains a lucid commentary and annotations. Maclean (1978) and Nelson (1963) follow Stein's lead (1934) in studying the whole volume. Specialized studies appear in Satterthwaite (1960) and Prescott (1978), who treat French source material, Manley (1982) and Herendeen (1981), who focus on the images of the city and the river, respectively, and Bender (1972), who devotes a chapter to the emblematic devices. Peter (1956) and Keller (1969) discuss the complaint form; Crampton (1977) deals with the complaints of *FQ* III iv.

### The Ruines of Time

MacLure (1973) uses *RT* to develop a suggestive profile of Sp's sense of his place and times. Satterthwaite (1960) (ch. 5), studies the poem's relationship to Du Bellay. DeNeef (1979) discusses the poem's unifying concern with the function of poetry. Rasmussen (1981) argues that Verulame's view is ironically undercut and that the concluding sonnet sequences provide a corrective to it. Orwen (1941) deals with the poem's treatment of the Elizabeth-Leicester relationship. Manley (1982) discusses the image of the city in *RT* and other Spenserian poems.

## Teares of the Muses

There has been little recent criticism of *TM*. The bibliographical and biographical concerns of *TM* are treated in Renwick (1928), the *Variorum*, and Stein (1934). Much of the earlier commentary concerns Sp's characterization of Clio and Calliope, Muses of History and Epic, as it illuminates the identity of the Muse that Sp invokes in the Proem of *FQ* I. On this see especially Bennett (1932), who usefully describes Sp's probable sources for the poem. In an indispensable article Snare (1969) discusses the larger meaning of the Muses as patrons of all knowledge.

## Virgils Gnat

Sp's practice as a translator attracts attention in Emerson (1918) and Lotspeich (1935), both of whom discuss in detail the Latin text Sp used. The most compelling solution of the "riddle rare" in the poem is offered by Greenlaw (1910;1932), though his argument fails to convince Stein (1934), or Mounts (1952) who furnishes an alternative explanation; Adler (1981) offers further insight into the historical situation of the poem. Rosenberg (1955) usefully treats Sp's relationship with Leicester as part of her larger study of an important patron, and Miller (1983) glances in passing at the poem's implication in the "literature of patronage" examined by van Dorsten (1981).

## Mother Hubberds Tale

The historical allegory of *Mother Hubberds Tale* has been treated most fully in Greenlaw (1910; 1932) and Stein (1934), whose conclusions disagree. Recent criticism has tended to concentrate on Sp's treatment of genre and narration in the poem as they articulate its concerns. Greene (1963) discusses the poem's use of epic topoi, and Atchity (1973) deals with the function of the poet in the poem's fallen world. Van den Berg (1978) discusses the narrator's changing relation to the fiction he tells.

## *Ruines of Rome: by Bellay*

There has been much recent work on Sp and Du Bellay. Renaissance attitudes toward Rome's greatness and fall are outlined by Allen (1960; 1968), and Sp's relation to Du Bellay is surveyed by Prescott (1978), ch. 2. Two recent studies of *Les Antiquitez de Rome*, Sp's source for *Ruines of Rome*, have considerable relevance to Sp as well: Greene (1982) points to tensions between Du Bellay and the Roman ruins and culture that inspired him, and Rebhorn (1980) deals with Du Bellay's projection of Rome as mistress. Hieatt (1983) shows how Shakespeare's beloved takes on characteristics of Sp's and Du Bellay's Rome. Ferguson (1982) sees Sp defining his own position both through and against Du Bellay. Manley (1982) provides the *RR* with a context in Sp's broader output. The best edition of Du Bellay is that of M. A. Screech (1966).

## *Muiopotmos*

Unlike earlier critics, such as Harris (1944), Allen (1960; 1968) treats the poem as moral allegory. Both Bond (1976) and Brinkley (1981) stress the applicability of the work to the Elizabethan political scene, whereas Anderson (1971) and Weiner (1985), in noting the inadequacy of the narrator's moralizations, emphasize its Protestantism. Hulse (1981) discusses the narrator's artfulness and Bender (1972), the poem's ecphrastic mode. Commentaries on *Muio* as a self-reflexive poem about art appear in Dundas (1975) and Grant (1979).

## *Visions of the Worlds Vanitie, Visions of Bellay, Visions of Petrarch*

Sp's relation to Du Bellay is considered by Satterthwaite (1960), who also considers *Vanitie* (ch. 6), and Prescott (1978). The background of *The Visions of Petrarch* is dealt with by Davis (1973).

## THEATRE FOR WORLDLINGS

Van Dorsten (1973) examines the Dutch background of the *Theatre*, and Foster (1967) provides detailed information on the Dutch exile community in London. Rasmussen (1980) studies the relationship between Sp's poetic translations and the *Theatre* itself. Satterthwaite (1960) studies the *Theatre* version of Du Bellay's *Songe* and argues (appendix 1) against Sp's authorship of sonets 12-15. Prescott (1978) examines the Du Bellay connection and argues for numerological significance in the sonets. The full text of the *Theatre* is available in facsimile (van der Noot 1939) and in *Early English Books 1475-1640* (University Microfilms), reel 347; the Dutch version is available on reel 716, and the French on reel 1147.

## DAPHNAÏDA

The biographical background of the poem is covered in an indispensable article by Sandison (1928) and its relation to the tradition of pastoral elegy in Lambert (1976). Since 1978 there have been three extended critical discussions of the poem, all similar in treating Alcyon as a flawed mourner. Harris and Steffen (1978) examine the meaning behind the book's difference from Chaucer's *Book of the Duchess*, Oram (1981) stresses Sp's fiction-making in the poem and DeNeef (1982) considers Alcyon as a bad "reader" of his situation. Cheney (1983) discusses Alcyon in the context of Sp's portraits of poets in the early 1590s.

## COLIN CLOUTS COME HOME AGAINE

### Colin Clout Comes Home Againe

The fullest treatment of the biographical relation between Sp and Ralegh is still Sandison (1934), supplemented by Meyer (1969). The poets Colin mentions under pseudonyms are convincingly identified by Gaffney (1982). Starting with Edwards (1971), and Hoffman (1977), much recent criticism has focussed on poet's relation to the world of power. Shore (1985) treats the poem as Sp's self-conscious examination of his poetic options; Cheney (1983) deals with the fictional self-portrait that Spenser creates, and Mallette (1979) discusses Colin's growth into an orphic poet. Burchmore (1977) concerns himself with the structure of the poem and the theme of concord. Colin's final hymn to love as a creator-God is illuminated by Ellrodt (1960) and Berger (1968). Williams (1974) compares the poem suggestively to the poetry of Pope.

### Astrophel

*Ast* has not received its share of serious attention. For the biographical and literary background, see Friedrich (1936). The major study of the poem is by O'Connell (1971). Tourney (1976) argues that Astrophel is criticized as a frustrated Petrarchan lover, and Bondanella and Conaway (1971) discuss the relation between *Ast* and Ronsard's *Adonis*. Sacks (1985) approaches the poem from a psychoanalytic perspective. The other elegies in the *Astrophel*-book are reprinted in De Selincourt (1910).

### AMORETTI AND EPITHALAMION

The *Variorum* contains much useful commentary, especially on continental models. For treatments of Petrarchism see Forster (1969), Warkentin (1975), Neely (1978), and Waller (1980); of Elizabethan psychology, Harvey (1975); of Protestantism, Sinfield (1983). A number of critics treat the work's relation to its generic tradition: on *Amor* see Hardison (1972) and Dasenbrock (1985); on the Anacreontics see Hutton (1941); on *Epith* see Greene (1957) and Welsford (1967). For discussion of calendrical and liturgical symbolism in *Amor* see Dunlop (1970), Johnson (1974 and 1976), and Prescott (1985), which touches significantly as well on other aspects of *Amor and Epith*. Calendrical symbolism in *Epith* is treated in a seminal work by Hieatt (1960); see also Hieatt (1961), Wickert (1968), Fowler (1970), and Eade (1972).

On the relationship between *Amor*, the Anacreontics, and *Epith* see Kaske (1978), Miola (1980), and Thompson (1985). Martz (1961) treats characterization and humor in *Amor*, Dunlop (1980) discusses its drama, and DeNeef (1982) its concern with metaphor. Cheney (1983) coments on Sp's fictional treatment of his life in *Amor and Epith* and Neuse (1966) argues that *Epith* emphasises a connection between poetry and magic.

## FOWRE HYMNES

The fullest list of analogues and possible sources is to be found in the *Variorum*. The primary treatment of Sp's use of Neoplatonic ideas in the *FH* is in Ellrodt (1960). Lewis's brief discussion (1954) is always enlightening. Welsford (1967) remains the best discussion of Sp's doctrine of love. The patterns of parallelism and contrast are studied by Nelson (1963), Paula Johnson (1972), and Einar Bjorvand (1975). Philip Rollinson (1971) discusses the generic background of the hymn. The unity of the hymns is discussed from various points of view by Peter Bayley (1971), Røstvig (1971), DeNeef (1982), and Oates (1983).

## PROTHALAMION

Ever since John Hughes complained, in his 1715 edition of the poem, of the disappearance of the swans after stanza seven, the unity of the *Prothalamion* has attracted critical discussion. Important contributions towards a modern reinterpretation have been made by Wine (1962), Woodward (1962), and Berger (1965). More recently, interesting observations have been offered by Prager (1976), Hollander (1985) and Manley (1985). A suggestive treatment of the mythology and the astrological and numerological structure can be found in Fowler (1975).

# Works Cited

Adler, Doris. "Imaginary Toads in Real Gardens." *ELR* 11 (1981): 235–60.

Alabaster, William. *The Elisaeis of William Alabaster*. Ed. and trans. Michael O'Connell. Studies in Philology. Texts and Studies. Chapel Hill: University of North Carolina Press, 1979.

Alciati, Andreas. *Emblemata*. Lyons, 1551.

Allen, Don C. *Image and Meaning: Metaphoric Traditions in Renaissance Poetry*. Baltimore: Johns Hopkins University Press, 1960; rev. and exp. 1968.

Allman, Eileen Jorge. "Epithalamion's Bridegroom: Orpheus-Adam-Christ." *Renascence* 32 (1980): 240–47.

Anderson, Judith. "'Nat worth a boterflye': *Muiopotmos* and the *Nun's Priest's Tale*." *JMRS* 1 (1971): 89–106.

Atchity, Kenneth John. "Spenser's *Mother Hubberd's Tale*: Three Themes of Order." *PQ* 52 (1973): 161–72.

Augustine. *Ennarrationes in Psalmos* and *De Trinitate*. *Patrologia Latina*. Vols. 37 and 42. Ed. J.-P. Migne. Paris, 1844–65.

———. *On the Holy Trinity*. Select Library of Nicene and Post Nicene Fathers. Ed. Philipp Schaff. Vol. 3. New York: Christian Literature Company, 1887.

Bartholomeus Anglicus. *Batman Uppon Barthelme, his Booke 'De proprietatibus rerum.'* Trans. Stephen Batman. London, 1582.

Bayley, Peter. *Edmund Spenser: Prince of Poets*. London: Hutchinson University Library, 1971.

Bender, John B. *Spenser and Literary Pictorialism*. Princeton: Princeton University Press, 1972.

Bennett, Josephine Waters. "Spenser's Muse." *JEGP* 31 (1932): 200–19.

——. "The Theme of Spenser's *Fowre Hymnes*." *SP* 28 (1931): 18–57.

Berger, Harry, Jr. "The Mirror Stage of Colin Clout: A New Reading of Spenser's *Januarye* Eclogue." *Helios* 10 (1983): 139–60.

——. "Mode and Diction in *The Shepheardes Calender*." *MP* 67 (1969): 140–49.

——. "Spenser's *Prothalamion*: An Interpretation." *EC* 15 (1965): 363–80; rpt. in *Essential Articles for the Study of Edmund Spenser*. Ed. A. C. Hamilton. Hamden, Ct.: Archon, 1972.

——. "The Spenserian Dynamics." *SEL* 8 (1968): 1-18.

Bernard, John D. "'June' and the Structure of Spenser's *Shepheardes Calender*." *PQ* 160 (1981): 305–22.

Bible. The Geneva Bible. Geneva, 1560. Facsimile ed. Ed. Lloyd E. Barry. Madison: University of Wisconsin Press, 1969.

Bjorvand, Einar. "Spenser's Defense of Poetry: Some Structural Aspects of the *Fowre Hymnes*." *Fair Forms: Essays in English Literature from Spenser to Jane Austen*. Ed. Maren-Sofie Røstvig. Cambridge: D. S. Brewer, 1975.

Boccaccio, Giovanni. *De Genealogia Deorum Gentilium XII*. Venice, 1472.

Bond, R. B. "*Invidia* and the Allegory of Spenser's *Muiopotmos*." *ESC* 2 (1976): 144–55.

——. "Supplantation in the Elizabethan Court: The Theme of Spenser's February Eclogue." *SSt* 2 (1981): 55–65.

Bondanella, Peter E., and Julia Conaway Bondanella. "Two Kinds of Renaissance Love: Spenser's 'Astrophel' and Ronsard's 'Adonis.'" *ES* 52 (1971): 311–18.

Boke of Common Prayer. London, 1549, 1552. Quoted from *The First and Second Prayer-Books of King Edward the Sixth*. Ed. E. C. S. Gibson. Everyman's Library. London: Dent, 1906.

Brinkley, R. A. "Spenser's *Muiopotmos* and the Politics of Metamorphosis." *ELH* 48 (1981): 668–76.

Burchmore, David W. "The Image of the Centre in *Colin Clouts Come Home Againe*." *RES* ns 28 (1977): 393–406.

Cain, Thomas H. *Praise in "The Faerie Queene."* Lincoln: University of Nebraska Press, 1978.

———. "Spenser and the Renaissance Orpheus." *UTQ* 41 (1971): 24–47.

Calvin, John. *Institutes of the Christian Religion*. Ed. John T. McNeill, trans. Ford Lewis Battles. The Library of Christian Classics, Vols. 20–21. Philadelphia: Westminster Press, 1960.

Camden, William. *Britannia*. London, 1586. Quoted in *Britain, or a Chorographicall Description of England, Scotland, and Ireland*. Trans. P. Holland. London, 1610.

Cartari, Vincenzo. *The Fountaine of Ancient Fiction*. 1599. Trans. Richard Linche. The Renaissance and the Gods, vol. 13. Ed. Stephen Orgel. New York: Garland Press, 1976.

Castiglione, Baldasare. *The Courtier*. 1561. Trans. Sir Thomas Hoby. Everyman's Library. London: Dent, 1928.

Cheney, Donald. "Spenser's Fortieth Birthday and Related Fictions." *SSt* 4 (1983): 3–31.

Chrétien de Troyes. *Arthurian Romances*. Trans. D. D. R. Owen. London: Dent, 1987.

Collinson, Patrick. *Archbishop Grindal 1519–1583: The Struggle for a Reformed Church*. Berkeley: University of California Press, 1979.

———. *The Elizabethan Puritan Movement*. Berkeley: University of California Press, 1967.

Comes, Natales. *Mythologiae, sive explicationis fabularum, libri decem*. Venice, 1568.

Cooper, Helen. *Pastoral: Mediaeval into Renaissance*. Totowa, N.J.: Rowman & Littlefield, 1977.

Crampton, Georgia Ronan. "Spenser's Lyric Theodicy: The Complaints of *The Faerie Queene* III iv." *ELH* 44 (1977): 205–21.

Cullen, Patrick. *Spenser, Marvell, and Renaissance Pastoral.* Cambridge, Ma.: Harvard University Press, 1970.

Cummings, R. M., ed. *Spenser: The Critical Heritage.* London: Routledge & K. Paul, 1971.

Curtius, Ernst R. *European Literature and the Latin Middle Ages.* Trans. Willard Trask. Bollingen Series 36. Princeton: Princeton University Press, 1973.

Dante. *The Divine Comedy.* Trans. Charles S. Singleton. Princeton: Princeton University Press, 1970–75.

———. *The New Life.* Trans. William Anderson. Baltimore: Penguin, 1964.

Dasenbrock, Reed Way. "The Petrarchan Context of Spenser's *Amoretti.*" *PMLA* 100 (1985): 38–50.

Davis, Charles Roger. "Petrarch's *Rime* 323 and Its Tradition through Spenser." Diss., Princeton University, 1973.

DeNeef, Leigh. "'The Ruins of Time': Spenser's Apology for Poetry." *SP* 76 (1979): 262–71.

———. *Spenser and the Motives of Metaphor.* Durham, N.C.: Duke University Press, 1982.

Du Bellay, Joachim. *Les Regrets et Autres Oeuvres Poetiques suivis des Antiquitez de Rome. Plus un Songe ou Vision sur le mesme subject.* Ed. M. A. Screech. Textes Litteraires Francais. Geneva: Droz, 1966.

Dundas, Judith. "*Muiopotmos*: A World of Art." *YES* 5 (1975): 30–38.

Dunlop, Alexander. "The Drama of *Amoretti.*" *SSt* 1 (1980): 107–20.

———. "The Unity of Spenser's *Amoretti.*" in *Silent Poetry.* Ed. Alastair Fowler. London: Routledge & K. Paul, 1970.

Eade, J. C. "The Pattern in the Astronomy of Spenser's *Epithalamion.*" *RES* 23 (1972): 173–78.

Edwards, Thomas R. *Imagination and Power: A Study of Poetry on Public Themes.* New York: Oxford University Press, 1971.

Ellrodt, Robert. *Neoplatonism in the Poetry of Spenser.* Travaux de Humanisme et Renaissance, 35. Geneva: Droz, 1960.

Emerson, O. F. "Spenser's *Virgil's Gnat*." *JEGP* 17 (1918): 94–118.

Erasmus, Desiderius. *Opuscula Aliquot*. Basel, 1514.

Ferguson, Margaret W. "'The Afflatus of Ruin': Meditations on Rome by Du Bellay, Spenser, and Stevens." in *Roman Images*. Selected Papers from the English Institute. New Series, No. 8. Ed. Annabel Patterson. Baltimore: Johns Hopkins University Press, 1982.

Ficino, Marsilio. *Commentary on Plato's Symposium on Love*. Trans. Sears Jayne. Dallas, Texas: Spring Publications, 1985.

Forster, Leonard. *The Icy Fire: Five Studies in European Petrarchism*. Cambridge: Cambridge University Press, 1969.

———. *Janus Gruter's English Years: Studies in the Continuity of Dutch Literature in Exile in Elizabethan England*. Leiden: The University Press for the Sir Thomas Browne Institute, 1967.

Fowler, Alastair. *Conceitful Thought: The Interpretation of English Renaissance Poems*. Edinburgh: Edinburgh University Press, 1975.

———. *Triumphal Forms: Structural Patterns in Elizabethan Poetry*. Cambridge: Cambridge University Press, 1970.

Friedrich, Walter G. "The Stella of *Astrophel*." *ELH* 3 (1936): 114–39.

Gaffney, Carmel. "Colin Clouts Come Home Againe." Diss., Edinburgh University. 1982.

Gascoigne, George. "Certayne Notes of Instruction." in *Elizabethan Critical Essays*. Ed. G. Gregory Smith. Vol. 1. London: Oxford University Press, 1904.

Gerard, John. *The Herball or General Historie of Plantes*. 1597. Rev. by Thomas Johnson. London, 1633.

Golding, Arthur. *Shakespeare's Ovid: Golding's translation of the 'Metamorphoses.'*1567. Ed. W. H. D. Rouse. London: Centaur Press, 1961.

Gottfried, Rudolph. "Spenser and the Italian Myth of Locality." *SP* 34 (1937): 107–265.

Grant, Patrick. *Images and Ideas in Literature of the English Renaissance*. Amherst: University of Massachusetts Press, 1979.

Greene, Thomas M. *The Descent From Heaven: a Study in Epic Continuity*. New Haven: Yale University Press, 1963.

———. *The Light in Troy: Imitation and Discovery in Renaissance Poetry*. New Haven: Yale University Press, 1982.

———. "Spenser and the Epithalamic Tradition." *CL* 9 (1957): 215–28.

Greenlaw, Edwin. "Spenser and the Earl of Leicester." *PMLA* 25 (1910): 535–61; rpt. in *Studies in Spenser's Historical Allegory*. Baltimore: Johns Hopkins University Press, 1932.

Hamilton, A. C. "The Argument of Spenser's *Shepheardes Calender*." *ELH* 23 (1956): 171–82.

———, ed. *The Faerie Queene*. Longmans Annotated English Poets. London: Longmans, 1977.

Hardin, Richard F. "The Resolved Debate of Spenser's *October*." *MP* 73 (1976): 257–63.

Hardison, O. B. Jr. "*Amoretti* and the *Dolce Stil Novo*." *ELR* 2 (1972): 208–16.

Harris, Brice. "The Butterfly in *Muiopotmos*." *JEGP* 43 (1944): 302–16.

Harris, Duncan, and Nancy L. Steffen. "The Other Side of the Garden: An Interpretive Comparison of Chaucer's *Book of the Duchess* and Spenser's *Daphnaida*." *JMRS* 8 (1978): 17–36.

Harrison, William. "Description of England." In Raphael Holinshed, *The Chronicles of England, Scotlande, and Irelande*. London: 1577, 1587.

Harvey, Gabriel. *Fowre Letters and certaine sonnets*. London, 1592.

———. *Gratulationes Valdinenses*. London, 1578.

Harvey, E. Ruth. *The Inward Wits: Psychological Theory in the*

*Middle Ages and the Renaissance*. London: University of London, Warburg Institute, 1975.

Helgerson, Richard. *Self-Crowned Laureates: Spenser, Jonson, Milton, and the Literary System*. Berkeley: University of California Press, 1983.

Heninger, S. K., Jr. "The Implications of Form for *The Shepheardes Calender*." *Studies in the Renaissance* 9 (1962): 309–21.

———. *Touches of Sweet Harmony: Pythagorean Cosmology and Renaissance Poetics*. San Marino: Huntington Library, 1974.

———. "The Typographical Layout of Spenser's *Shepheardes Calender* and Sansovino's Sannazzaro." in *The Word and the Visual Imagination. Studies in the Interaction of English Literature and the Visual Arts*. Ed. Karl Josef Höltgen et al. Erlangen: Universitatsbibliothek, 1988.

Herendeen, W. H. "Spenserian Specifics: Spenser's Appropriation of a Renaissance Topos." *M&H* ns 10 (1981): 159–88.

Hieatt, A. Kent. "The Daughters of Horus: Order in the Stanzas of *Epithalamion*" in *Form and Convention in the Poetry of Edmund Spenser*. Ed. William Nelson. New York: Columbia University Press, 1961.

———. "The Genesis of Shakespeare's *Sonnets*: Spenser's *Ruines of Rome: by Bellay*." *PMLA* 98 (1983): 800–14.

———. *Short Time's Endless Monument*. New York: Columbia University Press, 1960.

Hoffman, Nancy Jo. *Spenser's Pastorals: The Shepheardes Calender and Colin Clout*. Baltimore: Johns Hopkins University Press, 1977.

Holinshed, Raphael. *Chronicles of England, Scotland, and Ireland*. 6 vols. London, 1807–08. Rpt. New York, 1968.

Hollander, John. 'The Footing of His Feet: On a Line of Milton's" in *On Poetry and Poetics*. Ed. Richard Waswo. SPELL: Swiss Papers in English Language and Literature, 2. Tubingen: Gunter Narr, 1985.

_____. "Spenser and the Mingled Measure." *ELR* 1 (1971): 226–38.

_____. "Spenser's Undersong" in *Cannibals, Witches, and Divorce: Estranging the Renaissance*. Selected Papers from the English Institute. New Series, No. 11. Ed. Marjorie Garber. Baltimore: Johns Hopkins University Press, 1985.

Hughes, J., ed. *Spenser: Works*. London, 1715.

Hulse, Clark. *Metamorphic Verse: The Elizabethan Minor Epic*. Princeton, Princeton University Press, 1981.

Hume, Anthea. *Edmund Spenser: Protestant Poet*. Cambridge: Cambridge University Press, 1984.

Hutton, James. "Cupid and the Bee." *PMLA* 56 (1941): 1036–57.

Johnson, Paula. *Form and Transformation in Music and Poetry of the English Renaissance*. Yale Studies in English, 179. New Haven: Yale University Press, 1972.

Johnson, L. Staley. "Elizabeth, Bride and Queen: A Study of Spenser's April Eclogue and the Metaphors of English Protestantism." *SSt* 2 (1981): 75–91.

Johnson, William C. "Spenser's *Amoretti* and the Art of the Liturgy." *SEL* 14 (1974): 47–61.

_____. "'Sacred Rites' and Prayer-Book Echoes in Spenser's 'Epithalamion.'" *Ren and Ref* 12 (1976): 49–54.

Jones, R. F. *Ancients and Moderns: a Study of the Rise of the Scientific Movement in Seventeenth Century England*. Berkeley: University of California Press, 1961.

Jortin, John. *Remarks on Spenser's Poems*. 1734. Rpt. New York: Garland Publishing Co, 1970.

Kaske, Carol V. "Spenser's *Amoretti and Epithalamion* of 1585: Structure, Genre and Numerology." *ELR* 8 (1978): 271–95.

Keach, William. *Elizabethan Erotic Narratives*. New Brunswick, N.J.: Rutgers University Press, 1977.

Keller, Joseph. "The Triumph of Vice: A Formal Approach to the Medieval Complaint against the Times." *AnM* 10 (1969): 120–37.

Kellogg, Robert, and Oliver Steele, eds. *Books I and II of The Faerie Queene, the Mutability Cantos and Selections from the Minor Poetry*. New York: Odyssey, 1965.

King, John N. "Spenser's *Shepheardes Calender* and Protestant Pastoral Satire." in *Renaissance Genres*. Ed. Barbara Kiefer Lewalski. Cambridge, Mass.: Harvard University Press, 1986. [1986a]

———. "Was Spenser a Puritan?" *SSt* 6 (1986): 1–31. [1986b]

Knowlton, E.C. "'Oricalche' and 'Phoenice' in Spenser's *Muiopotmos*." *N&Q* 27 (1980): 138–39.

Koller, Katherine. "Identifications in *Colin Clouts Come Home Againe*." *MLN* 50 (1935): 155–58.

Landrum, Grace. "Spenser's Use of the Bible and his Alleged Puritanism." *PMLA* 41 (1926): 517–34.

Lambert, Ellen. *Placing Sorrow: A Study of the Pastoral Convention from Theocritis to Milton*. Chapel Hill: University of North Carolina Press, 1976.

Lewis, C. S. *English Literature in the Sixteenth Century Excluding Drama*. Oxford: Clarendon Press, 1954.

Lotspeich, H. G. *Classical Mythology in the Poetry of Edmund Spenser*. Princeton: Princeton University Press, 1942.

———. "Spenser's *Virgils Gnat* and Its Latin Original." *ELH* 2 (1935): 235–41.

Luborsky, Ruth Samson. "The Allusive Presentation of *The Shepheardes Calender*." *SSt* 1 (1980): 29–67.

———. "The Illustrations to *The Shepheardes Calender*." *SSt* 2 (1981): 3–53.

MacCaffery, Isabel G. "Allegory and Pastoral in *The Shepheardes Calender*." *ELH* 36 (1969): 88–109.

McCanles, Michael. "*The Shepheardes Calender* as Document and Monument." *SEL* 22 (1982): 5–19.

Macklem, Michael. *The Anatomy of the World: Relations between Natural and Moral Law from Donne to Pope*. Minneapolis: University of Minnesota Press, 1958.

McLane, Paul E. *Spenser's Shepheardes Calender: A Study in*

*Elizabethan Allegory*. Notre Dame, In.: University of Notre Dame Press, 1961.

Maclean, Hugh. "'Restlesse anguish and unquiet paine': Spenser and the Complaint, 1579–1590." in *The Practical Vision: Essays in English Literature in Honour of Flora Roy*. Ed. Jane Campbell and James Doyle. Waterloo, Can.: Wilfred Laurier University Press, 1978.

——. *Edmund Spenser's Poetry*. 2nd ed. New York: Norton, 1982.

MacLure, Millar. "Spenser and the ruins of time." in *A Theatre for Spenserians*. Ed. Judith M. Kennedy and James A. Reither. Toronto: University of Toronto Press, 1973.

Mallette, Richard. "Spenser's Portrait of the Artist in *The Shepheardes Calender* and *Colin Clouts Come Home Again*." *SEL* 19 (1979): 19–41.

Manley, Frank. *John Donne: the Anniversaries*. Baltimore: Johns Hopkins University Press, 1963.

Manley, Lawrence. "Spenser and the City: the Minor Poems." *MLQ* 43 (1982): 203–27.

Mantuanus, Baptista (Spagnuoli). *Eclogues*. Ed. Wilfred P. Mustard. Baltimore: Johns Hopkins University Press, 1911.

——. *Eclogues*. Translated by George Turberville (1567). Ed. Douglas Bush. New York: Scholars' Facsimiles and Reprints, 1937 (rpt. 1977).

Marot, Clément. *Œvres Lyriques*. Ed. C. A. Mayer. London: Athlone Press, 1964.

Martz, Louis L. "The *Amoretti*: 'Most Goodly Temperature'." in *Form and Convention in the Poetry of Edmund Spenser*. Ed. William Nelson. New York: Columbia University Press, 1961.

Meyer, Sam. *An Interpretation of Spenser's Colin Clout*. Notre Dame, Ind: University of Notre Dame Press, 1969.

Middleton, Thomas. *The Blacke Booke; a Satire*. London, 1604.

Miller, David L. "Authorship, Authority, and *The Shepheardes Calender*." *MLQ* 40 (1979): 219–36.

———. "Spenser's Vocation, Spenser's Career." *ELH* 50 (1983): 197–231.

Miola, Robert S. "Spenser's Anacreontics: A Mythological Metaphor," *SP* 77 (1980): 50–66.

Montrose, Louis Adrian. "'Eliza, Queene of Shepheardes,' and the Pastoral of Power." *ELR* 10 (1980): 153–82.

———. "'The perfecte paterne of Poete': The Poetics of Courtship in *The Shepheardes Calender*." *TSLL* 21 (1979): 34–67.

Mounts, Charles. "The Ralegh-Essex Rivalry and *Mother Hubberds Tale*." *MLN* 65 (1950): 509–13.

———. "Spenser and the Countess of Leicester." *ELH* 19 (1952): 191–202.

Nashe, Thomas. *Strange Newes of the Intercepting certaine letters*. 1592. in Vol. 1 of *Works* ed. Ronald B. McKerrow. 1903; rpt. Oxford: Basel Blackwell, 1958.

Neely, Carol Thomas. "The Structure of English Renaissance Sonnet Sequences." *ELH* 45 (1978): 359–89.

Nelson, William. *The Poetry of Edmund Spenser: A Study*. New York: Columbia University Press, 1963.

Neuse, Richard. "The Triumph over Hasty Accidents: A Note on the Symbolic Mode of the 'Epithalamion.'" *MLR* 61 (1966): 163–74.

Oakshott, Walter. "Carew Raleigh's Copy of Spenser." *Library* 5th Ser. 26 (1971): 1–21.

Oates, Mary. "Fowre Hymnes: Spenser's Retractions of Paradise." *SSt* 4 (1983): 143–69.

O'Connell, Michael. "*Astrophel*: Spenser's Double Elegy." *SEL* 11 (1971): 27–35.

Oram, William A. "*Daphnaida* and Spenser's Later Poetry." *SSt* 2 (1981): 141–58.

———. "Elizabethan Fact and Spenserian Fiction." *SSt* 4 (1983): 33–47.

Orwen, William R. "Spenser and the Serpent of Division." *SP*
38 (1941): 198–210.

Panofsky, Dora, and Erwin Panofsky. *Pandora's Box: the
Changing Aspects of a Mythical Symbol.* Bollingen Series 52.
Princeton: Princeton University Press, 1962.

Panofsky, Erwin. *Studies in Iconology: Humanistic Themes in
the Art of Renaissance.* 1939. New York: Harper, 1962.

Parkinson, John. *Paradisi in Sole Paradisus Terrestris.* London,
1629.

Patrides, C. A. "'Quaterniond into their celestiall
Princedomes': The Order of the Angels." *Premises and
Motifs in Renaissance Literature.* Princeton: Princeton
University Press, 1982.

Perionius, Joachim. *In Petrum Aretino oratio.* Paris, 1551.

Peter, John. *Complaint and Satire in Early English Literature.*
Oxford: The Clarendon Press, 1956.

Petrarch, Francesco. *Petrarch's Lyric Poems.* Ed. and trans.
Robert M. Durling. Cambridge, Mass.: Harvard University
Press, 1976.

Pico della Mirandola. *Commentary on a Canzone of Benivieni.*
Trans. Sears Jayne. New York: Peter Lang, 1984.

————. *Oration on the Dignitie of Man.* Trans. in *The
Renaissance Philosophy of Man.* Ed. Ernst Cassirer et al.
Chicago: University of Chicago Press, 1948.

Plato. *The Collected Dialogues.* Ed. Edith Hamilton and
Huntington Cairns. Bollingen Series, 71. Princeton:
Princeton University Press, 1961.

Prager, Carolyn. "Emblem and Motion in Spenser's
*Prothalamion.*" *Studies in Iconology* 2 (1976): 114–20.

Prescott, Anne Lake. *French Poets and the English Renaissance:
Studies in Fame and Transformation.* New Haven: Yale
University Press, 1978.

————. "The Thirsty Dear and the Lord of Life: Some
Contexts for Amoretti 67–70." *SSt* 6 (1985):
33–76.

Puttenham, George. *The Arte of English Poesie.* 1589. Ed.

Gladys D. Willcock and Alice Walker. Darby, Pa.: Darby Books, 1969.

Quitslund, Jon A. "Spenser's Image of Sapience." *Studies in the Renaissance*; 16 (1969): 182–213.

Rasmussen, Carl J. "'The Bonds of Man's Nature': Spenser's Vision Poems." Diss., University of Wisconsin, 1978.

———. "'How Weak Be the Passions of Woefulness': Spenser's *Ruines of Time*." *SSt* 4 (1981): 159–81.

———. "'Quietnesse of Minde': *A Theatre for Worldlings*." *SSt* 1 (1980): 3–27.

Reamer, Owen J. "Spenser's Debt to Marot — Re-examined." *TSLL* 10 (1969): 504–27.

Rebhorn, Wayne A. "Du Bellay's Imperial Mistress: *Les Antiquitez de Rome* as Petrarchist Sonnet Sequence." *RenQ* 33 (1980): 609–22.

Renwick, W.R., ed. *Complaints*. London: Scholartis, 1928.

———. *Daphnaida and Other Poems*. London: Scholartis, 1929.

———. *The Shepheardes Calender* London: Scholartis, 1930.

Richardson, J. M. *Astrological Symbolism in Spenser's Shepheardes Calender: The Cultural Background of a Literary Text*. Lewiston, N.Y.: Mellen Press, 1988.

Ringler, William. "Spenser and Thomas Watson." *MLN* 69 (1954): 484–87.

Rollinson, Philip. "A Generic View of Spenser's *Four Hymns*." *SP* 68 (1971): 292–304.

Ronsard, Pierre. "Adonis." in *Oeuvres Completes*. 2 vols. Ed. Gustave Cohen. Paris: Bibliothèque de la Pléiade, 1950.

Rosenberg, Eleanor. *Leicester, Patron of Letters*. New York: Columbia University Press, 1955.

Røstvig, Maren-Sofie. *The Hidden Sense*. Oslo: Universitetsforlaget, 1963.

———. "Images of Perfection." in *17th Century Imagery: Essays on the Use of Figurative Language from Donne to Farquhar*. Ed. Earl Miner. Berkeley: University of California Press, 1971.

Rowse, A. L. *Sir Walter Ralegh: His Family and Private Life*. New York: Harper and Row, 1962.

Sacks, Peter J. *The English Elegy: Studies in the Genre from Spenser to Yeats*. Baltimore: Johns Hopkins University Press, 1985.

Sandison, Helen Estabrook. "Arthur Gorges, Spenser's Alcyon and Ralegh's Friend." *PMLA* 43 (1928): 645–74.

———. "Spenser and Ralegh." *ELH* 1 (1934): 37–60.

Satterthwaite, Alfred W. *Spenser, Ronsard and Du Bellay: a Renaissance Comparison*. Princeton: Princeton University Press, 1960.

Shore, David R. *Spenser and the Poetics of Pastoral*. Kingston: McGill-Queen's University Press, 1985.

Sinfield, Alan. *Literature in Protestant England, 1560–1660*. London: Croom Helm, 1983.

Sjøgren, Gunnar. "Helena, Marchioness of Northampton." *History Today* 28 (1978): 596–604.

Smith, Sir Thomas. *De republica Anglorum*. London, 1581.

Snare, Gerald. "The Muses on Poetry: Spenser's *The Teares of the Muses*." *Tulane University Studies in English* 17 (1969): 31–52.

Spitzer, Leo. "Spenser, *Shepheardes Calender*, *March*, ll. 61–114, and the Variorum Edition." *SP* 47 (1950): 494–505.

Starnes, DeWitt T., and Ernest William Talbert. *Classical Myth and Legend in Renaissance Dictionaries: a Study of Renaissance Dictionaries in their Relation to the Classical Learning of Contemporary English Writers*. Chapel Hill: University of North Carolina Press, 1955.

Stein, Harold. *Studies in Spenser's Complaints*. New York: Oxford University Press, 1934.

Stern, Virginia F. *Gabriel Harvey: His Life, Marginalia, and Library*. Oxford: Clarendon Press, 1979.

Thompson, Charlotte. "Love in an Orderly Universe: A Unification of Spenser's *Amoretti*, 'Anacreontics,' and *Epithalamion*." *Viator* 16 (1985): 277–335.

Thompson, John. *The Founding of English Metre*. New York: Columbia University Press, 1961.

*Tottel's Miscellany*. Ed. H. E. Rollins. 2 Vols. Cambridge, Mass.: Harvard University Press, 1965.

Tourney, Leonard D. "Spenser's *Astrophel*: Myth and Critique of Values." *ELWIU* 3 (1976): 145–51.

Tuve, Rosemond. *Spenser, Herbert, Milton*. Ed. Thomas P. Roche, Jr. Princeton: Princeton University Press, 1970.

Van den Berg, Kent. "The Counterfeit in Personation: Spenser's *Prosopopoia*." in *The Author in his Work: Essays on a Problem in Criticism*. Ed. Louis Martz and Aubrey Williams. New Haven: Yale University Press, 1978.

Van der Noot, John. *Theatre for Worldlings*. London, 1569. Facsimile ed. Bibliographical note by William A. Jackson and introduction by Louis S. Friedland. New York: Scholars' Facsimiles and Reprints, 1939.

Van Dorsten, J. A. "Literary Patronage in Elizabethan England: The Early Phase." in *Patronage in the Renaissance*. Ed. Guy F. Lytle and Stephen Orgel. Princeton: Princeton University Press, 1981.

———. *The Radical Arts: First Decade of an Elizabethan Renaissance*. Leiden: The University Press for the Sir Thomas Browne Institute, 1973.

Waller, Marguerite R. *Petrarch's Poetics and Literary History*. Amherst: University of Massachusetts Press, 1980.

Warkentin, Germaine. "'Love's Sweetest Part, Variety': Petrarch and the Curious Frame of the Renaissance Sonnet Sequence." *Ren and Ref* 11 (1975): 14–23.

Warton, Thomas. *Observations on the Faerie Queen of Spenser*. London, 1807 (orig. 1752).

Weiner, Andrew D. "Spenser's *Muiopotmos* and the Fates of Butterflies and Men." *JEGP* 84 (1985): 203–20.

Welsford, Enid. *Fowre Hymnes; Epithalamion: a Study of Edmund Spenser's Doctrine of Love*. Oxford: Blackwell, 1967.

Wepley, W. H. "Edmund Spenser: Being an Account of

Some Recent Researches into his Life and Lineage, with some Notice of his Family and Descendants." *N&Q* 162 (1932): 110–14, 128–32, 146–50, 154–69, 182–87, 202–06, 220–24, 239–42, 256–60.

Wickert, Max A. "Structure and Ceremony in Spenser's *Epithalamion*." *ELH* 35 (1968): 135–57.

Williams, Arnold. *The Common Expositor: An Account of the Commentaries on Genesis 1527–1633*. Chapel Hill: University of North Carolina Press, 1948.

Williams, Kathleen. "Some Renaissance Themes in Pope." *ELH* 41 (1974): 578–601.

Wind, Edgar. *Pagan Mysteries in the Renaissance*. 1958. Second ed. Harmondsworth: Penguin, 1967.

Wine, M. L. "Spenser's 'Sweete *Themmes*': Of Time and the River," *SEL* 2 (1962): 11–17.

Woods, Susanne. *English Versification from Chaucer to Dryden*. San Marino, Ca.: The Huntington Library, 1984.

Woodward, Daniel H. "Some Themes in Spenser's *Prothalamion*." *ELH* 29 (1962): 34–46.

Yates, Frances A. *The French Academies of the Sixteenth Century*. Studies of the Warburg Institute, 15. 1947; rpt. Nendeln, Liechtenstein: Kraus Reprint, 1968.

50-5